THEGREENGUIDE
Spain

Casa Batlló, Barcelona © Rob Broek/iStockphoto.com

THE GREEN GUIDE **SPAIN**

Editor	Clive Hebard
Principal Writers	Vicky Hayward, George Semler, Suzanne Wales
Production Manager	Natasha G. George
Cartography	John Dear
Photo Editor	Yoshimi Kanazawa
Proofreader	Nicky Gyopari
Interior Design	Chris Bell
Cover Design	Chris Bell, Christelle Le Déan
Layout	Michelin Apa Publications Ltd. John Higginbottom
Cover Layout	Michelin Apa Publications Ltd.

Contact Us

The Green Guide
Michelin Travel and Lifestyle
One Parkway South
Greenville, SC 29615
USA
www.michelintravel.com

Michelin TravelPartner
Hannay House
39 Clarendon Road
Watford, Herts WD17 1JA
UK
✆01923 205240
www.ViaMichelin.com
travelpubsales@uk.michelin.com

Special Sales

For information regarding bulk sales, customized editions and premium sales, please contact our Customer Service Departments:
USA   1-800-432-6277
UK   01923 205240
Canada 1-800-361-8236

HOW TO USE THIS GUIDE

PLANNING YOUR TRIP

The blue-tabbed PLANNING YOUR TRIP section at the front of the guide gives you **ideas for your trip** and **practical information** to help you organise it. You'll find tours, practical information, a host of outdoor activities, a calendar of events, information on shopping, sightseeing, kids' activities and more.

INTRODUCTION

The orange-tabbed INTRODUCTION section explores Spain's **Nature** and geology. The **History** section spans the Carthaginians through Napoleon to the modern day. The **Art and Culture** section covers architecture, art, literature and music, while **Spain Today** delves into modern Spain.

DISCOVERING

The green-tabbed DISCOVERING section features Principal Sights by region, featuring the most interesting local **Sights**, **Walking Tours**, nearby **Excursions** and detailed **Driving Tours**. Admission prices shown are normally for a single adult.

ADDRESSES

We've selected the best hotels, restaurants, cafés, shops, nightlife and entertainment to fit all budgets. See the Legend on the cover flap for an explanation of the price categories. See the back of the guide for an index of where to find hotels and restaurants.

Sidebars

Throughout the guide you will find blue, orange and green-coloured text boxes with lively anecdotes, detailed history and background information.

😊 A Bit of Advice 😊

Green advice boxes found in this guide contain practical tips and handy information relevant to your visit or to a sight in the Discovering section.

STAR RATINGS ★★★

Michelin has given star ratings for more than 100 years. If you're pressed for time, we recommend you visit the ★★★, or ★★ sights first:

★★★ **Highly recommended**

★★ **Recommended**

★ **Interesting**

MAPS

- 🗺 National Driving Tours
- 🗺 Principal Sights map
- 🗺 Region maps
- 🗺 Maps for major cities and villages
- 🗺 Local tour maps

All maps in this guide are oriented north, unless otherwise indicated by a directional arrow. The term "Local Map" refers to a map within the chapter or Tourism Region. A complete list of the maps found in the guide appears at the back of this book.

PLANNING YOUR TRIP

INTRODUCTION TO SPAIN

DISCOVERING SPAIN

CONTENTS

Welcome to Spain

If this is your first trip to Spain, welcome to a land that boasts many different cultures and languages, virtually every kind of landscape, a wealth of heritage and history, world-renowned cuisine and quality wines.
Whether you opt for beach or mountains, city or countryside, the choices are enormous. If you are a returning visitor, you'll probably note with delight how rapidly Spain's towns and cities are reinventing themselves for modern times and how much easier travel around the country is today, whether by train, road or plane. Resorts offer new cultural attractions and levels of comfort, too. Meanwhile, reassuringly, large swathes of wild Spain – mountains, marshland and rolling olive groves – remain unchanged.

Cáceres Viejo, Cáceres, Extremadura, Central Spain

C. Labonne/MICHELIN

CENTRAL SPAIN (pp106–213)

The central tableland's rare grandeur and sense of history is best felt in its Medieval court and cathedral cities, such as Segovia, Ávila, Salamanca, Burgos, Valladolid and Toledo. Journeys between them take you across light-soaked plains where castles, often dramatically rearing up above the plains, are a reminder of Castille's embattled past. Yet the landscapes here can also be unexpected. La Mancha's flatlands – home to Don Quixote – contrast with Soria's soft green river valleys,

Extremadura's boulder-strewn hills and the high, rocky sierras north and west of Madrid. City sights allow you to travel back in time. Mérida, for example, preserves classical Roman monuments. But elsewhere, above all in Madrid, the country's political and business capital, there is a taste for vibrant modernity. Its hectic nightlife and shopping culture are as much part of any visit to the city as the time spent lingering in its splendid art galleries.

ATLANTIC SPAIN (pp214–305)

Atlantic Spain's shoreline stretches from France west to the deeply indented Galician coastline, then south to the Portuguese border. Rough seas break onto rocks, beaches and the coastal promenades of fishing villages, resorts and cities such as Donostia-San Sebastián, Bilbao, Santander, A Coruña and Vigo. Behind the coast lie verdant mountains and valleys in the País Vasco, Cantabria, Asturias and Galicia where traditional farming life survives along with local languages and dialects. Further inland in Navarra and La Rioja are historic vineyards, many now boasting state-of-the-art wineries such as Bodega Ysios and museums in Briones and El Ciego. The Medieval Camino de

Santiago pilgrimage route, still walked today, provides a popular way for exploring all these northern regions. Monasteries, hermitages and hostels lie on its path. So too, do cities such as Santiago de Compostela, its end point, and Pamplona, world-famous for its bull-running. Bilbao, with its spectacular Guggenheim Museum, and the gourmet mecca of Donostia-San Sebastián catch the eye of more visitors than ever before.

MEDITERRANEAN SPAIN
(pp306-449)

Spain's eastern Mediterranean coast and the Balearics are famed for their beaches. Benidorm's are the most crowded, but there is variety to satisfy all tastes: the Costa Brava offers coves; Murcia has fine scuba-diving waters; and Menorca boasts spectacular long sands. Inland, Aragón's empty mountains and flatlands, bisected by the giant River Ebro, and the hill country of Catalunya and Valencia are vast areas of unspoiled beauty. Their historic cities are made graceful by regional architectural styles. Highlights include Zaragoza's Mudéjar architecture, Tarragona's Roman monuments, Gerona's Gothic cathedral, Murcia's Baroque splendour, Palma de Mallorca's old town and Valencia's medieval quarter and striking Cuidad de las Artes y Ciencias, Europe's largest cultural centre. Yet it is the port city of Barcelona that reigns supreme as a destination, offering world-class museums, a cosmopolitan arts scene, football, nightlife and restaurants. Rural escapes are easily made from these cities into areas of outstanding beauty protected as natural parkland.

ANDALUCÍA AND THE CANARY ISLANDS *(pp450–497)*

Andalucía's coastline is the most heavily developed in the Iberian peninsula. Often the resorts and golf-courses of the Costa del Sol stretch miles inland. But away from the coast sit three great cities – Granada, Sevilla and Córdoba – with architectural wonders dating from the centuries of al-Andalus. The *pueblos blancos* (white villages) set among rolling olive groves, and ports of Almería, Cádiz and Huelva keep their character, too. Meanwhile Málaga, capital of the Costa del Sol, is rediscovering its rich cultural history. Far out in the mid-Atlantic, the volcanic-born Canary Islands are often picked as winter destinations for their balmy year-round climate.

Each island is a world apart. El Hierro and La Gomera offer rural simplicity, La Palma preserves old-fashioned colonial elegance while Gran Canaria, Tenerife and Lanzarote have grown around their tourism and unique landscapes into buzzing cosmopolitan communities.

Montañas de Fuego, Parque Nacional de Timanfaya, Lanzarote, the Canary Islands

© Deckard73/Dreamstime.com

Serving Txacolí in a bar, Donostia-San Sebastián, País Vasco
©Philippe Roy/hemis.fr/Photoshot

Michelin Driving Tours

Refer to the Driving Tours Map on the inside front cover and to Michelin maps nos. 571, 572, 574, 577 and 578 in order to make the most of the following driving tours.

1 GALICIA

Round trip of 1 031km/644mi from A Coruña/La Coruña – This tour provides an insight into a region with magnificent towns and cities, verdant landscapes, an indented coastline and villages full of character and charm, known in ancient times as *finis terra*, or "end of the world". Galicia is also renowned for its delicious seafood. After visiting **A Coruña/La Coruña**, with its old quarter and attractive seafront promenade *(avenida de la Marina)*, head south to **Santiago de Compostela**, one of Spain's finest cities, to marvel at the spectacular Praza do Obradoiro, dominated by the impressive cathedral – the final destination for thousands of pilgrims every year. The tour continues along the **Rías Baixas/Rías Bajas** via **Pontevedra** to the mouth of the Miño, forming a natural border with Portugal. Along this magnificent stretch of coastline, with the scenic fishing village of **Combarro** and the summer resort of **Baiona**, the sea has created a series of beautiful inlets. Having followed the Miño as far as the historic town of **Tui**, continue by motorway to **Ourense**. After visiting the town, the itinerary continues along the spectacular **Gargantas de Sil**, before following the same road into the province of León, and the town of Ponferrada, the gateway to the magical landscapes of **Las Médulas**. Heading back into Galicia, make your way to **Lugo**, which has managed to preserve its exceptional Roman walls. Continue north to the coast, driving along the **Rías Altas** before returning to A Coruña/La Coruña.

2 AROUND THE MONTES DE CANTABRIA

Round trip of 764km/477mi from Santander – The Cantabrian mountains form a natural boundary between Castilla y León and the autonomous communities of Cantabria and Asturias. To the north, the highest summits of the Picos de Europa rise up close to the stunning coast, while in the lands of Castilla to the south you won't want to miss some of the towns and villages along the **Camino de Santiago** (Way of St James), or two outstanding jewels of Gothic art, the cathedrals of León and Burgos. Leaving behind the elegant town of **Santander**, with its superb location on the **Costa de Cantabria**, head west to the charming medieval town of **Santillana del Mar**, making sure you visit the replica of the **Cuevas de Altamira**, a masterpiece of prehistoric cave art. Continue along the same road to the picturesque pueblo of **Comillas**, before reaching the seaside resort of **San Vicente de la Barquera**. From here, the tour heads into the mountains, passing through the northern section of the **Parque Nacional de los Picos de Europa** and the exquisite panorama from the **Mirador del Fito**, before driving along the **Costa Verde** to the coastal city of Gijón, renowned for its extensive beach, and then south to nearby **Oviedo**, with its well-maintained historical centre containing some outstanding examples of Asturian architecture. Continue inland to visit the historic city of **León**, and then east across the Meseta towards Burgos along the Camino de Santiago, visiting Villalcázar de Sirga, Carrión de los Condes and **Frómista** en route, the latter famous for the Iglesia de San Martín, a masterpiece of Romanesque architecture. Having spent time exploring **Burgos** and its magnificent religious heritage, the tour continues towards Aguilar de Campoo, overseen by its castle, and from here to Reinosa, at the foot of the Montes Cantábricos, an ideal departure point for an excursion to the **Pico de Tres Mares**; alternatively, make your way back to Santander, stopping at **Puente Viesgo** to admire the wall paintings in the Cueva del Castillo.

3 THE BASQUE COUNTRY, RIOJA AND NAVARRA

Round trip of 696km/435mi from Bilbao – This tour combines stunning coastline dotted with picturesque villages, the delightful inland landscapes of northern Spain and the Camino de Santiago pilgrimage route, as well as charming towns and cities renowned for their wonderful gastronomy. The tour starts with a visit to the stunning Guggenheim Museum in **Bilbao** before following the indented **Costa Vasca** eastwards through quaint fishing villages to **Donostia-San Sebastián**, with its majestic setting on one of Spain's most breathtaking bays. From here, continue the short distance to **Hondarribia/Fuenterrabía**, a pleasant resort and fishing port with an attractive old quarter, close to the French border. The magnificent **Valle del Bidasoa** provides the backdrop as you head inland to **Pamplona**, a medieval town built around its imposing cathedral and famous for the annual running of the bulls. The route then heads deeper into Navarra, past monasteries and important staging-posts on the **Camino de Santiago** (**Leyre**, **La Oliva**, **Sangüesa/Zangoza** and **Puente la Reina**) and historic towns such as Sos del Rey Católico and Olite/Erriberri, before reaching **Estella**, one of the most important stops along the famous pilgrimage route. After visiting the nearby Monasterio de Irache, the pilgrims' path continues southwest to Logroño, the capital of La Rioja, known for its cathedral and old streets, and then through the extensive vineyards for which this region is justifiably renowned; the most famous halts on this section of the path are undoubtedly **Nájera** and **Santo Domingo de la Calzada**. Between the two, nestled in a delightful valley, is the village of **San Millán de la Cogolla**, the cradle of the written Castilian language. Before returning to the País Vasco via its capital city, **Vitoria-Gasteiz**, with its atmospheric old quarter and several museums of interest, visit Haro and the Museo del Vino de La Rioja. Return to Bilbao via the motorway, which winds its way through an impressive mountain landscape.

4 CATALUNYA

Round trip of 1 020km/637mi from Barcelona – This driving tour through Catalunya is characterised by high Pyrenean peaks, rugged coasts with charming coves, long sandy beaches, picturesque villages, exquisite Romanesque churches, impressive monasteries, and towns and cities overflowing with history.

Once you've spent time in the region's capital, **Barcelona**, a city with a fascinating mix of modernity and history, begin your tour along the **Costa Brava**, a beautiful stretch of coastline dotted with authentic fishing villages and summer resorts. After visiting the old Roman colony of **Empúries**, the picture-postcard small town of **Cadaqués**, the **Monestir de Sant Pere de Rodes** and El Port de Llançà, head inland to **Figueres**, home of the Dalí Theatre and Museum, and **Girona/Gerona**, a city that still retains the vestiges of its Roman, Jewish, Moorish and Christian past. From here, the tour climbs up into the **Pirineos**

Monestir de Sant Pere de Rodes

© Yvon52/Dreamstime.com

Catalanes, a land of spectacular mountain roads, beautiful valleys and the charming villages of **Besalú**, with its Romanesque architecture, Camprodón, Ripoll and Puigcerdà. From Puigcerdà head west through the sunny **Cerdanya Valley** and the mountain city of **La Seu d'Urgell** with its lovely Santa María cathedral before setting off into the Noguera Ribagorçana valley and the **Parc Nacional d'Aigüestortes**. Continue north through the Val d'Aran, with its Atlantic climate and capital at Vielha to reach **Lleida/Lérida**, watched over by the remains of its former Moorish fortress and by the city's cathedral (La Seu Vella). The journey back to the Mediterranean provides an opportunity to visit **Poblet**, the most famous Cistercian monastery in Spain, as well as the walled town of **Montblanc**, before arriving in **Tarragona**, capital of Hispania Citerior Tarraconensis under the Romans. Have a fun day out at the **Port Aventura** theme park before heading back to Barcelona. The final leg of the tour runs past the attractive resort town of **Sitges** on the **Costa Dorada**.

5 CASTILLA Y LEÓN

Round trip of 756km/472mi from Salamanca – Historic towns and lofty castles dominate this tour through the lands of old Castile. If your trip coincides with Holy Week, head for Zamora or Valladolid to witness their solemn Semana Santa processions. After spending time exploring **Salamanca**, a lively university city teeming with sumptuous monuments, head north to **Zamora** to admire the scallop tiling on the cupola of the cathedral. The road east towards Valladolid passes through **Toro**, where the dome of the town's collegiate church is similar in style to the cupola of Zamora's cathedral, and Tordesillas, where the famous treaty dividing the lands of the New World between Spain and Portugal was signed. In **Valladolid**, renowned for fine examples of Isabelline art,

it is well worth visiting the National Sculpture Museum (Museo Nacional de Escultura). Continue your journey through an extensive landscape of cereal crops, passing through Medina de Rioseco en route to **Palencia**, with its magnificent cathedral. Heading east into the province of Burgos, the itinerary takes in charming small towns and villages such as Lerma and **Covarrubias**. One of the highlights of this tour is the **Monasterio de Santo Domingo de Silos**, the cloisters of which are a masterpiece of Romanesque art. From here, the itinerary heads south, skirting along the banks of the Duero, to visit a series of castles built to defend the lands conquered by Christians from the Moors, such as the ruined fortress at **Peñaranda de Duero**; the impressive castle at **Peñafiel**; **Cuéllar**; and the more unusual castle at **Coca**, in Mudéjar style. The tour continues to **Segovia**, famous for its aqueduct and fairytale castle, and on to **Ávila**, a city of convents and churches, encircled by its imposing walls. Before completing your circuit, it is well worth making a last stop in the small town of Alba de Tormes.

6 ZARAGOZA, SORIA, GUADALAJARA AND TERUEL

Round trip of 869km/543mi from Zaragoza – This tour travels across several inland provinces, passing through impressive mountain landscapes, villages crowned by old castles and towns full of character and charm. The journey begins from **Zaragoza** with a foray into Navarra to visit **Tudela**, with its interesting examples of Mudéjar architecture and its fine cathedral. Returning to the province of Zaragoza, head for Tarazona, famous for its old quarter and cathedral, and the **Monasterio de Veruela**, which is well worth a visit. From Tarazona, continue to **Soria**, a quiet provincial capital embellished with impressive churches, on the banks of the Duero. The itinerary then continues southwest, passing through Calatañazor, a picturesque village overlooked by a medieval castle, to **Burgo de Osma**, yet another charming town, renowned for its magnificent cathedral. Head across country to Berlanga de Duero, the site of another castle built to defend the Duero, and on to San Baudelio de Berlanga, a hermitage with an unusual 11C Mozarabic chapel. Once past Atienza, crowned by the ruins of its castle, continue to historic **Sigüenza**, whose highlights include the fortified cathedral with its impressive array of sculptures, and the castle (now a parador). Join up with the fast highway heading east towards Zaragoza, passing through attractive scenery along the banks of the Jalón, crossing the river briefly to visit the magnificent **Monasterio de Santa María de Huerta**, built in sober Cistercian style with a number of Renaissance additions. As the road passes Ateca, head directly south past La Tranquera Reservoir to the **Monasterio de Piedra** for a stroll through its delightful park.

The tour continues via Molina de Aragón, with yet another castle, before entering the **Sierra de Albarracín** en route to the charming medieval village of the same name. The next stop on the itinerary is **Teruel**, a town which enjoys a superb location, and adorned with a number of interesting examples of Mudéjar architecture. To complete the tour, head north to **Daroca**, with its 4km/2.5mi of walls, before joining the motorway for the final leg back to Zaragoza.

7 AROUND MADRID

Round trip of 689km/431mi from Madrid – The area around the Spanish capital is home to several towns of major interest, a number of royal palaces and the scenic, mountainous landscapes of the Sierra de Gredos and Sierra de Guadarrama. One of the closest towns to **Madrid** is **Alcalá de Henares**, the birthplace of Miguel de Cervantes, where the major attractions are the university buildings. From here, the route passes through **Chinchón**, with one of the country's prettiest main squares, and on to **Aranjuez**, nestled in a verdant setting on the banks of the Tagus. After visiting the royal palace and pavilions and strolling through the delightful gardens here, continue your journey southwest to the historic city of **Toledo**, magnificently perched in a loop of the Tagus, with the sumptuous vestiges of its rich past. Continue your journey west to Talavera de la Reina, famous for its ceramics, and then north along a mountain road through the **Sierra de Gredos** en route to Ávila, visiting along the way the **Cuevas del Águila**, an awesome 12 million-year-old underground cavern. Ávila, a city of churches and convents, and the shrine of St Teresa, has preserved intact its magnificent 11C walls. From Ávila, the tour heads east to the **Monasterio de El Escorial**, an immense monastery built by order of Philip II. On the way to Segovia, you may wish to branch off to the **Valle de los Caídos** (Valley of the Fallen) where Generalísimo Francisco Franco is buried in the stunning landscapes of the Sierra de Guadarrama foothills. In **Segovia**, admire the graceful 2 000-year-old Roman aqueduct, the city's Romanesque churches and the exotic Alcázar. Close to the city, at the foot of the Sierra de Guadarrama, are the palace and magnificent gardens of **La Granja de San Ildefonso**, built by Philip IV, the grandson of Louis XIV, in nostalgia for the Versailles of his childhood. Return to the mountains, and after crossing the Navacerrada Pass, head northeast through a valley to the **Monasterio de El Paular**. A twisting road further north traverses the Navafría Pass, before descending into **Pedraza de la Sierra**, a seigniorial town full of charm. Before returning by motorway to Madrid via the Somosierra Pass, the small town of Sepúlveda is worth a visit to admire its impressive site overlooking a deep gorge of the River Duratón.

8 EXTREMADURA AND THE PEÑA DE FRANCIA

Round trip of 780km/487mi from Plasencia – This tour through the region of Extremadura has a strong historic focus because of its links with the Romans, the great conquistadors and Emperor Charles V. The tour ends with the Peña de Francia, in the province of Salamanca.

After visiting the cathedral and old quarter of **Plasencia**, the tour starts in the verdant Valle de La Vera, the setting for the **Monasterio de Yuste**, to which Charles V withdrew following his abdication, and the 15C castle in Jarandilla de la Vera (now a parador). Leaving the valley along a country road that crosses the Valdecañas Reservoir, you come to the village of **Guadalupe**, huddled around its magnificent monastery.

Following a visit to this shrine, continue westwards to the monumental town of **Trujillo**, the birthplace of several of the famous conquistadors, including Francisco Pizarro, and the site of one of Spain's most impressive and original main squares. From Trujillo, the tour then heads southwest by fast highway to **Mérida** to admire the city's Roman remains and the Museo Nacional de Arte Romano, which bears witness to Mérida's importance during this period. The next stops on the itinerary are **Cáceres**, a monumental town with a stunning and superbly preserved old town where time seems to have stopped in the 16C and 17C, and **Alcántara**, whose main sights of interest are a monastery, the seat of the military order of the same name, and an exceptional Roman bridge spanning the Tagus. Head northeast to Coria to visit its cathedral, and then into the province of Salamanca, to **Ciudad Rodrigo**, a pleasant small town with several buildings of interest hidden behind its walls. The tour ends with a visit to the **Peña de Francia**, a crag rising to 1 723m/5 655ft, and the Sierra de Béjar, with its typical mountain village of the same name.

9 THE LANDS OF LA MANCHA

Round trip of 849km/531mi from Cuenca – For many, La Mancha conjures up a scene of seemingly endless fields of cereal crops and vines, interspersed with the occasional village or town and the evocative silhouette of a windmill or castle. Yet it is also an area of impressive mountains and landscapes that have little in common with this image.

Cuenca, with its spectacular position between the ravines of the Júcar and Huécar rivers, is the starting-point for this tour, which begins with a drive through the **sierra** of the same name, famous for sights such as the **Ciudad Encantada** (with its unusual stone formations), the source of the River Cuervo, and the **Beteta** Ravine *(Hoz)*. Returning to Cuenca, the itinerary then heads out along the flat landscapes to the southwest to **Belmonte**, with its castle and interesting collegiate church, and Campo de Criptana, a typical La Mancha village, whose houses are framed by the silhouette of its windmills. After passing through Alcázar de San Juan, the largest town in the area, continue on to **Consuegra**, where the castle and line of windmills on a hill overlooking the town offers one of the region's most enduring sights. From here, head south for a visit to the Parque Nacional de las Tablas de Daimiel, a wetland area at the confluence of the River Guadiana and River Cigüela. The next stop on the itinerary is in **Almagro**, a historic town that has preserved its delightful old quarter, including a magnificent main square and the Corral de Comedias, a 16C theatre. A short distance to the southeast stands Valdepeñas, the capital of La Mancha's wine industry. Continuing east, the tour passes through **Villanueva de los Infantes**, containing several fine examples of Renaissance and Baroque architecture, and the village of **Alcaraz**, with its outstanding main square lined by elegant buildings, protected by the mountain range in which the River Mundo has its source. The next stop is the city of Albacete, home to a provincial museum with an interesting archaeology section. From here, head north to **Alarcón**, impressively situated on a hill almost completely encircled by the River Júcar and crowned by an imposing medieval castle (now a parador), before returning to Cuenca.

1 0 THE LEVANTE REGION

Round trip of 715km/447mi from Valencia – This tour running along the coast and inland through the provinces of Valencia, Alicante and Murcia is characterised by long sandy beaches and charming villages and towns with a fascinating artistic and architectural heritage.

Having spent time exploring **Valencia**, start the tour along the Mediterranean, visiting El Saler, with its extensive sandy beaches, and the nearby Parque Natural de la Albufera, a large freshwater lake and important rice-growing area. The itinerary then passes through a series of large resorts such as Cullera, Gandía, home to the former palace of the Dukes of Borja, and Denia, watched over by its castle. **Xàbia/Jávea**, with its picturesque old quarter, is just a few miles north of the Cabo de la Nao headland, offering spectacular views of the coast, and Calp/Calpe, located close to the impressive Penyal d'Ifac rock. **Altea**, the next resort to the south, is one of the area's most attractive coastal towns with its steep and narrow streets. Continue along the coast to Benidorm, where the backdrop to the beach is a mass of high-rise hotels and apartment buildings, and from here to the **Terra Mítica** theme park. The tour then heads inland through the mountains to visit **Guadalest**, in a spectacular location on a rocky ridge, Alcoi/Alcoy, nestled in a fertile river valley, and to the south, Xixona, famous for its nougat, and reached via the Carrasqueta Pass. Returning to the coast, the next major city on the itinerary is **Alicante**, a pleasant and

relaxed provincial capital overlooked by an imposing fortress, the Castillo de Santa Bárbara. The itinerary continues southwards, skirting the resorts of Guardamar del Segura and Torrevieja, before arriving at Mar Menor, a shallow lagoon separated from the sea by a long sandbar, at the southern tip of which stands the resort of La Manga del Mar Menor. After a visit to Cartagena, on the curve of a deep bay, leave the coast for the town of **Murcia**, whose main sights are its fine cathedral and the Museo Salzillo, a museum dedicated to the 18C sculptor Francisco Salzillo. Continue northeast to **Orihuela**, a tranquil town with numerous churches of interest, and then to **Elx/Elche**, famous for its palm grove. From here the itinerary heads further inland by dual carriageway to Villena, protected by its imposing castle. The final stop on this driving tour is **Xàtiva**, the town of a thousand fountains and birthplace of two popes. Situated on a fertile plain, the town has preserved a number of buildings of architectural interest.

1 1 CÓRDOBA, SEVILLA, CÁDIZ AND MÁLAGA

Round trip of 890km/556mi from Córdoba – This tour takes in some of the finest cities of inland Andalucía, the delightful whitewashed villages (*pueblos blancos*) in the provinces of Cádiz and Málaga, and the famous Costa del Sol resorts.

Córdoba, one of the three emblems of Andalucía, along with Sevilla and Granada, is one of Spain's most beautiful cities with monuments such as the Mezquita, typical whitewashed streets and a history influenced by the Christian, Muslim and Jewish faiths. From here, head west to **Écija**, the so-called "frying pan" of Andalucía, a town of churches, convents, palaces and numerous bell towers. Further west stands the breathtaking city of **Sevilla**, a name that conjures up passion and colour, where several days are needed to explore it to the full. The itinerary then heads towards the Atlantic, pausing in the elegant town of **Jerez de la Frontera**, famous for its sherry, equestrian history and delightful architecture, before arriving in **Cádiz**, reached via an impressive causeway. This charming provincial capital and port is one of Spain's best-kept secrets, with its 18C architecture, historic squares, impressive monuments and superb beaches. Chiclana de la Frontera, to the south, is the closest town to the Playa de la Barrosa, a magnificent, and seemingly endless sandy beach. From here, the tour heads inland to **Medina Sidonia**, one of the oldest towns in Europe, steeped in history with a medieval quarter perched on a hill with expansive views of the surrounding plains. The white-washed town of **Arcos de la Frontera**, the next stop, has an even more out-standing location, straddling a ridge above a gorge of the River Guadalete. Arcos is one of the region's famous *pueblos blancos*, which include **Ronda**, renowned for its dramatic location, stunning architecture and tradition of bullfighting. From Ronda, the itinerary winds its way through stunning mountain scenery down to the coast, dominated by the impressive **Rock of Gibraltar**. The coast road east to Málaga passes through some of the **Costa del Sol**'s most famous resorts (**Estepona**, **Marbella**, Fuengirola, Benalmádena, etc.), with their luxury developments, hotels and apartments. From **Málaga**, follow the fast highway inland to **Antequera**, the ideal base from which to explore local nature, and from here to **Estepa**, crowned by the remains of a fortress. The hilltop town of **Osuna**, the last stage on the journey, has preserved an interesting architectural heritage with numerous palaces and noble mansions amid its old whitewashed centre. From Osuna, return directly to Córdoba.

1 2 GRANADA, ALMERÍA AND JAÉN

Round trip of 835km/522mi from Granada – This tour through

the eastern half of Andalucía is characterised by historic towns and cities with an outstanding artistic heritage, magnificent deserted beaches, breathtaking mountain scenery and a landscape carpeted with olive trees as far as the eye can see. For many, a visit to the Alhambra, overlooking **Granada**, is the highlight of a trip to Spain. It marks the starting-point for this driving tour, which begins with a journey across the spectacular **Alpujarras** mountain range, passing through verdant valleys and picturesque whitewashed small towns and villages to reach **Almería**, a provincial capital overlooked by a Moorish fortress perched on a hill above the city. The itinerary continues through the **Parque Natural de Cabo de Gata-Níjar** and along the Almerian coast, an area of luminous skies, sand dunes, wild beaches and impressive desert landscapes that conjure up images of nearby Africa; hill-top **Mojácar**, is the most attractive town in this area. From here, follow the fast highway north, cutting inland to the area known as Los Vélez, in the foothills of the Sierra de María, and the town of Vélez Blanco, overlooked by its unusual Renaissance castle. Once you have crossed the Sierra de María, a cross-country route leads to Pontones in the province of Jaén, at the heart of the **Parque Natural de las Sierras de Cazorla, Segura y las Villas**. The tour through the park as far as **Cazorla** passes through impressive mountain landscapes cut by deep ravines, rivers and streams. Following a restorative sojourn at the heart of nature, the tour continues to **Úbeda** and **Baeza**, two monumental towns renowned for their magnificent Renaissance architecture. The last leg of the tour traverses extensive olive groves before reaching **Jaén**, spread out at the foot of the Cerro de Santa Catalina, a hill crowned by the city's imposing Arab fortress. Apart from the castle, the other major sights of interest in Jaén are its sumptuous cathedral and the Arab baths in the Palacio de Villardompardo.

When and Where to Go

WHEN TO GO
SEASONS

As a guideline, the best two seasons to visit Spain are spring and autumn, when temperatures across the country are generally pleasant.

Spring is the best time to explore Extremadura, Castilla-La Mancha and Andalucía, which in summer are the hottest regions in Spain. Late spring is also a good time to visit the Mediterranean and Balearic Islands, as the sea temperature starts to warm up. In **summer**, the country's north coast comes into its own, offering a pleasant climate for sightseeing and relaxing on the beach without the oppressive heat of other parts of the country. This time of year is also ideal for discovering the magnificent mountains of the Pyrenees, Picos de Europa, and the Sierra de Gredos, Sierra de Guadarrama and Sierra Nevada ranges.

Autumn is a generally pleasant season across most of Spain.

In **winter**, skiing enthusiasts can head for the Pyrenees or the Sierra Nevada, while those preferring to escape the cold wet winter in northern Europe and America can travel south to the Canaries for some winter sunshine. For up-to-date information on **weather** in Spain, visit the Spanish Meteorological Office website at www.inm.es.

WHAT TO PACK

Since Spain has so many days of sunshine and its temperatures are generally warmer than many other European countries, pack as few clothes as possible. Unless you choose to visit in winter, lightweight clothing is usually an ideal choice. It's a good idea to pack a sturdy pair of walking shoes, or even hiking boots. An umbrella, rainwear, a lightweight jacket and suntan lotion are good to have with you. Try to pack everything in one suitcase and a carry-on bag. Take an extra tote bag for bringing new purchases back home.

IDEAS FOR YOUR VISIT
CITY BREAKS

Madrid

The back streets around Plaza Mayor and Plaza Santa Ana hold much of Madrid's most authentic charm. Paintings are Madrid's principal treasure and aside from the famous golden triangle – the Prado, the Thysssen-Bornemisza and the Centro Reina Sofía– the smaller repositories such as Descalzas Reales, Lázaro Galdano, Bellas Artes de San Fernando, the Sorolla Museums and Goya's tomb and frescoes in the Sant Antonio de la Florida church are not to be missed.

Bilbao

Frank Gehry's Bilbao Guggenheim transformed the city's economy from heavy industry to tourism, art and design, but don't overlook the Museo de Bellas Artes a few streets away. One of Spain's best museums, its permanent collection can rival the temporary exhibits at its headline-grabbing neighbour. The Casco Viejo, the oldest part of town, is filled with interesting architecture and the Museo Vasco, while the 19C Ensanche holds contemporary gems such as the culture and leisure Alhóndiga Bilbao centre.

Sevilla

Beyond the Alcázar, a stunning Moorish fortress, and the cathedral with its iconic Giralda bell tower, Sevilla's Barrio de Santa Cruz is filled with romantic corners and irresistible bars and taverns. Triana, the old gypsy and fishermen's quarter across the Guadalquivir river, has flamenco secrets and restaurants along the river, while the Barrio de la Macarena and its produce market, the Museo de Bellas Artes, and the Convento de Santa Paula complete the list of must-see sites.

Temperature chart (°C)

Maximum temperatures in black. Minimum temperatures in red.

Month	Jan	Feb	Mar	Apr	May	Jun	Jul	Aug	Sep	Oct	Nov	Dec
Barcelona	6	7	9	11	14	18	21	21	19	15	11	7
	9	11	15	18	21	27	31	30	26	19	13	9
Madrid	1	2	5	7	10	14	17	17	14	9	5	2
	12	12	15	15	17	20	22	22	21	18	15	12
Santander	7	6	8	9	11	14	16	16	15	12	9	7
	15	17	20	23	26	32	36	36	32	26	20	16
Sevilla	6	6	9	11	13	17	20	20	18	14	10	7
	15	16	8	20	23	26	29	29	27	23	19	16
Valencia	5	6	8	10	13	16	19	20	17	13	9	6

Valencia

The Ciutat de les Arts i les Ciències and the Museu de les Ciències Príncipe Felipe with its space-ship-like Hemisfèric observatory have become symbols of the new Valencia. However, the city's Gothic architecture – exemplified in buildings such as La Lonja – and the lively Modernist Mercado Central, still dazzle. The latter rivals Barcelona's Boqueria in size and aesthetics, while the Palau de la Generalitat, the Palacio del Marquès de Dos Aguas and the Estación del Norte railway station are key visits.

SPAIN'S COASTLINES

Mediterranean Coast

Spain has thousands of miles of beautiful coastline, with the Mediterranean continuing to attract millions of Spanish and foreign visitors every year to its delightful waters and magnificent beaches.

The rugged and indented **Costa Brava**, or Wild Coast, with its charming coves and lively resorts, extends from north of Barcelona as far as the French border.

The **Levante** coast, characterised by long sandy beaches and built-up resorts such as Benidorm, Cullera and Gandía, continues to be as popular as ever. This area is also favoured by Spanish families, and is occupied by a large number of second homes.

The **Costa del Sol**, in particular the stretch between Málaga and Estepona, is a succession of luxury developments and golf courses. Marbella is considered the leading resort here, reinforced by its reputation as the playground of the international jet-set.

The remainder of the Andalucían coast is generally quieter, attracting mainly Spanish visitors.

The **Balearic Islands** are one of the country's most popular tourist destinations. Of the three main islands, Mallorca and Ibiza attract large numbers of Spanish and foreign (particularly German) visitors, who come here to enjoy their magnificent landscapes and beaches and lively nightlife. Menorca tends to be quieter, finding popularity with those in search of a more relaxing holiday.

Atlantic Coast

Spain's North Atlantic coast stretches from the Basque Country in the east to Galicia in the west. In general, its resorts are popular with Spanish visitors attracted by the temperate climate, delightful beaches, excellent fish and seafood, impressive landscapes and fascinating towns and cities, including renowned resorts such as Donostia-San Sebastián and Santander. With the exception of a few places, the coast of northern Spain has escaped the frenetic development of the Mediterranean, and as such has managed to preserve its natural beauty. Although less popular with foreign visitors, the **Costa de la Luz** (Coast of Light), stretching between the southernmost tip of Spain and the Portuguese border, has some of the country's finest beaches, dotted with charming family resorts and historic cities such as Cádiz, the oldest in Spain.

Canary Islands

The Canary Islands come into their own in winter, when thousands of visitors flock here to escape the cold of northern Europe. High season in the Canaries runs from November to April. The main tourist centres on the archipelago can be found in the south of Gran Canaria (Maspalomas, Playa del Inglés and Playa de San Agustín) and on Tenerife (Playa de las Américas to the south, and Puerto de la Cruz to the north).

NATIONAL PARKS

Spain is a country that acts as a bridge between Europe and Africa, and as such has a wealth of different landscapes including salt marshes, conifer forests, high mountains, desert areas and Mediterranean woodland. The country's national parks protect those areas of major ecological interest to ensure their continuing survival. The main aim of these parks is to preserve their unique flora and fauna and to control public access. In total, Spain has fourteen national parks – nine on the mainland and five spread across the islands.

For many animal and plant species, Spain's mountain parks provide the most southerly habitat in Europe.

MOUNTAIN PARKS

The country's first national park was the Parque de Montaña de Covadonga, established in 1918. In 1995, this protected area was significantly extended (from 16 925ha/41 822 acres to 64 600ha/159 626 acres) and became known as the **Parque Nacional de los Picos de Europa**. This magnificent area is characterised by breathtaking landscapes with glacial lakes and extensive forests of beech (between 800m/2 624ft and 1 500m/4 920ft) as well as chestnut and oak, where water, in the shape of rivers, streams, lagoons and lakes, is an ecological factor of great importance. In terms of fauna, the main species found here are chamois, mountain cats, polecats, foxes, otters, squirrels, imperial eagles and partridges, with the occasional sighting of the brown bear. The main types of fish found in the park's rivers are trout and salmon.

Windsurfing in Tarifa, Costa de la Luz

©Nick Stubbs/Bigstockphoto.com

The **Parque Nacional de Ordesa y Monte Perdido**, at the heart of the Pyrenees in the province of Huesca, covers an area of 15 608ha/38 567 acres, and was also established in 1918.

The park is spread across four valleys, in which the landscape is dominated by rushing mountain rivers and streams, waterfalls, impressive precipices and forests of mountain pine, beech and fir, inhabited by mountain goats, wild boar, foxes, pine martens, otters and more.

The present-day appearance of the **Parc Nacional d'Aigüestortes i Estany de Sant Maurici**, covering 9 851ha/24 342 acres in the province of Lleida, in the Catalan Pyrenees, was created by the glaciers that invaded this area during the Quaternary era. The park's varied landscape includes lakes, forests of mountain pine and fir, and Alpine meadows, populated by mountain goats, wild boar, ermine, pine martens, dormice, imperial eagles, capercaillie and partridge.

The **Sierra Nevada** (90 000ha/222 390 acres) is a mountain park with several summits over 3 000m/9 840ft, including Mulhacén, the highest peak on mainland Spain at 3 478m/11 413ft. This range is also renowned for the variety of its flora and fauna, the result of the unique climatic conditions and topographical features.

The **Parque Nacional Monfragüe** (18 118ha/44 770 acres) runs westward along the River Tagus in Extremadura. The landscape varies from scrubland to mountainous ridges populated by deer, eagles and foxes.

Flatland Park

The **Parque Nacional de Cabañeros** is spread across a flatland area between two rocky formations in the Montes de Toledo. This protected national park covering some 40 000ha/98 840 acres is characterised by a Mediterranean-style wooded landscape abundant with deer, wild boar and birds of prey, in particular black and griffon vultures.

Wetland Parks

The Tablas de Daimiel and the Parque Nacional de Doñana are of vital ecological importance due to the protection they offer flora and fauna in danger of extinction, and their role as a breeding, migration and wintering area for numerous species of birds.

The **Tablas de Daimiel**, in the province of Ciudad Real is the smallest of Spain's national parks, with an area of just 1 928ha/4 764 acres. The flooding of the Cigüela and Guadiana rivers has resulted in the formation of areas of shallow bodies of water ideal for the creation of typical marshland vegetation that has been colonised by various species of birds, some of which migrate here for the winter or to nest (grey herons, lesser egrets, red-crested pochard, for example).

The extraordinary wealth of species in the **Parque Nacional de Doñana** (50 720ha/125 329 acres) is the result of its three distinct habitats: coastal dunes, salt marshes, and former hunting grounds or *cotos*. Its strategic location on the southern tip of Europe, almost within sight of the coast of Africa, has resulted in its development as an important wetland for migratory birds. Various birds and animals in danger of extinction can still be found here, such as the Iberian lynx, the ichneumon and the imperial eagle.

Tablas de Daimiel

Parks On The Spanish Islands

The **Parque Nacional Marítimo-Terrestre de Las Islas Atlánticas de Galicia** comprises the four archipelagos of Cíes, Ons, Sálvora and Cortegada, which lie off the coast of Pontevedra. The **Cabrera archipelago**, in the Balearics, stretches across an area of some 10 000ha/ 24 700 acres. The remaining four parks not on the Spanish mainland are found in the Canary Islands: the **Parque Nacional del Teide**, on Tenerife; the **Caldera de Taburiente**, on the island of La Palma; **Timanfaya**, on Lanzarote; and **Garajonay**, on the island of La Gomera.

OVER THE BORDER

If you're staying close to Spain's national borders, you may wish to consider a day trip into southwest France or Portugal to visit a number of sights of interest within easy distance. *The Green Guide* collection covers these areas (*Atlantic Coast; Languedoc Roussillon Tarn Gorges; and Portugal*), in addition to the **Michelin Guide France**, the **Michelin Guide España & Portugal**, and a comprehensive range of maps and plans to enhance your touring itineraries.

PLACES OF INTEREST CLOSE TO THE SPANISH BORDER

France

Across the border from the province of **Guipúzcoa**, the Basque Country of France boasts some of the country's most beautiful and most famous resorts such as St Jean de Luz, Biarritz and Bayonne.

Less than 30km/18.6mi from **Roncesvalles** (Navarra) is the town of St-Jean-Pied-de-Port, a famous staging-post on the Camino de Santiago. From various passes in the **Pirineos Aragoneses** such as Somport and Portalet, it is possible to drive into the Parc National des Pyrénées, a protected area within the French Pyrenees. From the **Pirineos Catalanes**, you can cross the border to admire the impressive landscapes on the French side of the range north

Parque Nacional de Garajonay, La Gomera

©Turespaña

of the Garonne headwaters in the Vall d'Aran and, further east, the Cerdanya Valley, which is half in France, half in Spain. From **Cerbère** (Girona), the coast road winds its way north to the delightful village of Collioure, cradle of the Fauvistes and where poet Antonio Machado died, and then inland to Perpignan, capital of French Catalunya.

Portugal

Opposite the Galician town of **Tui/ Tuy** and linked by a bridge designed by Gustave Eiffel over the River Miño, stands Valença do Minho, where you can ascend Monte do Faro to enjoy a magnificent view.

To the south lies **Puebla de Sanabria**, in the province of Zamora. It is well worth visiting the historic Portuguese city of Braganza, while from **Ciudad Rodrigo** you may wish to explore the fortified town of Almeida.

From **Cáceres**, the N 521 runs directly west into Portugal and the attractive mountain landscapes of the Serra de São Mamede, including the fortified town of Marvão and Castelo de Vide. The walled town of Elvas is located just across the border from **Badajoz**, with Estremoz and its attractive old quarter some 50km/31mi further west.

Ayamonte, the closest town to Portugal in southern Spain, is the perfect starting-point from which to explore the summer playground of the Algarve, with its beautiful beaches, lively resorts and quaint fishing villages.

What to See and Do

OUTDOOR FUN

As a result of its climate and varied landscapes, Spain is able to offer a whole range of activities for nature-lovers and outdoor sports enthusiasts.

WINTER SPORTS

There are 35 ski resorts in Spain including 19 in the Pyrenees, six in the Cordillera Cantábrica, four in the Cordillera Central, three in the Cordillera Ibérica, two in the Sierra Nevada (near Granada), one on La Rioja's Sierra de la Demada and an indoor ski slope in Madrid. Information on these is available from the **Federación Española de Deportes de Invierno** (*Avenida de los Madroños 36, 28043 Madrid; ℘913 76 99 30; www.rfedi.es*), or from **ATUDEM** (*Asociación Turística de Estaciones de Esquí y Montaña, Calle Padre Damián 43, 1°, office 11, 28036 Madrid; ℘913 59 15 17; snow conditions: ℘913 50 20 20; www.esquiespana.org*). Maps and brochures showing the major resorts, including their altitude and facilities (ski-lifts, downhill and cross-country runs), are available from tourist offices.

GOLF

There are over 400 golf courses across the country, a number that is steadily growing, particularly in coastal areas. For further information, contact the **Real Federación Española de Golf** (*calle Provisional Arroyo del Fresno Dos, 5°, 28035 Madrid; ℘915 55 26 82; www.golfspainfederacion.com*). A map of golf courses is also available from tourist offices. Golf courses and their telephone numbers are also listed in the current edition of the **Michelin Guide Portugal Madeira** under the nearest town or city.

HUNTING

Spain boasts the largest hunting area of any European country, populated by big game including wild boar, red stag, roe deer, moufflon, and smaller prey such as partridge, pheasant, woodcock, rabbits, hare and duck. The hunting season generally runs from September to February, although this varies from species to species. Hunting and fishing permits can be obtained from local autonomous community authorities.

For further details, as well as information on the official hunting calendar, contact the **Real Federación Española de Caza** (*Calle Francos Rodríguez 70, 2°, 28039 Madrid; ℘913 11 14 11; www.fecaza.com*).

FISHING

Spain's 76 000km/47 235mi of river courses provide a wealth of options for freshwater fishing enthusiasts, although seasons can vary from one region to another. Fishing permits are issued by the Environment Agency (*Ministerio de Medio Ambiente; www.marm.es*) in the relevant autonomous community. For further information on sea and freshwater fishing, contact the **Federación Española de Pesca y Casting** (*Calle Navas de Tolosa 3, 1°, 28013 Madrid; ℘915 32 83 53; www.fepyc.es*).

SAILING

The waters of the Mediterranean and Atlantic are one of Spain's major attractions. As a result, hundreds of sailing clubs and pleasure marinas have been established along the coastlines. For further information, apply to the **Royal Sailing Federation** (*Real Federación de Vela Calle, Luis de Salazar 9, 28002 Madrid; ℘915 19 50 08; www.rfev.es*).

SCUBA-DIVING

The Spanish coast, in particular the waters of the Mediterranean, is becoming increasingly popular with scuba-divers, with the development of diving sites such as the Cabo de Gata, the Islas Medes, on the Costa Brava, and resorts in the Balearic and Canary islands. For further information, contact the **Spanish Scuba-Diving**

Federation *(Federación Española de Actividades Subacuáticas, Calle Santaló 15, 3° 1ª, 0821 Barcelona; ☎932 00 67 69; www.fedas.es).*

HIKING AND MOUNTAINEERING

Hiking is becoming increasingly popular across Spain. For information on hiking routes and paths, as well as mountaineering, contact the **Spanish Mountaineering Federation** *(Federación Española de Deportes de Montaña y Escalada, Calle Floridablanca 84, 08015 Barcelona; ☎934 26 42 67; www.fedme.es).*

HORSE RIDING

A wide choice of options is available to horse-riding enthusiasts, ranging from short excursions to treks lasting several days. Every autonomous community has a large number of companies and organisations offering equestrian activities. For further information, contact the **Spanish Horse Riding Federation** *(Federación Hípica Española; calle Monte Esquinza 28, 3º, 28010 Madrid; ☎914 36 42 00; www.rfhe.com).*

OTHER SPORTS

Information on clubs offering paragliding, hang-gliding, microlight flying, rafting, etc. is available from local tourist offices.

SPAS

The hectic pace of modern life has resulted in an increasing number of people visiting the country's spa resorts for a few days in which to relax, recharge their batteries and help ease certain illnesses and ailments through treatments that are based on the medicinal qualities of the resorts' mineral-rich waters.

Generally speaking, spa complexes are found in areas of outstanding beauty where visitors and patients are also able to enjoy the surrounding nature and leisure facilities available. In Spain, there are a number of spa resorts dotted around the country, inheriting a tradition that has been passed down from the Greeks, Romans and Moors. For information on the treatments and facilities available at individual spas, contact the **National Spa Resort Association** *(Asociación Nacional de Balnearios, Calle Rodríguez San Pedro 56, 3º, 28015 Madrid; ☎915 49 03 00; www.balnearios.org).*

ACTIVITIES FOR KIDS

In this guide, sights of particular interest to children are indicated with a KIDS symbol (👥). Some attractions may offer discounted fees for children. In recent years, the number of leisure attractions popular with families has increased dramatically with the opening of several theme and water parks.

Horse riding in Sierra Nevada

©Turespaña

The following are just a few examples of places that will guarantee a fun day out for both children and their parents.

The country's best-known theme parks are **Port Aventura** *(near Reus Airport, Tarragona; www.portaventura.co.uk)*, **Terra Mítica** *(Benidorm; www.terra miticapark.com)*, **Isla Mágica** *(Sevilla; www.islamagica.es)* and **Warner Bros. Park** *(on the outskirts of Madrid; www.parquewarner.com)*.

Wildlife parks, such as the **Parque de la Naturaleza de Cabárceno** *(near Santander; www.parquedecabarceno. com)*, zoos and aquariums (Barcelona, Madrid, Benidorm, Donostia-San Sebastián, and O Grove, in Galicia), continue to be popular with youngsters of all ages, as do the bird and animal parks in the Canary Islands, including the Parque Ecológico Las Águilas del Teide, **Loro Parque** *(www.loroparque.com)* and Cactus and Animal Park (all on Tenerife); Palmitos Park, on Gran Canaria; and Tropical Park, on Lanzarote.

The Spanish coastline, particularly the Mediterranean, boasts numerous **water parks**, which are invariably full throughout the summer.

Interactive science museums, such as those in Valencia, Granada and A Coruña, offer an interesting and educational alternative to the leisure options above, as does a visit to the **Parque Minero de Riotinto** *(near Huelva; www.parquemineroderiotinto. com)*, where visitors are transported by miners' train to discover this fascinating site.

Lastly, for those families on holiday close to Almería, a visit to **Oasys**, a desert park where many of the early Spaghetti Westerns were filmed, is an absolute must for young and old alike.

WINE TOURS

La Rioja, El Penedès, El Priorat and the Rías Baixas wineries in Galicia all offer interesting wine tours through histric wineries, many of them endowed with contemporary architecture. Frank Gehry's wine spa at the **Marqués de Riscal** winery in Elciego in the Rioja Alavesa is the most spectacular encounter of hospitality, architecture and oenology, but there are other eye-knocking visits to be made, such as the **Bodegas Ysios** winery in Laguardia, designed by Pritzker prizewinner Santiago Calatrava, or the **Alvaro Palacios** winery in Gratallops in the El Priorat region south of Barcelona. Agustín Santolaya's Bodegas Roda, in Haro, not only makes one of Spain's top wines, Cirsión, but also showcases modern winemaking techniques. Jerez de la Frontera and Sanlúcar de Barrameda offer tours and tastings of sherry and cognac wineries, while in the Ribera de Duero district northwest of Madrid, mythical wineries such as Vega Sicilia, Pingus and Abadia Retuerta offer tastings and vineyard tours. **Cellar Tours** *(www.cellartours.com)* organises wine tourism in Spain, while **Epicurean Ways** *(www.epicureanways.com)* and A Taste of Spain *(www.atasteofspain. com)* are expert at contracting top British and American wine experts to accompany groups through the finest wineries and cultural destinations in any of Spain's ever-more-numerous winegrowing regions.

CYCLING

Spain offers a plethora of famous cycling routes in the mountains and on flatter terrain. From the Pyrenees to the Picos de Europa to the Alpujarras of Granada there is no shortage of scenic highland riding for the fit and ambitious. The **three-nation loop** through Spain, Andorra and France – beginning and ending in La Seu d'Urgell – is a physical challenge with stunning Pyreneen scenery.

For flatland cycling, the Delta del Ebro south of Tarragona and the Cerdanya Valley in the Pyrenees north of Barcelona have a remarkably level network of roads for easy riding. Cycling the Basque coast along the old corniche road that follows the edge of the Bay of Biscay is a perfect way to see fishing villages and rural farmhouses that motorists miss. The **Via de la Plata** route from Sevilla to Santiago de Compostela is a favourite cycling journey, while the Baix Empordà region in northern Catalunya has 19 bike routes through some of the Costa Brava's most picturesque and often overlooked inland villages. Spain also has 1 800km/1 120mi of abandoned railway lines that have been converted to **Vías Verdes** (green paths). Check www.viasverdes.com for itineraries.

HIKING

Long-distance hiking trails (designated GR for **Gran Recorrido**) can take you all over peninsular Spain as well as through the most scenic parts of the Balearic and Canary Islands. The GR11 is the six-to-seven-week trans-Pyrenean trail that begins at Cabo Higuer west of Hondarribia and ends at Cap de Creus, the Iberian Peninsula's easternmost point just north of Cadaqués.

The GR11 intersects with the HRP (Haute Randonnée Pyrénéenne) which follows the Pyrenean crest on either side of the France-Spain border. Other famous hikes include the **Alberes Mountains** walk from Puig Neulós above the Le Perthus French border crossing to Banyuls-sur-Mer (one day) or Cap de Creus (two days). The climb from Núria to the Coll de Núria followed by the traverse east over the Sierra de Catllar to the refuge at Ulldeter is an unforgettable challenge with panoramic views north and south from the crest of the Pyrenees. The **Parc Nacional d'Aiguestortes i Estany de Sant Maurici** offers excellent trekking between late May and September. Parque Nacional de Ordesa y Monte Perdido has a good day trip up to the Cola de Caballo waterfall and back or with an overnight up at the Refugio de Góriz overlooking Spain's Grand Canyon.

SHOPPING

Spain has a rich tradition of arts and crafts reflecting the character of each region as well as the influence of the civilisations – Iberian, Roman, Visigothic and Muslim – that have marked the country's history. Traditional wares such as pottery, ceramics, basketwork and woven goods are produced countrywide.

POTTERY AND CERAMICS

The difference between pottery and ceramics is that pottery has been baked just once. In Castilla, pottery is mainly made by women who use a primitive technique. Among their specialities are kitchen utensils, jars and water pitchers. The basic items of crockery used in farmhouses – dishes, soup tureens and bowls made of glazed earthenware *(barro cocido)* – appear in villages and on stalls in every market. Many of the techniques (metal lustre, *cuerda seca*, decorative motifs, and colour) used in ceramics have been influenced by Islamic traditions. There are two large pottery centres in the Toledo region. The first, **Talavera de la Reina**, is famous for its blue, green, yellow, orange and black ceramics, while the second, **El Puente del Arzobispo**, mainly uses shades of green. Pottery from **La Bisbal d'Empordà** in Catalunya has a yellow background with green decorative motifs. The Mudéjar tradition is evident in Aragón and the Levante region where blue and white pottery is made in **Muel**, green and purple ceramics in **Teruel** and lustreware in **Manises** (in the province of Valencia). Most of the figurines used as decoration for cribs at Christmas are produced in **Murcia**. Spain's richest pottery region is Andalucía, with workshops in **Granada** (glazed ceramics with thick green and blue strokes), **Guadix** (red crockery), **Triana** in Sevilla (polychrome animal figures, glazed and decorated), **Úbeda** in Jaén, **Andújar** (jars with cobalt blue patterns) and in **Vera** (white pottery with undulating shapes). In Galicia, porcelain and earthenware goods with contemporary shapes and designs have been factory-made since 1806 at the **Sargadelos** centre in the province of A Coruña, but there is also a craft industry at **Niñodaguia** in Ourense (where the yellow glaze only partially covers the pottery) and at **Bruño** (where yellow motifs set off a dark brown background). Mention should be made of the famous *xiurels*, whistles decorated in red and green from the Balearic Islands.

LACE, WOVEN AND EMBROIDERED GOODS

The textile industry prospered under the Muslims and several workshops still thrive today. Brightly coloured blankets and carpets are woven in the Alpujarras region, La Rioja, the area around Cádiz (Grazalema) and at Níjar near Almería (where *tela de trapo* carpets are made from strips of cloth). Blankets from Zamora, Palencia and Salamanca are well known.

The village of **El Paso**, on the island of La Gomera in the Canary Islands, is the only place in Spain that still produces silk fabrics.

In some villages in the province of Ciudad Real (particularly in **Almagro**) female lacemakers may still be seen at work in their doorways with bobbins and needles. Lacework from **Camariñas** in Galicia is also widely known. The most popular craft, however, is embroidery, often done in the family. The most typical, geometrically patterned embroideries, come from the Toledo region (**Lagartera** and **Oropesa**). Embroidery has been raised to the level of an art form in two thoroughly Spanish domains: firstly, in the ornaments used for *pasos* during Holy Week and secondly, in the bullfighters' costume, *traje de luces*.

METALWORK

Iron forging, a very old practice in Spain, has produced outstanding works of art such as the wrought-iron grilles and screens that adorn many churches. Blacksmiths continue to make the grilles for doors and windows so popular in architecture in the south of Spain (La Mancha, Extremadura and Andalucía).

Guadalupe, in Extremadura, is an important centre for copper production (boilers, braziers, etc.). Damascene weapons (steel inlaid with gold, silver and copper) are still produced, in **Eibar** (País Vasco) and in **Toledo** particularly, according to pure Islamic tradition. The best switchblades and knives in Spain are produced in **Albacete**, Las Palmas de Gran Canaria and Taramundi (Asturias).

Gold- and silver-smithing were developed in antiquity and throughout the Visigothic period and have retained some traditional methods. One example is filigree ornamentation (soldered, intertwined gold and silver threads) crafted in **Córdoba** and **Toledo**. Salamanca, Cáceres and Ciudad Rodrigo specialise in gold jewellery. **Santiago de Compostela** is the world's leading centre for black amber ornaments.

LEATHERWORK

Leather-making has always been an important trade, especially in Andalucía, and has become industrialised in some areas. The town of **Ubrique** (in the province of Cádiz) is the leading producer of leatherwork in Spain, followed by the Alicante area and the Balearic Islands. The production of famous **Córdoba** leather, including embossed polychrome leatherwork, continues to the same high standards.

Workshops specialising in the manufacture of harnesses and horse-riding and hunting accessories are predominantly found in Andalucía (Jerez de la Frontera, Alcalá de los Gazules, Villamartín, Almodóvar del Río and Zalamea la Real).

Typically Spanish gourds and wineskin containers are made in the provinces of Bilbao, Pamplona and Burgos and in other wine-growing areas. The wineskins produced in Valverde del Camino (Huelva) are known throughout Spain.

BASKETWORK

Basket-making remains one of the most representative of Spanish crafts. Although carried out countrywide, it is particularly rich on the Mediterranean coast and in the Balearic Islands.

The type of product and the material used vary from region to region. Baskets, hats and mats are made of reeds, willow, *esparto* grass, strips of olive-wood and birch and chestnut bark, while furniture may be rush or wickerwork. Willow is used in Andalucía and in the Levante, hazel and chestnut in Galicia and Asturias, and straw and *esparto* grass on the island of Ibiza.

SIGHTSEEING

Opening times and entrance fees for monuments, museums, churches, etc. are included in the *Discovering Spain* section of this guide. This information is given as a guideline only, as times and prices are liable to change without prior warning.

Prices shown are for individual visitors and do not take into account discounts for groups, who may also benefit from private visits.

As many monuments require frequent maintenance and restoration, it is advisable to phone ahead to avoid disappointment.

Information for churches is only given if the interior contains a sight of particular interest with specific opening times or if an entrance fee is payable. In general, religious buildings should not be visited during services, although some only open for Mass, in which case visitors should show appropriate respect.

BOOKS
Biography

Franco – Paul Preston (1994; 2004). A definitive life of the man who ruled Spain from 1936 until his death in 1975.

Reinventing Food – Colman Andrews (2010). The authorised biography of El Bulli chef Ferran Adrià.

REFERENCE

Barcelona – Robert Hughes (1992; 2001). An enthusiastic and scholarly celebration of the coming-out of Catalunya's distinct culture after Franco.

Barcelonawalks – George Semler (1992). Walking tours filled with anecdotes and reflections on Barcelona, Catalunya and life in the Med.

HISTORY

Moorish Spain – Richard Fletcher (1992; 2001). An illumination through literature and history of the culture that was expelled from Spain but never expurgated.

Homage to Catalonia – George Orwell (1938; 2003). An inside look at the Spanish Civil War from the Republican side, and the Communist purges that engulfed Barcelona in 1937.

FICTION

Don Quixote de La Mancha – Miguel de Cervantes Saavedra (1605; 2008). The classic novel of Castille and of Spanish character.

The Cathedral of the Sea – Ildefonso Falcones (2006). A *Pillars-of-the- Earth*-like historical novel about the construction of Barcelona's Santa María del Mar basilica.

The Sun Also Rises – Ernest Hemingway (1926). The Lost Generation takes on Pamplona's San Fermín festival.

For Whom the Bell Tolls – Ernest Hemingway (1938). Hemingway's story of a young American idealist fighting for the Republic in the Spanish Civil War.

Southern Seas – Manuel Vázquez Montalbán (1979; 1999). An acclaimed episode of the author's Pepe Carvalho series, involving murder, lust and nouvelle cuisine, set in Barcelona.

The Shadow of the Wind – Carlos Ruiz Zafón (2001; 2005). Contemporary allegory of post-Civil War Barcelona infused with Latin American magical realism.

TRAVEL

Death in the Afternoon – Ernest Hemingway (1932; 2007). A terse take on tauromarchy, tradition, and the Spanish soul.

Iberia – James A Michener (1968; 1989). Vintage Michener in a ramble through vintage Spain in the throes of entering modern Europe.

Driving over Lemons – Chris Stewart (1999). An account of unconventional living in rural Granada.

South from Granada – Gerald Brenan (1957; 2008). A literary and folkloric account of Spain in the last century.

Spain – Jan Morris (1970; 2008). The Morris take on Spain: history, encounters and pleasures.

The Way of St James – Alison Raju (2000; 2008). A modern guide to one of the first tourist routes.

ART

The Shameful Life of Salvador Dalí – Ian Gibson (1997). Brilliant portrait of a tortured soul.

Picasso – Timothy Hilton (1976). An attempt to define the Spanish master's place in world art.

FILMS

Un Chien Andalou (An Andalusian Dog; 1929). The surrealist masterpiece by Luis Buñuel and Salvador Dalí.

Las Hurdes (Land Without Bread, 1933). Buñuel charts the hard lives of peasants of an Extremaduran *comarca.*

Surcos (Furrows; 1951). A neo-realist drama by José Antonio Nieves Conde about the disintegration of a family unit in Franco's Madrid.

La Caza (The Hunt; 1966). A thriller by Carlos Saura about war veterans whose reunion turns to violence.

Cría Cuervos (Raise Ravens; 1976). A symbolic criticism of the Franco regime by Saura, with a haunting soundtrack by Jeanette.

Mujeres al Borde de un Ataque de Nervios (Women on the Verge of a Nervous Breakdown; 1988). Pedro Almodóvar's feminist comedy, marking his international breakthrough.

Jamón, Jamón (Ham, Ham; 1992). Bigas Luna's satire on Iberian machismo starring Penélope Cruz and Javier Bardem.

Los Amantes del Círculo Polar (The Lovers of the Arctic Circle; 1998). An homage to love and fate by Julio Medem.

Land and Freedom (1995). A Liverpudlian's experience of fighting for the Republic in the Civil War, with a narrative comparable to Orwell's *Homage to Catalonia.*

Hable con Ella (Talk to Her; 2002). An Oscar winner by Almodóvar about two men and their devotion to the comatose women who they love.

Mar Adentro (The Sea Inside; 2004). Amenábar's Oscar-winning biopic about Ramón Sampedro and his struggle with disability.

El Laberinto del Fauno (Pan's Labyrinth; 2006). In post-Civil War Spain, a young girl embraces her fantasy world, sumptuously brought to life by Guillermo del Toro.

Vicky Cristina Barcelona (2008). A Woody Allen comedy about two friends on a holiday in Spain and their entanglement with Javier Bardem's painter.

Biutiful (2010). Directed by México's Alejandro González Iñárritu, starring Javier Bardem, and set in Barcelona, this chronicle of a man in free-fall is a portrait of the city's seamy and steamy underbelly, the flip side of *Vicky Cristina Barcelona.*

Agnosia (2010). Eugenio Mira's psychological and romantic thriller about a woman suffering from agnosia (the inability to recognize faces) is set in an opulent late 19C Barcelona.

Pa Negre (Pan Negro or *Black Bread; 2010).* Beautifully filmed post-Spanish Civil War drama by Agustí Villaronga about a young boy drawn into the lives and lies of the adults around him, and the ideological purges of post-Civil War Spain.

Balada Triste de Trompeta (Sad Trumpet Ballad; 2010). Alex de la Iglesia's drama about two 1973 circus clowns fighting for the love of a dancer is borderline surreal but riveting.

Una hora más en Canarias (One More Hour in the Canaries; 2010). David Serrano's musical comedy set in the Canary Islands follows a guy on holiday with his new girlfriend, with his ex hot on his heels.

Calendar of Events

Spain's major festivals are mentioned in the list below. In order to confirm exact dates and times, which may vary slightly, contact the relevant local tourist office, which will be able to provide an up-to-date calendar of events. During the summer months, practically every small town and village in the country hosts a fiesta in honour of its own patron saint.

6 JANUARY
Three Kings Day
Sitges *(www.sitges.cat)*

20 JANUARY
San Sebastián Day: La Tamborrada
San Sebastián *(www.donostia.org)*

WEEK BEFORE ASH WEDNESDAY
Carnival festivities
Cádiz *(www.carnavaldecadiz.com)*
Santa Cruz de Tenerife
(www.santacruzmas.com)

1ST SUNDAY IN MARCH
International Vintage Car Rally
Sitges *(www.rallyesitges.com)*

3RD SUNDAY IN LENT
Feast of the Magdalen bullfights, processions
Castellón de la Plana
(http://fiestasmagdalena.es/blog)

12–19 MARCH
Las Fallas Festival
Valencia
(www.fallasfromvalencia.com)

HOLY WEEK
Processions
Cartagena, Cuenca, Málaga, Murcia, Sevilla, Valladolid, Zamora

FIRST WEEK AFTER EASTER
Spring Festival
Murcia *(www.murciaciudad.com/ ingles/fiestas)*

APRIL
April Fair
Sevilla *(http://feriadesevilla. andalunet.com)*

22–24 OR 24–26 APRIL
St George's Festival: "Moors and Christians"
Alcoi *(www.ajualcoi.org/festes)*

LAST SUNDAY IN APRIL
Romería (pilgrimage) to the Virgen de la Cabeza
Andújar *(www.ayto-andujar.es)*

LATE APRIL–EARLY MAY
Horse Fair
Jerez de la Frontera
(www.webjerez.com)
Las Cruces Festival
Córdoba
(www.turismodecordoba.org)

WEEK OF 15 MAY
San Isidro Festival
Madrid *(www.las-ventas.com)*

WHITSUN
Pilgrimage to the Nuestra Señora del Rocío shrine
El Rocío *(www.hermandad matrizrocio.org)*
La Caballada Festival
Atienza *(www.atienza.es)*

2nd SUNDAY AFTER WHITSUN
Corpus Christi Celebration.
Streets carpeted with flowers,
competitions, processions
Puenteareas
(*www.riasbaixas.depo.es*)
Sitges (*www.sitgestour.com*)
Toledo (*www.toledo-turismo.com*)

23–24 JUNE
"Hogueras" St John's Festival
Alicante (*www.hogueras.org*)
Midsummer's Day Festival
Ciutadella
(*http://santjoan.ajciutadella.org*)

1st SUNDAY IN JULY
"A Rapa das Bestas" Festival
A Estrada (*www.riasbaixas.depo.es*)

6–14 JULY
**San Fermín Festival, the running
of the bulls**
Pamplona
(*www.bullrunning.info/eng*)

1st SATURDAY IN AUGUST
Kayak races on the River Sella
Arriondas y Ribadesella
(*www.descensodelsella.com*)

14–15 AUGUST
Elche Mystery Play
Elche (*www.misteridelx.com*)

LAST WEDNESDAY IN AUGUST
La Tomatina
Buñol (*www.latomatina.es*)

7–17 SEPTEMBER
Fair (Feria)
Albacete (*http://feria-de-albacete.
albacity.org*)

21 SEPTEMBER
St Matthew's Festival
Oviedo (*www.ayto-oviedo.es*)

20–26 SEPTEMBER
La Rioja Wine Harvest Festival
Logroño (*www.logro-o.org*)

24 SEPTEMBER
**Festival of Our Lady of Mercy
(Virgen de la Merced)**
Barcelona
(*www.barcelonaturisme.com*)

8 OCTOBER
Procession of the Virgin
Guadalupe (*www.monasterio
guadalupe.com*)

WEEK OF 12 OCTOBER
Pilar Festival
Zaragoza (*www.zaragoza.es*)

CULTURAL FESTIVALS
HOLY WEEK
Sacred Music Festival
Cuenca (*www.smrcuenca.es*)

LATE JUNE–MID-JULY
**International Music and
Dance Festival**
Granada (*www.granadafestival.org*)

JULY
**International Classical
Theatre Festival**
Almagro
(*www.festivaldealmagro.com*)

MID-JULY
Jazz Festival
Vitoria (*www.jazzvitoria.com*)

LAST WEEK OF JULY
Jazz Festival
Donostia-San Sebastián
(*www.donostia.org*)

LATE JULY–LATE AUGUST
Classical Theatre Festival
Mérida (*www.festivaldemerida.es*)
Castell de Perelada Festival
Peralada
(*www.festivalperalada.com*)

LAST FORTNIGHT IN SEPTEMBER
**San Sebastián International
Film Festival**
Donostia-San Sebastián
(*www.sansebastianfestival.com*)

FIRST FORTNIGHT IN OCTOBER
**Catalunya International
Film Festival**
Sitges *(www.cinemasitges.com)*

LAST WEEK IN OCTOBER
Seminci (International Film Week)
Valladolid *(www.seminci.com)*

MID-NOVEMBER
Ibero-American Film Festival
Huelva *(www.festicinehuelva.com)*

Know Before You Go

USEFUL WEBSITES

www.spain.info
The official site of the Spanish
Tourist Board, providing
comprehensive information on all
aspects of the country, including
transport, accommodation, sport
and leisure activities.

www.tourspain.co.uk
The Spanish Tourist Board's site for
visitors from the UK.

www.okspain.org
The Spanish Tourist Board's site for
visitors from the US.

www.tourspain.toronto.on.ca
The Spanish Tourist Board's site for
Canadian visitors.

www.fco.gov.uk
The British Government's Foreign and
Commonwealth Office website provides
up-to-date information on travel.

www.state.gov
American visitors may check the
US State Department website for
travel advice.

www.fac-aec.gc.ca
Website of Foreign Affairs Canada
with relevant travel updates.

www.tourspain.es
The business-to-business site of the
Spanish Tourist Board is useful for
travel professionals.

TOURIST OFFICES

◆ **London**
2nd floor, 79 New Cavendish Street
London W1W 6XB
℘(020) 7317 2010

◆ **New York**
35th Floor, 666 Fifth Avenue
New York, NY 10103
℘212 265 8822

◆ **Chicago**
Water Tower Place, Suite 915 East
845 North Michigan Avenue
Chicago, IL 60611
℘312 642 1992

◆ **Los Angeles**
8383 Wilshire Blvd, Suite 960
Beverly Hills, CA 90211
℘323 658 7195

◆ **Miami**
1395 Brickell Avenue,
Miami, FL 33131
℘305 358 1992

◆ **Toronto**
2 Bloor St West, Suite 3402
Toronto, Ontario M4W 3E2
℘416 961 3131

INTERNATIONAL VISITORS
EMBASSIES AND CONSULATES

US Embassy
Serrano 75, 28006 Madrid
℘91 587 22 00 (emergencies
℘91 587 22 40). www.embusa.es

US Consulates
Paseo Reina Elisenda de
Montcada 23, 08034 Barcelona
℘93 280 22 27

In addition there are consular agencies in

Málaga ☎952 47 48 91
Sevilla ☎954 21 87 51
Valencia ☎963 51 69 73
Las Palmas ☎928 27 12 59
A Coruña ☎981 21 32 33
Palma de Mallorca ☎971 40 37 07

Australian Embassy

Torre Espacio, Paseo de la Castellana, 259D, Planta 24, 28046 Madrid
☎913 53 66 00
www.embaustralia.es

British Embassy

Calle Fernando el Santo 16
28010 Madrid
☎917 00 82 00
www.ukinspain.fco.gov.uk

British Consulate-General

Paseo de Recoletos 7–9, 4º
28004 Madrid
☎91 524 97 00

British Consular Offices

Alicante ☎965 21 60 22
Barcelona ☎933 66 62 00
Bilbao ☎944 15 77 22
Granada ☎ 669 89 50 53
Ibiza ☎971 30 18 18
Las Palmas, Canary Islands
☎928 26 25 08
Málaga ☎952 35 23 00
Palma de Mallorca, Mallorca
☎971 71 24 45
Santa Cruz de Tenerife, Canary Islands ☎922 28 68 63

Canadian Embassy

Calle Núñez de Balboa 35
28001 Madrid
☎914 23 32 50
www.espana.gc.ca

Canadian Consulate

Barcelona ☎934 12 72 36
Málaga ☎952 22 33 46

Embassy of Ireland

Ireland House, Paseo de la Castellana 46, 4ª
28046 Madrid
☎914 36 40 93

Honorary Irish Consulates

Alicante ☎965 10 74 85
Barcelona ☎934 91 50 21
Bilbao ☎944 23 04 14
El Ferrol ☎904 24 42 67
Lanzarote ☎928 81 52 62
Las Palmas, Canary Islands
☎928 29 77 28
Málaga ☎952 47 51 08
Palma de Mallorca
☎971 72 25 04
Sevilla ☎954 69 06 89
Santa Cruz de Tenerife
☎922 24 56 71

DOCUMENTS

Visitors must be in possession of a valid **passport**. Holders of British, Irish and US passports do not need a visa for a visit of up to 90 days. Visitors from some Commonwealth countries or those planning to stay longer than 90 days should enquire about visa requirements at their local Spanish consulate.

US citizens should view the International Travel Information for Spain online *(http://travel.state.gov/ travel)* for general information on visa requirements, customs regulations, medical care, etc.

CUSTOMS REGULATIONS

In the UK, **HM Revenue and Customs** *(www.hmrc.gov.uk;* ☎*0845 010 9000)* publishes *A Guide for Travellers* on customs regulations and duty-free allowances.

US Customs and Border Protection *(www.cbp.gov/xp/cgov/travel/vacation/ kbyg;* ☎*(877) CBP-5511)* offers a free publication *Know Before You Go* for download.

HEALTH

British and Irish citizens should apply for the European Health Insurance Card *(UK: ℰ0845 606 2030; www.ehic.org.uk or at a post office; Ireland: www.ehic.ie or at a local health office)* to obtain free or reduced-cost treatment in the EU. All visitors should consider insurance for uncovered medical expenses, lost luggage, theft, etc.

Pets (cats and dogs) – A general health certificate and proof of rabies vaccination should be obtained from your local vet before departure.

ACCESSIBILITY

Information on facilities for the disabled within Spain is available from Polibea, Ronda de la Avutarda 3, 28043 Madrid. ℰ917 59 53 72. www.polibea.com/turismo.

Getting There

BY PLANE

A number of Spanish and international airlines operate direct scheduled services to airports across Spain. These include:

- **Iberia Airlines:** ℰ902 400 500. www.iberia. com. Reservations within the UK: ℰ0870 609 0500; within the US and Canada: ℰ800 772 4642.
- **British Airways:** ℰ0844 493 0787. www.ba.com. Reservations within the US and Canada: ℰ800 247 9297.
- **Aer Lingus:** ℰ0818 365 000. www.aerlingus. com. Reservations within the UK: ℰ0870 876 2020.

A number of low-cost airlines also offer inexpensive flights to several Spanish cities from the UK and mainland Europe.
Some airlines only allow bookings to be made online, while others offer small discounts for internet bookings:

- **Bmibaby** www.bmibaby.com
- **EasyJet** www.easyjet.com
- **Flybe** www.flybe.com
- **Ryanair** www.ryanair.com
- **Vueling** www.vueling.com

Hundreds of weekly charter flights also operate from the UK to Spanish cities, particularly along the Mediterranean coast and in the Balearic and Canary islands.

BY SHIP

Brittany Ferries and P&O Ferries both operate services to northern Spain from the UK.

Brittany Ferries runs a ferry service from Plymouth (20hr journey time) and from Portsmouth to Santander (24hr journey) from mid-March to mid-November; for reservations, contact:

- **Brittany Ferries:** ℰ0871 244 0744 (UK); ℰ942 36 06 11 (Santander). www.brittany-ferries.com.

BY TRAIN

Eurostar (*ℰ08705 186 186; www.eurostar.com*) operates high-speed passenger trains from the UK to Paris, from where the overnight train-hotel services operate to Madrid via Orléans, Blois, Poitiers, Vitoria, Burgos and Valladolid; and Barcelona via Orléans, Limoges, Figueres and Girona. A coastal service between Montpellier and Valencia calls at Girona, Barcelona, Tarragona and Valencia. Services from Paris, as well as train tickets within Spain, can be booked through the Spanish State Railway Network's (RENFE) UK agent, the Spanish Rail Service: ℰ(020) 7725 7063; www.spanish-rail.co.uk. Alternatively, log-on to the official **RENFE** website at www.renfe.es. From Portugal, a daily service connects Lisbon with Madrid. The Sud Express train hotel between Paris and Lisbon calls at Irún on the French-

Spanish border, Burgos, Valladolid, Salamanca and Coimbra.
Useful websites for timetables, fares and online booking include *http://bahn.hafas.de and www.raileurope.co.uk*.

BY COACH/BUS

Regular long-distance bus services operate from London to all major towns and cities in Spain. For information, contact: **Eurolines**

UK: ✆08717 818 181. www.eurolines.co.uk.

Busabout (*✆08450 267 514; www.busabout.com*) offers a six-night seasonal hop-on-hop-off Explorer service from Madrid, with add-ons from European cities including London and Paris available. **Avanza** (*✆902 02 09 99; www.avanzabus.com*) runs two daily buses between Lisbon and Madrid.

Getting Around

BY PLANE

Spain has over 45 commercial airports, including 12 on the islands. Information on any of these is available from **AENA** (Aeropuertos Españoles y Navegación Aérea): ✆902 40 47 04.
www.aena.es.
The largest airports in the country are as follows:
* **Madrid-Barajas**
* **Barcelona**
* **Palma de Mallorca**
* **Málaga**
* **Gran Canaria**
* **Alicante**
* **Tenerife Sur-Reina Sofia**
* **Valencia**
* **Girona-Costa Brava**

MAJOR AIRLINE COMPANIES

* **Iberia:** Serviberia
  ✆902 400 500 (information and bookings).
  www.iberia.com.
* **Air Europa:**
  ✆902 40 15 01.
  www.aireuropa.com.
* **Spanair:**
  ✆902 13 14 15.
  www.spanair.com.

BY SHIP

Several ferry companies operate services between the Spanish mainland and the Balearics, Canaries, Italy and North Africa.

Trasmediterránea –
  Services between: Valencia to the Balearics; Barcelona to the Balearics, Livorno & Rome (Civitavecchia); Cádiz to the Canary Islands; Algeciras to Tanger & Ceuta; and Almería to Nador & Ghazaouet.
Information and reservations
  ✆902 45 46 45.
  www.trasmediterranea.es.
Regional offices:
* **Madrid** – Avenida Europa 10, Parque Empresarial La Moraleja, 28108 Madrid. ✆914 23 85 00.
* **Alicante** – Terminal MTMA del Sureste, 03001 Alicante.
  ✆965 20 08 41.
* **Barcelona** – Estació Marítima, Muelle San Beltrán, 08039 Barcelona.
  Fax 932 95 91 34.
* **Cádiz** – Estación Marítima Muelle Alfonso XIII, 11006 Cádiz.
  Fax 956 22 20 38.
* **Baleària** – Baleària operates services to and from the Balearics and from island to island. ✆902 160 180. www.balearia.com.
Regional offices:
* **Madrid** – Calle O'Donnell 38, 28009 Madrid.
  ✆914 09 14 42.
* **Barcelona** – Estació Marítima Drassanes, 08039 Barcelona.
  ✆933 24 89 80.
* **Denia (Alicante)** – Estación Marítima, 03700 Denia.
  ✆966 42 86 00.

BY TRAIN

RENFE ℘902 24 02 02; www.renfe.es.
AVE *(Alta Velocidad Española; www.renfe.es/ave)* high-speed trains run
from Madrid to:
    Sevilla (2hr30min)
    Valladolid (1hr)
    Barcelona (2hr45min)
    Huesca (2hr15min)
    Málaga (2hr45min)
and from Barcelona to:
    Sevilla (5hr40min)
    Málaga (5hr45min)

"Green" railway stations – Fifty stations are so designated *(estaciones verdes)* due to their location near

AVE high-speed train, Santa Justa station, Sevilla
G. Bludzin/MICHELIN

nature reserves, or because of their suitability for hikers, mountain-bikers or for nature lovers wishing to discover the beauty of rural Spain. Information about attractions near designated stations is available online at www.renfe.es/comunicacion/mundotren/medio_ambiente/index.html (Spanish).

TOURIST TRAINS

El Transcantábrico – This narrow-gauge train journeys from León to Santiago de Compostela via the shores of the Bay of Biscay.
The trip lasts eight days and combines rail and bus travel. The service operates from April to October. ⊗*Prices start from €2 600.* ℘902 55 59 02. www.transcantabrico.com.
El Tren de la Fresa – The Strawberry Train operates vintage carriages between Madrid and Aranjuez (50min), on Saturdays and Sundays

☺ **A Bit of Advice** ☺

In Spain, the word *calle* (or C., Castilian) or *carrer* (Catalan) for street is not generally denoted on maps or in addresses. Therefore, in the *Discovering* section, you may see street names without *calle* or *carrer* preceding them. However, *av.* (*avenida – avinguda* in Catalan), *ctra* (or *Ca.*, *carretera*), *pl.* (*plaza – plaça* in Catalan), *pso* (or *po.*, *paseo*) and *pas.* (*passeig – passatage* in Catalan) *are* indicated.

from 28 May to 30 September from the Museo del Ferrocarril near Atocha station (⊗€28; ℘902 24 02 02; www.renfe.es/trenfresa; www.museodelferrocarril.org).
El Tren de la Robla – Originally a coal carrier line from Bilbao to León and back in four days and three nights, offering spectacular scenery and old-world railroad luxe. There are also trains from Gijón to Ferrol and Santiago de Compostela (four days, three nights) or from Gijón to Ribadeo (two days, one night). ⊗*Prices range from €350 to €750.* ℘902 55 59 02. www.trenesturisticosdelujo.com.

BY METRO/TRAM

Eight cities in Spain host their own metro or light rail network and more are being constructed at the present time. The cities with networks are as follows: Alicante, Barcelona, Bilbao, Madrid, Valencia, Palma de Mallorca, Parma, and Santa Cruz de Tenerife (tram only).

BY COACH/BUS

The Spanish bus network is a comfortable, modern and relatively inexpensive way of travelling across the country. Numerous companies offer local and long-distance services. Information on routes, timetables and prices can be obtained from local bus stations.
Two of the companies with the largest networks are:

Alsa – Extensive routes across the country, particularly in the northwest, centre, and along the Mediterranean. *℘913 27 05 40. www.alsa.es.*

Avanzabus – Madrid-based company providing nationwide services. www.avanzabus.com.

BY CAR
ROAD NETWORK

Spain has over 343 000km/213 130mi of roads, including 9 000km/5 592mi of divided highways and expressways. **Speed limits** in Spain are as follows:

- **110kph/68mph** on expressways and divided highways
- **100kph/62mph** on the open road (with a hard shoulder of at least 1.5m/5ft)
- **90kph/56mph** on the open road (without a hard shoulder);
- **50kph/31mph** in built-up areas.

DOCUMENTS

In general, motorists need only have a current driving licence from their country of origin and valid papers (vehicle documentation and valid insurance) to drive in Spain, although in certain situations an International Driving Permit may be required. If in doubt, visitors should check with the AA *(www.theaa.com)* or RAC *(www.rac.co.uk)* in the United Kingdom or with the AAA *(www.aaa.com)* in the US.

DRIVING REGULATIONS

The minimum driving age is 18. Traffic drives on the right. It is compulsory for passengers in both front and rear seats to wear **seat belts**. Motorcyclists (on all sizes of machine) must wear safety helmets. It is now a legal requirement for motorists to carry two red warning triangles and reflective vests in addition to a spare tyre, first-aid kit and a set of replacement bulbs. ⊝Motorists should note that it is illegal to use a **cell/mobile phone** when driving, unless the vehicle is fitted with a hands-free unit. Heavy on-the-spot fines are frequent for those caught using hand-held phones.

INSURANCE

Those motorists entering Spain in their own vehicles should ensure that their insurance policy includes overseas cover. Visitors are advised to check with their respective insurance company prior to travel. Motorists are also advised to take out adequate **accident** and **breakdown** cover for their period of travel overseas. Various motoring organisations (AA, RAC, etc.) will be able to provide further details on options available. Bail bonds are no longer necessary, although travellers may wish to take this precaution (consult your insurance company). Members of the AAA should obtain the free brochure *Offices to Serve You Abroad*, which gives details of affiliated organisations in Spain. ⊝If the driver of the vehicle is not accompanied by the owner, he or she must have written permission from the owner to drive in Spain.

ROAD INFORMATION

The **National Traffic Agency** (Dirección General de Tráfico) is able to provide information in English on road conditions, driving itineraries, regulations, etc. *℘900 12 35 05.* www.dgt.es.

TOLLS

Tolls are payable on some sections of the Spanish highway network. On Michelin maps, these sections are indicated by kilometre markers in red; toll-free sections are marked in blue. Tolls are universally payable by credit card.

MAPS AND PLANS

Michelin's España & Portugal spiral **road atlas** and general **road maps** will assist you in the planning of your journey. These are listed in the **Maps and plans** section at the back of this guide.

MOTORING ORGANISATIONS

RACE (Royal Automobile Club of Spain) *℘902 40 45 45; 902 30 05 05 (roadside assistance). www.race.es.* **RACC** (Royal

Automobile Club of Catalunya) 📞902 106 106) and 902 307 307. (roadside assistance). www.racc.es.

CAR HIRE

Vehicles in Spain can be hired through the offices of all major international car hire companies around the world. Alternatively, cars can be hired at major airports, train stations, large hotels and in all major towns and cities around the country:

♦ **Avis** 📞902 18 08 54.
www.avis.com.

♦ **Europcar** 📞902 10 50 30.
www.europcar.com.
♦ **Hertz** 📞913 72 93 00.
www.hertz.com.

Visitors should bear in mind that although the legal driving age in Spain is 18, most companies will only rent out vehicles to drivers over the age of 21.

Where to Stay and Eat

Hotel and Restaurant recommendations are located in the Addresses sections of individual principal sights in the *Discovering Spain* **section of this guide. For coin ranges and for a description of the symbols used in the Addresses, see the Legend on the cover flap.**
Hotel and Restaurant listings fall within the description of each region in order to enhance your stay and enable you to make the most of your holiday. These have been recommended for their location, comfort, value for money and, in some cases, for their charm. We have also made a conscious effort to cover all budgets, although some regions (for example the Costa Brava, Costa del Sol and the Balearic Islands) are more expensive than others, and prices in Madrid and Barcelona can be as high as in other major cities in Europe. As a general rule, restaurants serve lunch from 1.30pm to 3.30pm and dinner from 9pm to 11pm.

FINDING A HOTEL

This guide lists a selection of hotels, *hostales* and *pensiones* based on the price of a double room in high season and generally excluding breakfast

and VAT, unless otherwise indicated. The difference in rates between high and low season can be significant, particularly on the coast and islands, so it is always advisable to receive confirmation of prices in writing at the time of booking.

PARADORS

Almost all of the state-run network of luxury hotels are in restored historic monuments (castles, palaces, monasteries, etc.) in magnificent locations. For more information, contact **Paradores de Turismo de España** *(calle Requena 3, 28013 Madrid; 📞915 16 67 00; www.parador.es).*

Parador de Santo Estevo, near Ourense, Galicia

©Paradores

The official UK representative is
Keytel International *(402 Edgware
Road, London W2 1ED; ℘(020) 7616
0300; www.keytel.co.uk)*. In the US,
contact **PTB Hotels** *(℘1 800 634 1188;
http://petrabax.com)*. Special weekend
offers are often available, in addition
to a five-night "go as you please"
accommodation card.

RURAL ACCOMMODATION

The number of visitors to Spain who
wish to stay in rural accommodation is
steadily increasing. Most autonomous
communities publish a practical
guide listing details of every type of
accommodation available, including
rooms in private houses, hostels for
groups, entire houses for rent, and
farm campsites. Contact local tourist
offices listed within the Principal
Sights for further details, or
www.ecoturismorural.com.

CAMPSITES

The Secretaría General de Turismo
publishes an annual campsite guide.
Further details on camping and
caravanning are supplied by the
Federación Española de Campings
*(calle Valderribas 48, Esc 3, 1ºC,
28007 Madrid; ℘914 48 12 34; www.
fedcamping.com)*. Book in advance for
popular resorts during summer.

YOUTH HOSTELS

Spain's 160 youth hostels are open to
travellers with an **international card**,
available from international youth
hostelling offices and youth hostels
themselves. For further information,
contact the **Spanish Youth Hostel
Network** *(Red Española de Albergues
Juveniles, Castello 24, 28001 Madrid;
℘915 22 70 07; www.reaj.com)*.

SPECIAL OFFERS

Many chains and hotels catering to
business travellers often offer reduced
rates at weekends. It is also possible to
purchase vouchers for one or several
nights at advantageous prices. For
further information on these special
offers, contact the following:

NH Hoteles ℘902 11 51 16. www.
nh-hoteles.es. ☞Sleep and Go rates
for 18–30 year olds for 50€.
Bancotel ℘902 87 78 77. 00 800 1001
1002 (from Europe). www.bancotel.
com/ing/index.htm. Bancotel sells
the *Bancotel checkbook* worth 150€
or 250€ for use in affiliated hotels
throughout the country. Good
discounts on standard rates.
Halcón Viajes ℘807 22 72 22.
(information and reservations)
www.halcon-viajes.es. Individual
vouchers (for a one-night stay for one
or two people) with a discount on the
official rate.
Hoteles Meliá ℘902 14 44 40.
www.solmelia.com. Discounts and
special weekend offers available via
the MAS rewards card.

DON'T FORGET THE
MICHELIN GUIDE

The red-cover **Michelin Guide
España & Portugal** is revised
annually and is an indispensable
complement to this guide with
additional information on hotels and
restaurants including category, price,
degree of comfort and setting.

WHERE TO EAT

The restaurants listed in the Addresses
in this guide have been chosen for
their surroundings, ambience, typical
dishes or unusual character. Coin

Bar with pintxos
©Turespaña

symbols (◔*see the Legend on the cover flap*) correspond to average cost of a meal and are given as a guideline only.

TAPAS

Given the country's reputation for tapas (*pintxo* in northern Spain), we have also included a list of tapas bars where visitors can enjoy an aperitif or meal throughout the day and late into the evening. Prices of tapas are often not listed, although as a general rule the cost of a reasonably priced tapas lunch or supper should not exceed 14€.

TAKING A BREAK, SHOPPING AND NIGHTLIFE

These headings, which appear periodically in the addresses sections throughout the guide, include a variety of addresses from cafés and bars to shops and theatres, as well as nightclubs and concert venues. Some may be quiet cafés during the day, transforming themselves into lively bars at night.

Useful Words and Phrases

The following phrases denote translations between English and **Castilian**, the official language of Spain and better known as Spanish in the wider world. Yet there are also four other languages officially recognised in various regions of Spain: **Catalan** (Catalonia, Valencia and the Balearics); **Basque** (Basque Country); **Galician** (Galicia); and **Aranès** (northwest Catalonia). These languages are widespread in these areas and many inhabitants see Castilian as their second language.

Common words

	Translation
Yes, No	Sí, No
Good morning	Buenos días
Good afternoon	Buenas tardes
Goodbye	Hasta luego, Adiós
Please	Por favor
OK	Vale
Agreed	De acuerdo
How are You?	¿Qué tal?
Thank you (very much)	(Muchas) Gracias
Excuse me	Perdone
I don't understand	No entiendo
Sir, Mr; You	Señor; Usted
Madam, Mrs	Señora
Miss	Señorita

Time

	Translation
When?	¿Cuándo?
What time?	¿A qué hora?
Today	Hoy
Yesterday	Ayer
Tomorrow	Mañana

Shopping

	Translation
How much?	¿Cuánto (vale)?
(Too) Expensive	(Demasiado) Caro
A Lot, Little	Mucho, Poco
More, Less	Más, Menos
Big, Small	Grande, Pequeño
Credit Card	Tarjeta de Crédito
Receipt	Recibo

Correspondence

	Translation
Postbox	Buzón
Postcard	(Tarjeta) Postal
Post Office	Correos
Telephone	Teléfono
Letter	Carta
Stamp	Sello
Telephone Call	Llamada
Tobacco Shop	Estanco, Tabaquería

On the road, in town

	Translation
Coche, Auto	Car
Gasolina	Petrol, Gasoline
A la derecha	On the right
A la izquierda	On the left
Obras	Roadworks

Peligro, Peligroso	Danger, Dangerous
Cuidado	Beware, Take care
Después de	After, Beyond

Numbers

	Translation
0	cero
1	uno/una
2	dos
3	tres
4	cuatro
5	cinco
6	seis
7	siete
8	ocho
9	nueve
10	diez
20	veinte
50	cincuenta
100	cien
1 000	mil

Food and drink

	Translation
Aceite, Aceitunas	Oil, Olives
Agua con/sin gas	Sparkling/still water
Ajo	Garlic
Albóndigas	Meatballs
Tengo alergia a...	I'm allergic to...
Arroz	Rice
Azúcar	Sugar
Boquerones	Anchovies
Café con leche	Coffee with hot milk
Black coffee	Café solo
Carne	Meat
Cebolla	Onion
Cerdo	Pork
Cerveza	Beer
Crema	Cream
Ensalada	Salad
Ensalada Rusa	Salad of diced vegetables in mayonaise
Gambas	Prawns
Helado	Ice cream
Huevo	Egg
Jamón	Ham
Lactosa	Lactose
Leche	Milk
Legumbres	Vegetables
Limón	Lemon
Mantequilla	Butter
Manzana	Apple
Mariscos	Seafood, shellfish
Mussels	Mejillones

Naranja	Orange
Nuez (Nueces)	Nut(s)
Pan	Bread
Patatas	Potatoes
Pescados	Fish
Pimienta (Negra)	(Black) pepper
Plátano	Banana
Postre	Dessert
Potaje	Soup
Queso	Cheese
Sal	Salt
Salchichas	Sausages
Setas/hongos	Mushrooms
Soja	Soya
Tortilla	Omelette
Trigo	Wheat
Vaca/buey	Beef
Vegetariano/a	Vegetarian
Vino blanco/rosado	White/rosé wine
Vino tinto	Red wine

Out and about

🐾 *Also See architectural terms in the Introduction.*

	Translation
Where is...?	¿Dónde está...?
May one visit...?	¿Se puede visitar...?
Key	Llave
Light	Luz
Guide	Guía
Porter, Caretaker	Guarda, Conserje
Open, Closed	Abierto, Cerrado
No Entry, Not allowed	Prohibido el paso
Entrance, Exit	Entrada, Salida
Wait!	Espere
Beautiful	Hermoso/a
Storey, Stairs, Steps	Piso, Escalera
Alcázar	Muslim Palace
Alrededores	Outskirts
Alto	Pass, High Pass
Audiencia	Audience, Court
Ayuntamiento	Town Hall
Balneario	Spa
Barranco	Gully, Ravine
Barrio	Quarter
Bodega	Wine Cellar/store
Boveda	Vaulting
Cabo	Cape, Headland
Calle	Street
Calle Mayor	Main street
Camino	Road, Track
Campanario	Belfry
Capilla	Chapel

Carretera	Main Road	Monasterio	Monastery
Casa	House	Monte	Mount, Mountain
Casa Consistorial	Town Hall	Museo	Museum
Castillo	Castle	Mudéjar	Moorish architectural style under Christian rule
Churrigueresco	Exuberant early baroque style named for the Churriguera brothers	Nacimiento	Source, Birthplace
		Palacio (Real)	(Royal) Palace
Ciudad	Town, City	Pantano	Artificial Lake
Claustro	Cloisters	Paseo	Avenue, Promenade
Colegio, Colegiata	College, Collegiate Church	Plaza	Square
Collado	Pass, High Pass	Plaza Mayor	Main Square
Convento	Monastery, Convent	Plaza de Toros	Bullring
Cruz	Cross	Pórtico	Portal, Porch
Cuadro	Picture	Presa	Dam
Cueva, Gruta, Cava	Cave, Grotto	Pueblo	Village, Market Town
Desfiladero	Defile, Cleft		
Embalse	Reservoir, Dam	Puente	Bridge
Ermita	Hermitage, Chapel	Puerta	Door, Gate, Entrance
Estación	Station		
Excavaciones	Excavations	Puerto	Pass, Harbour, Port
Finca	Property, Domain	Ría	Estuary
Fuente	Fountain	Río	River, Stream
Gargantas	Gorges	Santuario	Church
Gruta	Cavern, Grotto	Siglo	Century
Huerto, Huerta	Vegetable/ Market Garden	Talla	Carved Wood
		Tapices	Tapestries
Iglesia	Church	Techo	Ceiling
Imagen	Religious Statue/ Sculpture	Tesoro	Treasury, Treasure
		Torre	Tower, Belfry
Isla	Island, Isle	Torreón	Keep
Lago	Lake	Vidriera	Stained-glass window
Mezquita	Mosque		
Mirador	Belvedere, Viewpoint, Lookout Point	Viña	Vineyard
		Vista	View, Panorama

Getting by in Spain's other languages

English	Aranès	Basque	Catalan	Galician
good morning/hello	bon dia/ola/ adiu	egun on/kaixo	bon dia	boas días/ola
good evening	bona tarde	gabon	bona nit	boas noites
please	se vos platz	mesedez	per favor	por favor
thank you	gràcies/mercès	eskerrik asko	gràcies	grazas
today	auè	gaur	avui	hoxe
left	ara esquèra	ezker	esquerre(a)	esquerda
right	ara dreta	eskuin	dret(a)	dereita
open	obert	ireki	obert(a)	aberto
closed	tancat	hertsi	tancat	pechado
toilet	comuns	komuna	servies	servizos

Basic Information

BUSINESS HOURS

Shops are generally open 10am–2pm, 5–8.30pm, although an increasing number of larger stores and shopping centres do not close for lunch. The majority of shops close on Sundays, and some on Saturday afternoons.

DISCOUNTS

Consult the website of the **Instituto de la Juventud** (*Calle Marqués de Riscal 16, 28010 Madrid; ☎913 63 78 49; www.injuve.mtas.es*) for links to youth-orientated travel services.

The **Oficina Nacional de Turismo e Intercambio de Jóvenes y Estudiantes (TIVE)** (*Calle José Ortega y Gasset 71, 28006 Madrid; ☎913 47 77 00*) arranges hostel reservations, discounted transportation and language study, and sells certain student cards. There are offices in other major cities.

The **EURO<26 Card**, issued by student organisations in 27 countries, entitles young people between the ages of 14 and 25 to a whole series of discounts on travel, cultural events, accommodation, etc. In Spain, some 50 000 outlets participate in the scheme. For information, see www.eyca.org. In Spain, ☎91 363 76 85 or at TIVE offices.

The **Student Card**, available to those aged 12 and over, provides numerous discounts on a variety of services.

Senior citizens aged 65 and over qualify for significant discounts on transport, entrance fees to monuments, and events and shows (ID required). Many museums offer half-price entry, with free entrance to many national monuments.

City cards in most major cities offer discounts for transport, museums, restaurants, etc.

ELECTRICITY

220V AC (some older establishments may still have 110V). Plugs are two-pin.

EMERGENCIES

☎112 connects with all emergency services in Spain, when in Spain.

- **Police:** ☎091(national), 092 (local)
- **Medical emergencies:** ☎061
- **Fire:** ☎080, 085
- **Civil Guard:** ☎062
- **Mossos d'Esquadra**
- **(Catalan police):** ☎088
- **Directory Enquiries:** ☎11818
- **International Directory**
- **Enquiries:** ☎11825

MAIL/POST

Post offices (*correos*; www.correos.es) are open Mon–Fri 8.30am–2.30pm and Sat 9.30am–1pm. Stamps (*sellos*) can also be purchased at tobacconists (*estancos*).

MONEY

The unit of currency in Spain is the **euro** (€). Coin denominations are: 1, 2, 5, 10, 20 and 50 cents and 1 and 2 euro. Notes come in 5, 10, 20, 50, 100, 200 and 500 values.
There are no restrictions on the amount of currency foreigners may bring into Spain.

CHANGING MONEY

Traveller's cheques and foreign cash can be exchanged at banks and exchange offices (*cambios*). International credit cards are accepted in most shops, hotels and restaurants. Visitors can also obtain cash from bank machines using credit and debit cards; a pin number will be required.

Banks

Banks are generally open Mon–Fri 8.30am–2pm and Sat (Oct–May) 9am–1pm. Selected branches may also open on weekdays 4–5.30pm.

Credit Cards

In the event of a **lost or stolen credit card**, contact the relevant issuer as soon as possible:

- **Mastercard:** ☎900 97 12 31.
- **Visa:** ☎900 99 11 24
- **American Express:** ☎902 37 56 37
- **Diners Club:** ☎902 40 11 12

NEWSPAPERS

El País is Spain's "newspaper of record", though certain readers find it excessively pro-socialist. Barcelona's *La Vanguardia Española* is a respected daily distributed nationwide. *El Mundo* has sensationalist tabloid tendencies, but provides good information and entertainment. *El Periódico de Catalunya* is a Barcelona daily published in Spanish and Catalan. *ABC* is a monarchist and retro Madrid daily. Smaller regional newspapers around Spain have better information about local events. Free newspapers such as *20 Minutos*, *ADN* and *Que!* distributed in the metro are informative and time-saving. The English, French and German press is available at many newspaper kiosks in major cities and beach resorts.

PHARMACIES

Open Spanish pharmacies are marked by large illuminated green crosses on the street. Every neighourhood has a *farmacia de guardia* open around the clock. Lists of all-night and weekend pharmacies are published in the windows of all pharmacies.

PUBLIC HOLIDAYS

Municipalities may declare a maximum of 14 public holidays per year, up to 9 of which are selected by the national government. Therefore, the following list represents those public holidays that are taken throughout the country:

1 January	New Year's Day
6 January	Three Kings' Day
2nd day before Easter	Good Friday
1 May	Labour Day
15 August	Assumption Day
12 October	Hispanic Day
1 November	All Saints Day
6 December	Constitution Day
8 December	Immaculate Conception
25 December	Christmas Day

SMOKING

The new Spanish anti-smoking law came into effect on 1 January 2011: smoking is prohibited in all indoor spaces including on public transport, and at airports. Albeit in the open air these days, nearly a quarter of the population smoke, in a culture where smoking has been ingrained since Rodrigo de Jerez, a crew member of Columbus, became the first credited European smoker more than 500 years ago.

TELEPHONES

Spanish public pay phones cost 20 cents for a local call. Mobile phones usually require 00-34 before the nine-digit number. For **international calls** from Spain, dial 00, then dial the country code (44 for the UK, 353 for Ireland, 1 for the US and Canada), followed by the area code (minus the first 0 of the STD code when dialling the UK), and then the number.

♦ For calls **within Spain**, dial the full 9-digit number of the person you are calling.

♦ When calling Spain **from abroad**, dial the international access code, followed by 34 for Spain, then the full 9-digit number.

For more information, call ✆ 1004 (in Spain) or visit www.telefonica.com.

TIME

Spain is 1hr ahead of GMT. The Spanish keep different hours from either the British or North Americans: as a general rule, restaurants serve lunch from 1.30pm to 3.30pm and dinner from 9pm to 11pm.

TIPPING

Restaurants and other establishments in Spain usually include both taxes and service in prices. It is customary to leave an additional cash tip of from 5 to 10 per cent of a restaurant cheque or taxi fare. Tip porters 1€ per bag for assistance, and chambermaids 1€ per day. Guides may be tipped 3 to 5€ per day at your discretion.

CONVERSION TABLES

Weights and Measures

1 kilogram (kg)	**2.2 pounds (lb)**	**2.2 pounds**	*To convert*
6.35 kilograms	14 pounds	1 stone (st)	*kilograms*
0.45 kilograms	16 ounces (oz)	16 ounces	*to pounds,*
1 metric ton (tn)	**1.1 tons**	**1.1 tons**	*multiply by 2.2*
1 litre (l)	**2.11 pints (pt)**	**1.76 pints**	*To convert litres*
3.79 litres	1 gallon (gal)	0.83 gallon	*to gallons, multiply*
4.55 litres	1.20 gallon	1 gallon	*by 0.26 (US)*
			or 0.22 (UK)
1 hectare (ha)	**2.47 acres**	**2.47 acres**	*To convert*
1 sq kilometre	0.38 sq. miles	0.38 sq. miles	*hectares to*
(km²)	**(sq mi)**		*acres, multiply*
			by 2.4
1 centimetre (cm)	**0.39 inches (in)**	**0.39 inches**	*To convert metres*
1 metre (m)	3.28 feet (ft) or 39.37 inches		*to feet, multiply*
	or 1.09 yards (yd)		*by 3.28; for*
			kilometres to miles,
1 kilometre (km)	**0.62 miles (mi)**	**0.62 miles**	*multiply by 0.6*

Clothing

Women					Men			
	35	4	2½			40	7½	7
	36	5	3½			41	8½	8
	37	6	4½			42	9½	9
Shoes	38	7	5½		Shoes	43	10½	10
	39	8	6½			44	11½	11
	40	9	7½			45	12½	12
	41	10	8½			46	13½	13
	36	6	8			46	36	36
	38	8	10			48	38	38
Dresses	40	10	12		Suits	50	40	40
& suits	42	12	14			52	42	42
	44	14	16			54	44	44
	46	16	18			56	46	48
	36	6	30			37	14½	14½
	38	8	32			38	15	15
Blouses &	40	10	34		Shirts	39	15½	15½
sweaters	42	12	36			40	15¾	15¾
	44	14	38			41	16	16
	46	16	40			42	16½	16½

Sizes often vary depending on the designer. These equivalents are given for guidance only.

Speed

KPH	10	30	50	70	80	90	100	110	120	130
MPH	6	19	31	43	50	56	62	68	75	81

Temperature

Celsius (°C)	0°	5°	10°	15°	20°	25°	30°	40°	60°	80°	100°
Fahrenheit (°F)	32°	41°	50°	59°	68°	77°	86°	104°	140°	176°	212°

To convert Celsius into Fahrenheit, multiply °C by 9, divide by 5, and add 32.
To convert Fahrenheit into Celsius, subtract 32 from °F, multiply by 5, and divide by 9.
NB: Conversion factors on this page are approximate.

UNESCO WORLD HERITAGE SITES

In 1972, the United Nations Educational, Scientific and Cultural Organization (UNESCO) adopted a Convention for the preservation of cultural and natural sites. Over 800 sites "of outstanding universal value" are now on the World Heritage List. The protected cultural heritage may be monuments (buildings, sculptures, archaeological structures, etc.) with unique historical, artistic or scientific features; groups of buildings (such as religious communities, ancient cities); or sites (human settlements, examples of exceptional landscapes or natural sites that provide a habitat for threatened species, cultural landscapes) which are the combined works of man and nature of exceptional beauty. Spanish customs and activities featured in this guide that are inscribed on the Representative List of Intangible Cultural Heritage of Humanity include the Mystery Plays of Elche, Catalan human towers (Castells), and flamenco. Spain has more than 35 World Heritage Sites; those mentioned in the guide are below.

Alcalá de Henares: University and historic quarter
Aranjuez: Cultural landscape
Atapuerca (Burgos): Prehistoric remains
Ávila: Old town and extra-muros churches
Barcelona: Parc Güell; Palau Güell; Casa Milà; Casa Vicens; Casa Batlló; Palau de la Música Catalana; Hospital de Sant Pau; Colònia Güell Crypt
Burgos: Cathedral
Cáceres: Old town
Córdoba: Historic centre; Mosque-Cathedral
Cuenca: Historic fortified town
Doñana: National Park
Elx/Elche: El Palmeral palm grove
El Escorial: Monastery
La Gomera: Garajonay National Park
Granada: Alhambra; Generalife; Albaicín
Guadalupe: Monasterio Real de Santa María
Ibiza: Biodiversity and culture
Lugo: Roman walls
Mérida: Archaeological site
Oviedo: Monuments in the city; kingdom of Asturias
Poblet: Monastery
Salamanca: Old town
San Millán de la Cogolla: Monasterio de Yuso; Monasterio de Suso
Santiago de Compostela: Old town; Camino de Santiago; Cathedral
Segovia: Old town; aqueduct
Sevilla: Cathedral; Alcázar; Archivo de Indias
Tarragona: Roman town (Tarraco)
Tenerife: San Cristóbal de la Laguna; Parque Nacional del Teide
Teruel: Mudéjar architecture
Toledo: Historic city
Úbeda & Baeza: Renaissance monumental ensembles
Valencia: La Lonja de la Seda
Vall de Boí (Lleida): Romanesque churches

Windmills at Consuegra, Castilla-La Mancha
© Jordi Puig/age fotostock

Spain Today

Spain is living testimony that countries can change profoundly in modern times: from a closed society where views were rarely expressed in public to one where people speak their minds; from economically isolated to a dynamic economy that attracts immigrants; from a centralised government to a land that thrives on regional debate; from a repressive state to one whose prosecutors have won international prestige for their pursuit of human rights abuses. And yet all this transformation has come about while maintaining essential values and the Spanish family way of life. Elsewhere, the enthusiasm to be part of global culture will make the visitor feel at times as if he or she has never left home. But when you are in Spain, it is clear that you are nowhere else.

GOVERNMENT AND ADMINISTRATION

The Spanish Constitution, which was approved by referendum on 6 December 1978, defines the political status of the Spanish State as a constitutional monarchy in which sovereignty rests with the Spanish people. This political system can be broken down as follows: a **Head of State**, in the shape of the King, the **Cortes Generales** (Parliament) and a **Government**. The **Cortes** are elected by universal suffrage every four years. They are divided into two chambers: the **Congreso de los Diputados** and the **Senado**. The Government (Gobierno) performs executive functions and comprises a head of government (Presidente del Gobierno or prime minister), vice-presidents and ministers. Judicial power is an independent authority administered by judges and magistrates. The Supreme Court acts as the highest tribunal in the land.

Spain can be broken down into the following administrative divisions:

Autonomous Communities: Spain is divided into 17 Comunidades Autóno-mas, in addition to two autonomous cities (Ceuta and Melilla, in North Africa). These Communities may compose a single province or several provinces. Each Comunidad has its own Presidente and Cortes, who are elected by universal suffrage every four years. The level of decision-making of the Autonomous Communities varies and can change subject to the Constitution; however, in general terms, the Spanish system is one of the most advanced in Europe.

The Basque Country is designated as a historical region in Spain for its independent sense of identity. Extremists known as the **Euskadi Ta Askatasuna** (Basque Homeland and Freedom) or ETA have fought a violent campaign of murders and kidnappings since 1959 to press for an independent country. Alongside that a series of regional parties have campaigned for Basque autonomy and culture, symbolised by its language, Euskera, through democratic and peaceful means. Today international observors, asked by the Basque parties to guide a peace process, have opened a new period of dialogue.

Catalunya has developed a separate identity since the Middle Ages, with its own language (Catalan) and culture. Castilian opposition to Catalunya's identity came to a nadir during Franco's dictatorship, when the use of Catalan was forbidden in print and banned in public events. It is now an official language, taught publicly in schools and thrives alongside Spanish in the region's thriving capital, Barcelona.

Other Autonomous Communities such as Galicia, Valencia and Andalucía have also identified themselves as nationalities and promoted their own languages and regional administrations.

Provinces: The need for greater administrative efficiency led the governments under Isabel II (19C) to establish an initial division of the country into provinces. At present, Spain has 50 provinces.

Municipalities: The smallest territorial division, comprising a town council (ayuntamiento) headed by a mayor (alcalde). However, these town halls are often dynamic agencies of change.

Administrative boundaries :
— — — Autonomous community
.... Province

Given the administrative system now operating within Spain, communities and municipalities are able to administer and interpret national and European laws – for example, on town planning - in their territories in different ways.

A WAY OF LIFE

Whenever foreigners conjure up an image of Spain, their thoughts inevitably turn to a leisurely lifestyle, plentiful sunshine, noisy and lively towns and cities, and an extroverted, friendly people whose daily timetable is impossible to comprehend!

Yet, irrespective of the crazy rhythms imposed by the demands of modern life, the Spaniards always attempt to extract the very maximum from life; one maxim that often applies to them is that of having to work to live rather than living for work.

Despite the differences that exist between the north and south, the coast and inland areas, and towns and cities, it can be said that this is a common among all Spaniards in the manner in which they approach life.

The Iberian Peninsula, which is separated from the rest of Europe by the Pyrenees, is made up of continental Spain and Portugal. Spain covers an area of 504 030sq km/194 364sq mi, including the Canary Islands and Balearic Islands. It has over 4 000km/2 500mi of coastline lapped by the waters of the Mediterranean and Cantabrian Seas and Atlantic Ocean. Spain's population currently stands at more than 45 000 000.

LIFE IN THE STREET

There's no doubt that the excellent climate enjoyed by most parts of the country is one of the main reasons for the Spaniards' "passion" for living outdoors; there are of course others, of lesser or equal importance. Spain is a country of informal get-togethers and social gatherings, in bars, cafés, restaurants, at work, and of chance meetings of a couple of friends – any excuse is good enough to indulge in a friendly chat or animated discussion. This affection for going out

Plaça Reial, Barcelona

© Anna Serrano/hemis.fr

as a group, meeting friends for dinner, or enjoying tapas or a drink together, is to the Spanish a sign of identity, irrespective of their age or social standing. Nor is it uncommon for Spaniards to have a relaxed drink with friends or colleagues after work before heading home.

DAILY SCHEDULE

The daily schedule of the Spanish, shaped by the extreme summer heat, differs from the rest of Europe. Spaniards don't usually have lunch before 2pm or 2.30pm, or 3pm in summer, and they rarely have dinner before 9pm, a custom that results in long mornings and afternoons and provides ample time for them to indulge in a siesta or leisurely stroll, shopping or meeting up for a snack with friends and work acquaintances.

TAPAS AND APERITIF TIME

This gastronomic pastime is one of Spain's most popular modern traditions with youngsters, couples and entire families, who head for bars to *tapear*, either standing at the counter or, if time allows, visiting various bars to enjoy a tapa in each. An apéritif can be drunk with just a few olives, although by ordering a number of tapas you can quite easily create an alternative to lunch or dinner.

These small platefuls come in many guises and at many price levels, ranging from the small tapa itself to larger portions known as a *media ración* or *ración*. Choose a *media ración* of Manchego cheese or Serrano cured ham, a *ración* of chorizo sausage, or a selection of vegetarian, fish, seafood or meat dishes – washed down perhaps with a glass of draught beer *(una caña),* wine or, in southern Spain, a glass of fino sherry *(una copa de fino).* Every region has its own specialities and its own way of presenting tapas, though they often come with a basket of bread to round them out. In the north of Spain they are often called *pintxos.* Yet whether you're in the Basque Country, Andalucía or in the middle of the Meseta, you will always find a restaurant or bar where tempting tapas are coming out of the kitchen.

BARS

There are literally tens of thousands of bars in Spain, including in the smallest and most remote hamlets. They act as a focal point for locals, who congregate here with friends or family in the evening and at weekends, especially during football matches. During the afternoon and early evening in smaller towns and villages you may come across locals playing cards or indulging in a game of dominoes over a coffee or something stronger.

The mornings are busy in bars as well, with regulars stopping by for a pastry and coffee for breakfast. Smoking is now banned in bars though seats are often supplied just outside the door for smokers.

TERRACES

With the onset of fine weather, terraces spring up across Spain – outside restaurants, cafés, bars and ice-cream parlours, on pavements and patios and in gardens and narrow alleyways. During the warmer months, it is pleasant at any time of day to take the weight off your feet for a short while and watch the world go by in front of your table. Be aware, though, that you pay a small extra price for terrace service.

Many of the most crowded bars and clubs provide outdoor terraces for their customers till the early hours of the morning in summer. In winter they often open only at midday in good weather.

BEACH BARS

These typical features of resorts along the Spanish coast come in various guises, ranging from the cheap and cheerful to the expensive and luxurious. These *chiringuitos*, as they are known, have grown in popularity, particularly given that customers can enjoy a drink or have a meal wearing only their swim suits or meet here at night for a drink or dinner on the beach. In order to meet new legal requirements some are losing their charmingly old-fashioned air.

NIGHTLIFE

The lively character of Spanish towns and cities at night is often a cause of great surprise to visitors. Nowadays, the choice of venues is often overwhelming, with something to suit every budget and taste: quiet cafés for a drink and a chat with friends; lively bars packed to the rafters, with dance floors and music played at full volume; clubs offering a variety of shows; and nightclubs ranging from holes-in-the-wall to mega-venues where the pace doesn't stop until late the next morning. On Thursday and Friday nights and on weekends, as well as in summer and during holidays, the action is almost constant, with nightclubbers migrating from one club or bar to the next – don't be surprised if you get stuck in a traffic jam at three or four in the morning! An example of this is on the Paseo de la Castellana, in Madrid,

in summer when its numerous outdoor bars open until the small hours.

THE SIESTA

Although the demands of modern life prevent most people from perpetuating this healthy custom, most Spaniards like to have an afternoon nap and will make sure that they take a restorative siesta on weekends and when they're on holiday. Although less common nowadays, those Spaniards whose work schedule allows them three hours off from 2–5pm, or a workday ending at 3pm in summer, will try to make it home for lunch and a short sleep.

THE FAMILY

In line with other Latin countries, the family remains the bedrock of Spanish life, and is a determining factor in the behaviour and many of the habits of Spanish society at large.

Without a solid family base, it would be hard to understand how a country with a high rate of unemployment and one in which children continue to live with their parents until their late-20s and even early-30s could prosper without too many problems. It should also be added that numerous Spanish celebrations and fiestas are based upon these close family ties.

THE WORK ETHIC

Those foreigners who have chosen to live in Spain soon realise that the old image of Spain as a country where very little work is done – a view perpetuated by the country's way of life and daily schedule, and the Spaniards' well-documented liking for enjoying themselves to the full – is far removed from modern reality. Nowadays, Spaniards often work as intensively as in any other European country. Visitors may wonder how this is possible, given the unusual lifestyle. The answer is that they often start work very early or continue till very late in an improvised style. Equally, from an early age the Spanish are brought up used to sleeping less during the week and trying to catch up on lost sleep at the weekend.

FIESTAS, FOLKLORE AND POPULAR CULTURE

Spain has kept alive many old traditions, as can be witnessed by the huge number of fiestas fervently celebrated around the country throughout the year.

These unique and varied outpourings of local pride, religious feeling or simply a love of streetlife reflect Spain's rich cultural heritage and diversity.

A LAND OF FIESTAS AND TRADITIONS

Fiestas across Spain share huge crowds, ceremony and a sense of theatre. Beyond that, though, they are extraordinarily diverse.

A detailed list of major festivals in Spain can be found in the Planning Your Trip section of this guide.

Major festivals

To a greater or lesser degree, every Spanish town and city celebrates one main festival every year, normally in honour of its patron saint. These celebrations, many of which take place over the summer months, attract the entire local population, as well as inhabitants from outlying villages and rural areas.

Typical events vary from one region to the next: they may include religious celebrations and processions, floral offerings, fireworks or bullfights and bullrunning. Many people, though, attend just to indulge in animated discussions with friends until the early hours, or to enjoy rides on the fairground attractions, or to eat and drink together, often on the street. The most important festivals in Spain include:

Los Sanfermines de Pamplona, in honour of San Fermín (7 July), which starts on 6 July with the setting-off of a huge firework rocket or *chupinazo*.

For an entire week the city is the backdrop for a non-stop celebration that enjoys its most spectacular moments during the morning running of the bulls *(encierros)* and at the early-evening bull-fights. This ends at midnight on 14 July, with the candlelit singing of *Pobre de Mí* (Poor Me).

Las Fallas de Valencia, held in March in honour of San José, are renowned for bonfire sculptures and gunpowder bangs. This begins every day of the festival at 8am with *la despertà* (the wake-up call), a heady mix of brass bands and firecrackers. It culminates in the *Nit del foc* (Night of Fire) when the impressive *ninots* (bonfire sculptures) dotted around the city are set alight.

Andalucían fairs

Sevilla's *Feria de Abril* (April Fair) is the most famous of these spring and early summer festivals held in Andalucían cities. They are renowned for their exciting atmosphere, colourful costumes and spontaneous dancing of local sevillanas, with mountains of tapas consumed, accompanied by chilled dry sherry *(fino)* such as *manzanilla*.

The streets of the fairground area are a mass of colour as Andalucían men, women and children parade up and down on foot or on horseback dressed in the breathtaking long flounced flamenco dresses or horseriding suits.

Romerías

Romerías (pilgrimages) are an important aspect of religious life in Spain.

Although each has its own specific characteristics, the basic principle is the same: an annual pilgrimage on foot, and occasionally on horseback, to a hermitage or shrine to venerate a statue. Usually, this peregrination will also include a procession, music, dancing and a festive open-air meal.

The pilgrimage to El Rocío (Almonte, Huelva) is the largest and most deeply felt *romería* in the whole of Spain, attracting around one million pilgrims every year. Another pilgrimage of note is the St. John of the Mountain Festival in Miranda de Ebro dating from the 14C.

Semana Santa

Holy Week processions are another vivid expression of Spaniards' depth of religious sentiment.

Numerous villages, towns and cities around the country participate in these expressions of tragic feeling, which see thousands of people taking to the streets to accompany the passion of Christ and the pain of his mother. Semana Santa tends to be a more sober affair in Castilla, and more festive in Andalucía, although across Spain the beauty of the statues (often works of art in their own right), the solemnity of the processions, some of which take place against a magnificent backdrop, and the fervour of those involved, create an atmosphere that will involve and move believers and non-believers alike. Although Holy Week in Sevilla is the most famous, the processions in Valladolid, Málaga, Zamora, Cuenca and Lorca are also worthy of particular note.

Carnival

Carnival celebrations in Spain are generally extravagant and irreverent affairs. They often involve many months of hard work during which performances are rehearsed and costumes made. They remain liveliest on the periphery of Spain where Franco's 40-year ban on Carnival was avoided.

In the Canaries, particularly on Tenerife, Carnival is an important aspect of island tradition, involving a procession of floats and the election of the Carnival queen. Carnival in Cádiz is full of humour and music and Galician Carnival is famous for its folk costumes.

Christmas

The Christmas period in Spain is traditionally a time for family celebration.

At home, where the Christmas tree and crib are essential decorative features, families congregate for dinner either on Christmas Eve or on Christmas Day, depending on the custom of their region. An equally traditional aspect of Christmas is the procession of the Kings on the eve of Epiphany: the Three Wise Men and their pages ride through the streets of towns and cities on the night of 5 January, handing out sweets to excited children lining their path.

Bullfighting festivals

It is impossible to broach the subject of fiestas without mentioning bullfighting, a subject that raises passions and criticism in equal measure. Bullfighting festivals remain, despite modern protests, as much a part of Spanish culture as Holy Week processions, and their existence is often defended by those who do not wish to attend. Two regions, the Canary Islands and Catalunya, however, have banned bullfights.

Few cultural events are as ritualised as a bullfight; consequently, a basic understanding of the various moves and stages of the contest between man and bull is required to make any attempt to appreciate the spectacle.

The bullfighting season runs from the spring to the autumn, and the most important festivals are those in Sevilla, held during the April Fair, and the San Isidro festival in Madrid.

FOLKLORE AND POPULAR CULTURE

Aragón

Festivals and parties are often celebrated by a **jota**, a bounding, leaping dance in which couples hop and whirl to the tunes of a *rondalla* (group of stringed instruments), stopping only for the occasional brief singing of a *copla*.

Castilla and Extremadura

Few regions in Spain are as mystical or have such sober customs as Castilla. Traditional dances include the *seguidilla*, originating from La Mancha region, and the *paloteo*, also known as the *danza de palos*, which is accompanied by flute, tambourine, and sometimes by a bass drum or the most typical of Castilian instruments, the reed-pipe (*dulzaina*). Costumes may be richly embroidered with precious stones and silk thread.

Tablao Flamenco Los Gallos, Sevilla

R. Mattès/MICHELIN

Flamenco

Flamenco – a form of song, music and dance, but also a way of life – is one of Spain's most vibrant cultural expressions. The song, or *cante*, at its heart, took shape by the end of the 18thC in the Gypsy quarters of southern cities such as Cádiz and Jérez. At that time its dance, or *baile*, often remained behind closed doors. Flamenco guitar, or *toque*, then strikingly simple, has evolved in modern times to acquire great technical complexity.

All three are closely intertwined in live performance around flamenco's poetic sense of tragedy.

When in Spain, you may come upon flamenco as a stage show, as a recital in a classical auditorium, or as an acoustic session in a small club.

For aficionados it is worth timing a visit to coincide with one of the major events on the flamenco calendar. Seville's Bienal gives a sampling of pure and fusion flamenco; Jerez's annual spring festival is the main dance event; Murcia's midsummer Festival Nacional de Cante de las Minas, which grew around miners' flamenco, includes a song contest for young talent and gala performances by stars.

Performers may wear traditional flounced dresses, click castanets and play with fans, but do not be surprised if a show is contemporary in its aesthetics. Today's artists, keen to shrug off stereotypes, especially since flamenco won UNESCO World Heritage status, are often experimental. Symbolically, the national flamenco centre planned for Jerez's old town will be housed in a radically modern building, a good expression of the flamenco community's intent on renewing their art while remaining loyal to their roots.

Tablao Flamenco Cardenal, Córdoba

© John Frumm/hemis.fr

Catalunya and the Comunidad Valenciana

The **sardana** dance is still very popular in Catalunya where it is performed in a circle in main squares on Sundays. Inscribed on UNESCO's List of the Intangible Cultural Heritage of Humanity, **Castells**, are human towers which may be seen in festivals at El Vendrell and Valls. In the Levante, the baroque local costume notable for its colour and intricate embroidery is worn during colourful festivals. Valencia's **Fallas** in March bring city life to a halt; Alicante's **Foqueres** in June rival them on a smaller scale.

La Tomatina, which takes place in the Valencian town of Buñol every August, has become a renowned food fight at which participants come to throw overripe tomatoes in one of the briefest modern fiestas. Lastly, the **Moros y Cristianos** festivals – those of Alcoy (22–24 April) are the best known but there are many others around Alicante province – give a colourful costumed replay of the confrontations between Moors and Christians during the Reconquest.

Galicia, Asturias and Cantabria

Romerías in Asturias and Galicia are often accompanied by the shrill tones of the **gaita**, a type of bagpipe, and sometimes by drums and castanets. The *gaita* is played during events in honour of cowherds, shepherds, sailors and others who work in traditional occupations in these rural coastal regions. It is also part of all celebrations of Celtic music, which are held here during the summer. The most typical festivals are those held in summer for *vaqueiros*, or cowherds, in Aristébano and others for shepherds near the Lago de Enol. Common dances in Galicia include the *muñeira* or dance of the miller's wife, the sword dance performed only by men, and the *redondela*.

Bowls *(bolos)* is a very popular game, supposedly brought to the region by pilgrims on the Camino de Santiago.

Murcia

Flamenco flourishes in Murcia as does improvised rhyming poetry, or *trovos*. Cuban-influenced songs, called *habaneras*, are celebrated in an annual festival in Torrevieja. Murcia city hosts the International Festival of Mediterranean Folklore.

País Vasco and Navarra

The Basque Country and Navarra have preserved many of their distinct traditions. Men dressed in white with red sashes and the famous red berets dance in a ring accompanied by **zortzikos** (songs), a **txistu** (flute) and a *tamboril*. The most solemn dance, the *aurresku*, is a chain dance performed by men after Mass on Sundays. The **espata-dantza**, or sword dance, recalls warrior times while others, like the spinners' dance or another in which brooms are used, represent daily tasks. Basque men love contests, such as tug-of-war, trunk cutting, stone lifting and pole throwing. But by far the most popular sport is *pelota*, played in different ways: with a **chistera**, or wickerwork scoop, or with the very similar **cesta punta** in an enclosed three-walled court *(jai alai)*, or with a wooden bat or *pala* or, finally, simply with the hand, **a mano**. If you are lucky you may see *rebote*, considered the finest form, played on a large open court. The main competitive event of the year for enthusiasts is the Manomanista championship (April–May).

Balearic Islands

Mallorca's traditional dances include the *copeo*, the *jota*, the *mateixes* and the *bolero*. Dances and festivals are accompanied by a *xeremía* (local bagpipes) and a tambourine. In Menorca a festival that dates back to medieval times and calls for about 100 horsemen in elegant costumes is held at Ciutadella (The Feast of St John or *Sant Joan*, on 23–24 June). Popular dances in Ibiza have a poetical accompaniment.

Canary Islands

The folklore of the Canaries shows influences from the Spanish mainland, Portugal and South America (the last as a consequence of the strong links created by emigration); these in turn have become intertwined with local traditions. The **isa**, the **malagueña**, the *folía* and the *tajaraste* are the four best-known types of dance from the islands. The *salto del pastor* (shepherd's leap) is a traditional folk sport throughout the islands involving long pole vaults. On La Gomera there is a revival of the traditional *siblo*, or whistling, across valleys.

REGIONAL COOKERY

Spanish food varies enormously from region to region. A few dishes are served throughout the country: garlic soup, *cocido* (a type of stew accompanied by beans or chickpeas), tortilla, a thick potato omelette, cured pork products like lean *serrano* hams and chorizo (a sausage), and savoury rice dishes like paella. Fish and seafood are outstanding everywhere.

No description of Spanish food would be complete without a mention of tapas (see p52). A selection of tapas makes for a very pleasant lunch or supper accompanied by a glass (*caña*) of draught beer. Spain is also renowned for its magnificent wines, which include historic appellations such as La Rioja and Jerez.

GALICIA

Galicia's cuisine owes its delicacy to the quality of its **seafood**: hake, scallops (*vieiras*), mussels (*mejillones*), goose-barnacles (*percebes*), king prawns (*langostinos*) and mantis shrimps (*cigalas*). There is also **caldo gallego**, a local soup, **lacón con grelos** (hand of pork with turnip tops) and **pulpo gallego** (Galician-style octopus), cooked up in big copper pots at fiestas. The bakers' delicious flat empanada pies make good picnic food. All these may be accompanied by red or white Ribeiro or white Albariño wines. Desserts include *tarta de Santiago*, a frangipane tart, and *filloa* pancakes

ASTURIAS AND CANTABRIA

In both regions, fish and seafood are important but gourmets make the trip here just for the mountain cheeses, such as blue-veined Cabrales and plain Quesucos. A casserole called **fabada** made

with white beans, pork, bacon and sausages has many variations. Among sweet things Cantabrian cheesecake and Asturian rice pudding reign supreme. In Asturias it is fun to eat in the ciderhouses close to the apple orchards.

PAÍS VASCO

Cooking in the Basque Country has been raised to the level of a fine art. Traditional and avant garde styles are found at starred restaurants and in bars for pinxtos, or tapas.

Superb aged beef is woodgrilled while saltcod or hake is good in a green parsley sauce *(salsa verde)*. *Chipirones en su tinta*, a dish of baby squid in their own ink and *marmitako*, a fish soup, are good served with local *txacolí*, a tart white wine.

NAVARRA AND LA RIOJA

Navarra and La Rioja are famed for their game, market-garden produce and wines, especially reds. The food is varied and refined, with partridge, saltcod and grilled red peppers competing with trout for pride of place on local menus. In Navarra, delicious Roncal cheese is made in the valleys from ewe's milk.

ARAGÓN

Aragón is the land of **chilindrón**, a stew made with meat or poultry and peppers, and of **ternasco** (baby roast kid or lamb). These may be followed by delicious preserved peaches or pears in wine and washed down with wine from one of three vineyard areas: Cariñena, Somontano and Borja.

CATALUNYA

Catalunya's cuisine is Mediterranean. Look out for *pa amb tomaquet* (bread rubbed with a cut tomato and occasionally garlic and sprinkled with olive oil) and wonderful fish dishes with a variety of sauces such as *all i oli* (crushed garlic and olive oil) and *samfaina* (tomatoes, peppers and aubergines). Among pork meats are **butifarra** sausages and the *fuet* sausage from Vic. Dried fruit is used in a great many dishes or may be served at the end of a meal. The most

New Spanish Wines

While Spain's chefs rework regional flavours in their avant-garde dishes, the country's winemakers are turning old grapes into fine wines. Natural growing methods in the vineyards and state-of-the-art bodega techniques have revealed the potential of many overlooked grape varieties. To taste such wines as you travel, look for lesser known regional appellations – or *denominaciones de origen* – on wine lists. Examples include Bierzo (Castilla León), Bullas (Murcia), Montsant (Catalunya), Ribeira Sacra (Galicia) and Utiel Requena (Valencia), all offering outstanding quality and value. In all, Spain has over six dozen such DO wines to sample. It is also possible to plan a holiday around the growing number of wine museums, architect-designed bodegas, vineyard hotels and driving routes.

widespread dessert is **crema catalana**, a kind of crème brûlée. Catalunya's wines include sparkling *Cava*, like champagne, fruity whites made in Penedès and superb big reds in Priorato and Montsant.

CASTILLA AND EXTREMADURA

Castilian specialities using local produce include roast lamb (**cordero asado**), suckling-pig (**cochinillo tostón** or **tostado**) and **cocido**, all of which must be accompanied by a light, fresh Valdepeñas red. Other wines include Rueda's fresh fruity whites, Ribera del Duero's fruity reds and Toro's very big reds.

Both regions are also famed for their ewe's milk cheeses, including Manchego, which is good eaten with *membrillo*, a sweet quince paste. Among the region's sweets is Toledo marzipan (*mazapán*). Extremadura has the largest area of grazing pasture for black-footed pigs and enjoys an excellent reputation for its cured hams from Guijuelo (Salamanca) and Montánchez (Cáceres).

LEVANTE

The freshwater lake of l'Albufera just outside Valencia is said to be the birthplace of **paella**. A land of rice dishes, Levantine paella is prepared with seafood near the coast and with rabbit and green beans as you head inland. Further south at Jijona, **turrón**, a soft or hard almond and honey nougat, is made. Ice creams and iced drinks, such as *horchata de chufas*, made from tiger-nuts, water and sugar, are another speciality worth sampling.

BALEARIC ISLANDS

Soups are specialities in the Balearics; Mallorca's classic *sopa* has bread, leeks and garlic, while other soups are made with fish. **Tumbet** is a Mediterranean vegetable casserole and **sobrasada**, a soft lean spreading sausage. **Cocas**, a little like pizzas, and **ensaimadas**, light spiral rolls, make delicious desserts or breakfasts.

THE CANARY ISLANDS

Canarian specialities include **papas arrugadas**, small wrinkly potatoes with a dry, salty coating, served with green or red *mojos* or dipping sauces. Stoneground flour made from roasted maize, called *gofio*, is added to many foods. The Canary Islands are also known for Shakespearian sack wine, made from malvasia grapes.

ANDALUCÍA

The best-known dish is **gazpacho**, a cold raw cucumber and tomato soup made with oil and vinegar, but Andalucíans also love olive-oil fried food, especially seafood. Pigs are reared in the Sierra Nevada and Sierra de Aracena for making exquisite hams. Among local desserts, *tocino de cielo* custards and convent sweets are worth searching out. The region is well known for its **Jerez** or sherry wines, drunk with tapas.

History

Modern Spain represents the culmination of centuries of crossbreeding, political union, exclusion and division.
The country's history is a complex one, enlivened by myths and legends, and punctuated by significant historical and cultural landmarks. Today's imprints left by Carthiginian, Roman, Visigothic, Muslim and Christian cultures form a heritage that has made a profound impact on world history. From the flourishing of sciences during seven centuries of Muslim rule; the arts and literature in the Spanish Golden Age; the colonisation and identity of much of Latin America; to the Movida of the 1980s after the dictatorship, Spanish culture and history have combined to create a unique and proud people ready for their country to step up onto the world stage again.

TIME LINE
FROM ANTIQUITY TO THE VISIGOTHIC KINGDOM

BC

11C–5C Phoenician and Greek trading posts founded on the eastern and southern coasts of Spain, inhabited by **Iberians** and **Tartessians** respectively. In the 9C BC, the central-European Celts settle in west Spain and on the Meseta, intermingling with the Iberians (forming **Celtiberians**).

3C–2C The **Carthaginians** take over the southeast after conquering the Greeks and Tartessians. The capture of Sagunto by Hannibal leads to the Second Punic War (218–201 BC). Rome expels the Carthaginians and begins the conquest of peninsular Spain (with resistance at **Numancia**).

THE CHRISTIAN RECONQUEST OF THE IBERIAN PENINSULA

Kingdom of Asturias C.750
Recovered territory
C. 1040
C. 1270
C. 850
C. 1150
Between 1270 & 1492

Christian victories
Muslim victories
Muslim strongholds

1492

If there were only one important date to remember in Spanish history, it would be 1492. That year, after 781 years of Muslim occupation, the Reconquest ended with the fall of Granada on 2 January. This was also the year that the Jews were expelled, the Spaniard Roderic de Borja (Borgia) became Pope Alexander VI and, on 12 October, Christopher Columbus landed in the Americas.

Christopher Columbus (Cristóbal Colón) (1451–1506) and the discovery of America – Born in Genoa, the son of a weaver, Columbus began his seafaring career at an early age. He travelled to Lisbon in 1476 where he developed a passion for map-making on discovering Ptolemy's Geography and Pierre d'Ailly's Imago Mundi. Convinced that the Indies could be reached by sailing west, he submitted a navigation plan to João II of Portugal and to the Kings of France and England. He ultimately managed to gain the support of the Duke of Medinaceli and that of the Prior of the Monasterio de La Rábida, Ximenes de Cisneros, who was Isabel the Catholic's confessor. The Catholic Monarchs agreed to finance his expedition and, if he succeeded, to bestow upon him the hereditary title of Admiral of the Ocean Sea and the viceroyship of any lands discovered.

On 3 August 1492, heading a fleet of three caravels (the *Santa María*, under his command, and the *Pinta* and the *Niña* captained by the Pinzón brothers), he put out from Palos de la Frontera. On 12 October, after a difficult crossing, San Salvador (Bahamas) came into sight and a short time later Hispaniola (Haiti) and Cuba were discovered by the Europeans. On his return to Spain on 15 March 1493, Christopher Columbus was given a triumphant welcome and the means with which to organise new expeditions. This marked the beginning of the Spanish and European colonisation of the New World.

1C   Cantabria and Asturias are finally pacified in AD 19. Spain is now known as Iberia or Hispania.

AD

1C   Christianity reaches the Iberian Peninsula and begins to spread.

5C–6C   Early Suevi (Swabian) and Vandal invasions are followed by those of the **Visigoths** (456), who establish a powerful monarchy with Toledo as capital. The peninsula unites under King Leovigild (569–86).

MUSLIM SPAIN AND THE RECONQUEST

8C   **Moors** invade the Visigothic Kingdom after the **Battle of Guadalete** (711–18). Pelayo's victory at **Covadonga** in 718 heralds an 800-year-long Christian War of Reconquest. The first Muslim invaders are subjects of the Umayyad Caliphate in Damascus. **Abd al-Rahman I** breaks with Damascus by founding an independent emirate at Córdoba in 756.

9C   Settlement of uninhabited lands in north by Christians.

10C   Golden age of the emirate of Córdoba, which is raised to the status of a caliphate (1031) by **Abd ar-Rahman III**. A period of great prosperity ensues during which the expansion of Christian kingdoms is checked. Fortresses are built in the north along the Duero river.

11C   Christian Spain by 1100 includes the Kingdoms of León, Castilla and Navarra and the County of Barcelona and Valencia. The Caliphate of Córdoba disintegrates into about 20 *taifa* city-kingdoms (1031). Alfonso VI of Castilla conquers Toledo (1085), and the area around the Tajo river is resettled by Christians. The *taifa* kings call upon the **Almoravids** (Saharan Muslims) for assistance and in a short time the tribe overruns a large part of Spain. Pilgrims begin to tread the Camino de Santiago. **El Cid** conquers Valencia (1094).

12C Dissension stemming from a second age of *taifa* kingdoms assists the Reconquest, especially in the Ebro Valley (Zaragoza is taken in 1118, Tortosa in 1148 and Lleida in 1149), but after Yakub al-Mansur's victory in Alarcos (1195), the **Almohads** (who routed the Almoravids) recover Extremadura and check Christian expansion towards the Guadiana and Guadalquivir rivers. Sevilla, with Córdoba under its control, enjoys great prosperity.

Great military orders are founded (Calatrava, Alcántara and Santiago).

Dynastic union of kingdom of Aragón and county of Barcelona (1137).

13C The *taifa* kingdoms enter their third age. The decline of the Muslims begins with the **Battle of Las Navas de Tolosa** (1212). Muslim influence is reduced to the Nasrid Kingdom of Granada (modern provinces of Málaga, Granada and Almería), which holds out until its capture in 1492. Unification of Castilla and León under St Ferdinand III (1230).

The crown of Aragón under James I the Conqueror (1213–76) gains control over considerable territory in the Mediterranean.

THE CATHOLIC MONARCHS (1474–1516) AND THE UNIFICATION OF SPAIN

1474 Isabella, wife of Ferdinand, succeeds her brother Henry IV to the throne of Castilla. She has to contend with opposition from the supporters of her niece Juana la Beltraneja until 1479.

1478–79 The court of the **Inquisition** is instituted by a special Papal Bull and **Tómas**

El Cid

Rodrigo Díaz de Vivar was born to a noble family around 1040 in Vivar, near Burgos. He served under two kings in the Reconquista, during which time he earned the honorific title of "El Campeador" for his forward thinking and leadership which prompted jealousy amongst his peers. He was exiled by King Alfonso VI in 1079 for insubordination. The bloody Christian defeat at the Battle of Sagrajas (1086) prompted King Alfonso to repeal his decision, and El Cid was welcomed back. El Cid then raised an army and beseiged Valencia, finally conquering the city in May 1094. Though officially ruling in the name of King Alfonso, Valencia became his own independent Christian fiefdom. His legend has led him to be considered as Spain's national hero.

El Cid has inspired everything from epic poems ("The Song of the Cid") to Hollywood films (*El Cid*, 1961, starring Charlton Heston). His grave now lies as the centrepiece of Burgos Cathedral. Tizona, his legendary sword, can be found at the Museo de Burgos (&see BURGOS).

de Torquemada is later appointed Inquisitor-General.

The court, a political and religious institution directed against Jews, Moors and later Protestants, survives until the 19C.

Ferdinand becomes King of Aragón in 1479 and Christian Spain is united under Isabella and Ferdinand.

1492 Fall of Granada marks the end of the Reconquest. Expulsion of Jews.

12 Oct 1492 Christopher Columbus lands in the Americas.

1494 The **Treaty of Tordesillas** divides the New World between Spain and Portugal.

1496 Joanna (Juana), daughter of the Catholic Monarchs, marries Philip the Handsome (Felipe el Hermoso), son of Holy Roman Emperor Maximilian I of the Habsburgs.

1504 Death of Isabella. The kingdom is inherited by her daughter, Joanna (Juana la Loca), but Ferdinand governs as regent until Joanna's son Charles (1500–1558), future Emperor Charles V, comes of age to rule as Charles I.

1512 The Duke of Alba conquers Navarra, thus bringing territorial unity to Spain.

THE HABSBURGS (1516–1700) AND THE CONQUEST OF AMERICA

1516 – **The apogee: Charles I** (1516–56) and **Philip II** (1556–98). On the death of Ferdinand, his grandson becomes Charles I (Carlos I) of Spain. Through his mother, Charles inherits Spain, Naples, Sicily, Sardinia and American

A Life Less Ordinary

Miguel de Cervantes Saavedra was born in poverty at Alcalá de Henares in 1547, yet he went on to lead a life of adventure. From being a valet in Renaissance Rome, Cervantes would later fight against the Ottomans in the Battle of Lepanto (1571). He then spent five years in slavery in Algiers, before returning to Madrid as a purveyor and tax collector for the Spanish Armada. While being imprisoned for debts in La Mancha, it is said that he had the idea for his famous literary work, **Don Quixote de La Mancha**, *(vol I 1605, vol II 1615)*, now considered to be one of the greatest novels of all time. He died peacefully in 1616, having settled in Madrid.

territories. Cardinal Cisneros governs until the new king arrives for the first time in Spain in 1517.

1519 On the death of Maximilian of Austria, Charles I is elected Holy Roman Emperor under the name of **Charles V** (Carlos V). He inherits Germany, Austria, the Franche-Comté and the Low Countries.

1520–22 The Spanish, incensed by Charles V's largely Flemish court advisers and the increasing number of taxes, rise up in arms. The emperor quells **Comuneros** and **Germanías** revolts.

1521–56 Charles V wages five wars against France in order to secure complete control of Europe. In the first four he conquers Francis I (imprisoned at Pavia in 1525) and in the fifth he routs the new French king, Henri II, and captures Milan. The Conquistadores move across America. **Vasco Núñez de Balboa** discovers

THE EMPIRE OF CHARLES V

	Burgundian inheritance		Austrian inheritance		Other possessions
	Spanish inheritance		Charles V's conquests	– – –	The Holy Roman Empire

the Pacific; **Hernan Cortés** seizes Mexico in 1521; **Francisco Pizarro** and **Diego de Almagro** subdue Peru in 1533; **Francisco Coronado** explores the Colorado river in 1535; **Hernando de Soto** takes possession of Florida in 1539; and **Pedro de Valdivia** founds Santiago de Chile in 1541.

1555 Charles V signs the Peace of Augsburg with the Protestants in Germany after failing to suppress the Reformation.

1556 Charles V abdicates in favour of his son and retires to a monastery in Yuste. **Philip II** becomes king, inheriting Spain and its colonies, the kingdom of Naples, Milan, the Low Countries and the Franche-Comté, but not Germany and Austria, which are left by Charles to his brother

Ferdinand I of Austria. Philip II turns his attention to Spain and the defence of Catholicism. He chooses Madrid as his de facto capital in 1561. Spain goes through a serious economic crisis.

1568–70 Revolt of the Moriscos (Muslims who converted to Christianity) in Granada.

1571 The Turks are defeated in the **Battle of Lepanto** by a fleet of ships sent by the Pope, the Venetians and the Spanish, under the command of **Don John of Austria**, the king's natural brother. The victory seals Spain's mastery of the Mediterranean.

1580 The King of Portugal dies without an heir. Philip II asserts his rights, invades Portugal and is proclaimed king in 1581.

1588 Philip II sends the **Invincible Armada** against Protestant England, which supports the Low Countries. The destruction of the fleet marks the end of Spain as a sea power.

1598 Philip II dies, leaving a vast kingdom which, in spite of huge wealth from the Americas, is crippled by debt after 70 years of almost incessant war and monumental building projects like El Escorial.

1598–1621 – The decline – The last Habsburgs, **Philip III** (Felipe III, 1598–1621), **Philip IV** (Felipe IV, 1621–65) and **Charles II** (Carlos II, 1665–1700), struggle to maintain the kingdom. Paradoxically, Spain enjoys its **Golden Age** of art and culture. Philip III entrusts the affairs of state to the Duke of Lerma, who advises him to expel the Moriscos in 1609. By 1614, 300,000 Moriscos leave Spain with disastrous consequences for agriculture.

1640 Under Philip IV (Felipe IV), the Count-Duke of Olivares adopts a policy of decentralisation which spurs Catalunya and Portugal to rebellion. The Portuguese proclaim the Duke of Braganza King John IV, but their independence is not recognised until 1668.

1618–48 Spain wastes her strength in the **Thirty Years' War**. In spite of victories like that of Breda (1624), the defeat in the Netherlands at Rocroi (1643) signals the end of Spain as a European power. The **Treaty of Westphalia** gives the Netherlands independence.

1659 The **Treaty of the Pyrenees** ends war with France.

1665 Charles II, the final Habsburg monarch, of poor health, comes to the throne.

1667–97 Spain loses strongholds in Flanders to France during the **War of Devolution** (1667–68). The Dutch Wars (1672–78) end with the **Treaty of Nijmegen**. The **Treaty of Ryswick** (1697) concludes the war waged by the Confederation of Augsburg (Spain is a member) against France (1688–97).

THE BOURBONS, NAPOLEON AND THE WAR OF INDEPENDENCE (1808–14)

1700 Charles II dies without issue. He wills the crown to Philip, Duke of Anjou, grandson of his sister María Teresa and Louis XIV. Emperor Leopold, who had renounced his rights to the Spanish throne in favour of his son, the Archduke Charles of Austria, is displeased.

1702–14 War of the Spanish Succession – England, the Netherlands, Denmark and Germany support the Archduke of Austria against France and Philip of Anjou. Catalan, Valencian and Aragonese cities side with the Archduke and war spreads throughout Spain (1705). By the **Treaty of Utrecht (1713) ending the War**, Spain cedes Gibraltar and Menorca (taken by the English) and many of her Italian possessions to Austria. **Philip V** (Felipe V) is proclaimed King of Spain (1683–1746).

1759–88 The reign of **Charles III** (Carlos III), an enlightened despot, is the most brilliant of the Bourbon dynasty. He is assisted by competent ministers (Floridablanca and Aranda) who draw up important economic reforms. Expulsion of the

Jesuits from Spain and its empire in 1767.

1788 **Charles IV** (Carlos IV) succeeds to the throne. The country is largely governed by his wife María Luisa and her favourite, Manuel de Godoy.

1793 On the death of Louis XVI, Spain declares war on France (then in the throes of the Revolution).

1796–1805 Spain signs an alliance with the French Directorate against England (Second Treaty of San Ildefonso, 1796).

Napoleon enters Spain with his troops on the pretext that he is going to attack Portugal. The renewed offensive against England in 1804 ends disastrously with the **Battle of Trafalgar** the following year.

1805–08 Napoleon takes advantage of the disagreement between Charles IV and his son Ferdinand to engineer Charles IV's abdication.

2 May 1808 The Madrid uprising against French troops marks the beginning of the **War of Independence** (The Peninsular War), which lasts until Napoleon is exiled by Wellington in 1814. During the war Napoleon's brother, Joseph, rules Spain while provincial Juntas defend Ferdinand VII's rights, supported by British and Portuguese forces. Battles at Bailén (1808), Madrid, Zaragoza and Girona.

1812 The French are routed by Wellington in the Arapiles Valley; King Joseph flees from Madrid. Valencia is taken by the French General Suchet.

Spanish patriots convene the Cortes (parliament) and draw up the liberal **Constitution of Cádiz.**

1813–14 Anglo-Spanish forces expel Napoleon after successive victories.

Ferdinand VII (Fernando VII) returns to Spain, repeals the Constitution of Cádiz and so reigns as an absolute monarch until 1820. Meanwhile, the Latin American colonies struggle for independence.

THE DISTURBANCES OF THE 19C

1820–23 – The liberals oppose the king's absolute rule but their uprisings are all severely quelled. The 1812 constitution is reinstated after a liberal revolt led by **General Riego** in Cádiz in 1820, but only for three years.

In 1823 Ferdinand VII appeals to Europe for assistance and 100 000 Frenchmen are sent in the name of St Louis to re-establish absolute rule (which lasts until 1833).

1833–39 On the death of his brother Ferdinand VII, Don Carlos disputes the right to the throne of his niece Isabel II, daughter of the late king and Queen María Cristina. She comes to the throne. The traditionalist Carlists fight Isabel's supporters, who win the **First Carlist War** (Convention of Vergara 1839). In 1835, the new prime minister **Mendizábel** has a series of decrees passed which approve sale of church and religious orders' lands (*desamortización*).

1840 A revolutionary junta forces the regent María Cristina into exile. She is replaced by General Espartero.

1843–68 Queen Isabel II comes of age. The **Narváez** moderate uprising forces Espartero to flee. A new constitution is drawn up in 1845. The Second Carlist War (1847–49) ends in victory for Isabel II but her reign is troubled by uprisings on behalf of progressives and moderates, one of which, the 1868 revolt led by General Prim, puts an end to her reign. Isabel leaves for France and General Serrano is appointed leader of the provisional government.

1869 The Cortes passes a progressive constitution with universal male suffrage and a monarchy. Amadeo of Savoy is elected king.

1873 **The Third Carlist War** (1872–76). The king abdicates on finding himself unable to keep the peace. The National Assembly proclaims the **First Spanish Republic**.

1874 Brigadier Martínez Campos leads a revolt. The head of the government, Cánovas de Castillo, proclaims Isabel's son **Alfonso XII** King of Spain. The Bourbon Restoration and 1876 constitution open a long period of peace.

1885 Death of Alfonso XII (at 28). His widow María Cristina (who is expecting a baby) becomes regent.

1898 Cuba and the Philippines rise up with disastrous losses for Spain. The United States, which supports the rebel colonies, occupies Puerto Rico and the Philippines, marking the end of the Spanish Empire.

1902 **Alfonso XIII** (born after the death of his father

Alfonso XII) assumes the throne at 16.

THE FALL OF THE MONARCHY AND THE SECOND REPUBLIC (1931–36)

1914–18 Spain remains neutral throughout the First World War. A general strike in 1919 is severely put down.

1921 Insurrection in Morocco; General Sanjurjo occupies the north (1927).

1923 General **Miguel Primo de Rivera** abolishes the 1876 constitution and establishes a military dictatorship with the king's approval. Order and economic growth are restored, but opposition increases among the working classes.

1930 In the face of hostility from the masses, Primo de Rivera is forced into exile.

1931 April municipal elections bring victory to the Republicans in Catalunya, the País Vasco, La Rioja and the Aragonese province of Huesca. The king abdicates. The Second Republic is proclaimed and Generalitat of Catalunya created.

Jun 1931 A constituent Cortes is elected with a socialist Republican majority; a Constitution is promulgated in December. Agrarian reforms, such as compulsory purchase of large properties, meet strong right-wing opposition.

1933 The **Falange Party**, which opposes regional separation, is founded by **José Antonio Primo de Rivera**, son of the dictator. The right wins general elections.

Oct 1934 Catalunya proclaims its autonomy. Miners in Asturias spark a revolt against the government and are brutally repressed.

Feb 1936 The Popular Front wins general elections and in May Azaña becomes President of the Republic.

THE CIVIL WAR (1936–39)

17 Jul 1936 The Melilla uprising triggers the Civil War. The army takes control and puts an end to the Second Republic. Nationalist troops based in Morocco and led by General Franco cross the Straits of Gibraltar and make their way to Toledo, which is taken at the end of September. Franco is proclaimed Generalísimo of the armed forces and Head of State in Burgos. Nationalists lead an unsuccessful attack against Madrid. While Madrid, Catalunya and Valencia remain faithful to the Republicans, the Conservative agricultural regions – Andalucía, Castilla and Galicia – are rapidly controlled by the Nationalists. These regions out-supply the Republicans and the Republicans themselves are torn by dissension between the Anarchist CNT party, the Communist PCE and the Marxist POUM. They do, however, receive assistance from International Brigades.

1937 Industrial towns in the north are taken by Nationalist supporters in the summer (on 26 April, Gernika is bombed by German planes). The Republican Government is moved to Barcelona in November. In the battle of Teruel in December, the Republicans try to breach the Nationalist front in Aragón and thereby relieve surrounded Catalunya. Teruel is taken by the Republicans and recaptured by the Nationalists soon after.

1938 The Nationalist army reaches the Mediterranean, dividing Republican territory into two parts. The **Battle of the Ebro** lasts from July to November: Franco launches an offensive against Catalunya, which is occupied by the Nationalists in February 1939.

1 Apr 1939 The Spanish Civil War ends with the capture of Madrid.

THE FRANCO ERA

1939–49 Spain is declared a monarchy with Franco as regent and Head of State, and declares itself neutral in the Second World War. UN diplomatic boycott of Spain (1946).

1952 Spain joins UNESCO.

1955 Spain readmitted to the United Nations.

1969 Prince Juan Carlos is named as Franco's successor.

20 Dec 1973 Prime Minister Carrero Blanco is assassinated.

20 Nov 1975 Death of Franco. **Juan Carlos I** becomes King.

DEMOCRACY

1977 General elections – **Adolfo Suárez** is elected prime minister.

1978 A new constitution is passed by referendum. Statutes of autonomy are approved for Catalunya, the País Vasco (Euskadi) and Galicia.

1981–82 Suárez resigns. An attempted military coup takes place on 23 February 1981. **Felipe González** becomes prime minister after the Socialist Party wins election.

1 Jan 1986   Spain joins the **European Economic Community**.

12 Mar 1986   Spain's continued membership in NATO is voted by referendum.

1992   Barcelona hosts the Olympics, Sevilla hosts Expo, Madrid is Cultural Capital of Europe.

1996   **José María Aznar** of the Popular Party becomes prime minister.

1997   The Guggenheim Museum Bilbao opens.

2002   Spain adopts the **Euro**.

11 March 2004   The **Madrid train bombings** by terrorists leave 191 dead and 1 500 injured.

14 March 2004   **José Luis Rodríguez Zapatero** of the Socialist Party becomes prime minister.

22 May 2004   The Prince of Asturias, Felipe, heir to the Spanish crown, marries Letizia Ortiz Rocasolano, a journalist and divorcée.

2005   Princess Leonor is born in Madrid to Felipe and Letizia.

11 Apr 2008   Prime Minister Zapatero is re-elected.

July 2010   Spain wins the World Cup. Rafael Nadal wins Wimbledon.

2010   Unemployment, the highest in the EU, rises to over 20%.

2011   Earthquake in Lorca (Murcia) kills nine and damages 80% of the buildings.

Art and Culture

ARCHITECTURE AND THE VISUAL ARTS

Over the centuries, Spain has amassed artistic and architectural treasures. They range from diminutive Romanesque chapels, lofty Gothic cathedrals and exuberant Baroque churches to awe-inspiring Hispano-Arab monuments, imposing castles, magnificent paintings and outstanding modern architecture.

FROM PREHISTORY TO THE MUSLIM CONQUEST

Prehistoric art

Prehistoric inhabitants of the Iberian Peninsula have left some outstanding examples of their art. The oldest European hominid settlements are at Atapuerca, in Burgos (850–780,000 BC) but the earliest cave paintings are Upper Palaeolithic (40 000–10 000 BC) in Cantabria (Altamira and Puente Viesgo), Asturias (El Pindal, Ribadesella and San Román) and the Levante region (Cogull and Alpera). Megalithic monuments like the famous Antequera dolmens were erected during the Neolithic Era (7500–2500 BC), or New Stone Age, while in the Balearic Islands stone monuments known as **talaiots** and *navetas* were built by a Bronze Age people (2500–1000 BC).

First Millennium BC

Iberian civilisations produced gold and silverware treasures (Villena in its town museum and Carambolo in Sevilla's Museo Arqueológico), and fine sculpture. Some of their work, such as the Córdoba lions, the Guisando

Dama de Elche

©Photoojasson/Dreamstime.com

ARCHITECTURE A–Z

Words in italics are Spanish.

Ajimez paired window or opening separated by a central column.

Alfarje wooden ceiling, usually decorated, consisting of a board resting on cross-beams (a feature of the Mudéjar style).

Alfiz rectangular surround to a horseshoe-shaped arch in Muslim architecture.

Alicatado section of wall or other surface covered with sheets of ceramic tiles *(azulejos)* cut to form geometric patterns. Frequently used to decorate dados (a Mudéjar feature).

Alhondiga (almúdin) granary or food store, often Muslim in origin, but preserved after the Reconquest.

Aljibe Arab word for cistern.

Altarpiece (also retable). Decorative screen above and behind the altar.

Apse far end of a church housing the high altar; can be semicircular, polygonal or horseshoe-shaped.

Horseshoe (Moorish)

R. Corbel/MICHELIN

Apsidal or radiating chapel small chapel opening from the apse.

Arch (&see illustrations.)

Archivolt ornamental moulding on the outer edge of an arch.

Artesonado marquetry ceiling in which raised fillets outline honeycomb-like cells in the shape of stars. This decoration, which first appeared under the Almohads, was popular throughout the country, including Christian Spain, in the 15C and 16C.

Ataurique decorative plant motif on plaster or brick which was developed as a feature of the Caliphate style and was subsequently adopted by the Mudéjar.

Barrel

R. Corbel/MICHELIN

Azulejos glazed, patterned, ceramic tiles.

Barrel vaulting vault with a semicircular cross-section. (&see illustrations.)

Cabecera the east or apsidal end of a church.

Caliphate the architectural style developed in Córdoba under the Caliphate (8C–11C) of which the finest example is the mosque in that city.

Camarín a small chapel on the first floor behind the altarpiece or retable. It is plushly decorated and very often contains a lavishly costumed statue of the Virgin Mary.

Capilla mayor the area of the high altar containing the *retablo mayor* (monumental altarpiece), which often rises to the roof.

Coro a chancel in Spanish canonical churches often built in the middle of the nave. It contains the **stalls** *(sillería)* used by members of religious orders. When placed in a tribune or gallery it is known as the *coro alto*.

Churrigueresque in the style of the Churrigueras, an 18C family of architects. Richly ornate Baroque decoration.

Crucero transept. The part of a church at right angles to the nave which gives the church a cross shape.

Estípite pilaster in the shape of a truncated inverted pyramid.

Gargoyle projecting roof gutter normally carved in the shape of a grotesque animal.

Girola (also *deambulatorio*) ambulatory. An extension to the aisles forming a gallery around the chancel and behind the altar.

Groined vaulting vault showing lines of intersection of two vaults or arches (usually pointed).

Grotesque typical Renaissance decoration combining vegetation, imaginary beings and animals.

Kiblah sacred wall of a mosque from which the mihrab is hollowed, facing towards Mecca.

Lacería geometric decoration formed by intersecting straight lines making star-shaped and polygonal figures. Characteristic of Moorish architecture.

Arches

Pointed horseshoe   Raised

Ogee   Basket-handle   Rampant

Vaults

Arris

Barrel

Pointed

Fan

Cylindrical   Oven

R. Corbel/MICHELIN

Lombard bands decorative pilaster strips typical of Romanesque architecture in Lombardy.

Lonja commodity exchange building.

Mihrab richly decorated prayer-niche in the sacred wall (kiblah) in a mosque.

Minaret tower of the mosque (*mezquita*), from which the muezzin calls

the faithful to prayer.

Minbar pulpit in a mosque.

Mocárabes decorative motifs of Muslim architecture formed by

71

Tympanum

H. Choimet/MICHELIN

assembled prisms ending in concave surfaces. They resemble stalactites or pendants and adorn vaults and cornices.

Mozarabic the work of Christians living under Arab rule after the Moorish invasion of 711. On being persecuted in the 9C, they sought refuge in Christian areas bringing with them Moorish artistic traditions.

Mudéjar the work of Muslims living in Christian territory following the Reconquest (13C–14C).

Mullion slender column or pillar dividing an opening in a door or window.

Naveta megalithic monument found in the Balearic Islands, which has a pyramidal shape with a rectangular base.

Plateresque term derived from *platero* (i.e. silversmith); used to describe the early style of the Renaissance characterised by finely carved decoration.

Predella the lower part of an altarpiece.

Presbiterio the space in front of the altar (the presbytery is known as the *casa del cura*).

Púlpito pulpit.

Sagrario chapel containing the Holy Sacrament. May sometimes be a separate church.

Sebka type of brick decoration developed under the Almohads consisting of an apparently endless series of small arches forming a network.

Seo cathedral.

Sillería the stalls.

Soportales porticoes of wood or stone pillars supporting the first floor of houses. They form an open gallery around the plaza mayor of towns and villages.

Star vault vault with a square or polygonal plan formed by several intersecting arches.

Stucco type of moulding mix consisting mainly of plaster, used for coating surfaces. It plays a fundamental role in wall decoration in Hispano-Muslim architecture.

Talayot: megalithic monument found in the Balearic Islands, which takes the form of a truncated cone of stones.

Taula (*mesa* in the Mallorcan language) megalithic monument found in the Balearic Islands, which consists of a monolithic horizontal stone block placed on top of a vertical stone block.

Trasaltar back wall of the *capilla mayor* in front of which there are frequently sculptures or tombs.

Trascoro the wall, often carved and decorated, which encloses the *coro*.

Triforium arcade above the side aisles which opens onto the central nave of a church.

Tympanum inner surface of a pediment. This often ornamented space is bounded by the archivolt and the lintel of the doors of churches.

Venera scallop-shaped moulding frequently used as an ornamental feature. It is the symbol of pilgrimages to Santiago de Compostela.

Yesería plasterwork used in sculptured decoration.

---

bulls and, in the Museo Arqueológico in Madrid, the *Dama de Baza* and the *Dama de Elche*, influenced 20th-century art. Meanwhile, Phoenician, Carthaginian and Greek colonisers introduced their native art: Phoenician sarcophagi in Cádiz, Punic art in Ibiza and Cartagena, Greek art in Empúries.

Roman Spain (1C BC–5C AD)

Besides roads, bridges, aqueducts, towns and monuments, Roman legacies include the Mérida theatre, the ancient towns of Italica and Empúries, the Segovia aqueduct, Tarragona's magnificent Circus and Alcalà de Henares's Forum.

The Visigoths (6C–8C)

Christian Visigoths built small stone churches (Quintanilla de las Viñas, San Pedro de la Nave) adorned with friezes carved in geometric patterns with plant motifs. The apsidal plan was square and the arches were often horseshoe-shaped. The Visigoths were outstanding gold and silversmiths who made sumptuous jewellery in the Byzantine and Germanic traditions. Gold votive crowns (Guarrazar treasure in Toledo), fibulae and belt buckles adorned with precious stones, or *cloisonné* enamel, were presented to churches or placed in the tombs of the great.

HISPANO-ARABIC ARCHITECTURE (8C–15C)

The three major periods of Hispano-Arabic architecture correspond to the reigns of successive Arab dynasties over the Muslim-held territories in the peninsula.

Caliphate or Córdoba architecture (8C–11C)

This period is characterised by three types of building: **mosques**, built to a simple plan consisting of a minaret, a courtyard with a pool for ritual ablutions and finally a square prayer room with a mihrab (prayer-niche marking the direction of Mecca); **alcázares** (palaces), built around attractive patios and surrounded by gardens and fountains; and **alcazabas** (castle fortresses), built on high ground and surrounded by several walls crowned with pointed merlons – one of the best examples of these can be found in Málaga. The most famous monuments from this period are in Córdoba (the Mezquita and the Medina Azahara palace) and in Toledo (Cristo de la Luz) where, besides the ubiquitous horseshoe arch which virtually became the hallmark of Moorish architecture, other characteristics developed including ornamental brickwork in relief, cupolas supported on ribs, turned modillions, arches with alternating white stone and red-brick voussoirs, **multifoil arches** (*see illustration*) and doors surmounted with blind arcades. These features

Hispano-Moorish art

CÓRDOBA – Mezquita: Puerta de Alhakem II (10C)

Eight centuries of Moorish rule in Spain had a fundamental influence on Spanish art.

Crenellated merlons

Intercrossing horseshoe-shaped arches

Epigraphic decoration

Blind arcade

Foliation (leaf-like décoration)

Foliated arch

Geometric decoration

Lattice-work

Bicoloured art work

Brick

Stone

Alfiz: a rectangular surround to a horseshoe-shaped arch

Stucco: a moulding mix consisting mainly of plaster and glue (sometimes includes powdered marble)

GRANADA – La Alhambra (14C)

Mocárabes: decorative motifs of Muslim architecture formed by assembled prisms ending in concave surfaces. Used to adorn vaults, arches and cornices

A panel of **azulejos** with epigraphic and geometric decoration

H. Choimet/MICHELIN

R. Corbel/MICHELIN

Pointed

became popular in Mudéjar and Romanesque churches.

The Umayyads brought a taste for profuse decoration from Syria. As the Koran forbids the representation of human or animal forms, Muslim decoration is based on calligraphy (Cufic inscriptions running along walls), geometric patterns (polygons and stars made of ornamental brickwork and marble), and lastly plant motifs (flowerets and interlacing palm leaves).

Almohad or Sevilla architecture (12C–13C)

The religious puritanism of the Almohad dynasty, of which Sevilla was the capital, was expressed in architecture by a refined, though sometimes rather austere, simplicity. One of the characteristics of the style consisted of brickwork highlighted by wide bands of decoration in relief, without excessive ornamentation (the Giralda tower in Sevilla is a good example). The style was later used in the Mudéjar architecture of Aragón. Other features that emerged at

The Decorative Arts

Extremely rich and varied decorative artefacts from the Almohad period include geometric wood strapwork, brocades, weapons, ceramics with *esgrafiado* decoration and small ivory chests.

R. Corbel/MICHELIN

Multifoil

this time include *artesonado* ceilings and *azulejos*. Arches of alternate brick and stonework disappeared, the horseshoe arch became **pointed** and the multifoil arch was bordered by a curvilinear festoon (ornament like a garland) as in the Aljafería in Zaragoza. Calligraphic decoration included cursive (flowing) as well as Cufic script to which floral motifs were added to fill the spaces between vertical lines.

Nasrid or Granada architecture (14C–15C)

This period of high sophistication, of which the **Alhambra** in Granada (see illustration) is the masterpiece, produced less innovation in actual architectural design than in the decoration, whether stucco or ceramic, that covered the walls. Surrounds to doors and windows became focal points for every room's design and the spaces between them were filled by perfectly proportioned panels. Arch outlines were simplified – the stilted round arch became widespread – while detailed lacework ornamentation was used as a border.

Mudéjar architecture

This is the name given to work carried out in the Muslim style, usually by Muslim artesans, for Christian clients. It was fashionable from the 11C to the 15C in different regions depending on the area recovered by the Reconquest, although some features, like *artesonado* ceilings, continued as decorative themes for centuries.

Court Mudéjar, developed by Muslim artists (in buildings ordered by Peter the Cruel in Tordesillas and Sevilla, and in synagogues in Toledo), was an extension of the Almohad or contemporary Nasrid style. Popular Mudéjar, on the other hand, was produced by local Muslim workshops and reflects marked regional taste: walls were decorated with blind arcades in Castilla (Arévalo, Sahagún and Toledo) and belfries were faced with *azulejos* (see illustration) and geometric strapwork in Aragón.

PRE-ROMANESQUE AND ROMANESQUE ART AND ARCHITECTURE (8C–13C)

Asturian architecture

A highly sophisticated style of court architecture, characterised by sweeps of ascending lines, developed in the small kingdom of Asturias between the 8C and the 10C.

Asturian churches (Naranco, Santa Cristina de Lena) followed the precepts of the Latin basilica in their rectangular plan with a narthex, a nave and two aisles separated by **semicircular arches** (see illustration), a vast transept and an east end divided into three.

Decoration inside consisted of frescoes and borrowings from the East, including motifs carved on **capitals** (strapwork, rosettes and monsters, see illustration) and ornamental openwork around windows. Gold and silversmiths in the 9C and 10C produced rich treasures, many of which may be seen in the Cámara Santa in Oviedo Cathedral.

Mozarabic architecture

This term is given to work carried out by Christians living under Arab rule after the Moorish invasion of 711. Churches built in this style, especially in Castilla (San Miguel de Escalada, San Millán de la Cogolla), brought back Visigothic traditions (horseshoe arches) enriched by Moorish features such as ribbed cupolas and turned modillions.

Illuminated manuscripts provide the earliest known examples of Spanish medieval painting (10C). They were executed in the 10C and 11C by Mozarabic monks and have Moorish features such as horseshoe arches and Arab costumes. They portray St John's Commentary on the Apocalypse written in the 8C by the monk **Beatus de Liébana**, after whom the manuscripts were named.

Keystone
Voussoir
Springer
Semicircular

R. Corbel/MICHELIN

Romanesque

SANTIAGO DE COMPOSTELA – Cathedral: Interior (11C-13C)

Santiago cathedral is a typical example of a Spanish pilgrimage church and shows clear French influence.

Barrel vault

Barrel arch: formed of a single curved member, with no diagonal ribs

Tribune: a gallery above the side aisle and of a similar width

Paired arch: arches grouped in pairs

Wall arch: an arch parallel to the length of the nave, separating it from the side aisle

Raised round arch

Organ

Corinthian capital

Abacus: the uppermost slab of a capital or column

Pillar with engaged columns

H. Choimet/MICHELIN

Catalunya, home of the earliest Romanesque style in Spain

Catalunya had intimate links with Italy and France and consequently developed an architectural style strongly influenced by Lombardy from the 11C to the 13C. This evolved in the Pyrenean valleys, isolated from the more travelled pilgrim and trade routes. Sober little churches were often completed by a separate bell tower decorated with Lombard bands. Interior walls in the 11C and 12C were only embellished with frescoes which, in spite of their borrowings from Byzantine mosaics (heavy black outlines, rigid postures, and themes like Christ in Glory portrayed within a mandorla), proved by their realistic and expressive details to be typically Spanish. Altar fronts of painted wood, executed in bright colours, followed the same themes and layout.

European Romanesque art along the pilgrim routes

Northwest Spain opened its gates to foreign influence during the reign of Sancho the Great of Navarra early in the 11C. Cistercian abbeys were founded and French merchants allowed to settle rate free in towns (Estella, Sangüesa and Pamplona).

Meanwhile, the surge of pilgrims to Compostela and the fever to build along the routes brought about the construction of a great many religious buildings in which French influence was clearly marked (characteristics from Poitou in Soria and Sangüesa, and from Toulouse in Aragón and **Santiago de Compostela** (⚲ *see illustration*). The acknowledged masterpiece of this style is the Santiago de Compostela Cathedral.

In Aragón, Romanesque art was particularly evident in sculpture. The artists who carved capitals in the manner of their leader, the Maestro de San Juan de la Peña, had a seemingly clumsy style because their emphasis was more on symbolism than realistic portrayal. Disproportionate faces with bulging eyes were the means by which the sculptor illustrated the soul, while gestures such as outstretched hands conveyed religious meaning.

In the early 12C, reform of the **Cistercian Order** with emphasis on austerity brought an important change to architecture. The transitional style which heralded the Gothic (intersecting ribbed vaulting, squared apses) was introduced and the profusion of Romanesque decoration disappeared. Examples of this style may be seen in the monasteries of Poblet, Santes Creus, La Oliva and Santa María de Huerta.

THE GOTHIC PERIOD (FROM THE 13C)

The early stages

French Gothic architecture made little headway into Spain except in Navarra where a French dynasty had been in power since 1234. The first truly Gothic buildings (Roncesvalles church, Cuenca and Sigüenza cathedrals) were constructed in the 13C. Bishops in some of the main towns in Castilla (**León** (⚲ *see illustration*), Burgos, Toledo) sent abroad for cathedral plans, artists and masons. An original style of church, with no transept, a single nave (aisles, if there were any, would be as high as the nave), and pointed stone arches or a wooden roof resting on diaphragm arches, developed in **Valencia**, **Catalunya** and the **Balearic Islands**. The unadorned walls enclosed a large, homogeneous space in which there was little carved decoration, and purity of line supplied a dignified elegance.

Civil architecture followed the same pattern and had the same geometrical sense of space, used with rare skill particularly in the *lonjas* or commodity exchanges of Barcelona, Palma, Valencia and Zaragoza.

The Gothic style develops

During the 14C and 15C in Castilla, the influence of artists from the north, such as **Johan of Cologne** and **Hanequin of Brussels**, brought about the flowering of a style approaching Flamboyant Gothic. As it adapted to Spain, the style developed simultaneously in two different ways: in one, decoration proliferated to produce the Isabelline style; in the other, structures were simplified into a national church and cathedral style, which remained in favour until the mid-16C (Segovia and **Salamanca**, ⚲ *see illustration*).

The last of the Gothic cathedrals

Following the example of Sevilla, the dimensions of Gothic cathedrals became ever more vast. Aisles almost as large as the nave increased the volume of the building, while pillars, though massive, retained the impression of thrusting upward lines. A new plan emerged in which the old crescendo of radiating chapels, ambulatory, chancel and transept was superseded by a plain rectangle. Gothic decoration accumulated around doors, on pinnacles and in

Gothic

LEÓN – Cathedral: side façade (13C-14C)

In Gothic architecture, light was considered the essence of beauty and the symbol of truth. León cathedral is the brightest and most delicate of all the major Spanish cathedrals and is viewed as the best example of this concept. The beauty and magnificence of its stained glass attracts the admiration of its many thousands of visitors every year. French influence is clearly evident in its ground plan (Reims) and sculptures (Chartres).

Gable: ornamental triangular feature with solid or ornamental decoration

Gable: ornamental triangular feature with solid or ornamental decoration

Pinnacle

Rose window

Flying buttress

Tracery: decoration formed by geometric motifs, particularly used in rose windows and Gothic ogives

Tympanum

Buttress: a pillar built into a wall to reinforce those points subject to greatest stress

Pier: a vertical structure, often finely decorated, supporting a door or a wall

Mullion: a vertical feature which divides in two the opening or span of a portal or window

Archivolt: ornamental moulding on the outer edge of an arch

H. Choimet/MICHELIN

elaborate star vaulting; a style echoed in some Andalucían cathedrals.

Painting

Artists in the Gothic era worked on polyptyches and altarpieces which sometimes reached a height of more than 15m/49ft.

The Primitives, who customarily painted on gold backgrounds, were influenced by the Italians (soft contours), the French and the Flemish (rich fabrics with broken folds and painstaking detail). Nonetheless, as they strove for expressive naturalism and lively anecdotal detail, their work came across as distinctively Spanish.

There was intense artistic activity in the states attached to the Crown of Aragón, especially in Catalunya. The Vic, Barcelona and Valencia museums contain works by **Jaume Ferrer Bassá** (1285–

1348) who was influenced by the Sienese **Duccio**, paintings by his successor **Ramón Destorrents** (1346–91), and by the **Serra** brothers, Destorrents' pupils. Among other artists were **Luis Borrassá** (c. 1360–c. 1425), who had a very Spanish sense of the picturesque, **Bernat Martorell**, who gave special importance to landscape, **Jaime Huguet** (1412–92), who stands out for his extreme sensitivity and is considered to be the undisputed leader of the Catalan School, and finally **Luis Dalmau** and **Bartolomé Bermejo** (c. 1440–c. 1498), both influenced by Van Eyck (who accompanied a mission sent to Spain by the Duke of Burgundy).

In Castilla, French influence predominated in the 14C and Italian in the 15C until about 1450 when Flemish artists like **Roger van der Weyden** arrived. By the end of the 15C, **Fernando Gallego** (c.1440-1507) had become the main figure in the Hispano-Flemish movement in which **Juan de Flandes** was noted for his delicate touch.

Sculpture

Gothic sculpture, like architecture, became more refined. Relief was more accentuated than in Romanesque carving, postures more natural and details more meticulous. Decoration grew increasingly abundant as the 15C progressed and faces became individualised to the point where recumbent funerary statues clearly resembled the deceased. Statues were surmounted by an openwork canopy, while door surrounds, cornices and capitals were decorated with friezes of intricate plant motifs. After being enriched by French influence in the 13C and 14C and Flemish in the 15C, sculpture ultimately developed a purely Spanish style, the **Isabelline**.

Portals showed a French influence. Tombs were at first sarcophagi decorated with coats of arms, sometimes surmounted by a recumbent statue in a conventional posture with a peaceful expression and hands joined. Later, more attention was paid to the costume of the deceased; with an increasingly honed technique marble craftsmen were able to render the richness of brocades and the supple quality of leather. In the 15C, sculptors produced lifelike figures in natural positions, kneeling for instance, or even in nonchalant attitudes like that of the remarkable Doncel in Sigüenza Cathedral.

Altarpieces comprised a predella or plinth, surmounted by several levels of panels and finally by a carved openwork canopy. Choir stalls were adorned with biblical and historical scenes or carved to resemble delicate stone tracery.

The Isabelline style

At the end of the 15C, the prestige surrounding the royal couple and the grandees in the reign of Isabel the Catholic (1474–1504) provided a favourable context for the emergence of a new style in which exuberant decoration covered entire façades of civil and religious buildings.

Ornamentation took the form of supple free arcs, lace-like carving, heraldic motifs and every fantasy that imagination could devise. The diversity of inspiration was largely due to foreign artists: **Simon of Cologne** (son of Johan) – San Pablo in Valladolid, Capilla del Condestable in Burgos; **Juan Guas** (son of the Frenchman Pierre) – San Juan de los Reyes in Toledo; and **Enrique Egas** (nephew of Hanequin of Brussels) – Capilla Real in Granada.

THE RENAISSANCE (16C)

In the 16C, at the dawn of its Golden Age, Spain was swept by a deep sense of its own national character and so created a style in which Italian influence became acceptable only when hispanicised.

Architecture

Plateresque was the name given to the early Renaissance style because of its finely chiselled, lavish decoration reminiscent of silverwork (*platero*: silversmith).

Although close to the Isabelline style in its profusion of carved forms extending over entire façades, the rounded arches and ornamental themes (grotesques, foliage, pilasters, medallions and

Plateresque

SALAMANCA – University: façade (16C)

Although the exuberant decoration used to cover the entire façade is somewhat Gothic in style, the motifs used are Classical.

Cresting: the ornamental ridge crowning an architectural work

Frieze: decorative horizontal band

Pilaster: pillar attached to the wall

Golden Fleece: an ornamental collar and symbol of the Order of the Golden Fleece often seen on the escutcheon of Charles V

Medallion: an oval or circular decorative relief moulding

Scallop shell: scallop-shaped moulding used as an ornamental feature

Escutcheon

Bust

Grotesque: decoration combining foliation, imagin-ary creatures and animals

Basket-handle arch

H. Choimet/MICHELIN

cornices) were Italian. The Plateresque style was brought to a climax in **Salamanca** in the **façade of the Universidad** (see illustration) and that of the Convento de San Esteban.

Among architects of the time were **Rodrigo Gil de Hontañón**, who worked at Salamanca (Palacios de Monterrey and Fonseca) and at Alcalá de Henares (university façade), and **Diego de Siloé**, the main architect in Burgos (Escalera de la Coronería). Together with **Alonso de Covarrubias** (1488–1570), who worked mainly in Toledo (Alcázar and Capilla de los Reyes Nuevos in the cathedral), Diego de Siloé marked the transition from the Plateresque style to the Classical Renaissance. **Andrés de Vandelvira** (1509–75) was the leading architect of the Andalucían Renaissance (Jaén Cathedral). His work introduces the austerity which was to characterise the last quarter of the century.

The Renaissance style drew upon Italian models and adopted features from classical architecture such as rounded arches, columns, entablatures and pediments. Decoration became of secondary importance after architectonic perfection. **Pedro Machuca** (c. 1490–1550), who studied under Michelangelo, designed the palace of Charles V in Granada, the most classical example of the Italian tradition. Another important figure, **Bartolomé Bustamante** (1500–70), built the **Hospital de Tavera** in **Toledo** (see illustration).

The greatest figure of Spanish Classicism was **Juan de Herrera** (1530–93), who gave his name to an architectural style characterised by grandeur and austerity. He was the favourite architect of Philip II. The king saw in his work the sobriety that suited the Counter-Reformation and in 1567 entrusted him with the task of continuing work on El Escorial, his greatest achievement.

Sculpture

Sculpture in Spain reached its climax during the Renaissance. In the 16C, a great many choir stalls, mausoleums and

Renaissance

TOLEDO - Hospital Tavera: patio (16C)

The sense of proportion, visible on both the ground and first floors surrounding the double patio of this hospital, is a typical feature of pure Renaissance style.

Triglyph: three vertical bands separated by V-shaped grooves (characteristic of Doric frieze)

Spandrel or **pendentive** decorated with a rosette

Arris vault

Ionic column

Balustrade

Shaft

Base

Doric column

Superimposing of orders according to a classical plan (Doric on the lower gallery, Ionic on the upper gallery)

Metope: the triglyphs alternate with plain or sculpted panels

H. Choimet/MICHELIN

altarpieces (also known as **retables**: 👉 *see illustration*) were still being made of alabaster and wood. These latter were then painted by the *estofado* technique in which gold leaf is first applied, then the object is coloured and finally delicately scored to produce gold highlights. Carved altarpiece (*retablo*) panels were framed by Corinthian architraves (epistyles) and pilasters.

The sculptures of **Damián Forment** (c. 1480–1540), who worked mainly in Aragón, belong to the transition period between Gothic and Renaissance styles. The Burgundian **Felipe Vigarny** (c. 1475–1542) and the architect **Diego de Siloé**,

Retable or altarpiece

Frame

Wing panel

Second or middle tier

Predella

Crowning piece

Central panel

Side panels

First or lower tier

R. Corbel/MICHELIN

81

Ground plan

BARCELONA – Cathedral (13C-15C)

Ambulatory: an extension of the side aisles forming a gallery around the chancel and behind the altar

Pillar

Side chapel

Side aisle (Evangelist aisle)

Presbytery: the space in front of the altar, separated from the nave by some steps and a partition

Nave

Nave

Screen: often carved and decorated

Apsidal or **radiating chapels:** small apses radiating off the ambulatory

Chancel: the part of the church reserved for the clergy. In Spanish cathedrals it is often built in the middle of the nave. It can also be placed in a tribune or gallery

Transept: The part of the cathedral at right angles to the nave. It consists of the transept crossing and arms

R. Corbel/MICHELIN

who was apprenticed in Naples, both worked on Burgos Cathedral. **Bartolomé Ordóñez** (c. 1480–1520) studied in Naples and carved the *trascoro* (choir screen) in **Barcelona Cathedral** (*see illustration*) and the mausoleums of Joanna the Mad, Philip the Handsome (Capilla Real in Granada) and Cardinal Cisneros (Alcalá de Henares).

The home of the Renaissance School moved from Burgos to Valladolid in the mid-16C, by which time the Spanish style had absorbed foreign influences and Spain's two great Renaissance sculptors had emerged. The first, **Alonso Berruguete** (c. 1488–1561), who studied in Italy under Michelangelo, had a style which drew closely on the Florentine Renaissance and reflected a strong personality. He sought strength of expression rather than formal beauty and his tormented, fiery human forms are as powerful as those of his master (statue of San Sebastián in the Museo de Valladolid). The second, **Juan de Juni** (c. 1507–77), a Frenchman who settled in Valladolid, was also influenced by Michelangelo and founded the Catalan School of sculpture. His statues, recognisable by their beauty and the fullness of their forms, anticipated the Baroque style through the dramatic postures they adopted to express sorrow. Many of his works, such as the famous Virgen de los Siete Cuchillos (Virgin of the Seven Knives) in the Iglesia de las Angustias

Trascoro by Bartolomé Ordóñez, Barcelona Cathedral

© Yann Guichaoua/Pictures Colour Library

in Valladolid and the Entombments in the Museo de Valladolid and Segovia Cathedral, were subsequently copied. Most of the finely worked wrought-iron grilles closing off chapels and *coros* (chancels) were carved in the 15C and 16C. Members of the **Arfe** family, Enrique, Antonio and Juan, stand out in the field of gold and silversmithing. They made the monstrances of Toledo, Santiago de Compostela and Sevilla Cathedrals respectively.

Painting

Under Italian Renaissance influence, Spanish painting in the 16C showed a mastery of perspective, a taste for clarity of composition and glorification of the human body. These features found their way into Spanish painting mainly through the Valencian School, which had close links with Italian artists and patrons. **Fernando Yáñez de la Almedina** and **Hernando Llanos** introduced the style of Leonardo da Vinci, while **Vicente Macip** added that of Raphael and his son **Juan de Juanes** produced Mannerist works.

In Sevilla, **Alejo Fernández** painted the famous *Virgin of the Navigators* in the Alcázar. In Castilla, the great master of the late 15C was **Pedro Berruguete** (c. 1450–1503), whose markedly personal style drew upon all the artistic influences in the country. His successor, **Juan de Borgoña**, specialised particularly in landscape, architecture and decorative motifs. Another artist, **Pedro de Campaña** from Brussels, used *chiaroscuro* to dramatic effect while **Luis de Morales** (c. 1520–86), a Mannerist, gave his work a human dimension through the portrayal of feelings. Ordinary people with religious sentiments responded favourably to the spiritual emotion expressed in his paintings.

At the end of the 16C, Philip II sent for a great many Italian or Italian-trained artists to paint pictures for El Escorial. During his reign he introduced portrait painting under the Dutchman **Antonio Moro** (c. 1519–c. 1576), his cohort **Alonso Sánchez Coello** (1531–88) and **Juan Pantoja de la Cruz** (1553–1608).

El Greco (1541–1614), on the other hand, was scorned by the court and settled in Toledo.

BAROQUE (17C–18C)

Spanish art reached its apogee in the mid-17C. Baroque met with outstanding success in its role as an essentially religious art in the service of the Counter-Reformation and was particularly evident in Andalucía, then enriched by trade with America.

Architecture

Architects in the early 17C were still under the influence of 16C Classicism and the Herreran style to which they added decorative details. Public buildings proliferated and many continued to be built throughout the Baroque period.

Public buildings of the time in Madrid include the Plaza Mayor by **Juan Gómez de Mora**, built shortly before the *ayuntamiento* (town hall), and the most significant building of all, the present Ministerio de Asuntos Exteriores (Ministry of Foreign Affairs) by **Juan Bautista Crescenzi**, the architect of the Panteón de Reyes at El Escorial.

Church architecture of the period showed greater freedom from Classicism. A style of Jesuit church, with a cruciform plan and a large transept that served to

Virgin and the Child *(16C) by Luis de Morales, Museo Nacional del Prado*

Photo ©White Images/Photo Scala, Florence

83

Baroque

MADRID – Museo Municipal (Antiguo Hospicio): portal (18C)

The Baroque retable or altarpiece, which reached new architectural heights in Spain, was occasionally created on the façade of a building, rather than inside it.

Scallop shell

Vaulted niche: a hollow crowned by a quarter sphere, generally used to house a statue

Drapery effect

Escutcheon

Pilaster: a support with its narrowest part towards the base in the shape of a truncated inverted pyramid

Stone

Pediment: inserted in the cornice

Chiaroscuro: the use of relief and light to create contrasts in light and shade

Curved entablature

Volute

Oculus

Brick

H.Choimet/MICHELIN

light up altarpieces, began to emerge. Madrid has several examples including the Iglesia de San Isidro by the Jesuits **Pedro Sánchez** and **Francisco Bautista**, and the Real Convento de la Encarnación by **Juan Gómez de Mora**. In the middle of the century, architects adopted a less rigid style, changing plans and façades, breaking up entablatures and making pediments more elaborate. A good example of this Italian Baroque style is the Iglesia Pontificia de San Miguel (18C) in Madrid.

A new feature, the **camarín**, was introduced: at first simply a passage behind the high altar leading to the retable niche containing a statue venerated by the faithful, it developed into a highly ornate chapel.

Decoration of this kind may be seen in Zaragoza's Basílica de Nuestra Señora del Pilar designed by **Francisco Herrera el Mozo** (1622–85). The Clerecía in Salamanca is a magnificent Baroque creation with a patio that anticipates the audacity and superabundant decoration characteristic of the Churrigueresque style.

The Churrigueresque style

In this style, named after the Churriguera family of architects (late 17C), architecture became no more than a support for dense concentrations of ornament covering entire façades.

The style is typified by the use of *salomónicas*, or barley sugar columns entwined with vines, and *estípites*, or pilasters arranged in an inverse pyramid. Early examples of this extravagance, the altarpiece of the Convento de San Esteban in Salamanca and the palace in Nuevo Baztán near Madrid, were by **José de Churriguera** (1665–1725), who was the instigator of the style but did not make any architectural changes. His brothers **Joaquín** (1674–1724) and especially **Alberto** (1676–1750), who designed the Plaza Mayor in Salamanca, took greater liberties in their work.

Pedro de Ribera (1681–1742), a Castilian architect who worked mainly in Madrid, surpassed the Churriguera brothers in decorative delirium.

The other great Castilian, **Narciso Tomé**, is remembered for the façade of the Universidad de Valladolid (1715) and particularly for the *Transparente* in Toledo Cathedral (1721–32).

Regional variations

The popularity of the Baroque spread countrywide, differing from province to province. In **Galicia**, where the hardness of the granite precluded delicate carving, Baroque took the form of softer lines and decorative mouldings. The best example of the style was by **Fernando de Casas Novoa**, who designed the Obradoiro façade of Santiago de Compostela Cathedral (1750) at the end of his life.

In **Andalucía**, Baroque attained its utmost splendour, especially in decoration. Undulating surfaces characterised the façades of palaces (Écija), cathedrals (Guadix) and the doorways of countless churches and mansions (Jerez) in the 18C. As well as sculptor and painter, **Alonso Cano** was the instigator of Andalucían Baroque and designed the façade of Granada Cathedral. The major exponent of the style was, however, **Vicente Acero**, who worked on the façade of Guadix Cathedral (1714–20), designed Cádiz Cathedral and built the tobacco factory in Sevilla. Mention should also be made of **Leonardo de Figueroa** (1650–1730) for the Palacio de San Telmo in Sevilla and **Francisco Hurtado** (1669–1725) and **Luis de Arévalo** for La Cartuja in Granada; Hurtado worked on the monastery's tabernacle and Arévalo on the sacristy, the most exuberant Baroque works in Andalucía.

In the **Levante**, Baroque artists used polychrome tiles to decorate church cupolas and spires like that of Santa Catalina in Valencia. In the same town, the Palacio del Marqués de Dos Aguas by **Luis Domingo** and **Ignacio Vergara** is reminiscent of façades by Ribera, although its design is more like French Rococo. The cathedral in Murcia has an impressive façade by **Jaime Bort y Meliá**.

The golden age of Spanish painting

This was characterised by the rejection of the previous century's Mannerism and the adoption of Naturalism. The starting point was Caravaggio's tenebrism,

Detail of Las Meninas *(1656) by Diego Velázquez, Museo Nacional del Prado*

©World Illustrated/Photoshot

powerful contrasts of light and shade, and his stern realism. Painters took up portraiture and still life *(bodegón)*, while allegories on the theme of *vanitas* (still-life paintings showing the ephemerality of life) reflected a philosophical purpose by juxtaposing everyday objects with symbols of decay to illustrate the transience of wealth and the things of this world and the inevitability of death. Among 17C artists were two from the Valencian School – **Francisco Ribalta** (1565–1628), who introduced tenebrism into Spain, and **José de Ribera** (1591–1652), known for his forceful realism.

Some of the greatest Baroque artists worked in Andalucía.

One was **Francisco de Zurbarán** (1598–1664), master of the Sevilla School; light in his paintings springs from within the subjects themselves.

Other artists included **Bartolomé Esteban Murillo** (1617–82), who painted intimate, mystical scenes, and **Valdés de Valdés Leal** whose realism challenged earthly vanities.

Alonso Cano (1601–67), architect, painter and sculptor, settled in Granada and painted delicate figures of the Virgin. The Castilian painters, **Vicente Carducho** (c. 1576–1638) and portraitists **Juan Carreño de Miranda** (1614–85) and **Claudio Coello** (1642–93), all excellent artists, nonetheless pale beside **Diego Velázquez** (1599–1660), whose perspective, masterly sense of composition, sense of depth, technique and psychology are recognised as those of a universal master who influenced Spain's painters over the centuries to come.

Sculpture

Spanish Baroque sculpture was naturalistic and intensely emotive. The most commonly used medium was wood, and while altarpieces continued to be carved, *pasos* or statues specially made for Semana Santa processions proved a great novelty.

The two major schools of Baroque sculpture were in Castilla and Andalucía. **Gregorio Hernández**, Juni's successor, worked in Valladolid, the Castilian centre. His style was a lot more natural than

Detail of Mary Magdalene *(17C) by Pedro de Mena, Museo Nacional Colegio de San Gregorio, Valladolid*

Photo Scala, Florence

that of his master, and his Christ Recumbent for the Convento de Capuchinos in El Pardo was widely copied. Sevilla and Granada were the main centres for the Andalucían School.

Juan Martínez Montañés (1568–1649) settled in Sevilla and worked exclusively in wood, carving a great many pasos and various altarpieces.

Alonso Cano became famous for the grace and femininity of his Immaculate Conceptions while his best-known disciple, **Pedro de Mena** (1628–88), produced sculptures of great dramatic tension which contrasted with his master's understated style. The statue of Mary Magdalene (Museo Nacional de Escultura Policromada, Valladolid), St Francis (Toledo Cathedral) and the Dolorosa (Monasterio de las Descalzas Reales, Madrid) are telling examples of his work.

The 18C saw the rise to prominence of the great Murcian, **Francisco Salzillo** (1707–83), whose dramatic sculptures were inspired by Italian Baroque.

Churrigueresque excess in sculpture took the form of immense altarpieces which reached the roof. These huge constructions took on such grand proportions that they began to be designed by architects. Their statues seemed smothered by decoration, lost in an overabundance of gilding and stucco.

BOURBON ART

Spain's Catholic imperialism was succeeded by enlightened Bourbon despotism which resulted in artistic as well as political change in the 18C. Henceforth the rules of art were to be governed by official bodies like the Academia de Bellas Artes de San Fernando.

Architecture

During the first half of the century architecture still bore the stamp of Spanish Baroque, itself influenced at the time by French Rococo. The king and queen had palaces built in a moderate Baroque style (El Pardo, Riofrío, La Granja and Aranjuez) and began work on Madrid's Palacio Real modelled on Versailles. These buildings sought to ally French Classical harmony with Italian grace, and to this end most of the work was entrusted to Italian architects who generally respected the traditional quadrangular plan of *alcázares*, so typically Spanish. The vast gardens were generally given a French design.

Excavations of Pompeii and Herculaneum contributed to the emergence of a new, Neoclassical style which flourished between the second half of the 18C and 19C. It repudiated Baroque excess and aspired to Hellenistic beauty through the use of classical orders, pediments, porticoes and cupolas.

The Kings of Spain, Charles III in particular, set about embellishing the capital by building fountains (Cibeles, Neptune), gates (Alcalá and Toledo), and planting botanic gardens.

The first Spanish Neoclassical architect, **Ventura Rodríguez** (1717–85), who was actually apprenticed in Italian Baroque, quickly developed an academic Neoclassical style. His works include the façade of Pamplona Cathedral, the Paseo del Prado in Madrid and the Basílica de Nuestra Señora del Pilar in Zaragoza. **Francesco Sabatini** (1722–97), whose style developed along similar lines, designed the Puerta de Alcalá.

The leading architect was without doubt **Juan de Villanueva** (1739–1811),

Neo-Classical

MADRID - Observatorio Astronómico (18C)

This small building designed by Juan de Villanueva is a model of simplicity and purity which shows clear Palladian influence in its proportions and design.

Central part

Rotunda: based on a tholos design and surrounded by a circular colonnade

Ionic columns

Entablature

Hexastyle (entrance): a portico with six columns

Corinthian columns

Intercolumniation: the space between the columns

Arm (in buildings with a cruciform ground plan)

H. Choimet/MICHELIN

The Third of May *(1814) by Francisco de Goya, Museo Nacional del Prado*

©Imagestate/Tips Images

schooled in Classical principles during a stay in Rome. He designed the façade of the *ayuntamiento* in Madrid and, most importantly, the **Museo del Prado**.

Two notable town planners emerged during the 19C: **Ildefonso Cerdá** (1815–76) in Barcelona and **Arturo Soria** (1844–1920) in Madrid.

Painting

Bourbon monarchs took pains to attract the greatest painters to court and grant them official positions. In 1752 Ferdinand VI founded the Academia de Bellas Artes de San Fernando where it was intended that students should learn official painting techniques and study the Italian masters. Leading artists of the time were **Anton Raphael Mengs** (1728–79) from Bohemia and the Italian **Giambattista Tiepolo** (1696–1770), both of whom decorated the Palacio Real. There was also **Francisco Bayeu** (1734–95) from Aragón, who painted a great many tapestry cartoons, as did his brother-in-law **Francisco de Goya** (1746–1828). Goya's work, much of which may be seen in the Prado, Madrid, was to dominate the entire century.

Painters working in the post-Goya period did not follow in the master's footsteps as academic Neoclassical influences and Romanticism took over; Goya's legacy was not taken up until the end of the 19C. The following stand out among artists of the academic Romantic trend: **Federico de Madrazo**, representative of official taste in royal portraits and historical scenes, **Vicente Esquivel**, portrait-painter, and lastly **Leonardo Alenza**, and **Eugenio Lucas Velázquez**, the spokesmen for **Costumbrismo**, which had attained full status as a genre. (This was a style of painting illustrating scenes of everyday life which gradually developed from the simply anecdotal to a higher calling, the evocation of the Spanish soul.) Historical themes became very popular in the 19C with works by **José Casado del Alisal**, **Eduardo Rosales** and **Mariano Fortuny**. Impressionist features began to appear in naturalist paintings by **Ramón Martí Alsina** and in post-Romantic landscapes by **Carlos de Haes**. The style secured a definitive hold in the works of **Narciso Oller, Ignacio Pinazo Camarlench**, the best Valencian Impressionist, **Darío de Regoyos** and lastly, **Joaquín Sorolla**, who specialised in light-filled folk scenes and regional subjects.

The Basque artist **Ignacio Zuloaga** (1870–1945) expressed his love for Spain in brightly coloured scenes of everyday life at a time when Impressionism was conquering Europe.

The Decorative Arts

Factories were built under the Bourbons to produce decorative material for their royal palaces. In 1760, Charles III founded the Buen Retiro works, where ceramics for the famous Salones de Porcelana in the royal palaces of Aranjuez and Madrid were made. The factory was destroyed during the Napoleonic invasion.

In 1720, Philip V opened the Real Fábrica de Tapices de Santa Bárbara (in Madrid), the equivalent of the French Gobelins factory in Paris. Some of the tapestries were of Don Quixote while others depicted scenes of everyday life based on preparatory cartoons by Bayeu and Goya.

20C ART

From Modernism to Surrealism

The barren period that Spanish art in general experienced at the end of the 19C was interrupted in Catalunya by a vast cultural movement known as **Modernism**. This was particularly strong in architecture, with outstanding work by **Antoni Gaudí, Lluís Domènech i Montaner** and **Josep Maria Jujol**.

In the field of sculpture, **Pablo Gargallo** broke new ground through the simplicity of his shapes, the attention he gave to volume and the use of new materials like iron.

Painting was varied and prolific. The following stand out among the many artists of the time: **Ramón Casas**, the best Spanish Impressionist, whose works are suffused with an atmosphere of grey melancholy, **Santiago Rusiñol, Isidro Nonell**, instigator of Spanish Expressionism, and **Pablo Picasso** (1881–1973),

the dominant figure whose innovations were to mark the entire history of 20C painting. Picasso's attention was first devoted to academic Naturalism (Science and Charity). He subsequently became a Modernist and social Expressionist. Later, once he had moved to Paris (1904), his style developed through the successive blue and rose periods to Cubism (Les Demoiselles d'Avignon), Surrealism and Expressionism (Guernica), which in turn led to a totally personal and subjective lyrical style (La Joie de Vivre).

In the 1920s a movement began to emerge that was influenced by Cubism and, more particularly, by Surrealism. Its sculptors were **Ángel Ferrant, Victorio Macho, Alberto Sánchez Pérez** and lastly **Julio González**, who strove towards Abstract Expressionism through the use of iron and simple shapes. Painters of the movement included **Daniel Vázquez Díaz**, Juan Gris, Joan Miró and Salvador Dalí. **Juan Gris** (1887–1927), the most faithful analytical Cubist, worked in Paris. The works of **Joan Miró** (1893–1983), champion of Surrealism, are characterised by childlike spontaneity and an original attitude to everyday objects. Miró used very bright colours and magic symbols in all his paintings; today the Fundació Joan Miró in Barcelona houses his works (👁 see illustration). **Salvador Dalí** (1904–89), a quasi-Surrealist, dreamed up his

Inverted cupola of polychrome glass, Palau de la Música Catalana in Barcelona, designed by Domènech i Montaner

F. Vidal/MICHELIN

Modernism

BARCELONA –Casa Batlló (Antoni Gaudí: 1905-07)

Modernism is a colourful, decorative and sensual style which recreates organic forms in a world dominated by curves and reverse curves.

Cross (a decorative style frequently used by Gaudí)

Turret

Polychrome mosaic covering the façade

Columns: vertical piers ressembling bones

Ceramic roof resembling dragon skin

Opening for leaning out of the roof

Metal balconies

Large curved; windows

Stone columns and arches

Mediterranean Rationalist

BARCELONA – Fundació Joan Miró (JL Sert: 1972-75)

The building consists of a series of interrelated architectural features and open spaces in which natural light plays a fundamental role.

Skylights

No decorative features

Harmonious proportions

H. Choimer/MICHELIN

own creative method which he called the paranoic critical. Some of his best paintings were a result of his interest in the subconscious and his vision of a dream world.

Post-war art

Spanish art was crucially affected by the Civil War in two ways: firstly, the fact that artists, including Picasso, went into exile, and secondly, official taste in architecture developed a penchant for the monumental. This is clearly apparent in a number of colossal edifices. Many of Madrid's government buildings were designed in the manner of El Escorial, including the Ministerio del Aire complex by Moncloa's triumphal arch, and the nearby Museo de América. The most striking example is the monument of the Valle de los Caídos (Valley of the Fallen) outside Madrid. However, among exponents of the Nationalist style, there were several innovative architects like **Miguel Fisac**.

In 1950 the first signs of a new style, based on rational and functional criteria, began to emerge. Examples abound in Barcelona, including the Vanguardia building by **Oriol Bohigas** and **José María Martorell**, the residential block by **Ricardo Bofill Leví** in Carrer de Nicaragua, and in Madrid the Torres Blancas (White Towers) by **Francisco Javier Sáenz de Oíza**. Post-war sculpture and painting are basically academic but there are some notable artists such as **José Gutiérrez Solana**, whose paintings are full of anguish, and the landscape painters **Benjamín Palencia**, who glorifies the country and light of Castilla, and **Rafael Zabaleta**, who is more interested in painting the region's country folk.

Avant-Garde painters also began to emerge after the war. The first post-war Surrealists are members of a group called **Dau al Set** including **Modest Cuixart**, **Antoni Tàpies** and **Joan-Josep Tharrats**. Tàpies is a veritable pioneer, one of the major abstract artists.

Contemporary Art

In the 1950s two abstract groups with the common aim of artistic innovation were formed: the **El Paso** group in Madrid with **Antonio Saura**, **Manolo Millares** and **Rafael Canogar**, all representatives of what was known as action painting; and the **Equipo 57** group in Cuenca with **Eusebio Sempere**, **Ángel Duarte**, **Agustín Ibarrola**, **Juan Serrano** and **José Duarte**. The movement's sculptors included Basque artists **Jorge Oteiza** and **Eduardo Chillida**. He worked in iron and wood, stripping his sculptures of any figurative suggestion, a style that is still influential. Major international figures of the last decade, such as painter Miquel Barceló, sculptor Juan Muñoz (who died in 2001) and Ángela de la Cruz, nominated for the Tate Modern Award in 2010, increasingly make their careers outside Spain.

Photography, however, is especially strong on home ground, creating stars like Cristina Rodero and Albert García-Alix. Younger artists's work may be sampled at a clutch of outstanding regional modern art museums in Barcelona, Vitoria, Valladolid and La Palma.

SPANISH GARDENS

The gardens of Spain are a further example of the country's rich culture, and bear witness to an enviable ability to adapt to a varied climate. Although Spanish landscape gardening has inherited many of its traditions from within Europe, particularly from the Greco-Roman era, the long period of Muslim

Patio de la Acequia, El Generalife, Granada

© Geoffroy LEME/Fotolia.com

occupation added a new dimension as unique as that of its architecture.

THE GENERALIFE (14C), GRANADA

The Generalife is the Moorish garden par excellence. As a result of its extraordinary position it is a magnificent balcony, but above all it has been able to preserve the intimate, sensual character and evocation of paradise that was such a feature of Muslim gardens.

Despite alterations over the centuries it remains a feast for the senses and a harmonious whole which avoids grandiloquence. Nothing has been left to chance: the colour of the plants and flowers, their scent, and the omnipresence of water combine to create a serene ambience. The Generalife is laid out on several levels to ensure that the trees in one garden do not interfere with the views from another. In fact, the garden is best considered as a series of landscaped areas and enclosures, each with its own individuality, yet part of an overall design. The architectural features and vegetation, reflected in the water channels, blend together to create a perfect whole.

LA GRANJA (18C), LA GRANJA DE SAN ILDEFONSO, SEGOVIA

These magnificent Baroque palace gardens bring to mind those of Versailles, where Philip V spent his childhood. He was to make La Granja his personal retreat. While it lacks Versailles' grandiose perspectives it gains in its backdrop of peaked mountains whose snows feed magnificent fountains. The rigidity of the French garden is lost here as there is no clear central axis; instead, La Granja consists of a succession of parts, each with a certain independence, thus adopting hints of Moorish design.

Although the French gardeners Philip V invited south brought with them a variety of species, they were able to adapt them perfectly to the local landscape in the palace's nurseries while preserving some of its wildness.

Magnificent sculptures scattered in small squares and along avenues add a theatrical touch. The gardens are at their very best when the fountains are switched on for selected days in spring and early summer.

PAZO DE OCA (18C–19C), LA ESTRADA, LA CORUÑA

A *pazo* is a Baroque-style manor typically found in Galicia, built on a plot of land which generally comprises a recreational garden, a kitchen garden and cultivated farmland. The garden of the Pazo de Oca – or goose manor – is the oldest in Galicia and is a magnificent example of romantic garden design in green northern Spain. The damp climate has enabled vegetation to grow on rocks, creating an intimate relationship

La Granja de San Ildefonso, Segovia

© Turespaña

between its architectural and vegetable features. Water plays a vital role, appearing in basins or fountains or trickling through the garden.

The most romantic part, with its two ponds, is hidden behind a parterre. A delightful bridge, with benches enabling visitors to enjoy this enchanting spot, separates the two sections, overcoming the difference in height between them. The lower pond contains the *pazo*'s most representative and famous feature: the stone boat, with its two petrified sailors, planted with hydrangeas.

JARDINS DE MONFORT (19C), VALENCIA

The River Turia's ribbon of green parkland running through Valencia's city centre links three older gardens: the Jardins del Reial, which date back to Muslim times, the Jardí Botànic, founded in 1567, and finally the Jardins de Montfort, the smallest but perhaps the most beautiful of the three.

When the Marqués de San Juan, an ennobled businessman, created this romantic garden in the 1860s it lay between orchards and rural palaces. Today, protected by its old brick walls, it remains an ingenious oasis with a microclimate that fosters flowering plants and aromatics around the year. Close to a small pavilion a waist-high labyrinth of trimmed hedges is decorated by Italian marble statues and a graceful fountain. From here a bougainvillea bower leads through to a larger informal area which features olive and orange trees, a fragrant rose garden and oriental bamboo pond. As in other great Spanish gardens, you are never far from the sound of splashing water.

JARDÍN BOTÁNICO DE MARIMURTRA (20C), BLANES, GIRONA

Carlos Faust, the German impresario who settled on the Costa Brava, created this botanical garden in 1921 for research purposes and to preserve plants threatened with extinction. Situated in a delightful spot between the sea and the mountains, it offers

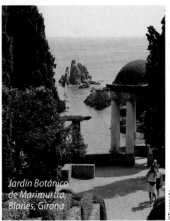

Jardín Botánico de Marimurtra, Blanes, Girona

©Turespaña

visitors magnificent views of the coast. Today Marimurtra is a fine example of a contemporary Mediterranean garden, although a number of exotic species from every continent have also adapted perfectly here. It contains an interesting cactus garden, an impressive aquatic garden, as well as a collection of medicinal, toxic and aromatic plants. The only architectural feature with a purely decorative function is the small temple built at the end of the steps running down to the sea.

LITERATURE

Errant knights, Don Juan characters, mystics and highwaymen occupy a hallowed place in Spanish letters. Spanish literature reached its peak during the Golden Age of the 16C and 17C, and has enjoyed a renewed period of acclaim since the beginning of the 20C through a new generation of writers from within Spain and across the Spanish-speaking world.

Roman Spain produced great Latin authors such as **Seneca the Elder** or the Rhetorician, his son **Seneca the Younger** and the poets **Martial** and **Lucan**. In the 8C, the monk **Beatus** wrote the Commentary on the Apocalypse, which gave rise to the outstanding illuminated beatus manuscripts. Arab writers, especially poets, won renown during the Muslim period. Works written in Castilian began to emerge only in the Middle Ages.

Statues of Don Quixote, Sancho Panza and Miguel de Cervantes, Plaza de España, Madrid

©Icefields/Dreamstime.com

THE MIDDLE AGES

The first milestone of Spanish literature appeared in the 12C in the form of *El Cantar del Mío Cid*, an anonymous Castilian poem inspired by the adventures of El Cid. In the 13C, the monk **Gonzalo de Berceo**, drawing on religious themes, won renown through his works of *Mester de Clerecía*, the learned poetry of clerics and scholars. **Alfonso X the Wise**, an erudite king who wrote poetry in Galician, decreed that in his kingdom Latin should be replaced as the official language by Castilian, an act subsequently followed throughout Spain, except in Catalunya, where Catalan remained the written language.

In the 14C, **Juan Ruiz**, **Archpriest of Hita**, wrote a brilliant satirical verse work titled *El Libro de Buen Amor*, which later influenced the picaresque novel.

THE RENAISSANCE

In the 15C, lyric poetry flourished under Italian influence with poets such as **Jorge Manrique** and the **Marquis of Santillana**. **Romanceros**, collections of ballads in an epic or popular vein, perpetuated the medieval style until the 16C when *Amadís de Gaula* (1508) set

the model for a great many romances or tales of chivalry. In 1499, *La Celestina*, a novel of passion in dialogue form by **Fernando de Rojas**, anticipated modern drama in a subtle, well-observed tragicomic intrigue.

THE GOLDEN AGE (SIGLO DE ORO)

Spain enjoyed its greatest literary flowering under the Habsburgs (1516–1700), with lyric poets such as **Garcilaso de la Vega**, disciple of Italian verse forms, mystic verse by **Fray Luis de León** and above all **Luis de Góngora y Argote** (1561–1627) whose obscure style won fame under the name of Gongorism.

The **picaresque** novel, however, was the genre favoured by Spanish writers at the time. The first to appear in 1554 was *Lazarillo de Tormes*, an anonymous autobiographical work in which the hero, an astute rogue (*pícaro* in Castilian), casts a mischievous and impartial eye on society and its woes.

There followed **Mateo Alemán**'s *Guzmán de Alfarache* with its brisk style and colourful vocabulary, and *La Vida del Buscón*, an example of the varied talents of **Francisco de Quevedo** (1580–1645), essayist, poet and satirist. The genius of the Golden Age, however, was **Miguel de Cervantes** (1547–1616), with his masterpiece, the universal **Don Quixote** (1605 and 1615). Dramatists proliferated, among them the master **Lope de Vega** (1562–1635), who perfected drama, working on it as an art for popular audiences. This "phoenix of the mind" wrote more than 1 000 plays, including *Fuenteovejuna*, and Europe's first manifesto on modern theatre. His successor, **Pedro Calderón de la Barca** (1600–81), wrote historical and philosophical plays (*El Alcalde de Zalamea* or *The Mayor of Zalamea*) in which he brilliantly reflected the mood of Spain in the 17C. **Tirso de Molina** (1579–1648) left his interpretation of Don Juan for posterity while **Guillén de Castro** wrote *Las Mocedades del Cid (Youthful Adventures of the Cid)*. Mention should also be made of works on the conquest of America by chroniclers **Cortés** and **Bartolomé de** las Casas among others. Finally, the moralist **Fray Luis de Granada** and the mystics **Santa Teresa de Ávila** (1515–82) and **San Juan de la Cruz** (St John of the Cross) (1542–91) wrote theological works equally inspiring for their writing.

18C AND 19C

The Enlightenment found expression in the works of essayists such as **Benito Jerónimo Feijoo,** a monk, and **Jovellanos**, while elegance dominated the plays of **Moratín**. The great romantic poet of the 19C was **Bécquer** (1836–70) from Sevilla, while **Larra** was a social satirist, **Menéndez Pelayo** a literary critic and **Ángel Ganivet** a political and moral analyst.

Realism was introduced to the Spanish novel by **Alarcón** *(The Three-Cornered Hat)* and **Pereda** *(Peñas arriba)*, who concentrated on regional themes. By the end of the 19C, the best realist was **Pérez Galdós** whose prolific, lively work *(National Episodes)* is stamped with a great sense of human sympathy.

20C

A group of intellectuals known as the Generation of '98, saddened by Spain's loss of colonies like Cuba, were provoked to produce writing with a new moral spirit, as reflected in the work of essayists such as **Miguel de Unamuno** (1864–1936) who wrote *El Sentimiento trágico de la vida (The Tragic Sense of Life)*, and **Azorín**, as well as the philologist **Menéndez Pidal**, the novelist **Pío Baroja** and the aesthete **Valle Inclán**, who created an elegant poetic prose style. Among their contemporaries were **Jacinto Benavente** (1922 Nobel Prize for literature winner), who developed a new dramatic style, and bestselling Valencian author **Blasco Ibañez**. Some great poets began to emerge, including **Juan Ramón Jiménez** (Nobel Prize 1956), who expressed his feelings through simple unadorned prose poems *(Platero y Yo)*, **Antonio Machado** (1875–1939), the bard of Castilla, and **Rafael Alberti**. **Federico García Lorca** (1898–1936), equally great as poet and dramatist *(Bodas de Sangre)*, anticipated magi-

Federico García Lorca

© Rafael Jáuregui/age fotostock

cal realism in his rich use of symbol and metaphor. His work was, perhaps, the most fascinating reflection of a Spain whose mystery **José Ortega y Gasset** (1883–1955), essayist and philosopher, spent his life trying to fathom.

POST-WAR WRITING

Several years after the Civil War, writing rose from its ashes with works by essayists (**Américo Castro,** in exile),playwrights (**Alfonso Sastre**) and novelists such as **Miguel Delibes**, **Camilo José Cela** *(La Familia de Pascual Duarte)* who won the Nobel Prize for Literature in 1989, and **Ramón Sender**, all preoccupied with social issues.

Contemporary Spanish writing has found international acclaim – **Javier Marías**, **Juan Goytisolo** and **Bernardo Atxaga** are examples – and produced bestselling authors like **Almudena Grandes**, **Carlos Ruiz Zafón** and **Arturo Pérez-Reverte**.

They followed a generation of writers who found recognition late at the end of the dictatorshop: **Juan Benet**, **Juan Marsé**, **José María Caballero Bonald** and **Manuel Vázquez Montalbán**. Women's writing has come into its own with **Mercè Rodoreda**, **Dulce Chacón** and **Ana María Matutes** leading the way for younger authors like **Lucía Etxebarria**. Some writers, notably **Atxaga** and **Manuel Rivas**, are writing in their own region's languages.

CINEMA AND MUSIC

Over the centuries, Spain has produced countless musicians and thespians of world renown. In more recent times, the genius of film directors such as **Luis Buñuel**, **Luis Berlanguer** and **Pedro Almodóvar**, composers such as **Manuel de Falla**, and guitarists such as **Antonio Segovia** and **Paco de Lucía** have thrilled audiences the world over.

PERFORMING ARTS

Opera, disliked by Franco, has made a comeback in Madrid's Teatro Real and Barcelona's historic Liceu. The revival of theatre is wider, with Catalunya's tradition of comedy joined by notable new work from Andalucía and Madrid.

CINEMA

Spanish cinema dates back to a short film in 1897 which shows people leaving the Basílica de Nuestra Señora del Pilar in Zaragoza after Mass. Studios for silent movies were later set up in Barcelona.

In the 1920s, several Surrealists tried their hand at the new art form. Among them were **Dalí** and above all **Luis Buñuel**, a master of Spanish cinema, who made *Un chien Andalou (An Andalusian Dog)* in 1928 and *Âge d'Or (The Golden Age)* in 1930.

When talking films appeared in the 1930s, Spain was in the throes of a political and economic crisis and so her studios lacked the means to procure the necessary equipment.

At the end of the 1930s, when films like *Sor Angélica (Sister Angelica)* by **Francisco Gargallo** tended to address religious themes, Juan Piqueras launched a magazine called *Nuestro Cinema*, which was strongly influenced by Russian ideas, and gave star billing to films such as *Las Hurdes (Land Without Bread)* by Buñuel in 1932, depicting poverty in a remote part of Spain.

During the Civil War and the ensuing Franco era, films were heavily censored and the cinema became one of the major vehicles for the ideology of the time, with historical and religious themes glorifying death and the spirit of sacrifice. One such success was *Marce-lino Pan y Vino (The Miracle of Marcelino)* by Ladislao Vajda in 1955. Change came with works by Juan Antonio Bardem like *Muerte de un Ciclista (Death of a Cyclist)* and, above all, *Bienvenido Mister Marshall (Welcome Mr Marshall*, 1953) and *El Verdugo (The Executioner*, 1963) by **Luis García Berlanga**.

The 1960s enjoyed a period of renewal with directors like **Carlos Saura**, whose first film, *Los Golfos (The Delinquents)*, came out in 1960. Mention should be made of Saura's *Ana y los Lobos (Anna and the Wolves*, 1973); *El Espíritu de la colmena (The Spirit of the Beehive*, 1973) and *El Sur (The South*, 1983) both by **Víctor Erice**; *La Colmena (The Beehive*, 1982) by **Mario Camus**, and films by **Manuel Gutiérrez Aragón** such as *La Mitad del cielo (Half of Heaven*, 1986) which illustrate the changes democracy brought to Franco's Spain.

Pedro Almodóvar broke with this serious, nostalgic type of cinema. His films show a completely different, modern Spain, often with a strong comic streak or powerfully dark melodrama behind the realism, and have won the hearts of critics and audiences around the world. *Mujeres al Borde de un Ataque de Nervios (Women on the Verge of a Nervous Breakdown*, 1988), *Volver* (2006) and *La Piel Que Habito (The Skin I Live In*, 2011) are three of a string of award-winning films. Like Almodóvar, contemporary filmmakers in Spain take on major social issues. Memorable examples from the last decade are **Alejandro Amenábar**'s *Mar Adentro (The Sea Inside*, 2004), Fernando León's *Lunes al Sol (Sunny Mondays*, 2002), **Icíar Bollaín**'s *Te Doy Mis Ojos (I Give You My Eyes*, 2003) and Mexican director Guillermo del Toro's *El Laberinto del Fauno (Pan's Labyrinth*, 2006), films which deal with euthanasia, unemployment, domestic violence and the legacy of the Civil War. While new talent emerges each year Almodóvar remains a key figure, having fostered the careers of actors Antonio Banderas, Javier Bardem and Penélope Cruz, director Isabel Coixet and Oscar-winning composer Alberto Iglesias. Animation flourishes. Young stars like Javier Recio work alongside experienced hands like Javier Mariscal.

MUSIC

Alongside its folk music, Spain has developed an extraordinarily rich musical repertory since the Middle Ages, marked by a large number of influences including Visigothic, Arabic, Mozarabic and French. Polyphonic chants were studied in the 11C and the oldest known piece for three voices, the *Codex calixtinus*, was composed at Santiago de Compostela c.1140. During the Reconquest, the church encouraged great musical creativity in the form of liturgical chants, plays *(autos)* like the *Elche Mystery* which is still performed today, and poetry like the 13C Cantigas de Santa María by **Alfonso the Wise**.

At the end of the 15C, the dramatist **Juan de la Encina** composed secular songs, thus proving that he was also an excellent musician. Music, like the other arts, however, reached its climax in the second half of the 16C, under the protection of the early Habsburgs. **Tomás Luis de Victoria** (1548–1611) was one of the most famous composers of polyphonic devotional pieces, while among his contemporaries, **Francisco de Salinas** and **Fernando de las Infantas** were learned musicologists and **Cristóbal de Morales** and **Francisco Guerrero** were accomplished religious composers. As for instruments, the organ became the invariable accompaniment to sacred music, while a favourite for profane airs was the *vihuela*, a sort of guitar with six double strings, which was soon replaced by the lute and eventually by the five-string Spanish guitar.

In 1629, **Lope de Vega** wrote the text for the first Spanish opera. **Pedro Calderón de la Barca** is credited with creating the **zarzuela**, a musical play with spoken passages, songs and dances, which, since the 19C, has based its plot and music on popular themes. The major composer of religious and secular music in the 18C was **Padre Antonio Soler**, a great harpsichord player.

In the 19C, the Catalan **Felipe Pedrell** brought Spanish music onto a higher plane. He opened the way for a new generation of musicians and was the first to combine traditional tunes with classical genres. In the early 19C, while works by French composers (Ravel's *Bolero*, Bizet's *Carmen*, Lalo's *Symphonie Espagnole* and Chabrier's *España*) bore a pronounced Hispanic stamp, Spanish composers turned to national folklore and traditional themes: **Isaac Albéniz** (1860–1909) wrote *Iberia*, **Enrique Granados** (1867–1916) became famous for his *Goyescas* and **Joaquín Turina** (1882–1949) for his *Sevilla Symphony*. This popular vein culminated in works by **Manuel de Falla** (1876–1946) including *Nights in the Gardens of Spain*, *El Amor Brujo* and *The Three-Cornered Hat*.

Among the best-known contemporary classical guitar players **Andrés Segovia** (1893–1987), **Joaquín Rodrigo** (1901–99), famous for his *Concierto de Aranjuez*, and **Narciso Yepes** (1927–97), have shown that this most Spanish of instruments can interpret a wide variety of music. Equally, flamenco maestros **Paco de Lucía** and Enrique Morente have shown the potential of flamenco guitar and song to create dialogues with jazz, North African and heavy metal music. Another Spaniard, **Pablo Casals** (1876–1973), was possibly the greatest cellist of all time. Spain holds a leading position in the world of opera with singers such as **Victoria de los Ángeles** (1923–2005), **Montserrat Caballé**, **Plácido Domingo**, **Alfredo Kraus** (1927–99), **José Carreras** and **Teresa Berganza**.

Today's music industry is plagued by piracy, but creatively lively. Artists range from classic crooners, like Julio Iglesias and his son Enrique, to radical fusion artist Manu Chao, cooperative Ojos de Brujo, jazzman Zenet and diva Concha Buika. Latin American stars like Shakira, Mana and Julieta Venegas have a huge following while younger Spanish talent is supported by the music festivals hosted by Spain. FIB – the Festival Internacional de Benicassím – is the most famous, but Barcelona's Sonar, Andalucía's Creamfields and Cartagena's La Mar de Músicas are all worth a special trip.

Nature

Because of its geographical location, Spain acts as a bridge between two continents – Europe and Africa. The country has myriad natural attractions, ranging from long sandy beaches, sheltered coves and steep cliffs to breathtaking mountain landscapes characterised by high peaks and enclosed valleys. By contrast, the centre of Spain, known as the Meseta, is marked by seemingly endless expanses of flat terrain.

LANDSCAPE

Relief – The average altitude in Spain is 650m/2 100ft above sea level and one sixth of the terrain rises to more than 1 000m/3 300ft.

The highest peak on the Spanish mainland is Mulhacén (3 422m/11 427ft) in the Sierra Nevada. The highest point in Spain, however, is Mount Teide on the Canary Islands, rising to a height of 3 718m/12 195ft.

The dominant feature of the peninsula is the immense plateau at its centre. This is the **Meseta**: a Hercynian platform between 600m/1 968ft and 1 000m/3 281ft high, which tilts slightly westwards. The Meseta is surrounded by long mountain ranges which form barriers between the central plateau and the coastal regions. All these ranges, the **Cordillera Cantábrica** in the northwest (an extension of the Pyrenees), the **Cordillera Ibérica** in the northeast and the **Sierra Morena** in the south, were caused by Alpine folding.

Other mountains rising here and there from the Meseta are folds of the original, ancient massif. They include the **Sierras de Somosierra**, **Guadarrama** and **Gredos**, the **Peña de Francia** and the **Montes de Toledo**.

The highest massifs in Spain, the **Pyrenees** (Pirineos) in the north and the **Sierras Béticas**, including the **Sierra Nevada**, in the south, are on the country's periphery, as are Spain's greatest depressions, those of the Ebro and Guadalquivir rivers.

CLIMATE

Although most of Spain enjoys 300 days of sunshine a year, the great diversity of its landscapes is partly due to the country's wide variety of climates.

The **Meseta** accounts for 40 per cent of the surface area of Iberia and includes Castilla y León, Castilla-La Mancha, Madrid and Extremadura. It has a continental climate with extremes of temperature ranging from scorching hot in summer to freezing cold in winter. These excesses are combined with modest and irregular rainfall to form an arid landscape that complements the seemingly infinite horizons in this part of Spain. The massif of the adjoining Pyrenees has a colder alpine climate. This is also prevalent in the Sierra Nevada (Snowy Range) in Andalucía.

The northern coast, which runs from Galicia to the País Vasco, is nicknamed **España verde** (Green Spain) due to its mild and very humid climate, with rainfall being much higher than in the heartlands of northern Europe. This is in stark contrast to the perceived image of Spain as an entirely dry country.

The Levante has a Mediterranean climate with rainfall being restricted mainly to autumn and spring, and warm temperatures in the winter giving way to high temperatures between June and August. This heat is tempered by the Levante, the cool wind by which this eastern coast, from Almería in the south to Catalunya in the north, is named.

A semi-arid or desert climate affects **Almería**, in southeastern Andalucía, with low rainfall to an extent that the Cabo de Gata near Almería is known as the driest region in Europe. The remaining coastline of **Andalucía** shares traits of a Mediterranean and subtropical region lending it a mild and sunny climate.

The climate of the **Balearic Islands** (Mallorca, Menorca, Ibiza, Formentera) in the Mediterranean Sea is characterised by mild and tempestuous winters, in between hot and bright summers.

The **Canary Islands** (Tenerife, Gran Canaria, Lanzarote, Fuerteventura, La Palma, La Gomera, El Hierro, 👁️ *see Discovering*

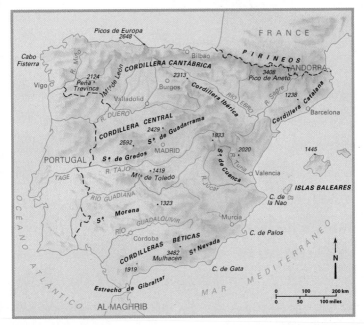

the Canary Islands) are characterised by a subtropical climate, due to their latitude in the Atlantic Ocean. They are well known for their year-round pleasant temperatures and low rainfall, making them a haven for winter sun-seekers.

CLIMATE CHANGE

Experts' warnings that large areas of Spain may be desertified by 2050 have stimulated tree-planting: the total of 18 million hectares of woodland is the fastest growing in Europe. Drought has been made more worrying by the demands of intensive farming and coastal tourism.

Desalination plants are likely to multiply to meet demand, like wind-farms, which produced 20 per cent of the country's energy in 2011, but water supplies now limit construction right along the Mediterranean coast.

Sierra Nevada, Andalucía

©Turespaña

99

Mezquita, Córdoba, Andalucía
©mtrommer/Fotolia.com

Central
Spain

Olive fields in Chinchón, Province of Madrid
© Francis Cormon/hemis.fr

Central Spain

0		50		100 km
0	30		60 miles

MADRID ★★★ Highly recommended

Cuenca ★★ Recommended

Soria ★ Interesting

Albacete Other sight described in this guide

N

TABRIA

Burgos

Covarrubias

Sto Domingo
de Silos

Peñaranda
de Duero

**PAÍS
VASCO**

LA RIOJA

NAVARRA

N 240

ARAGÓN

AP 1

AP 68

A 1

N 234

Soria

RÍO EBRO

AP 68

ZARAGOZA

BARCELONA

A 23

iel

**El Burgo
de Osma**

RÍO DUERO

A 2

AP 2

**Santa María
de Huerta**

N 234

A 23

Río Guadalope

Pedraza

Guadarrama

Sigüenza

A 2

RÍO TAJO

A

de

EL ESCORIAL

Guadalajara

BARCELONA

MADRID

**Alcalá
de Henares**

A 23

Aranjuez

Cuenca

N 420

Uclés

A 3

A 4

CM 42

Belmonte

Alarcón

VALENCIANA

VALENCIA

A 43

A 31

Río Júcar

A 43

LA-
CHA

A 43

▲ **La Ruta
Don Quixote**

A 31

Albacete

A 35

AP 7

Almagro

N 322

A 31

A 30

ALACANT/
ALICANTE

A 7

N 322

MURCIA

MURCIA

ANDALUCÍA

ALMERÍA

MADRID AND AROUND

Madrid stands at the geographical heart of Spain on the arid central tableland known as the *meseta*. Its central location contributed to Philip II's decision to settle his court here, but so, too, did its healthy climate and stunning mountain backdrop. It is one of the noisiest cities in Europe; it is also famed as a buzzing late-night metropolis, with traffic jams well into the small hours; it is the continent's richest city, alongside London, for art galleries; and, despite the fact that it is the highest European capital, at over 640m/2 100ft above sea level (and enjoys cooling breezes), Madrid is also the hottest capital with temperatures rising above 40°C (10°F) in August, when around one third of all Madrileños ("Madridians") flee the city. Madrid has not yet reached the popularity of Catalan capital, Barcelona, as a tourist destination, lacking its proximity to the sea and old-world charm. But it is an open-hearted dynamic city that is keenly recovering its historical past while refusing to let go of old-fashioned bars, restaurants and customs. City slickers, gourmets and clubbers appreciate Madrid as much as the culture vultures who relish its stunning art collections.

Highlights

1. Taking a walk and tapas in the **Plaza Mayor** (p111)
2. Gazing in wonder at the **Prado's** Spanish **art collection** (p119)
3. Seeing Picasso's *Guernica* in the **Museo de Arte Reina Sofía** (p124)
4. Enjoying dinner and a night out around **Plaza Sta Ana** (p127)
5. Strolling in the palace river gardens of **Aranjuez** (p139)

Paseo del Prado

This unique avenue, lined by lofty trees, is home to the Prado museum, which houses the Spanish royal collection of classical paintings including Velázquez's *Las Meninas*. Since the Paseo was laid out in the 18C it has attracted a host of other museums, galleries and art centres, including the famous Museo Thyssen-Bornemisza and the Reina Sofía contemporary art museum where Picasso's *Guernica* hangs.

Such is the richness of these and other art collections that many visitors choose to spend most of their days here, taking breaks in the green Retiro Park or Royal Botanical Garden nearby. At the Paseo's southern end, Atocha station is a central junction for the highspeed AVE train network.

Habsburg Madrid

Centring on the Plaza Mayor, the heart of the old town, also called the Barrio de los Austrias, combines narrow alleyways with squares, churches, convents and monasteries, traditional and modern shops, and a host of places to eat and drink. The grandiose 2 800-room Royal Palace, built over earlier Habsburg palaces and a Muslim Álcazar, will occupy half a day of your time alone. An evening stroll around the old Muslim town's winding streets is the easiest way to evoke the city's past.

Centro

The popular quarters around the wide arterial avenues of Alcalà and Gran Vía are a mosaic of bustling pedestrianised shopping streets and characterful old residential areas. Many of the city's hotels, theatres and cinemas are here and this is also the epicentre of its famed nightlife.

Day trips and excursions

A short trip out of Madrid allows you to visit El Escorial, the 16C royal pala-tial complex built by Philip II – a palace, church, monastery, mausoleum and museum all under one massive roof – or Alcalá de Henares, Cervantes' birthplace. Romantics and music lovers will want to make the trip to the palace of Aranjuez to see the gardens that inspired Rod-rigo's haunting guitar concerto.

Madrid★★★

Madrid is one of Europe's liveliest cities, with wide avenues, attractive parks and a general *alegría* or joie de vivre. It became capital of Spain in the 16C when Spain ruled a vast empire, and its many monuments span the 17C, 18C and 19C. The city is world-famous for its exceptional wealth of paintings.

THE CITY TODAY

Madrid today – Madrid is not only the judicial and political capital but also the country's main business centre.

The city's most noteworthy modern architecture includes the **Banco de Bilbao-Vizcaya** in the AZCA centre, the 250 m/820 ft highrise Cuatro Torres complex north of Plaza de Castilla, and the **Ciudad de Justicia** (City of Justice) complex on the city's eastern edge.

A BIT OF HISTORY

Madrid owes its name to the 9C fortress (*alcázar*) of Majerit. In 1085 it was captured by Alfonso VI, who discovered a statue of the Virgin by a granary (*almudín*). He converted the mosque into a church dedicated to the Virgin of the Almudena who was declared the city's patron. Emperor Charles V rebuilt the Muslim *alcázar* and in 1561 his son Philip II moved the court from Toledo to Madrid.

The town grew dramatically quickly in Spain's Golden Age (16C). King Philip IV gave court patronage to many artists including Velázquez and Murillo, as well as men of letters such as Lope de Vega, Quevedo and Calderón.

From a town to a city – Madrid, as we know it today, underwent its greatest transformations in the 18C under the Bourbons. Philip V built a royal palace; Charles III provided Madrid with a splendour hitherto unknown in the Paseo del Prado and the Puerta de Alcalá, magnificent examples of Neoclassical town planning.

The 19C began with occupation by the French and the Madrid rebellion of May 1808 and its brutal repression.

▸ **Population:** 3 273 049
 Michelin Map: 575 or 576 K 18–19 (town plan).
 Info: Plaza Mayor 27, ℘915 88 16 36; Ronda de Toledo 1, ℘913 64 18 76; Plaza de Colón, ℘915 88 16 36; Duque de Medinaceli 2, ℘914 29 49 51; Agustín de Foxá (Estación de Chamartín), ℘913 15 99 76; Estación de Atocha, ℘915 28 46 30; Aeropuerto de Barajas (T4 and T1), ℘913 05 86 56; tourist information, ℘902 10 00 07. www.esmadrid.com; www.turismomadrid.es.
 Location: Europe's highest capital (646m/ 2 119ft), at the centre of the Iberian Peninsula, with a dry climate: hot summers and cold, sunny winters.
 Parking: It's best to park for the duration and use the excellent Metro.
 Don't Miss: The Prado, crowds in Plaza Mayor.
 Timing: Start with the incomparable art museums, and take a siesta in order to enjoy Madrid's late-hours dining and bars.
 Kids: Faunia, the Casa del Campo's funfair, and Aquópolis water park will keep smaller visitors amused.

In 1857 the remaining ramparts were demolished and a vast expansion plan (*ensanche*) gave rise to the districts of Chamberí, Salamanca and Argüelles. At the beginning of the 20C, architecture was French-inspired, as in the Ritz and Palace hotels; the neo-Mudéjar style was also popular, as at the bullring. The **Gran Vía** linked Madrid's new districts in 1910. Since then its outer quarters have grown and spread in all directions around the metro underground and train system.

GETTING AROUND

Airport – Madrid-Barajas airport is located northeast of the city, 13km/8mi from downtown. The EMT24H bus operates between the airport's four terminals and city centre, ending at Atocha Station (€2). Departures every 35 minutes (between 11.30pm and 6am terminates in Plaza de Cibeles for night buses).

Metro line no. 8 connects the airport with the city. It's a 14-minute journey from Nuevos Ministerios to Terminal 1. Airport information: *902 40 47 04; www.aena.es.* Info-Iberia and bookings: *902 40 05 00.*

RENFE (Spanish State Railways) – The city's main railway stations are Atocha *(Pl. del Emperador Carlos V and Glorieta Carlos V)* and Chamartín *(Agustín de Foxa).* For information and reservations until 24 hrs before departure, call *902 24 02 02 (24-hr service);* or log on to *www.renfe.es.* AVE high-speed trains depart from Atocha, taking just 2hr35min to reach Sevilla via Córdoba (1hr50min); to Barcelona (2hr45min) via Zaragoza (1hr40min); to Toledo (30min); to Valencia (1hr38min) and to Valladolid (1hr5min) via Segovia (35min).

AVE services are planned for Cádiz, Alicante and the French frontier by the end of 2012. Madrid has a good suburban train network *(Cercanías)* which can be used to get to El Escorial, the Sierra de Guadarrama, Alcalá de Henares and Aranjuez.

Inter-city buses – Most buses to other cities depart from the Estación Sur *(Méndez Álvaro 83; *914 68 42 00; www.estacionautobusesmadrid.com).*

Car hire – All the familiar names are located at Barajas airport and Atocha railway station. **Pepecar (***Rda de Atocha 10. *91-5306103 8h-20h www.pepecar.com)* offers good value car hire with a wide range of models and 11 pick-up points, including the airport (Terminal 1). Prices start at €18 a day.

Bike hire – Bravo Bike (*Juan Alvarez Mendízábal, 19; *917 582945)* Cycle tours in and out of Madrid, plus bikes to hire by the day (from €20) or by the week (from €85).

Taxis – Madrid has a huge number of registered taxis with distinctive white paintwork with a red diagonal stripe on the rear doors. The green light indicates that the taxi is for hire.

Local buses – For information, call *902 50 78 50.* A good way of getting to know the city, although traffic jams may be a problem. Passengers should beware of pickpockets. Generally buses operate between 6am and 11.30pm. Night buses operate from 11.30pm onwards, with most departing from Plaza de Cibeles. In addition to single tickets, passengers can purchase a ten-trip **metro-bus** ticket *(un bono de 10 viajes; €9.30)* valid on both the bus and metro network, as well as a zone-based 1–7 day tourist season ticket *(abono turístico)* which is valid for an unlimited number of bus and metro journeys. Bicycles may be taken on the metro all day Sundays and for limited hours on other days.

Metro – *Metro stations are shown on the maps in this guide (*902 44 44 03; www.ctm-madrid.es).* The metro system is the fastest way to get around the city and consists of 13 lines. It operates from 6am to 1.30am. Passengers should beware of pickpockets.

SIGHTSEEING

The Guía del Ocio (*www.guiadelocio.com/madrid*) is a weekly guide containing a list of every cultural event and show in the city. It can be purchased at newspaper stands.

Bus turístico Madrid – This open-topped tourist bus offers two circular routes around the city (historic Madrid, modern Madrid). Tickets, which can be purchased on board, in hotels via a travel agent, or at newspaper kiosks, are valid for a day during which passengers can hop on and off both routes as much as they like. Services operate 10am–7pm in winter, 10am–9pm in spring and autumn, and 9.30am–midnight in summer. Stops include the Paseo del Prado, Plaza Colón, Gran Vía, Palacio Real and Puerta del Sol.

For information and prices, call ☎902-50 78 50 (www.emtmadrid.es).

DISTRICTS

Madrid is a city full of charm, with its magnificent parks and impressive buildings. It is a city best explored by strolling through its streets and squares, discovering the delights of its many districts or *barrios* and getting to know its friendly inhabitants.

Centro – This district is made up of several areas, each with their own individual character. It has a reputation for being the most popular, noisy and chaotic area, full of people, although visitors are often surprised by its quieter narrow alleyways and small squares. It includes **Sol-Callao,** the shopping area par excellence, packed with locals and visitors out for a stroll, heading for the main pedestrianised precinct (Preciados district), although today younger shoppers head for fashionable **Fuencarral**. A number of cinemas are also located in this area. Visitors should take particular care in the evening, especially in streets such as Valverde and Barco.

Barrio de los Austrias – Madrid's oldest district is wedged between Calles Mayor, Bailén, Toledo, Las Cavas and the Plaza de la Cebada. Its origins are Muslim and it still retains its evocatively named streets and Mudéjar towers. An excellent area for tapas, dinner or a drink. On Sundays, the famous **Rastro** flea market (&see Rastro) is starts near here, on Ribera de Curtidores.

Lavapiés – This district runs north from the square of the same name to Calle Atocha with many houses dating from the 17C. It is considered to be Madrid's most colourful district with a mix of locals, artists and a large immigrant population.

Huertas – Huertas was home to the literary community in the 17C. Nowadays, it is largely pedestrianised and packed with bars and restaurants. It is particularly lively at night, attracting an interesting mixture of late-night revellers.

Malasaña – This part of Madrid, which used to be known as Maravillas, is situated between Las Glorietas de Bilbao y Ruiz Jiménez and around Plaza del Dos de Mayo. In the mornings, this 19C *barrio* is quiet and full of local character, but it is transformed at night by the legions of young people who head for its bars, many of them classics from the 1980s Movida years. The district also has a number of more tranquil cafés and restaurants.

Alonso Martínez – The average age and financial standing of this district's inhabitants is somewhat higher than in neighbouring Bilbao and Chueca, as shown by the myriad upmarket bars, restaurants and food shops frequented by the city's rich and famous.

Chueca – This district's approximate outer limits are the Paseo de Recoletos, Calle Hortaleza, Gran Vía and Calle Fernando VI. At the end of the last century it was one of Madrid's most elegant districts. Today it is the city's gay area, focussed on the bohemian Plaza de Chueca, with a multitude of small and sophisticated boutiques, design shops and art galleries.

Salamanca – In the 19C the Marquis of Salamanca designed this smart residential area in the shape of a draughts board with wide streets at right angles. Nowadays, the district is one of the capital's most expensive areas and is home to some of Spain's leading designer boutiques (Serrano and Ortega y Gasset) and an impressive collection of stores selling luxury goods.

WALKING TOURS

1 OLD MADRID (CENTRO)★
See map of walking tour p 114–5.
Steep, narrow streets, small squares, 17C palaces and mansions, houses with wrought-iron balconies dating from the 19C and early 20C characterise Old Madrid, the very heart of the city.

Try to visit early, or late in the afternoon when the churches are open.

MADRID
Map I

Plaza Mayor★★

🚇 *Sol.*

The square built by Juan Gómez de Mora in 1619 is the centre of **Habsburg Madrid**. On the north side, the **Casa de la Panadería** (a former bakery, now a tourism centre) was reconstructed by Donoso in 1672. The plaza was the setting for *autos de fé*, mounted bullfights, and the proclamations of kings.

A stamp and coin market is held on Sunday mornings and fiestas (9am–2pm) while at Christmas stalls sell decorations. Shops around the square retain a yesteryear look.

Pass through the **Arco de Cuchilleros** (pl. Mayor 9) into the street fronted by

old houses with convex façades. The **Cava de San Miguel** provides a rear view of the houses on the square. This area is crowded with small restaurants (*mesones*) and bars (*tavernas*). The

Mercado de San Miguel, an indoor early 20C market, now a food emporium (*open 10am–10pm*) has an elegant iron structure.

▸ *Take Conde de Miranda. Cross Plaza del Conde de Barajas and Gómez de Mora to Plaza de San Justo or Puerta Cerrada, a city gate. Continue right on San Justo.*

Basílica Pontificia de San Miguel★

San Justo 4. ▣Tirso de Molina or Ópera. ◷Open 1 Jul–17 Sept Mon–Sat 10am–1pm, 6–9pm, public holidays 10am–1pm, 6.30–9pm; 18 Sept–30 Jun Mon–Sat 10am–2.15pm, public holidays 10am–2.15pm, 6–9.15pm. ℘915 48 40 11.

The basilica by Bonavia is a rare Spanish church inspired by 18C Italian Baroque. Its convex façade, designed as an interplay of inward and outward curves, is adorned with fine statues. The interior is graceful and elegant with an oval cupola, intersecting vaulting, flowing cornices and abundant stuccowork.

▶ Follow Puñonrostro and del Codo to Plaza de la Villa.

Plaza de la Villa★

▣Ópera. ⁕Guided tours Mon except public holidays 5pm. ⌑No charge. ℘915 88 16 36.

Buildings around the square include the **Ayuntamiento** (town hall), built by Gómez de Mora in 1617, the **Torre de los Lujanes** (Luján Tower), a rare examples of 15C civil architecture, and the 16C **Casa de Cisneros**, connected to the Ayuntamiento by an arch.

Mercado de San Miguel

© Ingolf Pompe hemis.fr

Map labels: B, C, M. de Santiago, Fuentes, Hileras, Arenal, Carmen, Sol, Santiago, Pl. de los Herradores, Pl. de la Puerta del Sol, Mayor, Sol, Casa de la Panadería, Pl. de S. Miguel, Marqués Viudo de Pontejos, Pl. de Pontejos, Casa de Pedro Calderón de la Barca, DE VILLA, Torre de los Lujanes, San Miguel, Espartería, POL, Ayuntamiento, Codo, Cava de San Miguel, PLAZA MAYOR, Zaragoza, Carretas, Cordón, Pl. del Conde de Barajas, Arco de Cuchilleros, Pl. de la Provincia, Pl. Jacinto Benavente, Pl. del Cordón, SAN MIGUEL, S. Justo, Cuchilleros, Palacio de Sta Cruz, Atocha, de Javier, Pl. Puerta Cerrada, Concepción, Jerónima, Segovia, Toledo, Colegiata, Conde de Romanones, San Pedro, Baja, S. Isidro, Plaza de Tirso de Molina, Museo de los orígenes, Cava, Alfa, Estudios, de Alba, Mesón, Jesús, Cabeza, Pl. Puerta de Moros, Cava, Duque, Juanelo, de, Paredes, María, Humilladero, T, La Latina, S. Millán, Pl. de la Cebada, Maldonadas, Plaza de Cascorro, MADRID, Map III, Toledo, Ruda, Embajadores, N, el Rastro, 0 200 m, 0 200 yds

Calle Mayor

🔵 *Ópera.*

The name, literally Main Street, gives an indication of its importance. At no. 61 is the narrow house of 17C playright **Pedro Calderón de la Barca**. The Antigua Farmacia de la Reina Madre (Queen Mother's Pharmacy) at no. 59, founded in 1576, previously an alchemist, keeps a collection of chemist's jars and pots. The **Instituto Italiano de Cultura** (no. 86) occupies a 17C palace.

The Palacio Uceda opposite, from the same period, is now the military headquarters of the **Capitanía General** (Captaincy General). In front of the **Iglesia Arzobispal Castrense** (17C–18C; ✆915 47 35 24), a monument commemorates an attack on Alfonso XIII and Victoria Eugenia in 1906. In the nearby calle de

San Nicolás is the Mudéjar tower of San Nicolás de los Servita.

▷ *Take del Sacramento to Plazuela del Cordón; return to del Cordón then continue to Segovia.*

Across the street rises the 14C **Mudéjar tower** of the **Iglesia de San Pedro el Viejo** (Church of St Peter), a rare example of the Mudéjar style in Madrid.

▷ *Go along del Príncipe Anglona.*

Plaza de la Paja

This was a commercial centre in the Middle Ages. The Palacio Vargas obscures the Gothic **Capilla del Obispo**, a 16C chapel. In Plaza de los Carros, the Capilla de San Isidro (chapel) is part of the 17C

115

Iglesia de San Andrés built in honour of Madrid's patron saint. The **Museo de los Orígenes** *(Pl. San Andrés 2; ⬤Latina; ◷open Tue–Fri 9.30am–8pm (Aug closes 2.30pm), Sat–Sun 10am–2pm; ◷closed public holidays; ⬤no charge; ℘913 66 74 15)*, a museum containing a miracle well and a fine Renaissance patio, is next to this complex of religious buildings. There is also an exhibit on Madrid from prehistory up until the installation of the Royal Court in the 16C.

◗ *Cross Bailén and take the first street on the right.*

Jardines de las Vistillas (Vistillas Gardens)

⬤ *La Latina.*
There are splendid **views to the west**, especially at sundown, of the Sierra de Guadarrama, Casa de Campo, the Catedral de la Almudena and the viaduct.

Basílica de San Francisco el Grande

San Buenaventura 1. ⬤ *La Latina.*
◷*Open Mon–Sat 11am–1pm, 4–7pm.*
⬤*€3.* ℘*913 65 38 00.*
The church's vast Neoclassical façade is by Sabatini; the circular edifice itself with six radial chapels and a large dome is by Francisco Cabezas. Walls and ceilings have 19C frescoes and paintings (18C in the chapels of St Anthony and St Bernardino).

The Capilla de San Bernardino holds an early Goya of St Bernardino of Siena preaching before the King of Aragón (1781). Plateresque **stalls**★ from the Monasterio de El Parral outside Segovia are in the chancel.
16C **stalls**★ in the sacristy and chapter house are from the Cartuja de El Paular, a Carthusian monastery near Segovia.

◗ *Walk along Carrera de San Francisco and Cava Alta to Toledo.*

Calle de Toledo

⬤ *La Latina or Tirso de Molina.*
This is one of the old town's liveliest streets. The **El Rastro** flea market is held here (◷*open Sun and public holidays 9am–2pm; ⬤beware pickpockets*).

◗ *Continue up Toledo for about 200m/656ft.*

Real Colegiata de San Isidro

Toledo 37. ⬤ *La Latina or Tirso de Molina.* ◷*Open daily 7.30am–1pm, 6–9pm.* ⬤*No charge.* ℘*914 54 64 00.*
Formerly the church of the Imperial College of the Company of Jesus (1622), it was the cathedral of Madrid from 1885 until 1993 and contains the relics of Madrid's patron saint, San Isidro.

◗ *Head north on Toledo then continue NE and along Esparteros. Turn right at Mayor then left.*

Paseo del Prado

With the 18C drawing to a close, Charles III wanted to develop a public area worthy of Madrid's position as capital of Spain and he called upon the court's best architects for his project. In an area outside the city at the time, Hermosilla, Ventura Rodríguez, Sabatini and Villanueva drained, embellished and built a curved avenue with two large fountains, Cybele and Neptune, at each end, and a third, Apollo, in the centre. To complete the project, the **Botanical Gardens**, **Natural History Museum** (now the Museo del Prado) and the **Observatory**, were also built. The result was a balanced combination of the functional and the ornate dedicated to science and the arts. Immediately the Paseo del Prado became a favourite place for Madrileños to meet and to relax. Today, the avenue retains its dignified air and a cluster of extraordinary museums that draw visitors from right around the world. A stroll along its tree-lined boulevard gives the chance to remember the vision and imagination of Charles III.

Plaza de Cibeles at night

F. Vidal/MICHELIN

Plaza de la Puerta del Sol

🚇 *Gran Vía or Callao.*

On the best-known square in Madrid, a small monument displays Madrid's coat of arms, next to an equestrian statue of Charles III. The clock on the former post office chimes midnight at New Year's Eve while a large crowd eats a grape between each chime, to bring luck the next year.

In nearby traditional shops with their colourful wood fronts customers can find fans and mantillas and delicacies.

▶ *Walk east through Plaza de la Puerta del Sol, then onto Alcalá.*

② **BOURBON MADRID**★★

&*See map of walking tour p121.*

Charles III's Paseo del Prado remains a grand tree-shaded avenue lined by world-class museums and from them it is a short walk to the Retiro Park.

Plaza de Cibeles★

🚇 *Banco de España.*

In the square is the 18C fountain of Cybele, goddess of fertility, emblematic of Madrid. Many an artist has been inspired to paint the perspectives opening from the square and the impressive buildings around, such as the **Banco de España** (1891), the 18C **Palacio de Buenavista** (Ministry of Defence), the late-19C **Palacio de Linares**, now the home of the Casa de América (*pas. de*

Recoletos 2; ➦ *guided tours Sept–Jul Sat–Sun 11am, noon, 1pm;* ⊙ *closed 10–11 Oct;* ⊜€7; ℘*915 95 48 00; www.casamerica.es*), and the **Palacio de Cibeles** (Post and Telegraph Office, 1919, now the Mayor's Office).

Paseo del Prado★

This tree-lined avenue runs from Plaza de Cibeles to Plaza del Emperador Carlos V, past the Ministerio de la Marina and Museo Naval, the **Plaza de la Lealtad** with an obelisk dedicated to the heroes of the 2 May, the Neoclassical **Bolsa** (Stock Exchange) and the emblematic **Hotel Ritz** (*www.ritzmadrid.com*).

▶ *Take the first left, Montalbán, after the Palacio de Cibeles.*

Museo Nacional de Artes Decorativas

Montalbán 12. 🚇 *Retiro.* ⊙ *Open Tue–Sat 9.30am–3pm, Thur 5-8pm, Sun and public holidays 10am–3pm.* ⊙ *Closed 1 Jan, 1 May, 24–25, 31 Dec.* ⊜€3; *no charge Sun, Thu afternoon, 18 Apr, 18 May, 12 Oct, 6 Dec.* ℘*915 32 64 99. http://mnartesdecorativas.mcu.es.*

This museum in a 19C mansion contains a splendid collection of furniture and decorative objects as well as a complete tiled 18C kitchen.

▶ *Return to the Paseo del Prado and continue south.*

Museo Naval

Pas. del Prado 5. 🚇 *Banco de España.* ⏰*Open Sept–Jul Tue–Sun 10am–2pm.* ⏰*Closed public holidays.* 💶*No charge.* ☎*915 23 87 89. www.armada.mde.es.*
On display are ship **models**★, nautical instruments, weapons, and paintings of naval battles. The **map of Juan de la Cosa**★★ (1500) is the first to show the American continent.

▷ *Continue south down the Paseo del Prado.*

Plaza de Canóvas del Castillo

🚇*Banco de España.*
This square, with its splendid Fuente de Neptuno (Neptune Fountain), is overlooked by the Neoclassical **Palacio de Villahermosa** housing the **Museo Thyssen-Bornemisza**★★★ (👁 *see Museo Thyssen-Bornemisza)* and the Hotel Palace.

▷ *Continue walking south, on the eastern side of the Paseo del Prado.*

Museo del Prado★★★

👁*See Museums.*
The Neoclassical building of one of the world's great art museums was built in the reign of Charles III, originally intended for the Institute of Natural Sciences. Behind it is Rafael Moneo's 2007 annexe, which incorporates the Jeronimos' monastery cloister and new iron doors by Cristina Iglesias. Behind the Prado is the recently renovated royal church, San Jerónimo el Real.

▷ *Continue south to the Pl. de Murillo facing the Museum's southern façade.*

Real Jardín Botánico

Pl. de Murillo, 2. ⏰*Open Nov–Feb 10am –6pm; Mar and Oct until 7pm; Apr and Sept until 8pm; May–Aug until 9pm.* ⏰*Closed 1 Jan, 25 Dec.* 💶*€2.50; no charge for children under 10.* ☎*914 20 30 17. www.rjb.csic.es.*
The Botanical Garden, opened in 1781, was commissioned by Charles III and planned by Juan de Villanueva, who also built the Museo del Prado. Today

one enters by just one gate facing the Museum's southern facade. Apart from its beautifully tended beds, lawns and variety of trees, the garden has a vine bower planted with grape varieties from around Spain and three greenhouses presenting ecosystems from desert to equatorial. The shop at the gate is small, but sells seeds and plants.

▷ *Cross the Paseo to its western side.*

Caixa Forum

Po. del Prado 36. ⏰*Open 10am-8pm.* ⏰*Closed 25 Dec, 1 and 6 Jan.* 💶*No charge.* ☎*913 307 300. www.laCaixa.es/ObraSocial.*
The latest addition to the Paseo del Prado, Caixa Forum, is well worth a visit for its architecture alone: Jacques Herzog and Pierre de Meuron artfully converted a Modernist power station and Patrick Blanc designed its stunning vertical garden. Inside, an arts centre mixes temporary shows with concerts, talks and, on the top floor, a café-restaurant.

▷ *Continue walking south, cross Calle Atocha and, 100m/110yd later, turn right into C. de Sta Isabel.*

The former **Hospital de San Carlos**, an austere but imposing granite block with a towering extension and agora designed by French architect **Jean Nouvel**, houses the **Museo Nacional Centro de Arte Reina Sofía**★ (👁 *see Museums).*

▷ *Cross the Pl del Emperador Carlos V to its southeastern side.*

Estación de Atocha (Atocha Railway Station)

Pl. del Emperador Carlos V. 🚇 *Atocha Renfe or Atocha.*
Atocha station's vast 19C glass and wrought-iron **lobby** dominates this square. Enter to view the tropical patio garden, where turtles swim in pools, and to glimpse the AVE high-speed train platforms. Walk through to the local train station (Cercanías) to visit the

underground memorial to those who died in the 2004 bombing of commuter trains: an opaque cylinder, engraved with messages to the dead from those who created a shrine here, rises above ground (⏰*open daily 10am–8pm*). The local train-station, nicknamed the "pill-box", was designed by Rafael Moneo. Opposite, on the north side of the Avda Ciudad de Barcelona, stands the elaborate late 19C Ministry of Agriculture.

▷ *Cross the Avda Ciudad de Barcelona and turn right to the junction with C. de Alfonso XII.*

Museo Nacional de Antropología

Alfonso XII, 68. ⏰*Open Tue–Sun 9.30am–8pm (Sun and hols 3pm).* ⏰*Closed 1 Jan, 1 May, 24, 25, 31 Dec.* ⬤€3; no charge Sat pm and Sun. ☎915 306 418.
www.mnantropologia.mcu.es.
Housed in a Neoclassical building this small museum, often unjustly overlooked, presents a fascinating ethnological collection of objects from around the world – the Americas, Philippines and Africa – arranged thematically around ways of life.

▷ *Follow Alfonso XII northeast, crossing to enter the park at the Puerta del Ángel Caído.*

Parque del Buen Retiro★★ (Retiro Park)

⏰*Open daily Oct–Apr 7am–10pm; May–Sept 7am–midnight.* ☎915 58 87 90.
The Retiro is close to the heart of every Madrileño. Once the garden of a Hapsburg summer palace, destroyed during the War of Independence, it keeps 130ha/321 acres of greenery with dense clumps of trees, a rose garden, fountains, temples, Modernist zoo buildings, colonnades and statues.
Beside the Lake (Estanque), where boats may be hired, is the imposing **Monumento a Alfonso XII**. Exhibitions are held in the graceful **Palacio de Cristal**★ (Glass Palace) which overlooks a shaded

pool (🏛 *Ibiza;* ⏰*open May–Sept Mon–Sat 11am–8pm, Sun and public holidays 11am–6pm; Oct–Apr Mon–Sat 10am–6pm, Sun and public holidays 10am–4pm;* ⏰*closed 1, 6 Jan, 1, 15 May, 24–25, 31 Dec;* ☎*915 74 66 14).*

▷ *After exploring the park, take the Avda Mejico from the Lake's northwestern corner to the Pl. de la Independencia.*

Puerta de Alcalá★ (Alcalá Arch)

Pl. de la Independencia. 🏛 *Retiro.*
The arch at the centre of Plaza de la Independencia was built by Sabatini between 1769 and 1778 to celebrate the triumphant entry of Charles III into Madrid and during the Movida years became the symbol of the city's new democracy. The perspective is particularly grand at night, taking in Plaza de Cibeles, Calle de Alcalá and the Gran Vía.

MUSEUMS
MUSEO NACIONAL DEL PRADO★★★

Allow 3–4 hours.
Pas. del Prado s/n (ticket office at northern entrance by Pl. Canovas del Castillo), 🏛 *Banco de España or Atocha.*
⏰*Open Tue–Sun and public holidays 9am–8pm (2pm 24, 31 Dec, 6 Jan). Last tickets for the permanent collection, 30min before closing; for temporary shows 1 hour before closing.* ⏰*Closed 1 Jan, Good Fri, 1 May and 25 Dec.* ⬤€8; €7 advance booking via Call Center; temporary exhibitions €10; no charge Tue–Sat 6–8pm, Sun 5–8pm, 2 May, 12 Oct, 19 Nov, 6 Dec. ☎913 30 28 00. Call Center information and advance booking 902-10 70 77.
www.museodelprado.es.
The Prado is the greatest gallery of Classical paintings in the world. The Neoclassical building was designed by Juan de Villanueva under Charles III for a science museum. After the Peninsular War, Ferdinand VII instead installed the Habsburg and Bourbon collections of Spanish painting, expanded over the years. In 2007 an extension, called the

Jerónimos building, incorporating a 16C monastery cloister, led to the collection being rehung with 19C work alongside classical painting schools.

Spanish Painting★★★ (1100-1910)

Bartolomé Bermejo (*Santo Domingo de Silos*; Rm 51A) and **Yáñez de la Almedina** cultivated an international style. Vicente Masip and his son **Juan de Juanes** (*The Last Supper*) are associated with Raphael. Morales' favourite subject, a *Virgin and Child*, is also outstanding.

In those rooms devoted to the **Golden Age**, two painters stand out: **Sánchez Coello**, and his pupil **Pantoja de la Cruz**, a portraitist at the court of Philip II. **El Greco** stands apart within the Spanish School. Works here date from his traits and still lifes of **Zurbarán** (Rm 10A) are peaceful compositions in which chiaroscuro and realism triumph. **Murillo** mainly painted the Virgin (*The Immaculate Conception*: Rm 29) but also plain folk (*The Holy Family with a Little Bird*). Works from Spanish historical painting include *The Last Will and Testament of Isabel the Catholic* by Rosales (Rm 61B), *Juana the Mad* by F Pradilla and *The Execution of Torrijos and his Colleagues on the Beach at Málaga* by A Gisbert.

Diego Velázquez (1599–1660)

The Prado possesses not only the greatest paintings of Velázquez, but the world's largest collection of his work. He spent time in Italy (1629–31) where he painted **Vulcan's Forge**. He began to use richer, more subtle colours and developed his figure compositions as in his magnificent **Christ on the Cross**. On his return he painted **The Surrender of Breda** (Rm 27) in which his originality emerges. The use of light in his pictures is crucial. Velàzquez strove towards naturalism in his royal hunting portraits of **Philip IV** and **Prince Baltasar Carlos as a Hunter** (1635, a wonderful rendering of a child) and his equestrian portraits of the royal family, in particular **Prince Baltasar Carlos on Horseback** with the sierra in the background. In 1650 he returned to Italy where he painted landscapes, **The Medici Gardens in Rome**. In his later masterpiece, **Las Meninas** (c. 1656; Rm 12), the Infanta Margarita is shown in the artist's studio in a magnificent display of light and colour. In **The Tapestry Weavers** (c. 1657), Velázquez combined myth and reality.

early Spanish period *(The Trinity)* to his maturity *(Adoration of the Shepherds;* Rm, 10B*)*. Other works are proof that he was a great portraitist, such as **The Nobleman with his Hand on his Chest**. **Ribalta** introduced tenebrism to Spain. **José (Jusepe) de Ribera (Lo Spagnoletto)** is represented by *Jacob's Dream* (Rm 9) in which the vigorous use of chiaroscuro reflects Caravaggio's influence. The por-

Goya (1746–1828)

Goya's portraits of the royal and famous, his war scenes, his depictions of everyday life, and his **Majas** (Rm 36) illustrate his extraordinary Realism and enthusiasm for colour. The museum contains 40 cartoons painted in oil between 1775 and 1791 for the Real Fábrica (Royal Tapestry Works). **The 3rd of May 1808 in Madrid: the Executions on Principe Pio Hill** (Rms 64-65) was inspired by the rebellion against the French occupation (see ARANJUEZ). His late works, the great series of so-called Black Paintings frescoed on the walls of his house, hang in Room 67.

Flemish Painting★★★ (1430–1700)

The exceptional collection of Flemish painting reflects Spain's history with the Low Countries.

Among the Flemish Primitives are Robert Campen, the Mester of Flemalle (St Barbara). **Van der Weyden** added great richness of colour, and a sense of composition (Descent from the Cross, Rm 58). Drama is interpreted through melancholy by his successor, **Memling** (Adoration of the Magi; Rm 58A). There follow the weird imaginings of **Hieronymus Bosch**, El Bosco (The Garden of Earthly Delights), which influenced his disciple Patinir (Crossing the Stygian Lake) – both these in Room 56A – and a **Bruegel the Elder** (Triumph of Death; Rm 56A).

The most Baroque of painters, **Rubens**, breathed new life into Flemish painting (The Three Graces; Rm. 25). There is a rich collection of his work completed by that of his disciples: **Van Dyck** and **Jordaens** (Rm. 168).

Dutch Painting (1700–1800)

Two interesting works by **Rembrandt** are a Self-Portrait and Artemis.

Italian Painting★★ (1300–1800)

The collection is especially rich in works by Venetian painters.

The Italian Renaissance brought with it elegance and ideal beauty as in paintings by **Raphael** (The Holy Family, The Cardinal; Rm 49), Roman nobility and monumental bearing in the work of **Mantegna** (The Death of the Virgin; Rm 56B) and melancholic dreaminess in **Botticelli** (Story of Nastagio degli Onesti). The spirituality of the magnificent Annunciation by **Fra Angelico** belongs to the Gothic tradition.

Colour and sumptuousness triumph with the Venetian school: **Titian** with his exceptional mythological scenes (Danae and the Shower of Gold; Rm 42, Venus with the Organist; Rm. 24) and his portrait of Charles V of Mühlberg; **Veronese** with compositions set off by silver tones; Tintoretto's golden-fleshed figures springing from shadow (Christ Washing the Disciples' Feet; Rm 44) and **Tiepolo**'s paintings intended for Charles III's royal palace.

French Painting (1600–1800)

The French are represented by **Poussin** (Rm 3) and by **Lorrain** (17C).

German Painting (1450–1800)

A selection includes **Dürer**'s figure and portrait paintings (Self-Portrait, Adam and Eve; Rm 55B) and works by Cranach. The Cáson del Buen Retiro, which housed Picasso's Guernica when it first returned to Spain, is now closed to the general public.

MUSEO THYSSEN-BORNEMISZA★★★

Po. del Prado 8. Banco de España, Atocha. Open Tue–Sun 10am–7pm (Sat temporary shows till 11pm; 24, 31 Dec till 3pm; last admission 30min before closing. Closed 1 Jan, 1 May, 25 Dec. €8; no charge for children under 12. 913 69 01 51. www.museothyssen.org.

The Neoclassical Palacio de Villahermosa houses an outstanding private collection acquired by the Spanish State from **Baron Hans Heinrich Thyssen-Bornemisza**. The museum displays some 800 works from the late 13C to the present day, exhibited in chronological order on three floors. Temporary exhibitions are shown in another wing of the museum.

Museo Thyssen-Bornemisza

© Maurizio Borgese/hemis.fr

Second floor

The visit begins with the Italian Primitives *(Gallery 1)*: **Duccio di Buoninsegna**'s *Christ and the Samaritan Woman*, with its concern for scenic realism. **Gallery 3** displays splendid examples of 15C Dutch religious painting such as **Jan van Eyck**'s *The Annunciation Diptych*. Next to it is the small *Our Lady of the Dry Tree* by **Petrus Christus**; Virgin and Child symbolise the flowering of the dry tree.

The museum possesses a magnificent **portrait collection**. **Gallery 5** contains superb examples of the Early Renaissance and its values of identity and autonomy. These come to the fore in the *Portrait of Giovanna Tornuaboni* by the Italian painter **D Ghirlandaio**. **Raphael**'s *Portrait of an Adolescent* can be seen in the Villahermosa Gallery *(Gallery 6)* while **Gallery 7** (16C) reveals **Vittore Carpaccio**'s *Young Knight in a Landscape* in which the protagonist's elegance stands out from a background heavy with symbolism. The *Portrait of Doge Francesco Vernier* by **Titian** shows sober, yet diverse tones. After admiring **Dürer**'s surprising *Jesus Among the Doctors* (1506, *Gallery 8*), move on to **Gallery 9**, with portraits from the 16C German School including **The Nymph from the Fountain**, one of several paintings by **Lucas Cranach the Elder**, and the *Portrait of a Woman* by **Hans Baldung Grien**. The 16C Dutch paintings in **Gallery 10** include **Patinir**'s *Landscape with the Rest on the Flight into Egypt*. **Gallery 11** exhibits several works by **El Greco** as well as **Titian**'s *St Jerome in the Wilderness* (1575), with its characteristic use of flowing brush-strokes.

One of the splendid early works of **Caravaggio**, the creator of tenebrism, *St Catherine of Alexandria*, hangs in **Gallery 12**. In the same gallery is a splendid sculpture (St Sebastian) by Baroque artist **Bernini**. Also here is the *Lamentation over the Body of Christ* (1633) by **Ribera**. The 18C Italian Painting section *(Galleries 16–18)* shows Venetian scenes by **Canaletto** and **Guardi**. Also on this floor *(Galleries 19–21)* are 17C Dutch and Flemish works. **Van Dyck**'s magnificent *Portrait of Jacques le Roy*, **De Vos**' *Antonia Canis*, and two memorable **Rubens**, *The Toilet of Venus* and *Portrait of a Young Woman with a Rosary*, all hang from the walls of **Gallery 19**.

First floor

Galleries 22–26 represent 17C Dutch painting with scenes of daily life and landscapes. Note **Frans Hals'** *Family Group in a Landscape*, a fine collective portrait.

Interesting portraits stand out from the 18C French and British schools while the 19C North American paintings, virtually unknown in Europe *(Galleries 29 and 30)* are exceptional. They include works by Romantic landscape artists Cole, Church,

Bierstadt and the Realist Homer. The European Romanticism and Realism of the 19C is expressed by **Constable**'s *The Lock*, **Courbet**'s *The Water Stream* and **Friedrich**'s *Easter Morning*, together with the three works by **Goya** *(Gallery 31)*.

Galleries 32 and **33** are dedicated to Impressionism and Post-Impressionism: magnificent works by Monet, Manet, Renoir, Sisley, Degas, Pissarro, Gauguin, Van Gogh, Toulouse-Lautrec and Cézanne. *At the Milliner* by **Degas** is one of his major canvases. Other works which stand out include **Van Gogh**'s *"Les Vessenots" in Auvers*, which displays the explosion of brush-strokes in some of his later works, *Mata Mua* by **Gauguin**, from his Polynesian period, and **Cézanne**'s *Portrait of a Farmer*, in which his use of colour to build volumes is a forerunner of Cubism.

Expressionism is represented in **Galleries 35–40**, following a small display of paintings from the Fauve movement in **Gallery 34**. The Expressionist movement, a highlight of this museum, supposes the supremacy of the artist's interior vision and colour over draughtsmanship. Two highly emblematic paintings by **Grosz**, *Metropolis* and *Street Scene*, hang in **Gallery 40**.

Ground floor

The first few galleries *(41–44)* contain exceptional Experimental Avant-Garde works (1907–24) from European movements: Futurism, Orphism, Suprematism, Constructivism (note the women artists' work), Cubism and Dadaism. **Room 41** displays Cubist works by **Picasso** *(Man with a Clarinet)*, **Braque** *(Woman with a Mandolin)* and **Juan Gris** *(Woman Sitting)*, while *Proun 1C* by **Lissitzky** and *New York City, New York* by **Mondrian** are in Room 43.

Gallery 45 shows post-First World War European works by **Picasso** *(Harlequin with a Mirror)* and **Joan Miró** *(Catalan Peasant with a Guitar)*, and a 1914 abstract composition by **Kandinsky** *(Picture with Three Spots)*. In the next gallery, mainly dedicated to North American painting, are *Brown and Silver I* by **Jackson Pollock** and *Green on Maroon*

by **Mark Rothko**, two examples of American Abstract Expressionism. The last two galleries *(47 and 48)* are given over to Surrealism, Figurative Tradition and Pop Art.

Carmen Thyssen-Bornemisza Collection

The more than 250 works on exhibit build on those in the original collection. Notable are 17C Dutch painting, Impressionism and Post-Impressionism, North American painting, and early Avant-Garde work.

MUSEO NACIONAL CENTRO DE ARTE REINA SOFÍA★★ (QUEEN SOFÍA ART CENTRE)

Santa Isabel 52. 🚇 *Atocha.* 🕐*Open Mon and Wed–Sat 10am–9pm, Sun 10am–2.30pm.* 🕐*Closed 1, 6 Jan, 1 May, 9 Sep, 9 Nov, 24–25, 31 Dec.* 💶*€6; €14.40 for Paseo del Arte Card (including Museo del Prado and Museo Thyssen); no charge Sat 2.30–9pm, Sun, 18 May, 12 Oct, 6 Dec.* 📞*917 74 10 00. www.museoreinasofia.es.*

The former Hospital de San Carlos was refurbished to house the city's museum of contemporary art. A modern extension, the work of Jean Nouvel, with large galleries designed for contemporary work, opened in 2005. The hanging of the permanent collection, mostly in the original Sabitini building, evolves around major themes.

Permanent collection★

First floor.

Galleries around the patio garden show a selection of modern international work, including **Juan Muñoz**'s *I Saw It in Bologna* (1991). The garden sculptures include pieces by Catalan artist **Joan Miró** and Basque sculptor **Eduardo Chillida**.

Second floor (galleries 201-210).

The museum's overview of Spanish art between 1900 and 1945 is structured around "micronarratives" which give the wider context of Europe's avant-garde movements. However, the centrepiece of this floor is undoubtedly Picasso's *Guernica*★★★, which hangs in gallery

206.6. (⊘Strictly no photography of any kind is allowed.) Considered one of the 20C's greatest paintings, commissioned for the Spanish Pavilion at the 1937 World Fair, it was inspired by the Fascist terror-bombing of Gernika and is renowned for its powerful Iberian symbolism and denunciation of the atrocities of war. Five other galleries give a narrative background to *Guernica*. Some galleries are dedicated to Spanish masters. Gallery 206.04 shows a retrospective of **Joan Miró**. **Dalí** is represented in Room 205, with early works and examples from his Surrealist period (*The Great Masturbator*). Gallery 208 is dedicated to the work of Juan Gris.
Fourth floor (Galleries 401–424).
Galleries dedicated to art since 1945 widen their scope to take in influences from elsewhere, especially North and Latin America, interwoven chronologically with Spanish and European work. Some galleries highlight the work of experimental Spanish pioneers such as Basque sculptor Oteiza (407). Another gallery (419) is dedicated to Picasso's and Miró's 1960s work. Photography and video are a strong suit throughout the collection, especially in this modern period. The main trends from the late 1940s are also delineated: the avant-garde in the early years of the dictatorship, abstract art in the 1950s, Neo-Realist photography and the realism of contemporary painters like Antonio López.

WALKING TOUR

③ ROYAL MADRID★★
⚲*See map of walking tour p120.*
Madrid is home to the Royal Palace, built where the Spanish Royal family lived for four centuries, and to convents and churches that sprung up around court life.

Plaza de la Armería
Along the vast arcaded square (south side) is the **Catedral de la Almudena** (⌂*Ópera;* ⏱ *open daily 10am–2pm, 5–8pm (Jul–Aug 9pm);* ⊗*no charge; €6 museum and dome Mon–Sat 10am–*

2.30pm; ℘*915 42 22 00*). The cathedral, begun in 1879, was finished in 1993. The neo-Baroque façade harmonises with the palace. The view towards the west extends over the Casa de Campo and the Campo del Moro gardens sloping down to the Manzanares river.

Palacio Real★★ (Royal Palace)
Bailén. ⌂*Ópera.* ⏱*Open Oct–Mar Mon–Sat 10am–6pm, Sun and public holidays 10am–4pm; Apr–Sept Mon–Sat 9am–7pm, Sun and public holidays 9am–4pm; changing of the guard Wed 11am and 2pm.* ⏱*Closed 1, 6 Jan, 1, 15 May, 12 Oct, 9 Nov, 24–25, 31 Dec and during State receptions.* ⊗*€10 palace, art gallery and armoury (⟳ currently closed); guide €7, no charge Wed (for EU citizens) and 18 May.* ℘*914 54 88 00. www.patrimonionacional.es.*
The best view of the palace is from Paseo de Extremadura and from the gardens of the **Campo del Moro**★ (⏱*open Oct–Mar Mon–Sat 10am–6pm (Apr–Sep 8pm)*. This imposing edifice, built by the Bourbons following a fire at the Habsburg Alcázar, was the royal residence until 1931. It is still used for major State occasions.
The palace is a quadrilateral made of Guadarrama granite and white stone, 140m/459ft on the sides, on a high bossaged base. The upper register, in which Ionic columns and Doric pilasters alternate, is crowned by a white limestone balustrade.
The north front gives onto the **Jardines de Sabatini**, the west the **Campo del Moro**. **Plaza de la Armería** stands to the south between the west and east wings of the palace. The east façade gives onto **Plaza de Oriente**.

Palacio★ (Palace)
A monumental staircase with a ceiling painted by Giaquinto leads to the Salón de Alabarderos (Halberdier Room), with a ceiling painted by Tiepolo.
This leads to the **Salón de Columnas** (Column Room) where royal celebrations and banquets are held. The **Salón del Trono**★ (Throne Room) retains decoration from the period of Charles III and is resplendent with crimson velvet hang-

ings and a magnificent ceiling by Tiepolo (1764) symbolising *The Greatness of the Spanish Monarchy*.

The consoles, mirrors and gilded bronze lions are of Italian design. The following three rooms were the king's quarters, occupied by Charles III in 1764. The Saleta Gasparini, the king's dining room, retains a ceiling painted by Mengs.

The Gasparini antechamber also has a ceiling by Mengs, and Goya portraits of Charles IV and María Luisa of Parma. The **Cámara Gasparini** is covered in pure Rococo decoration.

The Salón de Carlos III was the king's bedroom. The décor is from the period of Ferdinand VII. The **Sala de Porcelana** is, along with its namesake in Aranjuez Palace, the masterpiece of the Buen Retiro Porcelain Factory. Official banquets are held in the Alfonso XII **Comedor de Gala** or Banqueting Hall (for 145 guests), adorned with 16C Brussels tapestries.

The two music rooms contain instruments including several made by **Stradivarius**★. In the chapel are frescoes by Corrado Giaquinto and paintings by Mengs (*Annunciation*) and Bayeu (*St Michael the Archangel*).

Real Farmacia (Royal Pharmacy)

Several rooms display 18C–20C jars, including a fine 18C Talavera glass jar.

Museo de Colecciones Reales ★★

⚊The outstanding armoury is closed until 2013 for rebuilding work which will incoporate a 70m/230ft section of the wall of the Muslim city into the display of carriages, weapons and more than 100 tapestries.

▷ *The Royal Palace faces the Plaza de Oriente.*

Plaza de Oriente

This attractive square between the east façade of the Palacio Real and the Teatro Real is pleasant for a stroll. The magnificent equestrian statue of Philip IV is the work of Pietro Tacca (17C).

Teatro Real

Pl. de Oriente. 🚇 Ópera. 🚶Guided tours Mon–Fri 10.30am–1pm, Sat–Sun and public holidays 11am–1.30pm. 🕐Closed 1 Jan, 24–25, 31 Dec. ➾€5. 🕿915 16 06 96. www.teatro-real.com.
This hexagonal Neoclassical building was created as an opera house in 1850 for Isabel II. It has two façades.

▷ *On the western side of the Plaza de Oriente Calle Pavia leads to the Plaza de la Encarnación.*

Real Monasterio de la Encarnación★ (Royal Convent of the Incarnation)

Pl. de la Encarnación 1. 🚇 Ópera. 🚶Guided tours (45min) Tue–Thu and Sat 10.30am–12.45pm, 4–5.45pm, Fri 10.30am–12.45pm, Sun 11am–1.45pm. 🕐Closed 1, 6 Jan, Wed–Sat during Holy Week, 1, 15 May, 27 Jul, 9 Nov, 25 and 31 Dec. ➾€3.60 (combined with Monasterio de las Descalzas: €6); no charge Wed (for EU citizens) and 18 May. 🕿914 54 88 00. www.patrimonionacional.es.
The convent, on a delightful square near the former Alcázar, was founded in 1611 by Margaret of Austria. The collection of paintings from the 17C Madrid School is particularly rich and includes the interesting *Exchange of Princesses on Pheasant Island* in 1615 by Van der Meulen. There is a polychrome sculpture of *Christ at the Column* by Gregorio Hernández on the first floor.

The **Relicario**★, with ceiling painted by Vicencio Carducci, holds 1 500 relics. The church with quasi-Herreran portals was reconstructed in the 18C after the Alcázar fire.

▷ *Returning to the Teatro Real, turn left up Carlos III, then follow Arenal and turn left up San Martín.*

Monasterio de las Descalzas Reales★★

Pl. de las Descalzas. 🚇 Ópera. 🚶Guided tours (45min) Tue–Thu and Sat 10.30am–12.45pm, 4–5.45pm, Fri

10.30am–12.45pm, Sun 11am–1.45pm.
🕐*Closed 1, 6 Jan, Wed–Sat during
Holy Week, 1, 15 May, 9 Nov, 25, 31 Dec.*
👁*€5 (combined with Monasterio de la
Encarnación: €6); no charge Wed (for
EU citizens) and 18 May.* 📞*914 54 88 00.
www.patrimonionacional.es.*

Joanna of Austria, daughter of Emperor
Charles V, founded the convent of Poor
Clares in the palace where she was born.
It served as a retreat for nobles.

The magnificent grand **staircase**★ is
totally decorated with frescoes. In a
former dormitory is an extraordinary collection of **tapestries**★★ depicting the
Triumph of the Church, woven in Brussels in the 17C to cartoons by Rubens.
The **33 small chapels** are sumptuously
decorated; outstanding is that of the Virgin of Guadalupe.

Convent treasures include portraits of
the royal family by Rubens, Sánchez
Coello and others.

▷ *Take Postigo de San Martín to Plaza
del Callao and turn left down Gran Vía.*

Plaza de España

🏛 *Plaza de España.*

Gran Vía, built by Alfonso XIII before
his wedding, is now the city's busiest
shopping street. It leads west to the
Plaza de España, where a monument
to Cervantes in the middle of the city's
central esplanade is overwhelmed by
1950s skyscrapers. From here Calle
Princesa, popular with students, leads
towards Moncloa and the **Ciudad Universitaria**★ (University City). From its
southeastern corner Calle Bailen leads
back to the Royal Palace and splendid
formal **Jardines de Sabitini** (🕐*open
daily 9am–10pm; Oct–Apr 9pm*).

👣 **WALKING TOUR**

④ **LITERARY MADRID**

🕐*See map of walking tour p120.*

A network of characterful old streets on
the eastern side of Plaza de Santa Ana,
known as Huertas, or the Barrio de las
Letras, was home to great writers and
dramatists during Madrid's Golden Age.
Cervantes, Quevedo and Lope de Vega

lived here and were buried in the Iglesia
de San Sebastián. The quarter keeps
the **Teatro Español**, on Plaza Santa
Ana, and one of the country's finest,
as well as the **Círculo de Bellas Artes**
arts centre on Marqués de Casa Riera,
and some fine antequarian bookshops.
The quarter's bohemian nightlife also
remains as hectic as ever.

Around Plaza Santa Ana

Facing the Teatro Español the **Reina
Victoria** hotel, now the ME hotel, was
once a meeting place for bullfighters.
On the square's south side the **Cervecería Alemana**, a favourite haunt
of Ernest Hemingway and Ava Gard-
ner on their visits to Madrid, remains
unchanged.

Elsewhere you can enjoy decorative old
façades on a nightime stroll: the Villa
Rosa, an old flamenco *tablao* next door
to the Hotel ME, is splendidly tiled, as is
the nearby **Bar Madrid** and **Los Gabrieles** on Calle Echegaray (*free live shows
Tues after 10.30pm*).

▷ *Take Calle del Prado, turn right
down Calle de León and left down Calle
de Cervantes.*

Casa Museo de Lope de Vega★

Cervantes 11. 🏛 *Anton Martín.* 🕐*Open
for guided tours (45min) Tue–Sun 10am
–3pm.* 🕐*Closed national and local
public holidays.* 👁*No charge. Reserve in
advance:* 📞*91-429 92 16.*

Lope de Vega bought this house at the
heart of literary Madrid when he was
Spain's most famous playwright. The
top two floors and garden have been
recreated around an inventory and his
writings. Of special interest are the room
where he wrote such works as *Fuentove-
juna* and the chapel.

▷ *Turn left out of the house, take Calle
de San Agustín, first left, to come out in
the Plaza de las Cortes.*

When you emerge on the Plaza you
face the **Congreso de los Diputados**,
Spain's parliament, held up here at gun-
point during the attempted military

coup on 23 February 1981. Walking left up San Jeronimo, and then turning right down Calle Sevilla to Alcalá, you pass impressive embassies and old banks.

Real Academia de Bellas Artes de San Fernando★ (San Fernando Royal Fine Arts Academy)

Alcalá 13. 🚇 *Sevilla, Sol.* ⏱*Open Tue–Fri 9am–5pm, Sat 9am–3pm, Sun and public holidays 9am–2.30pm.* ⏱*Closed 1, 6 Jan, 1, 30 May, 24–25, 31 Dec.* 👁*€2.40; no charge Wed, 18 May, 12 Oct, 6 Dec.* ☎*915 24 08 64.*
Among the Royal Academy's valuable collection of 16C–20C paintings are works by Ribera, Zurbarán, Murillo, Alonso Cano *(Christ Crucified)* and Velázquez, but, above all, street scenes and a self-portait by Goya, a member of the Academy.

SALAMANCA – LA CASTELLANA
Museo Arqueológico Nacional★★ (Archaeological Museum)

Serrano 13. 🚇 *Serrano.* ⌐ *Currently closed for renovations. http://man.mcu.es.*
Shares a building with the **Biblioteca Nacional** *(National Library; Po. de Recoletos 20–22;* 🚇 *Serrano;* ⏱*exhibition galleries open Tue–Sat 10am–9pm, Sun and public hols 10am–2pm;* ⌐*guided tours of the library Tue 5.30pm, Thur 5pm (90min) may be booked;* 👁*no charge;* ☎*915 80 78 00; www.bne.es).*
The Museum's splendid collection runs from prehistoric art – in the garden is a reproduction of the **Cuevas de Altamira** and their paintings of bison – to treasures from churches along the pilgrimage route to Santiago. Currently it is being refitted within its old shell. When it reopens, it will keep the same collection. Among early pieces are the splendid bronze Costix **bulls**★ of the Megalithic culture (Talayots) of the Balearic Islands. Iberian sculpture is exhibited at its peak of artistic expression: the **Dama de Elche**★★★ *(Lady of Elche)* is an

outstanding stone bust, with a sumptuous headdress and corsage. The **Dama de Baza**★★ is a realistic goddess figure of the 4C BC. Medieval decorative arts include the magnificent **votive crowns of Guarrazar**★★ dating from the Visigothic period, made of embossed gold plaques, mixing Germanic and Byzantine techniques. Romanesque portals, engravings, grilles, tombs and capitals, and Gothic sculpture in subsequent galleries, show deep Moorish influence.
The collection also includes a reconstruction of a Mudéjar interior, with a magnificent **artesonado**★★ ceiling. North of the Museo Arqueológico is the Plaza de Colón (Columbus Square) with a statue of the navigator on a column.

Museo Lázaro Galdiano★★

Serrano 122. 🚇 *República Argentina.* ⏱*Open Wed–Mon 10am–4.30pm.* ⏱*Closed 1 Jan, 1 May, 9 Nov, 24–25, 31 Dec.* 👁*€4. Reserved guided tours 5.30–7pm. €8.* ☎*915 61 60 84. www.flg.es.*
This mansion houses **collections**★★ of editor and art lover José Lázaro Galdiano (1862–1947). On the **lower level**, are samples of outstanding paintings by the Master of Perea, Mengs, Zurbarán and Sánchez Coello.
The **main floor** – which retains ceilings painted by Villamil and some lovely items of furniture – is entirely devoted to 15C–19C Spanish Art with magnificent Gothic and Renaissance panels. On the **second floor** are works of the **Flemish School** and Italian works. The **third floor** houses decorative arts (some 4 000 items): **ivories and enamel**★★★, ceramics, numismatics, arms and fabric.

Museo Sorolla★

General Martínez Campos 37. 🚇 *Gregorio Marañón or Iglesia.* ⏱*Open Tue–Sat 9.30am–8pm, Sun and public holidays 10am–3pm.* ⏱*Closed 1 Jan, 1 May, 24–25, 9 Nov, 31 Dec.* 👁*€3.* ☎*913 10 15 84. http://museosorolla.mcu.es.*
The Madrid home of Joaquín Sorolla (1863–1923), the great Valencian painter

of local scenes filling with glowing Mediterranean light, is beautifully laid out, and includes his studio and a fine selection of his works. You can also relax in the garden.

Museo de la Cera

Po. de Recoletos, 41. Colón. *Open Mon–Fri 10am–2.30pm, 4.30–8.30pm, weekends and holidays 10am–8.30pm.* €16, under 10s and over 60s €10. 913 192 645. http://museocera madrid.com.

Among many wax models, often set against evocative backdrops, are historical figures such as Cleopatra and numerous actors (Penélope Cruz, Antonio Banderas). There is something here for everyone: Spain's football heroes for sports fans, Federico García Lorca and Picasso for culture-lovers, Barack Obama and George Clooney for those who would like to know them first-hand.

Real Casa de la Moneda (Royal Mint)

Doctor Esquerdo 36. O'Donnell. *Open Tue–Fri 10am–5.30pm, Sun and holidays 10am–2pm.* 915 66 65 44.

One of the world's largest royal mint collections, it covers not only coins, stamps and medals, but also lottery tickets and gambling.

MONCLOA – CASA DE CAMPO DISTRICT
Museo Cerralbo★

Ventura Rodríguez 17. Ventura Rodríguez. *Open Tue–Sat 9.30am–3pm, Sun and public holidays 10am–3pm.* Closed 1 Jan, 1 May, 24,25, 31 Dec. €3. 915 47 36 46. www.museocerralbo.mcu.es.

Housed in a late-19C mansion, recently restored, the Museo Cerralbo displays the collection of the Marquis of Cerralbo, a patron of the arts, including Spanish paintings, furniture, fans, clocks, armour and weaponry, porcelain, and archaeological finds.

Parque del Oeste★ (Park of the West)

This delightful garden, overlooking the Manzanares, was designed at the beginning of the 20C.

In the southern part stands the small 4C BC Egyptian **Temple of Debod** (*pas. del Pintor Rosales;* Argüelles; *open Apr–Sept Tue–Fri 10am–2pm, 6–8pm, Sat–Sun 10am–2pm; Oct–Mar Tue–Fri 9.45am–1.45pm, 4.15–6.15pm, Sat–Sun and public holidays 10am–2pm;* no charge; 913 66 74 15), rescued from Nubia when the Aswan Dam was being built.

The **Paseo del Pintor Rosales** nearby offers pavement cafés and views of Velázquez-like sunsets.

Ermita de San Antonio de la Florida★

Glorieta de la Florida 5. On the edge of the Parque del Oeste. Príncipe Pío. *Open Tue–Fri 9.30am–8pm.* 915 47 79 37. www.esmadrid.com/ museosdemadrid.

Goya was buried in this chapel, built in 1798 under Charles IV, at his own request. The chapel interior was frescoed by Goya with female angels around a central narrative scene on the cupola. One of the painter's first great works of realism, these **frescoes★★** illustrate the miracle of St Anthony of Padua.

Casa de Campo★

This extensive park is popular with Madrileños. Attractions include a lake, a swimming pool and an **amusement park★**.

Spain's biggest, with over 40 attractions, it is especially popular at night on summer weekends (*Ctra de Extremadura;* Batán; *open from noon;* €29.90; those under 1.2m €23; 902 34 50 09; www.parquedeatracciones.es).

The **Teleférico** (cablecar) connects to the city to the Casa de Campo with splendid views on the way (*Po. del Pintor Rosales–Cerro Garabita;* Argüelles; *open 12 noon–6–9.30pm seasonally, call for specific hours;* €5; round-trip €10; 915 41 11 18; www.teleferico.com).

The 🚋 **zoo-aquarium**★★ houses one of the largest assortments of animals anywhere in Europe *(Casa de Campo;* 🚇*Casa de Campo;* ⏱*open daily, Mon–Fri 10.30am–7pm; Sat, Sun, holidays 10.30am–8.30pm;* 💶*€19.40; children under 7 €15.70;* ☎*902 34 50 14; www.zoomadrid.com).*

Museo del Traje (Costume Museum)

Av. Juan Herrera 2. 🚇 *Moncloa.* ♿⏱*Open Tue–Sat 9.30am–8.30pm (Nov–Apr 6.30pm), Sun and public holidays 10am–3pm.* ⏱*Closed 1, 6 Jan, 1 May, 9 Sept, 24–25, 31 Dec.* 💶*€3; no charge Sat from 2.30pm, Sun, 18 Apr, 18 May, 12 Oct, 6 Dec.* ☎*915 50 47 00. http://museodeltraje.mcu.es.*

A showcase of fashion from the 18C to the 20C. Couturiers Mariano Fortuny and Balenciaga are featured among everyday designs.

Museo de América★ (Museum of the Americas)

Av. Reyes Católicos 6. 🚇 *Moncloa.* ⏱*Open Tue–Sat 9.30am–3pm, Sun and public holidays 10am–3pm.* ⏱*Closed 1 Jan, 6 Jan, 1 May, 24–25, 31 Dec.* 💶*€3; no charge Sat pm from 2.30pm, Sun, 18 Apr, 18 May, 12 Oct, 6 Dec.* ☎*915 49 26 41. http://museodeamerica.mcu.es.*

Over 2 500 objects, accompanied by maps, models, reconstructions of dwellings, etc, focus on the ties between Europe and America.

Outstanding are the Stele of Madrid (Mayan), the powerful **Treasure of Los Quimbayas**★ (Colombian), the *Tudela Manuscript* (1553) and the prized Maya **Tro Cortesiano Manuscript**★★★, one of only four remaining. The darkened map room memorably recreates early navigators' cartography.

El Faro de Moncloa (Moncloa Beacon)

Av. de los Reyes Católicos. 🚇 *Moncloa.* ⚒*Closed for renovation.* ☎*915 44 81 04* From its 76m/250ft high **observatory**★★, there is a wonderful view of Madrid and its surrounding area.

ADDITIONAL SIGHTS

Museo Municipal de la Historia de Madrid

C. Fuencarral 78. 🚇 *Moncloa.* ⚒*Closed for extensive renovation. www.esmadrid.com/museosdemadrid* Housed in a former city hospice, this small museum tracing the city's history keeps a superb carved 18C decorative **portal**★★ and, inside, old wells for storing ice from the sierra.

Museo Nacional de Romanticismo

C. San Mateo 13. 🚇 *Tribunal.* ⏱*Tue–Sat 9.30am–8.30pm (Nov–Apr 18.30pm), Sun and hols 10am–3pm.* 💶*€3, free Sat from 2pm and Sun.* ☎*914 481 045.* Built in 1776 for the Marqués de Matallana, this Neoclassical palace houses a 19C decorative arts collection gathered together by Benigno Valle-Inclán, the connoisseur who opened the museum in 1924. Two dozen rooms are beautifully furnished and a ground floor garden patio – access from the tea-room – is a lush oasis where water trickles from a graceful fountain.

Plaza Monumental de las Ventas★ (Bullring)

Alcalá 237. 🚇 *Ventas.* ⚒*Guided tours (40min) Tue–Sun 10am–2pm.* ☎*915 56 92 37.* 💶*€7. www.las-ventas.com.* Just to the east of Salamanca is Spain's largest bullring (built 1931), with a capacity of 22 300 spectators. Its **Museo Taurino** (Bullfighting Museum; 💶no charge) honours great bullfighters.

Museo del Ferrocarril (Railway Museum)

Po. de las Delicias 61. 🚇 *Delicias.* ⏱*Open Sept–Jul Tue–Sun 10am–3pm.* ⏱*Closed Aug, 1, 6 Jan, 1 May, 25 Dec.* 💶*€4.50; child €3.* ☎*902 22 88 22. www.museodelferrocarril.org.* The wrought-iron and glass Delicias railway station, from where trains ran 1880–1969, has a collection of steam and diesel engines, clocks, models and a delightful restaurant car for snacks. The Strawberry Train (🍓*see p.138*) leaves from here in the summer months.

Museo Nacional de Ciencas Naturales

C. José Gutiérrez Abascal 2. Gregorio Marañón. Open Tue–Fri 10am–6pm, Sats 10am–8pm (Jul–Aug closes at 3pm), Sun and hols 10am–2.30pm. €5, child €3. 91 411 13 28. www.mncn.csic.es

Madrid's Natural Sciences Museum has grown around an 18thC royal collection, still on show as a cabinet of curiosities. But today's huge collection of fossils and dinosaurs has been reoriented to delve into the world's past and exhibit its biodiversity.

Estadio Santiago Bernabeu

C. Concha Espina 1 (gate 20, tour tickets gate 10). Santiago Bernabeu. Open Mon–Sat 10am–7pm, Suns and public holidays 10.30am–6.30pm. Closed 5 hours before matches, 25 Dec, 1 Jan. €15, child €10. 902-311709.

For decades this stadium was home to the Real Madrid team. Today it still hosts epic matches. The tour takes you to the top of the stadium in a panoramic lift, into the Royal Box and changing rooms, and on to the pitch through the tunnel from which teams emerge before an 80,000-strong crowd.

Madrid Río (Madrid's Riverbanks)

River Manzanares. Príncipe Pío, Puerta del Ángel, Pirámides, Legazpi.

Half the full extension of the Manazares's planned riverside walkway has now been opened up to pedestrians and cyclists. Four new bridges link the left and right banks' sports and leisure areas. Parks and gardens are laid out around historic monuments like the city's old bridges, the Ermita Virgen del Puerto (1718) and Matadero Madrid, an arts centre inside a restored Modernist slaughterhouse. Plans to revive the river's water flow and to build a city beach are still to be carried out.

EXCURSIONS
PARQUE WARNER MADRID★

San Martín de la Vega. 25km/15.5mi SE of Madrid. Check seasonal schedule. €38 (€36 for tickets bought online); child €26.50; parking €8 per day. 902 02 41 00. www.parquewarner.com.

This park is a great family-oriented getaway. The themed areas include Hollywood Boulevard, Movie World Studios, DC Super Heroes World, Old West Territory and Cartoon Village, each with rides and activities.

Movie WB World Sutdios will appeal to those who love special effects and car chases. In Super Heroes World you can experience spectacular combats between Batman and the forces of evil, or a 110m/360 ft freefall.

For the youngest visitors, Cartoon Village offers watergames and recreates the magical world of old-fashioned heroes like Tom and Jerry. In summer take a hat: tree-shade is not yet abundant.

Faunia★

Av. de las Comunidades 28. 5km/3mi E of Parque El Retiro. Valdebernardo, Sierra de Guadalupe. Open from 10am, call to check specific hours. €24.70; child €19.10. 913 01 62 35. www.faunia.es.

A nature park which recreates the planet's ecosystems on a 140 000sq m/167 300sq yd site. It includes some 3 500 small- and medium-sized animals and birds, and over 70 000 trees and plants. One ecosystem is Europe's largest recreation of a polar ice-cap. Hugely popular with Madrileños and their children, Faunia may be visited time and again since the area is so large that it is difficult to explore it all on one visit.

PALACIO REAL EL PARDO★

Manuel Alonso, El Pardo. 17km/10.5mi NW of Madrid. Guided tours (35min) Oct–Mar Mon–Sat 10.30am–4.45pm, Sun and public holidays 10am–1.30pm; Apr–Sept Mon–Sat 10.30am–5.45pm, Sun and public holidays 9.30am–1.30pm. Closed 1, 6 Jan, 1, 15 May, 9 Nov, 24–25, 31 Dec and for State receptions. ⊷€4; Casita del Principe €3.40; no charge Wed (for EU citizens) and 18 May. ℘913 76 15 00. www.patrimonionacional.es.

The palace was built by Philip III (1598–1621) on the site of Philip II's (1556–98) palace which had been destroyed in a fire in 1604. Franco lived here for 35 years and King Juan Carlos spent his teenage years here; today, it is used by Heads of State on official visits.

Decorations include more than 200 **tapestries**★; the majority are 18C from the Real Fábrica de Tápices (Royal Tapestry Factory) in Madrid based on cartoons by Goya, Bayeu, González Ruiz and Van Loo. The Casita del Principe – Prince's House – is a richly decorated pleasure pavilion in the grounds.

A short walk or drive away (1km/0.6m), at the Convento de Capuchines (Camino del Cristo de Pardo s/n), is Gregorio Fernández's Cristo del Pardo (Christ Recumbent), a highpoint of Spanish baroque sculpture (◔open daily 8.30am–1pm, 4.30pm–8.30pm).

👤👤 Aquópolis

C. de la Mirasierra s/n, Villanueva de la Cañada. Bus 627 every 10 minutes from Moncloa, or 25min drive via N6. ◔Open Jun–Sep daily 12pm–8pm (Jun & Sep 7pm). ⊷€23.95, children under 1.4m €17.95. ℘91-8156911. www.aquopolis.es. Madrid's longest-established water amusement park with a wave pool, a dozen rides designed for all ages and tastes, a big swimming pool and bar-retaurants, is a blessing in the hot months. By car a trip can be combined with a visit to El Escorial (◔ see pp140–143).

👤👤 Parque de El Capricho

Avda de la Alameda de Osuna s/n. ◍ El Capricho. ◔Open weekends and public holidays 9am–9pm (Oct–Mar 6.30pm).

A stunning 18thC landscaped garden which reveals features such as a boating lake with oriental lakeside pavilion and boathouse, a giant beekeepers' hive, a romantic cottage and classical colonnade. Paths between these run under centennial trees and between beautifully kept lawns.

👤👤 Sierra de Guadarrama

Encircling the city to the north, the Guadarrama range provides splendid walking country. Starting points, at the foot of the slopes, may be reached by bus (Manzanares or Miraflores) or, in the case of Cercedilla, by train (from Atocha or Chamartín, about 1 hour's journey). A 20-minute walk above Cercedilla is the town's swimming pool, set among woods and filled by river water.

ADDRESSES

🍽 STAY

◒ **Hostal Gonzalo** – Cervantes 34 (Centro). ◍ Antón Martín. ℘914 29 27 14. www.hostalgonzalo.com. 15 rooms. Located close to the Prado, Reina Sofía and Thyssen-Bornemisza museums, this excellent hostal has a good family feel and soundproofed rooms for a night's rest before exploring the city.

◒ **Hotel Centro Sol** – San Jerónimo 5 (Centro). ◍ Sol. ℘915 22 15 82. www.hostalcentrosol.com. 35 rooms. A hotel very close to the Puerta del Sol occupying the second and fourth floors of a newly decorated building. Rooms, all with TVs and good bathrooms, are very reasonably priced.

◒◒ **Hostal Adriano** – Cruz 26 (Centro). ◍ Sol. ℘915 21 13 39. www.hostaladriano. com. 22 rooms. A good central choice in this price range, notable for its well-equipped rooms and original décor, with personalised rooms, especially no. 114, dedicated to soprano Maria Callas.

◒◒ **Hotel Mora** – Pas. del Prado 32 (Retiro). ◍ Atocha. ℘914 20 15 69. www.hotelmora.com. 62 rooms. The Mora enjoys a superb location in an impressive building opposite the botanical gardens on paseo del Prado. Comfortable, recently renovated rooms and reasonable rates.

◒◒ **Posada del Peine** – Postas 18 (Centro). ◍ Sol. ℘915 23 81 51. pos@hthoteles.com. 67 rooms. ⊟€7.50. Behind an elegant facade on a quiet pedestrian street just off the Plaza Mayor lies this comfortable modern hotel, one of a well-decorated modern chain.

Hotel Carlos V – *Maestro Vitoria 5 (Centro).* Callao. 915 31 41 00. www.hotelcarlosv.com. *67 rooms.* A good central option in a pedestrianised street away from the noise of the city. Although small, the English-style rooms are pleasant and well appointed. An eclectic cafeteria on the first floor.

Hotel Inglés – *Echegaray 8 (Huertas).* Sevilla. 914 29 65 51. www.hotel-ingles.net. *58 rooms.* There's no doubting the character of this hotel built in 1853. A good central and moderately priced option with the added attraction of its own garage parking. Clean, comfortable rooms.

Hotel Oskar – *Pl. Vázquez de Mella, 12 (Chueca).* Banco de España or Chueca. 917 011 173. www.room-matehotels.com. *74 rooms.* €9. Well-priced designer hotel in the middle of Chueca and close to the museums. There is contemporary art in the lobby, a minimalist pop café and glamorous rooftop terrace and pool.

Hotel Ritz – *Pl. de la Lealtad 5 (Retiro).* Banco de España. 917 01 67 67. .www.ritz.es. *137 rooms.* €30. *Restaurant* . The city's grandest hotel, a Belle Époque building, is superbly located near the Paseo del Prado. The Hotel Ritz has all the elegance, tradition and comfort you would expect from such a famous name, plus prices to match. The terrace-garden here is an additional delight.

⟡/ EAT

Bazaar – *Libertad 21 (Chueca).* Chueca, Banco de España. 913 69 35 57. www.restaurantbazaar.com. *Closed 24–25, 31 Dec, 1 Jan.* A stylish split-level restaurant serving good-value Mediterranean cooking with exotic modern touches. Lunchtime set menu. Go early as you can't reserve.

La Bola – *Bola 5 (Centro).* Santo Domingo. 915 47 69 30. www.labola.es. *Closed Sun, 24 Dec for dinner.* If you're hoping to try a traditional *cocido madrileño*, look no further than this famous tavern, which has been cooking it in earthenware pots on a charcoal fire for over a century.

Casa Lucio – *Cava Baja 35 (La Latina).* La Latina. 913 65 82 17. www.casalucio.es. *Closed Sat lunchtime and Aug.* One of Madrid's best-known addresses frequented by politicians, actors and visitors alike. Typical Castilian décor, and famous for its *huevos estrellados* (fried eggs).

La Vaca Verónica – *Moratín 38.* Antón Martín. 914 29 78 27. www.lavacaveronica.es. *Closed Sun for dinner.* The outstanding décor recreates a cosy, intimate space, with spider lamps, ceiling mirrors, candles and soft lighting. Posters recall Pop Art and Art Nouveau. Specialities include grilled meats and the delicious *pasta con carabineros*.

Zerain – *Quevedo 3 (Huertas).* Antón Martín. 914 29 79 09. www.restaurante-vasco-zerain-sidreria.es. *Closed Sun for dinner, 24–25 Dec.* A typical menu at this Basque cider bar near plaza de Santa Ana includes *tortilla de bacalao* (saltcod omelette) and *chuletón* (meat cutlets). Rustic, but pleasant décor. The cider here is served directly from the barrel.

Diverxo – *Pensamiento 28 (Tetuan).* Tetuan. 914 31 64 56. www.diverxo.com. *Closed Sun, Mon.* David Muñoz's Mediterranean and Japanese fusion cooking makes this one of Madrid's most exciting young eating places. Three set tasting menus.

Santceloni – *Po de la Castellana 57 (Castellano).* Serrano. 912 108840. www.restaurantesantceloni.com. *Closed Sat lunch, Sun and public holidays, Holy Week and Aug.* Exquisite, Michelin-star worthy Mediterranean cookery. Its tasting menu and legendary cheese trolley change daily. Prices match its fame as one of the city's best kitchens.

TAPAS

El Bocaito – *Libertad 6 (Chueca).* Chueca, Banco de España. 915 321219. www.bocaito.com. *Closed Sat lun, Sun, Aug, 24–25 Dec, 31 Dec–1 Jan.* One of the city's most complete and characterful tapas bars: excellent produce, wines and waiter service while you graze standing up. The restaurant at the back is good too.

Las Bravas – *Pje Matheu 5 (Centro).* Sol. 915 21 51 41. www.lasbravas.com. Taste the original spicy-hot patatas bravas, invented here, and you quickly grasp why they have travelled the world. The noisy café ambience and other tapas fit the popular mood.

Cervecería Cien Montaditos – *Pl. Mayor 22.* 🚇 *Sol.* ☎ *915 34 02 68.* The range of a hundred tapas, priced between one and two euros, at this popular chain make it a good choice in pricey quarters of town.

Casa Labra – *Tetuán 12 (Centro).* 🚇 *Sol.* ☎ *915 31 00 81. www.casalabra.es.* This old tavern dating back to 1860 is a Madrid institution. It was here that Pablo Iglesias founded the Spanish Socialist Party (PSOE) in 1879. Its house specialities are fried saltcod *(bacalao frito)* and saltcod croquettes, which you can enjoy standing up on the street or at the marble tables at the back. Always busy and has a restaurant menu.

Prada a Tope – *Príncipe 11 (Huertas).* 🚇 *Sevilla.* ☎ *914 29 59 21. www.pradaa tope.es. Closed 24–25 Dec, 31st Dec–1st Jan.* A warm locale in the spirit of El Bierzo, a traditional part of León. Outstanding rustic décor of wood and slate, with long bar, large tables, and walls covered with photos. Great variety of local products on sale.

Taberna de la Daniela – *General Pardiñas 21 (Salamanca).* 🚇 *Goya.* ☎ *915 75 23 29.* A bar with traditional decoration. *Azulejos* on the outside with vermouth on tap and a wide selection of canapés and *raciones* inside. Specialities here include *cocido madrileño*.

La Venenciana – *C Echegarray 7 (Huertas).* 🚇 *Sevilla.* ☎ *914 297 313.* Fabulous centennial Sherry bar that still serves Jerez's wines only from the cask with traditional tapas like *mojama* (cured tuna) and salted almonds. It is worth finding time to visit this unique bar just for the feel and décor.

🍷 CAFÉS

Café del Círculo de Bellas Artes – *Alcalá 42.* 🚇 *Banco de España or Sevilla.* ☎ *913 60 54 00. www.circulobellaartes.com. Closed 24–25 Dec, 31 Dec–1 Jan.* The marked 19C atmosphere of this great café with its enormous columns and large windows is in sharp contrast to its young, intellectual clientele. Outdoor terrace in summer. If you have time, visit the rooftop terrace for panoramic views. Highly recommended.

Café Gijón – *Pas. de Recoletos 21.* 🚇 *Colón or Banco de España.* ☎ *915 22 37 37. www.cafegijon.com.* This café, which has long been famous as a meeting point for writers and artists, continues the tradition to this day. Outdoor terrace with piano player in summer.

El Espejo – *Pas. de Recoletos 31.* 🚇 *Colón.* ☎ *913 08 23 47. www.restaurante elespejo.com.* An attractive, Modernist-style café close to the Café Gijón *(see above)*, with a charming wrought-iron and glass canopy. Usefully, it never closes.

Café de Oriente – *Pl. de Oriente 2.* 🚇 *Ópera.* ☎ *915 47 15 64. www.cafede oriente.es. Closed 24 Dec pm.* This classic institution, located in the Plaza de Oriente opposite the Royal Palace, is a delightful place for a drink at any time of day. Pleasant terrace.

🎭 NIGHTLIFE

Bar Café Clamores – *Albuquerque 14.* 🚇 *Bilbao.* ☎ *91 4457938. www.sala clamores.com.* Drop by here to see what is on by way of live jazz, Latin, flamenco or other sounds – the venue is a favourite with Spanish and international artists and prices are reasonable.

Café Central – *Pl. del Ángel 10.* 🚇 *Tirso de Molina.* ☎ *913 69 41 43. www.cafecentral madrid.com.* One of the city's main haunts for jazz lovers since the early 1980s; also open for coffee during the day.

Del Diego – *Reina 12.* 🚇 *Gran Vía.* ☎ *915 23 31 06. Closed Aug, Sun, Holy Week. Open 7pm–3am.* The house special is the vodka-based Diego in this elegant small cocktail bar.

Los Gabrieles – *Echegaray 17.* 🚇 *Antón Martín.* ☎ *913 69 07 57. Closed Sun evening.* Tapas by day and a bar by night. A favourite haunt for foreign students in Madrid, attracted, no doubt, by the historical chronicles on its *azulejo*-decorated panelling.

The Irish Rover – *Av. del Brasil 7.* 🚇 *Santiago Bernabéu.* ☎ *915 97 48 11. http://theirishrover.com. Closed Sun.* A huge Irish pub designed like a film set of a paved old Irish street. A section which looks as though it has come straight out of one of Joyce's novels and a tiny lounge are just two of the features of this Irish home-from-home. Daily performances, often of Celtic music, and a small market on Sundays. Young clientele.

Joy Madrid - Teatro Eslava – *Arenal 11.* 🚇 *Sol.* ☎*913 66 37 33. www.joy-eslava.com.* This well-known club, occupying a former 19C theatre, has been attracting a colourful crowd of club-goers and famous faces for several decades. One-off concerts can include major international names. On your way home, you can visit the famous Chocolatería de San Ginés, in the street of the same name.

Libertad 8 – *Libertad 8.* 🚇 *Chueca.* ☎*915 32 11 50. www.libertad8cafe.es.* A building over a century old is the setting for this atmospheric café, renowned for its poetry readings, storytellers and singer-songwriter performances which draw young, bohemian audiences.

Oui Oui Club – *Marqués de Santa Ana 11.* 🚇 *Noviciado. Open 11.30pm-3am.* One of the city's most fashionable clubs to start the night – has an electronic soundtrack and sofas for those who prefer not to dance.

Palacio de Gaviria – *Arenal 9.* 🚇 *Sol.* ☎*915 26 60 69. www.palaciogaviria.com. Open daily from 11pm.* An old palace converted into an elegant multispace club for an older crowd. The Thursday-night *fiesta internacional* is very popular with foreigners. This is also a mecca for lovers of ballroom dancing.

FLAMENCO

Madrid remains one of live flamenco's busiest showcases. Performances by top names, often on tour from Andalucía, are given in theatres and concert halls for which advance booking is a good idea, but the city's clubs, or *tablaos*, famed as the heart of the flamenco scene in the 1970s, still put on accessible though pricy nightly shows. Although unpredictable in quality, they are a good chance to sample the local scene. Traditionally shows start late; earlier ones tend to attract only tourists.

Las Carboneras – *Pl. del Conde de Miranda 1* ☎*915 42 86 77. www.tablaolas carboneros.com. Closed Sun.* Nightly shows in a venue with pleasantly simple décor. Young up-and-coming artists perform good modern pure flamenco. The ticket comes with dinner – not flamenco style – or, the better option, a drink.

Las Tablas– *Pl. de España 9.* ☎*915 420 520. www.lastablasmadrid.com.* As much a minimalist café as a *tablao*, this is one of flamenco's newest venues, offering a rooted live show every night and two at weekends (8pm and 10pm). A good option, and one of the most economic, to sample young flamenco.

Corral de la Morería – *Morería 17.* ☎*913 658 446. www.corraldelamoreria.com.* A long established large venue with traditional artists giving two shows a night. Many performers here are well-known names in the local flamenco scene, making this a good spot, though pricey, for a first taste of flamenco. The food is also good traditional cooking.

Café de Chinitas – *Torija 7.* 🚇 *Santo Domingo.* ☎*915 47 15 01. www.chinitas.com. Closed Sun.* This small central club just off Gran Vía, once a legendary name, is still very popular with tourists. The show varies: brilliant young artists have short residencies though the house group does not sparkle. Dinner shows (costly) also available.

Casa Patas – *Cañizares 10.* 🚇 *Antón Martín.* ☎*913 69 04 96. www.casapatas.com. Closed Sun.* One of the best venues in which to enjoy a night of young flamenco unplugged, with the option of tapas or supper first in the tiled dining room. The *tablao* itself is small and tightly packed, but it is a genuine part of the live scene. Prices vary depending on the artists performing.

La Candela – *Olmo 2.* 🚇 *Tirso de Molina.* ☎*914 673 382.* Legendary bar where artists go after shows (it remains open till 2.30am at weekends) or for a coffee in the afternoon – though today in truth it draws more onlookers and the artists often take refuge in the closed bodega downstairs. But the atmosphere still makes it unique

🎭 ENTERTAINMENT

Madrid's thriving cinema culture supports as many as six dozen subtitled screens showing *versión original* (VO) films. It also has an **Imax** cinema (*www.imaxmadrid.com*), over 30 theatres, numerous concert halls and one casino an hour's drive outside town. The **Auditorio Nacional** (opened in 1988; *www.auditorionacional.mcu.es*) has a varied programme of classical music performed in two spaces, the **Teatro de la**

Zarzuela (http://teatrodelazarzuela.mcu.es) hosts a wide range of dance, operettas (*zarzuelas*) and ballets, while the **Teatro Real** (www.teatro-real.com) offers opera though most seats are sold as season tickets.

The **Teatro Español,** a jewel of an old theatre on Plaza Santa Ana, and its spacious mixed arts extension in Leganés, **El Matadero** (www.mataderomadrid.org), have reliably interesting programming.

Veranos de la Villa (*Jul–Aug*), a varied music festival, and the **Festival de Otoño en Primavera** (*May–Jun; www.madrid. org/fo*) combining music, dance and opera, offer interesting international cultural line-ups. The **Festival Internacional de Jazz** is held during Oct–Nov.

Berlín Cabaret – *Costanilla de San Pedro 11.* 🖉*913 66 20 34.* 🚇 *La Latina. www.berlin cabaret.com*. One of Madrid's famous venues. Live acts (magicians, drag queens, etc.) and a fun atmosphere.

🛒 SHOPPING

Camper – *Gran Vía 54 (Centro).* 🚇*Gran Vía.* 🖉*915 475 223 www.camper. com.* The Mallorcan family shoe firm that blazed the way with design and comfort are popular with visitors taking advantage of the lower prices on home ground.

Capas Seseña – *Cruz 23 (Huertas).*🚇*Sevilla, Sol.* 🖉*915 31 68 40. www.sesena.com.* A family firm that dates from 1901, where traditional and contemporary **capes** are crafted by hand from fine fabric. Photos show such clients as Hemingway, Picasso, Catherine Deneuve, Rudolph Valentino and Michael Jackson.

Custo - *Fuencarral 29 (Gran Vía)* 🚇 *Gran Vía.* 🖉*913 60 46 36. www.custo-barcelona.com.* Catalan designer Custo's ravishing textile and clothes design is now found on catwalks round the world – it's worth seeing the full range.

La Duquesita – *Fernando VI 2.* 🚇 *Alsonso Martínez.* 🖉*913 08 02 31.* A family pâtissier and confectioners selling superb homemade chocolates, *mazapanes* (marzipan), biscuits, cakes, saints' days' sweets and *turrón*. In its Belle Époque shop-window food becomes art.

La Favorita – *Pl. Mayor 25.* 🚇 *Sol.* 🖉*913 66 58 77.* Basque berets, panama hats or made-to-measure fedoras are lined up in the window of this centennial hatshop, a favourite in Madrid.

La Violeta – *Pl. de Canalejas 6.* 🚇 *Sevilla.* 🖉*915 22 55 22. Closed Aug, Sat in Jul, Sun, public holidays*. This establishment has served such luminaries as King Alfonso XIII and writers Jacinto Benavente y Valle Inclán since 1915. The bonbons and caramels are popular but the *marron glacé* and violet products – glazed violets and violet jam are just two – take the cake.

Art Galleries – Look around the Centro de Arte Reina Sofía, in the Salamanca district (near the Puerta de Alcalá), on Paseo de la Castellana, close to calle Génova, and in and around Chueca.

FIESTAS

On 15 May the feast day of city patron, **San Isidro**, is celebrated with impromptu dancing, rock concerts and its famous bullfighting festival, which lasts for some six weeks.

Fiestas de San Isidro

© Bianka Kadic/age fotostock

Alcalá de Henares★

Alcalá has a **historic centre**★ of 16C–17C colleges and convents and spacious squares. Medieval calle Mayor is adorned with impressive gateways and the university and historic centre are a UNESCO World Heritage Site.

A BIT OF HISTORY

Under the Romans the city was an important centre known as **Complutum**, now being excavated, but the history of Alcalá is mainly linked to that of its university, founded by Cardinal Cisneros in 1498. It became famous for its language teaching and in 1517, Europe's first Polyglot Bible was published with parallel texts in Latin, Greek, Hebrew and Chaldean. The university was moved to Madrid in 1836.

Alcalá's most famous citizen is **Miguel de Cervantes**, Spain's greatest writer, whose memory is honoured by a week of celebrations every October. His birthplace, the Museo **Casa Natal de Cervantes** (C. Mayor s/n), recreated as a 16th-century house with a multi-lingual collection of editions of his novel *Don Quixote*, may be visited. (⊙ *open Tue–Sun 10am–6pm; ⊗no charge; ℘918 89 96 54*).

SIGHTS

Antigua Universidad or Colegio de San Ildefonso★

▲⌾⌐*Guided tours (40min) hourly Mon–Fri 10am-1pm, 4–7pm (5–8pm Aug); Sat, Sun and public holidays 11am–2pm, 4.30–7.30pm (4–7pm Nov–Feb).*
⊙*Closed 1 Jan, 25 Dec. ⊗€3 (includes Capilla de San Ildefonso, closed for restoration until 2012). ℘918 85 64 87.*
The original university, on plaza de San Diego, has a beautiful **Plateresque façade**★ (1543) by Rodrigo Gil de Hontañón crowned by a balustrade. The imperial escutcheon of Charles V decorates the pediment of the central section. The majestic 17C **Patio Mayor** was designed by Juan Gómez de Mora,

Alcalá de Henares — Info block

- ▶ **Population:** 203 645
- ⌾ **Michelin Map:** Michelin maps 575 and 576 K 19 – Madrid.
- ▤ **Info:** Plaza de los Santos Niños. ℘918 81 06 34.
- ◐ **Location:** Alcalá is east of metropolitan Madrid. ▭Plaza de la Estación.
- ⊘ **Don't Miss:** The old university.
- ♣♦ **Kids:** Casa Cervantes.
- ⊙ **Timing:** Take a day trip from Madrid.

pupil of Herrera and architect of the Plaza Mayor and ayuntamiento (town hall) in Madrid; at the centre is a well-head with a swan motif, emblem of Cardinal Cisneros. Across the 16C Renaissance Patio de los Filósofos stands the delightful **Patio Trilingüe** (1557) where Latin, Greek and Hebrew were taught. The **Paraninfoa** (1520), formerly used for examinations and degree ceremonies, now sees the solemn opening of the university year and the awarding of Spain's most important literary prize, the Cervantes. A gallery is in the Plateresque style, with superb Mudéjar **artesonado**★★ work.

Capilla de San Ildefonso★
Next to the university.
This early 16C chapel (closed for restoration till 2012) is crowned with magnificent **Mudéjar artesonado** ceilings. The delicate **stucco** on the Epistle side of the church is Late Gothic, while the Evangelist side opposite is Plateresque. In the presbytery is the Carrara marble **mausoleum**★★ of Cardinal Cisneros, by Domenico Fancelli and Bartolomé Ordóñez, one of the finest examples of 16C Spanish sculpture.

Catedral Magistral
Pl. de los Santos Niños. ⊙ *Open Mon–Sat 9am–1pm, 4–8.30pm, Sun and public holidays 10am–1.30pm, 6–8.30pm. ⊗€1.80 for cathedral, museum and tower. ℘918 88 09 30.*

Built between 1497 and 1515, the Cathedral has been remodelled several times. The central portal mixes Gothic, Plateresque and Mudéjar features. Outside stork-nesting season you can visit the church tower. The cloisters (calle Tercia) house a museum, closed until 2012.

Palacio Arzobispal

In the 13C, the bishops of Toledo, lords of Alcalá, erected a palace-fortress on Plaza de Palacio. The Renaissance **façade**, by Alonso de Covarrubias, once fronted a courtyard. The Baroque coat of arms was added later

On adjoining Plaza de San Bernardo, the 17C church of the **Convento de San Bernardo** is crowned by an elliptical dome. The **Museo Arqueológico de la Comunidad de Madrid** (archaeological museum), is in the 17C former **Convento de la Madre de Dios** (◯open Tue–Sat 11am–7pm(3pm Sun and hols); ℘91 879 66 66).

El Corral de Comedias★★

Pl. Cervantes 15. ⚲Guided tours (30 min) hourly Tue–Fri 11.30am–1.30pm, 5–6pm. Sat every 45 mins 11am-5.30pm. ⚲€3.

Spain's oldest working theatre – and, it is claimed, Europe's – was a stage for Golden Age drama performed by and for university students. Glass sections in the floor allow visitors to view the original theatre floor.

ADDRESSES

♈/ EAT

⚬⚬⚬ **Miguel de Cervantes** – Imagen 12. ℘918 83 12 77. www.hcervantes.com. Closed for dinner Sun and 24 Dec. This restaurant, behind Cervantes' birthplace in a restored town house, serves traditional cuisine in a Castilian setting. A few reasonably priced rooms are also available (⚬⚬⚬).

Aranjuez★★

Aranjuez, on the banks of the Tagus (Tajo), is an oasis in the Castilian plain, renowned for its green gardens and parkland, which are now a World Heritage landscape. The shaded walks immortalised by composers (the most famous being Joaquín Rodrigo's haunting guitar piece "Concierto de Aranjuez") and painted by artists are popular at weekends but wonderfully quiet during the week.

A BIT OF HISTORY

The Aranjuez Revolt (El motín de Aranjuez) – In March 1808, Charles IV, his queen and the prime minister, Godoy, were at Aranjuez. They were preparing to flee (on 18 March) first to Andalucía, then to America, in the face of popular opposition to the right-of-passage privileges granted to Napoleon's armies. On the night of 17 March, Godoy's mansion was attacked by followers of the heir apparent, Prince Ferdinand; Charles

▶ **Population:** 52 224
◔ **Michelin Map:** 575 and 576 L 19 – Madrid.
▯ **Info:** Plaza de San Antonio 9. ℘918 91 04 27. www.aranjuez.es.
▶ **Location:** Aranjuez is off the A 4 highway linking Madrid with Andalucía, 47km/29.2mi from both the capital and Toledo. ▭Plaza de la Estación.
◉ **Don't Miss:** The Palace and Prince's Garden.
▲▴ **Kids:** El Tren de la Fresa (℘902 228 822) runs May–Jun, Sep–Oct. An 1851 steam train carries you from Madrid's Museo del Ferrocarril at 10am to Aranjuez in style with costumed staff who serve you strawberries en route. Return journey at 6.25pm (⚲€24 return).

IV then abdicated in favour of his son, but Napoleon soon forced both royals to abdicate in his own favour (5 May). These intrigues and the presence of a French garrison in Madrid stirred the revolt of May 1808, the beginning of the War of Independence.

SIGHTS
ROYAL PALACE AND GARDENS★★

The Catholic Monarchs enjoyed the original 14C palace, enlarged by Emperor Charles V. The present palace is mainly the result of an initiative by Philip II who called on the future architects of the Escorial to erect a new palace amid gardens.

In the 18C, the town became a principal royal residence and was considerably embellished. It was, however, ravaged by fire in 1727 and again in 1748, after which the present façade was built. Ferdinand VI built the town to a grid plan; Charles III added two palace wings and Charles IV erected the delightful Labourer's Cottage.

Palacio Real★

Pl. de Parejas. ○ *Open Tue–Sun Oct–Mar 10am–5.15pm; Apr–Sept 10am–6.15pm.* ○ *Closed 1, 6 Jan, 1, 30 May, 5 Sept, 24–25, 31 Dec and during official ceremonies.* ○ €4.50, ○ *guided tour €5 (€7 with tour of private chambers); no charge Wed (for EU citizens).* ○ *918 91 07 40. www.patrimonionacional.es.*

This Classical-style royal palace of brick and stone was built in the 16C and restored in the 18C. In spite of many modifications it retains considerable unity of style. The entry and façades of the wings are marked by archways and domed pavilions mark the angles. The apartments have been left as they were at the end of the 19C.

The **Salón del Trono** (Throne Room), with crimson velvet hangings and Rococo furnishings, has a ceiling painted with an allegory of monarchy – ironically it was in this room that Charles IV abdicated in 1808.

The **Salón de Porcelana**★★ (Porcelain Room) is the palace's most notable room, covered in white garlanded porcelain tiles, illustrating in relief scenes of Chinese life, exotica and children's games, all made in the Buen Retiro factory in Madrid in 1763.

In the king's apartments a music room precedes the Smoking or Arabian Room – a reproduction of the Hall of the Two Sisters in the Alhambra. A fine Mengs *Crucifixion* hangs in the bedroom, and the walls of another room are decorated with **203 small pictures** on rice paper with Oriental-style motifs. A museum of palace life in the days of Alfonso XIII includes a gymnasium, and items such as a tricycle.

Parterre and Jardín de la Isla★ (Parterre and Island Garden)

○ *Open daily Nov–Feb 8am–6.30pm; Mar 8am–7pm; Apr–15 Jun and 16 Aug–Sept 8am–8.30pm; 16 Jun–15 Aug 8am–9.30pm; Oct 8am–7.30pm.* ○ *No charge.*

The **Parterre** is a formal garden laid out before the palace's east front by the Frenchman Boutelou in 1746. The fountain of Hercules brings a mythological touch to the balanced display.

The **Jardín de la Isla** was laid out on an island in the Tajo river in the 16C. Cross the canal to reach the park and its fountains hidden among chestnut, ash and poplar trees and boxwood hedges.

Jardín del Príncipe★★ (Prince's Garden)

Entrance in calle de la Reina.

This vast garden beside the Tajo (150 ha/371 acres) has four monumental gateways by Juan de Villanueva.

In 1763, Boutelou landscaped the park for the future Charles IV according to the romantic vision then in fashion. A farm, greenhouses with tropical plants, and stables for exotic animals were added.

Casa del Labrador★★ (Labourer's Cottage) –

○ *Guided tours by prior arrangement Tue–Sun and public holidays Oct–Mar 10am–5.15pm; Apr–Sept 10am–6.15pm.* ○ *Closed 1, 6 Jan, 24–25, 31 Dec.* ○ *€5; no charge Wed for EU citizens.* ○ *918 91 03 05.*

The so-called cottage at the eastern end of the Jardín del Príncipe, named after the humble cottages originally on the site, was built on the whim of Charles IV in Neoclassical style with sumptuous decoration.

Casa de Marinos (the Sailors' House) – *Reina.* ◐ *Open Tue–Sun and public holidays Apr–Sept 10am–6.15pm; Oct–Mar 10am–5.15pm.* ◐ *Closed 1, 6 Jan, 2, 3 May, 24–25, 31 Dec.* ◉€2, ⚬guided visits €3; no charge Wed for EU citizens. ☏918 91 03 05.
A museum beside the former landing stage exhibits **falúas reales**★★ (royal vessels) that ferried the royals and guests to the Labourer's Cottage.
One, a gift to Philip V from a Venetian count, is remarkable for its ornate decoration in gilded, finely carved wood.

EXCURSION
Chinchón★
◐ *21km/13mi NE along the M 305.*
Chinchón is famous for its aniseed spirit and, more importantly, the Countess of Chinchón, wife of a 17C viceroy of Peru, to whom the West owes quinine, extracted from the bark of a Peruvian tree (named chinchona in the countess' honour).

Plaza Mayor★★ – The picturesque arcaded square, dominated by its church, is surrounded by houses with wooden balconies. Bullfights are held in summer and a passion play on Easter Saturday.

ADDRESSES

⏃/EAT

⊜⊜⊜ **Rodriguez de la Calle** – *Antiguar Ctra de Andalucía 85, Aranjuez.* ☏918 910 807. www.restaurantedelacalle.com. *Closed Mon, 1–21 Aug.* De la Calle is a committed young cook known for his inspired style with vegetables, many from his own kitchen-garden, flowers and other delicate natural flavours. There are two tasting menus, or you can have tapas in the sleek wine bar here. Book ahead as the restaurant's fame fills the dining room.

Monasterio de
El Escorial★★★

This symbolic building on the slopes of the Sierra de Guadarrama, commissioned by Philip II and designed by Juan de Herrera, heralded a style that combined the grandeur of a palace with the austerity of a committed monastery.

A BIT OF HISTORY
In memory of San Lorenzo – On 10 August 1557, St Lawrence's Day, Philip II defeated the French at St-Quentin. The king decided to dedicate a monastery to the saint, to serve as royal palace and pantheon.
The stupendous project – nearly 1 200 doors and 2 600 windows, 1 500 workmen – was completed in only 21 years (1563–84), which explains the exceptional unity of style.

- ⚐ **Michelin Map:** 575 or 576 K 17 – Madrid.
- ▯ **Info:** Grimaldi 4, San Lorenzo de El Escorial. ☏918 90 53 13. ▭Calle Santa Rosa. www.san lorenzoturismo.org.
- ◐ **Location:** El Escorial is 56km/40mi NW of Madrid, at 1 065m/3 494ft.
- ◉ **Don't Miss:** The sumptuous royal apartments. The feast day of San Lorenzo (St Lawrence), the patron saint of the village and monastery, is celebrated on 10 August every year.
- ◐ **Timing:** El Escorial is a day trip from Madrid, the full monastery visit taking an estimated 4 hours.

Monasterio de El Escorial

©Turespaña

The general designs of Juan de Toledo were followed after his death in 1567 by **Juan de Herrera**.

In reaction to the excessive ornamentation of Charles V's reign, the architects produced a sober monument with clean, majestic lines.

There is a good **view**✶ of the monastery and countryside from **Silla de Felipe II** (Philip II's Seat), from where the king oversaw construction (▶*turn left after the monastery into the road marked Entrada Herrería-Golf*).

SIGHTS
Real Monasterio de San Lorenzo de El Escorial
Allow half a day.
Juan de Borbón y Battemberg.
🕐 *Open Tue–Sun and public holidays Oct–Mar 10am–5pm; Apr–Sept 10am–6pm. Recommended last entry time 4 hours before closure.*🕐*Closed 1, 6 Jan, 1 May, 10 Aug, second Sun and Mon Sept, 24–25, 31 Dec.* ⇔*€10 ticket includes monastery, palace and both casitas; guided tour €17.* ✆*918 90 59 02 www.patrimonionacional.es.*

It is said that the monastery's gridiron plan recalls St Lawrence's martyrdom. Measuring 206m x 161m (676ft x 528ft), the austerity of its grey granite emphasises the severity of the architecture. When the king commanded an increase in height, Herrera positioned windows asymmetrically to lessen monotony.

Palacios✶✶ (Royal Apartments)
While the Habsburgs remained on the Spanish throne, El Escorial was a place of splendour: the king resided in apartments encircling the church apse. The Bourbons preferred other palaces but when in residence, occupied suites on the north side of the church. The palace took on renewed glory in the 18C in the reigns of Charles III and IV.

A staircase built in the time of Charles IV goes up *(3rd floor)* to the **Palacio de los Borbones** (Bourbon Apartments), sumptuous with Pompeian ceilings and fine **tapestries**✶, many from the Real Fábrica (Royal Tapestry Works) in Madrid based on cartoons by Spanish artists, notably Goya. Elsewhere are Flemish tapestries.

The large **Sala de las Batallas** (Battle Gallery) contains frescoes (1587): the Victory at Higueruela in the 15C against the Moors and, on the north wall, the Victory at St-Quentin.

The restraint of the **habitaciones de Felipe II** (Philip II's apartments, *second floor*) is striking in comparison with the Bourbon rooms. Those of the Infanta Isabel Clara Eugenia comprise a suite of small rooms with dados of Talavera ceramic tiles. The king's bedroom is off the church. When he was dying of gangrene in 1598, he could contemplate the high altar from his bed.

The paintings in the apartments include a *St Christopher* by Patinir and a portrait of the king in old age by Pantoja de la Cruz. Facing the gardens and the plain, the Salón del Trono (Throne Room) is hung with 16C Brussels tapestries. The Sala de los Retratos (Portrait Gallery), which follows, holds royal portraits.

Panteones★★ (Pantheons)

Access through the Patio de los Evangelistas (Evangelists' Courtyard), with frescoes by Tibaldi and his followers.

A marble and jasper staircase leads down to the **Panteón de los Reyes**★★★ (Royal Pantheon) and the remains of monarchs from the time of Charles V, with the exception of PhilipV, Ferdinand VI and Amadeus of Savoy.

The octagonal chapel was begun in 1617 under Philip III and completed in 1654. Facing the door is the jasper altar; on either side stand 26 marble and bronze sarcophagi in wall niches. The kings are on the left and the queens whose sons succeeded to the throne, on the right. The ornate chandelier is the work of an Italian artist.

The 19C **Panteón de los Infantes**★ (Infantes' Pantheon) includes princes and princesses and queens whose children did not rule. The sculptures are delicately carved. Conditions are such that the room is well preserved.

Salas Capitulares★ (Chapter Houses)

Two fine rooms, with ceilings painted by Italian artists with grotesques and frescoes, form a museum of 16C–17C Spanish and Italian religious painting. The first room contains canvases by El Greco and Ribera, a St Jerome by Titian, and Joseph's Tunic by Velázquez. The second room has works from the 16C Venetian School, including paintings by Tintoretto, Veronese and Titian (Ecce Homo). A room at the back contains works by Bosch and his followers: the imaginative Haywain and the satirical Crown of Thorns (Los Improperios).

Basílica★★

Herrera based his final plan on Italian drawings. He introduced the **flat vault**, in the atrium. The interior owes much to St Peter's in Rome with a Greek Cross plan, a 92m/302ft high cupola above the transept crossing supported by four colossal pillars, and transept barrel vaulting. The frescoes in the nave vaulting were painted by Luca Giordano in Charles II's reign. Red marble steps lead to the sanctuary which has paintings on the vaulting of the lives of Christ and the Virgin by Cambiasso.

The massive **retable**, designed by Herrera, is 30m/98ft tall and is composed of four registers of jasper, onyx and red marble columns between which stand 15 bronze sculptures by Leone and Pompeo Leoni. The tabernacle is also by Herrera. On either side of the chancel are the royal mausoleums with funerary figures at prayer by Pompeo Leoni.

In the first chapel off the north aisle is the Martyrdom of St Maurice by Rómulo Cincinato, which Philip II preferred to that of El Greco (see Nuevos Museos, below). In the adjoining chapel is a magnificent sculpture of Christ by Benvenuto Cellini.

Patio de los Reyes (Kings' Courtyard)

One of the three Classical gateways opens onto this courtyard, named for the statues of the Kings of Judea on the west front of the church.

Biblioteca★★ (Library)

2nd floor.

The shelving, designed by Herrera, is of exotic woods; the ceiling, sumptuously painted by Tibaldi, represents the liberal arts with Philosophy and Theology at each end. There are also magnificent portraits of Charles V, Philip II and Philip III by Pantoja de la Cruz, and one of Charles II by Carreño. Philip II furnished the library with over 10 000 books, many of them lost in a 1671 fire. It is now a public library with over 400 00 books and historic manuscripts. The spines face inward for preservation purposes.

Nuevos Museos★★ (New Museums)

Paintings in the **Museo de Pintura** are on religious themes.

First room: canvases from the 16C Venetian School (Titian, Veronese and Tintoretto).

Second room: two works by Van Dyck and a small painting by Rubens.

Third room: works by Miguel de Coxcie, Philip II's Court Painter.

Fourth room: Rogier Van der Weyden's sober and expressive *Calvary*, flanked by an *Annunciation* by Veronese and a *Nativity* by Tintoretto.

Fifth room: canvases by Ribera including *St Jerome Penitent*, the *Chrysippus* and *Aesop*, with vividly portrayed faces, and Zurbarán's *St Peter of Alcántara* and the *Presentation of the Virgin*.

Last room: paintings by Alonso Cano and Luca Giordano.

On the ground floor, paintings include El Greco's **Martyrdom of St Maurice and the Theban Legionary**★, commissioned by Philip II but rejected by him. Nevertheless, it is now considered one of El Greco's greater works.

OTHER ROYAL BUILDINGS
Casita del Príncipe★ (Prince's or Lower Pavilion)

Jardín de los Moes. SE along the station road. ⏱*Same opening hours as Palacio, p.141.*

Charles III commissioned Juan de Villanueva to build a lodge for the future Charles IV. Its exquisite decoration makes it a jewel of a palace in miniature. There are painted **Pompeian-style ceilings**★ by Maella and Vicente Gómez, silk hangings, canvases by Luca Giordano, chandeliers, and a beautiful mahogany and marble dining room.

Casita del Infante (Infante's or Upper Pavilion)

Ctra de Ávila. 3km/1.8mi SW beyond the golf course. ⏱*Same opening hours as Palacio.*

This lodge was designed by Villanueva for the Infante Gabriel, Charles IV's younger brother. The interior is furnished in period style; the first floor was used by Prince Juan Carlos before his accession to the throne.

EXCURSION
Valle de los Caídos★★

▶ *16km/10mi NW on the M 600 and M 527.* ⚬➔ *Currently closed for extensive excavations, no due date for opening. Basilica open for mass Tue–Sun 11am.* 📞*918 90 56 11.* *www.patrimonionacional.es.*

The Valley of the Fallen is a striking monument to the dead of both sides of the Spanish Civil War (1936–39), built as a "national act of atonement" by Republican prisoners on the orders of Francisco Franco.

It is also the site of mass graves of prisoners who died here. These are now being opened and excavated.

Basílica★★

The Basilica is hollowed out of the rock face and dominated by a monumental Cross. Its west door is a bronze work crowned by a *Pietà* by Juan de Ávalos. At the entrance to the vast interior is a fine wrought-iron screen with 40 statues of Spanish saints and soldiers.

The 262m/859.5ft nave is lined with chapels between which are hung eight copies of 16C Brussels tapestries of the Apocalypse. Above the chapel entrances are alabaster copies of the most famous statues of the Virgin Mary in Spain.

A **cupola**★, 42m/137.8ft in diameter, above the crossing, shows in mosaic the heroes, martyrs and saints of Spain approaching both Christ in Majesty and the Virgin Mary. On the altar stands a painted figure of Christ Crucified, the work of Beovides. At the foot of the altar are the remains of Falangist Party founder José Antonio Primo de Rivera and Francisco Franco. Ossuaries hold remains of 40 000 soldiers and civilians from both sides.

La Cruz★

The Cross is 125m/410ft high (150m/492ft including the base), the width 46m/151ft. The immense statues of the Evangelists around the plinth and the four cardinal virtues above are by Juan de Ávalos.

Castilla-León occupies the northern part of Spain's great *meseta*, a plain around 1 000m/3 280ft above sea level. Wide terraced valleys and moors are dotted with rock pinnacles, narrow defiles and gentle hills. Vast spaces open up with a grandeur unusual in Europe. Some call it eerie and romantic, others label it harsh and monotonous. It is crossed from east to west by one of the country's great rivers, the Duero, a frontier territory during the medieval centuries that has retained its historic towns and cities. The region's history is certainly romantic; Castilla means land of castles and it was home to the legendary (and very real) El Cid, who fought both with and against the Moors. The weather is less romantic, with sub-zero winters and baking summers.

Highlights

1 Walking the **city walls** by night in **Ávila** (p145)

2 Climbing the **Roman road** at the **Puerto del Pico** (p148)

3 People-watching in **Plaza Mayor, Salamanca** (p149)

4 Relaxing in the **quiet village** of **La Alberca** (p158)

5 Exploring the **Romanesque churches** of Toro (p161)

A bit of geography

The striking Sierra de Gredos marks the southern border of Castilla y León, peaking at nearly 2 600m/8 530ft with glacial cirques and lakes. The towns at the foot of the southern slopes, which enjoy a benign climate, give access to gentle or adventurous walks up towards the peaks. Today's roads through the Sierra climb over historic passes that offer panoramic views to the south.

The cities of the north Meseta

Ávila, 107km/67mi northwest of Madrid, is a remarkable example of a town whose 11C walls and romantic towers have been neither removed nor exceeded. For a period in the 16C Ávila was the heart of Spanish religious life, thanks to its famous inhabitants, St Teresa of Ávila and St John of the Cross. The city keeps its famously chilly mountain air and an austerity of style that gives it a distinct personality.

Salamanca, northwest of that, sitting on the River Duero, is one of Spain's most beautifully preserved historic cities. Its university is as old as Oxford in England and its students make sure that the city buzzes. The double Cathedral and the central plaza – grand architectural set-pieces – alone make the visit worthwhile.

To the south and west of Salamanca the Meseta's stark landscapes soften as you drive into grazing lands where bulls and pigs graze under holm-oaks. Ciudad Rodrigo, just 25km/15.5mi east of the Portuguese border, set against that landscape, is another splendidly preserved town, where nobles' mansions and palaces bristle with bold carved standards.

Close to Castilla-León's southern border with Extremadura the plains turn into thickly wooded rolling hills that have kept a rural way of life and the popular architecture of past centuries. La Alberca, the best preserved of the towns and villages, makes a good base for exploring the national park of Las-Batuecas and Sierra de Francia.

Village of Candelario, La Alberca

C. Labonne/MICHELIN

Ávila★★

Ávila is one of the best-preserved fortified cities in Europe; its numerous convents and churches shelter behind magnificent 11C walls. The old town and churches outside the walls are a World Heritage Site.

THE CITY TODAY

Ávila is mostly a day-tripper's city but a night here is definitely worthwhile, preferably in the 16C parador occupying a former palace *(Calle Marqués Canales y Chozas 2; ℘92021 13 40)*. The town is hardly hopping, but there are enough tapas bars and drinking holes to make a night of it – try around the Plaza del Mercado Chico.

Wherever you go in town you will be reminded of the town's favourite daughter, Santa Teresa, if only by the *yemas de Santa Teresa*, a tooth-melting egg-yolk-and-sugar confection produced by the local nuns.

SIGHTS

Murallas★★ (City walls)

🕐Open Apr–Oct Tue–Sun 10am–8pm (July-Aug daily); Nov–Mar Tue–Sun and hols 10am–6pm. Last ticket 30min before closing.⌨€4. ℘ 920 25 50 88.
Europe's most striking medieval fortifications, with 90 bastions and towers and eight gateways, enclose an area 900m/ 2 953ft by 449m/1 476ft.

- **Population:** 56 144
- **Michelin Map:** 575 or 576 K 15 – Map 121 Alrededores de Madrid.
- **Info:** Plaza de Pedro Dávila 4. ℘920 21 13 87. www.avilaturismo.com.
- **Location:** Sitting at 1131m/ 3710ft, NW of Madrid, Ávila has a harsh and windy winter climate. ▭Avenida José Antonio.
- **Don't Miss:** The city walls.
- **Timing:** Start with the walls and Cathedral.

Most date from the 11C; and despite 14C modifications, maintain their unity. You can climb up on to the walls at various points to walk the sentry path along the top; the best **view** of the walls is from **Cuatro Postes**, on the Salamanca road.

Catedral★★

Pl. de la Catedral. 🕐*Cathedral and museum open mid-July–Sep Mon–Fri 10am–7.30pm (8pm Sat); Oct and Apr– Jun Mon–Fri 10am–6pm (7pm Sat); Nov –Mar 10am–5pm (6pm Sat); all year round Sun and public holidays 12–6pm. Last entry 45min before closing.* ⌨*€4.* ℘*920 21 16 41.*
The fortified **east end** of the Cathedral is set into the ramparts, crowned with

Murallas

© Alain Felix/hemis.fr

a double row of battlements. Granite and defensive design make it austere, despite window tracery, portal carvings and decoration along the upper tower, buttresses and pinnacles.

The 14C **north doorway** with French Gothic decoration, its stone eroded, was removed in the 15C from the **west front** during a renovation by Juan Guas. Its current placement, from the 18C, is more suitable for a palace.

The surprising **interior** has a high Gothic nave, a chancel with sandstone patches of red and yellow and many **works of art**★★. The **trascoro** (1531) holds lovely Plateresque statues (left to right): the Presentation of Jesus in the Temple, the Adoration of the Magi and the Massacre of the Innocents. The **choir stalls** are from the same period. There are two delicate wrought-iron **pulpits** – Renaissance and Gothic.

Construction lasted from 1135 to the 14C; windows in the apse are Romanesque. The large painted **altarpiece** (c. 1500) by Pedro Berruguete and Juan de Borgoña has a gilt wood surround with Isabelline features and Italian Renaissance pilasters.

Four carved panels on the high altar show the Evangelists and the four Holy Knights. The central panel is Vasco de la Zarza's masterpiece: the alabaster **tomb**★★ of Don Alonso de Madrigal, Bishop of Ávila in the 15C, called El Tostado (Swarthy). He is shown before a beautiful Epiphany.

Museo de la Catedral

The museum contains a notable 13C **sacristy**★★ with an eight-ribbed vault, massive 16C altarpiece and sculptures of the Passion in imitation alabaster. View a head of Christ by Morales painted on a tabernacle door, a portrait by El Greco, a huge Isabelline grille, late 15C antiphonaries and a colossal 1571 monstrance (1.7m/5ft 8in) by Juan de Arfe. The Gothic **cloisters** are restored. In plaza de la Catedral, the **Palacio de Valderrábanos**, now a hotel, has a fine 15C doorway with family crest.

Basílica de San Vicente★★

Pl. San Vicente 1. ◎ *Open May–Oct Mon–Sat 10am–6.30pm (Nov–Apr–1.30pm), Sun, hols 4–6.30pm (Nov–Apr 6pm)* ◎€2. ✆920 25 52 30.

This vast 12C–14C Romanesque basilica, with ogive vaulting, is on the reputed site of the 4C martyrdom of St Vincent of Zaragoza and his sisters. The ensemble includes the 14C south gallery with slender columns, a cornice over the length of the nave, the tall west front porch and two incomplete towers.

The **west portal**★★ is outstanding for the statue columns below the richly decorated cornice and lifelike covings. Beneath the 14C **lantern**★ is the **martyrs' tomb**★★, a late 12C masterpiece under a rare 15C Gothic canopy with pagoda top. The martyrdom of St Vincent and his sisters is attributed to the unknown sculptor of the west portal. The scenes of their capture, flaying and torture are particularly powerful.

Convento de Santo Tomás★

Pl. de Granada 1. ◎*Open daily 10am–1pm, 4–8pm. Last ticket 1 hour before closing.* ◎*Museum closed Mon.* ◎€3.50 (church, oriental museum, cloisters and choir). ✆920 22 04 00.

This late 15C Dominican monastery, at times a summer residence of the Catholic Monarchs, was also the university.

The **church** façade includes the common motifs of the monastery: details are emphasised with long lines of balls, and the yoke and fasces emblem of Ferdinand and Isabel.

The church has a single aisle, its arches on clusters of slender columns. Two galleries were accessible only from the cloisters by the monks. The fine **mausoleum**★ (1512) is of Prince Juan, only son of the Catholic Monarchs. Its alabaster table with delicate Renaissance sculpting is by Domenico Fancelli, who created the Catholic Monarchs' mausoleum in Granada. In a north chapel is the Renaissance tomb of Juan Dávila and his wife, the prince's tutors.

Claustro (Cloisters) – Beyond the plain 15C **Claustro de los Novicios** is the **Claustro del Silencio**★, intimate and generously carved on its upper gallery. The Catholic Monarchs' Cloister is larger and more solemn with spectacularly bare upper arching.

From the Claustro del Silencio, stairs lead to beautiful 15C Gothic **choir stalls** with pierced canopies and arabesques; and from the upper gallery, to the high altar gallery where one can see Berruguete's high relief masterpiece, the **retable of St Thomas Aquinas**★★ (c. 1495).

Iglesia de San Pedro

Pl. de Santa Teresa. 🕐 *Open daily Jul–Sep daily 10am–12.30pm, 6.30–8pm; Oct–Jun before and after Mass.* *No charge.* This Romanesque church on the vast **plaza Santa Teresa** has early Gothic pointed arches and a delicate rose window. Elsewhere, nearby, are a number of fine urban palaces with façades to view from the street: the Gothic Renaissance **Mansión de los Verdugo** (C. Lopez Núñe, closed to the public), marked with a family crest, is flanked by two stout square towers; the **Mansión de los Polentinos** (C. Vallespín), now a barracks, has a fine Renaissance entrance and patio; the **Torreón de los Guzmanes** (Pl. Corral de las Campanas), also called the Oñates Palace, has a massive square corner tower with battlements dating from the early 16C. Near the Cathedral the provincial Law Courts are housed in the **Palacio de Núñez Vela** (Pl. de la Catedral 10). This Renaissance palace of the Viceroy of Peru has windows framed by slender columns and coats of arms. The patio, accessible from the street, is lovely. Two 14C Gothic buildings with coats of arms give onto Plaza Pedro Dávila and two others, belonging to the Episcopal Palace, face Plaza de Rastro.

Museo Provincial de Arte

Pl. de Nalvillos 3. 🕐*Open Tue–Sun and public holidays 10am–2pm, 5–8pm (Oct–Jun 4–7pm).* *€1.20; no charge weekends and hols.* 📞*920 211 003.* The fine 16C Dean's House houses Ávila province's art collection. It is comprised of traditional objects, clothes and furniture; archaeological remains ranging from prehistoric to Visigothic times; and fine art. Among the paintings, in Room VII, hangs an outstanding primitive triptych by Hans Memling.

Iglesia Santo Tomé el Viejo

Pl. de Italia. Visit included in Museum of Provincial Art ticket. A 13C Romanesque church that serves as an annexe to the museum. On show are pieces from the archaeological collection and a fine Roman mosaic.

🚗 DRIVING TOUR

South of Ávila

120km/75mi. Allow half a day. ▷ *Drive northeast to Burgos, then follow the N403 south for 40km/25mi towards San Martín de Valdeiglesias.*

Embalse de Burguillo

This artificial lake on the River Alberche makes a splendid landscape set against the bare or scrubby hills.

▷ *Follow the N403 for another 10km/6mi before reaching San Martín de Valdeiglesias, then turn to your right where you see the signpost for the Toros de Guisando.*

Toros de Guisando

The granite Bulls of Guisando are surprisingly small. They stand in a enclosure just off the road. Many interpretations have been made of their meaning.

▷ *Drive through San Martín de Valdeiglesias and take the N501 towards Madrid for 5km/3mi.*

Pantano de San Juan

The winding road around the edge of the reservoir offers spectacular views down over the water though often in summer its upper reaches are left as bare hillside by drought. Between the pine-covered slopes are small watersport ports, bathing areas and restaurants. These are crowded in August but very pleasant spots to relax or picnic the rest of the year.

Sierra de los Gredos★★

The massif of the Sierra de Gredos includes Pico de Almanzor (2 592m/ 8 504ft), the highest peak in the Cordillera Central. The north face of the sierra is marked by glacial cirques and lakes; the south by a steep granite wall and gullies. Fertile valleys produce apples in the north and grapes, olives and tobacco on the sheltered south slope. Wildlife is protected in the Reserva Nacional de Gredos.

- **Michelin Map:** 575 or 576 K 14, L 14.
- **Info:** Plaza San Pedro, Ávila. ℘920 37 23 68.
- **Location:** The sierra is almost due west of Madrid (M 501 via San Martín de Valdeiglesias) and south of Ávila (N 502 to Puerto del Pico).
- **Timing:** Take a country drive of up to a day, stopping according to your interests.

SIGHTS

San Martín de Valdeiglesias

This old market town, with 14C castle walls built by the Lord High Constable Álvaro de Luna, is a starting point for explorations.

Toros de Guisando

6km/3.7mi NW.

The *Bulls of Guisando* are four roughly carved granite figures in an open field. Similar ancient figures, possibly Celt-Iberian, are found elsewhere in Ávila province. They are similar to the stone *porcas* (sows) seen in the Trás-os-Montes region of Portugal.

Embalse de Burguillo★ (Burguillo Reservoir)

20km/12.4mi NW.

See p147.

Pantano de San Juan

8km/5mi E.

See p147.

From San Martín de Valdeiglesias, take the N501 (which becomes the C501), towards Arenas de San Pedro.

Arenas de San Pedro

The main monument of this heavily developed town is the Gothic **Iglesia de Nuestra Señora de la Asunción** (Pl. Federico Fernández 8; ℘920 37 00 19).

Cuevas del Águila★ (Águila Caves)

9km/5.6mi S of Arenas de San Pedro. Take the C708 turn-off from the N502.

Open daily 21 Sept–21 Mar 10.30am –1pm, 3–6pm; 22 Mar–20 Sept 10.30am –1pm, 3–7pm. €7. ℘920 37 71 07. www.grutasdelaguila.com.

A single vast chamber is open to the public. Among the many concretions are lovely frozen streams of calcite, ochre crystals coloured by iron oxide and massive pillars still in the process of formation.

Puerto del Pico road★

29km/18mi NE of Arenas de San Pedro.

The road through the sierra crosses the attractive small town of **Mombeltrán** (15C castle with well-preserved exterior), then winds upwards, parallel to a Roman road. From the pass (1 352m/ 4 436ft) there are stunning **views**★ of the mountains, the Tiétar Valley (south) and, beyond, the Tajo.

The **Parador de Gredos**, first in Spain (1928), stands in a magnificent **setting**★★ with far-reaching views.

Laguna Grande★

12km/7.4mi S of Hoyos del Espino. Park at the end of the road.

A well-marked path leads up to Laguna Grande *(2hr)*, a glacial basin fed by mountain torrents. Halfway along is an unforgettable **panorama**★ of the Gredos cirque.

Salamanca★★★

Salamanca evokes its rich history through its venerable university, narrow streets, and splendid buildings of golden stone. Blessed with what is widely regarded as the most magnificent main square in Spain, Salamanca has long been a favoured destination for foreign students and visitors alike. The old town is a World Heritage site.

THE CITY TODAY

The University of Salamanca may no longer be in the same league academically as the Oxfords and Harvards of this world, but its 30 000 or so (international and Spanish) students bring a real joie de vivre to the city. If you are young, want to study Spanish for a couple of weeks and enjoy a lively typical Spanish social life, this is a good place to choose.

A BIT OF HISTORY

A tumultuous past – Salamanca flourished under the Romans who built the **Puente Romano** (Roman bridge). Alfonso VI took the city from the Moors in 1085. In 1218, Alfonso IX established a centre for study, later to become an important university. In 1520, Salamanca rose against the royal authority of Emperor Charles V (⌂ *see SEGOVIA*) and in the 16C it reached its artistic and intellectual zenith.

▶ **Population:** 155 740
⌖ **Michelin Map:** 575 and 576 J 12-13.
▣ **Info:** Plaza Mayor 32. ℰ923 21 83 42. www.salamanca.es.
▷ **Location:** Salamanca is in the western Castilla y León region, accessible from Ávila (98km/61mi SE on the N 501), Valladolid (115km/72mi NE on the A 62), and Zamora (62km/39mi N on the N 630).
⚑ **Kids:** A walk on the Ciudad Rodrigo ramparts.
⊕ **Timing:** There's easily enough to fill two days.
⊙ **Don't Miss:** The University and main square.

Los Bandos – During the 15C, rivalry between noble factions *(bandos)* saw the city's streets bathed in blood. The *bandos* remained active until 1476.
The university was founded in 1218 and grew under the patronage of kings of Castilla and high dignitaries.
Its great and famous members include the Infante Don Juan; St John of the Cross and his teacher, the humanist **Fray Luis de León** (1527–91); and **Miguel de**

Plaza Mayor

© Vincent Leduc/Author's Image/Photononstop

149

Unamuno (1864–1936), Professor of Greek, rector, and philosopher.

Art in Salamanca – In the late 15C and early 16C, two major painters were working in Salamanca: **Fernando Gallego**, one of the best Hispano-Flemish artists, and **Juan of Flanders** (c. 1465–1519), whose work is outstanding for the subtle delicacy of its colours.

The 15C also saw the evolution of the original Salamanca patio arch, in which the line of the Mudéjar curve is broken by counter-curves and straight lines.

The 16C brought Salamancan **Plateresque** art to an ebullient climax.

✺ WALKING TOUR

1 OLD CENTRE★★★

Allow one day. See map pp150-151.

Plaza Mayor★★★

The Plaza Mayor is the life and soul of Salamanca. All the city's major streets converge on the square, where locals and visitors alike meet. It was built by Philip V between 1729 and 1755 and is among the finest in Spain, designed principally by the Churriguera brothers.

Four ground-level arcades with rounded arches, decorated by a series of portrait medallions of Spanish kings and famous men such as Cervantes, El Cid and Columbus, support three storeys rising in perfect formation to an elegant balustrade.

On the north and east sides are the pedimented fronts of the **ayuntamiento** (town hall) and the Pabellón Real (Royal Pavilion).

▷ *Take Prior to Plaza de Monterrey, then Compañía.*

Casa de las Muertes (House of Death)

⌗ *Closed to the public.*

The early 16C Plateresque façade is attributed to Diego de Siloé; it's named after the skulls carved on the upper part of the façade.

▷ *Opposite stands the Ursuline Convent Museum.*

SALAMANCA

200 m
200 yds

ALBA DE TORMES, ÁVILA

Convento Museo de las Úrsulas (Ursuline Convent Museum)

Pl. de las Úrsulas 2.

🕐 *Open Tue–Sun 11.30am–1.30pm, 4.30–6pm.* 🚫*Closed last Sun in month.* ☎*923 21 98 77.* €2.

The 16C church contains the **tomb**★ of Alonso de Fonseca with delicate low reliefs attributed to Diego de Siloé. The **museum**, with its *artesonado* and coffered ceilings, houses panels and fragments of an altarpiece by Juan de Borgoña. There are also works by Morales the Divine, an *Ecce Homo* and a *Pietà*.

 Walk back along Calle de la Compañía.

Palacio de Monterrey
Pl. Monterrey 2.
Built in 1539, this typical Renaissance palace has an openwork balustrade crowning a long top-floor gallery, between corner towers.

 Opposite stands the Iglesia de la Purísima.

Iglesia de la Purísima (Church of the Immaculate Conception)
Pl. de las Agustinas. ○*Open for Mass (the church may be viewed before and afterwards).* ⌘*No charge.* ℘*923 21 27 38.*
The **Immaculate Conception**★ by Ribera hangs above the high altar.

 Take Ramón y Cajal straight to the end.

Colegio Arzobispo Fonseca★
C. Fonseca 4. ○ *Chapel and cloisters open daily 10am–1.30pm, 4–7pm.* ⌘€2. ℘923 29 45 70.
Built in 1535 by Archbishop Fonseca, this is the last of the surviving four university colleges, and is almost perfectly preserved. Theology, liberal arts and canon law were taught here. Designed by **Diego de Siloé** it was executed by Juan de Álava and Rodrigo Gil de Hontañon. The façade is strikingly simple. The main door is flanked by Ionic columns above which stand Saints Augustine and Ildefonso.
At the top a medallion freize shows Saint James at the Battle of Clavijo. The portico to the patio is decorated by 128 medallions mixing Biblical, mythological and historic personalities. In the chapel, immediately to the right of the entrance, a platabresque **retablo** by Alonso Berruguete, dated 1529, combines canvases with monumental statuary.

 Retrace your steps and turn right along Compañía to Rua Antigua, turn right and then left down Libreros.

Plaza de San Benito
On this delightful square are the **Iglesia de San Benito**, and mansions of Salamanca's old noble rival families.

Casa de las Conchas★ (House of Shells)
Compañía 2. ○ *Patio: open Oct–Mar Mon–Fri 9am–9pm, Sat 9am–2pm, 4–7pm, Sun and public hols 10am–2pm, 4–7pm; Apr–Sept Mon–Fri 9am–9pm, Sat 9am–2pm, 5–8pm, Sun and hols 5–8pm.* ⌘*No charge.* ℘*923 26 93 17.*
This late 15C house (now a library) is carved with 400 scallop shells in its golden stone wall. It has decorative Isabelline windows and beautiful wrought-iron grilles. The **patio** has delicate mixtilinear arches and openwork balustrades, carved lions' heads and coats of arms.

 Opposite stands the Jesuit College.

La Clerecía
Compañía 5. ○ *Open Mon–Fri 1.15pm, Sat 7.30pm, Sun and public holidays 12.30pm.* ⌘*No charge.*
This Jesuit College was begun in 1617; its Baroque towers were finished by Andrés García de Quiñones in 1755.

 Cross the Pl. de San Isidro and take Libreros.

Patio de las Escuelas★★★ (Schools' Square)
This small square, off the old Calle Libreros, is surrounded by the best examples of Salamanca Plateresque. The former university principals' residence is the **Casa-Museo Unamuno** (○ *open Tue–Fri 9am–1.30pm, 4–6pm, Sat–Sun and public holidays 10am–1.30pm;* ⌘€1.80; ℘923 29 44 00), a museum dedicated to the philosopher.

 Opposite the Patio, on Libreros, stands the University.

Universidad (University)

Patio de Escuelas. 🕐 *Open Mon–Fri 9.30am–1.30pm, 4–7pm, Sat 9.30am–1.30pm, 4–7pm, Sun and public holidays 10am–1.30pm. Last ticket 30min before closing. Limited access during academic events.* 🎟 *€4 ticket includes entrance to the Escuelas Menores; no charge Mon morning, 18 May.* 📞 *923 29 44 00. www.usal.es.*

The University's sumptuous 1534 **entrance**★★★ is a brilliant composition. Above the twin doors, covered by basket arches, the carving is in ever greater relief, to compensate for increasing height. A central medallion in the first register shows the Catholic Monarchs who presented the doorway; in the second are portrait heads in scallop-shell niches; in the third, flanking the pope supported by cardinals, are Venus and Hercules and the Virtues. The most famous motif is the Death's head surmounted by a frog (on the right pilaster, halfway up) symbolising the posthumous punishment of lust.

The lecture halls are around the **patio**: the **Paraninfo** (Great Hall) is hung with 17C Brussels tapestries and a portrait of Charles IV from Goya's studio; the hall where Fray Luis de León lectured in theology is as it was in the 16C.

The grand staircase rises beneath star vaulting, its banister carved with foliated scrollwork and, at the third flight, a mounted bullfight.

A gallery on the first floor has its original, rich **artesonado ceiling** with stalactite ornaments and a delicate low relief frieze along the walls. A Gothic door with a fine 16C grille opens into the 18C library, which contains books, incunabula and manuscripts, some of which date back to the 11th century.

Escuelas Menores (Minor Schools)

🕐 *Same opening hours as University.*

Standing to the right of the hospital, and crowned by the same openwork Renaissance frieze, is the entrance to the Minor (preparatory) Schools – a Plateresque portal decorated with coats of arms, roundels and scrollwork.

Façade of the university entrance

©Turespaña

The typical Salamanca **patio**★★ (1428) has lovely lines. To the right of the entrance is a new exhibition room with a fine Mudéjar ceiling; the **University Museum** opposite exhibits what remains of the ceiling painted by Fernando Gallego for the former university library. This section of the **Cielo de Salamanca**★ (Salamanca Sky) illustrates constellations and signs of the zodiac. Several works by Juan of Flanders and Juan of Burgundy stand out in the museum.

▷ *Off the patio to the left is the Museum of Fine Arts.*

Museo de Salamanca (de Bellas Artes)

C. Patio de Escuelas 2. 🕐 *Open Tue–Sat 10am–2pm, 5–8pm (Oct–May 4–7pm), Sun and public holidays 10am–2pm.* 🕐 *Closed 1, 6 Jan, 24, 25 and 31 Dec.* 🎟 *€1.20; no charge Sat and Sun.*

The contents of Salamanca's fine arts museum, housed inside a small urban palace, cover 2,000 years of history. Many of its artistic treasures come from convents or monasteries and others are on loan from Madrid's Prado Museum. Outstanding is a 14th-century **sarcophogus** richly decorated with a narrative of the stigmatisation of St Francis, and a Mannerist **Llanto por Cristo** (*Mourning at the tomb of Christ*). Its collection of modern paintings includes a portrait of

Don Miguel de Unamuno, by Basque painter Echevarria y Zunicalday, and **Corrida en Azul**★★★, a 1942 canvas by Luis de Horna, clearly influenced by Picasso's *Guernica*.

▷ *Take Libreros towards the river and take the first left, Calderón de la Barca, to reach Pl. Juan XXIII to enter the Cathedrals.*

Catedral Nueva★★ (New Cathedral)

Pl. Anaya. ○ *Open daily 9am–8pm.* ⊛*No charge.* ☏ *923 21 74 76. www.catedralsalamanca.org.*
Construction began in 1513, although additions continued to be made until the 18C – hence the variety of architectural styles.

The **west front**★★★ is divided into four wide bays outlined by pierced stonework, carved as minutely as the keystones in the arches, the friezes and the pinnacled balustrades. The Gothic decoration of the central portal, which includes scenes such as a Crucifixion between St Peter and St Paul, overflows the covings and tympanum.

The **north doorway**, facing the **Colegio de Anaya**, bears a delicate low relief of Christ's entry into Jerusalem. The restored lower section of the last archivolt contains the surprising figure of an astronaut as well as a mythological animal eating ice-cream.

The **interior** is notable for the pattern of the vaulting, the delicacy of the cornices and the sweep of the pillars. The eight windows in the lantern are given added effect by a drum with scenes from the Life of the Virgin painted in the 18C by the Churriguera brothers, who also designed the ornate Baroque stalls in the *coro*, the *trascoro* and the north organ loft.

Catedral Vieja★★★ (Old Cathedral)

Pl. Anaya. Access from the Catedral Nueva. ○ *Open daily 9am–8pm* ⊛*€4.25 (includes museum and cloisters).* ☏ *923 21 74 76. www.catedralsalamanca.org.*

▷ *Enter by the first bay off the south aisle in the new Cathedral.*

The builders of the new Cathedral respected the fabric of the old which is almost totally masked outside. It was built in the 12C and is a good example of the Romanesque, the pointed arching being a legitimate, if unusual, innovation; the **cimborrio** (lantern), or Torre del Gallo, with two tiers of windows and ribbing, is outstanding. Beneath the vaulting, capitals are carved with scenes of tournaments and imaginary animals.

The **altarpiece**★★ in the central apsidal chapel was painted by Nicholas of Florence in 1445 and comprises 53 compartments decorated in surprisingly fresh colours showing the architecture and dress of the times. The Virgin of the Vega is a 12C wooden statue, plated in gilded and enamelled bronze.

Recesses in the south transept contain French-influenced 13C recumbent figures and frescoes.

Claustro – Capitals from earlier Romanesque galleries destroyed during the 1755 Lisbon earthquake remain in these cloisters. The adjoining **Capilla de Talavera**, with a Mudéjar dome on carved ribs, was where the ancient Mozarabic rite was celebrated. A museum in three rooms and the Capilla de Santa Catalina contains works by Fernando Gallego and his brother Francisco and others by Juan of Flanders (St Michael altarpiece).

The **Capilla Anaya** contains the outstanding 15C alabaster **tomb**★★ of Diego de Anaya, archbishop first of Salamanca and then of Sevilla. Surrounding it is a magnificent Plateresque grille. There are also a 15C **organ**★ and superb 16C recumbent statues.

From the **Patio Chico** you can see the old Cathedral apse and the scallop tiling on the **Torre del Gallo** (Cockerel Tower). From here, Calle Arcediano leads to the delightful **Huerto de Calixto y Melibea**.

▷ *From Pl. Juan XXIII take Calle Tentenecio, then take the first left.*

Museo de Art Nouveau y Art Déco★★

Expolio 14. ⏰ *Open Tue–Fri 11am–2pm, 5–9pm (mid-Oct-Mar 4-7pm), Sat, Sun and hols 11am–9pm (mid-Oct–Mar 8pm).* 🚫*Closed 1, 6 Jan, 24–25, 31 Dec.* ✎€3. *Free Thurs 11am-2pm.* 📞 923 12 14 25. *www.museocasalis.org.*

This museum in the Modernist Casa Lis, dating from the beginning of the 20C, includes the house's own furnishings and bronzes, works by R Lalique, vases by E Gallé and sculptures by Hagenauer. Temporary shows focus on art of the period. There is a cafeteria and in summer there are live music events.

⏵ *From Calle Tentenecio take Po. de Rector Esperaba and C. Arroyo Sto Domingo*

Convento de San Esteban★ (St Stephen's Monastery)

⏰ *Pl. Concilio de Trento.* ⏰*Open daily Oct–Mar 9am–1pm, 4–6pm; Apr–Sept 10am–2pm, 4–8pm.* 🚫*Museum closed Sun pm–Tue am.*✎€3; *no charge Mon (except holidays) 9am–noon.* 📞 923 21 50 00.

Gothic pinnacles adorn the side buttresses of this 16C–17C Dominican monastery; the sculpture of the **façade**★★ is quintessentially Platervesque. A low-relief *Martyrdom of St Stephen* is by Juan Antonio Ceroni (1610).

In the 17C **cloisters**★, note the prophets' heads in **medallions** and grand staircase (1553).

The large **church** has star vaulting in the gallery and a main altarpiece by José Churriguera. Crowning it is a painting of *The Martyrdom of St Stephen*, by Claudio Coello.

⏵ *On the same square stands the Convento de las Dueñas.*

Convento de las Dueñas

Pl. Concilio de Trento. ⏰ *Open Oct–Mar daily 11.30am–12.45pm, 4.30–5.30pm; Apr–Sept Mon–Sat 10.30am–12.45pm, 4.30–6.45pm, Sun and public holidays 11am–12.45pm, 4.30–6.45pm.* ✎€2. 📞 923 21 54 42.

The Renaissance **cloisters**★★ have profusely carved capitals, extraordinarily forceful in spite of their small size.

⏵ *Take San Pablo towards the Plaza Mayor.*

Palacio de la Salina★

C. de San Pablo, 24. ⏰*Open 11am–11pm.* 📞 923 29 32 33.

The city's salt was once kept in this palace; hence its name. The **patio** combines Salamanca mixtilinear arches at one end with a corbelled gallery – supported by distorted atlantes – on the right and an arcade on the left.

⏵ *Take San Pablo, then turn right on to San Justo and right again down Consuelo.*

Torre del Clavero

Consuelo. ⛔*Closed to the public.*

The octagonal keep is all that remains of a castle built in 1450. Mudéjar trellis-work decorates its turrets.

⏵ *Return to San Justo, follow it to the Pl. T. Bréton, then turn right to find C. Santa Clara.*

Convento de Santa Clara★

C. Santa Clara 2. ⏰*Open Mon–Fri 9.30am–2pm.* 📞 923 269 623.

Although the convent was founded in the 13th century, the building dates from the 15th–18th centuries. Its church contains a fine retablo and, in the choir, frescoes. One wing of the convent is now an ethnographic museum.

EXCURSIONS
Alba de Tormes

⏵ *23km/14mi SE on the N 501 and C 510.*

Only the massive keep remains of the **Castle of the dukes of Alba** (⏰*open daily 10am–1.30pm, 4–7pm; €3*). The remains of St Teresa of Ávila are in the Carmelite Convent.

The **Iglesia de San Juan** (⏰*open daily 11am–1pm, 4–6.30pm (Oct–Feb 6pm);* ✎€1), featuring a Romanesque-Mudéjar east end, contains an outstanding 11C **sculpture ensemble**★ in the apse, showing a noble Christ and the Disciples. Elsewhere is a small museum of local prehistoric finds.

Ciudad Rodrigo★

Ciudad Rodrigo appears high on a hilltop, guarded by the square tower of its 14C Alcázar (now a parador) and medieval ramparts. A Roman bridge spans the río Águeda from the Portuguese side. After the Reconquest in the 12C, the town was repopulated by Count Rodrigo González for whom it is named; later it became a border stronghold and was involved in all the conflicts between Castilla and Portugal.

Wellington's success against the French in 1812 won him the title of Duke of Ciudad Rodrigo and Grandee of Spain. The area is planted with ilex trees, under which pigs and fighting bulls graze.

 WALKING TOUR

THE OLD TOWN

▷ *Start your visit at the plaza de las Amayuelas.*

Catedral★★

Pl. San Salvador. ◐ *Open Mon-Sat 11.30am–2pm and 4–7pm (closed Mon pm and Nov–Easter 6pm), Sun 12.30– 2pm, 4–6pm.* €3, *ticket includes museum entrance.* ℘923 48 14 24. *www.catedralciudadrodrigo.com*

The Cathedral was built in two stages, first from 1170 to 1230 and then in the 14C; in the 16C Rodrigo Gil de Hontañón added the central apse. Note the delicate ornamentation of the blind arcades. The 13C **Portada de la Virgen**★ (Doorway of the Virgin), masked outside by a Classical belfry, has a line of Apostles carved between the columns beneath the splayings and covings.

In the interior, the Isabelline choir stalls in the *coro* were carved by Rodrigo Alemán. The fine Renaissance **altar**★ in the north aisle is adorned with an alabaster masterpiece by Lucas Mitata.

The **cloisters**★ are made up of diverse architectural styles. In the west gallery,

the oldest part, Romanesque capitals illustrate man's original sin. Opening off the east gallery is a Plateresque door decorated with medallions.

The **Museo Catedralicio** is worth a visit. Note too the 16C **Palacio de los Miranda** on Plaza de San Salvador.

▷ *Return to the Cathedral; in front is the Capilla de Cerralbo.*

Capilla de Cerralbo

Cardenal Pacheco. ◐*Open for Mass Mon–Fri and Sat–Sun 11am–2pm, 4–7pm.* ℘923 49 84 00.

The chapel, built between 1588 and 1685, is pure and austere but harmonious.

▷ *The arcaded Plaza del Buen Alcalde is to the right. Take the street to the left to reach Plaza del Conde.*

Palacio de los Castro★ (or Palacio de los Condes de Montarco)

Pl. del Conde.

This late 15C palace, on Plaza del Conde (Count), has a long façade punctuated by delicate windows.

The Plateresque doorway is surrounded by an *alfiz* and flanked by two twisted columns showing Portuguese influence. It is now a restaurant; the patio may be visited when not in use.

▷ *Head to the Plaza Mayor, passing the 16C Palacio de Moctezuma to the right.*

Plaza Mayor★

Two Renaissance palaces stand on the lively main square: the first, now the **ayuntamiento** (town hall); *guided tours Sat–Sun 12noon;* ℘923 49 84 00) has a façade with two storeys of basket arcading forming a **gallery**★ and a loggia, while the second, the **Casa de los Cueto**, has a decorative frieze.

▷ *Continue to Juan Arias, lined by the Casa del Príncipe or Casa de los Águilas, a 16C building in Plateresque style.*

Murallas (Ramparts)

The walls, built on Roman foundations in the 12C, were converted to a full defensive system on the north and west flanks in 1710. There are several stairways up to the 2.25km/1.4mi-long sentry path.

▶ *The imposing keep of Henry of Trastámara's castle stands on the SW corner of the walls, alongside the Roman bridge spanning the Águeda river. Nowadays, the castle is the town's parador.*

ADDRESSES

◎ STAY

◎◎ **Hostal Catedral** – *Rua Mayor 46 1ºB. ℘923 27 06 14. www.hostalcatedral salamanca.com. Reservations recommended. 5 rooms. ☎ €3.* Occupying the first floor of an attractive stone building, some windows look directly over the Cathedral. The hostal is tastefully decorated with spotless bathrooms.

◎◎ **Hostal Plaza Mayor** – *Pl. del Corrillo 20. ℘923 26 20 20. www.hostal plazamayor.es. 19 rooms.* Ideally situated just behind Pl. Mayor, opposite the Romanesque church of San Martín. The hotel's interior design highlights the main features of the house, such as its attractive wooden beams. Garage parking.

◎◎ **Hosteria Casa Vallejo** – *San Juan de la Cruz 3. ℘923 28 04 21. www.hosteriacasavallejo.com. 13 rooms. Restaurant◎◎◎. Closed 2 weeks in Feb and Jul.* A small hotel located off Plaza Mayor. The refurbished interior, behind a 19C façade, includes a restaurant and tapas bar.

◎◎◎◎ **Hotel Rector** – *Po Rector Esperabé 10. ℘923 21 84 82. www.hotel rector.com. 13 rooms. ☎ €12.* A charming if pricy hotel with spectacular views of the Cathedral and elegant, well-appointed rooms.

◎ EAT

◎ **El Bardo** – *C. Compañía 8. ℘923 25 92 65 www.restauranteelbardo.com. Closed 1 Jan.* A typical student haunt with vaulted ceilings and a lively atmosphere. Vegetarian dishes available.

◎◎ **La Fonda del Arcediano de Medina** – *Reja 2. ℘923 21 57 12. www.lafondadel arcedianodemedina.com. Reservations recommended.* This restaurant has a solid local reputation for good foods, and wines. Pork, veal and saltcod are specialities. Pleasant décor.

◎◎◎ **Asador El Mesón** – *Pl. Poeta Iglesias 10. ℘923 27 13 53. Closed Sun in winter.* A restaurant with a high reputation within the city which has a traditional carvery menu, modern dishes and a tapas menu.

TAPAS

Mesón Cervantes – *Pl. Mayor 15. ℘923 27 13 53. www.mesoncervantes.com.* A bar with typical Castilian décor and fine views of plaza Mayor serving modern, innovative cuisine. Popular with Salamanca's young crowd at night. Try the house *sangría*.

Momo – *San Pablo 13. ℘923 28 07 98. www.momosalamanca.net. Closed Sun Aug.* The contemporary version of a tapas bar. Tapas and skewers come cold and hot, and in the basement dining room they serve meals of haute cuisine tapas.

◎ CAFÉS

Café Novelty – *Pl. Mayor 2. ℘923 21 49 56. www.cafenovelty.com.* Famous since 1905, Miguel de Unamuno used to meet here. The wooden chairs and marble tables conjure up his times and the terrace offers a wonderful view of one of Spain's finest squares. Home-made ice creams.

La Regenta – *Espoz y Mina 25. ℘923 12 32 30. www.cafelaregenta.com.* A much-loved café with a 19C atmosphere ambience you pay extra for, though it is worth it.

La Rayuela - *Rua Mayor 19. ℘923-26 32 16.* Students, locals and visitors drop by this classic day and night. Good *mojitos* and a friendly atmosphere.

La Alberca★★

La Alberca is a well-preserved village in the national park of Las Batuecas-Sierra de Francia. On 15 August each year a mystery play, or Loa, relating the triumph of the Virgin Mary over the devil, is performed. The sierra's rolling woodland is dotted by unspoiled villages with wooden-beamed architecture.

▶ **Population:** 1 177
◔ **Michelin Map:** 575 K 11.
▤ **Info:** La Puente 9. ✆923 41 52 91. http://laalberca.com.
▷ **Location:** La Alberca is 42km/26mi E of Cuidad Rodrigo and 77km/48mi S of Salamanca.

EXCURSIONS
Peña de Francia★★
▷ *15km/9.6mi W.*

The Peña, a shale crag, at 1 732m/5 682ft is the peak of the Peña de Francia range. The approach affords stunning **panoramas**★★ of the Hurdes mountains and the Sierra de Gredos. A 16C Dominican monastery with an excellent **hostelry** with restaurant is at the top (☺☺☻; 28 rooms; ✆923 16 40 00; www.hosteleria-peñadefrancia.com; open weekends from Easter and Jun–Oct).

Avenida de Las Batuecas★
▷ *To the S.*

This road climbs to the Portillo Pass (1 240m/4 068ft) then plunges into a deep, green valley where the Batuecas Monastery is situated.

🚗 DRIVING TOUR

Tour of The Sierra de Béjar and Sierra de Candelario

▷ *76km/47mi to the SE – allow one day.*

Meander through the gorges of the Alagón and Cuerpo de Hombre rivers amid walnut and oak forests.

▷ *Head east. After 2km/1.2mi, turn to Cepeda, then Sotoserrano. Head towards Lagunilla to reach the N 630 at Puerto de Béjar.*

Baños de Montemayor, a pleasant spa, and **Hervás**, with its old **judería** (Jewish quarter) are in this area.

▷ *Return to Puerto de Béjar. One road heads towards Candelario.*

Candelario★★
This picturesque village on the **sierra's flanks** retains traditional stone homes with elegant balconies.

Béjar
▷ *4km/2.5mi NW.*

Béjar, known for its textiles, stretches along a narrow rock platform at the foot of the Sierra de Béjar.

▷ *Leave Béjar along the SA 515.*

Miranda del Castañar
▷ *34km/21mi W.*

Pass the 15C **castle** and penetrate the old quarter through the Puerta de San Ginés **Mogarraz** (10km/6.2mi W) and **San Martín del Castañar** (10km/6.2mi N) are charming villages worth a visit.

▷ *Take the SA 202 back to La Alberca.*

ADDRESSES

🛏 STAY
☺☺ **Hotel Antiguas Eras** – *Avda Batuecas 29, La Alberca.* ✆923 415 113. www.antiguaseras.com. 9 rooms. ☲ €4.30. *Restaurant*☺☺☻. *Closed 1 week between Jun–Jul.* A rural hotel in the heart of La Alberca which occupies wooden-beamed homes with sierra views. The price includes breakfast.

🍴 EAT
☺☺ **Mesón La Romana** – *Nuñez Losada 4, Candelario.* ✆923 41 3272. *Reservations recommended. Closed Sun eve–Fri lunch.* A weekend-only restaurant situated next to the church. Wood-grilled meats, griddled fresh goat's cheese and wild mushrooms are specialities.

Zamora★

Zamora stands in a plain on the banks of the River Duero. The 12C and 13C saw the construction of the Cathedral and numerous Romanesque churches, which stand in the well-preserved old town.

A BIT OF HISTORY

Traces remain of the walls which made Zamora the western bastion along the Duero in the Reconquest. Zamora figured in repeated struggles for the throne of Castilla.

SIGHTS
Catedral★

Pl. de la Catedral. ○*Open daily Apr–Sep 10am–2pm, 4.30–8pm (Oct 6.30pm).* ⊕*Entry for cathedral and museum €4.* ℘*980 53 06 44.*

The Cathedral was built between 1151 and 1174 and subsequently altered. The north front is Neoclassical in keeping with the square in front; it contrasts, however, with the Romanesque bell tower and the graceful cupola covered in scallop tiling. The south front, the only original part, has blind arcades and a Romanesque portal with unusual covings featuring openwork festoons.

The aisles are transitional Romanesque-Gothic, the vaulting ranging from broken barrel to pointed ogive.

Slender painted ribs support the luminous **dome**★ on squinches above the transept. Late Gothic master woodcarvers worked here. Notable are fine **grilles** enclosing the presbytery, the *coro* and some chapels, two 15C Mudéjar pulpits, and **choir stalls**★★, decorated with biblical figures or with allegorical and burlesque scenes.

Museo Catedralicio (Cathedral Museum)

○*Open same hours as Cathedral.*

The museum, off the Herreran cloisters, displays 15C Flemish and 17C **tapestries**★★.

Also note the 16C Renaissance monstrance and a Virgin and Child and Little St John sculpted by Bartolomé Ordóñez.

▶ **Population:** 66 293
⊙ **Michelin Map:** 575 H 12.
▯ **Info:** Plaza de Arias Gonzalo. ℘980 53 36 94. http://zamoradipu.es.
▷ **Location:** Zamora is NW of Madrid, 65km/40mi N of Salamanca. ▭Carretera de la Estación.
▲▲ **Kids:** The Museo Ethnografico's costumes and shepherds' art will amuse children.
○ **Timing:** Allow a long morning to visit the old town and the afternoon for one of the excursions.

The **Jardín del Castillo** (Castle Garden) to the rear commands fine views.

Baltasar Lobo Centro de Arte★

Pl. de la Catedral. ○*Open Tue–Sun 12 –2pm, 7–9pm.* ⊕*No charge.* ℘*664 058 403. www.mbaltasarlobo.com.*

A monographical arts centre dedicated to the work of sculptor Baltasar Lobo, whose marble and bronze works are kept here. Born in Zamora province, he lived and worked in Paris, where his work evolved towards abstraction under the influence of Jean Arp and Henry Moore.

Romanesque churches★

○*Open Tue–Sun 2 Mar–Sept 10am– 1pm, 5–8pm; Oct–6 Jan 10am–2pm, 4.30–6.30pm.*

The 12C saw many original Romanesque churches built in Zamora. Features included portals without tympana, surrounded by multifoil arches and often possessing heavily carved archivolts.

Larger churches had domes on squinches over the transept crossing. The best examples in Zamora, open to the public with coordinated times, are the **Magdalena** *(los Francos)*, **Santa María la Nueva** *(Pl. de Santa María la Nueva)*, **San Juan de Puerta Nueva** *(Pl. Mayor)*, **Santa María de la Horta** *(Bar-*

rio de la Horta), **Santo Tomé** (Pl. Santo Tomé) and **Santiago del Burgo** (Santa Clara).

🏛 Museo Etnográfico de Castilla y Léon★

Del Sacramento, Pl. Viriato. ⏱*Open Tue–Sat 10am–2pm, 5–8pm, Sun and hols 10am–2pm.* €3. 980 531 708. www.museo-etnografico.com.
Outstanding collection of popular and folk art laid out in didactic displays with videos and written explanations.

Seigniorial Mansions
Palacio del Cordón
(Museo Provincial; Pl. de Santa Lucía 2; ⏱*open Tue–Sat 10am–2pm, 6–8pm (Oct–Jun 4–7pm, Sun and public holidays 10am–2pm;* €1.20; 980 51 61 50),* with archaeology and fine art, and the **Palacio de los Momos** (San Torcuato 7) have elegant Isabelline windows.

EXCURSIONS
San Pedro de la Nave★
▷ *19km/11.8mi NW. Leave Zamora on the N 122–E 82. Follow the N 122 for 12km/7.4mi then turn right.*
The late 7C Visigothic **church** (⏱*open Mar–Sept Tue–Sun 10am–1pm, 5–8pm; Oct–6 Jan Fri–Sat 10am–2pm, 4.30–6.30pm, Sun 10am–2pm;* no charge; ask for the keys at the nearby bar;*

San Salvador de los Caballeros, Toro
© Juan José Pascual/age fotostock

980 56 91 67), endangered by the damming of the Esla, was rebuilt at El Campillo.
It is remarkable for the Biblical carving on the transept **capitals**. The frieze, halfway up, presents Christian symbols including grapes and doves.

Arcenillas
▷ *7km/4.3mi SE on the C 605.*
In the village church (Nuestra Señora de la Asunción; *ask for key on arrival at bar*), 15 **panels**★ depicting the Life, Death and Resurrection of Christ have been reassembled from the late 15C Gothic altarpiece designed for Zamora Cathedral by **Fernando Gallego**, one of the great Castilian painters of the age.

Benavente
▷ *66km/41mi N along the N 630.*
The Renaissance **Castillo de los Condes de Pimentel** (Castle of the Counts of Pimentel; 980 63 03 00), now a parador, retains its 16C Torre del Caracol (snail tower), with a fine carved artesanado ceiling and valley **views**. The **Hospital de la Piedad**, once a pilgrims' hospital (C. de Santa Cruz 5), keeps a magnificent carved cloister (access 9am–8pm).
The transitional **Iglesia de Santa María del Azogue** (Pl. de Santa María; 980 66 42 58) has five apses and two Romanesque portals. A beautiful 13C *Annunciation* stands at the crossing.
The **Iglesia de San Juan del Mercado** (Pl. de San Juan 4; 980 63 00 80) has a 12C carving on the south portal illustrating the journey of the Magi.

Toro
▷ *33km/21mi E along the N 122–E 82.*
Toro, a wine-town on the River Duero, has preserved an exceptional cluster of Romanesque churches. **San Salvador de los Caballeros** is the finest example of the style: the brick Mudéjar Romanesque church was originally Templar, built on circular floorplans with elongated blind arcades on the curving facades; it keeps Mudéjar frescoes and an exquisite selection of art inside (⏱*open Tue–Sun, hours as for the Colegiata).* In the Museu de Sant Espir-

itu (Tue–Sun, 1 hour guided tours 10.30, 11.30, 12.30, 4.30 and 5.30) is an impressive collection of local Romanesque and other art. A number of the town's other recently restored monuments include the **Iglesia de San Lorenzo** (℘980 69 47 47) and the bullring, one of the oldest in Spain. The town's bodegas are open certain days of the week. Toro's magnificent red wines can be sampled in the tapas bars on the market place, which is especially lively on a Saturday.

Colegiata de Santa María La Mayor★
Pl. de la Colegiata. ◷Open Tue–Sun Mar–Sept 10.30am–2pm, 5–7.30pm; Oct–6 Jan 10am–2pm, 4.30–6.30pm. ◌2€. ℘980 69 47 47.

Construction began in 1160 with the elegant transept lantern and ended in 1240 with the west portal.

The Romanesque **north portal** illustrates the Old Men of the Apocalypse and angels linked by a rope. The Gothic **west portal★★**, repainted in the 18C, is the church treasure.

Statues on the pier and tympanum jambs have youthful faces. Start beneath the **cupola★**, one of the first of its kind in Spain, with two tiers of windows in the drum. Polychrome wood statues stand against the pillars at the end of the nave on consoles, one carved with an amusing version of the Birth of Eve (below the angel).

In the sacristy is the **Virgin and the Fly★**, a magnificent Flemish painting by either Gérard David or Hans Memling.

ADDRESSES

⌂ STAY

◌◌◌◌ **Parador Condes de Alba de Aliste** – Plaza Viriato 5, Zamora. ℘980 51 44 97. www.paradores.es. 52 rooms. ⌷€15. Immaculately preserved 15C Renaissance palace bursting with armour, tapestries, canopied beds and other baronial décor. Swimming pool. The restaurant serves traditional local dishes.

The central provinces of Spain's northern tableland offer landscapes of unexpected beauty. Segovia's mountains, the wheat plains of Valladolid and Soria's river valleys and gorges make superb driving and walking country. Segovia and Valladolid, both court cities long before Madrid, have preserved contrasting architectural and artistic legacies. Soria is less regal, but keeps medieval spiritual retreats and military monuments that date back to its time as a frontier between Christian and Muslim Spain.

Highlights

1 Wandering at the **Roman Aqueduct** of Segovia (p163)

2 Strolling in the gardens of **La Granja**'s royal palace (p168)

3 Admiring richly coloured Baroque sculpture in **Valladolid**'s museum (p171)

4 Calm in the cloisters of Santa María de Huerta, **Soria** (p176)

5 Visiting the Moorish ruins of **Gormaz castle**, the largest in Europe (p177)

Segovia

The Sierra de Guadarrama's hilltowns provide cool refuges from the summer heat: Pedraza de la Sierra, for example, a lovely village encircled by medieval walls, is popular as a weekend bolt hole.

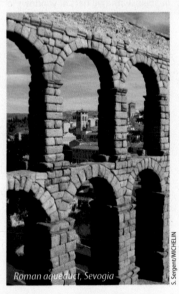

Roman aqueduct, Sevogia

S. Sergent/MICHELIN

At the foot of the sierra stands the Palacio de la Granja de San Ildefonso, where a splendid formal garden runs up into woodland. Just to the north, Segovia is famous for its Roman aqueduct – a triumph of art and engineering – and Romanesque churches.

Its fairytale castle (Alcázar) is actually a fanciful mid-19C recreation of the medieval original. However, most of this historic town is immaculately preserved within medieval walls.

Valladolid

By comparison Valladolid, once capital of Castille, is prosaic, although its Isabelline architecture and National Museum of Sculpture are outstanding. In Holy Week, church sculptures are processed through the streets in great solemnity. Elsewhere in the province is Tordesillas, where the famous treaty dividing the New World was signed.

The castles of Medina del Campo, Montealegre Peñafiel and Simancas, rising up above the wide-horizoned vineyards and fields, are a reminder of battles fought here long ago.

Soria

One of Spain's least populated provinces, much of Soria's beauty lies in its very emptiness. Medieval monasteries, such as San Juan de Duero, and hermitages may be seen against evocative rural backdrops. Castles built on an epic scale to defend a warring medieval frontier, such as Gormaz, loom up above dramatic bare red rock.

A trio of small towns – Burgo de Osma, Peñaranda and Berlanga – hold unexpected artistic wealth. Excursions to see them may be combined with walking in landscape of outstanding natural beauty.

Segovia★★★

This austere, imposing city, at 1 000m/3 280ft, rises on a triangular rock like an island in the Castilian plain. Its sturdy walls enclose a complicated maze of narrow streets dotted with Roman monuments and mansions. The old town and aqueduct are a UNESCO World Heritage Site.

A BIT OF HISTORY

Noble Segovia, residence of King Alfonso X, the Wise, and King Henry IV, played a decisive role in the history of Castilla. The 15C marked its golden age, when its population numbered 60 000.
Isabel the Catholic, Queen of Castilla – On the death of Henry IV in 1474 many grandees refused to recognise the legitimacy of his daughter, Doña Juana, known as **La Beltraneja**. In Segovia, the grandees proclaimed Henry's half-sister, Isabel, Queen of Castilla – thus preparing the way for Spain's unification (Isabel was married to Ferdinand, heir apparent of Aragón). La Beltraneja, aided by her husband, Alfonso V of Portugal, pressed her claim, but renounced it in 1479 after defeats at Toro and Albuera.
The "Comuneros" – In 1519, just three years after Charles I (Carlos I) had landed in Asturias to take possession of his Spanish dominions, he departed in order to be proclaimed Holy Roman Emperor (as Charles V).
An uprising started that was to become known as the revolt of the Comuneros. The catalysts included the absence of Charles V, his Flemish court, which overrode Castilian nobles, and his attempt to impose new taxes.
Behind the Comuneros movement lay the opposition of Castilian towns, the middle classes and merchants to the alliance between Charles V and the landed aristocracy. The Comuneros were finally crushed at Villalar in 1521.

WALKING TOUR

CIUDAD VIEJA★★(OLD TOWN)
4hr *See town plan.*

- ▶ **Population:** 56 858
- **Michelin Map:** 575 or 576 J 17 – map 121 Alrededores de Madrid – local map p 164.
- **Info:** Plaza de Azoguejo 1. *921 46 67 20. www. turismodesegovia.com.*
- ▶ **Location:** Segovia is 92km/57mi NW of Madrid. The AVE high-speed train service calls at Segovia-Guiomar, 6km/3.5mi from the town centre. Calle Obispo Quesada 1.
- **Don't Miss:** The Alcázar, and a meander along streets lined with palaces.
- **Timing:** Allow a full day in town, plus time for excursions.

Acueducto★★★
Pl. del Azogüejo.
This elegant structure was built during the reign of Trajan in the 1C to bring water from the River Acebeda to the upper part of town and remains one of the finest examples of Roman engineering still standing . It is 728m/2 388ft long, rising to 28m/92ft in Plaza del Azoguejo where the ground is lowest, and consists of two tiers of arches.

▶ *Take Calle Cervantes.*

Casa de los Picos
Juan Bravo 33. Open Apr–Oct daily noon–2pm, 7–9pm; Nov–Mar Mon–Fri noon–2pm, 6–8pm, Sat–Sun noon–2pm, 7–9pm. Patio open during exhibitions noon–2pm, 6–8pm No charge. 921 46 26 74.
The house, faced closely with diamond-pointed stones, is the most original of Segovia's 15C mansions. It is now Segovia's art school.

▶ *Take Juan Bravo and turn off to Pl. de Platero Oquendo.*

Casa del Conde de Alpuente

Pl. Conde Alpuente.

The elegant façade of this 15C Gothic house is adorned with *esgrafiado* designs.

▷ *Continue down Platero Oqueno.*

Alhóndiga

C. de Alhóndiga. ∞*No charge.*

This old 15C granary is now used as an exhibition room.

▷ *Return to Juan Bravo.*

Plaza de San Martín★

This lovely square in the heart of the old aristocratic quarter is the most evocative part of historic Segovia. Around the square stand the **Casa del Siglo XV** (15C House), also known as Juan Bravo's house, with a gallery beneath the eaves, the 16C tower of the **Casa de los Lozoya**, the Plateresque façade of

the **Casa Solier** (also known as Casa de Correas) and ornate entrances to other large houses.

In the middle of the square is the 12C **Iglesia de San Martín★** (○*open for Mass; 921 46 26 43*), a church framed on three sides by a covered gallery on pillars with carved strapwork and animal figures on the capitals.

▷ *The Pl. de las Bellas Artes opens off Pl. San Martín.*

Museo de Arte Contemporáneo Esteban Vicente

Plazuela de las Bellas Artes.

○ *Open Tue–Wed 11am–2pm, 4–7pm; Thu–Fri 11am–2pm, 4–8pm; Sat–Sun and public holidays 11am–8pm.* ∞€3; no charge Thu. *921 46 20 10. www.museoestebanvicente.es.*

The museum is in the palace of Henry IV in the Hospital de Viejos (Old People's Hospital). The only trace of the original building is the fine chapel with a Mudéjar ceiling, now an auditorium. The museum exhibits the work of artist Esteban Vicente (1904–2001) and is also used for concerts.

○ *Follow Juan Bravo past the town's old prison.*

Iglesia del Corpus Christi

Po. del Salón. ○ *Open Wed–Sun 10am–2pm.*
The convent church keeps the structure of the city's largest synagogue. Close by, a new centre for interpretation of the old Jewish quarter, centred here, has exhibits of other vestiges to be seen today (*C. Judería Vieja 12;* ○*open Wed–Sun 11am–2pm, 4–7pm;* ℘*921 46 23 96*).

○ *Take Isabel la Católica.*

Plaza Mayor

Dominated by the impressive Cathedral, the arcaded square with its terrace cafés is a popular meeting place. Among the buildings surrounding the square are the *ayuntamiento* (town hall) and the Teatro Juan Bravo.

Catedral★★

Pl. Mayor. ○ *Open daily Apr–Sept 9.30am–6.30pm; Oct–Mar 9.30am–5.30pm.* ○*Closed 1 and 6 Jan.* ◉€3; no charge Sun 9.30am–1.15pm. ℘*921 46 22 05.*
This was built during the reign of Emperor Charles V to replace a Cathedral destroyed during the Comuneros' Revolt in 1521. It is an example of the survival of the Gothic style in the 16C when Renaissance architecture was at its height. The beautiful golden stone, the stepped east end with pinnacles and delicate balustrades, and the tall tower bring considerable grace to the massive building. The width of the aisles combines with the decorative lines of the pillars and ribs in the vaulting to make the interior both light and elegant.
The chapels are closed by fine wrought-iron screens. The first off the south aisle contains as the altarpiece an *Entombment* by Juan de Juni. The *coro* stalls, in

View of the old town with the cathedral

C. Labonne/MICHELIN

late 15C Flamboyant Gothic style, are from the earlier Cathedral.
Claustro★ – The 15C cloisters from the former Cathedral, near the Alcázar, were rebuilt on the new site. In the Sala Capitular (chapter house) beautiful 17C Brussels **tapestries**★ illustrate the story of Queen Zenobia.

○ *Follow Mqués del Arco and Daioz to Pl. de la Reina Victoria Eugenia.*

Alcázar★★

Pl. de la Reina Victoria Eugenia. ○ *Open daily Apr–Sept 10am–7pm; Oct–Mar 10am–6pm (Fri–Sat in Oct till 7pm).* ◉€4.50; tower €2; no charge 3rd Tue of month (except holidays) for EU citizens. ℘*921 46 07 59.*
The Alcázar, on a cliff overlooking the valley, was built above a former fortress in the early 13C and modified in the 15C and 16C by Henry IV and Philip II. In 1764, Charles III converted the building into a **Real Colegio de Artillería** (Royal Artillery School), but in 1862 it suffered a devastating fire. Reconstruction was completed at the end of the 19C, hence its neo-Gothic look.
The furniture and richly decorated Mudéjar *artesonado* work, mostly from the 15C, are original and were brought from various Castilian towns. Its keep is flanked by corbelled turrets. The main rooms of note are the Chamber Royal

(Cámara Real) and the Sala de los Reyes (Monarchs' Room). The Sala del Cordón and terrace command a fine **panorama** of the fertile Eresma Valley, the Monasterio de El Parral, the Capilla de la Vera Cruz and the Meseta.

The artillery school houses a museum recalling the chemical laboratory located here in the 18C and the French chemist **Louis Proust**, who formulated his law of constant proportions in Segovia. The **views** from the keep (152 steps) stretch across the city to the Sierra de Guadarrama.

Take Velarde to Pl. San Esteban, passing through the medieval Porte de la Claustra.

Iglesia de San Esteban (St Stephen's Church)
Pl. de San Esteban. ⚫━ *Closed to the public.* 📞 *921 46 60 70.*
One of the latest (13C) and most beautiful of Segovia's Romanesque churches. The porticoes running along two of its sides have finely carved capitals.
The five-storey **tower**★ has elegant bays and slender columns on the corners. The interior is in Renaissance style. Inside, the altar in the south transept has a 13C polychrome Gothic figure of Christ.

Take Valdeláguila to Pl. de la Trinidad.

Iglesia de la Santísima Trinidad (Holy Trinity Church)
Pl. de la Trinidad 6. 🕐 *Open during Mass.* ⚫ *No charge.*
This austere Romanesque church has a decorated apse with blind arcading and capitals carved with imaginary beasts and plant motifs.

Take Trinidad and San Agustín, turning left down Zuloaga to Pl. de Colmenares.

Iglesia de San Juan de los Caballeros
Pl. de Colmenares. 🕐 *Open Tue–Sat 10am–2pm, 4–7pm, Sun and public holidays 10am–2pm.* ⚫ *€1.20;*

no charge weekends, or for under-14s. 📞 *921 46 33 48.*
This is Segovia's oldest Romanesque church (11C). Its portico (taken from the church of San Nicolás) has carvings of portrait heads, plant motifs and animals. The church, which was almost in ruins at the turn of the 20C, was bought by Daniel Zuloaga, who converted it into his home and workshop. Today it houses the **Museo Zuloaga**, exhibiting drawings by the artist and by his nephew, Ignacio Zuloaga.

Plaza del Conde de Cheste
On the square stand the palaces of the **Marqués de Moya**, the **Marqués de Lozoya**, the **Condes de Cheste** and the **Marqués de Quintanar**.

Iglesia de San Sebastián
Pl. de San Sebastián.
This small Romanesque church stands on one side of a quiet square.

OUTSIDE THE WALLS
Museo de Segovia★
Casa del Sol – Del Socorro, 11.
🕐 *Open Tue–Sat 10am–2pm, 5–8pm (Oct–Jun 4–7pm), Sun and public holidays 10am–2pm.* ⚫ *€1.20; no charge weekends.* 📞 *921 460 613.*
Segovia's archaeological, ethnological and fine arts museum collection ranges from exhibits on early hydraulic systems and present-day drovers' roads to some exceptional pieces of classical art. Galleries show prints by Rembrandt and Dürer, and fine sculpture and altarpieces from local monasteries and churches. The glass made at La Granja's Royal Factory since the 18C is also well represented.

Iglesia de San Millán★
Av. Fernández Ladreda. 🕐 *Open for Mass.* ⚫ *No charge.* ⚫ *Guided tours available in summer and Holy Week, please phone tourist office.*
📞 *921 46 09 63.*
The early 12C church stands in the middle of a large square, which allows a full view of its pure, still primitive Romanesque lines and two porticoes with finely carved modillions and capitals.

The three aisles have alternating pillars and columns as in Jaca Cathedral.
The apse has blind arcading and a decorative frieze. The transept has Moorish ribbed vaulting.

Monasterio El Parral★

Alameda del Eresma. ◷ *Open Tue–Sat 10am–12.30pm, 4.15–6.30pm (Sun 6pm).* ✉*Donation appreciated.* ✆*921 43 12 98.*

The monastery was founded by Henry IV in 1445 and later entrusted to the Hieronymites. The **church**, behind its unfinished façade, has a Gothic nave with beautifully carved doors, a 16C altarpiece by Juan Rodríguez and, on either side of the chancel, the Plateresque tombs of the Marquis and Marchioness of Villena.

Capilla de la Vera-Cruz★

Ctra de Zamarramala. ◷*Open Tue–Sun 10.30am–12.30pm, 4.15–6.30pm (Sun 6pm).* ✉*€1.75.* ✆*921 43 14 75.*
The unusual polygonal chapel was erected in the 13C, probably by the Templars; it now belongs to the Order of Malta. A circular corridor surrounds two small chambers, one above the other, where secret ceremonies were conducted. The Capilla del Lignum Crucis holds an ornate Flamboyant Gothic altar. There is a good view of Segovia.

Convento de Santa Cruz

Cardenal Zúñiga. ⚬*Closed to the public.* ✆*921 41 24 10.*
The convent pinnacles, the decorated Isabelline **entrance** with a Calvary, a *Pietà*, and the emblems of the Catholic Monarchs on this convent – now a business school – may be seen from the road.

Iglesia de San Lorenzo

Iglesia.
The Romanesque church with its unusual brick belfry stands in a picturesque square surrounded by corbelled half-timbered houses.

EXCURSIONS

Palacio Real de Riofrío★

▷ *Bosque de Riofrío, Navás de Riofrío. 11km/6.8mi S of Segovia on the N 603.* ◷*Open Apr–Sept Tue–Sun and public holidays 10am–6pm; Oct–Mar Tue–Sat 10am–1.30pm, 3–5pm, Sun and public holidays 10am–2pm.* ◷*Closed 23 Jan, 25 Aug, national holidays.* ✉*€4; no charge Wed for EU citizens.* ✆*921 47 00 19.*

The palace Riofrío was planned by Isabel Farnese as the equal of La Granja, which she had to vacate on the death of her husband, Philip V. Construction began in 1752 but though it was very big – it measures 84m x 84m (276ft x 276ft) – it was never more than a hunting lodge. It is built around a grand Classical-style courtyard. The green and pink façade reflects Isabel's Italian origins.

Castillo de Coca★★

▷ *Camino Antigua Cauca Romana, Coca. 52km/32mi NW of Segovia along the C 605 and SG 341.* ⚐*Guided tours daily 10.30am–1pm, 4.30–7pm (6pm Nov–Mar).* ◷*Closed 1st Tue in month, 15 Jan and national holidays.* ✉*€2.70.* ✆*921 57 35 54.*

This **castillo** (fortress), on the outskirts of Coca village, is the most outstanding example of Mudéjar military architecture in Spain. It was built in the late 15C by Moorish craftsmen for the archbishop of Sevilla, Fonseca, and consists of three concentric perimeters, flanked by polygonal corner towers and turrets with, at the centre, a massive keep. It is the epitome of all fortresses, but with the sun mellowing the pink brick and the interplay of shadows on battlements and watchtowers, it can be attractive as well as awesome.
The *torre del homenaje* (keep) and *capilla* (chapel), which contains Romanesque wood carvings, are open to the public.

Arévalo

▷ *60km/37mi NW along the C 605.*
Isabel the Catholic spent her childhood in the 14C **castle** with its massive crenellated keep which dominates the town. Of note also are Romanesque-

Mudéjar brick churches, and several old mansions.

Plaza de la Villa★, the former Plaza Mayor, is one of the best-preserved town squares in Castilla with its half-timbered brick houses resting on pillared porticoes. They blend in perfectly with the Mudéjar east end of the Iglesia de Santa María and its blind arcading.

Pedraza★★

▷ *40km/25mi NE of Segovia on N 110.*
🄸 *Real 40.* 🕾*921 50 86 66.*
www.pedraza.info.

Weekend visitors flock to Pedraza, encircled by medieval walls, to wander its enchanting streets.

The **Puerta de la Villa**, a fortified gateway, opens into a maze of alleys bordered by country-style houses. The first medieval building of interest is the **Cárcel de la Villa** (🕒*open Sat–Sun and public holidays 11.30am–2pm, 4–7.30pm; ⊛€2.50; 🕾921 50 86 66)*, the former jail.

The splendid **plaza Mayor** is surrounded by ancient porticoes topped by balconies and the slender Romanesque bell tower of San Juan. A 16C **castle** (⌾*guided tours (30min) Wed–Sun; please book in advance; 🕾921 50 98 25)* houses works by artist **Ignacio Zuloaga**.

From Pedraza you can continue on the N110, once a Roman road, to Riaza and Ayllón, attractive Castilian towns. Ayllón also gives access to **Tiermes archaeological sight**★★ *(via Montejo and the SO-P-4120; 🕾 975 18 61 56; www.tiermes. net)*. The Celtiberian town built into a sandstone rock cliff and its amphitheatre are set in an extraordinarily evocative landscape. Later Roman dwellings and a small museum stand nearby.

Sepúlveda

▷ *25km/15.5mi N of Segovia.*

You'll get a good view of the village's terraced **site**★ on the slopes of a deep gorge.

🄿*Park at the town hall square, overlooked by castle ruins.* Walk up to the **Iglesia de San Salvador** *(Subida al Salvador 10; 🕒open Apr–Sep 10am– 7pm,*

Oct–Mar 10am–6pm;⌾*free guided tours available in summer; 🕾921 54 02 37)* for a fine view. The church is typical Segovia Romanesque with one of the oldest side doors in Spain, dating from 1093.

Centro de Interpretación del Parque Natural del Río Duratón (Duratón Gorges)

🕒 *Open Oct–Jun daily 10am–5pm; Jul–Sept Sun–Fri 10am–2pm, 4–7pm; Sat and public holidays 10am–6pm.* 🕾*921 54 05 86.*

This centre provides information about hiking routes and canoe companies.

The **park** runs along the middle stretch of the river, hemmed in by spectacular 70m/230ft walls, under the simple Romanesque hermitage *(ermita)* of San Frutos.

🚗 DRIVING TOUR

From Segovia to Madrid via La Granja and El Paular

159km/99mi. Allow one day including visits to the palace and monastery, two days to walk in the mountains.

The **Sierra de Guadarrama**★'s bare peaks, visible from Segovia, rise above steep granite and gneiss slopes covered in oaks and pines. Mountain-born streams feed the province's reservoirs. At the foot of the sierra's slopes on the western side stands La Granja's royal summer palace. On the eastern side you can visit the restored medieval monastery of El Paular.

▷ *Take the CL 601 from Segovia to La Granja.*

Palacio Real de La Granja de San Ildefonso★★

Pl. de España 17. 🕒*Open Apr–Sept Tue–Sun 10am–6pm; Oct–Mar 10am– 1.30pm, 3–5pm. ⊛€4.50; ⌾guided tour €5; no charge Wed pm for EU citizens, 18 May. 🕾921 47 00 19.*

La Granja is a little Versailles at 1 192m/3 911ft, built in 1731 by Philip V, in pure nostalgia for the palace of his childhood. Philip V and his second wife, Isabel Farnese, are buried in the collegiate church.

The palace

Galleries and chambers, faced with marble or hung with velvet, are lit by chandeliers. A **Museo de Tapices**★★ (Tapestry Museum) contains principally 16C Flemish hangings, notably *(3rd gallery)* nine of the *Honours and Virtues* series and a 15C Gothic tapestry of *St Jerome* after a cartoon by Raphael.

Gardens★★

Open daily Oct and Mar 10am–6.30pm; Apr until 7pm; Nov–Feb until 6pm; May–15 Jun and Sept until 8pm; 16 Jun–Aug until 9pm. Fountains Holy Week, 30 May, 25 Jul, 25 Aug, and, water levels allowing, 5.30pm Sat–Sun and public holidays. €3.40; students and children €1.70.

The ground was levelled with explosives before the French landscape gardeners (Carlier, Boutelou) and sculptors (Dumandré, Thierry) started work. The woodland vistas are more natural, however. The chestnut trees, brought from France at great expense, are magnificent. The **fountains**★★ begin at the Neptune Basin, go on to the New Cascade (Nueva Cascada), a multicoloured marble staircase in front of the palace, and end at the Fuente de la Fama (Fame Fountain), which jets up a full 40m/131ft.

Real Fábrica de Vidrios y Cristales de La Granja (Royal Glass Factory)

Open 15 Jun–14 Sep Tue–Sun 10am–6pm, (Sat 7pm, Sun and public holidays 4pm). Closed 1, 6 Jan, 29 Sept, 25 Dec. €4. ℘921 01 07 00. www.fcnv.es.

The present building, erected in 1770 under Chalres III, contains magnificent exhibits of their contemporary glass and offers glass-blowing demonstrations.

Leave La Granja on the CL 601; it soon starts to climb steeply, with hairpin bends.

Puerto de Navacerrada★

1 860m/6 102ft. The pass, a ski resort on the borders of the two Castillas, commands a beautiful **view**★ of the Segovian plateau. A train runs to Cercedilla.

Take the M 604 at the junction on the pass.

Puerto de los Cotos

1 830m/6 004ft. The pass is a base for ski lifts. From the upper terminus at Zabala, hike in summer to the Laguna de Peñalara *(15min)*, a former glacial cirque, the Picos de Dos Hermanas (Summit of the Two Sisters) *(30min)* and Peñalara (2 429m/7 967ft), the highest point in the sierra *(45min)*. Trails for longer walks are also well marked; enquire at the information centre at Zabala.

Continue on the M 604 (the descent is gentler than the ascent).

Monasterio de Santa María de El Paular★

2km/1.2mi from Rascafría.

Guided tours (45min–1hr) Mon–Wed, Fri–Sat noon, 1pm, 5pm; Sun 1pm, 4pm, 6pm. Gregorian chant evensong daily 8pm; full sung Mass noon Sun and hols. No charge. ℘918 69 14 25.

Castilla's earliest Carthusian monastery (1390) stands in the cool Lozoya Valley. The reconstructed complex includes a hotel in a former palace. The **church** has a Flamboyant doorway by Juan Guas. There is a magnificent 15C alabaster **altarpiece**★★ illustrating the Lives of the Virgin and Christ. More than 50 canvases portraying Carthusian history, painted by Vicenzo Carduccio have recently been hung in the cloister for which they were painted in 1635. They were divided between museums around Spain at the time of the dissolution of the monasteries and were returned after extensive restoration. Close to the monastery stands the old stone Puente de Perdón (Pardon Bridge), so-called as those who walked to the gallows crossed it. Today the bridge gives access to a recreational area with summer river pools and walking paths to the sierra's foothills.

Rascafría

2km/1.2mi from El Paular

This lively small town, the capital of the Upper Lozoya valley, clustered close to an old bridge over the river, is built in traditional stone architecture. Restaurants and bars abound.

▷ *From Rascafría you can continue on the M 604 along the Lozoya valley, (32 km/20 mi) through small villages to join the A1 to Madrid, or take minor roads to Puerto de la Morcuera and Manzanares el Real.*

Puerto de la Morcuera

As you reach the pass (1 796m/5 892ft), an extensive view opens towards El Vellón reservoir. A descent through moorland brings you to the wooded Lozoya depression. The río Lozoya is a well-known trout stream.

Manzanares el Real

The **castillo**★ (◷*open Mon–Fri 10am–4pm, Sat–Sun 10am–6pm; ◉€3; ℘91 853 00 08; www.manzanareselreal.org)* was built by the Duke of Infantado in the 15C. This gem of civil architecture is well proportioned, the austerity of its lines relieved by bead mouldings on the turrets and the Plateresque decoration on the south front, possibly by Juan Guas.

▷ *The M 608 and M 607 lead to Madrid.*

ADDRESSES

STAY

⌂ **Hotel Don Jaime** – *Ochoa Ondategui, 8. ℘921 444 787. 24 rooms. ⊐ €4.* A charming Castilian house close to the aqueduct, converted into a hotel, this offers simple comfort at very reasonable prices.

⌂ **La Posada de Don Mariano** – *Mayor, 14, Pedraza ℘921 509 886. www.hoteldon mariano.com. 18 rooms. ⊐ €12.50.* Pretty bedrooms, helpful service and a terraced restaurant opening onto the Plaza Mayor make this one of the best choices among the village's hotels.

⌂ **Hotel Las Sirenas** – *Juan Bravo 30., Segovia. ℘921 46 26 63. www.hotel sirenas.com. 39 rooms.* A traditional hotel

in the old quarter with an elegant stone façade, feature staircase and an old hairdressing salon.

⌂ **Hotel La Posada de Alameda** – *Grande 34, Alameda del Valle. 6km/3.7mi NE of El Paular along the M 604 in the Sierra de Guadarrama. ℘918 69 13 37. 22 rooms. Restaurant ⌂.* This attractive rural inn started life as a dairy farm before its conversion to a modern-style hotel filled with designer furniture.

⌂ **La Casa Mudéjar** – *Isabel la Católica 8, Segovia. ℘921 46 62 50. www.lacasamudejar.com. 40 rooms. ⊐ €7.* Beautifully renovated hotel with a coffered mudéjar-style ceiling and delightful decorations. Enjoy Castilian and sephardic cuisine in the patio dining area.

⌂ **Parador la Granja** – *Los Infantes 3, Palacio de la Granja de San Idelfonso. ℘921 01 07 50. www.parador.es. 127 rooms. ⊐ €17.* Built in the 18C by Charles III, the princes' pavilion, once part of the royal palace, is now a luxury hotel with a spa and landscaped swimming pool. The largely traditional restaurant serves the town's famous *fabes* (beans), first grown in the palace gardens.

EAT

⌂ **La Fontana** – *Av Fernández Ladreda, 20. ℘921 461 806.* A tapas bar in the lower town, very popular locally, with a zinc bar and Belle Époque atmosphere in which to sample local flavours.

⌂ **Momo** – *San Agustín, 24. ℘921 463 242.* Modern European cooking in a relaxed atmosphere has given this restaurant, with its own bar for an aperitivo, a faithful local following.

⌂ **Narizotas** – *Pl. Medina del Campo 2, Segovia. ℘921 46 26 79. www.narizotas.net.* Traditional restaurant serving roast suckling pig and a tasting menu; pleasant street terrace with music.

⌂ **Asador Felipe** – *Mayo 2, Navacerrada in the Sierra de Guadarrama. ℘918 53 10 41. Closed Mon–Fri Oct–Jun.* The popular Asador Felipe is just a few metres from the Restaurante Felipe, owned by the same proprietor and in business for over 20 years. Delicious grilled meats cooked over an open fire, typically Castilian décor, and a pleasant terrace.

⌂ **Mesón de Cándido** – *Pl. del Azoguejo 5, Segovia. ℘921 42 59 11. www.mesondecandido.es.* The most famous restaurant in the province, set in a 15C house beneath the aqueduct, serving rich traditional Castilian cuisine.

Valladolid★

The former capital of Castilla and of a great empire, now a largely modern city, stands amid vineyards and cereal fields.

A BIT OF HISTORY

From the 12C, Castilla's kings frequently resided at Valladolid. Peter the Cruel married there, as did Ferdinand and Isabel; it was the birthplace of Philip IV and his sister Anne of Austria, mother of Louis XIV.

Castillo de Simancas *(11km/6.8mi SW;* ⏱*only open for study;* ☎*983 59 00 03)* – Charles V made this castle a repository for state archives. The collection is a history of Spanish administration from the 15C to the 19C.

SIGHTS

Colegio de San Gregorio

Cadenas de San Gregorio 1–2.
This is Valladolid's most impressive Isabelline building. On the sumptuous **entrance**★★★, attributed to Gil de Siloé and Simon of Cologne, fantasies from savages to interwoven thorn branches create a strongly hierarchical composition rising from the doorway.
The college is the seat of the **Museo Nacional de Escultura**★★★.

Iglesia de San Pablo (St Paul's Church)

Pl. de San Pablo 4. ⏱*Open before and after Mass.* ☞*No charge.* ☎*983 35 17 48.*
The **façade**★★★ is outstanding. The lower section, by Simon of Cologne, consists of a portal with an ogee arch all framed in a segmental arch, and above, a large rose window and two coats of arms supported by angels.

IN THE CENTRE

The historical centre of Valladolid is a blend of carefully tended plazas, lively pedestrian ways, and a pleasant park, the Campo Grande. The Plaza Mayor, the lovely and spacious focus of the city, dates from the 16C.

▶ **Population:** 318 461
Ⓖ **Michelin Map:** 575 H 15 (town plan).
🮐 **Info:** Acera de Recoletos (Pabellón de Cristal). ☎983 21 93 10. www.ava.es.
◑ **Location:** The city is at the centre of the northern section of the Spanish Meseta with AVE high-speed train service from Madrid to Valladolid-Campo Grande. 🚆Calle Recondo.
🮲🮲 **Kids:** The interactive Museo de la Ciencia.

Museo Nacional Colegio de San Gregorio★★★ (National Museum of Sculpture)

Cadenas de San Gregorio 1–2. ⏱*Open Tue–Sat 10am–2pm, 4–9pm (6pm Oct –Mar), Sun and public holidays 10am–2pm.* ⏱*Closed 1, 6 Jan, 1 May, 8 Sept, 24–25, 31 Dec.* ☞*3; no charge Sat pm, Sun am.* ☎*983 25 03 75.* http://museoesangregorio.mcu.es.
From the 16C to the 17C Valladolid was a major centre for sculpture, reflected in this museum's wonderful collection of religious statues and processional figures in polychrome wood, a material well suited to the expression of the dramatic.

On the ground floor of the Palacio de Villena, aside from paintings (including an attractive *Pietà* by Pedro Berruguete) are the magnificent sculptures of two 16C Mannerist masters: **Alonso Berruguete** (a remarkable altarpiece designed for the San Benito church) and **Juan de Juni** (*The Crucifixion* and the portentous ensemble **Burial of Christ**). Outstanding works by **Gregorio Fernández**, leading 16C exponent of Castilian Baroque, include *Passage to the Sixth Agony* and **Christ Recumbent**. There are also works of the Andalucían School (Martínez Montañés, Pedro de Mena, Alonso Cano).
On the second floor are works from the Renaissance by **Diego de Siloé**

(The Holy Family) and **Felipe Vigarny** *(Virgin and Child,* a model of grace and elegance). There is also an excellent painting by **Rubens** *(Democritus and Heraclitus).*

On the third floor are Late Baroque (18C) works, such as *St Francis of Assisi* by Salzillo and *Head of St Paul* by Juan Alonso de Villabrille y Ron. On the way down, admire a magnificent **Neapolitan nativity** of more than 180 figures.

Capilla del Colegio de San Gregorio★

Located within the Colegio.

Designed by Juan Guas, this lovely Gothic chapel with elevated choir contains an altarpiece by Berruguete, a tomb by Felipe Vigarny and carved choir stalls.

Catedral★

Arribas 1 (entry from Pl. de la Universidad). Open Tue–Fri 10am–1.30pm, 4.30–7pm, Sat–Sun and public holidays 10am–2pm. €2.50. 983 30 43 62. www.catedral-valladolid.com.

The Cathedral, commissioned in about 1580 by Philip II from Herrera, was distorted by the architect's 17C and 19C successors – in the octagonal tower, and the Baroque upper façade by Alberto Churriguera.

Never completed, the **interior** remains one of Herrera's triumphs. The altarpiece (1551) in the central apsidal chapel is by Juan de Juni.

Museo Diocesano y Catedralicio★

In the funerary chapels of the former Gothic Cathedral. Same entrance hours and ticket as the cathedral.

Note the Mudéjar cupolas in the Capilla de San Llorente. There is a **collection**★ of sculptures, paintings, silverware and ornaments.

Note two busts by Pedro de Mena *(Ecce Homo* and *Dolorosa),* two 13C tombs, two 13C Christs (one Protogothic with four nails), a dramatic *Ecce Homo* by Gregorio Fernández, the sculpture group *Lament for Christ* (c. 1500) and a 16C silver monstrance by Juan de Arfe.

Outside, note, on the Baroque University façade, sculptured and heraldic decoration by Narciso and Antonio Tomé.

Colegio Mayor de Santa Cruz

Cardenal Mendoza 1. Closed to the public. 983 42 30 32.

This lovely late 15C college is one of the first Renaissance buildings in Spain; the carved decoration at the entrance is Plateresque but the rusticated stonework is Classical. The Neoclassic balconies and windows are 18C additions.

Iglesia de Nuestra Señora de las Angustias

Angustias. 983 34 40 13.

The church, built by one of Herrera's disciples, contains Juan de Juni's masterpiece, the **Virgen de los Siete Cuchillos**★ (Virgin of the Seven Knives).

Palacio Pimentel★

Pl. San Pablo s/n; enter via Agustinas s/n.

Once a royal residence, where Charles V stayed, the building's façade has fine Plateresque details. Today it houses government offices. The meeting rooms (Salón de Plenos y Sala de Comisiones) have fine Mudéjar ceilings, which can be viewed in working hours (9am–3pm). The entrance hall, with a tiled frieze depicting key moments in Spanish history, is also left open in the afternoons.

Patio Herreriano – Museo de Arte Contemporáneo Español (Modern Spanish Art Museum)

Jorge Guillén 6. Open Tue–Fri 11am–8pm, Sat 10am–8pm, Sun 10am–3pm. Closed 25 Dec, 1 Jan. €3; Weds €1. 983 36 27 71. www.museopatio herreriano.org.

The lovely **Herreran patio**★ of the ex-monastery of San Benito and a newer annex house this collection of Spanish art since 1917.

Museo Oriental

Pas. Filipinos 7. Open Mon–Sat 4–7pm, Sun and public holidays 10am–2pm. €4. 983 30 68 00.

The museum, in a Neoclassical college (18C) designed by Ventura Rodríguez,

Castillo de Peñafiel

© Vincent Leduc/Author's Image / Photononstop

houses **Chinese art**★ (bronze, porcelain, lacquerware, coins and silk embroidery) and Philippine art with important **ivory pieces**★.

Casa de Cervantes

Rastro 2. ⊕*Open Tue–Sat 9.30am–3.30pm, Sun 10am–3pm; mid Jul–end Sep Tue–Sun 9.30am-9pm* ⊕*Closed 8 Sep and national holidays.* ⊕*€3; no charge Sun.* ✆*983 30 88 10. http://museocasacervantes.mcu.es.*
The author of *Don Quixote* lived in this house from 1603 to 1606; some of his simple furnishings remain.

BEYOND THE CENTRE
👥 Museo de la Ciencia (Science Museum)

Av. Salamanca 59. ⊕*Open Tue–Sun 10am–7pm; Jul–Aug 11am–9pm.* ⊕*€9; child €6, no charge for 1 child on Sat; planetarium €4.* ⊕*Closed national holidays.* ✆*983 14 43 00. www.museocienciavalladolid.es.*
Valladolid's interactive science museum includes a planetarium.

EXCURSIONS
Peñafiel★

▶ *55km/34mi E along the N 122.*
Peñafiel was a strongpoint along the Duero during the Reconquest and its massive 14C castle **Castillo**★ (⊕*open Oct–Mar Tue–Sun 11.30am–2pm, 4–7pm; Apr–Sept Tue–Sun 11.30am–2.30pm, 4.30 –8.30pm;* ⊕*closed 1, 6 Jan, 24–25, 31 Dec;*

⊕*€6 museum and castle, castle only €3;* ✆*983 88 11 99; www.museodelvino devalladolid.es*) is sited at the meeting point of three valleys.
Its imposing keep, reinforced by machicolated turrets houses the **Museo Provincial del Vino de Valladolid**, featuring local wines.
Also notable is the Convento de San Pablo (⊕*open daily 9.30am–2pm, 5–8pm;* 👥*guided tours available;* ⊕*no charge;* ✆*983 88 01 28*). Its church (1324) has a Mudéjar east end, with Renaissance vaulting in the 16C Capilla del Infante (Infante Chapel).

Tordesillas

▶ *30km/19mi SW along the A 62.*
The kings of Spain and Portugal signed the famous **Treaty of Tordesillas** here in 1494, dividing up the New World. **Juana the Mad (Juana la Loca)** locked herself away here on the death of her husband Philip the Fair in 1506.

Real Monasterio de Santa Clara★

▶ *Alonso del Castillo Solorzano.*
⊕*Open Tue–Sat 10am–1.30pm, 4–6.30pm, Sun and public holidays 10.30am–1.30pm, 3.30–5.30pm.*
⊕*€3.60; free Wed for EU citizens; €2.25 Arabic baths.* ✆*983 77 00 71.*
The palace built by Alfonso XI in 1350 was converted to a convent by Peter the Cruel. He installed María de Padilla here, to whom he might have been married. For María, homesick for Sevilla, he

commissioned Mudéjar decoration. The **patio**★ has multifoil and horseshoe arches, strapwork decoration and multicoloured ceramic tiles. In the **Capilla Dorada** (Gilded Chapel) are mementoes and works of art. The choir of the **church** has a particularly intricate **artesonado ceiling**★★.

Medina del Campo
◐ *54km/34mi SW along the A 62 and the A 6; 24km/15mi from Tordesillas.*
▬*Avenida de la Estación 27.*
In the Middle Ages Medina was famous for its fairs. A large market is held on Sundays. Isabel the Catholic died here in 1504.

Castillo de la Mota★
Av. del Castillo. ◐*Open Apr–Sept Mon–Sat 11am–2pm, 4–7pm, Sun and public holidays 11am–2pm; Oct–Mar daily 11am–2pm, 4–6pm.* ◐*Closed 2 Sep, 25 Dec, Jan 1.*⬤*No charge. Guided visits available.* ✆*983 80 10 24.*
Juana the Mad often stayed in this large 13C–15C castle. Cesare Borgia was imprisoned in the keep for two years.

Villa de Almenara-Puras: Museo de las Villas Romanas (Museum of Roman Villas)
◐ *51km/31.8mi S by the N 601. Turn at Almenara and continue 3km/1.9mi S.*
◐*Open Tue–Sun 10.30am–2pm, 4.30–8pm; (16 Oct–30 Dec and Mar 4–6pm).* ◐*Closed Jan 24–25, 31 Dec.*⬤*€4.* ✆*983 62 60 36. www.museodelas villasromanas.com.*
This museum features the remains of a sumptuous villa of the 4C and the underlying 3C structure. (This excursion may also take in a visit to Coca castle, 15km/8mi away.)

Castillo de Montealegre
◐ *35km/22mi NW from Valladolid along the VA 900 and the VA 912.* ◐*Open Apr–Oct Fri 5.30pm, weekends 11.30am and 5.30pm; guided visits (1hr).*⬤*€4.*
The imposing castle of Montealegre looms up above wide wheat fields. Twice besieged, by Peter the Cruel and later, in 1521, by Charles V, its stalwart

walls, 4m/13ft thick and 24m/79ft high, keep original Arab-medieval structures. In modern times it became a grain silo before restoration. Today it is home to the Centro de Interpretación del Medievo (Medieval Culture Centre).

Medina de Rioseco
◐ *40km/25mi NW along the N 601.*
The picturesque narrow main street, or **Rúa**, of this agricultural centre is lined by porticoes on wooden pillars.
The 16C Iglesia de Santa María *(Pl. de Santa María;* ◐*open Tue–Fri 10am–2pm, 4–8pm, Sat–Sun 10am–8pm; guided tours every 45min;* ◐*closed 1, 6 Jan, 25 Dec;* ⬤*€2.50;* ✆*983 72 03 19)* features a central altarpiece carved by Esteban Jordán. Other churches house Holy Week processional sculptures and religious art and the **Capilla de los Benavente**★ (Benavente Chapel, 16C) contains a 16C retable by Juan de Juni.

ADDRESSES

Soria★

This tranquil provincial capital stands on the banks of the Duero, a river that creates romantic and dramatic landscapes. The scenery and medieval atmosphere were immortalised by poet Antonio Machado. Many churches and monuments open for summer visits.

SIGHTS

Iglesia de Santo Domingo★

Pl. de los Condes de Lérida 3. Open daily 7am–9pm. No charge.

The west front of this church has two tiers of blind arcades and a richly carved **portal**★★. The church's founders were Alfonso VIII and his queen, Eleanor Plantagenet (they appear on either side of the portal), hence the French appearance. The figures on the archivolt are shown in great detail.

The scenes include the early chapters of Genesis (on the capitals of the jamb shafts), the 24 Elders of the Apocalypse playing stringed instruments, the Massacre of the Innocents, and Christ's childhood, Passion and Death (in ascending registers on the archivolt).

Palacio de los Condes de Gómara (Palace of the Counts of Gómara)

Pl. de Aguirre 3. 975 21 16 78.

The long façade, part Renaissance, part Classical, the bold tower and double patio exemplify late 16C opulence. Today the palace houses the city's law courts.

Iglesia de San Juan de Rabanera

Caballeros. Open for Mass. 15 Jul–15 Sept Tue–Sun 11am–2pm, 5–7pm. No charge.

The Romanesque portal taken from a ruined church dedicated to St Nicolas recalls the saint's life in the capitals on the slender columns on the right and on the tympanum. The decoration at the east end shows Byzantine and Gothic influences. Crucifixes inside are Romanesque over the altar and Baroque in the north transept.

▶ **Population:** 39 078

◔ **Michelin Map:** 575 G 22.

▤ **Info:** Medinaceli 2. 975 21 20 52. www.ayto-soria.org.

▶ **Location:** Soria lies in NE Spain at an altitude of 1 050m/3 445ft on a plateau buffeted by the winds of the Meseta. Calle Carretera Madrid.

Museo Numantino (Numancia Museum)

Pas. del Espolón 8. Open Tue–Sat 10am–2pm, 5-8pm (Oct–Jun 4–7pm), Sun and public holidays 10am–2pm. Closed 1 Jan, 26 and 29 Jun, 24–25 and 31 Dec. €1.20; no charge Sat–Sun, under 18s. 975 22 13 97.

The collections in the recently restored museum include an outstanding range of artefacts from Celt-Iberian necropolises and coloured pottery from Numancia.

Concatedral de San Pedro

Pl. de San Pedro. Open Sat 11am–2pm, 4–7pm, Sun 11am–2pm. No charge.

The 16C Gothic Cathedral is light and spacious; the **cloisters**★ are older, with three Romanesque galleries. The capitals have been delicately re-sculpted in a pure Romanesque style that recalls Santo Domingo de Silos.

Monasterio de San Juan de Duero★★

Pas. de las Ánimas. Open Tue–Sat 10am–2pm, 5–8pm (Oct–Jun 4–7pm), Sun and public holidays 10am–2pm. €0.60; no charge Sat–Sun. 975 23 02 18.

The monastery founded by the Hospitallers of St John of Jerusalem is in a rustic setting along the Duero. Only the graceful gallery arcading, with four different orders, remains of the 12C–13C **cloisters**★. The intersecting, overlapping arches owe much to Moorish art. The church contains a small lapidary museum. Two small chambers with beautiful historiated capitals stand at the entrance to the apse; the ciborium effect is unusual, as one might find in an Orthodox church.

Ermita de San Saturio

Pas. San Saturio. 1.3km/0.8mi S of N 122. Open Tue–Sat 10.30am–2pm, 4.30–7.30pm (6.30pm Nov–Mar, 8.30pm Jul–Aug), Sun 10.30am–2pm. No charge. 975 18 07 403.

A shaded path beside the Duero leads to the cave where the holy man sat in meditation. The 18C octagonal chapel is built into the rock.

DRIVING TOUR

SIERRA DE URBIÓN★★

Roads are liable to be blocked by snow Nov–May.

This hilly green part of the Sistema Ibérico mountain range rises to 2 228m/ 7 310ft. Streams rush through pinewoods and meadows; one is the source of the Duero, one of Spain's longest rivers *(910km/565mi).*

Laguna Negra de Urbión★★

53km/33mi NW of Soria via the N 234–allow about 1hr.

At Cidones bear right towards Vinuesa; after 18km/11mi head for Montenegro de Cameros. After 8km/5mi bear left onto the Laguna road (9km/5.6mi).

The **road**★★, after skirting the Cuerdo del Pozo reservoir *(embalse)*, continues through pines to **Laguna Negra** (alt 1 700m/5 600ft), a small glacial lake at the foot of a semicircular cliff over which cascade two waterfalls.

Laguna Negra de Neila★★

About 86km/53mi NW of Soria via the N 234.

At Abejar turn right towards Molinos de Duero; continue to Quintana de la Sierra then turn right for Neila (12km/7mi), then left for Huerta de Arriba; 2km/1mi on the left is the road to Laguna Negra.

The **road**★★ through picturesque countryside commands changing views of the valley and Sierra de la Demanda. The lake lies at 2 000m/6 561ft.

EXCURSIONS
Monasterio de Santa María de Huerta★★

The monastery stands close to the A 2 highway linking Madrid and Zaragoza (131km/82mi NE). It is 85km/ 53mi SE of Soria via the SC 20 A 15 and CL 116. Allow about 1 hr for the visit. Open Mon–Sat 10am– 1.30pm, 3.45–6pm, Sun and public holidays 11.30am–12.30pm, 3.45–6pm. €2. 975 32 70 02. www.monasteriohuerta.org.

In 1144, a Cistercian community came to this border region between Castilla and Aragón. Monks settled in Huerta in 1162. The monastery is entered through a 16C **triumphal arch**.

Cloisters and Claustro Herreriano (Herreran Cloisters)

16C–17C. The buildings around the cloisters are the monks' living quarters.

Claustro de los Caballeros★ (Knights' Cloisters)

13C–16C. The cloisters owe their name to the many knights buried there. The arches at ground level are elegant, pointed and purely Gothic; above, the 16C gallery, copied from Peñaranda del Duero's's Palacio de la Avellaneda, has all the exuberance and imagination of the Plateresque. The decorative medallions are of Prophets, Apostles and Spanish kings.

Sala de los Conversos (Lay Brothers' Hall)

12C. This is divided by stout pillars, crowned with stylised capitals. The **kitchen** is famed for its monumental central chimney.

The **Refectorio**★★ (refectory), a masterpiece of 13C Gothic, rises 15m/49ft above the 35m/114.8ft long hall and has a wonderful rose window. A beautiful staircase, its arches on slender columns, leads to the **reader's lectern**.

Iglesia

The church has been restored to its original state although the royal chapel has kept sumptuous Churrigueresque decoration. Between the narthex and the aisles is an intricate 18C wrought-iron screen. The **coro alto** (choir) is beautifully decorated with Renaissance panelling and woodwork. The Talavera *azulejos* on the floor are also worthy of note.

El Burgo de Osma★

56km/35mi SW of Soria and 139km/ 87mi SE of Burgos. 🏛 *Plaza Mayor 9. 975 36 01 16. www.burgosma.es.*

This attractive town with porticoed streets and squares has long been a bishop's seat. Its notable buildings include the San Agustín hospital and the imposing **Cathedral★** *(Pl. de la Catedral; open Tue–Sun 10.30am–1pm, 4–6pm (7pm Jul–Sep), guided visit (1 hour); no charge; 975 34 09 62).* This Gothic sanctuary was built after a Cluniac monk, Don Pedro de Osma, vowed to replace the former Cathedral.

The east end, transept and chapter house were built in the 13C; the late Gothic cloisters and chancel received Renaissance embellishments. The sacristy, royal chapel and 72m/236ft belfry are from the 18C.

There is magnificent Gothic decoration on the late 13C **south portal**.

The interior is remarkable for the elevation of the nave, the delicate wrought-iron screens (16C) by Juan de Francés, the **high altar retable** by Juan de Juni, and the 16C white marble **pulpit** and **trascoro altarpiece**.

The 13C polychrome limestone **tomb of San Pedro de Osma★** is in the west transept. In the **museum** are a richly illustrated 1086 **Beatus** and a 12C manuscript with the signs of the zodiac.

Returning to Soria *(25km/15.5mi NE on the N 122)* **Calatañazor** sits just off the main road. Time has stood still in its steep, stone-paved streets and castle ruins, where you can view the plains.

Peñaranda de Duero★

47km/29mi W of El Burgo de Osma along the N 122 and BU 924.

The small Castilian town is dominated by the ruins of its castle.

Around the 15C pillory in the **Plaza Mayor★** (square) are half-timbered houses on stone piers. To one side is the **Palacio de Avellaneda★** *(open Tue–Sun 10am–2pm, 4–7.30pm (Oct–Mar 3–6pm; last entry 1 hour before closing); guided tours every hour (30min); no charge; 947 55 20 13),* a palace with a Renaissance façade. A patio with a two-tier gallery, a grand staircase and chambers with **artesonado ceilings★** make this one of the finest Renaissance residences in Spain. An 18C pharmacy, the **Botica de Ximeno**, with books and instruments, may also be visited by arrangment with the tourist office.

Cañón del Río Lobos

15km/10mi N on the SO 920 (best access from the south). Centro de Interpretación del Parque Natural. 975 36 35 64.

The landscape along this 25km/15.5mi stretch of the Río Lobos is riddled with caves, depressions and chasms.

Castillo de Gormaz

14km/8.7mi S on the SO 160. 975 35 05 60.

These 10C Moorish castle ruins, overlooking the Duero, are the largest in Europe (446m/1 463ft in length, 26 towers).

Berlanga del Duero

28km/17.4mi SE on C 116 and SO 104.

Berlanga, below its massive 15C castle, was a strongpoint along the Duero frontier. There are guided tours of the Gothic **Colegiata** *(ring in advance; 975 34 30 57).* Some 8km/5mi southeast in **Casillas de Berlanga** is the **Iglesia de San Baudelio de Berlanga** *(open Wed–Sun 10am–2pm 5–9pm (Nov–Mar 3.30–6pm; Apr–May 4–7pm; Jun–Aug 5–9pm); €0.60; 975 22 13 97),* an unusual 11C Mozarabic chapel, its roof supported by a massive pillar.

All was covered with 12C frescoes, sold in the mid 20C, though their hunting scenes and geometric patterns can still be made out.

The southern *meseta*, which stretches south from Madrid through Castilla-La Mancha's flatlands, is a vast tableland slightly tilted towards the west, watered by two large rivers – the Tajo (Tagus), which cuts a deep gorge through the limestone Alcarria region, and the sluggish Guadiana.

The word La Mancha comes from the Arab *manxa* meaning dry land, which is particularly apparent in summer. Despite this there is considerable cultivation with wind-ruffled cereal fields, stretches of saffron turned purple in the flowering season, and serried ranks of olives and vines. Madrid's traditional table wines come from here, and the area is also renowned for its manchego cheese. La Mancha's most famous personality is Don Quixote, created by Cervantes 400 years ago. A Quixote trail leads in his (fictional) footsteps and includes (real) windmills and a glimpse of rural life here in past towns. Even today, small towns look more like large villages in which the arcaded Plaza Mayor (main square) is still the hub of activity and gossip.

Highlights

1. Gazing upon **Toledo** from the other side of the Tajo (p188)

2. The iconic "Don Quixote windmills" at **Consuegra** (p190)

3. The Museum of Abstract Art, set in a *casa colgada* in **Cuenca** (p197)

4. The spectacular natural formations of the **Serranía de Cuenca** (p198)

5. The sculptures in the cathedral and its museum at **Sigüenza** (p201)

Toledo and West

Toledo is the jewel of Castilla-La Mancha. It is surrounded, moat-like, on three sides by the Tajo, with parts of its city wall and gateways still intact, little changed in appearance over the centuries. Until 1560, when the capital moved to Madrid (70km/43.5mi north), the city was the nerve centre of not only Spain but of a burgeoning empire.

In the following years it declined rapidly and slid into the political backwaters. A happy circumstance of this was that "progress" bypassed Toledo, and its old town remained largely untouched. Today it is UNESCO World Heritage-listed with many very tangible reminders of its multi-faith past. The old city part of Talavera de la Reina, famous for the ceramic work which decorates its palaces, mansions and chapels, is well worth a visit. Nearby Oropesa is a charming village, home to a fine parador.

The South

The flat landscapes of the south conjure up the archetypal Don Quixote images of La Mancha. But there are surprises here too: Belmonte, with a fine 15C fortress and Almagro, once the headquarters of the Military Order of the Knights of Calatrava.

Cuenca city and province

This UNESCO World Heritage city's hanging houses, old town and superb Museum of Abstract Art place Cuenca high on most visitors' itineraries. Around the town a limestone plateau pitted with swallow-holes (*torcas*) and cut by gorges (*hoces*) makes for a spectacular and curious touring landscape.

Northeast

With fewer than 6 000 inhabitants, charming Sigüenza is remarkable for two imposing buildings set amid its medieval streets. The cathedral, which features some outstanding sculptures, would be more at home in a major metropolis. The mighty fortress was once a Moorish alcázar, then a Christian stronghold, home to most of the Castilian monarchs; today it is a parador, welcoming visitors who are happy to leave the beaten track.

Guadalajara is a more prosaic town, but still worth a visit for its late 15C Palace of the Duke of Infantado.

Toledo★★★

Golden Toledo rises dramatically on a granite eminence encircled by a steep ravine of the Tajo (Tagus). It is as spectacular in setting as it is rich in history, buildings and art. Every corner has a tale to tell. Taken as a whole, the city reflects a brilliant intertwining of east and west, of Christian, Jewish and Moorish cultures during the Middle Ages.

THE CITY TODAY

On busy days Toledo can resemble something of a medieval theme park with large groups of visitors on day trips from Madrid clogging up its narrow streets. In shop windows in the main streets are garish displays of Toledan steel, once the deadliest weaponry in the world, wielded by Spanish heroes from El Cid and the Conquistadores. Nowadays it is marketed as the "official" arms of epic films such as *Lord of the Rings*. Whenever you visit try to stay the night and do your exploration early (before the groups arrive) and late (after they have gone). Don't expect much nightlife as Toledo after dark is a fairly staid place.

A BIT OF HISTORY

Roman town to Holy Roman city – The Romans fortified the strategic settlement into a town they named Toletum. It passed into the hands of the barbarians, and in the 6C to the Visigoths, who made it a royal seat until they were defeated by the Moors at Guadelete in 711.

After the revolt of the taifas in 1012, Toledo was capital of an independent kingdom. In 1085 it was conquered by Alfonso VI, who soon moved his capital from León. Alfonso VII was crowned emperor in Toledo, hence the title of imperial city. The city of Moors, Jews and Christians began to prosper.

The Catholic Monarchs gave it the Monastery of St John but lost interest after they reconquered Granada in 1492. Emperor Charles V had the Alcázar rebuilt. In his reign the city took part in the Comuneros' Revolt led by **Juan de**

- ▶ **Population:** 80 810
- ⊙ **Michelin Map:** 576 M 17 (town plan) – map 121 Alrededores de Madrid – Castilla-La Mancha (Toledo) .
- 🛈 **Info:** Puerta de Bisagra. ℰ 925 22 08 43; Plaza del Ayuntamiento 1, ℰ 925 25 40 30. www.toledo-turismo.com.
- ▷ **Location:** Toledo is 71km/44mi SW of Madrid.
- 🅿 **Parking:** Try to park below the centre of the city, and walk or take a taxi up.
- ⊛ **Don't Miss:** El Greco's masterpiece, *The Burial of the Count of Orgaz*.
- ⊙ **Timing:** Monumental Toledo is compact. Walk around for an overview, then return for a visit to the sites of most interest.

Padilla, a Toledan. This was one reason why, in 1561, Philip II named Madrid as Spain's capital, relegating Toledo to the role of spiritual centre.

Toledo and the Jews – In the 12C the Jewish community numbered 12 000. **Saint Ferdinand III** (1217–1252) encouraged diversity which brought about a cultural flowering, and the city developed into a great intellectual forum. **Alfonso X the Wise** (1252–1284) gathered a court of learned Jews and established the *School of Translation*. In 1355 a pogrom was instigated by supporters of Henry IV of Trastamara. After repeated attacks, the Jews were expelled in 1492.

Mudéjar art in Toledo – The Mudéjar style established itself in Toledo after the Reconquest of the city, in palaces (Taller del Moro), synagogues (El Tránsito, Santa María la Blanca) and churches. Brick was widely used.

Moorish stuccowork, *artesonado* and *azulejos* became commonplace. In the 13C and 14C, most Toledan churches were given Romanesque semicircular **east ends**, blind arcades took on variations unknown elsewhere, and **belfries** were built square and decorated until they resembled minarets. The edifices often have a nave and two aisles – a Visigothic influence – Roman tripartite apses and Moorish wood vaulting.

SIGHTS
Catedral★★★

Pl. del Ayuntamiento. ⏱*Open Mon–Sat 10am–6.30pm, Sun and public holidays 2–6pm. Open 23 Jun and 15 Aug from mid-afternoon* ☞*€7.* ☎*925 22 22 41. www.catedralprimad.es.*

The Cathedral dominates the **Plaza del Ayuntamiento**. Construction began in the reign of Ferdinand III (St Ferdinand) in 1227. Unusually, the design was French Gothic, but as building continued until the end of the 15C, its architecture came to reflect Spanish Gothic. Despite late additions, the cathedral is outstanding for its decoration and works of art.

Exterior

The **Puerta del Reloj** (Clock Doorway), in the north wall, from the 13C, was modified in the 19C.

The **main façade** is pierced by three tall 15C portals; the upper registers were completed in the 16C and 17C. The central **Puerta del Perdón** (Pardon Doorway) is crowded with statues and crowned with a tympanum illustrating the Virgin Mary presenting the 7C bishop of Toledo with a chasuble.

The harmonious tower is 15C; the dome was designed by El Greco's son in the 17C. In the south wall is the 15C **Puerta de los Leones** (Lion Doorway) designed by Master Hanequin of Brussels and decorated by Juan Alemán. The Neoclassical portal is from 1800.

▷ *Enter through the Puerta del Mollete, left of the west front which leads you into the cloister.*

Interior

The size and sturdy character of the cathedral, with five unequal aisles and great pillars, are striking. Wonderful stained glass (1418–1561) colours the windows; magnificent wrought-iron grilles enclose the chancel, *coro* and chapels.

Capilla Mayor

The chancel, the most sumptuous section, was enlarged in the 16C.

The immense polychrome **retable**★★, carved in detail in Flamboyant style with the Life of Christ, is awe-inspiring.

The silver statue of the Virgin at the predella dates from 1418. The Plateresque marble tomb of Cardinal Mendoza on the left is by Covarrubias.

Coro

14C high reliefs and wrought-iron enclosed chapels form the perimeter of the choir, itself closed by an elegant iron screen (1547). The lower parts of the 15C and 16C **choir stalls**★★★ were carved by Rodrigo Alemán to recall the conquest of Granada; the alabaster 16C upper parts, by Berruguete *(left)* and Felipe Vigarny *(right)* portray Old Testament figures.

The central low relief, the Transfiguration, is also by Berruguete. The style of his work creates the impression of movement. Two organs and a Gothic eagle lectern complete the set. The 14C marble *White Virgin* is French.

Girola

The double ambulatory, surmounted by an elegant triforium with multifoil arches, is bordered by seven apsidal chapels separated by small square chapels. The vaulting is a geometrical wonder.

There is little room to step back for a good look at the **Transparente**★, the contentious but famous work by Narciso Tomé which forms a Baroque island in the Gothic church.

Illuminated through an opening in the ambulatory roof (made to allow light to fall on the tabernacle), the *Transparente* appears as an ornamental framework of angels and swirling clouds and rays surrounding the Virgin and the Last Supper. Elsewhere, in the **Capilla de San Ildefonso** (Chapel of San Ildefonso), the central tomb of Cardinal Gil de Albornoz (14C) is the most notable.

0   40 m

Capilla de los
Reyes Nuevos
Sixto   Ramón   Parro

Sala Capitular

Capilla
de Santiago
Capilla de
San Ildefonso

Roperia
Pérez

Girola

Cloakroom

Transparente ★

Sacristia
Maestro

Retablo ★★

CAPILLA MAYOR
Llana

Puerta del Reloj
CRUCERO
Puerta de
los Leones

Capilla de
San Pedro
CORO

Capilla de
San Blas
Puerta de
Sta Catalina

Silleria ★★★
Puerta

CLAUSTRO
Puerta Llana

Tesoro
Capilla Mozárabe
Puerta del Mollete
Puerta
del Perdón

Plaza del Ayuntamiento

Sala Capitular (Chapter House)

The antechamber has an impressive Mudéjar ceiling and two Plateresque carved walnut wardrobes. Remarkable Mudéjar stucco doorways and carved Plateresque panels precede the chapter house with its multicoloured **Mudéjar ceiling**★. Below frescoes by Juan de Borgoña are portraits of former archbishops including two by Goya.

Sacristía (Sacristy)

The first gallery, its vaulted ceiling painted by Lucas Jordán, includes **paintings by El Greco**★ of which **El Expolio** (The Disrobing of Christ, c. 1577) is outstanding. It sets an exalted personality against swirling robes to establish Baroque movement.

Other works include a remarkable portrait of Pope Paul III by Titian, a Holy Family by Van Dyck, a Mater Dolorosa by Morales and the Taking of Christ by Goya, which displays his skill in composition, use of light and in portraying individuals in a crowd. Pedro de Mena's (17C) famous sculpture, St Francis of Assisi, is in a glass case. In the vestry are portraits by Velázquez (Cardinal Borja), Van Dyck (Pope Innocent XI) and Ribera.

The old laundry (ropería) contains liturgical objects dating back to the 15C. The **Nuevas Salas del Museo Catedralicio** (Cathedral Museum's New Galleries; c/ Cardenal Cisneros; ⊘open same hours as cathedral; ⊘closed 1 Jan, Corpus Christi, 15 Aug, 25 Dec; €4.95) displays works by Caravaggio, El Greco, Bellini and Morales.

Tesoro (Treasury)

A Plateresque doorway by Covarrubias opens into the chapel under the tower. Beneath a Mudéjar ceiling note the splendid 16C silver-gilt **mon-**

strance★★ by Enrique de Arfe, weighing 180kg/392lb and 3m/10ft high, paraded at Corpus Christi. The pyx at its centre is fashioned from gold brought by Christopher Columbus.

Capilla Mozárabe (Mozarabic Chapel)

The chapel beneath the dome was built by Cardinal Cisneros (16C) to celebrate Mass according to the Visigothic or Mozarabic ritual which had been threatened with abolition in the 11C.

Claustro (Cloisters)

The simplicity of the 14C lower gallery contrasts with the bold murals by Bayeu of the Lives of Toledan Saints (Santa Eugenia and San Ildefonso).

⚡ WALKING TOUR

CENTRE OF OLD TOLEDO★★★

Allow 1 day – see town plan.

There is something to see and enjoy at every step in Toledo.

Ringing the square before the Cathedral are the 18C **Palacio Arzobispal** (Archbishop's Palace), the 17C **Ayuntamiento** (Town Hall) with classical façade and the 14C **Audiencia** (Law Courts).

Iglesia de Santo Tomé

Pl. del Conde. ⏱*Open daily mid 10am–7pm (5.45pm mid–Oct to Feb). Last ticket 30min before closing.* ✎€2.30; no charge Wed from 4pm for EU residents. ☏925 25 60 98. www.santotome.org.

The church, like that of San Román, has a distinctive 14C Mudéjar tower. Inside is El Greco's famous painting **The Burial of the Count of Orgaz**★★★ executed in about 1586. The interment is transformed by the miraculous appearance of St Augustine and St Stephen. Figures in the lower register are portraits of personalities of the day; the sixth from the left is said to be El Greco. Above, Christ prepares to receive the soul of the count.

Casa-Museo de El Greco★ (El Greco Museum)

Samuel Leví. ⏱*Tue–Sat 9.30am–8pm (Oct–Mar 6.30pm), Sun and hols 10am –3pm.* ✎€3. ☏925 22 40 46. http://museodelgreco.mcu.es.com.

In 1585, El Greco moved into a house similar to this one. In what would have been the artist's workroom is a signed *St Francis and Brother León*.

On the first floor are an interesting *View and Plan of Toledo* and the complete

Old Toledo and the Alcázar

©Turespaña

series of individual portraits of the Apostles and Christ (later and more mature than those in the cathedral).

The **capilla** on the ground floor, with a multicoloured Mudéjar ceiling, has a picture in the altarpiece of *St Bernardino of Siena* by El Greco.

Sinagoga del Tránsito★★ (Synagogue of El Transito)

Samuel Leví. ⏱*Opening hours as for Casa-Museo de El Greco, Sun and public hols 10am–3pm.* ⏱*Closed 1 Jan, 24, 25, 31 Dec.* ⌨*€3.* ✆*925 22 36 65. www.museosefardi.net.*

Of the ten synagogues that once stood in the Jewish quarter (Judería), only this and Santa María la Blanca remain. It was financed in the 14C by Samuel Ha-Levi, treasurer to King Peter the Cruel. In 1492 it was converted into a church.

Unpretentious outside, it is covered inside with amazing **Mudéjar decoration**★★.

Above the rectangular hall is an *artesonado* ceiling of cedarwood; just below are 54 multifoil arches, some blind, others pierced with delicate stone tracery. Below again runs a frieze, decorated at the east end with *mocárabes* and on the walls with inscriptions in Hebrew to the glory of Peter the Cruel, Samuel Ha-Levi and the God of Israel. In the east wall, inscriptions describe the synagogue's foundation. The women's balcony opens from the south wall.

The adjoining rooms, once a Calatrava monastery, are the **Museo Sefardí** *(Sephardic Museum;* ⏱*open Mar–Nov Tue–Sat 10am–2pm, 4–9pm; Dec–Feb Tue–Sat 10am–2pm, 4–6pm, Sun and public holidays 10am–2pm;* ⏱*Closed 1 Jan, 1 May, Corpus Christi, 24, 25, 31 Dec;* ⌨*€2.40, no charge Sat afternoons, Sun mornings, 18 May, 12 Oct, 6 Dec)* displaying tombs, robes, costumes and books. Several are gifts from descendants of Jews expelled in 1492.

Casa Museo Victorio Macho★

Pl. de Victor Macho. ⏱*Open Mon–Sat 10am–7pm, Sun 10am–3pm.* ⏱*Closed 1 Jan, 25 Dec.* ⌨*€3.* ✆*925 284 225. www.realfundaciontoledo.es.*

This impressively sited exhibition space, with views over the gorge of the River Tagus and San Martín bridge, occupies the home of avant-garde artist Victorio Macho, who went into exile in Peru on the outbreak of the Spanish Civil War. Alongside works on temporary show are numerous pieces by Macho, including an impressive portrait of his brother.

Sinagoga de Santa María La Blanca★

Reyes Católicos 4. ⏱ *Open daily 10am– 7pm (5.30pm Oct–Nov).* ⏱ *Closed 1 Jan, 25 Dec.* ⌨*€2.30.* ✆*925 22 72 57.*

This was the principal synagogue in Toledo in the late 12C. In 1405 it was given to the Knights of Calatrava as a church. Subsequent modifications incredibly left the Almohad-style nave untouched with five tiered aisles separated by octagonal pillars supporting horseshoe-shaped arches. The whitewashed pillars set off intricately carved **capitals**★ adorned with pine cones and strapwork. The polychrome wood altarpiece is 16C.

Monasterio de San Juan de los Reyes★ (St John of the Kings Monastery)

Reyes Católicos 17. ⏱*Open daily Apr– Oct 10am–7pm; Nov–Mar 10am–6pm.* ⌨*€1.90; free for EU citizens, and Wed 3.30–5.45pm.* ✆*925 22 38 02.*

The Franciscan monastery commemorates the victory over the Portuguese at Toro in 1476. The overall style is Isabelline: it fuses Flamboyant Gothic with Mudéjar and Renaissance art. The exterior is somewhat austere, relieved by pinnacles and a stone balustrade. Covarrubias designed the north portal, includ-ing in the decoration the figure of John the Baptist. The famous fetters depicted were taken from Christian prisoners freed from the Muslims.

Claustro

The cloisters are attractive with Flamboyant bays and the Plateresque upper galleries (1504) crowned with a pinnacled balustrade. The upper gallery has Mudéjar *artesonado* vaulting.

TOLEDO

0   200 m
0   200 yds

Iglesia

The church, burned by the French in 1808, has a typically Isabelline single wide aisle; at the crossing are a dome and a lantern. The **sculptured decoration**★ by Flemish architect Juan Guas provides a delicate stone tracery *(crestería)* which at the transept forms twin tribunes for

B ④ 🐂 ① **MADRID** ① **C**

HOSPITAL DE TAVERA

Av. de Los

Duques de Lerma

Honda

LAS COVACHUELAS

Tavera

Cardenal

PASEO DE MERCHÁN

Honda

P

PARQUE DE SAFONT

CIUDAD REAL ARANJUEZ ⌨

TAJO

Puente de Azarquiel

② **VALDEPEÑAS**

Pl. de Alfonso VI

Pta antigua de Bisagra

Puerta Nueva de Bisagra

LA ANTEQUERUELA

Real del Arrabal

Paseo de la Rosa

ARABES ④

Santiago del Arrabal

Subida Granja

Puerta del Sol

G. Lobo

J

Puente de Alcántara

PTA DEL VALMARDON

Cristo de la Luz

Núñez de Arce

Silleria

Venancio González

MUSEO DE STA CRUZ

Castillo de S. Servando

Alfileritos

San Vicente

P

⌨

Cadenas

Armas

CONVENTO DE LA CONCEPCIÓN

Santa Fe

Rónda de Juanelo

Esteban Illán

POL

10

Pl. de S. Vicente

Pl. de Zocodover

G

Plata

Card. Lorenzana

Cervantes

S. Román

S. ROMÁN

Comercio

San Ildefonso

Hombre de Palo

Toledo de Ohio

Pte Nuevo de Alcántara

Pedro

Alfonso XII

Pl.Padre Mariana

Tornerías

Circunvalación

Trav. Campana

Trinidad

Claustro

T

Alcázar

AUDITORIUM

B

Pl. del Ayuntamiento

Posada de la Hermandad

POLIDEPORTIVO

P

P

né

CATEDRAL

El Salvador

Cardenal Cisneros

Pl. S. Justo

Taller del Moro

P

Audiencia **Ayuntamiento**

Ramón Parro

Cuesta San Justo

Cabestreros

Carretera

de

Pl. del Consistorio

Ave. María

Pozo

Amargo

TAJO

Sola

San Torcuato

de

San

Paseo

CERRO DEL BU

Carreras

de

San Sebastián

del

Tajo

CIRCUNVALACIÓN ⌨

ERMITA DE LA VIRGEN DEL VALLE

| Palacio Arzobispal | **B** |
| Portada de S. Clemente | **K** |

B **C**

Ferdinand and Isabel. The transept walls are faced with a frieze of royal escutcheons, supported by an eagle, symbol of St John.

Not far away are a Visigothic palace and the **Puerta del Cambrón** (hawthorn gateway; *pas. de Recaredo*), once part of the town perimeter, rebuilt in the 16C.

Return to San Juan and take Ángel to Santo Tomé, then take the picturesque Travesía de Campana alley to the small Pl. del Padre Juan de Mariana. Cross the plaza past the monumental Baroque façade of the Iglesia de San Ildefonso and that of the Iglesia de San Pedro.

Iglesia de San Román: Museo de los Concilios y de la Cultura Visigoda★ (Museum of the Councils of Toledo and Visigothic Culture)

San Román. ○*Open Tue–Sat 10am–2pm, 4–6.30pm, Sun and public holidays 10am–1.45pm.* ○*Closed 1 Jan, 1 May, 25 Dec.* ▦€0.60. ℘925 22 78 72.

The 13C Mudéjar church, at the summit of Toledo's old town, has a tower resembling Santo Tomé's.

Aisles are divided by horseshoe arches. The walls are covered in 13C frescoes of the raising of the dead, the Evangelists and, on the far wall, one of the Councils of Toledo. The apse was modified in the 16C with a cupola by Covarrubias. Note the 18C **altarpiece**.

The collections include fine bronze jewellery and copies of Visigothic votive crowns decorated with cabochon stones from Guarrazar (originals in the Museo Arqueológico, Madrid). On the walls are steles, fragments from capitals, balustrades from the choir and pilasters.

In Plaza de San Vicente, note the Mudéjar east end of the **Iglesia de San Vicente**. Continue up Calle de la Plata with its houses with carved entrances.

Plaza de Zocodover

This bustling triangular square is the heart of Toledo. It was rebuilt after the Civil War as was the Arco de la Sangre (Arch of Blood), which opens onto calle de Cervantes.

Museo de Santa Cruz★★ (Santa Cruz Museum)

Miguel de Cervantes 3. ○*Open Mon and Sat 10am–6.30pm, Tue–Sat 10am–6.30pm, Sun and public holidays 10am–2pm.* ○*Closed 1 Jan, 1 May, 25 Dec.* ▦*No charge.* ℘925 22 14 02.

This fine group of Plateresque hospital buildings was begun by Enrique Egas and completed by Covarrubias, who was responsible for the **façade★★**.

On the gateway tympanum Cardinal Mendoza, the hospital's sponsor, kneels before the Cross supported by St Helena, St Peter, St Paul and two pages; on the arches are the cardinal virtues. Above, two windows frame a high relief of St Joachim and St Anne.

The museum is known for its **16C and 17C pictures★** including 18 paintings by **El Greco★**. The size of the nave and transept – forming a two-tiered Greek cross – and the beautiful coffered ceilings are outstanding.

Ground floor

The first part of the nave contains 16C Flemish tapestries, **primitive paintings★**, and the *Astrolabios* or *Zodiac* tapestry, woven in Flanders in the mid-15C for Toledo cathedral, still strikingly original. Note, in the south transept, the *Ascension* and the *Presentation of Mary in the Temple* by the Maestro de Sijena. In the second part of the nave hangs the immense pennant flown by Don Juan of Austria at the Battle of Lepanto. The north transept contains a *Christ at the Column* by Morales.

First floor

A staircase leads to the upper gallery of the north transept with **paintings by El Greco★**. There are gentle portraits of the Virgin and St Veronica as well as a version of the *Expolio*, later than the original in the cathedral.

Most famous is the late **Altarpiece of the Assumption★**, from 1613, with Baroque stylings and notably elongated figures. The south transept contains a *Holy Family at Nazareth* by Ribera, the specialist in tenebrism who here showed himself a master of light and delicacy.

In the first part of the nave are 16C Brussels tapestries showing the life of Alexander the Great; and 17C statues from the studio of Pascual de Mena.

The **Plateresque patio★** has bays with elegant lines complemented by the openwork balustrade and enhanced by Mudéjar vaulting and by the magnificent **staircase**★ by Covarrubias. Adjoining rooms house a museum of archaeology and decorative arts.

WITHIN THE CITY WALLS
Alcázar (Museo del Ejército)
Cuesta de Carlos V 2. ☏ *925 238 800. www.ejercito.mde.es.*
The Alcázar, destroyed and rebuilt so many times, is now the national army museum. Emperor Charles V converted the 13C fortress, of which El Cid had been the first governor, into an imperial residence. The work was entrusted to Covarrubias (1538–1551) and then Herrera, who designed the austere south front.

An eight-week seige in 1936 left the fortress in ruins. The Falangist commander defending it allowed his son to be shot rather than surrender.

The Alcázar is restored to its appearance at the time of Charles V. In 2010, after renovation, it opened as an ambitious army museum in which 6,500 exhibits tell the story of Spain's complex military past, so often at the centre of the country's life and even at the heart of government.

Posada de la Hermandad (House of the Brotherhood)
Hermandad 6.
This 15C building was once a prison.

Puerta del Sol
Carretas.
The Sun Gate in the second perimeter, rebuilt in the 14C, is a fine Mudéjar construction with two circumscribing horseshoe arches. At the centre a later low relief shows the Virgin presenting San Ildefonso with a chasuble.

At the top, the brick decoration of blind arcading incorporates an unusual sculpture of two girls bearing the head of the chief *alguacil* (officer of justice), allegedly a rapist, on a salver.

Mezquita del Cristo de la Luz (Christ of the Light Mosque)
Cta. de Carmelitas Descalzas. ⏱*Open Mon–Fri 10am–2pm, 3.30–6.40pm (5.40pm mid-Oct–mid-Mar), Sat–Sun 10am–6.45pm (5.45pm mid-Oct–mid-Mar).* ✆*€2.30.* ☏ *925 25 41 91.*
This 12C Mudéjar church succeeded a mosque which in turn replaced a Visigothic church. It is named for the miraculous appearance in a mosque of a lamp illuminating a Crucifix when Alfonso VI first entered Toledo. Arches of different periods, intersecting blind arcades, and a line of horizontal brickwork surmounted by Cufic characters make up the façade. Inside, Visigothic pillars support superimposed arches like those in the mosque in Córdoba. Nine domes, each different, rise from square bays.

The gardens lead to the Puerta del Sol. Enjoy the panorama from the top.

Iglesia de Santiago del Arrabal (St James on the Outskirts)
Real del Arrabal. ⚿*Closed to the public.* ☏ *925 22 06 36.*
San Vicente Ferrer is said to have preached from the Gothic Mudéjar pulpit of this beautifully restored church. Discreet visits may be made before or after evening mass.

Puerta Nueva de Bisagra (New Bisagra Gate)
Puerta de Bisagra.
The gate was rebuilt by Covarrubias in 1550 and enlarged under Philip II.
Massive round crenellated towers, facing the Madrid road, flank a giant imperial crest.

Puerta Antigua de Bisagra (Old Bisagra Gate)
Pas. Recaredo.
Alfonso VI entered Toledo in triumph through this Moorish gate in 1085.

Museo Taller del Moro

Taller del Moro. ⏰*Open Tue–Sat 10am–2pm, 4–6.30pm, Sun and public holidays 10am–2pm.* ⊷*No charge.* ℘*925 22 71 15.*

This workshop *(taller)*, a building yard for the cathedral, is an old palace. Mudéjar decoration can still be seen in rooms lit by small openwork windows.

ADDITIONAL SIGHTS

Hospital de Tavera★

Cardenal de Tavera 2. ⏰*Open Mon–Sat 10am–2.30pm, 3–6.30pm, Sun 10am–2.30pm.* ⤙*Guided tours every 45min from 10.15am.* ⊷*€4.50.* ℘*925 22 04 51.*

The hospital was begun by Bustamante in 1541 and completed by González de Lara and the Vergaras in the 17C. After the Civil War, the Duchess of Lerma rearranged her **apartments**★ in 17C style. These hold an outstanding collection of paintings.

In the vast library, the hospital archives contain volumes bound in leather by Moorish craftsmen. El Greco's *Holy Family* is arresting, the portrait of the Virgin perhaps the most beautiful by the artist. Note also the *Birth of the Messiah* by Tintoretto, the *Philosopher* by Ribera and, in an adjoining room, his strange portrait of the *Bearded Woman*.

On the first floor, in the reception hall, is El Greco's sombre portrait of *Cardinal Tavera*, painted from a death mask.

Talavera Ceramics

Since the 15C, the name Talavera has been associated with high-quality **ceramic tiles** used to decorate the palaces, mansions and chapels. Visit the town's Basilica and **Museo de Cerámica Ruiz de Luna** *(Pl. de San Agustín; ℘925 80 01 49)* to see ceramics dating from the 15C to modern times. Talavera now manufactures decorative crockery, and green-coloured items are made in **El Puente del Arzobispo**, a village (34km/21mi SW) specialising in pottery drinking jars.

Beside it are *Samson and Delilah* (Caravaggio) and two portraits of the *Duke and Duchess of Navas* (Antonio Moro).

A gallery leads to the **church** from the twin patio. The Carrara marble portal is by Alonso Berruguete, who also carved the tomb of Cardinal Tavera.

The retable at the high altar was designed by El Greco, whose last work, a **Baptism of Christ**★, is displayed. The artist's use of brilliant colours and elongated figures is at its most magnificent. The hospital pharmacy, facing the patio, has been restored.

Puente de Alcántara

At the ends of the 13C bridge are a Mudéjar tower and a Baroque arch. Across the Tajo, behind ramparts, is the restored 14C **Castillo de San Servando** (castle; *now a youth hostel;* ℘*925 22 45 54*). A plaque on the town wall by the bridge recalls how **St John of the Cross** (1542–1591) escaped through a window from his monastery prison nearby.

Puente de San Martín

The medieval bridge, rebuilt in the 14C, is marked at its south end by an octagonal tower; the north end is 16C.

Iglesia de Cristo de la Vega

Travesía Cristo de la Vega.

The Church of Christ of the Vega, formerly St Leocadia, stands on the site of a 7C Visigothic temple, the venue of early church councils. Although modified in the 18C, it retains a fine Mudéjar apse. A modern Crucifix replaces one which figures in many legends.

VIEWPOINTS

The city's incomparable **site**★★★ can be appreciated from the *Carretera de Circunvalación*, a ring-road which parallels the loop of the Tajo from the Puente de Alcántara (Alcántara Bridge) to the Puente de San Martín.

For truly memorable views, it is worth going to the **viewpoints** among olive groves on the surrounding hills. The terrace of the parador (⌕*see Addresses*), above the *carretera de circunvalación*, is a superb vantage point.

EXCURSION

Talavera de la Reina

▶ *80km/50mi W of Toledo on the CM-400.* 🏛 *Calle Palenque 2.* ☎*925 82 63 22.* *www.talavera.org.*

Talavera is synonymous with the azule-jos (ceramic tiles) which brought it fame and prosperity from the 15C when they became widely used to décorate chap-els and noble homes. On the right bank of the Tajo, spanned by a 15C bridge, it retains part of its medieval walls and Mudéjar churches.

Basílica de Nuestra Señora del Prado

Jardines del Prado 6. 🕐*Open daily 7am –2pm, 5–10pm (4–9pm during summer).* The church, virtually an *azulejos* museum, gives a good idea of the evolution of the local style. The earliest tiles, geometri-cally patterned and yellow in colour, may be found in the sacristy.
In the basilica itself later tiles (16C–18C) may be found with the classic blue nar-rative scenes. Nearby the Museo Ruiz de la Luna *(see box)* offers the chance to see more tiles in a museum setting.

Oropesa

▶ *32km/20mi W.*

This delightful hilltop village is crowned by its **castle**★ originally built in 1366 but rebuilt in 1402.
Part of it is open as a visitor attraction *(Pl. del Palacio 1;* 🕐*open Fri–Sat 10am-2pm, 4–6pm, Sun and public holidays 11am–2pm, 4–6pm;* 🎫*€2;* ☎*925 45 00 06)* while most of it now serves as a para-dor. It enjoys far-reaching views across to the Sierra de Gredos.

Montes de Toledo

Within the low wooded mountains lying southwest of Toledo, a central area of 1 000sq km /385sq m is protected as the Parque Nacional de Cabañeros, home to rare wildlife and shepherds' culture. To the east of it are villages and towns, some with castles, and the isolated early medieval church of Sta María del Melque, all set among olive groves pro-ducing some of Spain's finest olive oil.

ADDRESSES

🛏 STAY

🛏 **Hostal Santo Tomé** – *Santo Tomé, 13.* ☎*925 221 712. www.hostalsantotome.com 10 rooms.* 🍽*€10* 🅿 Ideally situated in the heart of the old town, with rooftop views from the top floor, this reasonably priced small hotel with spacious rooms and parking (extra cost) is an ideal base.

🛏 **Hotel La Almazara** – *3.5km/2mi SW along the Cuerva road.* ☎*925 22 38 66. www.hotelalmazara.com. 28 rooms.* 🍽*€5. Closed 10 Dec–30 Mar.* A former olive press, its walls clad with ivy, is reached via a lane planted with olive trees. Bedrooms are spacious and bright.

🛏🛏🛏 **Hostal del Cardenal** – *Pas. Recaredo 24.* ☎*925 22 49 00. www.hostal delcardenal.com. 27 rooms.* 🍽*€8.* This charming hotel, formerly a cardinal's residence, stands at the foot of the city walls. Behind the splendid stone façade, the rooms are elegantly decorated with wood furnishings and antiques. The restaurant is superb. Parking nearby.

🛏🛏🛏 **Parador del Toledo** – *Cerro del Emperador via Ctra de Circunvalaciónt.* ☎*925 225 166. www.parador.es. 74 rooms.* 🅿 🍽*€17.* As popular with locals as visitors, this parador, recently given a facelift, is a modern building, but its terraced dining room has a magnificent view of the city. Comfortable rooms and swimming pool.

🍴 EAT

🍽 **La Abadía** – *Nuñez de Arce 3 (Pl. de San Nicolás).* ☎*925 25 11 40. www.abadiatoledo.com.* Complex lighting and modern furniture in the basement of a 16C palace create a highly original overall effect and a pleasant, if enclosed, backdrop to creative cuisine.

🍽🍽 **Casón de los López de Toledo** – *Sillería 3.* ☎*925 25 47 74. www.cason toledo.com. Closed Sun evenings.* Time has stood still in this stone mansion built around a patio. A delightful setting for highly original cuisine.

🛍 SHOPPING

Toledo is renowned for **damascene ware** (black steel inlaid with gold, silver and copper thread).

🎉 FESTIVALS

The **Corpus Christi** procession is one of the largest in Spain *(www.corpus christitoledo.es).*

Ruta Don Quixote ★

The Quixote route, created to celebrate the 400th anniversary of the publication of Cervantes' great novel, in 1605, is the European Union's first approved cultural route dedicated to a literary figure. It provides a good guideline for meandering through La Mancha's flatlands to explore the villages and landscapes where Cervantes set the first volume of Don Quixote and Sancho Panza's imaginary adventures. Other historic towns also appear on the route.

- ▶ **Population:** 2 274 (Belmonte)
- ⌖ **Michelin Map:** 576 N 21 – Castilla-La Mancha (Cuenca).
- ▤ **Info:** C. Lucas Parra 20. ℰ967 17 07 41. http://perso.wanadoo.es/belmonte/ofitur.htm.
- ▷ **Location:** Belmonte is 157km/98mi NW) of Madrid and on the 250km/155mi Ruta Don Quixote.
- ▲▲ **Kids:** Consuegra's windmill-dotted hillsides are like something from a fairy story.
- ◴ **Timing:** You can easily spend two or three days exploring the region.

🚗 DRIVING TOUR

Consuegra

▷ *90km/56mi NE of Belmonte along the N 420.*

A row of 11 *molino de vientos* (windmills) stands alongside the 13C castle on a hill overlooking the town, making up the classic picture-postcard image of Don Quixote's La Mancha.
The castle (◴ *open daily 9am–2pm, 3.30–6pm (open 10.30am Sat and Sun, 4.30–7pm May–Sept);* ▭*€2;* ℰ*925 47 57 31)* once belonged to the Knights of St John and some of the rooms have been interpreted according to the time of their tenure. In the autumn it hosts the saffron festival after the local saffron crocus crop is handpicked, stripped of petals and dried.

Puerto Lápice

▷ *23km/14mi SE of Consuegra along the E S/A 4.*

Puerto Lapice keeps its rambling 17C inn though it is not known if it is the one that Don Quixote mistook for a castle believing the innkeeper to be a lord who knighted him. The inn holds a marvellous collection of Don Quixote memorabilia, ranging from tasteful to kitsch, and you can enjoy local food there too.

▷ *Take the N420 towards Cuenca for 32km/20mi.*

Campo de Criptana

Windmills: Barbero 1. ◴*Tue–Sat 10am–2pm, 4.30–6.30pm, Sun 10am–2pm.* ℰ*926 562 231.*
Three of the ten windmills on the hill above the town date back to the times of Don Quixote and one, which stands next to the windmill housing the tourist office, has its original working mechanism. The walk up to the windmills gives good views over the heart of La Mancha. Below the mill, a 16C miller's house, Las Cuevas de la Paz *(opening times as for the windmills;* ▭*€0.60)* may be visited. Alongside the highest windmill is a local collector's mass of wire models, as surreal as Don Quixote's universe.

▷ *Take the N420 for 2km /0.8mi towards Cuenca, turn left on to the CM 3162 for 18km/11mi towards Quintanar de la Orden.*

El Tobosco

Dulcinea, Don Quixote's distant love – though they saw each other only three to four times and their eyes never met – came from the small village of El Toboso. A wealthy woman of the time, Doña Morales, who may have inspired the character of Dulcinea, lived here in a 16C farmstead which is well preserved (*Museo Casa de Dulcinea;* ○*open Tue–Sun 10am–2pm, 4.30–7.30pm, Sun 10am–2pm;* ◉€0.60; ℘*925 19 72 88*). Nearby, the Convento de Trinitarias has a small museum of religious art.

For literary lovers of the novel, the late Gothic building which houses the Centro Cervantino (○*open Tue–Sat 10am–2pm, 4–7pm, Sun 10am–2pm;* ◉€2; ℘*925 568 226*) is well worth a visit. It houses a polyglot collection of editions of *Don Quixote* from around the world. Recent additions include Thai and Kurdish translations, and copies signed by Nelson Mandela and Silva de Lula (earlier editions include one signed by Hitler).

▷ *Take the CM 3162, then the N301 towards Cuenca.*

Belmonte★

Belmonte's whitewashed houses are overlooked by an imposing church and castle.

Iglesia Colegial de San Bartolomé★

Iglesia. ○ *Open Tue–Sun 11am–2pm, 4–6.30pm (8pm Apr–Sept).* ◉€2. ℘*967 17 02 08.*

This 15C collegiate church holds 15C–17C **altarpieces. Choir stalls★** from the cathedral in Cuenca starkly illustrate scenes from Genesis and the Passion.

Castillo★

○*Open Tue–Sun 10am–1.30pm, 4–7.30pm.* ○*Closed 1 Jan and 25 Dec.* ◉€6. ℘*678 64 64 86.*

Recently reopened after years of restoration, this 15C fortress with six circular towers was built by the Marqués de Villena, and long abandoned.

In 1870 the new owner, Eugenia de Montijo, installed an ugly brick facing in the patio. The empty rooms hold beautiful Mudéjar **artesonado★** ceilings – the audience chamber is outstanding – and delicately carved stone window surrounds. Follow the curtain walls to the stepped merlons for views of the village and countryside.

▷ *6km/3.7mi NE along the N 420.*

Villaescusa de Haro

The magnificent 1507 **Capilla de la Asunción★** (Chapel of the Assumption) of the parish church boasts a Gothic-Renaissance altarpiece and a wrought-iron screen with florid Gothic arches *(open for Mass only).*

▷ *Take the N420 and CM 3103 S.*

Argamasilla de Alba

This quiet town is thought to be where Cervantes invented Don Quixote while he languished in prison for fraud during his brief working life as a tax collector. At the time, Don Rodrigo de Pacheco, a fantasist like Cervantes's fictional character, lived here, perhaps inspiring Cervantes.

You can visit the basement prison under the tourist office (*Cervantes 7;* ○*open Tue–Sat 10am–2pm, 5–8pm (4–7pm Oct–Mar);* ℘*926 52 32 34*), and in the Iglesia de San Juan Bautista you can see Don Rodrigo's portrait hanging in the chapel of the Virgen de la Caridad. The church, begun in 1542, was never finished.

▷ *Take the CM3109 towards La Solana, then the CM 3127 to Villanueva.*

Villanueva de los Infantes

Perhaps the most charming town on the Quixote route, Villanueva claims to be the " certain village in La Mancha, which I do not wish to name" in the famous opening sentence of Cervantes's novel. Here, it is said, the knight lived before setting out on his adventures and here he returned to die.

For sure it is where the great Spanish poet **Francisco de Quevedo** (1580–1645) came to die in the **Convento de Santo Domingo**, founded in 1526. You can see the cell inside the convent, now a historic hotel. But this gracious little town deserves a visit in its own right. The spacious Plaza Mayor sits to one side of the old town, a network of small streets with stone houses decorated by over 200 carved shields. The **alhóndiga**, or granary, and late Renaissance Iglesia de San Andrés stand out.

Almagro★

Set in the red earth of La Mancha, Almagro's stone-paved streets and façades with coats of arms recall the Military Order of the Knights of Calatrava. The 16C Convento de San Francisco is now a parador.

A BIT OF HISTORY

The impressive architecture of this charming town, the birthplace of the explorer Diego de Almagro (1475–1538), can be explained by its eventful history. From the 13C until the end of the 15C, Almagro was the stronghold of the Military Order of the Knights of Calatrava and the base from which they administered their possessions.

Between 1750 and 1761, the town became the capital of the province as a result of the favours of the Count of Valparaíso, the then Minister of Finance under Ferdinand VI. From the 16C to the 19C, a number of religious orders established convents and monasteries here.

SIGHTS

You will walk along cobbled streets past whitewashed houses and convents and monasteries with fine stone doorways.

Plaza Mayor★★

This long square, one of the most beautiful in Castile, was the scene of bullfights and tournaments. A stone colonnade frames two sides, under two rows of windows with green surrounds.

The 17C **Corral de Comedias**★ (Pl. Mayor 18; ⏰ open daily 10am–2pm, 4–7pm (Apr–Sep 5–8pm, Jul 6–9pm); ⌨ €3, performances €3.50; ☎ 926 86 15 39) is the only intact original theatre in Europe. Wooden porticoes, oil lamps, stone well and scenery wall combine in a superb example of popular architecture. Summer performances are part of the annual International Festival of Classical Drama (www.festivaldealmagro.com).

From near the statue of Diego de Almagro, take calle de Nuestra Señora de las Nieves (note fine doorways) to the left, to the triangular Plaza Santo Domingo,

- ▶ **Population:** 18 581
- **Michelin Map:** 576 P 18 – Castilla-La Mancha (Ciudad Real).
- **Info:** Plaza Mayor 1. ☎ 926 86 07 17. www.ciudad-almagro.com.
- **Location:** Almagro is on the plain south of Madrid. ▭ Paseo de la Estación.
- **Don't Miss:** A walk through streets frozen in time.

surrounded by mansions. Turn left into Calle de Bernardas, to face the spectacular Baroque doorway of the **Palacio de los Condes de Valparaíso**. Follow Calle de Don Federico Relimpio; go left on Calle de Don Diego de Almagro, dominated by the 16C **Convento de la Asunción de Calatrava** (⏰ open daily noon–2pm, 4–7pm (winter noon–2pm, 4–6pm); ⌨ €1.50; ☎ 926 86 07 17), with its fine Renaissance staircase.

At the Plaza Mayor, turn right at the end onto calle Gran Maestre and the **Museo Nacional del Teatro** (⏰ open Mon–Sat 10am–2pm, 6–8pm (5–7pm Apr–Jun and Sep, 4–6pm Oct–May) Sun and public holidays 11am–2pm; ⏰ closed 1 Jan, 5 and 24 Aug, 24–25 and 31 Dec, and some local hols; ⌨ €3, no charge for under 18s; no charge Sat pm and Sun; ☎ 926 26 10 14; http://museoteatro.mcu.es), in an 18C palace, showing old documents, costumes, and models of theatre sets.

EXCURSIONS

Parque Nacional de las Tablas de Daimiel

▶ 31km/19mi N by the CM 4107 and N 420. From Daimiel, take a tarmac road to the right (7km/4.5mi).
⏰ Centro de Información, 9am–sunset. ☎ 926 69 31 18. ⌨ Guided tours 9am and 11am, ⌨ no charge (book ahead). These wetlands cover 1 928ha/4 764 acres in the heart of dry La Mancha. The tablas are floodplains where marshes of the Rivers Guadiana and Cigüela provide a habitat for a huge variety of birds

in winter and dry out in summer. The underlying soaked subsoil, threatened by irrigation on surrounding farmland, currently survives thanks to winter rainfall

Parque Natural Lagunas de Ruidera

▶ *67km/42mi NE. Centro de Información, Avda Castilla La Mancha s/n.*

This park, covering 3 772ha/9 320 acres, comprises 15 lagoons linked by streams, gullies and waterfalls, which are linked by a country road along which you can explore them.

San Carlos del Valle★

▶ *46km/29mi E.*

The 18C **Plaza Mayor**★ is charming, with a Baroque church with four lantern turrets. The house at no. 5, a former hospice, retains a stone doorway and typical patio.

Valdepeñas

▶ *34km/21mi SE along the CM 412.*
🚂 *Paseo de la Estación.*

This wine centre is at the southern tip of the vast grape-growing area of La Mancha. Blue- and white-coloured houses rise above shady porticoes on the spacious Plaza de España.

The late Gothic **Iglesia de la Asunción** (Church of the Assumption), has a Plateresque upper gallery. The Ermita de la Veracruz, once a synagogue *(hermitage usually closed to the public; ℘926 33 82 35)* is locally venerated.

Visit the **Museo del Vino**, *(C. Princesa 39;* 🕐*open 10am–2pm, 4–9pm (Jun–Sep 5–8pm);* ℘*926 32 11 11)*, installed in one of the town's oldest bodegas, to enjoy the atmosphere and aromas of wine culture.

Sacro Castillo y Convento de Calatrava la Nueva★

▶ *32km/19.8mi SW. 7km/4.3mi SW of Calzada de Calatrava, turn right onto a paved road (2.5km/1.5mi).* 🕐*Open Oct–Mar Tue–Fri 11am–2pm, 4–6pm, Sat 10am–2pm, 4–6pm, Sun 10am–6pm;*

Apr–Sept Tue–Fri 11am–2pm, 5.30–8pm, Sat–Sun 10am–2pm, 5.30–8.30pm.
👓*No charge.* ℘ *926 26 21 20.*
🖐*Call ahead to confirm castle is open.*

This semi-ruined citadel occupies a magnificent **hilltop site** which dominates the route to Andalucía.

The gateway leads into vaulted stables. The second perimeter, built into rock, houses religious buildings, including the impressive **church**, lit by an immense rose window, and brick swallow's nest vaulting, probably the work of Moorish prisoners. Views from the towers include the ruined **Castillo de Salvatierra**. The cracks caused by the 1755 Lisbon earthquake are clearly visible.

Viso del Marqués★★

▶ *El Viso de Marqués.* 🕐*Open Tue–Sun 9am–1pm, 4–6pm (Jul–Aug 9am–2pm). Last entrance 30min before closing.*
👓*Guided tours every 30min.*
👓*No charge.* ℘ *926 33 75 18.*

The Renaissance Palace of Alvaro de Bazán, the Marqués de Santa Cruz, Philip II's admiral, is an imposing building unexpectedly sited in a small village. As you approach you can see the damage left by the 1755 Lisbon earthquake, which destroyed the palace's corner towers. Behind its austere façade are magnificent frescoes in the ground floor patio, reception rooms and monumental double staircase. Upstairs in the living rooms, also frescoed, are a collection of model boats. A crocodile hangs on the wall in the entrance to the chapel where the Marqués was buried on his death in 1588 just weeks before he was due to take command of the Invincible Armada; he brought it back from one of his expeditions.

Close to the Palace, alongside the tourist office, a small **Museo de Ciencias Naturales** *(*Natural Sciences Museum; 👓*no charge;* ℘*926 33 68 15)* houses a remarkable collection of butterflies.

Albacete

Albacete (from *Al Basite*, "plain" in Arabic), capital of the province of the same name, stands on a dry plateau that juts into the fertile east. Heritage structures are grouped with modern buildings and residential districts.

SIGHTS

Museo Provincial de Albacete

Parque Abelardo Sánchez. ⏱*Open Tue–Sat 9am–2pm, 4.30–7pm, Sun and public holidays 9am–2pm.* ⏱*Closed 1 Jan, Maundy Thu, Good Fri, 25 Dec.* ✆*€1.20; no charge Sat–Sun.* ✆*967 22 83 07.*

This modern building is in Abelardo Sánchez Park. Its Fine Arts Museum (Museo de Bellas Artes) collects works of landscape artist Benjamín Palencia (1894–1980). The Joaquín Sánchez Jiménez Archaeology Museum displays finds from sites in the province: Iberian sculptures including the **sphinx of Haches**, the **hind of Caudete**, the lion from Bienservida, and above all **Roman dolls with movable joints**★.

Catedral de San Juan Bautista

Pl. de la Virgen de los Llanos. ⏱*Open daily 8.30am–1pm, 6–9pm.* ✆*967 21 53 42.*

Construction began in the late 16C. The façade and side doorway are additions. Three naves are separated by large Ionic columns. Mannerist paintings decorate the sacristy. The Capilla de la Virgen de los Llanos is a fine chapel dedicated to the Virgin of the Plains, the city's patron. The Renaissance altarpiece is by the Maestro de Albacete. Recent restoration has returned the original colours to the 19C ceiling frescoes.

Pasaje de Lodares

This narrow conservatory passageway, lined by shops and homes, links Calle Mayor with Clle del Tinte. Its Modernist architecture, dating from 1925, is emblematic of Albacete and was inspired by Milanese decoration. Allegorical figures proliferate.

▶ **Population:** 166 909

⚲ **Michelin Map:** 576 O-P 24 – Castilla-La Mancha (Albacete).

ℹ **Info:** Calle Tinte 2, Edificio Posada del Rosario. ✆967 58 05 22. www.albacete.es.

◐ **Location:** The A 35 and A 30 lead to Valencia (NE) and Murcia (SE); the A 32 runs SW to Andalucía. AVE high-speed trains use the central station. ▬Calle Ferrocarril.

◉ **Don't Miss:** Stroll Pasaje de Lodares for a taste of old Albacete.

◷ **Timing:** Spend a morning, then see caves and castles nearby.

EXCURSIONS

Alarcón★

◐ *103km/65mi NW.*

◐ *Take the A 31 to Honrubia, then turn right onto the A 3.*

Alarcón, named for Alaric, its Visigothic founder, rises above a loop of the Júcar river.

The 13C–14C castle is now a parador. The **location**★★★ made the fortress practically impregnable. It follows a triangular plan, with a double protective enclosure. **Don Juan Manuel** (1282–1348) wrote many of his cautionary tales while living there.

Amid the whitewashed façades of Albacete, note the **Iglesia de Santa María** *(Dr Agustín Tortosa)*, a Renaissance church with an elegant Plateresque doorway and a fine sculpted 16C altarpiece.

On **Plaza de Don Juan Manuel** are the *ayuntamiento* (town hall), with its porticoed façade, the Iglesia de San Juan Bautista, a Herreran church, and the Casa-Palacio, adorned with splendid grilles.

Alcalá del Júcar★

◐ *60km/37.3mi NE along the CM 3218.*

The road winds through steep **gorges**. The Júcar river encircles the magnificent **site**★ of the village between its castle and church overlooking a fertile plain on the bottom of the gorge, unusual for arid La Mancha.

A walk through Alcalá's maze of steep alleyways reveals nooks, crannies and lookout-points at every turn. Dwellings hollowed out of rock have long corridors leading to cliffside balconies; some can be visited.

Cueva de la Vieja

▶ *70km/43.5mi E along the A 35, via Alpera.* ⏱*Open Mon–Fri 10am–2pm.* *€2.50.* ✆*967 33 00 01 (ayuntamiento).*

This easily accessible cave retains clearly visible prehistoric paintings. Stylised human silhouettes are shown alongside hunting stags with bows and arrows. Note females in robes and a figure with a plumed headdress.

Almansa

▶ *74km/46mi E along the A 35.* 🚉*Plaza 1° de Mayo.*

Almansa's maze of streets and lanes spreads around a limestone crag crowned by a medieval castle.

Iglesia de la Asunción – *Below the castle.* The church owes its mix of styles to a remodelling. The Renaissance portal is attributed to Vandelvira.

Palacio de los Condes de Cirat *(Pl. de Santa María)* – The fine Mannerist-style doorway of this mansion, the **Casa Grande**, bears an escutcheon flanked by crude figures.

Castle – *(Castillo;* ⏱*open Jun–Sep daily 10am–2pm, 6–8pm, (Oct, Apr–May 5–7pm; Nov–Mar 4–6pm); last entrance 30min before closing;* ⏱*closed public holidays;* *€3;* ✆*967 31 12 59)* Restored 15C ramparts, perched along the rock ridge, command a view of the plain. Keystones in the keep *(torre de homenaje)* bear the coat of arms of the Marqués de Villena, once the feudal lord of the town.

Alcaraz

▶ *79km/49mi SW along the A 32.*

Alcaraz, the historic capital of the sierra of the same name, stands isolated on a red clay rise. The town grew rich manufacturing carpets and retains its Renaissance character in buildings influenced by the great **Andrés de Vandelvira**, born here in 1509.

Plaza Mayor – On the main square are: the 15C Pósito, once a granary; the 16C **ayuntamiento** (town hall) with emblazoned façade; the 17C **Lonja** del Corregidor, standing against the **Torre del Tardón** (clock tower); and the 15C **Iglesia de la Santísima Trinidad**. Old houses front the **Calle Mayor**. Note a façade with the two warriors and the Plateresque **Puerta de la Aduana** (Customs Doorway) of the Casa Consistorial. Stepped alleys head from the right-hand side of the square.

Guided visits to the old town, including the town's revived craft carpet workshops, need to be reserved In advance (✆*967 34 47 71)*. The visit takes 90min (*€2)*.

The path to the cemetery passes under two arches to attractive views of brown rooftops and the countryside. A short walk or drive outside town you can visit the 18C Santuario de la Virgen de Cortés *(N322 towards Albacete;* ⏱*open daily 10.30am–8pm)*.

From Alcaraz you can make a picturesque **excursion** 46km/28.5mi south to the **source of the River Mundo** where there are wooded valleys, springs, caves and falls.

Source of the Rio Mundo

▶ *62 km/38.5mi S of Alcaraz on the CM 412.*

Where the Rio Mundo, a tributary of the Segura, emerges above ground a spectacular waterfall tumbles from a sheer wall of rock into pools below at the foot of the Sierra del Calar.

The source's flow varies greatly from spring to high summer, when it is best visited early in the day before coaches arrive. From the carpark, numerous signposted footpaths lead into the surrounding countryside.

Cuenca★★

Cuenca's spectacular **setting**★★ is a rocky platform hemmed in by the Júcar and Huécar ravines *(hoces)* in defiance of the laws of gravity. The magnificently preserved old city is on UNESCO's World Heritage List. Its beauty drew artists to work here in the 1960s and they have left superb collections to the city.

◦◦◦ WALKING TOUR

CIUDAD ANTIGUA★★ (OLD TOWN) *2hr30min.*

▷ *From the car park, pass through the 16C Renaissance-style Arco del Bezudo, follow San Pedro to the San Pedro church, then turn left onto ronda de Julián Romero.*

Ronda Julián Romero

This delightful stepped alley runs above the Huécar gorge to the cathedral.

Convento de las Carmelitas

This ex-Carmelite convent houses the **Fundación Antonio Pérez** (*see entry*) and Museo Internacional de Electrografía *(Rda Julián Romero, 20; ◷ open Mon–Sat 11am–9pm, Sun and public holidays noon–2pm; ◷ closed 18–21Sep; ◦◦ no charge; ☎969 17 91 15).*

Catedral de Nuestra Señora de Gracia★

Pl. Mayor. ◷ Open daily 10.30am–1.30pm, 4–6.30pm. ◷ Closed 1 Jan, 25 Dec. ◦◦ €2.80. ☎969 22 46 26.
The Cathedral was started in the 13C in Norman-Gothic style. One of two towers collapsed after an early 20C fire. The interior, a mix of Gothic architecture and Renaissance decoration, has superb wrought-iron chapel **grilles**★, a twin **ambulatory**, a **triforium** and an elegant Plateresque **door**★ into the chapter house with carved walnut panels by Alonso Berruguete.

▷ *Walk along the right-hand side of the Cathedral and take Canónigos.*

▶ **Population:** 54 600
◉ **Michelin Map:** 576 L 23 – Castilla-La Mancha (Cuenca)
ℹ **Info:** Alfonso VIII 2. ☎969 24 10 51; Avenida Cruz Roja 1. ☎969 24 10 50. www.cuenca.org.
◐ **Location:** Cuenca lies 164km/102mi E of Madrid in the Montes Universales, on the edge of the central Meseta. AVE high-speed train services from Madrid and Valencia call at Cuenca Fernando Zóbel station on the edge of town. ▭ Calle Mariano Catalina.
🅿 **Parking:** Follow signs for the *casco antiguo*. Cross Plaza Mayor and leave your car in the free car park.
☺ **Don't Miss:** Hanging houses and vertiginous canyon views.

This street is lined by the Bishops Palace, housing the **Museo Diocesano**★ (◷ *open Tue–Sat 11am–2pm, 4–8pm, Sun 11am–2pm; ◦◦ €2,* and the **Museo de Cuenca** (*see Sights*).

Casas Colgadas★ (Hanging Houses)

These restored 14C houses contain the **Museo de Arte Abstracto** (*see Sights)* and a restaurant. The best **view**★ of these gravity-defying buildings can be enjoyed from across the **Puente de San Pablo**, an iron bridge that leads to the city's parador. This panorama is enchanting when illuminated.

▷ *Return to the Cathedral and head along José T Mena.*

Iglesia de San Miguel

Bajada de San Miguel.
◷ *Open for events and performances. ☎969 23 21 19.*
This Gothic-style former church is one of the main venues for Cuenca's Religious Music Week.

The museum grew around the friend-ships of the Cuenca Group formed in the 1960s among abstract artists, one of whom, Gustavo Torner, was born in Cuenca. Today it is the best of its kind in Spain.

Museo de Cuenca★

Obispo Valero 6. Open Tue–Sat 10am –2pm, 5–7pm (4pm Nov–Mar), Sun and public holidays 11am–2pm. €1.20; no charge Sat–Sun. 969 21 30 69.
This museum displays prehistoric objects, sculpture, coins and ceramics found in Roman excavations. Note the top of a **Roman altar**★ found at Ercávica illustrating ritual items.

Espacio Tomer★★

Hoz del Huécar. Open Tue–Sat 11am– 2pm, 4–6pm, Sun 11am–2.30pm. 969 23 83 73. www.espacio.torner.com.
A superb fine art space within the shell of a Gothic church, conceived and designed by Gustavo Torner, a Cuenca-born artist, whose works hang here. Their abstract geometry perfectly matches the elegance of the church and reveals influences ranging from poet Quevedo to artists Cranach, Duchamp and Brancusi.

Fundación Antonio Peréz★

Rda Julián Romero, 20. Mon–Sat 11am–9pm, Sun and public holidays 12 noon– 2pm. Closed 18–21 Sep. No charge. 969 23 06 19.
Within a 17C Carmelite friary, well worth a visit in its own right, works of modern Spanish art donated by local collector Antonio Pérez hang against a plain backdrop. Large canvases by Millares and Saura, among others, sit alongside works of found objects composed into small installations.

Casa Museo Zavala

Pl. de San Nicolás 4. 969 23 60 54.
Among the city's quartet of outstand-ing contemporary art spaces, this one, within a 17C palace with views over the Júcar gorge, is used for temporary shows.

Casas Colgadas
© Maurizio Borgese/hemis.fr

▶ *Return to the Plaza Mayor. Follow calles Severo Catalina and Pilares.*

Plaza de las Angustias★

An 18C Franciscan monastery and a Baroque hermitage, the Virgin in Anguish, stand in this quiet square between the town and the ravine.

▶ *Return to San Pedro and continue to the San Pedro church. Bear left into an alley which ends at the edge of the Júcar ravine, for a good view.*

SIGHTS
Museo de Arte Abstracto Español★★

Casas Colgadas, Canónigos s/n. Open Tue–Sat and public holidays 11am–2pm, 4–6pm (8pm Sat), Sun 11am–2.30pm. Closed 1 Jan, Maundy Thursday (afternoon), Good Friday, 18– 21 Sep, 24, 25, 31 Dec. €3; no charge children under 10. 969 21 29 83. www.march.es/arte/cuenca.
The views from the Museum of Abstract Spanish Art are veritable works of art in themselves. The collection, hung in a series of small plain galleries within stripped-back traditional houses, some overhanging the gorge, includes works by Chillida, Tàpies, Saura, Zóbel, Cuixart, Sempere, Rivera and Millares.

Museo de las Ciencias de Castilla-La Mancha

Pl. de la Merced 1. ⏰Open year-round Tue–Sat 10am–2pm, 4–7pm, Sun 10am –2pm; , Sun 10am–2pm. ⏰Closed 1 Jan, Maundy Thu, Good Fri, 25 Dec. ⊚€1.20; no charge Sat–Sun, 18, 31 May, 12 Oct. ✆969 24 03 20. www.jccm.es/ museociencias.

This lively modern science museum also has a planetarium.

EXCURSIONS
Las Hoces (Ravines)

Roads parallel to the river circling Cuenca's rock spur afford amazing views of the hanging houses. The **Hoz del Júcar** is the shorter, more enclosed ravine. The **Hoz del Huécar** course swings from side to side between gentler slopes given over to market gardening.
Round tour of 15km/9.6mi.

▷ *Turn left at the end of the ravine for Buenache de la Sierra and left again for the Convento de San Jerónimo.*

In a right bend, there's a **view**★ of grey rock columns and, in the distance, Cuenca. Enter through the gateway.

Las Torcas★

▷ *Take the N 420 then bear left after 11km/6.5mi.*

The road crosses a conifer wood where the *torcas*, odd and occasionally spectacular depressions, can be seen.

🚗 DRIVING TOUR

SERRANÍA DE CUENCA★
270km/168mi . Allow 1 day.

Wind and water have formed whimsical landscapes in limestone, amid pines and numerous streams.
Continuing northwards, you reach a Roman settlement and Renaissance monastery lying close to the main route from Madrid to the Mediterranean coast since Classical times.

Ventano del Diablo

▷ *25.5km/15.8mi from Cuenca along the CM 2105.*

The Devil's Window, an opening in rock, overlooks the depths of the **Garganta del Júcar** (Júcar Gorges).

Ciudad Encantada★

▷ *Follow the road signposted to the right of the CM 2105.*

A circuit directs visitors through this Enchanted Forest, to the Tobogán (Toboggan Slope) and the Mar de Piedras (Sea of Stones). To reach the **Mirador de Uña** *(2km/1mi)*,

▷ *Take the road from the car park.*

Enjoy the **view** of the Júcar Valley and Uña's green lake dominated by towering cliffs.

Los Callejones
▷*3km/1.8mi from Las Majadas.*
🚗*Leave your car on the esplanade.*
This isolated spot is a maze of eroded blocks, arches and the narrow alleyways which lend their name to the area: The Alleyways.

Nacimiento del Río Cuervo★ (Source of the Cuervo)
▷*30km/18.6mi N of Las Majadas towards Alto de la Vega.*
🚗*Leave your car after the bridge and walk up 500m/547yd.*
A footpath leads to **waterfalls**★ and mossy grottoes at the beginnings of the Cuervo river.

Hoz de Beteta★ (Beteta Ravine)
▷*30km/18.6mi NW along the CM 2106 and CM 2201 towards Beteta.*
This impressive ravine was cut by the River Guadiela. From Vadillos, a road to the left leads to the spa of Solán de Cabras. The road (CM 210) continues through the **River Escabas valley**. Before reaching Priego *(3km/1.8mi)*, a

branch to the right leads to the **Convento de San Miguel de las Victorias**, in an impressive **setting**★.

▶ *Take the N320 E, then turn S along the CM 2006 and CM200 to the A40, which leads you to the A3. From there follow signs to Uclés.*

Uclés

The massive Monasterio d'Uclés was the seat of the Order of Santiago from 1174 to 1499).

Castillo Monasterio d'Uclés

🕐*Open daily 10am–6pm (8pm Jul–Sep).* 🕐*Closed 1 Jan, 25 Dec.* ◉◉€3. 🕿*969 13 50 58.*
This massive castle-like monastery was begun in 1529 in Plateresque style. Most of the work was undertaken by Herrera's disciple, **Francisco de Mora** (1553–1610), hence its nickname, the Little Escorial. The entrance is via a beautiful Baroque **portal**★★.
Note the Baroque well and the magnificent **artesonado**★ ceiling in the refectory. The ramparts command a fine view.

Roman Segóbriga

▶ *In Saelices, 14km/8.7mi S of Uclés. Leave the A 3 at exit 103/104 and follow signs towards Casas de Luján.*
The **museum** *(ctra de Saelices a Villamayor de Santiago;* 🕐*open Tue–Sun Apr–Sept 10am–9pm; Oct–Mar 10am–6pm;* ◉◉€4; *no charge 18, 31 May, 12 Oct, 6 Dec)* in **Saelices** provides an overview of the 5C BC Celtiberian site which became an important Roman crossroads town. By the 1C AD, it had a theatre and an imposing **amphitheatre**★, with a capacity for 5 000 spectators. Parts of the baths and walls also remain.

ADDRESSES

🏠 STAY

🛏️🛏️ **Posada Huécar** – *Pas. del Huécar 3.* 🕿*969 21 42 01. www.posadahuecar.com. 22 rooms.* 🍽️*€3.* Behind the sober, salmon-coloured façade is a pleasant hotel with simply furnished but perfectly

adequate rooms, all with TV, and a delightful garden. A good location in the old part of Cuenca.

🛏️🛏️🛏️ **Posada San José** – *Rda Julián Romero, 4.* 🕿*969 21 13 00. www.posada sanjose.com.* A delightful hotel within one of the old-fashioned beamed hanging houses. The large comfortable rooms and bathrooms are simply decorated. The public spaces – sitting room and cafeteria for breakfast and dinner – hang over the gorge below.

🛏️🛏️🛏️🛏️ **Parador** – *Paseo del Huéscar (road up to San Pablo).* 🕿*969 23 23 20. www.parador.es.* 🍽️*€17.* Sitting on the far bank of the River Huéscar, the parador can been seen from afar. Built within a 16C convent, it offers a superb view back over the old town and its hanging houses. The tasteful décoration includes superb old tiles in the dining room.

🍴 EAT

🍽️🍽️ **Mesón Mangana** – *Pl. Mayor 3.* 🕿*969 22 94 51. Closed 15 Oct–15 Nov, Thu.* The perfect spot for a meal when visiting the old quarter. Good home cooking and local specialities, excellent sausages, mature Manchego cheese and grilled meats. Good value set menu.

🍽️🍽️🍽️ **Figon del Huécar** – *Ronda Julián Romero 6.* 🕿*969 24 00 62. www.figondel huecar.com.* A good choice when you are in search of modern market cooking, with international as well as local flavours. The dining room offers fine views over the gorges at the back of the old hanging house.

🍽️🍽️🍽️ **Mesón Casas Colgadas** – *Canónigos.* 🕿*969 22 35 09. www.meson casascolgadas.com. Closed Mon eve, Tue.* A well-known local landmark housed in one of the city's famous hanging houses *(casas colgadas)*, with a stupendous view of the Huécar Ravine. Carefully cooked traditional cuisine.

🎉 FESTIVALS

The city's Holy Week processions are spectacularly set against the steep narrow streets of the old town. Best known is The Procesión de las Turbas, which sets out at dawn (5.30–6.00am) to the sound of drumbeats through silent crowds streets as it winds its way up to the Calvary Around this time of year is also a festival of holy music.

Guadalajara

Guadalajara ("river of stones" in Arabic) in the 14C became the fief of the **Mendozas**, an illustrious family in Spanish history. It includes the poet Íñigo López de Mendoza, first **Marquis of Santillana** (1398–1458); his son, **Cardinal Pedro González de Mendoza** (1428–95); and the second Duke of Infantado, who built the palace at the north entrance to the town in the 15C.

SIGHTS
Palacio del Infantado★ (Palace of the Duke of Infantado)

Pl. de los Caídos. ◷*Open Tue–Sat 10am –2pm, 4–7pm, Sun and public holidays 10am–2pm.* ◷*Closed 1, 6 Jan, Good Fri, 1 May, 25 Dec.* ✆€1.20. ✆949 21 33 01.

The late 15C palace, by Juan Guas, is a masterpiece of Isabelline civil architecture fusing Gothic and Mudéjar styles. The **façade**★ is adorned with diamond stonework and the Mendoza coat of arms. The upper gallery is a series of paired ogee windows interposed between corbelled loggias.

The effect is splendid in spite of windows added in the 17C.

The two-storey **patio**★ is just as remarkable with multifoil arches on turned columns and extremely delicate Mudéjar

Façade of Palacio del Infantado
C. Labonne/MICHELIN

- **Population:** 81 221
- **Michelin Map:** 576 K 20 – map 121 Alrededores de Madrid – Castilla-La Mancha (Guadalajara).
- **Info:** Plaza de los Caídos 6. ✆949 21 16 26. www.guadalajara.es.
- **Location:** Guadalajara is NE of Madrid along the A 2 motorway. High-speed AVE trains link to Madrid and Barcelona (station 9km/5.5mi from town centre). ▭Calle Francisco Aritio.
- **Don't Miss:** The Palacio del Infantado.

ornamentation. The once-sumptuous interior was damaged during the Spanish Civil War.

Francis I of France, captured at Pavia in 1525, was received here with pomp on his way to imprisonment in Madrid.

The palace houses the **Museo Provincial de Guadalajara** (◷*open Oct–Apr Tue–Sat 10.30am–2pm, 4.15–7pm, Sun and public holidays 10.30am–2pm; May–Sept Tue–Sat 10.30am–2pm;* ✆€1.20, no charge Sat–Sun; ✆949 21 27 73).

EXCURSION
Pastrana

▷*42km/26mi SE on the N 320.*

This picturesque town was the seat of the **Princess of Eboli**, involved in intrigues in the time of Philip II. She was imprisoned by her husband for the last five years of her life in the palace which stands on the Plaza de la Hora, so called because she was allowed to show herself at the window for an hour a day.

The 16C **Colegiata** (*Melchor Cano 1;* ◷*open daily–11.30am–2pm (Sun and public holidays 1–2.30pm), 4.30–6.30pm; no charge for church;* ✆€2.50 for entry to crypt, church and museum; ✆949 37 00 27), a collegiate church, contains, in the sacristy, four Gothic **tapestries**★ woven in Tournai after cartoons by Nuno Gonçalves which illustrate the capture of

Arzila and Tangier by Alfonso V of Portugal in 1471. They reveal a mastery of composition, love of detail (armour and costume) and talent for portraiture.

Sigüenza★

🕒 75km/46mi NE on the E 90 N 2 then the CM-1101. 🗊 Serrano Sanz 9.
🕾 949 34 70 07. www.siguenza.es.
Sigüenza descends in pink and ochre tiers below a cathedral fortress and castle. The old quarter is a maze of narrow streets lined by Romanesque mansions.

Catedral★★

Serrano Sanz. ⌇Guided tours Tue–Sat 10am–2pm, 4.30pm–8pm; Sun 10am–2pm. ⊕€4. 🕾 619 36 27 15.
The nave, begun in the 12C, was completed in 1495. In the **north aisle**, the **doorway**★ into the Capilla de la Anunciación is decorated with Renaissance pilasters, Mudéjar arabesques and Gothic cusping.

In the **north transept** is a fine **sculptured unit**★★: a 16C **porphyry doorway** opens onto cloisters of marble. The **sacristy ceiling**★ by Covarrubias is a profusion of heads and roses between which peer thousands of cherubim.

The **chancel** (presbiterio) has a beautiful 17C wrought-iron grille framed by alabaster **pulpits**★. The **Doncel tomb**★★, in the south transept features a realistic figure of a youth which is a major work of sepulchral art.

The **Museo de ArteAntiguo**'s outstanding holdings, many drawn from small churches in the countryside around Sigüenza, include a 14C alabaster Virgin, a Pietà attributed to Morales, a Salzillo statue of the prophet Eli and a fine canvas, The Immaculate Conception, by Zurbarán (Plaza Obispo Don Bernardo; 🕒 open Tue–Fri 11am–2pm, 5–8pm (4–7pm Oct–Mar), Sat 11.30am–1.30pm, 5–8pm, Sun 11am–2pm; ⊕€3; 🕾 949 39 10 23).

Valverde de los Arroyos★

🕒 68km/45mi N via CM 1003 AND 1006.
Around Ocejón (2 048m/6 700ft) are clustered the so-called pueblos negros or black slate villages. Among them Valverde is especially attractive, its houses with long wooden balconies, and its plaza retaining the old drinking fountain. A footpath leads to the splendid **Despeñal Agua** waterfall that tumbles 100m/110ft in its fall down the rock faces.

ADDRESSES

🛏 STAY

⊝ **Hotel España** – Tenient Figueroa 3, Guadalajara. 🕾 949 21 13 03. 45 rooms. A simple two-star hotel, this long-established local favourite is ideally situated close to the Plaza Mayor. Its rooms are plainly decorated, while a cafeteria offers meals and coffee throughout the day.

⊝⊝ **Hotel Tryp** – Autovía A 2, km 55, Guadalajara. 🕾 902 44 66 66. www.hotel gudalajara.com. 159 rooms. Sitting on the edge of the town, the Tryp hotel, one of a large chain, is a tall modern building with good views. The decoration is clean and modern, and the cafeteria and restaurant serve elegant food.

⊝⊝⊝ **Parador de Sigüenza** – El Castillo. 🕾 949 39 01 00. www.parador.es. 79 rooms. A fine example of the parador chain's level of historical restoration, this vast hilltop castle keeps an air of sobriety as well as comfort. The inner patio, with a garden where you can relax with a drink, is full of atmosphere. Safe parking.

🍴 EAT

⊝ **El Mesón** – Seminario 14, Sigüenza. 🕾 949 39 06 49. Lots of regional specialities, several of them based on the delicious local lamb, are served here to lots of families spreading over large tables. The homemade puddings are delicious.

⊝⊝ **Calle Mayor** – Mayor 21, Sigüenza. 🕾 949 39 17 48. www.restaurantecalle mayorcom. Traditional and creative dishes are combined on the menu of this countrified restaurant in the centre of old Sigüenza.

⊝⊝⊝ **Amparito Roca** – Toledo 19, Guadalajara. 🕾 949 21 46 39. www.amparito roca.com. The setting of the elegant restaurant in a house with garden goes with the high-end feel to the menu, which mixes traditional and avant-garde Spanish cooking.

EXTREMADURA

Extremadura – it means "beyond the River Douro" – forms much of the boundary between Spain and Portugal. In Roman times it was at one with present-day Portugal, making up the Roman territory known as Lusitania. This was the heyday of the region, when Mérida, the home of Emperor Augustus, was its capital. Some 1 500 years later Charles V also chose to retire here, far from the cares of the world. Like La Mancha, Extremadura is dominated by the harsh, unforgiving arid climate of La Meseta.

Add to this its isolation from the rest of Spain (even today it is known as the back of beyond) and an unrewarding system of absentee landlord farming, and it is no wonder that over the centuries so many Extremadurans chose to make their fortune elsewhere. The region's most famous sons were its Conquistadores: Cortés, conqueror of Mexico; Pizarro, conqueror of Peru; Hernando de Soto, first European discoverer of the Mississippi, and many more. This is one of Spain's least densely populated regions; in many areas sheep outnumber humans while storks wheel majestically overhead and nest on tall buildings and towers. Summers are punishingly hot, while spring and autumn are exceptionally beautiful times of year.

Highlights

1. Wandering the time-capsule streets of Old **Cáceres** (p373)

2. Paying homage to the Virgin in the Monasterio de **Guadalupe** (p376)

3. Sitting in **Mérida**'s Teatro Romano, imagining the past (p379)

4. Taking a coffee in the Plaza Mayor in charming **Trujillo** (p381)

5. Crossing the Puente Romano bridge near **Monfragüe**'s natural parkland (p204)

Medieval Majesty

Upper Extremadura has the most fertile land in the region, especially in the verdant Valle de la Vera, where crops include cotton and around 80 per cent of all Spain's tobacco. The hilltop town of Plasencia, an important market town, is a highlight. Built mostly between the 12C and 14C, its old mansions and churches retain their atmosphere and the cathedral is one of Extremadura's finest. Close by is the monastery of Yuste, the retirement home of Charles V, a haven of tranquility at the foot of the mountains. In the centre of the region, the ancient walled city of Cáceres, designated a World Heritage site, has a feast of medieval architecture, including one of Spain's finest assemblies of Gothic and Renaissance mansions.

Conquistador Towns

Guadalupe is famous for its Mudéjar monastery, the second most important Marian shrine in the country, home to the venerated effigy of the Virgin of Guadalupe. The cult of the Virgin and the village's name was exported by the Conquistadores and is widespread throughout Latin America. Trujillo is a charming small town, redolent of Conquistador wealth with mansions built from the riches accumulated by Pizarro (his four half brothers, also from Trujillo), de Orellana and other adventurers.

Small cities and towns in the south have kept extraordinary architecture and art. Mérida was the headquarters of Western Roman Iberia and retains many important monuments including the Roman Theatre, where plays are staged each summer. Olivenza, close to the Portuguese border, keeps the imprint of its Manueline architecture in quiet plazas. Its 15C castle is now a sumptuous parador. Stay the night here and you will be following in the footsteps of Hernán Cortés, who lodged in the castle before setting off for the New World.

Extremadura boasts historic paradores at Plasencia, Trujillo, Guadalupe and Cáceres, that allow you to really feel part of the region's rich history.

Plasencia★

In this tranquil provincial town are interesting Renaissance buildings such as the New Cathedral. Between February and July migrating storks nest on rooftops and towers.

SIGHTS
BARRIO VIEJO (OLD QUARTER)

Houses with wrought-iron balconies make up the neighbourhood.

Catedral★

Pl. de la Catedral. ⏱*Open Mon–Sat Apr–Oct 9am–1pm, 5–7pm; Nov–Mar 4–6pm, Sun 9am–1pm.* ⏱*Closed during Mass and on public holidays in the afternoon.* ⊙€1.50. ☏927 41 48 52.

Enter by the north door which has rich Plateresque decoration. A door left of the *coro* opens into the 13-14C **old cathedral** (parish church of Santa María). The cloisters have pointed arches and Romanesque capitals while the chapter house is covered by a fine dome. In the shortened nave is a museum of religious art.

Inside the 15C *Catedral Nueva* (New Cathedral), the tall pillars and slender ribs illustrate the mastery of architects Juan de Java, Diego de Siloé and Alonso de Covarrubias.

The **altarpiece**★ is decorated with statues by the 17C sculptor Gregorio Fernández; the **choir stalls**★ were carved in 1520 by Rodrigo Alemán.

Start from Plaza de la Catedral and leaving on your right the **Casa del Deán** (Deanery) with its unusual corner window, and the **Casa del Dr Trujillo**, now the Law Courts (Palacio de Justicia), head towards the Gothic **Iglesia de San Nicolás**, a church which faces the beautiful façade of the **Casa de las Dos Torres** (House with Two Towers).

Continue to the **Palacio Mirabel**. This palace, flanked by a massive tower, contains a two-tiered patio and the Museo de Caza (Hunting Museum). A passage beneath the palace *(door on right-hand side)* leads to **Calle Sancho Polo** and a quarter near the ramparts of stepped alleys, white-walled houses and washing hanging from the windows. Turn right for **Plaza Mayor**, an asymmetrical square surrounded by porticoes and full of busy cafés.

EXCURSIONS
Monasterio de Yuste★

▶ *1.8km/1mi from Cuacos de Yuste.* ⏱*Open Tue–Sun Apr–Sept 10am–6.15pm; Oct–Mar 10.30am–1.30pm, 3–5.15pm.* ⊙€2.50. ☏927 17 21 97. *www.yustedigital.com.*

In 1556, a weary Emperor **Charles V** retired to this modest Hieronymite monastery in a serene setting against a mountain backdrop.

The monastery, devastated during the War of Independence, is partially restored. Of Charles V's small palace one sees the dining hall, the royal bedroom adjoining the chapel, the Gothic church and, lastly, the two fine cloisters, one Gothic, the other Plateresque. Leave time to wander down to Cuacos de Yuste, the picturesque village below the monastery where Charles V's illegitimate son, Don Juan of Austria, grew up.

Coria★

▶ *42km/26mi W.*

▶ *Take the N 630 S. After 7km/4.3mi turn right onto the EX 108.*

This atmospheric town overlooking the Alagón Valley retains Roman walls and gateways, rebuilt in the Middle Ages. Walk through its old streets to reach the cathedral.

▶ **Population:** 40 105
⏱ **Michelin Map:** 576 L 11 – Extremadura (Cáceres).
🅘 **Info:** Plaza de la Torre de Lucía. ☏927 01 78 40. www.aytoplasencia.es.
▶ **Location:** Plasencia stands where the Sierra de Gredos meets the Extremadura plain. 🚂Calle Alfonso Camargo.

Catedral de la Asunción de Nuestra Señora★

Plaza de la Catedral. ⏱*Open daily 15 May–31 Oct 10.30am–2pm, 4.30–7pm.* ⏱*Closed Sun am.* 🎟€2 museum. 𝄞927 50 39 60.

The Gothic cathedral, embellished with elegant Plateresque decoration in the 16C, is crowned with a Baroque tower and has a sculptured frieze.

The tall single aisle has vaulting adorned with lierne and tierceron ribs typical of the region. Note the 18C altarpiece and, in the *coro*, the wrought-iron grilles and the Gothic choir stalls. Within the cathedral is a museum of religious art, much drawn from other churches in the area, with some fine pieces.

EXCURSION
Parque Nacional de Monfragüe

The National Park of Monfragüe, lying southeast of Plasencia, protects 500sq km/19 sq mi of rolling hill country around the dammed valleys of the River Tagus and Tiétar.

The Mediterranean scrub and woodland here, unbroken by large towns or farmland, has become a refuge for wildlife, particularly rare birds, which can be seen here, at a distance, often from the road or lookout points, with remarkable ease. The entry point to the park, is **Villarreal de San Carlos**,

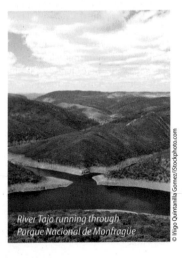

River Tajo running through Parque Nacional de Monfragüe

© Iñigo Quintanilla Gomez/iStockphoto.com

where there are two information centres: one explains the park's ecosystems, and the other its fauna (Centro de Información, Villareal de San Carlos, off the EX208 from Plasencia; ⏱open 9am–7.30pm, 6pm Sep–Mar; 𝄞927 19 91 34; www.extremambiente.es). The little town offers simple accommodation and eating places and is the starting point of hiking and driving routes. One road route (12km/7.5mi) takes you to the lake formed by the dam, which overlooks the farmland outside the park, where fighting bulls and black pigs graze under holm-oaks.

The second (8km/5mi) leads through the hills, past a lookout point to the Salto del Gitano (Gypsy's Leap), a peak where imperial eagles, black storks and kites breed. Shortly afterwards you can park and climb Monfragüe fortress, which gives a splendid 360° view from the top. Some of the other wildlife in the park, such as its Iberian lynx, are more difficult to see, but driving slowly through its roads often surprises red deer and wild boar.

ADDRESSES

🛏 STAY

🛌 **Casa Rural Al-Mofrag** – *Villareal de San Carlos, 19.* 𝄞*927 199 205. www.casaruralalmofrag.com. 6 rooms.* Simple but comfortable rural accommodation, with a kitchen available, designed for those who want to explore the nature park on foot.

🛌🍽🖥🛏 **Parador de la Vera** – *Avda de García Prieto 1, Jarandilla de la Vera, Cáceres.* 𝄞*927 56 00 88. www.parador.es.* One of the most beautiful rural paradors inside a modest 15C castle, entered through a long courtyard, this hotel offers tranquility, gardens, mountain walks nearby and an ideal summer base for exploring the Plasencia area.

🍴 EAT

🍽 **La Pitarra del Gordo** – *Pl Mayor, 8.* 𝄞*927 41 45 05. www.lapitarradelgordo.com.* A useful stopping-off point for a tapa or lunch of various raciones, this popular bar serves excellent charcuterie, including ham, and the rough red pitarra wine made from local grapes.

Cáceres★★★

The Almohad walls of this World Heritage Site, a provincial capital, enclose a rare ensemble of Gothic and Renaissance noble houses.

THE CITY TODAY

Cáceres was a thriving commercial site as far back as 25 BC under Roman rule and contains a heady mix of Roman, Moorish, Sephardic and Renaissance architecture enclosed by its medieval walls.

☙ WALKING TOUR

CÁCERES VIEJO★★★ (OLD CÁCERES)

1hr30min.

Within Moorish walls lies a group of Gothic and Renaissance mansions beyond compare in Spain. The shields on the unadorned, ochre façades of the 15C and 16C reflect their owners, the Ulloas, the Ovandos and the Saavedras, who in battles won prestige, not wealth. The fortified towers of Cáceres were demolished on the command of Queen Isabel in 1477.

Pass beneath the **Arco de la Estrella** (Star Arch; *Pl. Mayor*), which was built into the wall by Manuel Churriguera in the 18C.

Plaza de Santa María★

On all sides are golden ochre façades. The front of the **Palacio Mayoralgo** (Mayoralgo Palace; ○━*closed to the public*) has elegant paired windows while the **Palacio Episcopal** (Bishop's Palace; *free access is available to the patio portico*) has a 16C bossed doorway with medallions of the Old and New Worlds on either side.

Iglesia de Santa María

Pl. Santa María. ◷*Open Mon–Sat 10am –2pm, 5–8pm, Sun and public holidays 9.30–11.50am, 5–6.15pm.* ◓*€1.* ✆*927 21 53 13.*

This 16C church has three Gothic aisles of almost equal height, with lierne and tierceron vaulting from which ribs

descend into slender columns engaged in the main pillars. The fine carved high altar retable (16C) is difficult to see.

▷ *Continue to the top of Calle de las Tiendas.*

Casa y Torre de los Caravajal

Amargura. ◷*Open Mon–Fri 10am– 2pm, 5–7pm, Sat–Sun and public holidays 10am–2pm, 5–8pm.* ◓*No charge.* ✆*927 25 55 97.*

Built between the 15C and 16C, blending Gothic and Renaissance styles, this palace, flanked by a medieval tower, houses an information centre sketching out what you can see in Cáceres province. Of special interest is the architectural model of Cáceres old town.

▷ *Take the narrow alley opposite, Adarve Obispo Álvarez de Castro.*

Palacio Toledo Moctezuma

This 14–16C palace is now the city's history archive. Its curious name derives from the marriage of conquistador Juan Cano de Saavedra with the daughter of Aztec king Moctezuma II. Visits may be made on request.

▷ *Return to Plaza Sta María.*

▸ **Population:** 92 187
⚲ **Michelin Map:** 576 N 10 (town plan) – Extremadura (Cáceres).
▯ **Info:** Plaza Mayor. ✆927 01 08 34. www.turismocaceres.org.
◉ **Location:** Cáceres is strategically situated at the heart of Extremadura in west-central Spain. ▭Avenida Juan Pablo II nº 6.
◈ **Don't Miss:** The city walls and mansions, especially at night.
◷ **Timing:** Allow a half-day in Cáceres, then explore the region.

Palacio de los Golfines de Abajo★ (Lower Golfines Palace) Pl. de Santa María.

⊶Closed to the public.

This splendid late 15C Gothic-Plateresque mansion is of stone. The paired window derives from the Moorish *ajimez*; the fillet, delicately framing the windows and door, recalls the *alfiz*.
A Plateresque frieze with winged griffons was added in the 16C.

▷ *Plaza San Jorge is adjacent to Plaza Sta María.*

Plaza San Jorge

Note the austere 18C façade of the Jesuit church of **San Francisco Javier.**

▷ *Take Cuesta de la Compañía to Pl. San Mateo.*

Iglesia de San Mateo

Plaza de San Mateo. ⏲Open for Mass.
The church's high Gothic nave, begun in the 14C, abuts a 16C *coro alto* set on a vaulted arcade. Inside are a Baroque altarpiece and side chapels with tombs with decorative heraldic motifs.
In the Calle Orellana the 15C **Torre de la Plata** (Silver Tower) and **Casa del Sol**

(Sun House, for the Solís family crest over the arch) have unusual parapets.

▷ *Walk back to Plaza San.*

Casa de las Cigüeñas

Plaza de San Mateo. ⏲Open daily 11am–1pm, 5–8pm. ⊗No charge.
The Stork House retains the town's only 15C battlemented tower.

▷ *Turn left towards Plaza de las Veletas.*

Casa de las Veletas (Weather Vane House)

Pl. de las Veletas s/n. ⏲Open Jun–Sept Tue–Sat 9.30am–2.30pm, 5–8.15pm, Sun and public holidays 10.15am–2.30pm. ⊗€1.50; free for EU citizens. ✆927 01 08 77.
This 18C mansion houses, built on the site of the Alcazar, the **Museo de Cáceres**. Collections include Bronze Age steles, Celt-Iberian statues of wild boar (*verracos*) and local dress and crafts.
The 11C **aljibe** (cistern) is still fed from the roof and sloping square. It is covered by five rows of horseshoe-shaped arches supported by granite capitals.

▷ *Take Calle Ancha oppositee Iglesia San Mateo.*

Casa del Comendador de Alcuéscar Ancha 6.

This palace, also called the **Palacio de Torreorgaz**, with fine Gothic tower, delicate window surrounds and an unusual corner balcony, is a Parador.
Down the alley within the ramparts is the **Palacio de los Golfines de Arriba** (⏾*see entry*) with plain façade and attractive patio. Further on, on Santa Ana, the **Casa de la Generala** is the law school.

Map of Cáceres Viejo:

Barrio Nuevo · Sancti Espíritu · Camberos · Santiago · Villalobos · N · Palacio de Godoy · Pl. de la Concepción · Gen. Ezponda · Pl. Mayor · Palacio de los Toledo-Moctezuma · Arco de la Estrella · P · Palacio episcopal · Torre de los Espaderos · Torre del Horno · Palacio Carvajal · Parra · Pintores · H · Palacio Mayoralgo · Sta María · Pl. STA MARÍA · Casa de la Generala · Casa de los Becerra · PALACIO DE LOS GOLFINES DE ABAJO · Adarve de Sta Ana · Cuesta de la Compañía · Pl. San Jorge · Pl. de San Juan · Torre de los Plata · S. Francisco Javier · Palacio de los Golfines de Arriba · Olmos · Casa del Sol · Adarve del Padre Rosalío · S.Mateo · Casa de las Cigüeñas · Ancha · Pl. S. Mateo · Pl. de las Veletas · Fuente Concejo · F. Pizarro · Hornos · Casa del Comendador de Alcuéscar · Casa de las Veletas · S. Roque · CÁCERES VIEJO · Pl. de Sta Clara · 100 m · 100 yds

---

▷ *Go through the ramparts opposite.*

The steps to Plaza Mayor del General Mola afford an interesting view of the walls.

ADDITIONAL SIGHTS

Iglesia de Santiago (St James' Church)
Pl. de Santiago. ☞*No charge.*
The Romanesque church is the birthplace of the Military Order of the Knights of Cáceres who in turn founded the Order of the Knights of St James.
The altarpiece by Berruguete (1557) bears scenes from the Life of Christ. These surround a vigorous, finely portrayed St James the Moorslayer.
The **Palacio de Godoy** opposite has an impressive coat of arms on the corner and a fine inner patio.

EXCURSIONS

Santuario de la Virgen de la Montaña
▷ *Sierra de la Mosca. 3km/1.8mi E.*
🕐*Open daily 8.30am–2pm, 5–9pm.*
🕐*Closed 22 Apr–1st Sun in May.*
℘*927 22 00 49.*
In this 17C Baroque shrine in a lovely setting among olive trees is a statuette of the Virgin (*romería*, or pilgrimage, the first Sunday in May). The esplanade offers a **view**★ of the plateau.

Museo Vostell-Malpartida
▷ *15.2km/9.3mi E along the N 521 to Malpartida de Cáceres; the museum is 3km/1.8mi beyond (follow signposts).*
🕐*Open Tue–Sat 10.30am–1.30pm, 5–8pm (Mar–Jun 7.30pm, Sep–Mar 6.30pm), Sun 10am–2.30pm.* 🕐*Closed public hols.* ☞*€2; no charge Wed.*
℘*927 01 08 12. www.museovostell.org.*
The museum in an 18C wool-washing plant was created by Hispano-German artist Wolf Vostell, co-founder of the 1960s art movement Fluxus. It includes late 20C works by Canogar, the Crónica team, Saura, Maciunas and Brecht.

Arroyo de la Luz
▷ *20km/12.4mi W along the N 521 and C 523.*

To find the **Iglesia de la Asunción**, head for the tower. The 16C altarpiece has 16 **painted tablets**★ and four medallions by **Morales the Divine**, a stunning assemblage of his works in one place. The tourist office (🕐*open Tue–Fri, Sun 9.30am–2pm, 4.30–7.30pm (5–8pm Jun–Sep); Sat 10am–1pm*), which stands directly opposite the church, opens the church for visitors.

Alcántara
▷ *65km/40mi NW via the N 521 and C 523.*
Alcántara is famed for its Roman bridge from which it took its ancient name (*Al Kantara* in Arabic).

Puente Romano★
▷ *2km/1.2mi NW on the road to Portugal.*
This magnificent bridge (106 AD), of massive unmortared granite blocks, has withstood formidable floodwaters. Note the small temple at one end and the central triumphal arch.

Convento de San Benito
Regimiento de Argel. ☞*Guided tours (45min) daily Apr–Sept 10am–2pm, 5–8pm; Oct–Mar 4–6.30pm.*
☞*No charge.* ℘*927 39 00 80.*
The old headquarters of the Military Order of Alcántara stands high above the Tajo. The 16C monastery has a Plateresque church with star vaulting, a Gothic patio and a well-restored refectory. The graceful Renaissance amphitheatre is used as the backdrop for plays.

ADDRESSES

♟/EAT

⊜☺☺ **Atrio** – *Av de España 30 (pasaje)*
℘*927 24 29 28. www.restauranteatrio.com*
Closed last 2 weeks of Jul, Sun pm, Mon.
A gourmet place of pilgrimage where chef-proprietor Toño Pérez has slowly created a unique repertoire updating regional flavours and produce in creative modern dishes. The wine cellars are astonishing in range and quality.

Trujillo★★

Modern Trujillo conceals the charm of the old town, on a granite ledge above. It was hastily fortified by the Moors in the 13C, and embellished over centuries with mansions built by those who had made their fortunes in the Americas.

A BIT OF HISTORY

Cradle of the Conquistadores – From Trujillo **Francisco de Orellana** left in 1542 to explore the country of the Amazons. Native son **Francisco Pizarro** (c. 1475–1541) plundered the riches of the Inca Emperor Atahualpa and was murdered amid untold riches in his own palace.

SIGHTS
OLD QUARTER

Trujillo's mansions, built later in the 16C and 17C, decorated with arcades, loggias and corner windows, form changing compositions along steep alleys.

One of the most beautiful squares in Spain, the **Plaza Mayor★★** is irregular, lined by mansions, its levels linked by wide flights of steps. By night, it is positively theatrical. The 16C **Iglesia de San Martín** (◔open daily 10am–2pm, 4–6.30pm; ☞€1.40) encloses a vast nave chequered with funerary paving stones.

The 17C **Palacio de los Duques de San Carlos★** (Palace of the Dukes of Saint Charles) is now a convent. The granite façade, decorated in Classical Baroque style, has a corner window topped by a crest with a double-headed eagle, and with chimneys on top inspired by American cultures. Calle Sillería leads away from the souteastern corner of the square. A Renaissance loggia, the **Palacio de los Marquess de Piedras Albas** (Palace of the Marquises of Piedras Albas) has been accommodated into the original Gothic wall. On the other side of the square stands the **Palacio de los Marqueses de la Conquista** (Palace of the Marquises of the Conquest), in reality the palace of Hernando Pizarro, the conquistador's brother. To the left of a

▷ **Population:** 9 860
◔ **Michelin Map:** 576 N 12 – Extremadura (Cáceres).
▯ **Info:** Plaza Mayor. ✆927 32 26 77. www.trujillo.es.
▷ **Location:** Trujillo is situated on the A 5 linking Madrid and Badajoz.
◉ **Don't Miss:** The Plaza Mayor and old town's alleys.

Plateresque corner **window★**, added in the 17C, are busts of Francisco Pizarro and his wife; on the right are Hernando and his niece, whom he married.

Other buildings on the plaza include the Old Town Hall, now the town's law courts, fronted by Renaissance arcades and the Casa de las Cadenas (House of Chains), where Christians freed from the Moors traditionally left their chains, with a tower including a Mudéjar belfry, a favourite spot for storks.

Sometimes used as a venue for council meetings in the Middle Ages is the **Iglesia de Santiago** (◔open daily 10am–2pm, 5–8pm (4–7pm Oct–May); ☞€1.40). The church's 13C Romanesque belfry and the tower of the Palacio de los Chaves frame the Arco de Santiago (St James Arch), one of seven gateways to the town.

Trujillo's pantheon is the 13C **Iglesia de Santa María★** (Pl. de Santa María; ◔open daily Apr–Sept 10am–2pm, 5–8pm; Oct–Mar 10am–2pm, 4–7pm; ☞€1.25; ✆927 32 30 05). The panels of the Gothic **retable★** are by Fernando Gallego.

From the top of the belfry there is a delightful **view** of brown tile roofs, the Plaza Mayor arcades and the castle.

The **castle** (Cerro Cabeza de Zorro; ◔open daily Jun–Sept 10am–2pm, 5–8.30pm; Oct–May 10am–2pm, 4–8pm; ◔closed 1 Jan, Easter Monday, 29–31 Aug afternoons, 25 Dec; ☞€1.30; ✆651 86 96 51) stands out on a granite ledge, its massive crenellated wall reinforced by heavy towers. Above the keep is the patron of Trujillo, Our Lady of Victory. View Trujillo from these walls.

Guadalupe★★

Guadalupe's monastery bristles with battlements and turrets above a picturesque village with brown tile roofs. Richly endowed by rulers and deeply venerated by the people, the Virgin of Guadalupe, in the monastery's church, thought to be miraculous, made this a place of pilgrimage with great influence by the 16C and 17C. Ferdinand and Isabelle received Christopher Columbus here and the first American Indians were brought to the church for baptism. Today the Virgin remains a symbol of Hispanidad, the community of Spanish cultures in the Old and New Worlds. The road above the **old village**★ commands a good **view**★ of the magical setting.

SIGHTS
Monasterio★★

Guided tours (1hr) daily 9.30am –1pm 3.30–6pm. €4. *Entrance includes Embrodiery Museum, and Painting and Sculpture Museum.* ☏927 36 70 00.

The monastery complex dates from the late 14C–early 15C, but there are numerous additions within the fortified perimeter. The monastery contains artistic treasures, many of which reflect the Hieronymite monks' craftmanship – embroi-dery, gold, silversmithing and illumination.

Façade

Golden in colour, exuberant in its Flamboyant Gothic decoration, the 15C façade overlooks a picturesque square. Moorish influence can be seen in the sinuous decoration. Bronze reliefs on the 15C doors illustrate the Lives of the Virgin and Christ.

Iglesia (Church)

14C. One of the first buildings, the church received 18C additions. An intricate 16C grille by Valladolid iron-smiths closes the sanctuary, which has a large Classically ordered 17C retable

> ▶ **Population:** 2 114
> ⚲ **Michelin Map:** 576 N 14 – Extremadura (Cáceres).
> 🛈 **Info:** Plaza Santa María de Guadalupe. ☏927 15 41 28. www.puebladeguadalupe.net.
> ▶ **Location:** Guadalupe is SW of Madrid, on the slopes of the Guadalupe range.
> ☺ **Don't Miss:** The monastery, and, if you visit on 12 Oct, processions to celebrate the Day of Hispanidad.

by Giraldo de Merlo and Jorge Manuel Theotocopuli, son of El Greco. The Virgin of Guadalupe in the altarpiece **(1)** can be seen more clearly from the **camarín**★.

Camarín★

This 18C chapel-like room is where the Virgin of Guadalupe rests.

Riches of every description abound: jasper, gilded stucco and marble and precious wood marquetry frames for nine canvases by Luca Giordano. The Virgin sits on an enamelwork throne (1953), a small 12C figure carved in darkened oak, obscured beneath embroidered veil and mantle.

Camarín, Monasterio de Guadalupe
©Turespaña

Sala Capitular (Chapter House)

The chapter house contains a remarkable collection of 87 **antiphonaries** and **books of hours with miniatures**★ by the monks of Guadalupe.

Claustro Mudéjar

The 14C–15C cloisters are remarkable for their size and the two storeys of horseshoe arches. Note a small Mudéjar Gothic temple and, in a corner, a lavabo faced with multicoloured tiles.

Sacristía★★ (Sacristy)

Canvases by Carreño de Miranda hang in the antechamber. The 17C sacristy combines Classical architecture and ornate Baroque decoration. The unexpected harmony and rich colouring set off **paintings by Zurbarán**★★ to perfection. The 11 canvases, painted in a serene yet forceful style between 1638 and 1647, are of Hieronymite monks and scenes from the Life of St Jerome which include *The Temptation*.

Relicario (Reliquary Cabinet)

This contains the Virgin of Guadalupe's processional mantles and crown.

Claustro Gótico (Gothic Cloisters)

In the *hospedería* (hostelry). The cloisters were built in the 16C in Flamboyant Gothic style to serve as a dispensary for the monastery's four hospitals.

Museo de Bordados (Embroidery Museum)

The museum, in the former refectory, displays a fine collection of **copes** and **altarfronts**★★, embroidered by the monks between the 15C and the 19C. The richness of their work and artistry are exceptional.

Museo de Pinturas y Esculturas★ (Painting and Sculpture Museum)

Works include a 16C triptych of the *Adoration of the Magi* by Isembrandt, an ivory Christ attributed to Michelangelo, an *Ecce Homo* by Pedro de Mena, eight superb small canvases of the monks by Zurbarán, and Goya's *Prison Confession*.

EXCURSION

Puerto de San Vicente (San Vicente Pass)

▶ *40km/25mi E on the C 401.*

The **road**★ to the pass crosses the Las Villuercas range. The climb *(8km/5mi)* beyond the Guadarranque Valley affords wonderful **views**★ of jagged green mountain ranges above the wild moorland.

ADDRESSES

STAY

Hospedería del Real Monasterio – *Pl. Juan Carlos I. ℰ927 36 70 00. www.monasterioguadalupe.com. 47 rooms. ⬚ €6.50. Restaurant⬚⬚. Closed 15 Jan–15 Feb.* The hotel's superb setting, around the monastery's Gothic cloisters, and its comfortable, quiet rooms ensure a memorable stay. Excellent value for money plus a good restaurant. Highly recommended.

Parador de Guadalupe – *Marqués de la Romana, 12. ℰ927 36 70 75. www.parador.es. 41 rooms.* An exquisite parador occupying the old monastery hospital, once famed as a school of humanities and medicine. The cloister, planted with lemon trees, the garden and swimming pool place luxury within the historic shell. Charming bedrooms keep the buildings' old structure. The restaurant allows you to sample traditional cooking.

Badajoz

Once an Arab fortress, Badajoz crowns a hill along the Guadiana river and the border with Portugal. Much of the old city was destroyed during the Spanish Civil War, but original walls, a fortress and ramparts, the 16C Puente Royal bridge, Mudéjar houses and a fine gateway are reminders of the past.

A BIT OF HISTORY

In the 11C Badajoz became capital of a Moorish kingdom. Because of its frontier location, however, it was besieged and pillaged in the 16C Wars of Succession between Spain and Portugal.

SIGHTS

The 13C **Gothic Catedral de San Bautista** was considerably remodelled during the Renaissance (*Pl. de España; ⓒopen Mon–Fri 10am–10.30am; ⇔no charge; Museo Catedralicio Tue–Sat 11am–1pm, 5–8pm (7pm Oct–Mar); ⇔€3; ℘924 22 39 99*). Its fortress tower boasts delicate Plateresque friezes and window surrounds. The impressive *coro* has 16C stalls and the sacristy holds six fine 17C Flemish tapestries. In the cathedral museum, the canvases include a number by Luis de Morales.

The **Museo Arqueológico Provincial** is a modern museum in the 16C Palacio de la Roca in the *alcazaba (Pl. de José Álvarez y Sáenz de Buruaga; ⓒopen Tue–Sun 10am–3pm; ⓒclosed 1 Jan, 25, 31 Dec; ⇔no charge; ℘924 00 19 08)*. It displays prehistoric and protohistoric steles and figurines; Roman mosaics and bronze tools; Visigothic **pilasters** carved with plant and geometric motifs; medieval artefacts; and Islamic pieces. Unique are the finds from Cancho Ruano, the only excavated Tartessan site in Spain.

The **Museo de Bellas Artes** in two elegant 19C mansions holds a collection of paintings, sculpture and sketches, particularly from the 19C and 20C (*Duque de San Germán 13; ⓒopen Tue–Sat 10am–2pm, 4–6pm (8pm Jun–Aug), Sat–Sun 10am–2pm; ⓒ closed public holidays; ⇔no charge; ℘924 21 24 69)*.

▶ **Population:** 146 832
⚙ **Michelin Map:**
   576 P 9 (town plan) – Extremadura (Badajoz).
🅸 **Info:** Pasaje de San Juan. ℘924 22 49 81. www.turismobadajoz.es.
◗ **Location:** The A 5 links with Mérida (62km/39mi W), the EX 100 connects the town with Cáceres (91km/57mi NE). ▭▭Avenida Carolina Coronado.

The contemporary art museum, the **Museo Extremeño e Iberoamericano de Arte Contemporáneo**, inside its old prison, displays cutting-edge exhibits (*ⓒopen Tue–Sat 10.30am–1.30pm, 5–8pm, Sun 10am–1.30pm; ⓒclosed public holidays; ⇔no charge; ℘924 01 30 60. www.meiac.org)*.

EXCURSIONS

Olivenza

◗ *25km/15.5mi SW.*
www.ayuntamientodeolivenza.com.
Olivenza, given in dowry to King Denis of Portugal at the end of the 13C was returned to Spain in 1801. Portuguese influence shows in its graceful white-walled town centre set in olive groves, not least in its early 16C Manueline style of architecture, late Gothic, with Renaissance and Moorish elements and maritime motifs. Its main monuments are the Ayuntamiento (town hall), and the **Iglesia de Santa María Magdalena★★**

Albuquerque★

◗ *49km/30mi N of Badajoz on EX110.*
Albuquerque, close to the Portuguese frontier, has a well-preserved 13C castle standing on a rocky promontory. Visits to the castle are guided and include the terrace with its water cistern, dungeon, living quarters and tower, from the top of which you can look over to Portugal. You can also wander around the medieval quarter that lies below its walls.

Mérida★

This historic town in Extremadura, capital of Roman Lusitania, retains an extraordinary series of classical monuments that have earned it World Heritage status. Today it is also Extremadura's regional capital.

SIGHTS
ROMAN MÉRIDA★★
In 25 BC, the Romans founded *Emerita Augusta* on the River Guadiana and at the junction of major Roman roads. They lavished upon it temples, a theatre, an amphitheatre and even a circus.

Museo Nacional de Arte Romano★★ (National Museum of Roman Art)
José Ramón Mélida. ◷*Open 1 Jul–30 Sep 9.30am–3.30pm, 5.30–8.30pm; 8 Dec–14 Feb 10am–2pm, 4–6pm; 15 Feb–30 Jun and 1 Oct–7 Dec 10am–2pm, 4–9pm.* ◷*Closed 1 Jan, 1 May, 24–25, 31 Dec.* ✆€3. ✆924 31 19 12. *www.museoromano.com.*
An imposing brick **building**★ by Rafael Moneo Vallés, reminiscent of a Roman amphitheatre, displays Mérida's rich archaeological collections.
Sculptures include the head of Augustus *(at the end of the second bay).* In the last bay are statues, caryatids and giant medallions (Medusa and Jupiter) which made up the frieze of Mérida's forum. Wonderful **mosaics**★ may be viewed up close.
In the basement are remains of Roman villas and tombs.

♟♟Teatro Romano★★ (Roman Theatre)
Av. de los Estudiantes. ◷*Open daily 9.30am–2pm, 5–7.30pm (Oct–May 4–6pm).* ✆€8. ✆924 00 49 08. *www.consorciomerida.org.*
The theatre, built by Agrippa in 24 BC, seated 6 000. A high stage wall was decorated in Hadrian's reign (2C AD) with colonnade and statues. Great granite blocks over the passages are skilfully secured without mortar.

▶ **Population:** 55 568
⊙ **Michelin Map:** 576 P 10 – Extremadura (Badajoz).
🛈 **Info:** Paseo José Álvarez Saénz de Buruaga. ✆924 33 07 22. www.merida.es. A combined entrance ticket (✆12€), on sale at all the city's major monuments, allows entry to the theatre, amphitheatre, Roman houses, Alcazaba and the Iglesia de Santa Eulalia.
▶ **Location:** Mérida is close to the A 5 highway to Portugal. ▬Calle Cardero.
⊙ **Don't Miss:** Roman sites and museum.

Anfiteatro★ (Amphitheatre)
Pl. José Álvarez Saenz de Buruega. ◷*Open same hours as Roman Theatre.* ✆€4.
The 1C BC arena held 14 000 spectators. It staged chariot races and was flooded for mock sea battles. Original steps remain; a few tiers are reconstructed. A wall crowned by a cornice protected noble spectators from beasts during gladiatorial combats.

Casa Romana del Anfiteatro (Roman Villa)
Adjacent to Amphithetare.
☞*Closed until 2013 for excavations.* ✆€4. ✆924 31 20 24.
Water channels, pavement foundations and mosaics remain in this large Roman villa.

Casa del Mitreo
Oviedo. ◷*Open Tue–Sun 10am–1.45pm, 4–7.15pm (6.15pm Oct–May).* ✆4€.
The patios of this 1C villa served to distribute light and collect rainwater. Visible remains include the **Cosmological Mosaic**★.

Templo de Diana
Santa Catalina. ✆*No charge.*
Corinthian columns and fluted shafts of this temple are visible. Its stones were

used in the 16C to build the palace of the Count of Corbos.

Two Roman **bridges** still span the Albarregas and Guadiana. Polychrome arches remain from two **aqueducts**.

Alcazaba

Graciano. ⏰*Open same hours as Roman Theatre.* ⊜€4. ☏924 31 73 09.
The Moors built this fortress in the 9C to defend the 792m/866yd **Puente Romano**★ (Roman Bridge) across the Guadiana. Inside the walls is a **cistern**.

Zona Arqueológica de Morería★

Po. de Roma. ⏰*Same opening hours as Casa del Mitreo.* ☏924 31 33 53.
The riverside Morería archaeological site includes finds from Classical to modern times, ranging from sections of Roman wall to 15C–17C craftsmen's workshops.

Basílica de Santa Eulalia★

Av. de Extremadura 15. ⏰*Same opening hours as Casa del Mitreo.* ⏰*Closed religious holidays.* ⊜€4.
☏*924 31 20 24.*
The site, occupied in turn by a palaeo-Christian necropolis, a 5C basilica and this 13C Romanesque church, has been excavated and can be visited on its different levels.

EXCURSIONS

Zafra

◐ *SW of Madrid 27m/4.3mi W of the N 630.*
A 15C *alcázar* (now a parador) guards this white-walled town, one of the oldest in Extremadura. It was built by the Dukes of Feria with nine round towers, a white marble Renaissance patio and delightful gilded salon.
The large 18C **Plaza Grande**★ and the adjoining smaller 16C **Plaza Chica**★ are lined by fine arcaded houses.
The 16C transitional Gothic-Renaissance **Iglesia de la Candelaria** (*Rotonda de la Candelaria;* ☏924 55 01 28) has a massive red-brick belfry. In the south transept is an **altarpiece** by Zurbarán painted in 1644.

Llerena

◐ *42km/26mi from Zafra SE along the N 432.*
The **Plaza Mayor** of this country town is one of the most harmonious in Extremadura. The composite façade of the **Iglesia de Nuestra Señora de la Granada** (Church of Our Lady of Granada; *Pl. San Juan;* ☏924 87 23 25) built of white limestone and brick has superimposed arcades which contrast with the mass of a great Baroque belfry.

Jerez de los Caballeros

◐ *42km/26mi SW along the EX 101 and EX 112.*
Jerez de los Caballeros is the birthplace of **Vasco Núñez de Balboa** (1475–1519), who crossed Panama and in 1513 discovered the Pacific Ocean. The town's name, tradition and atmosphere stem from the Knights Templar – Caballeros del Temple – to whom the town was given in 1230 by Alfonso IX of León on its recapture from the Moors.
Jerez's stands on a hillside and its steep lanes lined by white-walled houses are a foretaste of Andalucía. On the summit is the ornate San Bartolomé *(Pl. de San Bartolomé)*. This is a centre of ham-making, hosting a world congress every year, and the aroma of ham hangs in the streets and surrounding hillsides where black-footed pigs snuffle.

ADDRESSES

🛏 STAY

⊜⊜⊜⊜ **Parador de Hernán Cortés** – *Pl Corazón de María, 7, Zafra* ☏924 55 45 40. *www.parador.es. 51 rooms.* ⊡ €15. Housed inside the town's old Alcázar, this parador gives a chance to stay where Hernán Cortés, controversial conquistador, passed time before sailing to conquer Mexico. Useful central parking.

🎉 FESTIVALS

From late July to late August the Roman theatre reverts to its original function to host the prestigious Merida Classical Theatre Festival which has been running since 1953. www.festivaldemerida.es.

Atlantic Spain

View of Donostia-San Sebastián - Isle of Santa Clara in the bay of La Concha

Atlantic Spain

PICOS DE EUROPA ★★★ Highly recommended

Burgos ★★ Recommended

Lugo ★ Interesting

Reinosa Other sights described in this guide

---------- Camino de Santiago
(Chemins de St-Jacques)

La Rochelle

BORDEAUX

FRANCE

NO ATLÁNTICO

Costa de Cantabria

Santillana
del Mar   Santander

Costa de Vizcaya   Costa de Guipúzcoa

PICOS DE   Bilbao   Donostia/   Fontarabie/
EUROPA   Guernica   San Sebastián   Hondarribia/
                                           Fuenterrabía
CANTABRIA   S. Ignacio
Reinosa   de Loiola   LA RHUNE

NERVIÓN   Tolosa   Pau

ICO DE   Vitoria-   Oñati   Valle del   Orreaga/
S MARES   Gasteiz   Baztan   Roncesvalles

Aguilar de   P. N. de   Pamplona
Campoo   Valderejo   Estella
                        Labastida   NAVARRA
LLA   Burgos   Laguardia
ÓN   Haro   Viana   Leyre
GO   Sto Domingo   Nájera   Puente-   Sangüesa
        de la Calzada   la-Reina   Olite
lencia   Covarrubias   Logroño   Tudela
                            La Rioja
Valladolid   Sto Domingo
            de Silos   Soria
                                    ZARAGOZA

CASTILLA
Y LEÓN   CASTILLA
        LA MANCHA
Segovia   ARAGÓN

                Río Tajo
            Embalse de   R. Guadalope
            Entrepeñas

MADRID

                            Teruel

                Embalse de
                Alarcón

NAVARRA

Navarra (Navarre) forms part of Spain's northeastern frontier and is probably the most geographically diverse of the peninsula's northern regions, sweeping from the lush and mountainous belt facing France to a semi-arid desert in the south. In the Middle Ages the towns and villages of Navarra found fame and wealth as staging points on the Camino de Santiago, leaving a rich legacy of churches, monasteries and pilgrims' hospices. Navarran gastronomy is one of Spain's finest: cheese is produced with milk from the sheep you see grazing on its green pastures, and although lesser known than neighbouring La Rioja, local wine is good, cheap and plentiful.

Highlights

1. Watching the bull running at **Pamplona** from a safe distance! (p219)

2. Spooky witches caves near **Zagarramurdi** (p222)

3. Hiking between villages on the **Camino de Santiago** (p226)

4. Discovering the rich royal and pilgrimage legacies of **Estella/ Lizarra** (p230)

5. Staying at the parador **Castillo de los Reyes de Navarra**, Olite/Erriberri (p232)

Pamplona/Iruña

Pamplona/Iruña – most famous outside Spain for the hair-raising "running of the bull" San Fermín festival (held the first week of July) – has been the capital of Navarra for more than a thousand years. Its characterful medieval old town, crumbling citadel and fine Cathedral

make a good base from which to discover the rest of this surprising region.

East of Pamplona

Estella/Lizarra was not only a medieval royal capital but also one of the main halts on the Camino de Santiago – it still is today – and it retains a rich medieval legacy. Like Estella, Sangüesa/Zangoza was once an important pilgrim's pit-stop and has all the historic religious trimmings to prove it, including some remarkable church stone carvings. Just outside the town stands the impressive Castillo de Javier, and it's worth journeying beyond to the Monasterio de Leyre, which not only occupies a magnificent position but also possesses an atmospheric church and crypt.

South of Pamplona

Olite/Erriberri and Tudela are two more charming medieval towns. Olite castle was once the fortress of the kings of Navarra; today it is a magnificent parador. Stay here, then continue to Tudela to see its superb cathedral and then onto the spectacular Bardenas Reales, a desert landscape of rock, clay and gypsum formations home to numerous birds and animals.

North of Pamplona

North of the capital, roads lead to the lush pre-Pyrenees, a popular day-trip destination for *Pampaloneses* fleeing the city heat for hikes in the countryside around the gorgeous Valle de Bidosa's charming "five villages". One of the finest garden estates in Spain, the Jardín de Señorío de Bertiz, is nearby at the threshold to the national park of the same name, where you might spot a Pyrenean salamander if you're lucky.

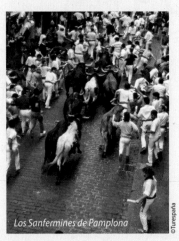

Los Sanfermines de Pamplona

©Turespaña

Pamplona/ Iruña★

The old quarter of Pamplona (Iruña in Basque) keeps its narrow medieval streets and arcaded squares. Streets around the plaza del Castillo are named for trades: Zapatería (shoemaker) and Tejería (tilemaker).

A BIT OF HISTORY

Pamplona is said to have been founded by Pompey, who gave his name to the town. The Moors briefly took over in the 8C but were repelled by Charlemagne, who demolished the walls. The townspeople in turn massacred Charlemagne's rearguard.

In the 10C Pamplona became the capital of Navarra, though it was torn for a time between proponents of Castilla and of French rule.

SIGHTS
Catedral★★

Pl. de la Catedral. Open Mon–Fri 10am–1.30pm, 4–7pm, Sat 10am–1.30pm. Extended hours in summer. €4. 948 21 25 94. www.iglesianavarra.org.

The Gothic Cathedral was built in the 14C and 15C. At the end of the 18C, Ventura Rodríguez rebuilt the west front.

Interior★

The nave has wide arches and windows and great bare walls, typical of Navarra Gothic. In front of the finely wrought grille closing the sanctuary stands the alabaster **tomb**★★, commissioned

- ▶ **Population:** 197 275
- ⌖ **Michelin Map:** 573 D 25 (town plan).
- **Info:** Eslava 1 (corner with Plaza San Francisco). 848 42 04 20. www.pamplona.es.
- ▶ **Location:** Modern Pamplona extends south from the riverside old town. Roads lead to Roncesvalles in the Pyrenees and to Hendaye, both in France. Plaza Estación.
- **Parking:** Don't even try to park in the old city.

in 1416 by Charles III, the Noble. The reclining figures and **mourners** were carved by Janin Lomme. Note the late 15C Hispano-Flemish altarpiece (south ambulatory chapel).

Claustro★

The 14C–15C cloisters appear delicate, with elegant Gothic arches surmounted, in some cases, by gables. Sculptured tombs and doors add interest. Off the east gallery is the Capilla Barbazán with beautiful 14C star vaulting.

On the south side, the doorway of the Sala Preciosa is a masterwork of the period, its tympanum beautifully carved with scenes from the Life of the Virgin and two statues forming a fine Annunciation. In the southeast corner, a lavabo is turned into a shrine commemorating the Battle of Las Navas de Tolosa.

Epic Poems

According to legend, Roncesvalles was the site where the Basques of Navarra massacred the rearguard of Charlemagne's army in 778 as Roland was leading it back through the Pyrenees to France. The late 12C to early 13C poem of **Bernardo del Carpio** describes Bernardo as a national hero who fought alongside his Basque, Navarran and Asturian companions in arms to avenge the Frankish invasion of Spain; the 12C **Song of Roland**, the first French epic poem, on the other hand, glorifies the heroic but ultimately despairing resistance of a handful of valiant Christian knights against hordes of Saracen fanatics.

Museo Diocesano★

Dormitalería 3–5. ⏱*Open Mon–Fri 10am–2pm, 4–7pm, Sat 10am–2pm.* ⟲*Guided tours available with prior booking.* ✎€4. ✆948 21 25 94.

The Diocesan Museum is in the old refectory and kitchen, which date from 1330. The refectory, a lofty hall with six pointed arches, contains a rostrum decorated with an enchanting scene of a unicorn hunt.

The square kitchen has a central lantern rising to 24m/79ft. Displays include a 13C *Reliquary of the Holy Sepulchre* donated by St Louis (Louis IX of France) and polychrome wood statues of the Virgin and Christ. *Follow the narrow, picturesque del Redín to the ramparts.*

Murallas (Ramparts)

La Cuenca de Pamplona zone.
A bastion, now a garden, commands a view of the Puerta de Zumalacárregui (a gate below and to the left), and a stretch of the old walls and a bend in the rivers Arga and Monte Cristóbal.

Museo de Navarra★

Santo Domingo 47. ⏱*Open Tue–Fri 10am–3pm, Sat 11am–7pm.* ⏱*Closed 1 Jan, Good Fri, 7 Jul, 25 Dec.* ✎€2; no charge Sat afternoons and Sun. ✆948 42 64 93. www.cfnavarra.es/cultura/museo.

This museum is on the site of the 16C Hospital de Nuestra Señora de la Misericordia. Only a Renaissance gateway and the chapel remain.

The Roman period *(basement and first floor)* is represented by funerary steles, inscriptions and **mosaic**★ pavements from 2C and 4C villas.

The main exhibit in the Hispano-Moorish section *(Room 1.8)* is an 11C ivory **casket**★ from San Salvador de Leyre sculpted in Córdoba. Romanesque **capitals**★ are from the former 12C cathedral of Pamplona, brilliantly carved with the Passion, the Resurrection and the Story of Job.

The museum also contains **Gothic wall paintings**★ from Artaíz (13C), Artajona (14C), Pamplona (14C), and elsewhere in the province. They share an unobtrusive emphasis on faces and features reminiscent of French miniaturists.

The reconstruction of the interior of the **Palacio de Oriz** is decorated with 16C monochrome panels depicting Adam and Eve and the wars of Charles V.

On the third floor are 17C–18C paintings by Luis Paret and Francisco de Goya (portrait of the *Marqués de San Adrián*).

Iglesia de San Saturnino★

Ansoleaga 21. ⏱*Open Mon–Sat 9am–12.30pm, 6–8pm, Sun and public holidays 10.15am–1.30pm, 5.45–8pm.* ✎*No charge.* ✆948 22 11 94.

This church in a tangle of narrow streets in the old quarter mingles Romanesque brick towers, 13C Gothic **portals**★ and vaulting and later additions.

Ayuntamiento (Town Hall)

Pl. Consistorial. ⊶*Closed to the public.*
This has a reconstructed **Baroque façade**★ (originally late 17C) with statues, balustrades and pediments.

EXCURSIONS
Museo Oteiza

▶ *Cuesta 7, Alzuza. 7 km/4.3mi E. Take the NA 150, then immediately turn left.* ⏱*Open Tue–Fri 10am–3pm, Sat 11am–7pm, Sun 11am–3pm; extended hours in summer.* ✎€4. ✆948 33 20 74. www.museooteiza.org.

Jorge Oteiza (1908–2003) was a key figure of modern Spanish abstract sculpture. The museum is beside his house.

Santuario de San Miguel de Aralar★

▶ *45km/28mi NW. Follow the A 15, then shortly before Lecumberri, turn onto the NA 751. The NA 751 crosses the Sierra de Aralar through beech woods to this sanctuary.* ⏱*Open daily 10am–2pm, 4–7pm.* ✎*No charge.* ✆948 37 30 13. www.aralarkosanmigel.info.

The sanctuary consists of an 8C Romanesque **church** which encloses a totally independent chapel. The gilt and enamel **altar front**★★ is one of the major works of European Romanesque gold- and silverwork, attributed by some to a late 12C Limoges workshop. It con-

The "Sanfermines"

The *feria* of San Fermín is celebrated with joyous ardour from 6 to 14 July each year. Visitors pour in, doubling the town's population, to see the great evening bullfights and enjoy the carefree atmosphere (described by Hemingway in *The Sun Also Rises*). The most spectacular event, and the one most prized by "Pamploneses", however, is the **encierro** or early morning *(around 8am)* running of the bulls. The beasts selected to fight in the evening are let loose with a number of steers to rush through the streets along a set route leading to the bullring.

sists of gilded bronze plaques adorned with enamel and mounted precious stones, arranged as an altarpiece. The outstanding multicoloured honeycomb enamelwork is adorned with arabesques and plant motifs.

Roncesvalles/Orreaga★

▶ *47km/29mi NE along the N 135.*
This 12C ensemble of buildings served as an important hostelry for pilgrims to Santiago de Compostela. Its square funerary chapel is now the Capilla del Sancti Spiritus (Chapel of the Holy Spirit). A collegiate church is rich in relics.

Iglesia de la Real Colegiata

Única. ◐*Open daily 10am–2pm, 3–6pm. Extended hours in summer.* ◐*Closed Jan.* ◐*€4.10.* ◐*Guided tours available.* ℘ *948 79 04 80. www.roncesvalles.es.*
This Gothic collegiate church, inspired by those of the Paris region, was consecrated in 1219. Beneath the high altar canopy is the silver-plated statue of **Nuestra Señora de Roncesvalles**, created in France in the late 13C.

Sala Capitular (Chapter house)

The beautiful Gothic chamber contains the tombs of the founder, Sancho VII, the Strong (1154–1234), King of Navarra and his queen.

Museo★

Única. ◐ *Same opening hours as Iglesia de la Real Colegiata.* ◐*Closed Jan.* ◐*€4.10.* ℘ *948 79 04 80.*
The museum contains fine pieces of ancient plate: a Mudéjar casket, a Romanesque book of the Gospel, a 14C

enamelled reliquary known as "Charlemagne's chessboard", a 16C Flemish triptych, an emerald, said to have been worn by Sultan Miramamolín el Verde in his turban on the day of the Battle of Las Navas de Tolosa in 1212, and a lovely *Holy Family* by Morales.

🚗 DRIVING TOUR

TOUR THROUGH THE VALLE DEL BIDASOA ★

134km/83mi. Allow one whole day.

The Bidasoa Valley cuts through the lower foothills of the western Pyrenees, where villages of typical Basque houses lie amid lush meadows. The Bidasoa river is renowned for its salmon and trout.

▶ *Exit Pamplona from the PA-30 ring road towards Ezcaba. Then take the the N -121A. Near the exit to Oricáin, take the N-121B and exit at Oronoz then follow the signs to the Parque Natural de Señorío Bértiz.*

Señorío Bértiz Natural Park

Access beside the petrol station, on the edge of town. ℘ *948 592 421. www.parquedebertiz.es.*
A natural park since 1984, this area covers 2040 ha/5 000 acres, about half of which is forest (mainly oak and beech). Woods and meadows are home to diverse wildlife, from salamanders to Pyrenean desman (a type of mole). Pedro Ciga was its last lord, custodian of the land formerly given as a gift from King Charles III in the 14C. He planted exotics in the garden (situated at the entrance to the

park and now open to the public) and built a new palace in the Art Nouveau style, while restoring the old. He donated all the deputation of Navarra in 1949, provided everything was left as is. The palace overlooks the Aizkolegi, offering under a wide panorama of the park and the surrounding valleys.

Several marked trails leave from the park entrance (ask for the plan at the gate). The shortest (700m/765yd) and easiest bears left to follow the River Bidasoa. The others go into the forest along the path marked Aizkolegi *(the only one on which you can cycle – follow the green signage).*

 From the centre of Oronoz, take the N 121B, towards Elizondo.

Elizondo, the capital and gateway of the **Valle del Baztán**, has numerous 18–19C houses decorated with armorial bearings known as *caserios*. It's a pleasant place to wander around, soaking up the atmosphere and perhaps buying some of the village's local speciality – hazelnut chocolate.

 From Elizondo head to Elbete and take the N 121B (from here on the road contains many hairpin bends). At Otxondo take the NA 4402 to Leoriaz and then the NA 4401 to Zugarramurdi.

The sleepy enclave of Zugarramurdi is home to one of the most extraordinary places in the region – the so-called "witches caves". At over 120m/130yd long and set over various levels deep in the woods, they are an eerie sight, made even more evocative by the fact that they were an alleged meeting place for Medieval witches.

Many who were caught here were tortured and executed in an inquisition that targeted women and children from the fringe of society (open Tue–Sun 11am–sundown; €3.50).

 Take the N 4401 to Urdax then follow the signs to the N 121B. Close to Oronoz follow the signs to the N121A towards Bera/Vera de Bidasoa.

Bera (or Vera) de Bidasoa is the largest of the ancient confederation of the **Cinco Villas**, comprising **Etxalar**, **Arantza**, **Igantzi** and **Lesaka**. Like the others, Bera's houses bear coats of arms, particularly along its main street. The typically Basque façades have deep eaves over balconies with delicate balustrades.

ADDRESSES

STAY

 Hotel Europa – *Espoz y Mina, 11.* 948 22 18 00. www.hreuropa.com. *25 rooms.* €9. This renovated hotel is a good choice in the centre of Pamplona. Comfortable and functional rooms and a good location near the bullring. As with everywhere in the city at fiesta time, not easy to get a room here.

 Hotel Yoldi – *Av. de San Ignacio, 11.* 948 22 48 00. www.hotelyoldi.com. *50 rooms.* €10.65. Small but well equipped rooms with marble bathrooms. On-site restaurant.

 Hotel Albret – *Ermitagaña 3* 948 17 22 33. www.hotelalbret.net. *107 rooms.* €12.50. Modern rooms lead off a spacious reception area. Free Wi-Fi throughout.

 Hotel Leyre – *Leyre, 7* 948 22 85 00. www.hotel-leyre.com. *55 rooms.* €9. Centrally located with rooms at a variety of prices, all of which are spacious with parquet flooring.

EAT

 Rodero – *Emilio Arrieta 3.* 948 22 80 35. www.restauranterodero.com. *Closed Sun and Holy Week*. This luxury restaurant behind the bullring is one of the best in the whole province. Family-run with high-quality service and creative, innovative cuisine with prices to match.

TAPAS

Baserri – *San Nicolás 32.* 948 22 20 21. www.restaurantebaserri.com. The Baserri is widely recognised as being one of the best place for tapas in Pamplona, as witnessed by its numerous prizes and the huge number of locals who come here. Make sure you try the sirloin with roquefort *(solomillos al roquefort)*.

Monasterio de San Salvador de Leyre★

At the end of a winding road, a splendid **panorama**★★ opens up: limestone crests form majestic ramparts on whose slopes appear the ochre walls of the monastery.

A BIT OF HISTORY

By the early 11C, the Abbey of San Salvador de Leyre was the spiritual centre of Navarra, and the final resting place of kings.

In the 12C, after union with Aragón, Leyre was neglected. By the 19C it had been abandoned. In 1954, however, a Benedictine community from Silos took over. They restored the 17C and 18C conventual buildings which have now been converted into a hostelry.

IGLESIA★★

⊙*Open Mon–Fri 10.15am–2pm, 3.30–6pm, Sat–Sun 10.15am–2pm, 4–6.30pm extended hours in summer* ⊚€1.95.

East End – Built in the 11C. Three apses of equal height, together with the nave wall surmounted by a turret and a square tower make a delightful group. The absence of decoration, apart from several modillions, suggests the building's age.

Crypt★★ – The robust 11C crypt, built to support the Romanesque church above, looks even older. The vaulting is relatively high but divided by arches with enormous voussoirs curving down onto massive plain capitals.

Interior★ – In the 13C the Cistercians rebuilt the central aisle with a bold Gothic vault, while retaining earlier Romanesque bays with barrel vaulting, engaged pillars, and perfectly hewn stone. In the north bay a wooden chest contains the remains of the first kings of Navarra.

West Portal★ – 12C. The portal is called the Porta Speciosa for its decorative richness. Carvings cover every available space. On the tympanum are archaic

▶ **Population:** 575
◔ **Michelin Map:** 573 E26.
▯ **Info:** ℘948 88 41 50. www.monasterio deleyre.com.
▷ **Location:** Near the Yesa reservoir; 50km/31mi SE of Pamplona and 16km/10mi NE of Sangüesa.
◔ **Timing:** The monks perform Gregorian chants inside the church daily at 7pm.
▣ **Parking:** Spaces available at the end of the road near the monastery buildings.

statues – Christ (centre), the Virgin Mary and St Peter *(on His right)* and St John *(on His left)*; the covings are alive with monsters and fantastic beasts.

EXCURSIONS
Hoz de Lumbier★

▷ *14km/8.7mi W.*

The Irati gorge between Lumbier and Liédana is barely 5km/3mi long and so narrow that it appears at either end as a crack in the cliff face. There is a good **view** of the gorge from a lookout point on the road (N 240).

Hoz de Arbayún★

▷ *31km/19.2mi N along the N 240 and NA 211.*

The River Salazar is steeply enclosed within limestone walls. From a point north of Iso there a splendid **view**★★ to the end of the canyon where the cliff walls are clad in lush vegetation.

ADDRESSES

🏠 STAY

⊜⊜🛎 **Hotel Señorío de Monjardín** – *Carret. de Leyre, Yesa.* ℘948 884 188. *40 rooms.* ▣ ⌑ *9.50€. Closed 20 Dec–20 Jan.* Located on an isolated site at the foot of the road, this hotel offers spacious rooms with modern bathrooms. Traditional Navarra-Basque cuisine is served in the restaurant.

Sangüesa/ Zangoza★

Situated on the Río Aragón, Sangüesa (Zangoza in Basque) still stands guard over the bridge which in the Middle Ages brought the region and the city so much prosperity. Its monumental and artistic heritage stems from its location on the Way of St James.

SIGHTS

Iglesia de Santa María la Real★

Mayor. ⏱*Open daily Holy Week–Oct 10.30am–1.30pm, 4–6pm; rest of the year by appointment.* ☞€1.95. ☎*620 110 581.*

Portada Sur★★ (South Portal) – Late 12C to 13C. The portal is amazingly crowded with sculpture. The Master of San Juan de la Peña worked on this masterpiece.

The **statue columns**, already Gothic, derive from those at Chartres and Autun. On the **tympanum**, God the Father at the centre of a group of angel musicians receives the chosen at His right, but with his down-pointing left arm reproves sinners. The **covings** swarm with motifs; the second innermost shows the humbler trades: clog-maker, lute-maker and butcher.

The older **upper arches**, marked by an Aragonese severity of style, show God

▶ **Population:** 5 130
⚙ **Michelin Map:** 573 E 26.
🛈 **Info:** Mayor, 2. ☎948 87 10 84. Guided tours Sangüesa Tour, ☎978 87 10 84. www.sanguesa turismo.com.
▷ **Location:** Sangüesa is 5km/3mi from the N 240, linking Jaca with Pamplona, 36km/22mi away.
👪 **Kids:** Exploring Castillo de Javier.
🕐 **Timing:** A couple of hours.

surrounded by the symbols of the Evangelists, two angels and the disciples.

EXCURSIONS

Castillo de Javier★

▶ *Javier. 7km/4.3mi NE on the NA 541.* ⏱*Open daily Mar–Oct 10am–1.30pm, 3.30–6.30pm; rest of the year closure one hour earlier.* 🕐*Closed 1 Jan, 24–25, 31 Dec.* ☞€2.50. ☎*948 88 40 00.*

St Francis Xavier, the patron saint of Navarra was born in this picturesque fortress in 1506. He founded the Society of Jesus (with Ignatius Loyola), died in 1552 and was canonised in 1622.

The castle was in part destroyed by Cardinal Cisneros in 1516. Its **oratorio★** (oratory) contains a 13C Christ in walnut and an unusual 15C fresco of the Dance of Death.

Detail of the south portal, Iglesia de Santa María la Real

S. Sauvignier/MICHELIN

Sangüesa and the Camino de Santiago

Fear of the Moors compelled Sangüesans to live until the 10C on the Rocaforte hillside; by the 11C, however, the citizens had moved down to defend the bridge and clear a safe passage for pilgrims. Sangüesa reached its zenith at the end of the Middle Ages when prosperous citizens began to build elegant residential mansions. These contrasted with the austere Palacio del Príncipe de Viana (Palace of the Prince of Viana), residence of the kings of Navarra, now the ayuntamiento (town hall), with its façade (seen through the gateway) flanked by two imposing battlemented towers. The main street, the former Calle Mayor which was once part of the pilgrim road, is lined with comfortable brick houses with the Classical carved wood eaves and windows featuring rich Gothic or Plateresque surrounds. In the second street on the right coming from the bridge can be seen the Baroque front of the Palacio de Vallesantoro, a palace protected by monumental overhangs carved with imaginary animals.

Sos del Rey Católico★

 13km/8mi SE along the A 127.

It was here, in the **Palacio de Sada** (Sada Palace; *pl. Hispanidad; location of tourist office;* *948 88 85 24*), that Ferdinand the Catholic, who was to unite Spain, was born in 1452. The town still has a medieval air.

On the **Plaza Mayor** stand the imposing 16C ayuntamiento (town hall), with large carved wood overhangs, and the Lonja (Exchange) with wide arches.

Iglesia de San Esteban★

Pl. de la Iglesia *Open mid-Jun–mid-Sept Mon–Sat 10am–1pm, 3.30–6pm, Sun 10am–noon, 3.30–6pm; mid-Sept–mid-Jun Mon–Sat 10am–1pm, 3.30–5.30pm, Sun 10am–noon, 3.30–5.30pm.* *No charge; €1 crypt.* *948 88 82 03.*

The Church of St Stephen is reached through a vaulted passageway. The 11C **crypt**★ is dedicated to Our Lady of Forgiveness (Virgen del Perdón). Two of the three apses are decorated with fine 14C **frescoes**.

The central apse contains outstanding capitals carved with women and birds. The statue columns at the **main door** have the stiff and noble bearing of those at Sangüesa.

The church, in transitional style, has a beautiful Renaissance **gallery**★. A chapel contains a 12C Romanesque Christ with eyes open.

Uncastillo

 34km/21mi SE; 21km/13mi from Sos del Rey Católico.

The Romanesque **Iglesia de Santa María** *(Pl. de la Villa)* has an unusual 14C tower adorned with machicolations and pinnacle turrets. The delicate carving on the **south portal**★ makes it one of the most beautiful doorways of the late Romanesque period. The church gallery with Renaissance **stalls**★ and the **cloisters**★ are 16C Plateresque.

Cáseda

 12km/7.5mi SW. Head from Sangüesa towards Sos del Rey Católico and turn right after 1km/.06mi onto the NA 5341.

Perched on a hillside and surrounded by fields and the Aragon River, this picturesque village is dominated by a Gothic church and a medieval stone bridge.

Upstream and 10km/6mi W via the NA5321, **Gallipienzo**/Galipentzu's hilltop church perches above the remains of fortified walls, from where you can enjoy a **view**★ of the surrounding fields.

ADDRESSES

STAY

 Yamaguchi Hotel – *Ctra Sangüesa was Javier, s/n.* *948 870 127. www.hotel yamaguchi.com. 41 rooms.* *€6.30.*
This family-run hotel is a good choice for its category. Rooms are varied, with the most modern located on the first floor.

El Camino de Santiago★★★

The Way of St James

The discovery of the body of the Apostle James transformed Santiago de Compostela into the most important pilgrimage desination in Europe in the Middle Ages. From the 11C onwards, the veneration of these saintly remains gave rise to the Way of St James and today thousands of pilgrims (and interested tourists) walk the same path, called "El Camino de Santiago" in Spanish. The Camino Francés that crosses Navarra and many monuments en route have UNESCO World Heritage Status.

- **Michelin Map:** 573.
- **Info:** www.caminode santiago.org. Confraternity of St James. www.csj.org.uk.
- **Location:** El Camino de Santiago runs east to west from the Pyrenees to Santiago de Compostela across northern Spain.
- **Timing:** If you're fit and healthy, you can cover about 25km/15mi a day, and therefore walk between Roncesvalles and Santiago de Compostela in about a month.

A BIT OF HISTORY

The discovery of the remains of St James (Santiago) in the 9C had an enormous effect on early pilgrims. By the 11C taking the journey to his shrine ranked on the same level as visiting Rome or Jerusalem. St James had a particular appeal for the French, who at the time were united with the Spanish against the Moors, but others made the long pilgrimage along routes organised by the Benedictines, Cistercians and the Knights Templars. Purpose-built hospitals and hospices received the sick and the weary and all travelled in the same pilgrim's uniform consisting of a heavy cape, 2.4m/8ft staff with a hollowed-out gourd attached to carry water, sturdy sandals and broad-brimmed felt hat marked with three or four scallop shells. A *Pilgrim Guide* of 1130, the first tourist guide ever written, describes the inhabitants, climate, customs and sights on the way. Churches and towns along the route prospered, receiving between 500 000 and two million pilgrims a year. Those from England who "took the cockleshell" often sailed from Parson's Quay in the Plymouth estuary to Soulac and followed the French Atlantic coast, or otherwise landed at La Coruña or in Portugal. Routes through France from Chartres, St-Denis and Paris joined at Tours.

Villages along the main route grew into towns and some were settled by foreigners, often from France, or Jews. With time, the faith that impelled the pilgrims began to diminish; crime, particularly from bandits, increased; and infighting amongst Christians reduced the faithful. In 1589, Drake attacked La Coruña and the bishop of Compostela removed the relics from the cathedral. They were then lost and for 300 years the pilgrimage was virtually abandoned. In 1879 they were recovered, recognised by the pope and the pilgrimage was reborn. In Holy Years, on 25 July, when the feast day of St James falls on a Sunday, elaborate religious and cultural celebrations in the major halts of St James Way attracts even more pilgrims.

THE WAY IN SPAIN – MAIN HALTS

The Camino Francés is the most popular of the handful of *caminos* to Santiago de Compostela. Routes from France converge at either Roncesvalles or Somport and then cross the Pyrenees Mountains. The easier southerly route (from Somport) goes via **Jaca**, **Santa Cruz de la Serós**, **San Juan de la Peña**, the **Monasterio de Leyre** and **Sangüesa** and features churches and monasteries in which the French architectural influence is obvious. Both routes converge at Puente la Reina.

Puente la Reina★

The 11C humpbacked bridge was built for pilgrims. A bronze pilgrim marks where routes converged.

The wide N 111 circles the old town outside whose walls stands the **Iglesia del Crucifijo** (Church of the Crucifix; ◷ *open daily 9am–8.30pm;* ⊜ *no charge*). A second nave was added to the 12C main aisle in the 14C and now contains the famous Y-shaped Cross with a profoundly Expressionist **Christ**★ carved in wood, said to have been brought from Germany in the 14C.

◗ Walk along the narrow, elegant main street, calle Mayor, fronted by houses of golden brick with carved wood eaves, to the bridge. You will see the **Iglesia de Santiago** (Church of St James; ◷ *open Mon–Fri 10am–2pm, 5–8pm, Sat–Sun 10am–1pm;* ⊜ *no charge*), its **doorway**★ crowded with carvings now almost effaced.

The nave, remodelled in the 16C, was adorned with altarpieces. Note two statues facing the entrance: St James the Pilgrim in gilded wood, and St Bartholomew.

Iglesia de Santa María de Eunate★★

◗ *Muruzábal. 5km/3mi E of Puente la Reina.* ◷ *Open spring–summer; Tue–Sun 10.30am–1.30pm, 4–7pm. Check ahead for other dates.* ⊜ *No charge.* ℘ *948 34 08 45.*

Human bones indicate that this delightful, isolated 12C **Romanesque** building might have been a funerary chapel like that of Torres del Río (◷ *see entry*). The

plan is octagonal, with a pentagonal apse outside and a semicircular one inside.

Cirauqui★

Steep, winding alleyways are crowded by houses with rounded doorways, their upper fronts adorned with iron balconies, coats of arms and carved cornices. At the top of the village *(difficult climb)* stands the **Iglesia de San Román** with a multifoil 13C **portal**★.

Estella★ and Monasterio de Irache★

◷ *See ESTELLA/LIZARRA*

Los Arcos

The **Iglesia de Santa María de los Arcos** (Church of St Mary of the Arches; *Pl. de Santa María;* ◷ *open noon–1pm, 5–6.30pm;* ℘ *948 64 00 21*), with its high tower, is Spanish Baroque inside, with overpowering stucco, sculpture and painting covering every available space. Above the high altar rises the 13C polychrome wood statue of the Black Virgin of Santa María de los Arcos. The cloisters illustrate the elegance and lightness of 15C Gothic.

Torres del Río

The **Iglesia del Santo Sepulcro**★ (Church of the Holy Sepulchre; *Mayor;* ℘ *948 64 00 21*) is a tall, octagonal Romanesque building, which might be a funerary chapel, dating from about 1200. The Mudéjar-inspired, star-shaped **cupola** is geometrical perfection. Note also the fine 13C crucifix.

Nájera and Santo Domingo de la Calzada★ ⓒ See La RIOJA

Burgos★★★ ⓒ See BURGOS

Iglesia de Frómista★★
ⓒ See PALENCIA

Villalcázar de Sirga
The vast Gothic **Iglesia de Santa María la Blanca** (ⓒ open weekends only, call ahead for other times; ⊙€2; ℘979 88 80 41) has a fine carved **portal**★ and two outstanding Gothic **tombs**★.
The recumbent statues of the brother of Alfonso X (who had the king murdered in 1271), and his wife Eleanor, are carved in great detail.

Carrión de los Condes
The 11C **Monasterio de San Zoilo**, rebuilt during the Renaissance, has **cloisters**★ (San Zoilo 23; ⓒ open Tue–Sun 10.30am–2pm, 4.30–8pm; ⊙€2; ℘979 88 09 32) designed by Juan de Badajoz with distinctive vaulting. The keystones and bosses are adorned with figurines and medallions.
The **Iglesia de Santiago** (Rúa; ⓒ open Holy Week–Oct daily 11am–2pm, 5–8pm. Call ahead for other times; ⊙€1; ℘979 88 09 32) has beautiful 12C carvings on the façade including, on the central coving, an architect with his compass, a barber with his scissors, and other tradesmen. High reliefs above show Gothic influence.

León★★ ⓒ See LEÓN

Astorga
🚃 Plaza Estación.
Astorga is renowned for its delicious mantecadas, a type of rich, oily biscuit.

Catedral de Santa María★
Pl. de la Catedral. ⓒ Open Mon–Sat 9am–10.30am, Sun 11am–1pm. ⊙€2. ℘987 61 58 20.
Building, begun with the east end in Flamboyant Gothic style in the late 15C, was not completed until the 18C, which explains the rich Renaissance and Baroque façade and towers. The front **porch**★ low reliefs illustrate the Expulsion of the Moneylenders and the Pardoning of the Adulterous Woman, among other events. Above the door is a beautiful Deposition.
The **interior** is surprisingly large, with an upsweeping effect created by innumerable slender columns. Behind the high altar is a 16C **retable**★. Gaspar de Hoyos and Gaspar de Palencia were responsible for the painted, gilt decoration, and **Gaspar Becerra** (1520–70), an Andalucían who after study in Italy developed a style of humanist sensitivity far removed from the Expressionism of his contemporaries.
The **Museo de la Catedral** contains a 13C gold filigree Holy Cross reliquary and a 10C reliquary of Alfonso III, the Great (⊙ combined entrance with the Museo de los Caminos €4).

Palacio Episcopal
Pl. de Eduardo de Castro.
This fantastic pastiche of a medieval palace was dreamed up by **Gaudí** in 1889. The original, brilliant interior decoration, especially in the neo-Gothic chapel on the first floor, is a profusion of mosaics, stained glass and intersecting ribbed vaults. In the **Museo de los Caminos** (Museum of the Way of St James; ⓒ open Oct–Apr Tue–Sun 11am–2pm, 4–6pm; Apr–Sept daily 10am–2pm, 4–8pm; ⓒ closed Mon and Sun afternoon; ⊙ €2.50 combined with Museo de la Catedral €4; ℘987 61 68 82), medieval art reflects the theme of pilgrimage.

Ponferrada
🚃 Avenida del Ferrocarril 9.
The centre of a mining area, Ponferrada owes its name to an 11C iron bridge built across the Sil for pilgrims. Above the town are the ruins of the **Castillo de los Templarios** (Templars' Castle; ⓒ open Nov–Feb Tue–Sat 10.30am–2pm, 4–6pm; extended hours at other times; ⊙ €2.50; ℘987 40 2 44).

Peñalba de Santiago★
▶ 21km/13mi SE.
Peñalba stands in the heart of the so-called Valle del Silencio (Valley of

Silence). Its houses are schist-walled with wooden balconies and slate roofs. The Mozarabic **Iglesia de Santiago** (🕐*open Oct–Apr Tue–Sat 10am–2pm, 4.30–8pm, Sun and public holidays 10am–2pm; May–Sept Tue–Sat 10am–2pm, 5–9pm, Sun and public holidays 10am–2pm;* 🕐*closed 1, 6 Jan, 2 May, 24–25, 31 Dec;* 👁*no charge)*, is all that remains of a 10C monastery. The paired horseshoe portal arch is set off by an *alfiz*.

Las Médulas★

▶ *22km/14mi SW.*
World Heritage Site.
Debris from a Roman gold mine has transformed slopes of the Aquilianos mountains into a magical landscape of rocky crags and strangely shaped hillocks of pink and ochre, covered over the ages by gnarled chestnut trees. A new information centre for the park can be found in the village of El Bierzo.

Cebreiro

Cebreiro, not far from the Puerto de Piedrafita (Piedrafita pass, 1 109m/3 638ft), reflects the hardship of the pilgrim journey.
Drystone and thatched houses *(pallozas)* descend from ancient Celtic huts; in one is an **Ethnographic Museum** (Museo Etnográfico; 🕐*open daily 11am–2pm, 3–7pm;* 👁*no charge)*. A pilgrim inn remains beside the small 9C mountain church where pilgrims venerated the relics of the miracle of the Holy Eucharist (c. 1300), when bread was turned to flesh and wine to blood. Relics in silver caskets presented by Isabel may be seen with the miraculous chalice and paten.

Portomarín

Before centuries-old Portomarín was drowned by a dam, the **church**★ (🕐*open Tue–Sun 10.30am–1pm, 4.30–7pm;* 👁*no charge)* of the Knights of St John of Jerusalem was moved stone by stone. It is square, fortified and ornamented with massive arches and Romanesque doors with delicately carved covings. The west door depicts Christ in Majesty with the 24 Old Musicians of the Apocalypse.

Vilar de Donas

▶ *6.5km/4mi E of Palas de Rei.*
Enter the **church** (🕐*open Tue–Sun 11am –2pm, 3–6pm;* 👁*no charge)*, slightly off the main road, through a Romanesque doorway. Lining the walls are tombs of the Knights of the Order of St James, slain in battle.

15C **frescoes**★ decorate the apse, illustrating Christ in Majesty with St Paul and St Luke on his left and St Peter and St Mark on his right and, on the chancel walls, the faces of the elegant young women who gave the church its name (*donas* in Galician).

Santiago de Compostela★★★

👣*See SANTIAGO DE COMPOSTELA*

ADDRESSES

🛏 STAY

🍴 **Hotel Madrid** – *Av. de La Puebla 44, Ponferrada.* ☎*987 41 15 50. www.hotel madridponferrada.com. 45 rooms.* 🍽*€5.50. Restaurant*🍽. A good central location, friendly staff and clean, comfortable rooms.

🍴🍴 **Hotel Real Monasterio San Zoilo** – *Obispo Souto, Carrión de los Condes.* ☎*979 88 00 49. www.sanzoilo.com. 49 rooms.* 🍽 *€8.90. Restaurant*🍽🍽. This former Benedictine monastery is now a delightful, welcoming hotel with elegant architecture. Great value.

🍴🍴 **Hotel Rural Bidean** – *Mayor 20, Puente la Reina.* ☎*948 34 04 57. www.bidean.com. 20 rooms.* This cosy little hostelry has many period features and is popular with pilgrims, who get a special rate.

🍴 EAT

🍴🍴 **La Peseta** – *Pl. San Bartolomé 3, Astorga.* ☎*987 61 72 75.* This popular, family-run restaurant has a simple dining room, where the cuisine is traditional and reasonably priced.

🍴🍴🍴 **Mesón del Peregrino** – *Irunbidea 10, Puente la Reina. 1km/0.6mi NE of Puente la Reina on the Pamplona/Iruña road.* ☎*948 34 00 75. Closed Sun for dinner, Mon.* A charming restaurant housed in a magnificent stone mansion with dining rooms overlooking the garden and swimming pool. Creative cuisine is served in tasteful rustic surrounds.

Estella/ Lizarra★★

The brick and rough stone façades remind us that Estella (Lizarra in the Basque language) was the 12C capital of the kings of Navarra and the 19C base of the Carlists. It is also an important staging post on the Camino de Santiago.

SIGHTS

Plaza de San Martín

The once-bustling small square was originally the heart of the freemen's parish. On one side is the **former ayuntamiento** (town hall) dating from the 16C. On the other side of the Río Ega on Calle de la Rúa (Pilgrim Road) stands the **Casa de Cultura Fray Diego de Estella** (𝒫 948 55 17 47), built in 1565, at no. 7, with an emblazoned Plateresque façade.

Palacio de los Reyes de Navarra★ (Palace of the Kings of Navarre)

San Nicolás 1. Open Tue–Sat 11am–1pm, 5–7pm, Sun and public holidays 11am–1.30pm. Closed 1 Jan, 25 Dec. No charge. 𝒫 948 54 60 37. www.museogustavodemaeztu.com.
This rare 12C Romanesque civil building is punctuated by arcades and twin bays with remarkable capitals. The palace now houses a contemporary art museum the **Museo Gustavo de Maeztu y Whitney** (open Tue–Sat 11am–1pm, 5–7pm, Sun and public holidays 11am–1.30pm; no charge; 𝒫 948 54 60 37;

▶ **Population:** 14 029
◔ **Michelin Map:** 573D 23.
🄸 **Info:** San Nicolás 3. 𝒫 948 55 63 01. www.estella-lizarra.com.
▶ **Location:** Estella lies in NE Spain near the Pyrenees on the slopes of the Sierra de Andía, along the N 111 linking Pamplona and Logroño (48km/30mi SW).
◕ **Timing:** Allow time for aimless wandering in this old town.

www.museogustavodemaeztu.com).
This museum holds the works of the painter Gustavo de Maeztu y Whitney (1887–1947). Son of a Cuban father and French mother, he grew up in Bilbao and then moved to Paris, but travelled extensively through Spain. In 1936 he settled in Estella until his death.
His œuvre, which focuses on landcapes and portraits, is marked by colour and attention to detail. The first floor of the museum holds portraits of women, and the second drawings, sketches and rural scenes.

Iglesia de San Pedro de la Rúa

San Nicolás 2. Closed until 2012 for rennovations.
The church stands facing the royal palace on a cliff spur formerly crowned by the city castle. It retains outstanding 12C and 13C features.
The unusual **doorway**★ at the top of a steep stairway in the north wall has an equilateral scalloped arch, Caliphate influenced. Similar portals can be seen in Navarra and in the Saintonge and Poitou regions of France. Inside note the transitional Romanesque Virgin and Child, a Gothic Christ and an unusual column of intertwined serpents in the central apse, and a Romanesque Crucified Christ in the apse on the left.
The Romanesque **cloisters** lost two galleries when the nearby castle was blown up in the 16C. The skill and invention of the masons are evident in the remain-

Palacio de los Reyes de Navarra

S. Sauvignier/MICHELIN

ing **capitals**★★; the north gallery series illustrates scenes from the lives of Christ, St Lawrence, St Andrew and St Peter, while plant and animal themes enliven the west gallery.

Iglesia del Santo Sepulcro (Church of the Holy Sepulchre)

Curtidores. ⚬ *Not open to public.*
The portal is purely Gothic. Superimposed above are the Last Supper, the three Marys at the Holy Sepulchre and Hell, and Calvary. The niches contain somewhat mannered figures of saints.

Iglesia de San Miguel

Mayor 46. 🔍 *Guided tours (30min) with prior booking Mon–Sat 11am-1pm, 5-8pm; Sun 5-8pm.* 🎫 *No charge for entry.* ✆ *948 55 04 31 .*

The church dominates a quarter that retains narrow streets and a medieval atmosphere. On the tympanum of the north **portal**★ is a figure of Christ surrounded by the Evangelists and mysterious personages. The covings are full of sculptures. The capitals illustrate the childhood of Christ.

On the upper register of the walls are eight Statue columns of the Apostles; on the lower register, two **high reliefs**★★, accomplished and expressive, show St Michael slaying the dragon (left) and the three Marys coming from the Sepulchre. The noble bearing, the elegant drapery and the facial expressions make the carving a Romanesque masterpiece.

EXCURSION

Monasterio de Irache★

▶ *Irache. 3km/1.8mi SW of Estella.*
🕐 *Open Wed–Fri 9.30am–1pm, 5–7pm, Sat, Sun 8.30am–1.30pm, 4–7pm.*
🕐 *Closed Dec 1–Jan 7.* 🎫 *No charge.*
✆ *948 55 44 64.*

A Benedictine abbey occupied the site in the 10C. Later, this was a major pilgrimage halt and a Cistercian community before becoming a university under the Benedictines, in the 16C.

Iglesia★ – This 12C–13C church's apse is purely Romanesque with rib-vaulted nave. The dome on squinches and the *coro alto* are Renaissance; the façade and most of the structures were rebuilt in the 17C. Brackets and capitals illustrate the lives of Christ and St Benedict in the **claustro**.

🚗 DRIVING TOUR

TOUR THROUGH THE SIERRA DE ANDÍA AND SIERRA DE URBASA★
94km/58mi. About 3hr.

▶ *Leave Estella on NA 120 north towards the Puerto (pass) de Lizarraga. The road crosses beechwoods and rises to a pass that affords extensive views.*

Monasterio de Iranzu

9km/5.6mi N of Estella. Signposted from NA 120. 🕐 *Open daily May–Sept 10am–2pm, 4–8pm; Oct–Apr 10am–2pm, 4–6pm.* 🎫 *€2.80.* ✆ *948 52 00 47. www.monasterio-iranzu.com.*

The 12C Cistercian monastery, isolated in a wild **gorge**★, is now a college. It is a good example of the Cistercian transitional style from Romanesque to Gothic combining robustness and elegance. The cloister bays, where they have not been given a later florid Gothic fenestration, have Romanesque blind arcades, oculi and wide relieving arches.

The church, with primitive vaulting, has a flat east end decorated with three windows, symbolising the Trinity, a common Cistercian feature.

Puerto de Lizarraga Road★★

Once out of the tunnel (alt 1 090m/ 3 576ft) pause at the **viewpoint**★ overlooking the Ergoyena Valley before the descent through woods and pastures.

▶ *Continue to Etxarri-Aranatz; take N 240 W to Olatzi; turn left to Estella.*

Puerto de Urbasa road★★

The road climbs steeply between great boulders and clumps of trees. Beyond the pass (alt 927m/3 041ft) tall limestone cliffs add character to the landscape before the road enters the gorges of the sparkling river Urenderra.

Olite/Erriberri★

Olite (Erriberri in Basque), the favourite residence of the kings of Navarra in the 15C, possesses a restored fairytale castle the size of a city in itself. Olite's activities and setting attract numbers of summer visitors.

SIGHTS

Castillo de los Reyes de Navarra★★ (Fortress of the Kings of Navarra)

Pl. Carlos III El Noble. ○*Open daily Jul–Aug and Holy Week 10am–8pm; Oct–Mar 10am–6pm; Apr–Jun and Sept 10am–7pm.* ○*Closed 1, 6 Jan, 25 Dec.* ◗*Guided tours available* ◌€3.10. *℘948 74 00 35.* http://guiartenavarra.com/es.

The Palacio Viejo (Old Palace) is Olite's parador. The Palacio Nuevo (New Palace) was ordered built by Charles III, the Noble, in 1406. The French origins of the prince – Count of Evreux and native of Mantes – explain the fortifications, a transition between the massive stone constructions of the 13C and the royal Gothic residences of the late 15C with galleries and courtyards.

During the Peninsular War, a fire almost completely destroyed the building. Behind the 15 or so towers marking the peri-meter were hanging gardens, along

▶ **Population:** 3 754
◔ **Michelin Map:** 573 E 25.
▯ **Info:** Plaza de los Teobaldos 10. ℘948 74 17 03. www.olite.es.
◔ **Location:** Olite stands at the heart of the Navarran plain, 4km/2.5mi from the A 15 motorway linking Zaragoza and Pamplona/Iruña (43km/26mi S).
▲▲ **Kids:** Castillo de los Reyes de Navarra.
◔ **Timing:** In the last week of August, Olite celebrates with a theatre festival.

with inner halls and chambers decorated with *azulejos*, painted stuccowork and coloured marquetry ceilings.

The most impressive rooms are the Guardarropa (Wardrobe), now housing an exhibition, the Sala de la Reina (Queen's Room) and the Galería del Rey (King's Gallery).

Iglesia de Santa María la Real

Pl. de los Teobaldos. ○*Open half an hour before Mass; Sun 11am and 6.30pm.*

The church is the former chapel royal. An atrium of slender multifoil arches precedes the 14C **façade**★, a fine example

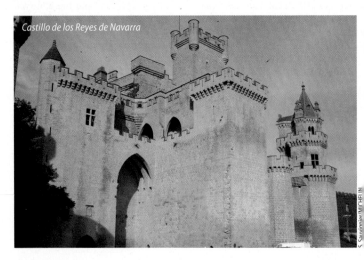
Castillo de los Reyes de Navarra

S. Sauvignier/MICHELIN

of Navarra Gothic sculpture. The only figurative carving illustrates the lives of the Virgin and Christ. A painted 16C retable frames a Gothic statue of Our Lady.

Iglesia de San Pedro

El Fosal 2. ⏱*Open half an hour before Mass; Sun 10am and 12.30pm.*

The church façade below the tapering octagonal spire is somewhat disparate. The portal covings are set off by tori (large convex mouldings). Eagles on either side symbolise Gentleness and Violence.

Museo del Vino★

Plaza de los Teobaldos 4. ⏱*Open Holy Week–12 Oct Mon–Sat 10am–2pm, 4pm–7pm, Sun 10am–2pm; rest of the year Mon–Sat 10am–2pm, 3–4pm, Sun 10am–2pm.* ✆*€3.50.* ✆*948 741 273. www.guiartenavarra.com.*

Sharing the same building as the tourist office, this modern museum promotes the teaching and culture of Navarra's renowned wines. Each floor introduces a different theme: the history of wine; vineyard management; bottling and aging. Perhaps most interesting of all is the section that teaches us to appreciate wine and numerous varietals.

EXCURSIONS
Ujué★

▶ *19km/11.8mi NE of Olite, along NA 5 300 (Ctra de San Martin de Unx) to San Martín de Unx, then follow the NA 5310.*

Ujué, overlooking the Ribera region, remains, with its winding streets, much as it was in the Middle Ages.

Iglesia de Santa María

⏱*Open daily 9am–7pm.* ☛*Guided tours of church and fortress available with prior booking.* ✆*948 73 92 57.*

A Romanesque church was built at the end of the 11C. In the 14C, Charles II, the Bad, began a Gothic church, but the Romanesque chancel remains to this day. The central chapel contains the venerated **Santa María la Blanca**, a plated Romanesque statue honoured with a **romería** (pilgrimage) the Sunday after St Mark's Day (25 April).

Fortaleza (Fortress)

The church towers command a view which extends to Olite, the Montejurra and the Pyrenees. Of the medieval palace there remain lofty walls and a covered watch path circling the church.

Monasterio de La Oliva★

▶ *Ctra de Lerida, Carcastillo, 27km/ 16.7mi S of Ujué.* ⏱*Open Mon–Sat 9am–12.30pm, 3.30–6pm, Sun and public holidays 9am–11am, 4–6pm.* ✆*€1.80.* ✆*948 72 50 06. www.monasteriodelaoliva.eu.*

La Oliva was one of the first Cistercian monasteries built outside France.

The buildings, stripped of treasure and trappings, retain a pure Cistercian beauty.

Iglesia★★ – The façade of this late 12C church is mostly unadorned, a perfect setting for the interplay of lines of the portal and two rose windows. The interior is surprisingly deep with pillars and pointed arches lined with thick polygonal ribs in austere Cistercian style.

Claustro★ – The bays in these late 15C cloisters appear exceptionally light. Gothic elements were grafted onto an older construction: Ogival vaults rise from Romanesque capitals at the entry to the 13C **Sala Capitular** (chapter house).

Lagunas de Pitillas★

▶ *13km/8.7mi SW of Olite, along the N-121 to Pitillas*

This marshy area covers 87ha/216 acres at the foot of a range of mountains crowned with wind turbines.

The average water depth is 3m/9.8ft, and a dyke regulates the level when needed. The site was declared a nature reserve in 1987 because of its ecological importance. It lies on the migratory routes of many species of birds, who use the marshes as a breeding ground, so the best time to discover it is in winter. A free bird observatory (*Observatorio de Aves*) provides telescopes to watch their activities among wetland flora.

Tudela/Tutera★

Tudela was once part of the Córdoba Caliphate, which is evident from its large Moorish quarter, the Morería. Interesting churches were built following the 12C Reconquest. Irrigation has made the surrounding Ribera region a market-gardening centre.

▶ **Population:** 35 268
 Michelin Map: 573 F 25.
Info: Juicio 4 ℘948 84 80 58. www.tudela.es.
▶ **Location:** Tudela is on the right bank of the River Ebro in NE Spain, 50km/31mi S of Olite via N 121 and N 134. Plaza Estación.
Kids: Bárdenas Reales.
Timing: During the Festival de Santa Ana at the end of July is a great time to visit.

SIGHTS
Catedral★
Pl. Vieja. ◐*Open Mon–Sat 10.30am–1pm, 4–7pm, Sun 10am–1pm.* ⊛€3.10 *museum and cloisters.* ℘948 40 21 61.
The 12C–13C cathedral exemplifies the transitional Romanesque-Gothic style. The **Last Judgement Doorway**★ (Portada del Juicio Final), though difficult to see, is incredibly carved with nearly 120 groups of figures.

The **interior** is Romanesque in the elevation of the nave, Gothic in its vaulting and clerestory. Gothic works include early 16C choir stalls, the high altar retable and the Byzantine-looking 13C stone reliquary statue of the White Virgin. In the **Capilla de Nuestra Señora de la Esperanza**★ (Chapel of our Lady of Hope), 15C masterpieces include the tomb of a chancellor of Navarra and the main altarpiece.

The 12C–13C **cloisters**★★ *(claustro)* are harmonious. Romanesque arches rest alternately on columns with historiated capitals with scenes from the New Testament and the lives of the saints in a style inspired by the carvings of Aragón. A door of an earlier mosque remains.

St Anne's Feast Day

(26 July). Celebrated annually, as at Pamplona/Iruña, with several days of great rejoicing including *encierros* and bullfights. During Holy Week, an event known as the Descent of the Angel takes place on the picturesque **Plaza de los Fueros**, which served as a bullring in the 18C.

Iglesia de San Nicolás de Bari
La Rúa.
In the 18C façade of this church in calle Rúa is a 12C Romanesque tympanum showing God the Father holding his Son, amid symbols of the Evangelists.

Palacio Episcopal y Meuo de Tudela
Plaza Vieja 2. ◐*Mon–Fri 10am–1.30pm, 4–7pm, weekends and public holidays 10am–1.30pm.* ⊛€3; under 18s €1.50. ℘948 40 21 61. www.ciudadtudela.com /decansal.
The former bishop's palace built in the 16th century houses the Museum of Tudela and acts as a threshold to the cathedral. Before entering the museum, which includes a visit to the cloisters, take time to admire the magnificent Plateresque portico adorning the facade. Inside the museum you will discover a collection of sacred art.

Plaza Fueros
This richly-decorated Baroque square –originally built to stage bull fights– stands on the threshold of the old and new city and is used for large-scale community and political events.

Plaza de la Judería
Until 1498 Tudela was home to a sizable Jewish population, including the mathematician and philosopher Abraham ibn Ezra and the poet Yehuda Ha Levi.
On one of the square's flanks resides the 16th-century Renaissance Palacio del

Bardenas Reales

© Jean-Luc Armand/Photononstop

Marqués de San Adrián. Note the Aragonese style arches and eaves, which were carved by the sculptor Esteban de Obray in 1519. The interior houses a Renaissance courtyard.

Plaza Vieja
Bordered by the 15C *ayuntamiento* (city hall) and the Museum of Modern Art Muñoz Sola.

Museum of Modern Art Muñoz Sola
Plaza Vieja 2. ⊙*Open Tue–Fri 10am– 1.30am, 4–7pm, weekends and public holidays 10am–1.30pm;* €1 (under 16s free), combined ticket with the Museum of Tudela €3. *℘948 402 640. www.museomunozsola.com.*
A native of Tudela, the painter César Muñoz Sola (1921-2000) amassed an extensive collection of French, mid to late 19th century paintings during his lifetime. Represented in this museum are works from Girodet Roucy, Hugard Tower, Julien Tavernier and Foubert amongst others, and there is also a room of works by Muñoz Sola himself.

EXCURSIONS
Bardenas Reales★★
▶ *N 15km/9mi north of Tudela on the NA 134; 800m/875yd before the village of Arguedas you will see signs.*
⊙*Take water and food as there are few* facilities in the park for either. Beware of snakes. Access is permitted 8am to sundown.

The incredible and awe-inspiring Bardenas Reales consists of 42 500ha/105 000 acres of arid gypsum, clay and sandstone formations. The park is divided into several areas according to the vegetation found there. The northern swathe and the southern *Bardena Negra* are characterized by pines and oaks, whilst the central *Bardena Blanca* has the most spectacular landscape.

The diversity of terrain and flora in the area allows for the coexistence of many species of birds, and by ancient decree sheep are allowed to graze here during the cooler months, an event celebrated every September 18.

Coming in via the road from Arguedas, you will first pass a military base before the surreal beauty of the Bardenas begins. From here, you can take a loop around the *Bardena Blanca*, where centuries of erosion created by wind and water have created an unforgettable, lunaresque landscape.

Enter by Nuestra Señora del Yugo, a shrine housing a 15C Madonna, to access the best known of the Bardenas, that of Blanca, where sites such as Pisquerra, Sanchicorrota and the Ralla Rallón will guarantee a change of scenery from the alluvial greenery of nearby Tudela.

EL PAÍS VASCO AND LA RIOJA

The Basque Country (País Vasco) forms part of Spain's northeastern frontier, facing the Atlantic. The region of La Rioja borders on its southern edge. In the Middle Ages the towns and villages of País Vasco and Rioja found fame and wealth as staging points on the Camino de Santiago, leaving a rich legacy of religious buildings. Today, with the exceptions of the towns of Donostia-San Sebastián and Bilbao, few people outside Spain are aware of what lies within these regions. Like the rest of northern Spain, the Basque Country and Rioja are mostly rural with none of the sun-blessed imagery or icons of the south. This is a land where isolated farms and small villages nestle in verdant valleys. Rioja is synonymous with high-quality Spanish wine and Haro is the place to learn more about it. The Basque Country is renowned for its local cuisine and is famed for its *pinxtos*, delectable bite-size tapas.

Highlights

1 Eating and drinking your way around **San Sebastián** (p237)

2 Pottering along the scenic **Costa de Vizcaya/Bizcaya** (p239)

3 Gazing on and visiting Bilbao's **Museo Guggenheim** (p242)

4 Archeological treasures in **Vitoria-Gasteiz** (p248)

5 Wine tasting in a state-of-the-art winery in **La Rioja** (p251)

Costa Vasca

The Basque coastal region is known as Vizcaya (Biscay) and is famous for its capital, Bilbo, better known as Bilbao. Just as the 1992 Olympics led to the reinvention of Barcelona, in 1997 Frank Gehry's stunning Guggenheim Museum was the launch pad for the renaissance of a fading port city.

The city's splendid fine arts museum and characterful old quarter were here long before then. Queen of the Costa Vasca is Donostia-San Sebastián, European Captial of Culture 2016. It boasts one of Spain's finest natural settings on a glorious sandy bay, attracting Spanish holidaymakers, a fashionable international set and gourmets; it is often referred to as Spain's food capital with more Michelin stars than Madrid or Barcelona, and an atmospheric old quarter chock-a-block with eating and drinking options.

Plaza de la Virgen Blanca, Ciudad Vieja, Vitoria-Gasteiz

© José Fuste Raga/age fotostock

País Vasco interior

The inland Basque regions of Guipúzcoa and Álava are so frequently overshadowed by the delights of the coast and overlooked by most visitors.

Those who do make the effort to seek out Vitoria (Gasteiz), the sophisticated Basque capital, are rewarded with a splendid old walled town boasting fine museums and galleries.

The old university town of Oñati (Oñate), and nearby Santuario de Arantzazu are worth the trip for the scenic countryside settings alone.

La Rioja

Irrigated by the Ebro river, a good proportion of Rioja's 5 034sq km/1 944sq mi is devoted to producing some of Spain's finest wines. Many of its towns and villages were (and still are) on the Camino de Santiago, so there are numerous tangible reminders of a rich past. The capital, Logroño, has an atmospheric old town bursting with superb tapas bars.

Donostia-San Sebastián★★

San Sebastián (Donostia in Basque) is in a glorious setting on a scallop-shaped bay framed by two hills and the Isle of Santa Clara. Two vast sand beaches follow the curve of the bay: La Concha and fashionable Ondarreta. Gardens, promenades and statuary decorate the town, most notable of which is *El Peine del Viento XV* (Windcomb 15), by Eduardo Chillida.

A BIT OF HISTORY

Pioneer of tourism – Queen María Cristina of Habsburg chose Donostia-San Sebastián as her summer residence in the 19C, establishing it as a leading resort. The *belle époque* atmosphere is alive today at the stellar urban beach.

A gastronomic capital – The all-male members of 30 gourmet clubs prepare excellent meals which they consume with cider or *txacolí* wine. Specialities include hake, cod, bream and sardines and squid *(chipirones)*.

SIGHTS

Old Town

The narrow streets of the old town (rebuilt after an 1813 fire) contrast the wide avenues of modern Donostia. The area comes alive at the apéritif hour when locals and tourists (especially the French) crowd the bars and small restaurants in the *calles* Portu, Muñoa, 31 de Agosto and Fermín Calbetón to enjoy tapas and the excellent seafood.

Basílica de Santa María

Mayor. ⏱*Open Jun–Sept 8am–2pm, 4–8pm; Oct–May 8.30am–2pm, 5–8pm.* ⬤*No charge.* ☎*943 42 31 24.*
The church has an exuberant late 18C portal and Baroque altars.

Museo de San Telmo

Pl. Zuloaga 1. ⏱*Open Mon–Sun 10am–8pm.* ⏱*Closed 1 and 20 Jan, 25 Dec.* ⬤*€5.* ☎*943 48 15 81. www.museosantelmo.com.*

▶ **Population:** 186 122
⬤ **Michelin Map:** 573 (town plan or 574 C 23-24.
▣ **Info:** Boulevard 8. ☎*943 48 11 66. www.san sebastianturismo.com.*
◯ **Location:** Donostia-San Sebastián is on the Gulf of Vizcaya, 25km/15.5mi W of the French border, 102km/63.3mi E of Bilbao. ▭Paseo de Francia 22.
🅿 **Parking:** Space is limited in the old quarter; walking is preferable.
◉ **Don't Miss:** A walk in the old quarter, and a fine seafood repast.
◯ **Timing:** Take a day for San Sebastián and drives nearby.
👥 **Kids:** The Aquarium.

The museum is in a 16C monastery. The Renaissance cloisters hold Basque stone funerary crosses from the 15C–17C carved in traditional Iberian style. The upper gallery is the ethnographic section, with a reconstructed Basque interior.

Paintings include a Ribera, an El Greco, and 19C artists. The chapel was decorated by **José María Sert** with scenes from the city's history.

Paseo Nuevo (Pasealekua Berria)

This promenade almost circles Monte Urgull and affords good **views**.

👥 Aquarium San Sebastián★

Pl. Carlos Biasca de Imaz 1. ⏱*Open Jul–Aug daily 10am–9pm; Oct–Holy Week Mon–Fri 10am–7pm, Sat–Sun and public holidays 10am–8pm; Holy Week–Jun and Sept Mon–Fri 10am–8pm, Sat–Sun and public holidays 10am–9pm.* ⏱*Closed 1 Jan, 25 Dec.* ⬤*€12; child €6.* ☎*943 44 00 99. www.aquariumss.com.*
One of the best in Europe, this aquarium also includes a natural sciences museum

and naval museum. Visitors can cross its **Oceanarium**★ via a tunnel with 360° views.

Museo Naval (Naval Museum)

Pasealekua 24. Open Sat 10am–1.30pm, 4–7.30pm, Sun and public holidays 11am–2pm. €1.20; free Thu. 943 43 00 51. http://um.gipuzkoakultura.net. Small Basque-oriented museum, showing a traditional way of life at sea.

Mercado de la Bretxa

Alameda del Boulevard 3 Open Mon–Sat 10am–10pm. In order create a stellar local cuisine, you need top-rate produce, and many of the city's star chefs can be seen perusing the stalls of this covered marketplace that dates from 1870. It's a great place to pick up ingredients for a picnic, or try some *pintxos* at the handful of bars inside.

Kursaal

Zurriola, 1. Open hours vary depending on programme. 943 00 30 00. www.kursaal.com.es. Spanish architect Rafael Moneo's cube-shaped concert hall is a modernist landmark. Performances vary, from pop to classical.

EXCURSIONS
View from Monte Ulía★

7km/4.3mi E. Follow the N 1 towards Irún and take a right before the summit. The twisting drive up affords good **views** of the town and its setting.

Astigarraga-Sagardoetxea

N 10km/6mi S towards Hernani.
Basque Cider House (Sagardoetxea)
In the centre of town on a hillside, look for the barrel on the street. Open Jul–Aug Mon–Sat 11am–1.30pm, 4pm–7.30pm, Sun 11am–1.30pm; Sep–May Tue–Sat 11am–1.30pm, 4pm–7.30 pm, Sun 11am–1.30pm. €3.50; under 10 free. 943 550 575. www.sagardoetxea.com. The Basque Country has 53 varieties of apples. In order to make cider, you need

80% acidic varieties and 20% sweet. Here you will discover such manufacturing secrets as well as the history of this popular regional beverage through strolling the orchards where the apple trees are grafted, and the museum itself, where all stages of manufacturing are explained. A tasting caps off the visit.

≗♿ Eureka! Zientzia Museoa (Science Museum)

Bus 28, from the city centre (allow 20min). Allow 2hr for visit. Mikeletegi, 43 Open 1 Jul–end Aug Mon–Fri 10am–8pm, Sat, Sun 11am–7pm. Rest of the year Tue–Fri 10am–7pm, Sat, Sun 11am–7pm. €7. 943 012 478. www.miramon.org.

Each room of this large, modern museum focuses on a different scientific principle – be it light, energy, the senses or mechanisms – and experiments and demonstrations are offered to illustrate each one. Children will enjoy visiting this museum as it is both didactic and entertaining.
The building also houses a planetarium (open Tue–Fri; sessions in Spanish and Basque; €3.50, children €2.50).

Parque de Aiete ★★

Can be accessed on foot, though it's a long , uphill walk. Otherwise by car or bus 19, 31.
This beautiful park – situated on a hilltop at the heart of a residential neighbourhood – is arguably the most attractive in the entrie city.
Designed by the French landscape gardener Pierre Ducasse, it surrounds a Neoclassical palace which was built in 1878 for the Duke and Duchess of Bailen and later in 1941 became summer residence for General Franco. Opened to the public in 1977, it currently serves as a cultural centre.
The gardens themselves are a haven of greenery and peace, composed of Atlas cedars, ginkgo biloba, plane trees, redwoods, shrubs and flowerbeds. There are playgrounds for children, benches for resting up with a good book and green streches of lawn for a picnic.

Tolosa

▶ *26kms/16mi south on the N1.*

A stronghold of Basque separatism, Tolosa has grown prosperous through the production of paper and has a fine historic centre replete with old houses, palaces, churches and a recently restored mill. A stroll around it will reveal colourful Basque houses, markets, shops and cafés with the bubbling River Oria never far out of view.

Sites to seek out include the **Plaza de Triángulo** (so named because of its unusual shape), and the Plaza Zarra where the Basque flags flap high on the balconies of the 17C red-brick *Ayuntamiento* (City Hall).

Chocolate lovers should not miss the nearby **Museo de la Confitería** (*Lechuga 3;* ◷ *by appointment only;* ✆ *943 697 413; www.gorrotxategi. com*) a museum dedicated to the Mayan Gold that is run by a famous family of chocolatiers. The **Plaza Berdura★** has yet more charming coloured houses and cafés. A flower market is held here every Saturday.

Tolosa's most notable church is the Baroque Santa Maria, situated on the square of the same name.

From here, wander along typically Basque Kale Nagusia, stopping at the Palacio Atodo No. 33 to admire the handsome coat of arms and eaves in the vernacular Basque style before heading to the 15C Torre Andia.

Other emblematic streets and squares include the arcaded, Neoclassical Plaza Euskal Herria (which also hosts a market every Saturday morning) and the streets parallel to Kale Korreo.

Tolosa is famous for its beans (*alubias*), which you can try in soups and stews while here.

Costa de Guipúzcoa★★

The Basque Coast (Costa Vasca) stretches from the Golfo de Vizcaya (Bay of Biscay) to the headland of the Cabo de Machichaco. The steep shoreline, lined by cliffs and indented by estuaries, is a line of fishing villages nestling in inlets.

🚗 DRIVING TOUR

FROM HONDARRIBIA TO BILBAO

70km/43mi. Allow one day.

Hondarribia/Fuenterrabía★

Fuenterrabía (Hondarribia in Basque) is a resort. **La Marina** is the fishermen's quarter with characteristic wood balconies and bars and cafés. On 8 September, a parade and festival honour the Virgen de Guadalupe, who is said to have delivered the town from a two-month siege by the French in 1638. Overlooking the River Bidasoa, the **Old Town**, an old fortified town with steep streets, retains its 15C walls. These are punctuated by the **Puerta de Santa María**, a gateway surmounted by the town's coat of arms and twin angels venerating the Virgen de Guadalupe. Picturesque **calle Mayor** is lined with houses with wrought-iron balconies.

The **Iglesia de Santa María** (*Mayor;* ✆ *943 64 54 58*), a Gothic church with massive buttresses, was remodelled in the 17C and given a Baroque tower. It

---

- ♿ **Michelin Map:** 574 B-C 21 to 24 – País Vasco (Guipúzcoa, Vizcaya).
- 🛈 **Info:** www.bizkaiacosta vasca.com.
- ▶ **Location:** The Basque Coast runs from the French border to Bilbao.
- 👫 **Kids:** Museo del Ferrocarril Vasco.
- ◷ **Timing:** The Basque Coast can suffer from extreme weather. Bring waterproofs, even in August.

was the site of a proxy wedding in 1660 between Louis XIV and the Infanta María before the real marriage in France. The **Castillo de Carlos V**, a fortress *(pl. de Armas 14; now a parador)* was constructed in the 10C by Sancho Abarca, King of Navarra, and restored by Charles V in the 16C.

▷ *Leave Fuenterrabía on the harbour road.*

Cabo Higuer★
4km/2.5mi N.
Turn left; as the road climbs, you get a **view**★ of the beach, the town and the quayside and from the end of the headland, the French coast and the town of Hendaye.

▷ *Leave Fuenterrabía on the Behobia road; take the first right after the Palmera factory and bear left at the first crossroads.*

Ermita de San Marcial
9km/5.6mi SE.
A narrow road leads up to the wooded hilltop (225m/738ft). The **panorama**★★ from the hermitage includes Fuenterrabía, **Irún** and **Isla de los Faisanes** (Pheasant Island) in the mouth of the River Bidasoa on the border. In the distance are Donostia-San Sebastián and Hendaye beach.

Jaizkibel Road★★
The **drive**★★ along this road *(GI 3440)* is impressive at sunset. After 5km/3mi you reach the Capilla de Nuestra Señora de Guadalupe (Chapel of our Lady of Guadalupe) where there is a lovely **view**★ of the French coast.
Past pines and gorse is the Hostal de Jaizkibel *(www.hoteljaizkibel.com)* at the foot of a 584m/1 916ft peak and a lookout with a superb **view**★★. The road down affords **glimpses**★ of the indented coast, the Cordillera Cantábrica range and the mountains above Donostia-San Sebastián.

▷ *Travel 17km/10.5mi W along the Jaizkibel road.*

Pasaia/Pasajes
Pasaia comprises three villages around a sheltered bay. **Pasai Antxo** is a trading port, **Pasai Donibane★** and **Pasai San Pedro** are both deep-sea fishing ports, processing cod. To get to **Pasai Donibane**★, either park at the village entrance or take a motorboat from San Pedro. The **view** from the water is picturesque – tall houses with brightly painted wooden balconies, boats and docks, and a single street. A path runs to the lighthouse (45min).

Donostia-San Sebastián★★
See DONOSTIA-SAN SEBASTIÁN

▷ *Take the N 1; 7km/4.3mi S of Donostia-San Sebastián take the N 634 towards Bilbao.*

Zarautz
Queen Isabel II made this her summer residence in the 19C. Two **palaces** stand in the old quarter: the 16C property of the Marqués de Narros *(Elizaurre Kalea 2; ☎943 13 09 60)*, and the Luzea tower, on Plaza Mayor, with mullioned windows and a machicolated corner balcony. The tower of the church of Santa María *(Guipúzcoa 51; ☎943 83 21 61)* can be seen to one side.
The modern **Photomuseum** *(San Ignacio 11; ☎943 130 906; www.photomuseum.es)* is devoted to the art of photography, from landscapes to portraits and its application in the Surrealism movement as well as its history from lithography to the digital age.
Beyond Zarautz, the road rises to a picturesque **corniche section**★★.

Getaria-Guetaría
Getaria is known for its *chipirones*, or squid, and its rock – el ratón, or Monte de San Antón – linked by a causeway. Native son **Juan Sebastián Elcano** set out with Magellan and was the first sailor to circumnavigate the world (1522). A narrow street, lined with picturesque houses, leads to the 13C–15C **Iglesia de San Salvador** (Church of our Saviour; *Nagusia;* open Mon–Sat 10am–7.30pm *(8pm in summer),* Sun 10am–12.30pm;

943 14 07 51). its chancel rests on an arch above an alleyway. The gallery is Flamboyant Gothic.

The **Cristóbal Balenciaga Museoa** *(Aldamar Parkea 6; open Tue–Sun 10am–8pm (Tue–Thur 5pm), Fri–Sun and public holidays 10am–7pm Oct–May; €8; 943 00 88 40; www.cristobalbalenciagamuseoa.com)* showcases key designs from the couturier's career in a purpose-built structure here in his home town.

Zumaia

Zumaia has two fine beaches: Itzurun, between cliffs, and Santiago. Near the latter is the house of painter **Ignacio Zuloaga** (1870–1945), converted into a **casa-museo** *(open Holy Week–mid-Sept Wed–Sun 4pm–8pm; rest of the year by appointment; €8 (Oct–Mar), €6 (Apr–Sept). 943 86 23 41; www.ignaciozuloaga.com)* showing his works – realistic and popular themes with brilliant colours and strong lines – and his collection of paintings by El Greco, Goya, Zurbarán and Morales.

The 15C **Iglesia de San Pedro** contains a 16C altarpiece by Juan de Anchieta.

> *Past Zumaia, go left onto the GI 631.*

Santuario de San Ignacio de Loyola

Zumaia. Open daily 10am–12.30pm, 3–6.45pm. Santa Casa €2; no charge for the rest. 943 02 50 00. www.santuariodeloyola.org.

This **sanctuary** was built by the Jesuits to plans by Italian architect Carlo Fontana around the Loyola family manor near Azpeitia at the end of the 17C. It is an important place of pilgrimage especially on St Ignatius' day (31 July).

The basement casemates of the 15C tower are vestiges of the original Loyola manor house, the **Santa Casa**. The rooms in which Ignatius was born, convalesced and converted have been transformed into profusely decorated chapels. The Baroque **basilica** is more Italian than Spanish in style, circular with a vast cupola (65m/213ft high) attributed to Churriguera.

Museo Vasco del Ferrocarril

Azpeitia. Open Jul–Aug Tue–Sat 10.30am–2pm, 4pm–7.30pm, Sun 10.30am–2pm. Shorter hours rest of the year. Museum €3, train rides €3. 943 150 677. www.euskotren.es

A disused railway station is the perfect setting for a railway museum, with all buildings used – including the platforms and warehouses – for the exhibits, which include lovely old locomotives dating from the late 19C. From 22 Apr–1 Nov you can take a 5km/3.1mi ride through the verdant countryside, making this museum highly appealing to children.

> *Return to the coast. The journey by road to Deba is one of the most beautiful in the Basque Country.*

Deba

The **Iglesia de Santa María la Real** *(pl. Zaharra 7; open daily 9am–1pm; no charge; 943 12 24 52)* in this fishing port conceals, beneath the porch in its fortified front, a superb Gothic portal decorated with extremely lifelike statues. The cloister galleries have intricate tracery. There is a splendid **view**★ of the coast from the **cliff road**★ between Deba and Lekeitio.

Mutriku has one of the region's most delightful beaches, **Saturraran**.

ADDRESSES

STAY

Hotel Obispo – *Pl. del Obispo, Hondarribia. 943 64 54 00. www.hotelobispo.com. 17 rooms.* Charming hotel housed in a 14C–15C palace located in the upper section of the old quarter. Cosy and atmospheric.

EAT

Iribar – *Nagusia 34, Getaria. 943 14 04 06. Closed a fortnight in Apr and Oct.* Traditional restaurant serving reasonably priced grilled fish in the centre of this fishing village.

Bilbao★

Bilbao has renewed itself with a new metro system, with distinctive glazed station entrances by Sir Norman Foster; a new footbridge and airport terminal, both by Santiago Calatrava; and a riverside development by Cesar Pelli (of London's Canary Wharf tower). But Bilbao's jewel is the Guggenheim, its spectacular modern art museum designed by Frank Gehry. Bilbao was the birthplace of writer and humanist Miguel de Unamuno (1864–1936).

A BIT OF HISTORY

The city – Founded in the early 14C, old Bilbao is on the right bank of the Nervión, under the Santuario de Begoña (Begoña Sanctuary). It was originally named *las siete calles*, or seven streets, for its layout. The modern *El Ensanche* business district (*ensanche* means "enlargement"), across the river, developed in the 19C. The wealthy residential quarter spreads around Doña Casilda Iturriza park and along Gran Vía de Don Diego López de Haro.

Industry – Industry developed in the middle of the 19C when iron mined nearby was shipped to England. Iron and steelworks were subsequently established.

Greater Bilbao and the ría – Since 1945 Greater Bilbao has included the towns from Bilbao itself to Getxo on the sea. Industry is concentrated along the left bank in **Baracaldo**, **Sestao**, **Portugalete** with its **transporter bridge** built in 1893, and in Somorrostro where there is an oil refinery.

Santurtzi, a fishing port, is known for its sardines.

Algorta, a residential town on the right bank, is a contrast to heavy industry; **Deusto** is famous for its university.

MUSEO GUGGENHEIM★★★

Av. Abandoibarra 2. ⏱*Open Jul–Aug daily 10am–8pm; Sept–Jun Tue–Sun 10am–8pm.* ⏱*Closed 1 Jan, 24 (5pm), 25, 31 (5pm) Dec. Ticket office closes*

- ▶ **Population:** 355 731
- ⏱ **Michelin Map:** 573 C 21 (town plan) – País Vasco (Vizcaya)
- ℹ **Info:** Plaza del Ensanche 11. ℘944 79 57 60. www.bilbao.net.
- ▶ **Location:** Bilbao is in northeastern Spain's Basque Country. Vitoria-Gasteiz is 69km/43mi to the S, Donostia-San Sebastián 102km/63mi to the E, and Santander 103km/64mi to the W. 🚈Plaza Circular 2.
- 🅿 **Parking:** It can be difficult to find street parking.
- ⊚ **Don't Miss:** The Guggenheim is a must-see for Spain, not just Bilbao.
- ⏱ **Timing:** Spend a few hours at the Guggenheim for starters, try out the metro and stroll the riverside.
- 👪 **Kids:** Museo Marítimo Ría del Bilbao.

30min before museum. ⊚*€13.50; under-12 free. Bono Artean ticket (Guggenheim and Bellas Artes) €13.50. ℘944 35 90 80. www.guggenheim-bilbao.es.*

This is the European showcase for the collection founded in New York by art patron Solomon R. Guggenheim (1861–1949), the youngest of the prestigious museums managed by the Guggenheim Foundation. With this stunning museum complex, inaugurated in 1997, acclaimed architect **Frank Gehry** created one of the great buildings of the late 20C, a counterpart to Frank Lloyd Wright's famous 1950 spiral housing the Guggenheim's Fifth Avenue museum.

Emblem of the City

The museum rises from the banks of the Nervión like a complex ship with billowing sails. Formal geometry and symmetry are abandoned to free forms, creating harmony and lines flowing

Museo Guggenheim

Photo: David M. Heald © The Solomon R. Guggenheim Foundation, New York

gracefully out of potential chaos. The composition, shimmering in titanium, demands to be seen from all angles and alters with every change of light. The south entrance, of golden limestone, opens to a soaring **central atrium** (50m/164ft high) which echoes Wright's great spiral, transformed here into a whirl of smoothly moulded shapes and natural light.

Access to the galleries is by glass-fronted lifts or vertiginous suspended walkways and staircases. The largest measures 130m/426.5ft long and 25m/82ft wide, running the length of the riverside site, culminating in a V-shaped metal and stone tower.

Collections

Drawing on the vast Guggenheim collections (more than 6 000 paintings, sculptures and works on paper), the latest Guggenheim museum focuses on art from the 1950s to the present. Well represented are Modern masters (Picasso, Mondrian, Kandinsky) and major movements such as Abstract Expressionism (Rothko, De Kooning, Pollock), Pop art (Oldenburg, Rosenquist, Warhol), and Conceptual and Minimalist art (Carl André, Donald Judd). Contemporary artists likely to be on view include Anselm Kiefer, Francesco Clemente and Damien Hirst.

The museum's own acquisitions include a vast mural by Sol LeWitt and Richard Serra's Snake, three gigantic sheets of undulating steel. Notable Spanish works are by Antoni Tàpies, Eduardo Chillida, Francesc Torres, Cristina Iglesias and Susana Solano. Space is reserved for **Picasso**'s *Guernica*, now in Madrid's Reina Sofía museum.

SIGHTS

Museo de Bellas Artes★

Pl. del Museo 2. ○*Open Tue–Sun 10am –8pm.* ○*Closed 1, 6 Jan, 25 Dec.* ∞*5.50€; free Wed; Bono Artean ticket (Guggenheim and Bellas Artes)* €*13.50.* ℘*944 39 60 60. www.museobilbao.com.* The fine arts museum is in two buildings in Doña Casilda Iturriza park.

The **ancient art section**★★ *(old building, ground floor)* exhibits 12–17C Spanish paintings. Romanesque works include a 12C Crucifixion from the Catalan School. The 16C–17C Spanish Classical section has works by Morales, El Greco, Valdés Leal, Zurbarán, Ribera and Goya.

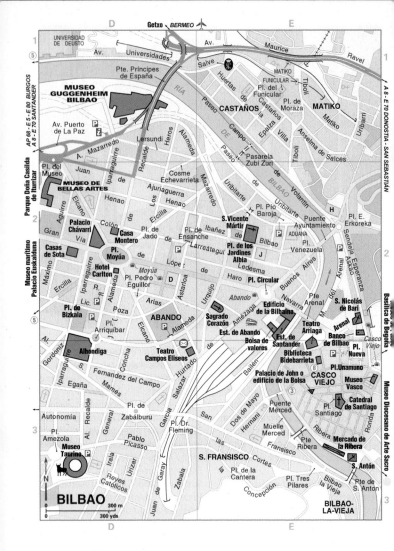

Dutch and Flemish canvases (15C–17C) include *The Usurers* by Quentin Metsys, a *Pietà* by Ambrosius Benson and a *Holy Family* by Gossaert.

The **Basque art section** (*first floor*) holds works by the great Basque painters: Regoyos, Zuloaga, Iturrino etc.

The **contemporary art section** (*new building*) displays works by artists both Spanish – Solana, Vázquez Díaz, Gargallo, Blanchard, Luis Fernández Otieza, Chillida and Tàpies – and foreign – Delaunay, Léger, Kokoschka and Bacon.

Museo Vasco (Basque Museum)

Pl. Miguel de Unamuno 4.
🕐*Open Tue–Sat 11am–5pm, Sun 11am–2pm.* 🕐*Closed public holidays.* ✆*€3; free Thu.* ✆ *944 15 54 23. www.euskal-museoa.org.*

The museum, in the ex-**Colegio de San Andrés** in the old town, provides insight into traditional Basque activities (linen weaving, arts and crafts, fishing). In the centre of the Classicist cloisters stands the primitive, animal-like **idol of Mikeldi**.

Museo Diocesano de Arte Sacro (Sacred Art Museum)

Pl. de la Encarnación 9. ○*Open Tue–Sat 10.30am–1.30pm, 4–7pm, Sun 10.30am–1.30pm.* ○*Closed public holidays.* ∞€2; free Thu. ✆944 32 01 25. www.eleizmuseoa.com.

This museum, in the former Convento de la Encarnación (16C), contains a Basque silverware collection and 12C–15C sculptures of the Virgin and Child.

Basílica de Begoña

Virgen de Begoña 38. ⬧*You can drive up but it's easier to take the lift from Esperanza Ascao.*

There is a fine **view of Bilbao** from the upper terminus footbridge. From Mallona park, take the main street on the right to the sanctuary (○*open Mon–Sat 10.30am–1.30pm, 4.30–8.30pm, Sun Mass only;* ✆944 12 70 91).

The church contains the venerated figure of Nuestra Señora de Begoña, patron of the province.

👥 Museo Marítimo Ría de Bilbao★★

Muelle Ramón de la Sota. ○*Open Jun–Oct Tue–Sun 10am–8pm, Nov–May Tue–Fri 10am–6pm, Sat, Sun 10am–8pm. Shorter hours rest of the year.* ∞€5. ✆902 131 000. www.museomaritimo bilbao.org.

This playful and didactic museum explains Bilbao's important maritime history and culture.

Located inside the outbuildings of the old shipyards (or in *astilleros* Spanish), the ground floor focuses on the development of and changes to the city's estuary, with an entire room devoted to **Evaristo de Churruca** (1841–1917), the engineer who constructed the city's first port.

The second level focuses on Bilbao's commercial and industrial maritime prominence and the industrialisation of the city through historic maps, documents and models.

Outside in the dry docks, the tour ends with a display that includes a life boat, old wooden fishing boats and a tug from 1928, which visitors can board.

🚗 DRIVING TOUR

Costa de Vizcaya/Bizkaia

The beaches and coves that dot the Costa de Guipuzcoa are backed by rolling green hills and make for an ideal escape from busy Bilbao, with genuine corners of untouched paradise, particularly around the pristine Urdaibai Biosphere Reserve. Touring the coastline will enable you to discover towns and villages brimming with Basque history and culture. For outdoor enthusiasts there are ample opportunities for sport or just soaking up the great outdoors.

▷ *Exit Bilbao W along the A-8 in the direction of Vitoria-Gasteiz. At exit 14 take the N-624 towards Donostia-San Sebastián then the GI-638 towards Mutriku. Once there, take the Bi-633.*

Ondárroa

10km/6.2mi W of Deba along GI 638.
The church, standing like a ship's prow, tall Basque houses with washing at the windows, and the encircling river, make an attractive **picture**★. Canning and fish salting are the main industries.

Onward, on rounding a point you have a good **view**★ of Lekeitio, its beach and the island of San Nicolás, joined to the mainland at low tide.

▷ *Leave W along BI 3438.*

Lekeitio

12km/7.4mi W.
A deeply indented bay at the foot of Monte Calvario, divided by an island, is Lekeitio's fishing harbour. There are good beaches. The 15C **iglesia** (*Independentzia Enparantza;* ○*open daily 8am–noon, 5–7.30pm;* ∞*no charge;* ✆946 84 09 54) guarding the harbour has three tiers of flying buttresses and a tall Baroque belfry.

Ispaster/Ispáster

This atmospheric town has retained an ensemble of old buildings, including a pretty 15th-century church, some Renaissance, Baroque mansions and the Arana Homestead (1700), which is easily recognisable by its two towers. To get to the coast, take the road on your right just before the cemetery on the outskirts of the village. It runs though the forest before reaching Ogeyi Beach.

▷ *Continue NW BI 3438.*

Ea
11km/6.8mi NW of Lekeitio
This miniature harbour stands between two hills at the end of a quiet creek.
Old houses follow the banks of the river, which is spanned by stone bridges and affords a pleasant, shady walk.
To the left of the church of Nuestra Señora de Jesús at the entrance of the village follow the yellow-white markings. The walk continues through woods and meadows. Once you reach two houses overlooking the main road, take the path at the side of the second as it provides access to the forest. Back on the road, follow it left to the houses where you return to the main path. It leads to the coast and the hermitage of Talako Ama, revealing a beautiful sea **view★** (90min).

▷ *Continue NE along BI 3438.*

Elantxobe★
7km/4.3mi NW of Ea.
Fishermen have long used the bay as a natural harbour and built their houses overlooking the water, against steep-sided Cabo Ogoño (300m/1 000ft).
Beyond rose-coloured **Playa de Laga**, a beach circling Cabo Ogoño, you can see **Gernika ría★** (Estuary), Izaro island, the white outline of the town of Sukarrieta on the far bank, and Chacharramendi island. The resort of **Playa de Laida**, on the *ría*, is popular with Gernika residents.

▷ *Go SW and bear left at Kortezubi.*

Cuevas de Santimamiñe
Barrio Basondo, Kortezubi.
Guided tours pre-booked through the Interpretation Centre, daily 10am–1.30pm, 3–7pm. ☞5€. ℘944 65 16 57. santimamine@bizkaia.net.

Wall paintings and engravings from the Magdalenian period were discovered in these caves in 1917.

▷ *Return to the main road and bear S.*

Gernika
14km/8.7mi S of Elantxobe.
Picasso's painting, *Guernica* (see *MADRID*), immortalised a Spanish Civil War atrocity: on 26 April 1937, Nazi planes bombed the town, killing more than 1 000 people.
In the Middle Ages, the Gernika oak was one of the four places where newly created lords of Biscay came to swear that they would respect the local *fueros* or privileges. The remains of the 1 000-year-old tree are in the small temple behind the **Casa de Juntas** (*Allendesalazar;* ⏱open daily 10am–2pm, 4–6pm *(7pm Jun and Oct);* ⏱closed 1, 6 Jan, 16 Aug, 24–25, 31 Dec; ☞no charge; ℘946 25 11 38).
This extremely moving **Museo de la Paz** is divided into three environments: the first attempts to define the concept of peace through quotes from famous people such as Martin Luther King, Gandhi and Chateaubriand, while the second discusses Guernica's tragic history. The third addresses the concept of peace today, focusing on the Basque conflict, political prisoners and torture *(Foru Plaza 1;* ⏱open Jul–Aug *Tue–Sat 10am–8pm, Sun 10am–3pm; rest of year Tue–Sat 10am– 2pm, 4pm– 7pm, Sun 10am–2pm;* ⏱closed Mon; ☞ €4 (under 12 free); ℘946 27 02 13; www.museodelapaz.org).
18km/11mi south *(via the BI 2224 and BI 3231),* the **Balcón de Vizcaya★★** (Balcony of Biscay) viewpoint overlooks a chequerboard of meadows and forests.

▷ *Return to Gernika.*

Two viewpoints before Mundaka enable you to take a last look back over still waters. As the road drops downhill, you get a magnificent **view★** of Bermeo.

Bermeo

15km/9mi NW of Gernika along BI 2235.
The fishermen's quarter, still crowded onto the Atalaya promontory overlooking the old harbour, was protected by ramparts (traces remain), and the grim granite Torre de Ercilla, now the **Museo del Pescador** *(pl. Torrontero;* ○*open Tue–Sat 10am–2pm, 4–7pm, Sun 10am–2.15pm;* ∞*€3 (under 12 no charge);* ✆*946 88 11 71)* dedicated to local fishermen.
A reconstruction of a 17C whaling boat transports the visitor to Bermeo's golden age of fishing at **Whale Ship Aita Guria** (○*open Tue–Sat 10am–2pm, 4pm–7pm, Sun 11am–2pm;* ∞*€2 from Tourist Office, 4–14 €1;* ✆ *946 17 91 21; www.aitaguria.bermeo.org).*
A voice-over introduces the captain's cabin, galleys and the hold, and helps you understand the living conditions on board. Call before visiting as access depends on the tides.

▷ *Turn left towards Mungía.*

Alto del Sollube★ (Sollube Pass)

The road up to the low pass (340m/1 115ft) affords a good view of Bermeo.

▷ *Return to Bermeo, follow the coast road left for 3km/1.8mi then turn right.*

Faro (Lighthouse) de Machichaco

From just left of here there is a good view west. The road winds to a **viewpoint★** over the **San Juan de Gaztelugache** headland and its hermitage (*access via a pathway)*, the goal of a *romería* (pilgrimage) on Midsummer's Day *(23 Jun)*; there are extensive views from the **corniche road★** between Bakio and Arminza. A belvedere commands an interesting **view★** of the coast, Bakio, valley farms and wooded hinterland.

Arminza

Arminza is the only harbour along a section of wild coast.

▷ *Continue SW.*

Gorliz

7km/4.3mi SW of Arminza.
Gorliz is an attractive beach resort at the mouth of the River Butrón. **Plentzia** nearby *(2km/1.2mi)* is an oyster farming centre and resort.

Castillo de Butrón

⊶*Closed for restoration.*
This fantasy castle, built on the remains of a 14C–15C construction, is a good example of eclectic, picturesque 19C architecture, and provides insight into medieval castle life.

Getxo

13km/8mi SW of Gorliz.
A **paseo marítimo** (sea promenade) overlooks the coast. From the road up to Getxo's well-known golf course there is a view of the Bilbao inlet and on the far bank, Santurtzi and Portugalete.

Bilbao★

♨*See BILBAO*

ADDRESSES

🏠 STAY

🛏 **Bilborooms** – Victor 3, 1st Floor. ✆ 944 79 35 91. www.bilborooms.com. 7 rooms. ⌇
This charming, sober little pension offers a simple but comfortable and quiet place to rest your head. Frugal breakfast.

🛏 **Hotel Plaza San Pedro** – Luzarra, 7. ✆944 76 31 26. www.hotelplazasanpedro.com 19 rooms. ⌇€3.50. Family-run place located in the university district. The rooms are nice for their class.

🍴/EAT

🍽 **Gatz** – Sta Maria, 10. ✆944 15 48 61. www.bargatz.com. Closed second fortnight Sept. ⊟. Old-town bar with prize-winning pintxos.

🍽🍽🍽🍽 **Goizeko Kabi** – Particular Estraunza, 4. ✆946 42 11 29. www.goizeko catering.com. Closed first 2 weeks Aug, Sun. Located near the Museo de Bellas Artes, this gastronomic institution serves high-quality and innovative dishes. The way fish is cooked and presented is the stuff of legend among gourmands.

Vitoria-Gasteiz★

Vitoria-Gasteiz is the capital of the largest Basque province and the seat of the Basque government, sited in a cereal-covered plateau. It was founded in the 12C and was surrounded by walls. The old quarter is in the upper section.

CIUDAD VIEJA★★

Concentric streets – each named after a trade – ring the cathedral in the old town. The liveliest streets are to the left of the plaza de la Virgen Blanca.
The **Iglesia de San Pedro** (*Fundadora de las Siervas de Jesús 2*), with its Gothic façade, can also be found in this part of the old town.

Plaza de la Virgen Blanca

The square, dominated by the Iglesia (church) de San Miguel, is surrounded by house fronts with glassed-in balconies, or *miradores*.
The massive monument at the square's centre commemorates Wellington's decisive victory on 21 June 1813, putting to flight King Joseph Bonaparte and his army. It communicates with the nobly ordered 18C **Plaza de España** (or Plaza Nueva).

Iglesia de San Miguel

Escaleras de San Miguel 1.
Guided tours available Jul–Sept, organised by the tourist office.
In a jasper niche in the church porch is a polychrome Late Gothic statue of the Virgen Blanca, the city's patron. In the late 14C portal, the tympanum shows the Life of St Michael. In the chancel are an altarpiece by Gregorio Fernández and a Plateresque sepulchral arch.

Plaza del Machete★★

This small, long square lies behind the **Arquillos**, an arcade which links the upper and lower towns. A niche in the east end of San Miguel church contains the *machete* or cutlass, on which the procurator general had to

▶ **Population:** 240 580
⚙ **Michelin Map:** 573 D 21-22 (town plan) – País Vasco (Álava).
Info: Plaza España 1 ℘945 16 15 98. www.vitoria-gasteiz.org.
▶ **Location:** The city is at 524m/1 718ft in NE Spain. A 2h30min walking tour of the historic district departs from the Tourist Office. Eduardo Dato 46.
Kids: Museo de Armería.
🕑 **Timing:** Vitoria hosts a jazz festival in July.

swear to uphold the town's privileges *(fueros)*. The 16C **Palacio de Villa Suso** (🕑*open Mon–Fri 8.30am–1.30pm, 9pm in summer)*, on the right side, is now a meeting centre.

▶ *Climb the steps adjoining the palace.*

A stroll along **calle Fray Zacarías Martínez**, with wood-framed houses and palaces, is pleasant. The Renaissance north doorway of the Palacio de los Escoriaza-Esquivel (*5–7; ℘945 24 76 01*), built on the old town walls, is worthy of special note; if it is open, enter to view the lovely covered courtyard.

Catedral de Santa María

Cuchillería 95–97. 🕑*Open daily 11am– 1pm, 5–7pm.* 🕑*Closed 1 Jan, 25 Dec.* *Guided tour (60min) available with prior booking.* €6. ℘945 25 51 35. *www.catedralvitoria.com.*
The construction of the Gothic church-fortress, part of the city's first defensive ring, began at the end of the 13C.
In the 16C wood and brick. **Casa Godeo-Guevara-San Juan** is home to a small archaeological museum. The **Casa del Portalón**, opposite, is a typical late 15C-early 16C shop, now a well-known restaurant. The **Torre de los Anda**, part of the medieval defences, forms a triangle with the two houses.

In calle Cuchillería, in the **Palacio de Bendaña**, a building noted for its corner turret and doorway with *alfiz* surround, is a museum devoted to playing cards. Part of the delightful **Renaissance patio** has been preserved. The **Casa del Cordón** *(Cuchillería 24)*, a 16C house, is used for exhibitions.

CIUDAD NUEVA

As Vitoria-Gasteiz grew in the 18C, neo-Classical constructions began to appear such as the **Arquillos** arcade in what is referred to as the modern town.

In the 19C, the town expanded southwards with the **Parque de la Florida** (Florida Park), the **Catedral Nueva** (New Cathedral, 1907) in neo-Gothic style and two wide avenues: paseo de la Senda and paseo de Fray Francisco, the latter lined by mansions, such as the Palacio de Ajuria Enea, seat of the Lehendakari, or Basque government, and two museums, the Museo de Armería and the Museo de Bellas Artes.

Near Plaza de España is the modern Plaza de los Fueros, the work of architect José Luis Peña Ganchegui and sculptor Eduardo Chillida.

Restoration Work at Catedral de Santa María★★

See Cathedral entry for details.

The diocese has stuggled for centuries to keep this Gothic cathedral from subsiding and tumbling. A programme to realign its walls will run to at least 2010. An innovative hard-hat tour along walkways and passages reveals the secrets of this temple fortress.

Museo Artium★

Francia 24. Open Tue–Fri 11am–2pm, 5pm-8pm; Sat- Sun 11am–9pm. Closed Sept. €6. 945 20 90 20. www.artium.org.

This museum and cultural centre focuses on the foundations of modern art.

A significant selection from its **magnificent collection**★ is shown on a rotating basis.

The museum owns more than 1 800 works of Spanish artists, from the Avant Garde of the twenties and thirties (most of the collection) to the most recent. Names are of the stature of Miró, Gargallo, Tàpies, Canogar, Palazuelo, Oteiza and Chillida.

Museo de Armería★ (Museum of Arms and Armour)

Pas. de Fray Francisco 3. Open Tue–Fri 10am–2pm, 4–6.30pm, Sat 10am–2pm, Sun and public holidays 11am–2pm. Closed 1 Jan & Good Friday. No charge. 945 18 19 25.

The well-presented collection housed in a modern building traces the tradition and evolution of weaponry in the Basque Country from prehistoric axes to early 20C pistols. Note the 15C–17C **armour**, including suits of 17C **Japanese armour**.

Museo Diocesano de Arte Sacro (Diocesan Sacred Art Museum)

Monseñor Cadena y Eleta s/n . Open Tue–Fri 10am–2pm, 4–6.30pm Sat 10am–2pm, Sun and public holidays 11am–2pm. No charge. 945 15 06 31

This museum in the ambulatory of the **Catedral Nueva** exhibits Gothic images, Flemish works (*Descent from the Cross* by Van der Goes, *The Crucifixion* by Ambrosius Benson), 16C–18C canvases (*St Francis* by El Greco, several Riberas, *The Immaculate Conception* by Alonso Cano) and silverware.

Museo de Bellas Artes (Fine Arts Museum)

Pas. de Fray Francisco de Vitoria 8. Open Tue–Fri 10am–2pm, 4–6.30pm, Sat 10am–2pm, Sun 11am–2pm. Closed 1 Jan & Good Friday. No charge. 945 18 19 18.

The museum, housed in the early 20C Historicist Palacio de Agustí, displays Spanish art of the 18C and 19C and a comprehensive selection of Basque *costumbrista* painting by such artists as Iturrino, Regoyos and Zuloaga. Highlights include the *La Cuidad con Sol* by Fernando de América.

BIBAT: Museo Fournier de Naipes y Museo de Arqueología ★ (Archaeological Museum)

Cuchillería 54. ⏰*Open Tue–Fri 10am–2pm, 4–6.30pm, Sat 10am–2pm, Sun and public holidays 11am–2pm.* ✍*No charge.* ✆*945 20 37 07.*

Two museums – the Museo de Arqueología and Museo de Álava Fournier Naipes – are viewed together here in an exciting complex that fuses a Renaissance palace with cutting-edge architecture.

The Naipes (playing cards) collection occupies the older building. Founded in 1868 by Heraclio Fournier, a descendant of a Parisian family of printers of famous of playing cards. Anxious to preserve their heritage, he amassed an incredible collection, which was acquired by Alava's Provincial Council. It currently comprises of over 20 000 sets of cards from around the world, from the 14C to the present day. They cover a wide variety of topics (such as history, geography, art, caricatures and customs) and a diversity of print media, including paper, parchment, leaves, fabric and metal.

The Archeological Museum occupies a modern annex (work of architect Patxi Mangado) and displays finds from excavations in Álava province. Note the dolmen collections and Roman monuments.

EXCURSIONS
Santuario de Estíbaliz

▷ *10km/6.2mi E. Leave Vitoria-Gasteiz via the Avenida de Bruselas then take the A 132 towards Argadoña. Bear left after about 4km/2.5mi.*

⏰*Open daily 8am–8pm.* ⏰ *No visits during religious services.* ✍*No charge.* ✆*945 29 30 88.*

This Late Romanesque pilgrim shrine has an attractive wall belfry on the south front, and a 12C Romanesque statue of the Virgin.

EAST OF VITORIA-GASTEIZ: MEDIEVAL PAINTINGS

▷ *25km/15.5mi along the E5-N1 motorway as far as junction 375.*

Gazeo

🎧*Guided tours of Gazeo and Alaiza Sept–Jun Thu and Fri; Jul–Aug and Holy Week daily.* ✆*945 31 25 35.* ✍*2€.*

Superb 14C **Gothic frescoes**★★ decorate the chancel of the church (iglesia). The south wall shows Hell as a whale's gullet, the north, the Life of the Virgin. On the roof are scenes from the Life of Christ.

Alaiza

▷ *Follow the A 4111 for 3km/1.8mi, turn right, then left after a few metres.*

Obscure **paintings**★ on the walls and roof of the church (iglesia) apse probably date from the late 14C. Strange red outlines represent castles, churches, soldiers and many other personages.

Oñati/Oñate

▷ *At the foot of Monte Alona (1 321m/4 333ft), 45km/28mi NE of Vitoria-Gasteiz and 74km/46mi SW of Donostia-San Sebastián*

Oñati, with its seigniorial residences, monastery and old university, nestles amid the wild beauty of the Udana Valley. It figured prominently in the First Carlist War.

The **old university**★ (*Universitate Etorbidea 8.* ⏰*Open Sept–Jul Mon–Thu 9am–4.30pm, Fri 9am–2pm; Aug Mon–Fri 9am–2pm.* 🎧*Guided tours available Holy Week and August.* ✆*943 78 34 53*), now administrative headquarters of Guipúzcoa province, was founded in 1542 and functioned until the early 20C. The gateway, by Pierre Picart, is surmounted by pinnacles and crowded with statues.

The **ayuntamineto**★ is housed in a fine 18C Baroque building designed by Martín de Carrera.

The Gothic church, **Iglesia de San Miguel**, facing the university was modified in the Baroque period.

A Renaissance chapel off the north aisle, closed by beautiful iron grilles, contains an interesting gilded wood altarpiece. The golden stone cloister exterior with is Isabelline Plateresque (🎧*guided tours Mon–Fri 9am and 7.15pm, Sat 7pm, Sun 11am and 1pm;* ✍*2€;* ✆*943 78 34 53*).

Santuario de Arantzazu★

▶ *9km/5.5mi S of Oñati/Onnate along the GI 3591.* 🕐*Open daily 8.30am–8pm.* 🎧*943 71 89 11.*

The **scenic cliff road**★ follows the the River Arantzazu, which flows through a narrow gorge. The **shrine** at 800m/2 625ft in a mountain **setting**★ faces the highest peak in the province, Mount Aitzgorri (1 549m/5 082ft).

Dominating the church is an immense bell tower 40m/131ft high, with diamond-faceted stone symbolising the hawthorn bush (*arantzazu* in Basque) in which the Virgin appeared to a local shepherd in 1469.

ADDRESSES

🏨 STAY

🛏️🍽️ **Hotel Dato** – *Dato 28.* 🎧*945 14 72 30. www.hoteldato.com. 14 rooms.* The Dato is centrally located with traditional but out of the ordinary (for the price category) décor. The rooms are impeccably maintained.

La Rioja★

The Ebro Valley in La Rioja is carpeted with vineyards and vegetable fields under the peaks of the Sierras de Cantabria and de la Demanda. La Rioja flourished thanks to its position on the pilgrim route to Santiago de Compostela, and later became famous for its wine.

A BIT OF GEOGRAPHY

Bustling **Rioja Alta** (Upper Rioja), to the west around Haro, is devoted to wine-growing while **Rioja Baja** (Lower Rioja), with **Logroño** and Calahorra as its main towns, is given over to the early growing of vegetables.

SIGHTS
Logroño

The capital of the Rioja region is on the banks of the Ebro. Pilgrims to Santiago de Compostela would have entered this

🛏️🍽️🍽️ **Hotel Palacio de Elorriaga** – *Elorriaga 15, 1.5km/1mi E along Av. de Santiago and the N 104.* 🎧*945 26 36 16. www.hotelpalacioelorriaga.com. 21 rooms. Restaurant*🛏️🍽️🍽️. This 16C–17C mansion has been completely restored. Behind the sober walls of stone and brick, the overall effect is delightful with tasteful small touches and an abundance of wood and antique furniture. Guest rooms are cosy with en-suite bathrooms.

🍽️ EAT

🛏️🍽️🍽️ **Gurea** – *Pl. de la Constitución 10.* 🎧*945 24 59 33. Closed Sun–Wed for dinner, 2nd fortnight in Aug.* The attractive wood façade leads to rustic dining areas where traditional foods are served.

TAPAS

El Rincón de Luis Mari – *Rioja 14.* 🎧*945 25 01 27. Closed Mar and Sept, Tue .* A simple bar with a large choice of tapas and *raciones*, a fine selection of cured hams, and a good location near the old quarter.

- ▶ **Population:** 321 702
- ⓘ **Michelin Map:** 573 E 20-23, F 20-24 – La Rioja, Navarra, País Vasco (Álava).
- ▪ **Info:** Logroño: Portales 50. 🎧941 27 33 53; Nájera: Plaza San Miguel 10. 🎧941 36 00 41; San Millán de la Cogolla: Monasterio de Yuso. 🎧941 37 32 59; Santo Domingo de la Calzada: Mayor 44. 🎧902 106 637. www.lariojaturismo.com. 🚌Plaza Europa, Logroño.
- ▶ **Location:** La Rioja (from Río Oja, a tributary of the Ebro) covers approximately 5 000sq km/1 930sq mi in the provinces of La Rioja, Álava and Navarra.
- 🕐 **Timing:** Three or four days to tour the vineyards.

TAPAS

The small **calle del Laurel** is without doubt one of the main attractions in Logroño with its huge choice of bars serving delicious local specialities (sweet peppers, mushrooms, etc.).

pleasant town through the stone gateway, overlooking the cathedral.

Santa María la Redonda

Portales 14. ⊙*Open Mon–Sat 8am–1pm, 6–8.45pm, Sun 9am–2pm, 6.30–8.45pm.* ⊛ *No charge.* ℘*941 25 76 11.*
Dating from 1435, the church has three naves, three polygonal apses and chapels in its side aisles. These include the Plateresque Chapel of Our Lady of Peace (Nuestra Señora de la Paz), founded in 1541 by Diego Ponce de León.

Museo de la Rioja

Pl. de San Agustín. ⟋*Closed for renovation until 2012.* ℘*941 29 12 59.*
This regional museum is in a fine 18C Baroque palace.

Laguardia/Biasteri/Guardia★

Hillside Laguardia is perhaps the most attractive town in Rioja Alavesa, with two imposing towers visible as you approach: San Juan to the south, and the 12C tower of the abbey to the north, once connected to the Gothic Iglesia de Santa María de los Reyes.

Iglesia de Santa María de los Reyes

Mayor. ⟋*Guided tours Tue–Fri 10am–2pm, 4–7pm, Sat 10am–2pm, 5–7pm, Sun 10.45am–2pm.* ⊛*€2.* ℘*945 60 08 45.*
A superb late 14C **portal**★★ retains its 17C polychrome decoration. The tympanum is divided into three scenes relating the life of the Virgin. Note the figure of Christ holding a small child in his hands representing the soul of the Virgin.

Labastida

◗ *20km/12mi W of Laguardia via A 124*
So-called capital of Rioja Alavesa, this frontier town perched on a rocky outcrop has a pretty old town, **La Mota★**, with narrow streets lined with charming, albeit faded, stone houses with studded doors.

Bodega Ysios

◗ *Due north of Laguardia on the Camino de la Hoya.* ⟋*Guided tours Mon–Fri 11am, 1pm, 4pm, Sat–Sun 11am, 1pm with prior booking.* ℘*945 60 06 40. www.ysios.com.*
Designed by renowned Valencian architect Santiago Calatrava and nestled at the base of the Sierra de Cantabria Mountains the outline of this *bodega* (winery) evokes both the shape of wine barrels and the mountains' curves in its undulating form. Inside, vats and bottles are stored in soaring wall-less, arc-like spaces that allow air to circulate.
The upstairs tasting room is characterised by a high ceiling and an incredible view onto the vineyards.

Ciudad del Vino (Wine City)

◗ *5km/3.1mi S of Laguardia on the A2310.* ⟋*Guided tours (1hr30min) Mon–Fri 8am–8pm, Sat 9am–5pm with prior booking.* ⊛*€10.* ℘*945 18 08 88. www.marquesderiscal.com.*
In the tiny village of El Ciego, Frank Gehry, of Guggenheim fame, has designed a stunning hotel and spa for the Marqués de Riscal wine makers.
On the same grounds, the group's cellars are open to the public, a visit that ends at "the cathedral", where a bottle of wine from each year of the company's long history is kept.

Centro Temático del vino Villa Lucía (Villa Lucía Wine Centre)

On the way to Logroño.
⊙*Open Tue–Sun 9am–2pm, 4–8pm.* ⊛*€8.50.* ℘*945 60 00 32. www.villa-lucia.com.*
The museum on this lovely estate traces the elaboration of wines. The **panorama** from the **Balcón de Rioja**★★ or Rioja Balcony 12km/7.4mi northwest of Laguardia near the Puerto de Herrera (Herrera Pass, 1 100m/3 609ft), is extensive.

Wines of La Rioja

In 1902, Rioja was the first Spanish appellation with the Denominación de Origen Calificada (DOC) quality label and today over 500 *bodegas* (wineries) dot the region. The wine is the result of more than seven centuries of tradition and a superb position in the Ebro Valley between the Sierra de la Demanda and the Sierra de Cantabria. The wine region is traditionally divided into three sub-zones: Rioja Alavesa, Rioja Baja and Rioja Alta. Although seven grape varieties are permitted, the two most commonly used are Tempranillo and Grenache. Red wine accounts for 75 per cent of production and is produced according to two different processes: **carbonic maceration**

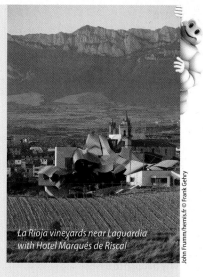

La Rioja vineyards near Laguardia with Hotel Marqués de Riscal

John Frumm/hemis.fr © Frank Gehry

and **ageing**. The first produces young, fresh wines which are best consumed in the year of production, whereas the ageing process, in Bordeaux oak barrels, results in three different wines, classified according to the time spent in the barrel and the time which has elapsed between the harvest and the moment the wine leaves the cellars: **Crianza** (12 months in the barrel, one year in the bottle), **Reserva** (12 months in the barrel, two years in the bottle) and **Gran Reserva** (24 months in the barrel, three years in the bottle).

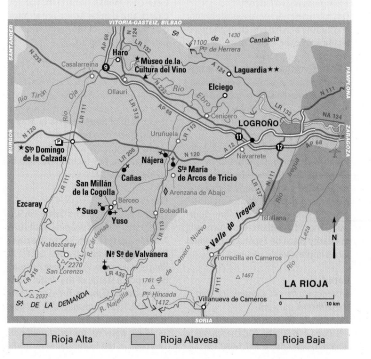

Rioja Alta Rioja Alavesa Rioja Baja

Haro

This centre is famous for its wines. Elegant 16C and 18C façades recall a prestigious past. In **plaza de la Paz** note the simple lines of the Neoclassical town hall (ayuntamiento), built by Juan de Villanueva in 1769; also note the Baroque tower of the **Iglesia de Santo Tomás** (pl. de la Iglesia; ℘941 31 16 90).

Centro de Interpretación del Vino de la Rioja

Bretón de los Herreros 4. ◯Open Fri–Sat 10am–2.30pm, 3.30–6pm, Sun and public holidays 10am–2pm. ◯Closed Dec 24, 25, 31, Jan 1–6. ◉€3. ℘941 31 05 47. www.vinodelarioja.org.
This information centre/museum is devoted to wine, from cultivation all the way through to the bottling process.

Museo de la Cultura del Vino – Dinastía Vivanco★

◗5km/3mi from Haro, in Briones (442km/275mi on the N 232).
Guided tours by arrangement Tue–Fri 1am, 4pm. ◉€7.50. ℘902 32 00 01. www.dinastiavivanco.com.
This splendid museum covers the history and culture of wine and changing wine technology over 10 000 years.

Santo Domingo de la Calzada★

This staging post on the Camino de Santiago was founded in the 11C and owes its name to a hermit, Dominic, who built a bridge for pilgrims. Parts of the 14C ramparts can still be seen.
The **old town**★ huddles around the **Plaza del Santo**, dominated by the Cathedral and the ex-hospital, now a parador. The streets around the square, particularly the calle Mayor, retain 16C and 17C stone houses with fine doorways. The 18C ayuntamiento (town hall), in nearby plaza de España, is crowned by an impressive escutcheon.

Catedral★

Entrance via the 14C cloisters, housing the cathedral museum.
Pl. del Santo. ◯Open Mon–Sat 9.30am –1.30pm, 4–6.30pm. ◯Closed public holidays. ◉€3.50. ℘941 34 00 33.

The church is Gothic, apart from the ambulatory and apsidal chapel, which are Romanesque (second half of the 12C). The saint's tomb (13C), beneath a 1513 canopy, is in the south transept, and opposite is a sumptuous **Gothic cage**. This contains a live white cock and hen in memory of a miracle attributed to the saint – a cock about to be eaten sprang up and proclaimed the innocence of a convicted thief.
The **retable**★★ at the high altar (1538) is an unfinished work by Damián Forment. The Cathedral also contains the **Capilla de la Magdalena**★ (Evangelist's nave) with fine Plateresque decoration and magnificent screen.

Abadía de Cañas

Real, Cañas. ◗13km/8mi SE of Santo Domingo de la Calzada. ◯Open Nov–Mar Tue–Sat 10.30am–1.30pm, 4–6pm, Sun 11am–1.30pm, 4–6pm; Apr–Oct Tue–Sat 10am–1.30pm, 4–7pm, Sun 11am–1.30pm, 4–7pm. ◉€3. ℘941 37 90 83. www.abadiadecanas.com.
This monastery has been inhabited by Cistercian monks since 1170. The 16C church and chapter house are extraordinary examples of the purity and simplicity of Cistercian art.

Ezcaray

This delightful village is a summer resort and ski area. It has houses with stone and wood porticoes, mansions and the church of **Santa María la Mayor** (guided tours available through tourist office; ℘941 35 46 79) as well as a former tapestry factory founded by Charles III in 1752.

Nájera★

Reconquered by Sancho Garcés I in 920, Nájera was Navarra's capital until 1076. The **Monasterio de Santa María la Real**★ was founded by Don García III, King of Navarra, in 1032, where he stumbled upon a statue of the Virgin (Pl. de Santa María; ◯open Tue–Sat 10am–1pm, 4–5.30pm, Sun and public holidays 10am–12.30pm, 4–5.30pm. ◉€3; ℘941 36 10 83; www.santamarialareal.net). The bays in the lower galleries of the

cloisters★ are filled with Plateresque stone tracery (1520).

Beneath the gallery of the **church**★ is the **Panteón Real**★ (Royal Pantheon) of princes of Navarra, León and Castilla of the 11C and 12C.

Basílica de Santa María de Arcos de Tricio

▷ *3km/2mi SW of Nájera.* ◷*Open Jul–Sept Tue–Sat 10.30am–1.30pm, 4.30–7.30pm, Sun 10.30am–1.30pm; Oct–Jun Sat–Sun and holidays only 10.30am–1.30pm.* ⊗*€1.50.* ✆*941 36 16 57.*

This unusual church, with basilical plan, was built in the 5C.

San Millán de la Cogolla

The most attractive approach is via the turn-off from the LR 113 at Bobadilla.

A World Heritage Site, San Millán de la Cogolla was already famous in the 5C when Millán or Emilian de Berceo and his followers settled as hermits. Here the first manuscripts were written in Castilian Spanish.

Monasterio de Suso★

⊸*Guided tours daily year-round 9.30am–1.30pm, 3.30–6 /6.30pm. Booking essential 3€* ⊗*.* ✆*941 37 30 82. www.monasteriodeyuso.org.*

Housed in a Mozarabic building partly hollowed out of the rock, the monastery overlooks the Cárdenas Valley.

Monasterio de Yuso

◷*Open Tue–Sun Holy Week–end Sept 10.30am–1.30pm, 4–6.30pm Oct–start Holy Week 10am–1pm, 3.30–5.30pm.* ◷*Closed Sun pm during winter.* ⊗*€5.* ✆*941 37 30 49. www.monasterio deyuso.org.*

In the treasury are splendid **ivories**★★ from two 11C reliquaries.

Monasterio de Nuestra Señora de Valvanera

Anguiano. Access via the LR 113. ◷*Open daily 9am–7pm.* ⊗*No charge.* ✆*941 37 70 44.*

This monastery is in a delightful, isolated wooded mountain **setting**★★. The church houses a 12C statue of the patron saint of La Rioja, the Virgen of Valvanera. The complex includes a hostel.

Valle del Iregua★

▷ *50km/31mi S of Logroño on the N 111.*

Near Islallana appear the **rock faces**★ of the Sierra de Cameros, overlooking the Iregua Valley from more than 500m/1 640ft. In the village of **Villanueva de Cameros**, half-timbered houses are roofed with circular tiles.

ADDRESSES

⌂ STAY

⊖⊜⊜ **Hotel Echaurren** – *Padre José García 19, Ezcaray.* ✆*941 35 40 47. www.echaurren.com. 25 rooms.* ⊐*€8. Restaurant*⊖⊜⊜⊜*.* This hotel is best known for its cuisine, with traditional and creative menus.

⊖⊜⊜⊜ **Parador de Santo Domingo de la Calzada** – *Pl. del Santo 3, Santo Domingo de la Calzada.* ✆*941 341 150. www.parador. es. 59 rooms.* ⊐*€15. Restaurant*⊖⊜⊜. This parador is housed in a former pilgrims' hospital along the Camino de Santiago. Features Gothic-style stone walls and arches.

⌁ EAT

⊖⊜⊜ **Marixa** – *Sancho Abarca 8, Laguardia.* ✆*945 60 01 65. www.restaurante marisa.com.* Popular and known for traditional cooking. Good views from the dining room, plus comfortable rooms (*10 rooms*⊖⊜⊜).

⊖⊜ **El Bodegón** – *Calle Frontin, 31, Labastida.* ✆*945 33 10 27 or 629 829 775.* Enjoy grilled chops in a rustic compound of stone walls, exposed beams and old photographs.

⊖⊜ **Héctor Oribe** – *Gasteiz, 8, Páganos.* ✆ *945 60 07 15. www.hectororibe.es. Closed 1 Jul, 15, 20 Dec–10 Jan, Sun and Mon night.* À la carte and daily set menus from a chef who's worked in the kitchens of some of the region's Michelin-starred establishments.

CANTABRIA AND ASTURIAS

Asturias, to the east, and Cantabria, to the west, make up the central part of Spain's northern Atlantic coastline. The countryside, watered and made verdant by the highest rainfall in the country, rises sharply inland, and the region is frequently compared to more northern climes; perhaps a scaled-down maritime Switzerland, or a version of misty Ireland.

Whichever, it is a far cry from the classic sun-baked Spanish images of the south. Roads wind along valley floors hemmed in by lush meadows with cider apple orchards and grazing dairy cows. Olive oil may be king elsewhere in Spain but here butter is the norm. Maize is an important crop, evident in the large number of distinctive *hórreos* (squat drying sheds), so typical of Asturian villages. The coast is indented by deep inlets *(rías)* and lined by low cliffs, and it boasts many beautiful beaches.

Highlights

1 Marvelling at the prehistoric paintings at **Cueva de Altamira** (p257)

2 Relaxing on the broad golden sands at **El Sardinero** (p259)

3 Exploring the old town of **Santillana del Mar** (p262)

4 The Mirador del Cable view point at **Fuente Dé** (p264)

5 The panormaic views unfolding along the **Navia Valley** (p274)

Asturias

Asturias is the only part of Spain never to have been conquered by the Moors. Aside from the bragging rights that this gives its independently minded natives – who have their own Romance language as well as many indigenous customs – it also influenced the development, or rather non-development, of the region as it became a backwater for several centuries. One of the consequences of this isolation was the development of a unique art and architectural form known as Asturian Pre-Romanesque art which can still be seen in 14 buildings, mostly churches, built between the 8C and 10C. They symbolise the birth and development of the Asturian Monarchy and of the first Christian kingdom on the Iberian Peninsula.

Other idiosyncratic Asturian features include bagpipes – keep an ear open for students practising in city squares – emphasising the region's historic Gallic influences, and cider *(sidra)* thanks to the large number of orchards. This is drunk in *sidrerías* (cider bars), where there is always a protocol: a small amount of cider is theatrically poured from a height of around 30cm/1ft in order to aerate it; this is known as "throwing the cider" to produce an *estrella*, or star. The ideal temperature is cool but not (like lager-style beer) chilled. Asturias is also renowned for its cheeses, particularly the blue-veined *cabrales*. It goes particularly well with a glass of *sidra*.

Cantabria

Cantabria is the stretch of land sandwiched between the Bay of Biscay and the mountains of the Cantabrian Cordillera; in fact the mountains are so dominant that elsewhere in Spain Cantabria is known as La Montaña.

It is too cool and wet for most northern Europeans to holiday here (it receives less than 60 per cent of the sunshine hours of the south), but for that very reason it has long been popular with the Spanish, as a respite from the summer heat.

Santillana del Mar, labelled "the prettiest village in Spain" by Jean-Paul Sartre, is the jewel of the Cantabrian coast.

The medieval centre is a preserved national-historic monument, showcasing architectural styles from the 14C to the 18C. Nearby is the world-famous Altamira Cave, "the Sistine Chapel of Prehistoric Art" with its amazing ancient drawings of animals.

Beautifully located on a sandy bay, Santander is the regional capital and main port of arrival for both Cantabria and Asturias.

Paintings at Cueva de Altamira

©Turespaña

The Altamira Caves

More than anywhere in the world, Cantabria has the richest heritage of Palaeolithic cave art. All over the region, underground caverns hold treasure troves of paintings rendered by the ancients, often dazzling in detail, colour and vivacity.

The most famous of these sites is the Cueva de Altamira. The complex consists of a series of galleries with wall paintings and engravings thought to date back to the Solutrean Age, 20 500 years ago. The most impressive paintings are in the Sala de los Polícromos (Polychrome Chamber). It has an outstanding ceiling painted mainly during the Magdalenian period (15 000–12 000 BC). Numerous polychrome bison are shown asleep, crouched and galloping with extraordinary realism. They were discovered in 1880 by a local amateur archaeologist Marcelino Sanz de Sautuola who was led to the entrance of the caves by his young daughter. Due to the painting's sophistication, their authenticity was immediately challenged and Sanz de Sautuola was even charged with forgery. The paintings forever changed our perception on the "primitiveness" of the ancients, and even led Picasso to proclaim: "After Altamira, all is decadence".

The caves were open to the public in the 1960s and 70s, but studies showed that human breath damaged their delicate state. Reopened in 1982 with a heavily restricted number of visitors, they were again closed in 2002 but at the same time a replica (called the Neocueva) near the site was installed. Using the latest in technology, it simulates the forms of the cave itself and the images on its walls while an adjacent museum covers the evolution of humans and daily life in the Upper Palaeolithic period. More recently, a panel of experts are in lengthy discussions about how many people can enter the caves at a time without causing degradation, giving hope that these thrilling artworks will one day be open to all. The local government has invited US president Barrack Obama to be the first visitor when they do.

▷ *2km/1.2mi SW of Santillana del Mar.*
🕐 *Open May–Oct Tue–Sat 9.30am–8pm, Sun and public holidays 9.30am–3pm; Nov–Apr Tue–Sat 9.30am–6pm, Sun and public holidays 9.30am–3pm.*
🕐 *Closed 1, 6 Jan, 1 May, 24, 25 , 31 Dec.*
€3; child €1.50; no charge Sat afternoon, Sun, 18 Apr, 18 May, 12 Oct, 6 Dec. 📞 *942 81 88 05. http://museo dealtamira.mcu.es.* *Purchase tickets in advance at Banco de Santander.*

Santander ★

Santander enjoys a magnificent location★★ on a bay bathed by the azure waters of the Cantabrian Sea. It is best enjoyed on foot, with its long maritime front – one of the finest in Spain – lined by attractive gardens offering incomparable views. Superb beaches draw summer visitors.

THE CITY TODAY

The constant movement of passengers to and from the boat terminal of Santander in summer, and the throng of students at the international university for the rest of the year, gives the town a buzzing atmosphere.

Most visitors stay at the nearby beach resort of **El Sardinero**.

SIGHTS

The **paseo de Pereda**★, along the seafront, is lined by the imposing Banco de Santander building and the Palacete del Embarcadero, an exhibition centre.

Museo de Prehistoria y Arqueología de Cantabria★

Closed for restoration.

The archaeological museum in the Diputación shows finds from prehistoric caves in Cantabria, and remains of extinct animals from the Quaternary era. The richest period is the Upper Palaeolithic from which there are bones engraved with animal silhouettes and **batons**★ (from El Pendo) made of horn and finely decorated.

Three large circular steles, used for funerary purposes, are representative of the apogee of the Cantabrian culture (Bronze Age). Roman finds are mostly from Julióbriga (*see AGUILAR DE CAMPOO – Driving Tours*) and Castro Urdiales, and include coins, bronzes and pottery figurines. A medieval Mozarabic belt clasp made from bone is dated from the 10C.

▶ **Population:** 184 788
Michelin Map: 572 B 18.
Info: Jardines de Pereda.
 ℘942 20 30 00.
 www.ayto-santander.es.
Location: Santander sprawls to the west of the bay. The A 8 motorway runs SE to Bilbao (116km/72mi). Plaza de las Estaciones.
Kids: Museo Marítimo de Cantábrico.
Timing: The International Music and Dance Festival (*www.festivalsantander. com*) is held around the city every year in August.

Catedral de Nuestra Señora de la Asunción

Pl. del Obispo José E Eguino. Entry is through the restored Gothic cloisters.
Mon–Fri 10am–1pm, 4.30–7pm. Sat 10am–1pm, 4–8pm, Sun 10am–1.30pm, 5–9pm *Guided tours Jul–Aug.*
No charge. ℘942 22 60 24.

The fortress-like cathedral was badly damaged in a 1941 fire, but has been rebuilt in its original Gothic style.

A Baroque altarpiece dominates the presbytery; the **font** to the right of the ambulatory was brought here from Sevilla by soldiers of the Reconquest.

Iglesia del Cristo★ – Access to the fine 13C crypt is through the south portal. Excavations in the Evangelist nave have brought to light the remains of a Roman house with the relics of St Emeterio and St Celedonio, patron saints of the city. The Baroque Christ at the high altar is from the Castilian School.

Museo de Bellas Artes (Fine Arts Museum)

Rubio 6. Open 15 Sept– Jun Mon–Sat 10.30am–1pm, 6–9pm, Sun 11am-1.30pm; end Jun–14 Sept Mon–Sat 10am–1pm, 5.30–9pm, Sun 11am–1.30pm. Closed public holidays. No charge.
℘942 20 31 20.

Works include a portrait of Ferdinand VII by **Goya**; a series of Goya etchings – *Disasters of War, La Tauromaquia* and *Caprichos* – and several 16C-18C paintings by Flemish and Italian artists.

👥 Museo Marítimo del Cantábrico

San Martín de Bajamar. ◷ *Open May 1– end Sept Tue–Sun 10am–7.30pm; Oct– end April 10am–6pm.* ◷ *Closed 1, 6 Jan; 24, 25, 31 Dec.* €6. ℘ *942 27 49 62. www.museosdecantabria.com.*
This new museum on the seafront covers all aspects of the region's maritime past and present. It includes an aquarium and a very impressive blue whale skeleton.

Biblioteca de Menéndez Pelayo

Rubio 6 ◷ *Mon–Sat 9am–1.30pm* ➤ *Guided tours (20min) Sat–Sun 10am.* ◷ *Closed public holidays.* ℘ *942 23 45 34. www.bibliotecademenendez pelayo.org.*
Marcelino Menéndez y Pelayo (1856–1912), one of Spain's greatest historians, bequeathed this fabulous library of nearly 43 000 books and manuscripts by great Castilian authors.

Península de la Magdalena★★

With its magnificent position and sublime views, this peninsula is one of Santander's major sights. The small 👥 **zoo** (seals, penguins, polar bears etc.; *no charge*) on the El Sardinero side, and the replicas of the galleons in which Francisco de Orellana explored the Amazon are popular with children. The **Palacio de la Magdalena** was a summer residence for Alfonso XIII. Today, it is occupied by the Menéndez Pelayo International University.

Walk to Cabo Mayor★

🚶 *Allow 2hr; 4.5km/3mi round trip from the junction of Calle García Lago and calle Gregorio Marañón, at the far end of El Sardinero. By car, 7km/4.3mi N.*
This attractive walk, adjoining the Mataleñas golf course, runs along the coast, offering magnificent views all the way.

EXCURSIONS
El Sardinero★★

With its three magnificent **beaches**, the residential and resort area of El Sardinero is one of Santander's main attractions.

👥 Parque de la Naturaleza de Cabárceno

Obregón.15km/9.3mi S. ◷ *Open Jul– Aug daily 9.30am–7pm; Sept–Oct, Mar– Jun daily 9.30am–6pm; Nov–Feb Mon– Fri 10am–5pm, Sat–Sun and public holidays 10am–6pm.* ◷ *Dec 24, 25, 31; Jan 1* *Mar–Oct* €20.50, child €1.20; *Nov–Feb* €14.50 child €9.60 ℘ *902 21 01 12. www.parquedecabarceno.com.*
An old iron mine in the Sierra de Cabarga is part of an environmental rehabilitation project which includes a superb **game park**.

Castañeda

▷ *24km/15mi SW via N 623 and N 634.*
The **Colegiata** (◷ *open 15 Jul–15 Sept Tue–Sun 11.30am–1.30pm, 4–7.30pm, Sun Mass at noon ; no charge*), a former collegiate church from the end of the

12C, stands in a pleasant valley. The unusually deep doorway is simple and elegant.

Puente Viesgo★
▶ *26km/16mi SW along the N 623.*

The were inhabited in prehistoric times. **Cueva del Castillo★** (*guided tours (45min) mid June–mid Sept daily 9.30am–2.30pm, 3.30–6.30pm; slightly reduced hours rest of year; €3; 942 59 84 2; www.culturadecantabria.com).* Cave dwellers began engraving and painting the walls towards the end of the Palaeolithic Age.

🚗 DRIVING TOUR

Costa de Cantabria★

The Cantabrian coast is a succession of gulfs, capes, peninsulas, *rías*, splendid bays (most notably at Santander and Santoña), traditional summer beach resorts and delightful towns dotted with impressive mansions.
This area is also rich in caves bearing traces of human habitation in the Palaeolithic Age.

Castro Urdiales
The medieval heart of this attractive town-cum-resort, set above a vast bay, clusters round its mighty Gothic church **Iglesia de Santa María de la Asunción** (open Mon–Fri 10am–noon, 4–6pm; Sat 10am–noon; no charge; 942 86 15 86), plus a ruined castle and lighthouse. Beaches lie to east and west.

Laredo
▶ *25km/15.5mi W of Castro Urdiales off N 634.*

The **old town** adjoins a long beach lined by modern buildings.

Limpias
▶ *8km/5mi S of Laredo.*

The fishing village on the banks of the ría Asón is known for a miracle which occurred in 1919, when a deeply venerated Baroque Crucifix attributed to Juan de Mena shed tears of blood.

Santuario de Nuestra Señora de la Bien Aparecida
▶ *12km/7.4mi SW of Limpias.*

A road winds up to the Baroque shrine. offering a splendid **panorama**★.

Santoña
▶ *17km/10.5mi NW of Laredo.*

This fishing port facing Laredo was a French headquarters in the Peninsular War. The **Iglesia de Nuestra Señora del Puerto** (*Alfonso XII 11;* open daily 10am–1pm, 4–8pm; 942 66 01 55), remodelled in the 18C, has, in addition to Gothic aisles, Romanesque features including carved capitals and a font.

Bareyo
▶ *14km/9mi W of Santoña off CA 141.*

The tiny **Iglesia de Santa María**, overlooks the ría de Ajo. It retains original Romanesque moulded arches and historiated capitals. The **font** is probably Visigothic.

Peña Cabarga
▶ *35km/22mi SW of Bareyo off E 70.*

A steep road rises to the summit (568m/1 863ft) and a monument to the Conquistadores and the Seamen Adventurers of Castilla. From the top there is a splendid **panorama**★★.

▶ *Return to the E 70 and follow signs to Santander★ (see above). Leave the town centre heading W on the A 67 to Santillana del Mar★★ (see below), where you can visit the Museo de Altamira★★.*

Comillas★
▶ *54km/33.5mi W of Santander off E 70.*

Comillas is a pleasant seaside resort with a delightful plaza, a beach and easy access to the extensive sands at Oyambre – 5km/3mi west.
It was a royal residence at the time of Alfonso XII. In its large park is the neo-Gothic **Palacio de Sobrellano,** the **Capilla Panteón de los Marqueses de Comillas** (Capilla closed for restoration palace open daily 15 Jun–14 Sept 9.40am–2.30pm, 3.30–7.20pm; reduced hours rest of year; last tickets sold 30min

before closing; €3; 942 72 03 39; www.comillas.es) and Gaudí's outland-ish **El Capricho**, now a restaurant.

San Vicente de la Barquera★

⟩ *11km/6.8mi W of Comillas on N 634.*
This resort attracts visitors to its vast **beach**★, across the inlet. The hilltop **Iglesia de Nuestra Señora de los Ángeles** has two Romanesque portals, Gothic aisles and tombs from the 15C and 16C. On the Unquera road is a fine **view**★ of San Vicente.

Cueva el Soplao★

⟩ *Near Rábago, 20km/12.4mi S of San Vicente de la Barquera.* Open Apr–Sept daily from 10am (Oct–Mar Tue–Sun). Reservations advised. €10.50. 902 82 02 82. www.elsoplao.es.
Visit this impressive cave as a regular tourist, or in adventure mode with boots, helmet and the rest.
Entry is through mining tunnels. Notable are oddly shaped stalactites and salag-mites and ghost figures.

ADDRESSES

STAY

Pensión La Sota – *La Correría 1, Castro Urdiales.* 942 87 11 88. 19 rooms. €3.50. Closed last week of Dec. This small pensión stands on the main square of Castro Urdiales in the heart of the old quarter. Though small, the guest rooms are well furnished with modern bathrooms.

Hotel Gerra Mayor – *Los Llaos, Gerra. 5km/3mi NE of San Vicente de la Barquera.* 942 71 14 01. www.hgerra mayor.com. 20 rooms. €4. Closed Dec 15–Mar 1. This simple hotel, formerly a farmhouse, is superbly located between the sea and the mountains. It is perfect for peace and quiet and makes a pleasant base from which to explore the coastline.

Las Brisas – *La Braña 14, El Sardinero.* 942 27 50 11. www.hotellas brisas.net. 13 rooms. Closed Nov–Mar. An attractive building with a tower, in the El Sardinero district next to the beach. Sitting rooms have lovely details, and the service and attention in this small establishment are personalised.

Palacio del Mar – *Av. de Cantabria 5, El Sardinero.* 942 39 24 00. www.hotel-palaciodelmar.com. 66 rooms. €13. Restaurante Neptuno. A modern building with attractive design and comfortable rooms, including some with hydro-massage baths. The restaurant has its own distinctive ocean theme.

EAT

Mesón Rampalay – *Daoíz y Velarde 9, Santander.* 942 31 33 67. www.meson-rampalay-santander.com. Closed 2nd fortnight in Dec, Tue. This bar-restaurant is located in a street running parallel to paseo Pereda, next to the Iglesia de Santa Lucía. A long bar and a number of tables, where you can enjoy traditional specialities such as red peppers with tuna, seafood salad, and mushrooms with cod.

El Serbal – *Andrés del Rio 7, Santander.* 942 22 25 15. Closed Sun eve, Mon. Run with professionalism and sporting modern décor, this restaurant and bar is known for its seasonal, creative menus.

Maruja – *Av. Generalísimo, San Vicente de la Barquera.* 942 71 00 77. www.restaurantemaruja.es. Closed fortnight in Jun and Nov; Wed and Sun for dinner Sept–Jun. This small restaurant is one of the best-known along the Cantabrian coast, with traditional dishes using local produce.

Mesón Marinero – *La Correría 23, Castro Urdiales.* 942 86 00 05. www.mesonmarinero.com. This famous name in Cantabrian gastronomy specialises in seafood of excellent quality. The choice of tapas at the bar is equally impressive.

FESTIVALS

Santander hosts the fiesta of St James (Santiago) in July, with its bullfights and range of popular concerts and performances.

BOAT TRIPS

Throughout the year, vessels known as *reginas* provide a shuttle service between Santander and Somo and Pedreña (two districts on the other side of the bay). In summer, excursions around the bay and along the Cubas river are also available for visitors, with departures from the **Embarcadero del Palacete dock on paseo de Pereda** (942 216 753; www.losreginas.com).

Santillana del Mar★★

Santillana del Mar ("of the sea") is in fact located a few kilometres inland. It retains a medieval appearance, with mansions embellished with family coats of arms.

A BIT OF HISTORY

Santillana developed around a monastery which sheltered the relics of St Juliana, who was martyred in Asia Minor – the name Santillana is a contraction of Santa Juliana. Throughout the Middle Ages, the monastery was famous as a place of pilgrimage and was particularly favoured by the Grandees of Castilla. In the 11C it became powerful as a collegiate church; in the 15C, the town, created the seat of a marquisate, was enriched by the fine mansions which still give it so much character.

◂⦁◦ WALKING TOUR

The **town**★★ has two main streets, both leading to the collegiate church. Start in **calle de Santo Domingo**, with the 17C Casa del Marqués de Benemejís to the left and the Casa de los Villa, with its semicircular balconies, to the right.

▷ *Turn left into Juan Infante.*

Along the vast, pleasing triangular square of **Plaza de Ramón Pelayo** are the **Parador Gil Blas** and the 14C **Torre de Merino** (Merino Tower, *right*); the **Torre de Don Borja**, with its elegant pointed doorway; and *(left)* the 18C ayuntamiento (town hall), Casa del Águila and Casa de la Parra.
Calle de las Lindas *(end of the square on the right)* runs between massive houses with austere façades to **calle del Cantón** and **calle del Río**, which lead to the collegiate church.
As you approach the church, you will see several noble residences on the right-hand side. On the left, the house of the Archduchess of Austria is decorated with three coats of arms.

▷ **Population:** 4 040
◔ **Michelin Map:** 572 B17.
▯ **Info:** Calle Jesús Otero.
   ✆942 81 82 51.
   www.santillanadel
   marturismo.com.
◖ **Location:** Santillana is surrounded by verdant hills, between Santander and Comillas (16km/10mi W).

The **Colegiata**★ (collegiate church) dates from the 12 and 13C. The design of the east end is pure Romanesque, as is the 12C **claustro**★ (*Pl. del Abad Francisco Navarro;* ◷open Tue–Sun 10am–1.30pm, 4–7.30pm; ◉€3 (includes visit to the Claustro); ✆942 84 03 17).

▷ *Return to your starting-point.*

The restored 16C Convento de Clarisas (Convent of the Poor Clares) is the **Museo Diocesano** (◷open Tue–Sun 10am–1.30pm, 4–7.30pm or 6.30pm Oct–end May; ◉€3, free 15 and 30 of every month; ✆942 84 03 17; www.santillanamuseo diocesano.com), a museum with a collection of paintings, sculptures and religious gold and silver. The Baroque carvings and ivory are noteworthy.

SIGHT
Museo el Solar
Escultor Jesús Otero, 1. ◷*Open mid-Jun –mid-Sept daily 10am–9pm; rest of the year daily 10.30am–8pm.* ◔*Closed 1 Jan, 25 Dec.* ◉€3.60. ✆942 840 273.
The range of punishment used by the Inquisition or deployed against the agitators of the public from the Middle Ages to the modern era is well represented in this museum with some 70 instruments of torture on display.
On the left, just before the college, the house of the Archduchess of Austria is decorated with three coats of arms. In front, the house-museum of sculptor Jesús Otero (free admission).

Picos de Europa★★★

The Picos de Europa, highest range in the Cordillera Cantábrica and just 30km/18.6mi from the sea, include deep gorges cut by gushing mountain rivers and snow-capped peaks jagged with erosion.
The south face is less steep than the north, where the higher peaks are concentrated, and looks out over a harsh terrain of outstanding beauty. The **Parque Nacional de los Picos de Europa**, covering 64 660ha/159 775 acres, protects the region's flora and fauna.

▶ **Population:** 2 379
⛰ **Michelin Map:** 572 C 14-15-16.
ℹ **Info:** Cangas de Onís: Avenida de Covadonga. ℘985 84 80 05; Covadonga: El Repelao. ℘985 84 61 35. www.cangasdeonis.com.
◐ **Location:** The Picos de Europa rise along the northern coast, between Gijón and Santander.
👪 **Kids:** A ride on the cableway at Fuente Dé.
🕐 **Timing:** Roads are very busy during Jul and Aug.

DRIVING TOURS

☐1 DESFILADERO DE LA HERMIDA (LA HERMIDA DEFILE)★★

From Panes to Potes
27km/16.7mi. Allow about 1hr.

A **ravine**★★, 20km/12.4mi long, extends to either side of a basin containing the hamlet of La Hermida. The narrow gorge is bare and lacking in sunlight.

Iglesia de Nuestra Señora de Lebeña
Lebeña. ◐*Open summer Tue–Sun 10am–1.30pm, 4.30–7.30pm. Winter by appointment,* ✍*€1.* ℘*942 74 43 32.*
The small 10C Mozarabic church stands amid poplars at the foot of tall cliffs. The belfry and porch are later additions. The church houses a venerated 15C sculpture of the Virgin Mary.

Tama
This charming little mountain town is situated in a lush basin and surrounded by the sharp peaks of the Central Range. As well as many operators offering adventure activities, it also has an excellent **visitor centre** (◐*open daily Jul–Sept 9am–8pm, Oct–Jun 6pm;* ℘*942 738 109*).

Potes
9km/5.6mi S of Lebeña along N 621.
Potes is a delightful village in a pleasing **site**★ in a fertile basin set against jagged crests. From the bridge, view old stone houses and the 15C **Torre del Infantado** (tower), now the town hall.

☐2 THE CLIMB TO FUENTE DÉ★★
30km/19mi on the N 621.
Allow about 3hr.

Monasterio de Santo Toribio de Liébana
Approach along a signposted road on the left. ◐*Open daily 10am–1pm, 4–7pm.* ✍*No charge.* ℘*942 73 05 50*
The monastery was founded in the 7C and grew to considerable importance when a fragment of the True Cross was placed in its safekeeping. A *camarín* contains the largest known piece of the True Cross in the *lignum crucis* reliquary, a silver gilt Crucifix. The transitional Romanesque church is restored to its original harmonious proportions.
The monastery was the house of **Beatus**, the 8C monk famous for his **Commentary on the Apocalypse**, copied in the form of illuminated manuscripts. There is a **view**★ of Potes and the central range from the lookout point at the end of the road.

Fuente Dé★★

21km/13mi W of Liébana.
The parador is at 1 000m/3 300ft.
Nearby, the 🚠cableway (**teleférico**)
rises 800m/2 625ft to the top of the
sheer rock face (🕐*only weather permitting, Oct–Jun 10am–6pm; Jul–Sept 9am–
8pm; ⊷€15.50; ☏942 73 66 10*). During
the **ascent** you may see wild chamois.
The **Mirador del Cable**★★ commands
a splendid panorama of the upper valley of the Deva and Potes. A path leads
to the Aliva refuge. Erosion of the karst
limestone produces stony plateaux and
huge sink-holes known as **hoyos**.

③ PUERTO DE SAN GLORIO (SAN GLORIO PASS)★

From Potes to Oseja de Sajambre
83km/52mi. Allow about 3hr.
The road crosses the Quiviesa Valley,
then climbs through pastures.

Puerto de San Glorio★

Alt 1 609m/5 279ft.
A track leads north from the pass (*1hr
there and back*) to near the Peña de
Llesba and the **Mirador de Llesba**, a
magnificent **viewpoint**★★.
To the right is the east range; to the
left, the steep south face of the central
massif. In the left foreground is Coriscao
peak (2 234m/7 330ft).

▷ *At Portilla de la Reina, bear
right onto LE 243.*

Puerto de Pandetrave★★

19km/11.8mi NW of Puerto de San Glorio.
This pass (1 562m/5 125ft) affords a
panorama of the three ranges: in the
right foreground, the Cabén de Remoña
and Torre de Salinas, both in the central
massif. In the distance, in a hollow, is the
village of Santa Marina de Valdeón.
🚗 *The road between Santa Marina de
Valdeón and Posada de Valdeón is narrow but passable.*

Puerto de Panderruedas★

21km/13 mi NW.
The road climbs to pastures at 1 450m/4
757ft. 🚶Walk up the path to the left

(*15min there and back*) to the **Mirador
de Piedrahitas**★★ (*viewing table*) for an
impressive view of the immense cirque
which closes the Valdeón Valley.
To the northeast is the Torre Cerredo
peak (2 648m/8 688ft), highest in the
range.

Puerto del Pontón★

8km/5mi SW of Puerto de Panderruedas.
Alt 1 280m/4 200ft. From the pass, get a
fine **view**★★ of the Sajambre Valley.
The descent to Oseja de Sajambre begins
with hairpin bends below the western
range; it continues as a spectacular road
tunnelled into the mountainside.

RIBADESELLA
N 634
Unquera
SANTANDER
R. Deva
N 621
Panes
AS 114
Carreña
Las Arenas
de Cabrales
AS 114
R. Cares
6
R. Casaño
★ Desfiladero
AS 264
Gargantas ★
N 621
de Enol ★
L. de la Ercina ★
Poncebos
Desfiladero
de la Hermida ★★★
1
★★Garganta Divina
Funicular de Bulnes
Bulnes
Nª Sª de Lebeña
NACIONAL
Cares
Caín
Naranjo de Bulnes
2519
2648
Centro de
visitantes
Tama
del
DE LOS PICOS DE EUROPA
Piedrahitas ★★
El Cable ★★
R. Deva
Valle alto
Posada de Valdeón
Mogrovejo
2
Potes
Fuente Dé ★★
Sto Toribio
de Liébana
Sta Marina
de Valdeón
CA 185
Valle de Camaleño
3
LE 244
1450
de
Pto de Pandetrave ★★
1562
N 621
anderruedas ★
LE 243
Coriscao
2234
CA 184
Llesba ★★
Llánaves
de la Reina
1609
R. Quiviesa
Puerto de S. Glorio ★
Portilla de la Reina
Gargantas
N
R. Yuso
PICOS DE EUROPA
0   15 km
0   9 miles
PALENCIA

4 DESFILADERO DE LOS BEYOS★★★ (LOS BEYOS DEFILE)

From Oseja de Sajambre to Cangas de Onís
8km/23.6mi. Allow about 1hr along N 625.

Mirador de Oseja de Sajambre★★

There is an awe-inspiring **view**★★ of the Oseja de Sajambre Basin: the sharp Niaja peak at its centre rises to 1 732m/5 682ft, and of the Los Beyos defile opens between walls of broken rock strata.

Desfiladero de Los Beyos★★★
4km/2.5mi NW of the Mirador de Oseja de Sajambre.

This is one of the most beautiful gorges in Europe, 10km/6.2mi long, cut by the Sella. The limestone is exceptionally thick here; an occasional tree clings to its sides.

Cangas de Onís
26km/16mi N of the Desfiladero de Los Beyos.

A humpbacked **Roman bridge** *(puente romano)* crosses the Sella to the west. The Capilla de Santa Cruz *(⏲ open Jun–*

Desfiladero de Los Beyos

Sept Mon–Fri 10am–2pm, 4pm–7pm, Sat 10am–2pm, 4pm–7.30pm; rest of the year, consult the Tourist Office), also west, in Contranquil, commemorates the victory of Covadonga. It houses the region's only dolmen (megalithic tomb).

Aula del Reino de Asturias (Church of Santa María de Cangas de Onis, at the end of Calle Evaristo Sanchez; ☞ €1.50). A small museum which traces the modern history of the city.

Monastery of San Pedro de Villanueva *(on the outskirts of the village towards Arriondas)*. This former Benedictine monastery from the 17C includes a Romanesque church. It has been converted into a *parador* but is open to the public. The church is opened for a short time before and after the hours of worship.

Villanueva
4km/2.5mi N of Cangas de Onís.
The 17C Benedictine **Monasterio de San Pedro** stands at the end of the village. The monastery was built around a pre-existing Romanesque church of which there remain the apse and an elegantly decorated side portal.

5 THE ROAD TO COVADONGA AND THE LAKES★★

From Cangas de Onís to Covadonga
35km/22mi. Allow about 3hr.

Cueva del Buxu
Guided tours (30min) Wed–Sun 10.30am, 11.30am, 12.30pm, 3.15pm. 4.14pm; Max. 25 people, reservations essential ☞ €3; *no charge Wed.*
☎ 608 17 54 67.
The cave in the cliff face contains charcoal drawings and rock engravings from around 14 000 years ago, including a stag, horse and bison.

Covadonga
16km/10mi SE of La Cueva del Buxu.
This famous shrine, a landmark in Spanish history, is nestled in a magnificent **setting**★★ at the bottom of a narrow valley surrounded by impressive peaks. **Don Pelayo** defeated the Moors at Covadonga (722), marking the beginning of the Spanish Reconquest.

La Santa Cueva
Open daily 8.30am–8pm.
☎ 985 84 61 15.
The cave, dedicated to the Virgin of the Battlefield, holds the deeply venerated 18C wooden statue of the Virgin, patron of Asturias, **La Santina**.

Basílica

Explanada Basílica, Cangas de Onís.
🕐*Open daily 9am–8pm.* 🚫*No charge.*
📞*985 84 60 35. www.santuariode
covadonga.com.*

Before the neo-Romanesque Basilica built between 1886 and 1901 stands a statue of Pelayo. The **museo** (🕐*open daily 10.30am–2pm, 4–7.30pm;* 🚫*€3;* 📞*985 84 60 96*) contains gifts to the Virgin including a magnificent **crown**★ with more than 1 000 diamonds.

Lago de Enol★ and Lago de la Ercina★
(Lake Enol and Lake Ercina)

Lakes Enol and Ercina (alt. 1 232m/ 4 042ft), are two of the most visited places in the *sierra*, as evident in the parking facilities, paved roads, walking trails, restaurant and museum that surround them.

There is a walking trail around both of the lakes (3km/1.86mi, 1h) or you can follow a longer circuit (8km/5mi) for a less crowded experience. From mid-July to early September, access to the lakes is restricted for cars between 8.30am and 8.30pm. Shuttle buses depart regularly from Cangas de Onis.

Pedro Pidal Information Centre, Buferrera (🕐*open Apr–mid-Dec 10am–6pm;* 🚫*no charge*) has several thematic exhibitions on the Picos de Europa explaining their different ecosystems. Outside, there is a reproduction of a small shepherd's hut.

▷ *Continue to the lakes along the C0 4. The road is steep; look back to an extensive panorama. After 8km/5mi, you reach the **Mirador de la Reina**★★ with a view of the rock pyramids which make up the Sierra de Covalierda. Beyond the pass, two rock cirques are the settings of Lago de Enola and Lago de la Ercina (lakes, alt. 1 232m/4 042ft).*

6 GARGANTAS DEL CARES (CARES GORGES)★★

From Covadonga to Panes
90km/56mi. Allow one day.

Just out of Portillo la Estazadas village there is a splendid **panorama**★★ of the rock wall, which closes off the Río Casaño Valley. From a viewpoint on the right, shortly after Carreña de Cabrales, there is a glimpse of the fang-like crest of **Naranjo de Bulnes** (2 519m/8 264ft).

Las Arenas de Cabrales

▷ *10km/6.2mi E of Las Estazadas along the AS 114.*

This is the main production centre for *cabrales*, a blue ewes' milk cheese. The 🛈tourist office (*Crta de Cabrales;* 🕐*open 5 May–15 Nov Wed–Sun 10am–2pm, 4–8pm;* 🕐*closed rest of the year;* 📞*985 846 484; www.cabrales.org*) offers information on hiking trails in the area.

Beyond Arenas the **gorges**★ are green with moss and the occasional tree. Humpbacked bridges and fragile footbridges span the emerald waters.

▷ *Bear right onto AS 264, which runs through the Upper Cares Valley.*

Upper Cares Valley

The Poncebos road leads south, through a pleasant **ravine**★. After the embalse de Poncebos (reservoir), a track (*3hr there and back on foot*) leads up to the village of Bulnes.

Bulnes funicular (Access at Poncebos at the intersection of the Sotres road; 🕐*open Jun–Sept 10am–8pm, rest of year 10am–12.30pm, 2–6pm;* 🚫*€15.80 one-way, €19.90 return, under 12 €3.90 one-way, €6 return;* 📞*902 42 22 42; www.alsa.es*).

This funicular will whip you up to the Bulnes ski station (alt. 400m/1 312ft) in a mere 7 minutes, where (on a clear day) the best views of the Uriellu peak are afforded. Walking back down will take one and half hours.

🚶 From Poncebos to Caín (*3hr30min one way*) a path follows the Cares and plunges into the **gorge**★★ to the foot of the central massif (🚕*here you can take a taxi back to Poncebos*).

▷ *Return to Arenas de Cabrales.*

Oviedo★★

The capital of Asturias has a long and eventful history. Its old quarter is sprinkled with enchanting plazas and streets lined with sculptures. Strolling about this World Heritage Site is a delight.

THE CITY TODAY

Oviedo is excellent for shopping and is particularly well known for its leather goods.

Despite its World Heritage status it is not afraid to keep its public monuments up to date, dedicating a prominent statue to Woody Allen (calle de Milicias Nacionales), who won the Prince of Asturias Arts prize in 2002.

Allen visited the city to collect his award and said of it, "Oviedo is a delicious city, exotic, beautiful: it's as if it didn't belong to this world, as if it didn't exist at all... Oviedo is a fairytale."

A BIT OF HISTORY

The capital of the Kingdom of Asturias (9C–10C) – Alfonso II, the Chaste (791–842), moved his court to Oviedo and rebuilt the former Muslim town. The heir to the throne of Spain is still called the Prince of Asturias.

Two Battles of Oviedo – In 1934, Oviedo was heavily damaged in fighting between miners and right-wing government forces. In 1936, Oviedo was the scene of a three-month siege when the garrison rose in revolt against the Republican government during the Spanish Civil War.

Prince of Asturias Awards – have been presented from here since 1981, for achievements in sciences, humanities or public affairs.

SIGHTS

OUTSIDE THE OLD QUARTER
Antiguo Hospital del Principado

Leave Oviedo on Conde de Toreno (marked on the plan).

The façade of the 18C former principality hospital, now the Hotel Reconquista, bears a fine Baroque **coat of arms**★.

▶ **Population:** 225 210
⚲ **Michelin Map:** 572 B 12
❚ **Info:** Calle Marqués de Santa Cruz 1. ℘985 22 75 86. http://turismo. ayto-oviedo.es
▶ **Location:** The A 66 links Oviedo to the north coast at Gijón (29km/18mi) and to León (121km/75mi S). Calle Uría
🅿 **Parking:** Avoid looking for a space in the old quarter.
🕑 **Timing:** Stroll the old town first.

Iglesia de San Julián de los Prados★

Selgas 1. Open May–Sept Mon 10am –12.30pm, Tue–Fri 10am–12.30pm, 4–5.30pm, Sat 9.30am–12pm, 3.30– 5pm; Oct–Apr Mon 10am–12.30pm, Tue–Sat 9.30–11.30am. Last ticket sold half an hour before closure. Guided tours (30min). €1.20. ℘607 35 39 99. This outstanding early 9C work has a characteristic porch, twin aisles, wide transept and, at the east end, three chapels with barrel vaults. The walls are covered in **frescoes**★ of Roman influence. A fine transitional Romanesque **Christ in Glory**★ is in the central apse.

Santuarios del Monte Naranco★ (Mount Naranco Church and Chapel)

4km/2.5mi along Av. de los Monumentos to the NW.

The former audience chamber (now a church) and part of the chapel are what remain of the 9C summer palace of Ramiro I.

Centro de Recepción e Interpretación del Prerrománico Asturiano

Just above the parking area, to the left. Open Mon, Wed–Fri 11am–6pm (7.30pm Jun–Sept), Sat–Sun 10am– 6.30pm (8pm Jun–Sept). No charge. ℘985 11 49 01.

Panels explain Asturian art (in Spanish only); a video is narrated in English, Spanish, French and German.

Iglesia de Santa María del Naranco★★

Monte del Naranco. ○*Open Apr–Sept Tue–Sat 9.30am–1pm, 3.30–7pm, Sun–Mon 9.30am–1pm; Oct–end Mar Tue–Sat 10am–12.30pm, 3–4.30pm, Sun–Mon 10am–1pm.* ∞*€3; no charge Mon morning.* ℘*638 260 163. www.santamariadelnaranco. blogspot.com.*

This harmonious church is supported by grooved buttresses and lit by vast bays. The lower floor is a vaulted crypt. On the upper floor (a former reception hall), two loggias open off the great chamber. Decoration is delicate and unified. From outside, there is a fine **view** of Mount Aramo, with Oviedo in the foreground.

Iglesia de San Miguel de Lillo★

Monte del Naranco. 15min on foot. ○*Open same hours as Iglesia de Santa María.* ∞*€3; no charge Mon.* ℘*985 29 56 85.*

What remains is probably only a third of the original church, which probably collapsed in the 13C.
The aisles are narrow. Several claustral-type windows remain. The delicate carving is a delight: on the door **jambs**★★ are identical scenes in relief of arena contests. An Asturian cord motif is repeated on the capitals and on vaulting in the nave and gallery.

⚘ WALKING TOUR

OLD TOWN
Allow 1hr30min.

○ *Enter by San Francisco, and proceed along the right side of the street.*

Antigua Universidad

The austere 17C stone-fronted university was restored after the Civil War. Opposite the façade is *Mujer Sentada (Seated Woman)* by Manolo Hugué, one of many sculptures set in the old town.

Plaza de Porlier

View the cathedral in the next plaza. The **Palace of the Count of Toreno** *(right)* dates from 1673; the **Camposagrado** *(opposite)*, an 18C edifice, houses the Law Courts (note spread eaves).

○ *Continue along C. San Francisco.*

Plaza de de Alfonso II el Casto (Plaza de la Catedral)

Note the coat of arms on the façade of the 17C **Palacio de Valdecarzana**. The majestic Cathedral rises at the far end of the square. The **Palacio de la Rúa** was built at the end of the 15C.

○ *The cathedral is on the eastern side of the square.*

Catedral★

Pl. de la Catedrál. ○*Open July–mid-Sept Mon–Fri 10am–2.30pm, 4–8pm, Sat 10am–2.30pm, 4–6pm. Slightly shorter hours rest of the year; last visit 45min before closure.* ∞*€3.50 (combined ticket cathedral, Santa Camera and claustro); Thurs pm no charge.* ℘*985 20 31 17.*

The main work was carried out between 1412 and 1565 in Flamboyant Gothic style. The south tower tapers into a delicate openwork spire. Three 17C Gothic portals pierce the asymmetrical façade; figures of the Transfiguration are above the central portal. On the walnut-panelled doors (also 17C) are figures of Christ and St Eulalia.

Interior – The Cathedral has three aisles, the triforium surmounted by tall stained-glass windows, and an ambulatory. A splendid 16C polychrome **high altarpiece**★★ shows scenes from the Life of Christ. On either end of the transepts are 18C Baroque panels, and in the south transept, next to the main chapel, the 17C polychromed stone image of The Saviour.

The **Capilla de Alfonso II El Casto** (Alfonso II The Chaste), on the site of the original church, is the pantheon of Asturian kings. The decoration inside the gate *(end of north transept)* is Late Gothic. In the embrasures are figures of the Pilgrim St James, St Peter, St Paul and St Andrew, and on a mullion, a Virgin of Milk. Renaissance and Baroque elements intermingle.

Cámara Santa

Access by the south transept of the Cathedral. ⏱*Open daily, same hour as cathedral.* 🎫*Combined ticket cathedral, Santa Camera and claustro €3.50; no charge Thu evening.*

The Cámara Santa was built by Alfonso II early in the 9C and reconstructed in the Romanesque period.

These 12 **statue columns**★★ representing the Apostles are among the most masterly sculptures of 12C Spain. The artist was obviously influenced by the Pórtico de la Gloria (Doorway of Glory) in Santiago Cathedral. Capitals illustrate the marriage of Joseph and Mary, the Holy Women at the Tomb and lion and wild boar hunts.

The **tesoro**★★ (treasury) in the apse includes outstanding ancient gold and silver plate: the **Cruz de los Ángeles** (Cross of the Angels), a gift from Alfonso II in 808, studded with precious gems, Roman cabochons and cameos; and the **Cruz de Victoria** (908), faced with chased gold, precious stones, and enamel, supposedly carried by Pelayo at Covadonga.

Claustro

⏱*Open same hours as Cámara Santa.*

The Gothic cloisters (14C–15C) have intersecting pointed arches and delicate tracery in the bays. The **Capilla de Santa Leocadia** *(to the left on entering)* contains an altar, tombs from the time of Alfonso II and an unusually small stone altar. The **sala capitular** (chapter house) contains fine 15C stalls.

▷ *Return to Pl. de Alfonso II El Casto.*

To the right of the Cathedral (*leaving*), low reliefs and busts compose a homage to the kings of Asturias. To the left, at calle Santa Ana, note the unexpected Moorish *alfiz* window enclosure in the remaining east wall of the 9C **Iglesia de San Tirso** (🎫*no charge;* 📞*985 22 07 02*).

▷ *Turn left onto Tránsito de la Virgen alongside the Cathedral.*

Beyond the arch that connects the Cathedral to the Palacio Arzobispal (archbishop's palace, *left*) is the Romanesque former cathedral.

Just ahead in Plaza de la Corrada del Obispo is the rather loud façade of the **Palacio Arzobispal** (late 16C) and the imposing 18C **Puerta de la Limosna** (alms gate).

▷ *Continue along San Vicente.*

Museo Arqueológico

San Vicente 5. ⏱*Open Wed–Fri 9.30am –8pm, Sun and public holidays 9.30am –3pm.* 📞 *985 20 89 77, www.museo arqueologicodeasturias.net.*

This archaeological museum is in the former Convento de San Vicente (16C–18C). Two galleries off the 15C Platesque cloisters display pre-Romanesque art. Fragments and reproductions evidence the sophistication of Asturian art. Among exhibits are the Naranco altar; low reliefs showing Byzantine influence, and column bases from San Miguel de Lillo.

After the museum, go under the arch and cross the Plaza de Feijoo, past the **Iglesia de Santa María la Real de la Corte** *and the palace-like façade of the 18C* **Monasterio de San Pelayo.**

▷ *Turn right onto Jovellanos and look back at the city wall. Return to Santa Ana.*

Museo de Bellas Artes de Asturias (Fine Arts Museum)

Santa Ana 1–3. ⏱*Open Sept–Jun Mon– Fri 10.30am–2pm, 4.30–8.30pm, Sat 11.30am–2pm, 5–8pm, Sun and public holidays 11.30am–2.30pm; Jul–Aug Tue–Sat 10.30am–2pm, 4–8pm, Sun and public holidays 10.30am–2.30pm.* 🎫*No charge.* 📞*985 21 30 61. www.museobbaa.com.*

The museum is in three buildings. The core collection of Spanish painting is enriched by Italian and Flemish works. There is also a sculpture collection.

Among the works in the 18C **Palacio de Velarde** are a complete **Apostolado** by **El Greco** (ground floor); the Gothic panels of the *Santa Marina Retable* (on the stairway); the *Triptych of Don Alvaro de Carreño* by the master of the *Legend of Mary Magdalene;* a *Burial of Christ* and a magnificent *Apostle* by **Ribera;** a *Crucifixion* by **Zurbarán**; a *San Pedro* by Murillo; the portrait of *Charles II at Ten Years* by Carreño de Miranda, and two portraits by **Goya** (*Jovellanos* and *Charles IV*) on the first floor. The second floor is devoted to Asturian and Spanish art of the 19C and early 20C.

A passageway leads to the second floor of the 17C **Casa Oviedo-Portal**. Worth seeing are a gallery dedicated to **J Sorolla**; a *Musketeer with Sword and Cupid* by **Picasso**; and paintings by Gutiérrez-Solana, Regoyos and Nonell. As you leave, take a look at the enchanting Plaza de Trascorrales, with its brightly coloured houses and its sculpture of *The Milkmaid*.

◯ *Take Cimadevilla to reach Plaza de la Constitución.*

Along **Plaza de la Constitución** are the **ayuntamiento** (City Hall), with 17C and 18C porticoes, and the Iglesia de San Isidoro, from the same era.

◯ *Take Fierro, where there is a covered market, to Fontán.*

Fontán is a picturesque area. Porticoed houses have enchanting courtyards, reached by multiple archways.

◯ *Leave by the archway that faces Plaza de Daoíz y Velarde.*

The first sight in **Plaza de Daoíz y Velarde** is the sculpture ensemble, **Las vendedoras del Fontán**, in honour of women who have sold goods in the outdoor market of these streets over the years. The beautiful tree-set plaza is the site of the noble **Palacio de Camposagrado**. Beside it is the Biblioteca de Asturias (library), with its unusual façade.

Iglesia de Santa Cristina de Lena★

◯ *34km/21mi S on the A 66 (junction 92) At Pola de Lena, head for Vega del Rey then take the signposted road.* 🅿 *Park before the rail viaduct and walk up the steep path (15min).* ◷*Open Tue–Sun Apr–Oct 11am–1pm, 4.30–6.30pm; Nov–Mar 11.30am–1pm, 4.30–6pm.* ⊛*€1.50; no charge Tue.* ☏*985 49 05 25.*

Santa Cristina de Lena (9C) is a well-proportioned church built of golden stone. It stands on a rocky crag, with a **panorama**★ of the Caudal Valley.

The little building has a Greek cross plan unusual in Asturias, and traditional stone vaulting, with blind arcades, and columns with pyramid-shaped capitals emphasised by a cord motif. The nave is separated from the raised choir by an iconostasis in which the superimposed arches increase the impression of balance. The low reliefs in the chancel are Visigothic sculptures (note geometric figures and plant motifs).

Teverga

◯ *43km/27mi SW on the N 634 and AS 228.*

The road follows the River Trubia, which, after Proaza, enters a narrow gorge. Glance back for a **view**★ of the Peñas Juntas cliff face. Beyond the Teverga fork the road penetrates the **desfiladero de Teverga**★ (Teverga Defile).

The **Colegiata de San Pedro de Teverga** (*La Plaza;* ◷ *open Mon–Fri noon–2pm, 4–6pm, Sat–Sun 11am–2pm, 4–7pm;* ⊛*€2.* ☏*985 76 42 75*), a late 12C collegiate church, is just outside La Plaza village. Built in a continuation of pre-Romanesque Asturian style, it includes a narthex, a tall narrow nave and a flat east end, originally three chapels. The narthex capitals are carved with stylised animal and plant motifs.

Costa Verde★★

The Green Coast of Asturias is named for the colour of the sea, pine and eucalyptus trees along the shore, and wooded pastures inland. Towns and villages are nestled in picturesque coves, where fishing is the main activity. On a clear day the Picos de Europa and Cordillera Cantábrica are a stunning backdrop.

🚗 DRIVING TOURS

Along the rocky coast, low cliffs are interrupted by sandy inlets; the estuaries are narrow and deep. West of Cudillero, the coastal plain ends in sheer cliffs overlooking small beaches.

1 FROM LLANES TO GIJÓN
145km/90mi.

Llanes
The clifftop promenade affords a good view of the once fortified port, the rampart ruins and castle and the squat Iglesia de Santa María. In mid-August, see the St Roch festival dances (the *Pericote* and the children's *Prima* dance; *www.san-roque.com*) in brilliant local costume. 20km/12.5mi E along the E 70 Caratera del Cantábrico is the **Museo de la Emigración - Fundación de Indianos**, in Colombres *(San Vicente de la Barquera;* 🕐*open Jun–Sep Mon–Sun 11am–2pm, 5–8pm; rest of the year Tue–Sat 10am–2pm, 4–7pm, Sun 10am–2pm;* €4; 🏛*985 412 005).* Housed in the sumptuous Quinta Guadalupe palace, this museum tells the story of hundreds of thousands of Asturians who emigrated to Latin America in the 19C, an event that shaped the region and its culture.

 ▷ *Take the E70 W back to Llanes, where it turns in to the Autovía del Cantábrico. Continue to Ribadesella.*

Ribadesella
The town and port of Ribadesella are on the right side of the estuary opposite a holiday resort.

 ▷ **Population:** 65 136
 ⛲ **Michelin Map:** 571 and 572 (town plan of Gijón) B8-15.
 ℹ **Info:** Gijón: Rodriguez Sampedro. 🏛985 34 17 71; Llanes: Alfonso IX (La Torre building). 🏛985 40 01 64; Luarca: Los Caleros 11. 🏛985 64 00 83. www.infoasturias.com.
 ▷ **Location:** The N 634 runs along the northern coast of Asturias, affording sea and mountain views.
 👨‍👦 **Kids:** MUJA, the Jurassic Museum, is unmissable.

👨‍👦 Cuevas de Tito Bustillo★
🐾*Guided tours (1hr) Apr–end Oct, Wed–Sun 10am–5pm.* €7; no charge Wed (reservations required). 🏛985 86 12 55 (Wed–Sun 10am–2.30pm, 4-7pm). These caves are famous for their **wall of paintings**★ by Palaeolithic inhabitants (20 000 BC) of horses, stags and a doe.

 ▷ *26km/16mi W of Ribadesella on the A-8. Squat drying sheds or hórreos, typical of Asturias, stand beside the houses in the small, attractive village of* **La Isla**.

👨‍👦 MUJA (Museo del Jurásico de Asturias – Jurassic Museum)
🕐*Phone or see website for opening hours.* 🕐*Closed 1 Jan, 24, 25, 31 Dec.* €6.70; child €4.10. Final admission 1hr before closing. 🏛902 30 66 00. www.museojurasicoasturias.com Between Colunga and Lastres is this dinosaur footprint of a building dedicated to these creatures. Dinosaur prints are found in the area.

 ▷ *12km/7.4mi SE of La Isla on AS 260.*

Mirador del Fito★★★
This viewpoint has a spectacular panorama of the Picos de Europa and the coast.

 ▷ *17km/10.5mi W of Fito.*

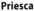

Priesca

The capitals in the chancel in the **Iglesia de San Salvador** (*℘ 985 89 32 02*) resemble those at Valdediós (*see entry below*)

◐ *11km/6.8mi W of Priesca via N 632.*

Villaviciosa

Emperor Charles V arrived here in 1517 to take possession of Spain.

The **Iglesia de Santa María** (*◐open Tue–Sun 11am–1pm, 5–7pm*) is decorated with a Gothic rose window.

◐ *3km/1.8mi S of Villaviciosa.*

Amandi

The bell gable of the **Iglesia de San Juan** (*o—closed to the public*) stands on high ground. The remodelled church retains a 13C portal with sophisticated **decoration**★. Inside the **apse**★, the frieze from the façade reappears to form a winding ribbon that follows the curves of the intercolumniation.

◐ *7km/4.3mi S of Villaviciosa.*

Valdediós★

The **Iglesia de San Salvador** (*◐open May–Oct Tue–Sun 11am–3.30pm, 4.30–7pm, Nov–Apr Tue–Sun 11am–1pm, Sat–Sun 4–5.30pm; ∞€1; ℘985 89 23 24*), consecrated in 893 and known as *El Conventín*, dates from the end of the Asturian period of architecture (8C–10C). The **Monasterio de Santa María** (monastery) consists of a 13C Cistercian church and cloisters dating from the 15C, 17C and 18C (*◐open Apr–Sept Tue–Sun 11am–1pm, 4.30–6pm; Oct–Mar Tue–Fri 11.15am–1pm, Sat–Sun 11.15am–1pm, 4–5.30pm; ◐closed 1 Jan, Easter Sun and 25 Dec; ∞€1; ℘985 89 23 24; www.valdedios.org*).

◐ *Take the AS 112, A 66 and Autoveia Minera N to Gijón.*

Gijón

36km/22mi NW of Valdediós.
▭ *Avenida Juan Carlos I.*

Gijón is a lively city with a population of over 275 000. On **Plaza del Marqués** is the late 17C **Palacio de Revillagigedo** (*◐open depending on exhibition inside, but generally 11am–2pm; ∞no charge; ℘985 34 69 21*), with an elegant façade. Nearby is the fishermen's quarter, Cimadevilla.

Vestiges of a Roman past, include the **Termas Romanas del Campo Valdés** (Roman baths) in the old quarter (*Campo Valdés; ◐open Tue–Fri 9.30am–2pm, 5-7.30pm, Sat–Sun 10am–2pm, 5–7.30pm; ◐closed 1, 6 Jan, 15 Aug, 24, 25, 31 Dec; ∞€2.50; ℘985 18 51 51*).

The **Torre del Reloj** (*Recoletas 5; ◐open Mon–Fri 9am–2pm; ∞no charge; ℘985 181 329*) is also well worth a visit, for its history displays and splendid views.

② FROM GIJÓN TO CASTROPOL

179km/118mi.

Luanco

The charming port-village of Luanco mixes a workaday fishing with tourist development, as seen in the new buildings multiplying on the watefront. Calle La Riva is the main street, where you'll find three Baroque monuments: the Torre del Reloj (clock tower), the Palacio de los Menéndez Pola and, overlooking the beach, Santa Maria church.

Afterwards, stroll the Paseo del Muelle where lively restaurants overlook the charming bay Luanco.

Avilés

With 85,000 inhabitants, Avilés is the third-largest city in Asturias. Industrial and set just back from the coast, it is worth a visit for its old neighbourhood, concentrated around the town hall, and a new cultural centre designed by Brazilian architect Oscar Niemeyer.

Plaza de España is the heart of the old city, dominated by the City Hall, a former palace built in 17C and modelled on that of Oviedo (the clock tower was added in the 19C). Facing this, the **Palacio Ferrera** is a beautiful example of baroque architecture. In the adjacent Calle San Francisco the 17C **Fuente de los Canos**

de San Francisco, was once the city's main water source.

Partly opened in mid 2011, the **Centro Niemeyer** is situated 500m/550yd from the Plaza de España, just over the river via a footbridge. A curious avant-garde landmark given the location, Oscar Niemeyer's clean, white rationalist forms spread out over a giant swathe of reclaimed industrial land. Exhibitions, generally tied to the prestigious annual Príncipe de Asturias awards, are held in the dome-like hall, while other buildings accommodate dance, theatre, a cinema and a restaurant atop a sci-fi lookout tower. Even if you don't have a ticket, you are free to wander around the complex and admire what is probably one of the last works from the grandfather of the Modernist movement (○*open Tue–Thur and Sun 11am–midnight, Fri, Sat 11am–2am; www.niemeyercenter.org).*

Avilés' nearest beach, **Salinas**, is a rapidly expanding resort. The rock islet of La Peñona affords a **view** of the beach, one of the longest on the Costa Verde.

Ermita del Espíritu Santo
Muros de Nalón. 19km/11.8mi W of Salinas.
The hermitage commands an extensive **view**★ west along the coastal cliffs.

Cudillero★
9km/6mi W of la Ermita.
The fishing village makes an attractive **picture**★: tall hillside houses in pastel shades and white cottages with brown-tiled roofs lead down to the harbour full of fishing boats. Continue west for some of the area's best beaches: Playa Concha de Artedo (4km/2.5mi), Playa de San Pedro (10km/6.2mi) and, best of all, Playa del Silencio (15km/9.3mi).

Cabo Vidio★★
14km/8.7mi NW of Cudillero.
Catch the coastal **views**★★ from near the lighthouse on this headland.

Excursion to the Narcea River
▷ *91km/57mi to Cangas del Narcea along the N 634 and AS 216, branching S at the Cabo Busto.*

Tineo
▷ *50km/31mi SW of Cabo Vidio.*
Perched 673m/2 208ft up the mountainside, the town of Tineo commands an immense mountain **panorama**★★.

Monasterio de Corias
▷ *28km/17mi SW of Tineo.*
⌖ *Closed until 2012. ℘985 81 01 50.*
The 11C monastery, rebuilt after a 19C fire, was occupied for 800 years by Benedictines.

▷ *Return to the coast road (N 632).*

Luarca★
Luarca is in a remarkable **site**★ at the mouth of the winding río Negro, spanned by seven bridges. A lighthouse, church and cemetery stand on the headland once occupied by a fort. For an interesting **view**★, take the lighthouse road left, then circle the church to the right and return to the harbour.

Excursion along the Navia Valley
▷ *82km/51mi along the AS 12 (2hr30min each way).*
The River Navia flows along a wild valley below several peaks. After Coaña, turn right at the sign "castro". Circular foundations and paving remain from a **Celtic village**. For a striking **panorama**★★ of the **Arbón dam**, pause at the viewpoint. Past Vivedro, there is another **panorama**★★, and as the road climbs, the **confluence**★★ of the Navia and the Frío is impressive from a giddy height. Beyond Boal, the valley is blocked by the high **Doiras dam**. The **Museo Etnográfico** at Granda de Salime *(av. del Ferreriro; ◉€1.50, no charge Tue; ℘985 62 73 31; www.museodegrandas.com)* traces Asturian life through re-created rooms and artefacts.

▷ *Return to Navia, then continue W along the N 634.*

From Figueras on the ría Ribadeo you can view **Castropol**, which resembles an Austrian village, with its whitewashed main square. Opposite stands Ribadeo, its Galician counterpart.

This remote region, around the size of Belgium, or Maryland in the US, fronts the Atlantic on Spain's northern and western borders. In appearance and culture it is akin to the Celtic regions of Ireland, Wales and Brittany; far removed from the archetypal images of southern Spain. Geologically speaking, Galicia is an ancient eroded granite massif, and the overall impression is that of a hilly and mountainous region. The climate is influenced by the sea: temperatures are mild and rainfall is abundant, providing the verdant landscapes which give the whole of Spain's northern coast its nickname "Green Spain". The interior is primarily an agricultural region where mixed farming is the norm: maize, potatoes, grapes and rye, and cattle in Orense province. Galicia is Spain's chief fishing region and is renowned for its seafood even though most of the catch is canned. The Galician natives are a fiercely independent people – even by Spanish standards – with their own heritage, folklore and Galician language, *gallego*, not unlike Portuguese.

La Coruña and the Rías Bajas

Former capital of Galicia, the port of A Coruña is a bustling centre of industry, with a charming cobbled old town of narrow alleyways and pretty plazas.

The Rías Altas, deep inlets backed by pine and eucalyptus, stretching eastwards from La Coruña, shelter some fine beaches and low-key resorts.

By contrast, many a ship has been dashed against the rocks at the western Costa de la Muerte, but is worth a visit for its drama and (occasionally) calm beauty.

The Rías Bajas, its inlets, creeks and coastline more spectacular than its counterpart north, is Galicia's major holiday area. There are several good resorts, chief among them A Toxa/La Toja. The best beaches are to be found on the Ilas Cíes, reached by boat from Vigo. Vigo is Spain's leading fishing port, with a picturesque harbour location. The area's other city, Pontevedra, has a charming and historic old quarter.

Camino de Santiago

There is no official starting point for the arduous Camino de Santiago (Way of St James), though the Spanish leg (measuring around 750km/465mi) begins at the French border, runs across the Pyrenees, then west through Navarra, Rioja, Castile and Galicia, waymarked by the pilgrim's symbol of a scallop shell.

Over the centuries numerous, often rudimentary, inns providing refreshments and shelter have opened along the route.

Highlights

1 Standing in front of the Cathedral at **Santiago de Compostela** (p276)

2 Relaxing in a wonderful setting on the beach at **A Toxa/La Toja** (p282)

3 Touring the **Ría de Vigo** and taking in the wonderful views (p283)

4 Strolling through the delightful Old Quarter at **Pontevedra** (p285)

5 Walking atop the Roman city walls at **Lugo** (p288)

View towards Islas Cíes, Ría de Vigo

© Nano Calvo/age fotostock

It ends at Santiago de Compostela, whose narrow atmospheric streets and extraordinary cathedral rank among Spain's highlights.

Santiago de Compostela★★★

In the Middle Ages Santiago de Compostela attracted pilgrims from all of Europe in search of eternal salvations. Today around 100 000 pilgrims make a similar trek to the city, declared a UNESCO World Heritage Site, each year.
Whatever the spiritual benefits gained en route, the sightseeing highlight is fittingly, and literally, the final step of the journey: the wondrous Cathedral, which is the focal point of a city that celebrates life and piety in equal measures.

▶ **Population:** 94 339
 Michelin Map: 571 D 4 (town plan).
 Info: Rúa do Vilar 63. ℘981 55 51 29. www.santiagoturismo.com.
◐ **Location:** This pilgrimage city in NW Spain is connected by the AP 9 to Vigo (84km/52mi S) and La Coruña/A Coruña (72km/45mi N) and by the N 547 with Lugo (107km/67mi E). The AP 53 runs SE to Ourense/Orense (111km/69mi). Calle Hórreo 75 A.
 Don't Miss: The Cathedral.

THE CITY TODAY

Despite its large number of visitors, Santiago de Compostela remains one of Spain's most enchanting cities with its old quarters and maze of narrow streets containing numerous bars and restaurants. The city's 40 000 or so university students mix with the hundreds of thousands of annual visitors from all over the world and ensure a lively cosmopolitan atmosphere, which has only increased since Santiago was European City of Culture in 2000.

A BIT OF HISTORY

History, tradition and legends – The Apostle **James the Greater** crossed the seas to convert Spain to Christianity. He returned to Judaea where he fell victim to Herod Agrippa. His disciples fled to Spain with his body. A star is believed to have pointed out the grave to shepherds early in the 9C.

In 844 during an attack against the Moors at **Clavijo**, a knight on a charger, bearing a white standard with a red cross, appeared on the battlefield and brought victory. The Christians recognised St James, naming him *Matamoros* or Moorslayer. The Reconquest and Spain had found a patron saint.

In the 11C devotion spread until a journey to St James' shrine ranked with one to Rome or Jerusalem.

Catedral de Santiago de Compostela

C. Labonne/MICHELIN

SIGHTS

Plaza del Obradoiro

The majesty of the square makes it a fitting setting for the Cathedral.

Catedral★★★

Pl. del Obradoiro. ⏰*Open daily 7.30am –9pm.* ⊗*No charge.* ☎*981 58 35 48. www.catedraldesantiago.es.*

The present cathedral dates mostly from the 11C to the 13C, although from the outside it appears Baroque.

Fachada do Obradoiro★★★ (Obradoiro façade) – This Baroque masterpiece by **Fernando Casas y Novoa** was completed in 1750. The central area, given true Baroque movement by the interplay of straight and curved lines, rises to what appears to be a long tongue of flame.

Pórtico de la Gloria★★★ (Doorway of Glory) – Behind the façade stands the narthex and the Pórtico de la Gloria, a late 12C wonder by **Maestro Mateo**. The statues of the triple doorway are exceptional both as a composition and in detail.

The doorway is slightly more recent than the rest of the Cathedral and shows Gothic features. Mateo, who also built bridges, had the crypt reinforced to bear the weight of the portico. The central portal is dedicated to the Christian Church, the one on the left to the Jews, that on the right to the Gentiles. The central portal tympanum shows the Saviour surrounded by the Evangelists while on the archivolt are the 24 Elders of the Apocalypse.

The engaged pillars are covered in statues of Apostles and Prophets. Note the figure of Daniel with the hint of a smile, a precursor to the famous Smiling Angel in Reims Cathedral in France. The pillar beneath the seated St James bears finger marks; traditionally, on entering the Cathedral, exhausted pilgrims placed their hands here in token of safe arrival. On the other side of the pillar, the statue known as the saint of bumps is believed to impart memory and wisdom.

Interior – The immense Romanesque cathedral displays all the characteristics of medieval pilgrim churches: a Latin

Cross plan, vast proportions, an ambulatory and a triforium. The side aisles are covered with 13C groin vaults. At major festivals a huge incense burner, the **botafumeiro** *(displayed in the library),* is swung from the transept dome keystone by eight men.

The **altar mayor** or high altar, surmounted by a sumptuously apparelled 13C statue of St James, is covered by a gigantic baldaquin. Beneath the altar is the **cripta**, a crypt built into the 9C church. It enshrines the relics of the saint and his disciples, St Theodore and St Athanasius.

The Gothic vaulting of the Capilla Mondragón (1521), and the 9C Capilla de la Corticela, formerly separate, are beautiful. The Renaissance doors to the **sacristía** (sacristy) **(1)** and *claustro* (cloisters) **(2)** on the right arm of the transept are noteworthy.

Museo – ⏲ *Open Jun–Sept Mon–Sat 10am–2pm, 4–8pm, Sun and public holidays 10am–2pm; Oct–May daily 10am–1.30pm, 4–6.30pm, public holidays 10am–1.30pm.* ⏲ *Closed 1, 6 Jan, 25 Jul, 15 Aug, 25 Dec.* ●€5. ℘981 56 93 21.

Enter the **tesoro** (treasury), in a Gothic chapel to the right of the nave, from inside of the cathedral.

Exhibits include a gold and silver monstrance by Antonio de Arfe (1539–66). To visit the 11C **cripta**★ (crypt), exit to Plaza del Obradoiro. This is in fact a small Romanesque church with a Latin cross plan. Use the side entry for the rooms devoted to archaeological excavations, the **biblioteca** (library), the **sala capitular** (chapter house) with its granite vault and walls hung with 16C Flemish tapestries, and the rooms with **tapestries**★★ by Goya, Bayeu, Rubens and Teniers.

Claustro – *Access via the museum.* This Renaissance cloister was designed by Juan de Álava, who combined a Gothic structure with Plateresque decoration.

Puerta de las Platerías★★ **(Silversmiths' Doorway)** – This is the only intact 12C Romanesque doorway. Not all of the entrance is original. The most impressive figure is David playing the viola on the left door. Adam and Eve can be seen being driven out of the Garden of Eden; the Pardoning of the Adulterous Woman is on the right-hand corner of the left tympanum.

The **Torre del Reloj** (Clock Tower) was added at the end of the 17C. To the left stands the **Torre del Tesoro** (Treasury Tower). The 18C Baroque façade of the **Casa del Cabildo** is opposite the *fuente de los caballos,* or horse trough.

Palacio Gelmírez and Cathedral roof

Pl. del Obradoiro. 🔊 *Guided tours (45min) Tue–Sun 10am–2pm, 4–8pm.* ⏲ *Closed 1, 6 Jan, 25 Jul, 15 Aug, 25 Dec.* ●€10. ℘981 55 29 85 *(reservations recommended).*

This is the bishops' palace (left of the cathedral). The **Salón Sinodal**★ (Synod Hall) is more than 30m/98ft long and has sculptured ogive vaulting.

A guided tour includes a trip to the roof, which offers a surprising view of the Cathedral and affords unforgettable views of the city.

Hostal de los Reyes Católicos★ (Hostelry of the Catholic Monarchs)

Pl. del Obradoiro. www.parador.es.

This former pilgrim inn and hospital, now a parador, has an impressive **façade**★ with a splendid Plateresque doorway and four elegant patios. Even now the first ten pilgrims to arrive every day receive three free meals in the hotel, the most luxurious in the city.

Casco Antiguo★★ (Old Town)

The old part of the city is a maze of delightful narrow streets which open out onto lively squares.

Rúa do Franco

This street is lined by old colleges, such as Renaissance-style Colegio de Fonseca, and shops and bars. The Porta de la Faxeiras leads to paseo de la Herradura, the hill that is the setting for fairs. The excellent **view**★ includes the cathedral and the rooftops of Santiago.

Fundación Eugenio Granell

Pl. del Toral. *Open Oct–May Tue–Sat 11am–2pm, 4–9pm, Sun 11am–2pm; Jun–Sept Tue–Sat 11am–9pm, Sun 11am –2pm.* *Closed public hols.* €2; no charge Sun and all June. *981 57 63 94. www.fundacion-granell.org.*

Inside the Pazo de Bendaña, a 18C noble building, the Fundación Eugenio Granell displays surrealist art.

Rúa do Vilar

The street leading to the cathedral is bordered by arcaded and ancient houses, as is the parallel **rúa Nova**.

Plaza de la Quintana★★

Along this square at the east end of the Cathedral, which was once a cemetery, but now bustles with students, are the former **Casa de la Canónica** (Canon's Residence) and the 17C Monasterio de San Paio de Antealtares.

Inside is the **Museo de Arte Sacra** (Sacred Art Museum; *open Mon–Sat 10.30am–1.30pm, 4–7pm.* €1.50. *981 58 31 27).*

Opposite, the doorway in the Cathedral's east end, known as the **Puerta del Perdón**★ (Door of Pardon), designed by Fernández Lechuga in 1611 and opened only in Holy Years (when the feast day of St James, 25 July, falls on a Sunday, next occurring in 2016), incorporates all the statues of the Prophets and Patriarchs carved by Maestro Mateo for the original Romanesque *coro*. At the top of a large flight of stairs is the **Casa de la Parra,** House of the Bunch of Grapes, a fine late 17C Baroque mansion.

Monasterio de San Martín Pinario★

Pl. de la Inmaculada 5. *Open winter Tue–Sun 11am–1.30pm, 4–6.30pm; summer Tue–Sun 10am–1.30pm, 4–6.30pm.* *981 58 30 08. www.seminariomayorcompostelano.com*

The monastery church has an ornate Plateresque front.

The interior, with coffered barrel vaulting, is lit by a Byzantine-style lantern without a drum. The Churrigueresque high altar **retable**★ is by the great archi-

tect Casa y Novoa (1730). A grand staircase beneath a cupola leads to 16C–18C cloisters.

The façade overlooking Plaza de la Inmaculada is colossal with massive Doric columns. Plaza de la Azabachería opposite is named for the jet ornament craftsmen *(azabacheros)* who had workshops in this square.

Museo do Pobo Galego (Museum of the Galician People)

Open Tue–Sat 10am–2pm, 4–8pm, Sun and public holidays 11am–2pm. *Closed 1 Jan, 25 Dec.* €3. *981 58 36 20. www.museodopobo.es.*

This regional museum, in the former Convento de Santo Domingo de Bonaval (17C–18C), provides an introduction to Galician culture. Rooms are devoted to the sea, crafts, painting and sculpture. The building has an impressive triple **spiral staircase**★.

The **Centro Gallego de Arte Contemporáneo** (Galician Contemporary Art Centre; *open summer Tue–Sun 11am– 8pm; winter Tue–Sun 12pm–9pm; no charge; *981 54 66 19; www.cgac.org),* designed by the Portuguese architect Álvaro Siza, is situated opposite.

Museo de las Peregrinaciones (Pilgrimage Museum)

San Miguel 4. *Open Tue–Fri 10am– 8pm, Sat 10.30am–1.30pm, 5–8pm, Sun and public holidays 10.30am–1.30pm.* *Closed 1, 6 Jan, 1 May, 25 Jul, 1 Nov, 8, 24–25, 31 Dec.* €2.40. *981 58 15 58. www.mdperegrinacions.com.*

This small museum is devoted to the pilgrimages to Santiago. Hardly any of its original medieval features remain.

Colegiata de Santa María la Real del Sar★

Pl. de la Colegiata de Sar. *Open Mon– Sat 10am–1pm, 4–7pm, Sun (Mass) 10.30am and 12.30pm.* €4. *981 56 28 91.*

The 12C Romanesque collegiate church has 18C buttresses – a glance inside at the astonishing slant of the pillars explains why. The only cloister gallery to remain is elegant, with paired **arches**★ decorated with floral and leaf motifs. A museum displays gold and silverwork.

EXCURSIONS
Pazo de Oca★
◐ *25km/15.5mi S on N 525.*
◔ *Gardens: open daily Nov–Mar 9am–6.30pm; Apr–Oct 9am–8.30pm.*
◉ *€5.* ☏ *986 58 74 35.*
www.fundacionmedinaceli.org.
This austere Galician **manor**, or *pazo*, with a crenellated tower, lines two sides of a vast square.

The romantic **park**★★ behind comes as a complete surprise (◔*see INTRO-DUCTION – Spanish Gardens*). There are shady arbours, terraces covered with rust-coloured lichen, pools, and a lake with a stone boat.

Monasterio de Santa María de Sobrado
◐ *Pl. Portal. 56km/35mi W.*
◔ *Open Mon–Sat 10am–1pm, 4.30–7pm, Sun 12.15pm–1pm, 4.30–7pm.*
◉ *€1.* ☏ *981 78 75 09.*
Sobrado is a vast weatherworn **monastery**, built between the Renaissance and Baroque periods.

Despite the severe church façade the interior displays fertile imagination in the design of the **cupolas** in the transept, the sacristy and the Rosary Chapel. Medieval parts of the monastery include the kitchen, chapter house and Mary Magdalene Chapel.

ADDRESSES

⌂ STAY

◉ **Hostal Mapoula** – *Entremurallas 10, 3º.* ☏ *981 58 01 24. www.mapoula.com. 11 rooms.* A small, family-run hostal in the old quarter. Good service and clean rooms with en-suite bathrooms.

◉◉ **Hotel San Clemente** – *San Clemente 28* ☏ *981 56 93 50. www.pousadasde compostela.com. 10 rooms.* ⌸ *€6.45.* An enviable central location a couple of minutes' walk from the Plaza del Obradoiro; rooms are decorated in brick and wood. Highly recommended.

◉◉◉ **Casa Grande de Cornide** – *Cornide 82, Calo-Teo. 11.5km/7mi SW of Santiago.* ☏ *981 89 30 44. www.casagrande decornide.com. 11 rooms.* ⌸ *€7.05.* This large, traditional-style Galician house offers peace and quiet. Décor and furnishings are a fusion of the classic and the modern, and offer a cosy atmosphere. The house is set in a lovely garden complete with a swimming pool.

◉◉◉◉ **Parador Hotel Reyes Católicos** – *Pl. del Obradoiro 1.* ☏ *981 58 22 00. www.parador.es. 137 rooms.* ⌸ *€21. Two restaurants* ◉◉◉◉. The former Royal Hospital founded by the Catholic Monarchs in 1499 has now been converted into a parador. Particularly worthy of note are its inner patios, which trace the typology of such hospitals in the 16C. Some rooms have four-poster beds.

⊗ EAT

◉◉ **O Dezaseis** – *R. de San Pedro 16.* ☏ *981 56 48 80. www.dezaseis.com. Reservations recommended. Closed Sun.* Impressive local gastronomy with delicious tapas and excellent wines, beneath the vines on the terrace or in a décor of wood and local stone.

◉◉◉ **Calderón** – *Car. del Conde 8.* ☏ *981 55 43 56. www.calderoncatering.com. Closed Aug 3 wks, Sun.* Garden terrace, cosy dining rooms and tapas bar.

◉◉◉ **Don Quijote** – *Galeras 20.* ☏ *981 58 68 59. www.quijoterestaurante.com.* A stronghold of traditional Galician cuisine with a popular bar.

◉◉◉◉ **Casa Marcelo** – *Hortas 1.* ☏ *981 55 85 80. www.casamarcelo.net. Closed Sun, Mon.* A charming restaurant serving innovative cuisine.

TAPAS

Bierzo Enxebre – *Troia 10.* ☏ *981 58 19 09. www.bierzoenxebre.com.* Fine tapas bar with three rustic dining rooms including stone columns and timber rafters.

La Bodeguilla de San Roque – *San Roque 13.* ☏ *981 56 43 79. www.labodeguilladesan roque.com.* This bodega has a good reputation for its *revuelta* dishes, chorizos and wines. Pleasant restaurant on the first floor.

Caney – *Hotel Meliá Araguaney, Alfredo Brañas 5.* ☏ *981 59 02 87.* An elegant tapas bar alongside the adjoining Meliá Hotel.

Rías Bajas★★

This coastline of deep inlets affording safe anchorages is Galicia's most attractive region for holidaymakers, who enjoy beaches and resorts like those of A Toxa/La Toja.

🚗 DRIVING TOURS

1 RÍA DE MUROS Y NOIA★★
From Muros to Ribeira
71km/44mi. About 1hr15min.

The *ría* is delightfully wild, its low coastline strewn with rocks. The northern bank is wooded. **Muros** is a seaside town with local-style houses. **Noia** is notable for its square looking out to sea, upon which stands the Gothic **Iglesia de San Martín**★ (*Pl. Suárez Oviedo; ℰ981 82 01 31*) with a magnificent carved portal and rose window.

2 RÍA DE AROUSA
From Ribeira to A Toxa/La Toja
115km/71mi. About 3hr

Ría de Arousa, at the mouth of the Ulla, is the largest and most indented inlet. **Ribeira** is a large fishing port with vast warehouses. **Mirador de la Curota**★★ is 9km/5.6mi northeast of Ribeira.

▷ *Take the LC 302 W towards Oleiros and after about 4km/2.5mi turn right onto a narrow road up to the viewpoint.*

From a height of 498m/1 634ft there is a magnificent **panorama**★★ of the four inlets of the Rías Bajas.

Padrón
41km/25.5mi NE of Ribeira.
The legendary boat brought St James to this village. Its mooring stone (*pedrón*) can be seen beneath the altar in the parish church. The town, renowned for its green peppers, was home to poet **Rosalía de Castro** (1837–85). Her house is a **museum** (*⚪open Summer 10am–2pm, 4–8pm; winter 4pm–*

- ⚒ **Michelin Map:** 571 D-E-F 2-3-4 and p282.
- ℹ **Info:** Baiona: Paseo da Ribeira. ℰ986 68 70 67; Vigo: Canovas del Castillo 3. ℰ986 22 47 57; Tui: Colón 2. ℰ986 60 17 89. www.riasbaixas.depo.es.
- ▶ **Location:** The Rías Bajas are four inlets: the Ría de Muros y Noia; the Ría de Arousa; the Ría de Pontevedra; and the Ría de Vigo, all along the northern coast.
- 🧒 **Kids:** Acuario de O Grove welcomes small marine explorers.

8pm, Sun and public holidays 10am–1.30pm; closed Mon. ☞€1.50; ℰ981 81 12 04; www.fundacionrosaliadecastro.es).

Vilagarcía de Arousa
32km/19.8mi SW of Padrón off AP 9.
A garden-bordered promenade overlooks the sea. The **Convento de Vista Alegre**, founded in 1648, on the outskirts, is an old *pazo* with square towers, coats of arms and pointed merlons.

Mirador de Lobeira★
4km/2.5mi S. Take a signposted forest track at Cornazo.
The view from the lookout takes in the whole *ría* and the hills inland.

Cambados★
12km/7.4mi SW of Vilagarcía de Arousa along PO 549.
The alleys of the old quarter are bordered by beautiful houses. At the northern entrance is the magnificent **Plaza de Fefiñanes**★, lined on two sides by the emblazoned Fefiñanes *pazo*, on the third by a 17C church with lines harmonising with the *pazo*, and on the fourth by a row of arcaded houses. On the other side of the village are the romantic ruins of **Santa Mariña de Dozo**, a 12C parish church which is now a cemetery.

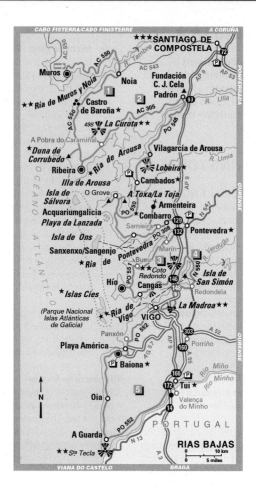

Map: RIAS BAJAS

CABO FISTERRA/CABO FINISTERRE · A CORUÑA
★★★SANTIAGO DE COMPOSTELA
Muros
Noia
Fundación C. J. Cela
Padrón
★★Ría de Muros y Noia
Castro de Baroña ★
La Curota ★★
498
A Pobra do Caramiñal
★Duna de Corrubedo
Vilagarcía de Arousa
Ribeira
Ría de Arousa
★Lobeira★
Illa de Arousa
Cambados★
Isla de Sálvora
O Grove
A Toxa/La Toja
Acquariumgalicia
Armenteira
Playa da Lanzada
Combarro
Isla de Ons
Samieira
Pontevedra★
Sanxenxo/Sangenjo
★ Ría de Pontevedra
Marín
Bueu
★★Coto Redondo
Hío
Cangas
Isla de San Simón
Redondela
★Islas Cíes
La Madroa ★★
(Parque Nacional Islas Atlánticas de Galicia)
Ría de Vigo
VIGO
Panxón
Porriño
Playa América
Baiona ★
Oia
Tui ★
Valença do Minho
PORTUGAL
A Guarda
RIAS BAJAS
0   10 km
0   5 miles
★★Sta Tecla
VIANA DO CASTELO · BRAGA

Isla de la Toja★

20km/12.4mi SW of Cambados off PO 550.

A sick donkey abandoned on the island was the first creature to discover the health-giving properties of the spring in La Toja. The stream has run dry but the pine-covered island in a wonderful **setting**★★ remains the most elegant resort on the Galician coast, with luxury villas and an early 20C palace. A small church is covered in scallop shells. The seaside resort and fishing harbour of **O Grove** on the other side of the causeway is renowned for its seafood.

♣♨ Acuario de O Grove

Punta Moreiras, Reboredo. From O Grove head towards San Vicente and turn off at Reboredo. ◷*Open 10am–6pm;* €10; *child* €8. ℘986 73 15 15.
The only aquarium in Galicia, has over 150 species on display in 18 tanks. The complex also includes a marine farm where turbot and gilthead are raised. The **road**★ from A Toxa/La Toja to Canelas affords views of sand dunes and rock-enclosed beaches such as **La Lanzada**.

③ RÍA DE PONTEVEDRA★

From A Toxa/La Toja to Hío
62km/39mi. About 3hr.

Sanxenxo is a lively summer resort with one of the best climates in Galicia. Further east at Samieira, a small road leads to the Monasterio de Santa María de Armenteira (◷*open daily 9am–sunset.*

No charge. 𝒫986 71 83 00), a Cistercian monastery, where a 12C church and 17C Classical-style cloister can be visited. Some 12km/7.4mi east of Sanxenxo along PO 308 is Combarro★, a fishing village with winding alleyways, that has a good many Calvaries, and is famed for its **hórreos**★ (drying sheds). Beyond Combarro is Pontevedra★ ⓗ See PONTEVEDRA.

Around 8km/5mi southwest of Pontevedra along PO 11 is Marín, headquarters of the Escuela Naval Militar (naval academy).

A further 19km/11.8mi southwest of Marín along AP 9 is Hío, a village at the tip of the Morrazo headland that has a famous and intricately carved **Calvary**★.

4 RÍA DE VIGO★★

From Hío to Baiona
70km/43mi. About 3hr.

The Vigo inlet is deep and sheltered inland by hills and out to sea by the Islas Cíes. By Domaio, where the wooded banks draw together and the narrow channel is covered in mussel beds, it becomes really beautiful.

From Cangas and Moaña you can see the white town of Vigo covering the hillside across the inlet.

Vigo
38km/23.6mi SE of Hío.

Vigo is Spain's principal transatlantic port and leading fishing port. Vigo's **setting**★ is outstanding: an amphitheatre on the south bank of the ría surrounded by parks and pinewoods.

There are magnificent **views**★★ from El Castro hill. Berbés is the picturesque fishermen and sailors' quarter. Adjacent is the A Pedra market where fishwives sell oysters; try them in the local bars. **MARCO (Museo de Arte Contemporáneo)** *(Príncipe 54;* ⓞ*open Tue–Sat 11am–9pm, Sun 11am–3pm;* ⓝ*no charge;* 𝒫*986 11 39 00; www.marcovigo.com)* displays the works of avant-garde artists, sculptors and architects.

At Punta de Muíño are splendid **views** of the *ría* and the **Museo do Mar** *(Av. Atlántida 160;* ⓞ*open 15 Jun–15 Sept Tue–Fri*

11am–2pm, 5–8pm, Sat, Sun 11am–9pm; 15 Sept–14 Jun Tue–Fri 10am–2pm, Sat, Sun 11am–7pm; ⓔ*€3;* 𝒫*986 24 77 50; www.museodomar.com)*, where the history of Vigo and the sea is explored.

Islas Cíes★

By boat from Vigo or Cangas (30min). 𝒫986 22 52 72. www.mardeons.com.
The beautiful archipelago of crystalline water and white sand guards the entrance to the Ría de Vigo.
The archipelago is part of **Parque Nacional de las Islas Atlánticas de Galicia**, including three islands and Playa de Rodas beach.

Mirador la Madroa★★
6km/3.7mi. Exit Vigo along the airport road. After 3.5km/2mi turn left, following signposts to the "parque zoológico" (zoo). The esplanade commands a fine **view**★★ *of Vigo and the ría.*

The Alcabre, Samil and Canido beaches stretch down the coast south of Vigo.

Panxón
14km/9mi SW along the C 550.
A seaside resort at the foot of Monte Ferro.

Playa América
2km/1.2mi S of Panxón.
A very popular, elegant resort in the curve of a bay.

Baiona/Bayona★
5km/3mi SW of Playa América.
It was here, on 10 March 1493, that the caravel *Pinta* – one of the three vessels in Christopher Columbus's fleet – captained by **Martín Alonso Pinzón,** gave the first reports of the New World.
Today, Baiona is a lively summer resort with a harbour fronted by a promenade of terrace cafés. In the old quarter houses may still be seen with coats of arms and glassed-in balconies.
The **ex-colegiata**, former collegiate church *(Pl. de Santa Liberata 1;* ⓞ*open 11am–12.30pm, 4.30–6.30pm;* 𝒫*986 68 70 67)* at the top of the town was built in a transitional Romanesque-Gothic style.

Monterreal

🕐 *Open daily 10am–dusk.* 🚶*€1;*
€5 vehicles. 📞*986 35 50 00.*

The Catholic Monarchs had a wall built around Monterreal promontory at the beginning of the 16C. The fort within is now a parador, surrounded by pinewood. **A walk round the battlements**★ *(about 30min),* rising above the rocks, affords splendid **views**★★ of the bay, Monte Ferro, the Estela islands and the coast stretching to the Cabo Silleiro headland.

⑤ THE ROAD FROM BAIONA TO TUI★

58km/36mi

The coast between Baiona and La Guarda is flat and semi-deserted.

Virgen de la Roca

🕐 *Open 10am–2pm, 3.30–8pm.* 🚶*€1.*

This huge granite statue (15m/50ft high) of the Virgin holding a boat in her right hand was built by architect Antonio Palacios in 1930. It can be climbed via a spiral staircase. The view over the bay and the ocean from the top is impressive.

Oia

Houses in the fishing village cluster around the former Cistercian abbey of **Santa María la Real** *(www.monasterio deoia.com)* with its Baroque façade.

La Guarda/A Guarda

13km/8mi S of Oia along PO 552.

This fishing village stands at the southern end of the Galician coastline. To the south, **Monte Santa Tecla**★ (341m/1 119ft) rises above the mouth of the Miño, affording fine **views**★★.

▶ *Follow signs for Citania de Santa Trega.*

On the slopes are the extensive remains of a **Celtic city**, inhabited from the Bronze Age to the 3C AD.

▶ *From La Guarda, the PO 552 heads inland parallel to the Miño river.*

Tui/Tuy★

27km/17mi NE of La Guarda along PO 552.

Tui stands just across the border from Portugal in a striking **setting**★. Its old quarter, facing the Portuguese fortress of Valença, stretches down the rocky hillside. The **Parque de Santo Domingo**, including a Gothic church of the same name, commands a good view of Tui and the Portuguese coast.

The town is one of the oldest in Galicia; its emblazoned houses and narrow stepped alleys climbing towards the Romanesque-Gothic **Cathedral**★ *(*🕐*open 10.30am–2pm, 4–8pm;* 📞*986 60 05 11),* consecrated in 1232.

ADDRESSES

🏨 STAY

🛏 **Canaima** – *Av. de García Barbón 42, Vigo.* 📞*986 43 09 34. www.hotelcanaima.es. 52 rooms.* 🍽*€4. Restaurant* 🛏🛏.
Some rooms at this centrally located and well priced hotel have balcony views.

🛏🛏 **Tres Carabelas** – *Ventura Misa 61, Baiona.* 📞*986 35 51 33. www.hoteltres carabelas.com. 10 rooms.* Family-run hotel in the centre of town.

🛏🛏🛏 **Pazo de Hermida** – *Trasmuro 21, Lestrove. 1km/0.6mi SW of Padrón.* 📞*981 81 71 10. www.pazodehermida. com. 6 rooms.* A 17C Galician manor in a tranquil setting.

🍴 EAT

🍽 **La Oca** – *Purificación Saavedra 8 (opposite Teis market), Vigo.* 📞*986 37 12 55. Closed Holy Week, late Jul–early Aug, and for dinner Mon–Thur.* Small family-run restaurant serving innovative food with notable French influences.

🍽 **Posta do Sol** – *Ribeira de Fefiñáns 22, Cambados.* 📞*986 54 22 85. www.postado sol.com.* An attractive little restaurant, decorated in regional style. The speciality is seafood. Also try the *empanadas* and house desserts.

🍽🍽 **O Fogón da Ría** – *Fontecarmoa 3, Vilagarcia De Arousa.* 📞*986 50 79 62. www.ofogondaria.com. Closed Mon for dinner, Tue.* This lovely establishment has two dining rooms with rustic décor with a varied menu and good wine list.

Pontevedra★

Quiet Pontevedra has a pleasant mix of fine buildings, plain arcades, cobbled streets and attractive parks and gardens. Terrace cafés teem in summer while bars are a cosy retreat in winter.

CASCO ANTIGUO★

The **old quarter** is tucked between calles Michelena, del Arzobispo Malvar and Cobián, and the river. Glass-covered passages and picturesque squares (**Plaza da la Leña; del Teucro, de la Pedreira**) are enchanting. There are endless places to stop for a drink and busy shopping streets such as **Sarmiento**.

The delightful asymmetrical **Plaza de la Leña★** is surrounded by beautiful façades. Two 18C mansions have been converted into a museum.

The ground floor of the **Museo de Pontevedra** holds Bronze Age **Celtic treasures**★ from A Golada and Caldas de Reis, and that of Foxados (2C and 1C BC), and a pre-1900 silverware collection with pieces from a number of countries. The first floor, which is dedicated to paintings, has several 15C Aragonese Primitives.

The second mansion includes a reconstruction of a stateroom from a 19C Spanish frigate, the *Numancia*. On the upper floor are an antique kitchen and 19C Sargadelos ceramics. The museum *(Pasantería 2-12; ◑open Tue–Sat 10am–9pm, Sun and public holidays 11am–2pm; ◷ closed 1 Jan, 25 Dec; ◔ no charge; ✆986 85 14 55; www.museo.depo.es)* encompasses the ruins of Santo Domingo and the Sarmiento building (ex-collegiate church of la Compañía de Jesús), beside the Iglesia de San Bartolomé.

Old alleyways and gardens surround the delightful 15C–16C Plateresque **Basílica de Santa María la Mayor★** *(Av. de Santa María 24; ◑open Mon–Fri 10am–1pm, 5.30–9pm, Sat 10am–1pm, Sun 10am–2pm, 5.30–9pm; ◔no charge; ✆986 86 99 02; www3.planalfa.es/santamarialamayor)*. The **west front**★ is carved like an altarpiece, divided into separate superimposed registers on

▶ **Population:** 80 749
◔ **Michelin Map:** 571 E 4.
▮ **Info:** Pl. Santa María.
  ✆986 88 62 11.
  www.riasbaixas.depo.es.
◑ **Location:** Pontevedra,
  near the northern coast, is
  linked by motorway with
  Vigo (27km/17mi S) and
  Santiago de Compostela
  (57km/35mi N). ▭ Plazá
  Calvo Sotelo.

which are reliefs of the Assumption of the Virgin and the Trinity. At the summit is the Crucifixion at the centre of an openwork coping finely carved with oarsmen and fishermen. The **interior** mingles Gothic (notched arches), Isabelline (slender cabled columns) and Renaissance (ribbed vaulting) styles.

San Bartolomé is an 18C Baroque church with fine scupltures, including some by Pedro de Mena *(Sarmiento 51; ◑open Tue–Sun 9am-1pm, 6-10pm; ✆986 85 13 75; www.archicompostela.org/san bartolome)*.

Overlooking the gardens of Plaza da Ferrería is the simple Gothic façade of **San Francisco** church *(Jardines de Castro San Pedro; ◑open Mon–Sat 7.30am–12.45pm, 5.10–8.15pm, Sun and public holidays 8.30am–2pm, 5.30–8.30pm; ◔no charge; ✆986 85 11 13)*. The interior features timber vaulting.

A small 18C Pilgrim's Chapel *(Capilla de la Peregrina; Pl. de la Peregrina; ◑open daily 9am–2pm, 4–7pm; ✆986 85 13 75)*, with scallop-shaped floor plan and convex façade, contains a venerated statue of the patron saint of Pontevedra.

The **Ruinas de Santo Domingo** *(Pas. de Montero Ríos; ◑open Jun–Sept Tue–Sun 10am–2pm, 5–8.30pm; ◷closed 31 May, 1 Oct; ◔no charge; ✆986 84 32 38)* are a perfect example of medieval romanticism. The Gothic east end is overgrown with ivy. Arranged inside, from the Museo de Pontevedra, are Roman steles, Galician coats of arms and tombs of craftsmen showing the tools they used, and tombs of noblemen.

Ourense/Orense

Since Antiquity, Orense/Ourense has been famous for its hot springs. Its Roman bridge is a crossing for pilgrims to Santiago de Compostela. The pedestrianised old town is packed with cafés and restaurants, whose terraces spill out on to the streets, shaded by the numerous churches and *casonas*, solid Baroque residences.

SIGHTS

Catedral★

Pl. del Trigo 1. 🕐 *Cathedral: open Mon–Sat 8.30am–1.30pm, 4.30–8.30pm, Sun 9am–1.30pm, 4.30–9pm; Museum: open Mon–Sat noon–1pm, 4.30–7pm, Sun 4.30–7pm.* €1. 📞 *988 22 09 92. www.obispadodeourense.com.*

The 12C–13C cathedral has been repeatedly modified. The **Portada Sur** (South Door), in the Compostelan style, lacks a tympanum, but is profusely decorated with carvings. The **Portada Norte** (North Door) has two statue columns and, beneath a great ornamental arch, a 15C Deposition framed by a *Flight into Egypt* and statues of the Holy Women.

The interior is noteworthy for its pure lines. At the end of the 15C, a Gothic-Renaissance transitional-style **lantern**★ was built above the transept. The ornate Gothic high altar retable is by Cornelius de Holanda. The 16C and 17C **Capilla del Santísimo Cristo** (Chapel of the Holy Sacrament), off the north transept, is decorated with exuberant sculpture in the Galician Baroque style. The triple-arched **Pórtico del Paraíso**★★ (Paradise Door), at the west end, has beautiful carvings and bright medieval colouring. The central arch shows the 24 Old Men of the Apocalypse; to the right is the Last Judgement. The pierced tympanum above, like the narthex vaulting, is 16C.

A door in the south aisle opens onto the 13C chapter house, now a **museum (Museo Catedralicio)** which includes church plate, statues, chasubles and a 12C travelling altar.

▸ **Population:** 107 057
⌚ **Michelin Map:** 571 E 6, F 6 (town plan) – Galicia (Orense).
🔖 **Info:** Isabel La Católica 2. 📞 988 36 60 64. www.turismodeourense.com.
▶ **Location:** Orense is 101km/ 62.7mi E of Vigo along the A 52 motorway; 100km/ 62mi SE of Pontevedra via the N 541; 105km/65mi SE of Santiago de Compostela on the N 525 and the AP 53. 🚌 Calle Eulogio Gómez Franqueira.

Museo Arqueológico y de Bellas Artes

Pl. Mayor. 🕐 *Tue–Sat 9–2.30pm, 4–8.30pm, Sun 9am–2.30pm.* *No charge.* 📞 *988 22 38 84. www.musarqourense.xunta.es*

Collections in the former bishop's palace on Plaza Mayor include prehistoric specimens, cultural objects (mainly statues of warriors) and an early 18C woodcarving of the **Camino del Calvario**★ (Stations of the Cross). The museum is partly closed for renovation, but one room remains open with a selection of the holdings.

EXCURSIONS

Monasterio de Osera★

▶ *34km/21mi NW. Leave Orense on the N 525. After 23km/14mi turn right towards Cotelas.* 🕐 *Phone for opening hours.* €3. 📞 *988 28 20 04. www.mosteirodoseira.org.*

The grandiose 12C Cistercian monastery, called the Escorial of Galicia, was founded by Alfonso VII. It stands isolated in the Arenteiro Valley, a region that once abounded in bears (*osos*) as the name suggests.

The **façade** (1708) is in three sections. In a niche below the statue of Hope, which crowns the doorway, is the figure of a Nursing Madonna with St Bernard at her feet. Of note inside are an **escalera de honor** (grand staircase) and the **Claustro de los Medallones** (Medallion Cloisters), which is decorated with 40 busts of historic personages.

The **church** (12C–13C), hidden behind the Baroque façade of 1637, has retained the customary Cistercian simplicity modified only by frescoes in the transept, painted in 1694.

The **chapter house**★ dates from the late 15C and early 16C and is outstanding for its beautiful vaulting of crossed ribs descending like the fronds of a palm tree onto four spiral columns.

Verín

▶ *69km/43mi SE along the A 52.*

Verín is a lively, picturesque town with narrow paved streets, houses with glassed-in balconies, arcades and carved coats of arms. It is best known for its thermal springs, which were already famous during the Middle Ages and reputed for their treatment of rheumatic and kidney disorders.

Castillo de Monterrei

▶ *6km/3.7mi W.* ⏰ *Phone for opening hours.* ⊛*No charge.* 𝒫*675 567 911.*

There is a parador next to the castle, which was a frontier redoubt throughout the Portuguese-Spanish wars.

It was more than a castle, however, with a monastery, hospital and a town which was abandoned in the 19C.

The approach is up an avenue lined with lime trees, which commands a full **panorama**★ of the valley below.

To enter the castle you will pass through three walls, the outermost of them dating from the 17C. At the centre stand the square 15C Torre del Homenaje (Keep) and the 14C Torre de las Damas (Lady's Tower); the courtyard is lined by a three-storey arcade and is less austere than the rest of the building.

The 13C church has a **portal**★ delicately carved with a notched design and a tympanum showing Christ in Majesty between the symbols of the Evangelists.

Celanova

▶ *26km/16mi S on the N 540.*

The large, imposing **monastery** on Plaza Mayor was founded in 936 by San Rosendo, Bishop of San Martín de Mondoñedo. The **church** (📷⊶*guided tours (1hr, phone to check times);* ⊛*€2;* 𝒫*988 43 22 01; www.concellodecelanova.com)* is a monumental late 17C edifice built in Baroque style. The coffered vaulting is decorated with geometrical designs, the cupola with volutes. An immense altarpiece (1697) occupies the back of the apse. Note the choir stalls, Baroque in the lower part and Gothic in the upper, as well as the fine organ.

The **cloisters**★★, among the most beautiful in the region, took from 1550 until the 18C to complete. The majestic staircases here are particularly worthy of note.

The **Capilla de San Miguel** (*opening hours and visits as church;* ⊛*€1),* a chapel behind the church, is one of the monastery's earliest buildings (937) and one of the rare Mozarabic monuments still in good condition.

Santa Comba de Bande

▶ *52km/32.5mi S along the N 540 (26km/16mi S of Celanova). 10km/6.2mi beyond Bande, head along a road to the right for 400m/440yd.*

The small 7C Visigothic **church**★ *(call to arrange a visit;* 𝒫*988 44 31 40)* overlooks the lake. The plan is that of a Greek cross, lit by a lantern turret. The apse is square and is preceded by a horseshoe-shaped triumphal arch resting on four pillars with Corinthian capitals.

TOUR ALONG THE RÍO SIL★

▶ *65km/40.3mi E. Head along the C 536; after 6km/3.7mi, turn left towards Luintra; continue for a further 18km/11mi.*

The ex-Benedictine monastery, the **Parador de Santo Estevo**, is signposted. Note the majestic **setting**★ and the church's Romanesque east end and cloisters, built to grandiose proportions largely in the 16C. Return downhill on the road on the left towards the Sil. Two dams control the waters of the Sil, which flow through **deep gorges**★. whose sides are dotted with vineyards.

Lugo★

Lugo was capital of Roman Gallaecia, the legacy of which includes the town walls, old bridge and thermal baths. The old quarter huddles around the cathedral.

OLD TOWN
Murallas★★
Ronda de la Muralla.
The Roman walls were built in the 3C, although they have been significantly modified. They are made of schist slabs levelled at a uniform 10m/32.8ft in a continuous 2km/1.2mi perimeter with 10 gateways and are listed as a UNESCO World Heritage site.

Catedral★
Pl. Santa María. ⏱*Open daily 8am–8.30pm; museum daily 11am–1pm.* ✆*No charge; museum €2.* ☎*982 23 10 38.*
The Romanesque church (1129) has Gothic and Baroque additions. The Chapel of the Wide-Eyed Virgin at the east end, by Fernando Casas y Novoa (who built the Obradoiro façade of the Cathedral in Santiago de Compostela) has a Baroque rotunda and stone balustrade. The north doorway has a fine Romanesque **Christ in Majesty**★. The figure is above a capital curiously suspended, carved with the Last Supper. The nave is roofed with barrel vaulting and lined with galleries, a feature common in pilgrimage churches. There are two immense wooden Renaissance altarpieces at the ends of the transept – the south one is signed by Cornelis de Holanda (1531). A door in the west wall of the south transept leads to the small but elegant **cloisters**.

City squares
The 18C **Palacio Episcopal**, facing the north door of the cathedral on **Plaza de Santa María**, is a typical *pazo*, one storey high with smooth stone walls, advanced square wings framing the central façade and decoration confined to the Gil Taboada coat of arms on the main doorway.

▶ **Population:** 95 416
● **Michelin Map:** 571 C 7 (town plan) – Galicia (Lugo).
▮ **Info:** Prazo do Campo 11. ☎982 23 13 61. www.lugo turismo.com.
▷ **Location:** Lugo is 96km/59.6mi SE of La Coruña/A Coruña along the A6, 94km/58.4mi NE of Ourense/Orense on the N 540, and 135km/83.8mi SW Santiago de Compostela on the A 6 and A P9. ▭Plaza de Conde Fontao.
◈ **Don't Miss:** The sundials at Museo Provincial.
◔ **Timing:** See the Cathedral and walls first, then explore the surrounding area.

Plaza del Campo, behind the palace, is lined by old houses. Calle de la Cruz with its bars and restaurants, and **Plaza Mayor**, dominated by the 18C **town hall**, with its gardens and esplanade, are popular meeting places. The Alejo Madarro sweet shop (*Reina 13;* ☎*982 22 97 14; www.madarro.net*) first opened its doors in the middle of the 19C.

Museo Provincial
⏱*Open Jul–Aug Mon–Fri 11am–2pm, 5–8pm, Sat 10am–2pm, Sun 11am–2pm; Sept–Jun Mon–Fri 10.30am–2pm, 4.30–8.30pm, Sat 10.30am–2pm, 4.30–8pm, Sun and public holidays 11am–2pm.* ⏱*Closed 1 Jan, 22 May, 24, 25, 31 Dec.* ✆*No charge.* ☎*982 24 21 12. www.museolugo.org.*
This museum of regional art, is housed in the former Monasterio de San Francisco. A room is devoted to ceramics from Sargadelos, and there are sundials and other objects from the Roman period. The former cloister of San Francisco contains an interesting collection of sundials, as well as several altars and sarcophagi.
The connecting **Museo Nelson Zúmel** is dedicated to Spanish paintings from the 19C and 20C.

La Coruña/ A Coruña★

This pleasant Galician city is set on a rocky islet, linked to the mainland by a strip of sand. At the northern end of the harbour, the charming Ciudad old quarter of small squares and Romanesque churches is a contrast to the wide streets of the business centre on the isthmus. The warehouses and industry of the Ensanche district are a reminder that La Coruña is Spain's sixth largest port and the main economic engine of the region.

A BIT OF HISTORY

Spanish Armada – Philip II's ill-fated "Invincible Armada" set out for England from La Coruña in 1588. A year later, Elizabeth I sent Drake to burn La Coruña but the town was saved by **María Pita**, who gave the alarm.

The 19C – During the Peninsular War, Marshal Soult of France defeated the English in the Battle of Elviña in 1809. In the late 19C, La Coruña consistently supported liberal insurgents and suffered severe reprisals.

SIGHTS

Colegiata de Santa María del Campo

Pl. Santa María 1. ⏲*Open Tue–Sat 9.30am–1pm, 5–7pm, Sat 10am–1pm, Sun and public holidays 9.30am– 1.30pm.* ✆*No charge.* ✆*981 20 31 86.*
This Romanesque church has a triple barrel-vaulted nave strengthened by arches with plaster borders. Note the fine 13C–14C portal, Gothic rose window and tower. A **Museum of Sacred Art** (*Arte Sacro*) is on one side of the church. In the square stands a 15C Calvary.

Iglesia de Santiago

Parrote 1. ⏲*Open Mon–Fri 8am–1pm, 5.30–7pm, Sat–Sun 10am–1pm, 4.30– 7pm.* ✆*No charge.* ✆*981 20 56 96.*
The church is a mix of Romanesque and Gothic. The stone pulpit is beautifully carved.

▶ **Population:** 245 164
⏲ **Michelin Map:** 571 B 4 (town plan) – Galicia (La Coruña).
▤ **Info:** Pl. María Pita 6. ✆981 92 30 93. www.turismocoruna.es.
▶ **Location:** La Coruña, on the north coast, links to Santiago de Compostela by the AP 9 motorway. The A 6 heads SE past Lugo (97km/60mi SE) and on to Madrid. ▬Joaquín Planelles Riera.
👪 **Kids:** Aquarium Finisterrae.

EL CENTRO (CENTRAL DISTRICT)
Avenida de la Marina★

The avenue, facing the harbour, is lined by tall houses with glassed balconies. Along one side is the paseo de la Dársena and on the other the **Jardines de Méndez Núñez**, gardens with a variety of flowering trees.

Plaza de María Pita

The vast café-lined square honours a local 16C heroine. It has a great many terrace cafés.

Castillo de San Antón: Museo Arqueológico e Histórico

Pas. del Parrote. ⏲*Open Jul–Aug Tue–Sat 10am–9pm, Sun and public holidays 10am–3pm; Sept–Jun Tue–Sat 10am–7.30pm, Sun and public holidays 10am–2.30pm.* ✆*€2.* ✆*981 18 98 50.*
This fortress dates from the period of Philip II and now houses an archaeological museum, including exhibits of prehistoric gold and silver.

Museo de Bellas Artes

Avenida Zalaeta. ⏲*Open Tue–Fri 10am–8pm, Sat 10am–2pm, 4.30–8pm, Sun 10am–2pm.* ⏲*Closed hols.* ✆*€2.40; no charge Sat afternoon and Sun.* ✆*881 88 17 00.*
http://museobelasartescoruna.xunta.es.

Light and spacious exhibition rooms are dedicated to art from the 16C to the 20C, including sketches by Goya.

Domus-Casa del Hombre

Santa Teresa 1. ◷*Open Jan–Apr Mon–Fri 10am–6pm, Sat, Sun and public holidays 11am–7pm; May, June, Sept–Dec Mon–Fri 10am–7pm, Sat, Sun and public holidays 11am–7pm; July, Aug 10am–8pm.* ∞€2. ℘981 18 98 40. www.mc2coruna.org.

This museum **building**★ designed by **Arata Isozaki**, is emblematic of the city. The façade is a double curve shaped like a sail, covered in slate. The other wall uses an old quarry to create a screen of large stone blocks. Displays deal with the human species and genetics through texts and interactive displays.

♣♣ Aquarium Finisterrae

Pas. Marítimo. ◷*Open Jan–Apr Mon–Fri 10am–6pm, Sat, Sun and public holidays 11am–8pm; May, June, Sept–Dec Mon–Fri 10am–7pm, Sat, Sun and public holidays 11am–8pm; July, Aug 10am–9pm.* ∞€10; child €4. ℘981 18 98 42. www.mc2coruna.org.

This excellent aquarium highlights local marine ecosystems.

Torre de Hércules (Hercules Tower or Lighthouse)

Avenida de Navarra. ◷*Open Sept–June 10am–5.45pm, July, Aug 10am–8.45pm.* ∞€3. ℘981 22 37 30.

This is the oldest functioning lighthouse in the world, dating from the 2C AD. The original outer ramp was enclosed in 1790. From the top (104m/341ft), there is a good **view** of the town and the coast.

EXCURSIONS
Costa de la Muerte (Coast of Death)

The coast between La Coruña and Cabo Finisterre is wild, harsh and majestic, whipped by storms, the graveyard of many a ship smashed against its rocks. Tucked in its more sheltered coves are fishing villages like **Malpica de Bergantiños**, protected by the Cabo de San Adrián (opposite the Islas Sisargas, with a bird sanctuary) or **Camariñas**, a lively port town famous for its bobbin-lace, which can be bought in various shops ranged around the harbour.

Museo do Encaixe

Plaza Insuela. ◷*Open 16 Sept–14 June Tue–Sun 11am–2pm, 4–7pm; 15 June–15 Sept Tue–Sun 11am–2pm, 5–8pm.* ∞€2. ℘981 73 63 40.

Two rooms display Camariñas lace and embroidery in pieces such as veils, mantillas and shawls, some dating from the 17C.

Cabo Finisterre or Fisterra★ (Cape Finisterre)

Legend has it that the Romans arrived here and christened it Finis Terrae ('the end of the earth'). **Cabo Finisterre** vies for the distinction of westernmost point of mainland Spain with Touriñan 29km north. The lighthouse on the headland commands a fine **panorama**★ of the Atlantic and the bay.

The coast **road**★ to the cape looks down over the Bahía de Cabo Finisterre, a bay enclosed by three successive mountain chains. **Corcubión**★, west of Cabo Finisterre, is an old harbour town of emblazoned houses with glassed-in balconies.

South of here the coast is a succession of coves, harbours and beaches against a backdrop of hills dotted with windmills. At **Ezaro**, you can make a detour on the Rio Xallas, turning left onto the CA 2308, then right towards the **Noveira** waterfall. You will find several small waterfalls and natural pools up towards the Fervenza reservoirs.

Other nearby highlights include the long beaches 8km south of Ezaro at **Caldebarcos**. One is 6km long and 1km deep – to access it, go down the small road that runs past the church and continue straight to the car park.

Carnota

7km/4mi south of Caldebarcos, the village of Carnota is home to the longest **"hórreo"**★ (typical barn on stone pillars) in Galicia. Built in 1760, it is 35m/115ft long.

Rías Altas ★

Although indented by *rías* – inlets of the Atlantic – the northern coast of Galicia is generally low-lying. Rocks and granite houses suggest a grim climate – yet holidaymakers arrive with the summer season for the scenery and sandy creeks. Galicia's *rías* are described below from east to west. The Rías Altas are deep inlets backed by thick forests of pine and eucalyptus.

- **Michelin Map:** 571 A 5-7, B4-8, C 2-5, D 2 – Galicia (Lugo, La Coruña/A Coruña).
- **Info:** Ferrol: Magdalena 12. ℘981 31 11 79; Foz: Edificio Cenima, Avda de Ribeira. ℘982 13 24 26; Viveiró: Avenida de Ramón Canosa. ℘982 56 08 79. www.turgalicia.es.
- **Location:** This series of inlets is in the far north-west corner of the Iberian Peninsula.

SIGHTS

Ría de Ribadeo

See also COSTA VERDE

The ría de Ribadeo is the estuary of the Eo, which slackens its pace to wind gently between wide banks.

There is a beautiful **view**★ up the estuary from the bridge across the mouth of the river.

The old port of **Ribadeo** is an important regional centre and summer resort.

Praia das Catedrais★

The "Beach of the Cathedrals" is so-called for the curious shape of its cliffs, carved by the sea to resemble buttresses. Pass under the arches and you'll also find caves to explore, but beware high tides – check with the tourist office first.

Ría de Foz

Foz, at the mouth of its *ría*, is a small port with a fishing fleet. Its two good beaches are popular in summer.

Iglesia de San Martín de Mondoñedo

Barrio Caritel, Foz. 5km/3mi S of Foz. Take the Mondoñedo road, then immediately turn right. Open 15 Sept –15 June Tue–Sun 11am–1pm, 4–6pm, 16 June-14 Sept Tue–Sun 11am–1pm, 4–7pm. No charge. ℘982 13 26 07.

Standing almost alone on a height, this archaic church was once part of a monastery and an episcopal seat until 1112. Unusually in this region, it shows no sign of Compostelan influence. The east end, with Lombard bands, is supported by massive buttresses; the transept **capitals**★ are naively carved and rich in anecdotal detail: one shows a table overflowing with food while a dog licks the feet of a suffering Lazarus. The capitals, believed to date from the 10C, show Visigothic plant motifs.

Mondoñedo

23km/14mi SW along the N 634.

Mondoñedo rises out of the hollow of a lush valley. Streets are lined with balconied white houses bearing coats of arms. The cathedral square is delightful with its arcades and *solanas* (glassed-in galleries).

The immense façade of the **cathedral**★ *(Pl. Catedral;* open daily 10am–1pm, 4.30–8pm; €2 museum; ℘982 52 10 06) combines the Gothic grace of the three large portal arches and the rose window, all dating from the 13C, with the grandiose Baroque style of towers added in the 18C.

Late 14C frescoes decorate the interior, one above the other (below the extraordinary 1710 organ) illustrating the Massacre of the Innocents and the Life of St Peter. There are a Rococo retable at the high altar and a polychrome wood statue of the Virgin in the south ambulatory. It is known as the English Virgin, as the statue was brought from St Paul's, London, in the 16C.

The classical **cloisters** were added in the 17C.

Ría de Viveiro

All **Viveiro** retains of its town walls is the Puerta de Carlos V (Charles V Gateway), emblazoned with the emperor's arms. In summer, the port is a holiday resort. On the fourth Sunday in August, visitors from all over Galicia come for the local Romeria do Naseiro festival.

Ría de Santa María de Ortigueira

The *ría* is deep and surrounded by green hills while **Ortigueira** port has quays bordered by well-kept gardens.

Santuario de San Andrés de Teixido★★

🕐*Open June–Sept 9am–10pm; Oct–May 9am–6pm.* 📞*981 48 24 96.*
This stone hermitage has long been a site of pilgrimage and is worth a visit for the views alone.

Ría de Cedeira

A small, deeply enclosed *ría* with beautiful beaches. The road gives good **views** of **Cedeira** (summer resort).

Ría de Ferrol

The *ría* forms a magnificent harbour entered by a channel guarded by two forts. In the 18C, **Ferrol** (🚍 *Avenida de Compostela)* became (and remains) a naval base. The symmetry of the old quarter dates from the same period.

Betanzos★

Betanzos, a one-time port which has now silted up, stands on a hill at the end of a *ría*. Its old quarter retains three richly ornamented Gothic churches and old houses with glassed-in balconies.

Iglesia de Santa María del Azogue★

Pl. de Fernán Pérez de Andrade. 🕐*Open May–Aug 10am–1pm, 4.30–7.30pm; Sept–Apr 10am–1pm, 4.30–6.30pm.* 🎟*No charge.* 🎧*Guided tours available:* 📞*981 77 66 66.*
The name of the 14C–15C church comes from *suk* (marketplace in Arabic). The asymmetrical façade is given character by a projecting central bay pierced by a rose window and a portal with sculp-

tured covings. Niches on either side contain archaic statues of the Virgin and the Archangel Gabriel. Three aisles of equal height, beneath a timber roof, create an effect of spaciousness.

Iglesia de San Francisco★

Pl. de Fernán Pérez Andrade. ♿🕐*Open May–Aug Mon 10am–1pm, Tue–Sun 10am–1pm, 4.30–7.30pm; Sept–Apr Mon 10am–1pm, Tue–Sun 10am–1pm, 4.30–6.30pm.* 🎟*No charge.* 🎧*Guided tours available :* 📞*981 77 66 66.*
This Franciscan monastery church, in the shape of a Latin Cross, with a graceful Gothic east end, was built in 1387 by the powerful Count Fernán Pérez de Andrade, Lord of Betanzos and Puentedeume. It is remarkable for the many tombs along its walls, the carved decoration on its ogives and chancel arches and the wild boar sculpted in the most unexpected places. Beneath the gallery to the left of the west door is the **monumental sepulchre**★ of the founder, supported by a wild boar and a bear, his heraldic beasts. Scenes of the hunt adorn the sides of the tomb.

Iglesia de Santiago

Pl. de Lanzós. 🕐*Open May–Aug 10am–1pm, 4.30–7.30pm; Sept–Apr 10am–1pm, 4.30–6.30pm.* 🎟*No charge.* 🎧*Guided tours available:* 📞*981 77 66 66.*
The church, built in the 15C by the tailors' guild, stands on higher ground. Above the main door is a carving of St James Matamoros (Moorslayer) on horseback. The arcaded 16C **ayuntamiento** (town hall) is alongside.

Museo das Marinas

Emilio Romay 1. 🕐*Open Sept–June Mon–Fri 10am–1pm, 4–8pm; July, Aug Mon–Fri 9am–2pm, Sat 10.30–1pm.* 🎟*€1.29.* 📞*981 77 66 66.*
Local history museum housed in a former convent, with displays of Roman archaeology, national dress and local art.

Ría de La Coruña
⛵*See La CORUÑA/A CORUÑA*

CASTILLA-LEÓN: *Burgos, León and Palencia*

These three provinces of Castilla-León occupy the northern part of Spain's semi-arid *meseta*. Fortified towns such as Léon and Palencia rise above vast plains of cereal crops and remind today's visitors of this area's importance in the establishment of the kingdom of Castille and its power during the Reconquest. In addition to thriving university towns are numerous isolated and sparsely populated villages where life continues uninterrupted by many aspects of modern life. The decline in rural population is resulting in an increase in forested land, though the importance of cereal cultivation and creation of pasture means that the oaks and juniper bushes that carpeted the *meseta* before the agrarian age are found only in the most secluded pockets.

Reclics of a glorious past

León was once the capital of a kingdom that covered nearly a quarter of present-day Iberia and its old centre retains splendid monuments from this period. King Ferdinand and Queen Isabella were keen patrons of the arts to promote the restoration of royal authority and primacy of Catholicism. León's Cathedral, with the richest stained glass in Spain, and its Pantéon Real, are emblematic of this, and unmissable sights today. The old town's buzzing bars entertain a sizeable student population.

The ancient capital of Castilla for almost 500 years, **Burgos** is a pleasant city, famous for its magnificent Cathedral, the third largest in Spain, which contains relics (and the remains) of El Cid.

A candiate city for European Capital of Culture, it has benefited from a recent restoration programme that has made the old town's riverfront an even more attractive place to wander.

Summer festivals, such as that of San Pedro y San Pablo and the Día de las

Highlights

1   Stunning **Burgos cathedral**, a showcase of European Gothic sculpture (p294)

2   Panorama from the **Pico de Tres Mares** (p300)

3   The 900-year-old church **San Martín de Frómista** (p301)

4   Ancient and modern artwork at **León**'s Museo and MUSAC (p304)

5   Rock formaitons at the **Cuevas de Valporquero** (p305)

Peñas, are celebrated with processions, bullfights and traditional Castilian dishes including *morcilla*, blood sausage mixed with rice.

Aguilar de Campoo marks the northeast border of the region, and from the nearby Pico de Tres Mares there is a wonderful panorama across to the Picos de Europa in Cantabria.

View of Burgos with its cathedral

© Vincent Leduc/Author's Image / Photononstop

Burgos★★

Burgos sits on the banks of the River Arlanzón, on a windswept plateau at the heart of the Spanish Meseta. The most famous of its monuments is the magnificent Cathedral, whose lofty Gothic spires dominate the city's skyline.

A BIT OF HISTORY

Founded by Diego Rodríguez in 884, Burgos was capital of Castilla and León from 1037 until the fall of Granada in 1492. Yet commerce and the arts flourished afterwards: the town became a wool centre for the sheep farmers of the Mesta (⌕ see SORIA); architects and sculptors from northern Europe transformed monuments. Burgos became Spain's Gothic capital with outstanding works including the Cathedral, the Monasterio de las Huelgas Reales (Royal Convent of Las Huelgas) and the Cartuja de Miraflores (Carthusian monastery). The end of the 16C brought the decline of the Mesta and of the town's prosperity. Burgos was the seat of Franco's government from 1936 to 1938.

Land of El Cid (c. 1040–99) – The exploits of Rodrigo Díaz of Vivar (9km/5.5mi N of Burgos) light up the late 11C history of Castilla. The brilliant captain first supported the ambitious King of Castilla, Sancho II, then Alfonso VI, who succeeded his brother in dubious circumstances. Alfonso, jealous of his exploits against the Moors, banished the hero.

Díaz entered service first with the Moorish King of Zaragoza and subsequently fought Christian and Muslim armies with equal fervour. Most famously, he captured Valencia at the head of 7 000 men, chiefly Muslims, after a nine-month siege in 1094. He was finally defeated by the Moors at Cuenca and died soon after (1099). His widow held Valencia against the Muslims until 1102 when she set fire to the city, then fled to Castilla with El Cid's body. The couple were buried in San Pedro de Cardeña (10km/6.2mi SE of Burgos), but their ashes were moved to Burgos Cathedral in 1921.

▶ **Population:** 177 879
⌕ **Michelin Map:** 575 E 18 –19 (town plan).
ℹ **Info:** Plaza de Alonso Martínez 7. ☎947 20 31 25. www.turismoburgos.org.
▶ **Location:** Burgos is in the north of Spain, 88km/54.6m from Palencia, 117km/73mi from Vitoria-Gasteiz and 120km/74.5mi from Valladolid; at 856m/2 808ft, it's exposed to bitter winds in winter. ▰Avenida Principe de Asturias.
⊘ **Don't Miss:** The Cathedral, monasteries and circular main square.
⊙ **Timing:** A least a day of exploration.

Legend has transformed the stalwart but ruthless 11C warrior, the Campeador (Champion) of Castilla, El Cid (Seid in Arabic), into a knight of exceptional valour. The epic poem El Cantar del Mío Cid appeared in 1180 and was followed by ballads. In 1618 Guillén de Castro wrote a romanticised version of El Cid, Las Mocedades del Cid (Youthful Adventures of El Cid), upon which Corneille, in 1636, based his drama Le Cid.

SIGHTS
CATHEDRAL★★★
Pl. de Santa María. ⊙Open 20 Mar–Oct 9.30am–6.30pm; Nov–19 Mar 10am–6pm. ⊛€5. ☎947 20 47 12. www.catedraldeburgos.es.
The third-largest Cathedral of Spain (after Sevilla and Toledo) illustrates the transformation of French and German Flamboyant Gothic into an exuberant Spanish style.

Ferdinand III laid the first stone in 1221. At the beginning of the 13C, under Maurice the Englishman, then Bishop of Burgos, who had collected drawings during a journey through France (at that time very much influenced by the Gothic style), the nave, aisles and portals were built by local architects.

The 15C saw the building of the west front spires and the Capilla del Condestable (Constable's Chapel) and the decoration of other chapels.

Architects and sculptors from Flanders, the Rhineland and Burgundy were brought by another Burgos prelate, Alonso de Cartagena, on his return from the Council of Basel.

These artists found new inspiration in Mudéjar arabesques and other Hispano-Moorish elements.

The most outstanding, the Burgundian **Felipe Vigarny**, the Fleming **Gil de Siloé** and the Rhinelander **Johan of Cologne**, integrated rapidly and with their sons and grandsons – Diego de Siloé, Simon and Francis of Cologne – created what was essentially a Burgos school of sculpture.

The cloisters were built in the 14C, while the magnificent lantern over the transept crossing – the original of which collapsed after some particulary daring design work by Simon of Cologne – was rebuilt by Juan de Vallejo in the mid-16C.

Exterior – A walk round the Cathedral reveals how the architects took ingenious advantage of the sloping ground (the upper gallery of the cloisters is level with the Cathedral pavement) to introduce delightful small precincts and closes.

West front – The ornate upper area, with its frieze of Spanish kings and two openwork spires, is the masterwork of Johan of Cologne.

Interior – The design of the interior is French inspired, while the decoration bears an exuberant Spanish stamp.

Portada de la Coronería – The statues at the jambs have the grace of their French Flamboyant Gothic originals, though their robes show more movement. The Plateresque **Portada de la Pellejería** (Skinner's Doorway) in the transept was designed by Francis of Cologne early in the 16C.

Around by the east end it becomes obvious that the Constable's Chapel, with its Isabelline decoration and lantern with pinnacles, is one of the Cathedral's later additions.

Portada del Sarmental – The covings are filled with figures from the Celestial Court. The tympanum is a remarkable showing of each Evangelist in a different position as he writes.

Crucero, Coro and Capilla Mayor★★ – The splendid star-ribbed lantern of the transept crossing rises on four massive pillars to 54m/177ft above the funerary stones of El Cid and Ximena, inlaid in the crossing pavement. The imposing unit of 103 walnut choir stalls, carved by Felipe Vigarny between 1507 and 1512, illustrates biblical stories on the upper, back rows and mythological and burlesque scenes at the front. The handsome recumbent statue of wood, plated with enamelled copper, on the tomb at the centre, from the 13C, is of Bishop Maurice. The high altar retable is a 16C Renaissance work in high relief against an intrinsically Classical background of niches and pediments.

Claustro – The 14C Gothic cloisters present a panorama of Burgos sculpture in stone, terracotta and polychrome wood.

The **Capilla de Santiago** (St James' Chapel) contains the Cathedral treasure of plate and liturgical objects.

In the **Capilla de Santa Catalina** (St Catherine's Chapel) are manuscripts and documents, including the marriage contract of El Cid. On the 15C carved and painted consoles, Moorish kings pay homage to the King of Castilla.

The **sacristía** (sacristy) houses the *Christ at the Column* by Diego de Siloé, a supreme example of Spanish Expressionism in post-16C Iberian sculpture.

The **sala capitular** (chapter house) displays, besides 15C and 16C Brussels tapestries symbolising the theological and cardinal virtues, a Hispano-Flemish diptych, a *Virgin and Child* by Memling and, above, a painted wood Mudéjar *artesonado* ceiling (16C).

Capilla del Condestable★★ – A magnificent grille closes off the area. The Isabelline chapel, founded by Hernández de Velasco, Constable of Castilla, in 1482 and designed by Simon of Cologne, is lit by a lantern surmounted by an elegant cupola with star-shaped vaulting.

All the great early Renaissance sculptors of Burgos cooperated in the decoration of the walls and altarpiece. The heraldic displays in the chapel are striking. On either side of the altar, the Constable's escutcheon, held by male figures, seems suspended over the balustrades of the tribune.

Statues of the Constable and his wife lie on their tomb, carved in Carrara marble, and beside them is an immense garnet-coloured marble funerary stone for the names of their descendants. To the right is a Plateresque door to the sacristy (1512) where there is a painting of *Mary Magdalene* by Pietro Ricci.

Girola★ – The *trasaltar* (at the back of the high altar), carved partly by **Felipe Vigarny**, includes an expressive representation of the Ascent to Calvary.

Escalera Dorada or Escalera de la Coronería – The majestically proportioned golden or coronation staircase was designed in pure Renaissance style by Diego de Siloé in the early 16C. Twin pairs of flights are outlined by an ornate, elegant gilded banister by the French master ironsmith, Hilaire.

Each of the side chapels is a museum of Gothic and Plateresque art: **Gil de Siloé** and Diego de la Cruz worked together on the huge Gothic altarpiece in the **Capilla de Santa Ana★** which illustrates the saint's life. In the centre is a Tree of Jesse with, at its heart, the first meeting of Anne and Joachim, and at the top, the Virgin and Child.

At the beginning of the Cathedral nave, near the roof, is the **Papamoscas** or **Fly-catcher Clock**, with a jack which opens its mouth on the striking of the hours.

In the **Capilla del Santo Cristo** (Chapel of Holy Christ) is a Crucifixion with the particularly venerated figure complete with hair and covered with buffalo hide to resemble human flesh.

The **Capilla de la Presentación** (Chapel of the Presentation) contains the tomb of the Bishop of Lerma, carved by Felipe Vigarny, and the **Capilla de la Visitación** (Chapel of the Visitation), the tomb of Alonso de Cartagena by Gil de Siloé.

Monasterio Santa María Real de las Huelgas★★ (Royal Convent of las Huelgas)

Compases. 1.5km/1mi W of Burgos; take Avenida del Monasterio de las Huelgas.
🕐*Call for opening times and charges.*
📞*947 20 16 30.*

Las Huelgas Reales, the summer palace of the kings of Castilla, was converted in 1180 into a convent by Alfonso VIII and his wife Eleanor, daughter of Henry II of England. The nuns were Cistercians of high lineage, the abbess all-powerful; by the 13C the convent's influence, both spiritual and temporal, extended to more than 50 towns and it had become a place of retreat for members of the house of Castilla and even became the royal pantheon.

Rearrangement over the centuries has resulted in a somewhat divided building, featuring the Cistercian style of the 12C and 13C, alongside Romanesque and Mudéjar features (13C–15C) as well as Plateresque furnishings.

The clean lines of this **church** are pure Cistercian. The interior is divided by a screen: from the transept, open to all, you can see the revolving pulpit (1560), in gilded ironwork, which enabled the preacher to be heard on either side. Royal and princely tombs, originally coloured, rich in heraldic devices and historical legend, line the aisles, while in the middle of the nave, the nuns' *coro*, is the tomb of Alfonso VIII and Eleanor of England. The rood screen retable, delicately carved and coloured in the Renaissance style, is surmounted by a fine 13C Deposition. The altar is flanked on each side by two handsome 13C and 14C tombs.

13C–15C. Enough fragments of Mudéjar vaulting stucco remain in these **Gothic cloisters** to suggest the delicacy of the strapwork inspired by Persian ivories and fabrics.

The **chapter house** holds the **pendón★**, a trophy from the Battle of Las Navas de Tolosa, decorated with silk *appliqué*.

Late 12C. In these **Romanesque cloisters**, slender paired columns, topped by highly stylised capitals, combine to create an effect of elegance. Several rooms in this part of Alfonso VIII's former palace were decorated by Moors.

The **Capilla de Santiago** (Chapel of St James) retains an *artesonado* ceiling with original colour and stucco frieze. According to legend, the statue of the saint with articulated arms conferred knighthoods on princes of royal blood. The fabrics, court dress and finery displayed in the former loft of the **Museo de Telas Medievales**★ provide a vivid view of royal wear in 13C Castilla.

Of the clothes (tunics, pelisses and capes) found in the tombs, the most valuable come from that of the Infante Fernando de la Cerda (who died in 1275), son of Alfonso X, the Wise. This tomb, which escaped French desecration in 1809, contained a long tunic, *pellote* (voluminous trousers with braces) and a large mantle, all of the same material embroidered with silk and silver thread. There is also a *birrete*, a silk crown adorned with pearls and precious stones.

Cartuja de Miraflores (Miraflores Carthusian Monastery)

Ctra de la Cartuja. 4km/2.5mi E.
○*Open Mon, Tue, Thur–Sat 10.15am–3pm, 4–6pm, Sun and public holidays 11am–3pm.* ◌*No charge.*
✆*947 25 25 86. www.cartuja.org.*

This former royal foundation, entrusted to the Carthusians in 1442, was chosen by Juan II as a pantheon for himself and his second wife, Isabel of Portugal. The church was completed in full Isabelline Gothic style in 1498.

Iglesia★ – The sobriety of the façade, relieved only by the buttress finials and the founders' escutcheons, gives no indication of the elegant interior vaulting and gilded keystones.

Sculpture ensemble in the Capilla Mayor★★★ – Designed by the Fleming Gil de Siloé at the end of the 15C, it comprises the high altarpiece, the royal mausoleum and a funerary recess.

The polychrome **altarpiece**, the work of Siloé and Diego de la Cruz, is striking. The usual rectangular compartments are replaced by circles crowded with biblical figures.

The white marble **mausoleo real** (royal mausoleum) is in the form of an eight-pointed star in which are recumbent statues of Juan II and Queen Isabel, parents of Isabel the Catholic. Dominating the exuberant Flamboyant Gothic decoration of scrolls, canopies, pinnacles, cherubim and armorial bearings, executed with rare virtuosity, are the four Evangelists. In an ornate **recess** in the north wall is the tomb of the Infante Alfonso, whose premature death gave the throne to his sister Isabel the Catholic. The statue of the prince at prayer is technically brilliant but impersonal (compare with that of Juan de Padilla in the Museo de Burgos ◖ *see Sights*). Also in the church are a 15C Hispano-Flemish triptych (to the right of the altar) and Gothic **choir stalls** carved with an infinite variety of arabesques.

SIGHTS

Museo de Burgos★

Miranda 13. ○*Open Jun–Sept Tue–Sat 10am–2pm, 5–8pm, Sun and holidays 10am–2pm; Oct–May Tue–Sat 10am–2pm, 4–7pm, Sun and public holidays 10am–2pm.* ◌€*1.20; no charge Sat–Sun, 18 May.*
✆*947 26 58 75.*

This excellent museum showcases the ethnography of the region.

Prehistoric and Archaeological Department – In the Casa de Miranda, a Renaissance mansion with an elegant patio, this section holds objects from the Prehistoric to Visigothic periods. Of particular interest are the rooms devoted to Iron Age sites, to the Roman settlement of Clunia and the Roman funerary steles.

Fine Arts Department – The Casa de Ángulo houses art from the region covering the period from the 9C to the 20C. There are several precious items from the Santo Domingo Monastery at Silas: an 11C **Hispano-Moorish casket**★, delicately carved in ivory in Cuenca and highlighted with enamel plaques, the 12C **Frontal** or **Urn of Santo Domingo**★ in beaten and enamelled copper, and a 10C **marble diptych**. On the **tomb**★ of Juan de Padilla, Gil de Siloé beautifully rendered the face and robes of the deceased. The collection of 15C paintings includes a *Christ Weeping* by Jan Mostaert.

Museo de la Evolución Humana★

Paseo Sierra de Atapuerca. ⏰*Open Tue –Fri 10.30am–2.30pm, 4.30–8.30pm, Sat, Sun 10am–8pm.* ✇€6, combined with archaeological remains (see p299) €10. ☏ 902 024 246. www.museo evolucionhumana.com

This magnificent museum, opened in summer 2010, occupies the central part of a large modern building designed by architect, sculptor and painter Juan Navarro Baldeweg.

One floor is devoted to the archaeological site of Atapuerca; another to Darwin's evolutionary theories; a third the differences and similarities of modern man with the hunter-gatherer 9 000 years ago, while another looks at the ecosystems fundamental to the course of evolution.

Arco de Santa María★

Pas. del Espolón. ⏰*Open Tue–Sat 11am–2pm, 5–9pm, Sun 11am–2pm.* ⏰*Closed public holidays.* ✇No charge. ☏ 947 28 88 68.

The 14C gateway in the city walls was modified to form a triumphal arch for Emperor Charles V and embellished with statues of the famous including (top right) El Cid with Charles V.

Inside are the **Sala de Poridad**, with magnificent Mudéjar cupola, and the pharmacy of the ex-Hospital de San Juan.

Iglesia de San Nicolás

Fernán González. ⏰*Open Jun–Sept Mon–Fri 10.30am–1.30pm, 4–6pm; Oct–May Mon–Fri 12.30–1.30pm, 5–7pm, Sat 9.30am–2pm, 5–7pm, Sun and public holidays only open before or after Mass.* ✇€1.50. ☏ 947 20 70 95.

The large, ornate **altarpiece★** of this Gothic church, carved by Simon of Cologne in 1505, has over 465 figures.

Iglesia de San Esteban: Museo del Retablo

San Esteban 1. ⏰*Call for opening hours.* ✇€1.20. ☏ 947 27 37 52.

The Retable Museum is in this delightful 14C Gothic **church★**. The interior is a magnificent setting for the 18 retables, exhibited according to their religious significance in the church's three naves. The *coro alto* contains a small collection of gold and silverwork.

Iglesia de San Gil

San Gil 12. ⏰*Open Tue–Sun Jul–Sept 10am–2pm, 5–8pm; Oct–Jun only open before or after Mass.* ✇No charge. ☏ 947 26 11 49.

One of the city's most beautiful churches. Hidden behind its sober façade is a late Gothic temple. Noteworthy are the Nativity Chapel and Buena Mañana chapels, the latter containing a retable by Gil de Siloé.

Casa del Cordón

Pl. de la Libertad. ⏰*Patio open Mon– Fri 9am–2.30pm.* ✇No charge. ☏ 947 25 81 00.

The 15C palace of the Constables of Castilla (now housing a bank, the Caja de Ahorros) displays a thick Franciscan cord motif, hence the name. It is where Columbus was received by the Catholic Monarchs on his return from his second voyage to America, and where Philip the Fair died suddenly of a chill.

Museo de Pintura Marceliano Santa María

Pl. de San Juan. ⏰*Open Tue–Sat 11am–2pm, 5–9pm, Sun 11am–2pm.* ⏰*Closed public holidays.* ✇No charge. ☏ 947 20 56 87.

Impressionist canvases by Marceliano Santa María (1866–1952) are shown in the ruins of the former Benedictine monastery of San Juan.

Hospital del Rey

Hospital del Rey. ⏰*Open same hours as university.* ☏ 947 25 87 77.

Founded by Alfonso VIII as a hospital for pilgrims, it retains its entrance, the Patio de Romeros, with its fine 16C

Plateresque façade. Today, it is the seat of the University of Burgos.

Castillo

🕐 *Open Oct–Jun Mon–Fri 11am–1.30pm, 4–6.30pm, Sat–Sun and public holidays 11am–2pm (and 4–7pm Apr–Jun); Jul–Sept daily 11am–1.30pm, 4–7.30pm.* ✎€3.70. ☎*947 28 88 74.*
This restored hilltop fortress dominates Burgos. Dating from the 9C, it was destroyed by troops of Napoleon. Views are magnificent.

EXCURSIONS
Sierra de Atapuerca

▶ *Take the N 120 towards Logroño. In Ibeas de Juarros (13km/8mi), head to the Emiliano Aguirre hall (beside the main road).* ☛*Guided tours (2hr) of the caves and Museo Emiliano Aguirre by prior arrangement.* ✎€4. ☎*902 02 42 46. www.atapuerca.com.*
This is one of the world's most important palaeontological sites. Excavations at **La Dolina** have uncovered remains of hominids who lived around 800 000 years ago. The fossil register at the **Sima de los Huesos** (Chasm of Bones) is the largest in Europe, dating from between 400 000 and 200 000 years ago. Visitors can walk along the trench and visit a small archaeological museum.

Covarrubias★

This historic Castilian village of half-timbered houses and a Renaissance palace is partly surrounded by medieval ramparts. Covarrubias is the burial place of Fernán González, one of Castilla's great historic figures and the catalyst behind the kingdom's independence.
The Gothic collegiate church, the **Colegiata★** contains 20 medieval tombs, including those of Fernán González and the Norwegian Princess Cristina who married the Infante Philip of Castilla in 1258 *(Pl. Rey Chidasvinto 3; 🕐 open Mon, Wed–Fri 10.30am–2pm, 4–7pm, Sun and public holidays 10.30am–noon, 4–7pm, organ Mass Sun noon;* ✎€2; ☎*947 40 63 11).*
Note paintings by Pedro Berruguete and Van Eyck in the Museo Paroquial

(Pl. Rey Chindasvinto 3; 🕐 *open Mon and Wed–Sun 10.30am–2pm, 4–7pm;* ✎€2*).*
A 15C Flemish **triptych★**, with central relief of the Adoration of the Magi, is said to be by Gil de Siloé.

Monasterio de Santo Domingo de Silos★★

Valle de Tabladillo. ▶ *18km/11mi SE.* 🕐*Phone for opening times.* ✎€3. ☎*947 39 00 68. www.abadiadesilos.es.*
This site, originally Visigothic, was occupied by Benedictine monks from France in 1880. The monastery is renowned for its concerts of Gregorian chants. The **cloisters★★★** are among the most beautiful in Spain.

Garganta de la Yecla

▶ *3km/1.8mi SW of Santo Domingo de Silos via the BU 910 –* 🚶 *20min.*
A footpath follows a narrow gorge.

Lerma

▶ *23km/14.3mi W along the C 110.*
Lerma owes its splendour and Classic town plan to the extravagance and corruption of the **Duke of Lerma**, Philip III's early 17C favourite.
The quarter built by the duke retains steep cobbled streets and houses with wood or stone porticoes. The ducal palace, with its austere façade, stands on the spacious **Plaza Mayor★**.
The **Colegiata** church *(☛guided tours organized by tourist office;* ☎*947 17 70 02; www.citlerma.com)* has a 17C gilded bronze statue by Juan de Arfe of the duke's nephew, Archbishop Cristóbal de Rojas.

Quintanilla de las Viñas

▶ *24km/15mi N. Take the C 110, the N 234 towards Burgos, then bear right onto a signposted road.*
The road follows the Arlanza Valley. Below and to the right, are the ruins of the **Monasterio de San Pedro de Arlanza**.
Though only the apse and transcept of the **Iglesia de Quintanilla de las Viñas★** remain, it is of great archaeological importance *(🕐phone for opening hours;* ☎*947 39 20 49).*

Aguilar de Campoo

The Castillo de Aguilar stands on a desolate outcrop typical of this part of the Meseta. Below the castle stretches the medieval old town, with its handsome main square, gateways, walls, and mansions adorned with coats of arms.

▶ **Population:** 7 196
Michelin Map: 575 D 17.
Info: Plaza de España 30. ℘979 12 36 41. www.aguilardcampoo.com.
Location: Aguilar is 115km/71mi NE of Burgos. ▭Calle Camesa de Valdivia
Don't Miss: A drive to the Pico de Tres Mares.
Timing: Take half a day.

SIGHTS
Colegiata de San Miguel
Pl. de España. ◔*Open Holy Week, Jul–15 Sept Tue–Sun 10am–1pm, 5–8pm; 16 Sept–June Mon–Sat 12-1pm, 5–8pm.* ◉€1.50. ℘979 12 26 88.
This Gothic church has Romanesque elements and two fine 16C tombs which bear statues of the Marquesses of Aguilar at prayer. Look for the lifelike sculpted tomb of archpriest García González.

Monasterio de Santa María la Real
Ctra de Cervera. On the edge of town towards Cervera de Pisuerga. ◔ *Open Jul–Aug daily 10.30am–2pm, 4.30–8pm. Sept–Jun Tue–Fri 4–7pm, Sat–Sun and public holidays 10.30am–2pm, 4.30–7.30pm.* ◉€1.80 (museum included). ◉Guided tours €3. ℘979 12 30 53. www.santamarialareal.org.
This fine, thoroughly restored transitional (12C–13C) monastery houses a Romanesque interpretation centre.

🚗 DRIVING TOUR

Pico de Tres Mares via Reinosa
66km/41mi N.

Cross a vast plain and ascend the south face of the Cordillera Cantábrica.

▷ *Follow the A 67.*

Cervatos
The **antigua colegiata**★(◔ *open daily 10am–2pm)*, a Romanesque former collegiate church, bears imaginative carved **decoration**★. The portal tympanum bears a meticulous openwork design. There is a frieze of lions , while varied figures decorate the modillions.
The carving on the capitals and consoles supporting the arch ribs is dense and sophisticated and the 14C nave has intersecting rib vaulting.

▷ *Continue 5km/3mi, then turn right.*

Retortillo
Only an oven-vaulted apse and arch with two finely carved capitals illustrating warriors remain of a small Romanesque **church**. Adjacent are the ruins of a villa of the Roman city of **Julióbriga.**

▷ *Return to the A 67.*

Reinosa
The nearby Embalse del Ebro (a reservoir) and the Alto Campoo ski resort (℘942 77 92 23; www.altocampoo.com) make this a growing tourist centre. 6km/3mi W via the AC 825 is an interpretation centre for Romanesque art (in Villacanti).

▷ *From Reinosa, take the CA 183 to the Pico de Tres Mares (27km/17mi).*

Pico de Tres Mares★★★
On the way, paths from Fontibre lead to a greenish pool, the **source of the Ebro** (Fuente del Ebro), Spain's largest river, at an altitude of 881m/2 890ft.
To the Pico de Tres Mares by chairlift (Dec–Apr). Rivers flow from the peak (2 175m/7 136ft) to three seas. At the crest is a splendid **panorama**★★★.

Palencia

Palencia is a tranquil provincial capital situated in the fertile Tierra de Campos region. It was here that Alfonso VIII created the first Spanish university in 1208. Irrigation of the region has opened up an important horticultural industry.

▶ **Population:** 82 626
Michelin Map: 575 F 16.
Info: Mayor 105.
℘979 74 00 68.
www.palenciaturismo.es.
Location: Palencia is close to the A 62 heading NW to Burgos (88km/55mi) and SE to Valladolid (50km/31mi) and Salamanca (166km/104mi).
Plaza de los Jardinillos.
Don't Miss: The Cathedral.

CATHEDRAL★★

Pl. de la Inmaculada. Open May–Oct 10am–1.30pm, 4.30–7.30pm; Nov–Apr 10am–1.30pm, 4–7pm. €2; €3 with museum; €3 guided tours. ℘979 70 13 47.

Palencia's little-known Cathedral is a 14C–16C Gothic edifice with Renaissance features. The original 7C Visigothic chapel lay forgotten during the Moorish occupation, until Sancho III de Navarra came upon it while hunting.

Interior★★

The Cathedral contains an incredible concentration of art in all the styles of the early 16C: Flamboyant Gothic, Isabelline, Plateresque and Renaissance. The monumental high altar **retable** (early 16C) was carved by Felipe Vigarny, painted by Juan of Flanders and is surmounted by a Crucifix by Juan de Valmaseda.

The 16C tapestries on the sides were commissioned by Bishop Fonseca. The *coro* grille, with a delicately wrought upper section, is by Gaspar Rodríguez (1563); the choir stalls are Gothic, the organ gallery, above, is dated 1716.

The **Capilla del Sagrario** (Chapel of the Holy Sacrament) is exuberantly Gothic with a rich altarpiece by Valmaseda (1529), and the central **triptych**★ is a masterpiece, painted in Flanders by Jan Joest de Calcar in 1505 – the donor, Bishop Fonseca, is shown at its centre.

Museo Catedralicio★

To the right of the west door. Open May–Oct 10am–1.30pm, 4.30–7.30pm; Nov–Apr 10am–1.30pm, 4–7pm. €3. ℘979 70 13 47.

The collection includes a *St Sebastian* by El Greco and four 15C Flemish **tape-**stries★ of the Adoration, the Ascension, Original Sin and the Resurrection of Lazarus.

EXCURSIONS

Iglesia de San Martín de Frómista★★

 29km/18mi NE along the N 611. Open daily Apr–Sept 10am–2pm, 4.30–8pm; Oct–Mar 10am–2pm, 3.30–6.30pm. €1.50. ℘979 81 01 28. www.fromista.com.

Pilgrims on the way to Santiago de Compostela used to stop here. The only vestige of the famous Benedictine **Monasterio de San Martín** is a church, built in 1066, with beautifully matched stone blocks of considerable size. This was a model for many others in the region.

Baños de Cerrato

 14km/8.7mi SE.

 Cross the railway at Venta de Baños; turn right towards Cevico de la Torre. Bear left at the first crossroads.

Iglesia de San Juan Bautista★

 Open Nov–Mar Tue–Sun 10.30am–1.30pm, 5–8pm; Apr–Oct Tue–Sun 10.30am–1.30pm, 4–6pm. €1; no charge Wed. ℘979 77 06 88.

This, the oldest church in Spain, was built by Visigothic King Recceswinth, while he was taking the waters in Baños de Cerrato, in 661.

León★★

León, once the capital of a kingdom, was an important pilgrim stop on the Camino de Santiago and retains fine Romanesque and Gothic monuments.

THE CITY TODAY

León is a lively city, thanks in no small part to its 14 000-strong student population with lots of good places to eat drink and party. The centre of attention by night is the Plaza de San Martin in Barrio Húmedo on the edge of the historic centre. For a more old-fasioned elegant drinking stage try the Plaza Mayor. León is also good for shopping, particularly in its many small arts and crafts and antiques shops.

A BIT OF HISTORY

The medieval town – In the 10C, the kings of Asturias moved their capital from Oviedo to León, and fortified it. By the 11C and 12C León had become virtually the centre of Christian Spain. Ramparts and peeling stucco over old brick in the east of the city recall the early medieval period.

The most evocative quarter, the Barrio Húmedo (the "wet quarter", named for for its proliferation of small bars), lies between the **Plaza Mayor** and the **Plaza de Santa María del Camino**, an attractive square with wooden porticoes.

The modern city – modern León is a sprawling industrial city. But its artistic tradition continues in Gaudí's neo-Gothic palace, **Casa de Botines** on plaza de San Marcelo.

Puerta del Castillo

A good starting point for exploring León is the Puerta del Castillo, the only remaining entrance arch along the ancient city walls.

Built between the 1st and 3rd centuries and rebuilt in the 12th and 15th centuries, the walls originally formed a quadrangle, punctuated by 72 semicircular towers in addition to the eight towers that flanked the entrances. There are now 36, from the Torre de los Ponces

▶ **Population:** 135 119
🕐 **Michelin Map:** 575 E 13.
▯ **Info:** Plaza de la Regla 3.
📞 987 23 70 82.
www.leon.es.
▶ **Location:** León is on the northern edge of the Meseta.
The AP 66 motorway runs north to Oviedo (121km/75mi). Palencia (128km/79.5mi) and Valladolid (139km/86.3mi) are to the southeast.
🚌 Calle Astorga.
👁 **Don't Miss:** The Cathedral.

behind the Plaza Mayor to the tower of San Isidoro.

CATHEDRAL★★★

Pl. Regla. 🕐*Open Jul–Sept Mon–Sat 8.30am–1.30pm, 4–8pm, Sun 8.30am–2.30pm, 5–7pm; Oct–May Mon–Sat 8.30am–1.30pm, 4–7pm, Sun 8.30am–2.30pm, 5–7pm.* 🕐*Closed public holidays.* ⊸*Guide €4; Cloisters €2.* 📞 987 87 57 70.
www.catedraldeleon.org.

The Cathedral, built mainly between the mid-13C and late 14C, is true Gothic in style even to the very high French-inspired nave with vast windows.

The **façade** is pierced by three deeply recessed and richly carved portals. The gently smiling Santa María Blanca *(a copy: original sculpture in the apsidal chapel)* stands at the pier of the central doorway; on the lintel is a Last Judgement.

The left portal tympanum illustrates scenes from the Life of Christ; the right portal includes the Dormition and the Coronation of the Virgin.

The statues decorating the jambs of the central doorway on the south façade are extremely fine.

Inside, the cathedral's outstanding **stained-glass windows**★★★ – 125 windows and 57 oculi with an area of 1 200sq m/12 917sq ft – are unique in Spain; by their sheer number they weaken the walls.

The west front rose and the three central apsidal chapels contain 13C–15C glass; the Capilla de Santiago (St James Chapel) shows Renaissance influence.

The Renaissance **trascoro**★, by Juan de Badajoz, includes four magnificent alabaster high reliefs framing Esteban Jordán's triumphal arch.

The high altar **retable**, painted by Nicolás Francés, is a good example of the 15C international style. To the left is a remarkable **Entombment**★, showing Flemish influence, attributed to the Master of Palanquinos.

A silver reliquary contains the remains of San Froilán, the city patron. Several Gothic tombs can be seen in the ambulatory and transept, in particular that of Bishop Don Rodrigo – in the Virgen del Carmen Chapel to the right of the high altar – which is surmounted by a multifoil arch.

The galleries of the **claustro**★ are contemporary with the 13C–14C nave but the vaulting, with ornate keystones, was added at the beginning of the 16C. The galleries are interesting for the frescoes by Nicolás Francés and for the Romanesque and Gothic tombs.

Museo Catedralicio

Guided tours (1hr) Oct–June Mon–Fri 9.30am–1.30pm, 4–7pm, Sat 9.30am–1.30pm; July–Sept daily 9.30am–1.30pm, 4–7pm. €5 (includes entrance to cloisters).

Among items in the museum are a French-inspired 15C statue of St Catherine, a Christ carved by Juan de Juni in 1576 (meant to be viewed from below), and a Mozarabic Bible. Entrance is by guided tour only, except during the months of July, August and September, when the public is free to wander.

SIGHTS

Real Colegiata de San Isidoro de León★★

Pl. de San Isidoro 4. Open Sept–Jun Mon–Sat 10am–1.30pm, 4–6.30pm, Sun and public holidays 10am–1.30pm; Jul–Aug Mon–Sat 9am–8pm, Sun and public holidays 9am–2pm. Closed 1 Jan, 25 Dec. €4; no charge Thu afternoon. 987 87 50 88. www.sanisidorodeleon.net.

The **basilica**, built into the Roman ramparts, was dedicated in 1063 to Isidore, Archbishop of Sevilla, whose ashes had been brought north for burial in Christian territory. Of the 11C church only the pantheon remains. The apse and transept of the present basilica are Gothic; the balustrade and the pediment on the south front were added during the Renaissance.

Panteón Real★★★

In the Colegiata Real de San Isidoro de León.

The Pantheon is one of the earliest examples of Romanesque architecture

12C frescoes, Panteón Real

in Castilla. The **capitals**★ on the short, thick columns bear traces of the Visigothic tradition yet at the same time exhibit notable advances in sculpture, showing scenes for the first time.

The 12C **frescoes**★★★ are outstanding. They illustrate not only New Testament themes but also country life.

The pantheon is the resting place of 23 kings and queens and many children.

Tesoro★★

Colegiata Real de San Isidoro de León.

The 11C reliquary containing the remains of San Isidoro is made of wood, faced with embossed silver and covered in a Mozarabic embroidery. The famous **Cáliz de Doña Urraca**★ (Doña Urraca chalice) comprises two Roman agate cups mounted in the 11C in a gold setting inlaid with precious stones.

The plaques of the 11C **Arqueta de los Marfiles**★ (Ivory Reliquary) each represent an Apostle. The library contains over 300 incunabula and a 10C Mozarabic Bible.

Convento de San Marcos★ (Former Monastery of St Mark)

Pl. de San Marcos 7. ℘987 23 73 00. www.parador.es.

This former monastery, connected with the Knights of the Order of Santiago (St James) since the 12C, is now a parador. The 100m/328ft long **façade**★★ has a remarkable unity of style in spite of the addition of an 18C Baroque pediment. It has two storeys of windows, niches friezes and cornices, engaged columns, pilasters and medallions in high relief illustrating biblical and Spanish personages. The **church** front (on the extreme right), emblazoned with scallop shells, symbols of the pilgrimage to Santiago de Compostela, remains incomplete.

MUSAC (Museo de Arte Contemporáneo de Castilla y León)

Av. de los Reyes Leoneses 24. ◷Open Tue–Fri 10am–3pm, 5–8pm; Sat, Sun 11am–3pm, 5–9pm. ◷Closed 1 Jan, 25 Dec. ◉No charge. ℘987 09 00 00. http://musac.es.

This evocative building by Mansilla + Muñón, a centre for modern art, is covered in coloured crystals and focuses on living, working artists.

Museo de León★

Pl. de Santo Domingo 8. ◷Open Oct–Jun Tue–Sat 10am–2pm, 4–8pm, Sun and public holidays 10am–2pm; Jul–Sept Tue–Sat 10am–2pm, 5–8pm, Sun and public holidays 10am–2pm. ◉€1.20. ℘987 23 64 05. http://turismo.iranon.org/museodeleon.

This museum displays the 10C Votive Cross of Santiago de Peñalba and an outstanding 11C ivory crucifix, the **Cristo de Carrizo**★★★. Byzantine influence is apparent in the small figure. The **cloister** galleries, built between the 16C and 18C, serve as a lapidary museum. The northeast corner contains a low relief of the Nativity with an interesting architectonic perspective by Juan de Juni. The **sacristy**★ is a sumptuous creation by Juan de Badajoz (1549) with decorated ribbed vaulting.

Casa de Botines★

Pl. de San Marcelo 5. ℘987 29 27 12.

Currently home to the offices of a Spanish bank (and therefore not open to the public), the neo-Gothic Casa de los Botines was one of Gaudí's few buildings outside Catalonia. It was commissioned by wealthy textile firm Fernández y Andrés (its official name is Casa Fernández-Andrés), and construction began in 1891. Impressively, it was completed the following year.

Unlike most of Gaudí's fantastical buildings, it is a heavy, squared-off affair which uses iron pillars inside to give the sensation of light and space. Above the entrance there is a statue of Saint George slaying the dragon by Antonio Cantó and Vicenç Matamala.

In front of the building is a bronze statue of Gaudí, perched upon a bench.

Palacio de los Guzmanes★

Pl. de San Marcelo 6. ◷Open Sept–Jun daily 10am–2pm; July, Aug 10am–2pm, 4–8pm. ◉No charge. ℘987 29 21 01. www.dipuleon.es.

Built in the late 16C by the wealthy and influential Guzmán family, this Renaissance palace is the work of two great architects, Rodrigo Gil de Hontañón (famous for the university buildings in Alcalá de Henares, among others) and Juan del Ribero. Flanked by two towers, and built on three levels, the palace bears heraldic decoration, such as the Guzmáns' shield – a cauldron with snakes crawling out of it – and warriors adorning the front façade either side of the balcony located above the main entrance. There is also a relief of St Agustín washing Christ's feet, and the façade bears various Classical allusions, with Ionic, Doric and Corinthian columns.

The Plateresque patio has a spectacular galleried upper storey, and also of note is a magnificent staircase.

EXCURSIONS
San Miguel de Escalada★

▶ 28km/17.4mi W. Leave León via N 601.
🕙 Open year-round Tue–Sat 10.30am–1.15pm/1.45pm, 4.30–6pm/8pm, Sun and holidays 10.30am–1.15pm/1.45pm.
🕙 Closed 1, 6 Jan, 2 May, 24, 25, 31 Dec.
🚫 No charge.

In the 11C Alfonso III gave this abandoned **monastery** to refugee monks from Córdoba. Today the surviving church is the best-preserved Mozarabic building in Spain.

The **outside gallery★**, built in 1050, has horseshoe-shaped arches resting on carved capitals at the top of smoothly polished columns. An earlier church (**iglesia★**) from 913 has wooden vaulting, and a balustrade of panels carved with Visigothic (birds, grapes) and Moorish (stylised foliage) motifs.

Cuevas de Valporquero★★ (Valporquero Caves)

▶ 47km/29mi N on the LE 311.
📷 Guided tours (1hr 15min) daily Mar–May and Oct–Dec 10am–5pm; Jun–Sept 10am–2pm, 3.30–7pm.
🚫 €6.10. 📞 987 57 64 08.

Neutral lighting sets off extraordinary shapes – there is a stalactite "star" hanging from the roof of the large chamber

Cuevas de Valporquero

© Quim Llenas/Getty Images

– and there are 35 tones of red, grey and black in the mineral oxide-stained stone.

Puebla de Sanabria

Puebla de Sanabria is an attractive mountain village along the A 52 motorway, close to the Embalse de Cernadilla (reservoir), near the Portuguese border. The 15C castle of the Count of Benavente overlooks its white houses and late 12C church.

Valle de Sanabria

▶ 19km/11.8mi NW. Follow the lake road; turn right after 14km/8.7mi; after a further 6km/3.7mi turn left.

This valley of glacial origin, now a nature reserve, was hollowed out at the foot of the Sierras de Cabrera Baja and Segundera. It is a delightful area, well known for its hunting and fishing.

Lago de Sanabria is the largest glacial lake in Spain, at 1 028m/3 373ft. It is used for water sports, and for salmon-trout fishing.

There are attractive **views★** of the rushing Tera and the mountain-encircled lake all the way to the Galician-looking village of **San Martín de Casteñada**, with an 11C Romanesque **church** (Pl. de la Iglesia; 📞 980 62 67 55).

Mediterranean Spain

La Pedrera/Casa Milà, Barcelona
©Turespaña

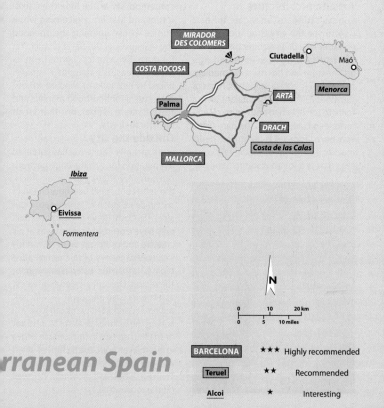

BARCELONA AND AROUND

Barcelona – the capital of Catalunya and favourite Spanish city of foreign visitors – shows no signs of flagging in the popularity stakes. It really is one of the few metropolises in the world that is all things to all people: atmospheric cobbled streets lined with cosmopolitan boutiques; medieval and Modernist masterpieces; art galleries and museums; colourful street theatre; beaches and buzzing restaurants, bars and nightlife. If it all gets a little too much, its revamped coastline and serene hinterland can provide some sun-kissed downtime.

Highlights

1 Barcelona's atmospheric **Barri Gòtic** and **Cathedral** (p314)

2 The roof terrace of Gaudí's **La Pedrera/Casa Milà** (p319)

3 Strolling the 19C splendour of the **Eixample** (p. 319)

4 Admiring the wealth of artworks at the **MNAC** (p328)

5 Getting away from it on the beach at **Sitges** (p 334)

Art and architecture

Compact and easy to navigate, the best way to see the city is on foot. This is certainly true of its architectural assets. The city has long been endeared with architecture and has used the medium to make civic improvements at times of prosperity. When feisty Catalans were a force to be reckoned with on the Mediterranean trade routes, the Barri Gòtic was born. Today it is an atmospheric, moody ensemble of Medieval buildings that is a joy to wander. Similarly, the *modernisme* period, with its keynote buildings by Antoni Gaudí, was ushered in when Catalans started a brisk trade with the newly discovered Americas. Barcelona's museums are world class. The one-time resident Pablo Picasso bequeathed an extensive collection of his early work while Joan Miró's purpose-built museum illustrates the genius of this groundbreaking abstract surrealist. A millennium's-worth of Catalan art, from ancient Romanesque frescoes to modernista decorative pieces can be seen at the MNAC. Spaces showcasing some of the world's best contemporary art include the Caixa-forum and MACBA, a gleaming white edifice whose opening spearheaded the makeover of the Raval district. Yet for most, Barcelona's charms lie in its smaller pleasures: delightful squares linked by networks of winding streets, colourful neighbourhood markets and the palatable exuberance that locals have for their city.

Outside the city

More recently Catalunya has garnered a reputation for cutting-edge gastronomy, mainly thanks to Ferran Adrià, the self-taught chef and figurehead of *cocina de vanguardia* (avant-garde cuisine). His Costa Brava restaurant El Bulli may have closed while Adrià was at his creative and professional peak, but his influence is everywhere, from creative tapas bars to haute-eateries throughout the region. One of Barcelona's greatest assets is its ease of escape. An efficient regional transport network can have you scaling the bulbous peaks of Montserrat or soaking up rays in fashionable Sitges in less than an hour. A little further afield and you are in the Catalan heartland of Terrassa, a bustling provincial city well off the tourist trail.

Sagrada Família lit up at night

©Turespaña

Barcelona★★★

Combining urban sophistication with Mediterranean warmth, Barcelona is open and welcoming, melding both tradition and the avant-garde.

THE CITY TODAY

Barcelona is not only southern Europe's most popular city, it is also an industrial centre and major port, a university town and seat of the Generalitat de Catalunya government. Moreover, it has a thriving cultural life for its own citizens with an opera house, theatres and concert halls. In all but name it is a capital city.

The 1992 Olympic Games brought large-scale planning projects that radically changed the face of Barcelona, and since then the city regeneration and improvements have continued apace. The Forum of Cultures in 2004 led to the redevelopment of the Sant Adrià del Besòs waterfront.

A BIT OF HISTORY

The growth of the city – Founded by the Phocaeans, the city grew as Roman **Barcino**, within a 3C fortified wall. In the 12C, Barcelona became the capital of Catalunya and seat of the expanding kingdom of Aragón-Catalunya. Catalan Gothic architecture blossomed.

Catalunya sided with the Archduke of Austria in the War of the Spanish Succession (1701–14), and in defeat lost its autonomy. Montjuïc hill was fortified by the victors, and construction was prohibited except in the old city. Building outside the walls began again in the mid-19C. Industrialisation followed, along with two International Exhibitions, in 1888 and 1929. Modernist architecture flowered.

Catalan identity and cultural life – Catalan, banned under the Franco regime, is the language along with Castilian Spanish, used on all street names and in literature. Painters Picasso, Miró, Dalí, Tàpies, sculptor Subirachs and the architects Gaudí, Josep Lluís Sert, Bofill and Bohigas all lived here. Barcelona remains a hub for great artists.

▶ **Population:** 1 615 908
⊙ **Michelin Map:** 574 H 36 (town plan) – map 122 Costa Brava. Michelin City Plans Barcelona 40, 41 and 2040 – Catalunya (Barcelona).

🛈 **Info:** Pl. de Catalunya 17; Ciutat 2 (Pl. de Sant Jaume); Pl. dels Països Catalans (Estació de Sants); Rambla dels Estudis 115 (Cabina Rambla); Pl. Portal de la Pau (Mirador de Colom). www.barcelonaturisme.com.

⊙ **Location:** Seaside Barcelona is the hub of northeastern Spain. The AP 7 motorway runs from Murcia to Girona and France; the C32 heads to the resorts to the north and south to Tarragona; the C 16 veers inland to Manresa (59km/37mi NE) and the C 17 to Vic. 🚆Plaça Canonge Rodó (Clot Aragó); Av. Marquès de l'Argentera (Estació de França); Pas. de Gràcia; Pl. de Catalunya Estació; Pl. Estació (Sant Andreu Comptal); Pl. dels Països Catalans (Sants).

🅿 **Parking:** Don't even think about driving in Barcelona. Use the excellent Bus Turistic to get about (www.tmb.net/en_US/turistes/busturistic/busturistic.jsp).

👓 **Don't Miss:** Sagrada Família church and Modernist masterpieces of architecture along Passeig de Gràcia.

🕓 **Timing:** Start from the Gothic Quarter, and see the Ramblas, Passeig de Gràcia and Sagrada Família before all else.

👫 **Kids:** El Poble Espanyol; Parc Güell; the Aquarium; the Chocolate Museum.

GETTING THERE

Airport – *℘902 40 47 04.*
www.aena.es. 18km/11mi from the city centre. Can be reached by local train from Terminal 2 (*Línea 2, Cercanías; ℘900 202 220*) every 30min from 5.32am to 11.38pm, or by the bus service from the Plaça de Catalunya and Plaça d'Espanya, departing every 15min from 5.30am to 12.15am (*€5; ℘902 07 50 27*). By taxi, the fare from the city centre will be approximately €25

Taxis – The city's black and yellow taxis are an efficient, inexpensive way of getting around the city. Radio Taxi Barcelona: *℘932 25 00 00* Radio Taxi 033: *℘933 03 30 33 (www.taxibarcelona.cat).*

Metro – *Metro stations are shown on the maps in this guide (⊜).* For further information: *℘902 07 50 27* or visit www.tmb.net. Information on access for the disabled can be obtained on *℘934 12 44 44.*
The network is open Mon–Thu and Sun 5am–midnight; Fri 5am–2am; Sat and days preceding public holidays 24 hours. A free metro guide is available.
Metro **tickets and cards** can also be used on buses, the "Tramvía Blau" (a tourist tram in the Diagonal section of the city) and train services operated by Ferrocarriles de la Generalitat de Catalunya. In addition to single tickets, multi-journey cards include the T-1 (valid for ten trips), T-DIA (unlimited travel for one day), T50/30 (50 trips in 30 days) and the T-MES (unlimited travel for one month).

Tram/Streetcars – There are four lines (T1, T2, T3 and T4).

Regional railway network – *Ferrocarriles Catalanes train stations are shown on the maps in this guide (℘932 05 15 15; www.fgc.cat).* Free connections to the metro system may be made at these stations: Avinguda Carrilet /L'Hospitalet, Espanya, Catalunya and Diagonal/Provença.

Bus Turístic – This excellent service offers visitors a variety of bus itineraries throughout the city. Daily departures from Plaça de Catalunya starting at 9am (*€23 1 day; €27 2 days*).

Boat trips – The Las Golondrinas company organises trips around the port *(approx 35min)*. Departures from Portal de la Pau, opposite the Columbus monument. *℘934 42 31 06. www.lasgolondrinas.com.*

SIGHTSEEING

Publications – The **Guía del Ocio** (*www.guiadelociobcn.com*) is a weekly guide on sale at newspaper stands containing a list of every cultural event in the city. The city's airport and tourist offices are also able to provide visitors with a full range of booklets and leaflets produced by the Generalitat de Catalunya's Department of Industry, Commerce and Tourism.

COMBINED TICKETS AND DISCOUNTS

Barcelona Card: (2, 3, 4 or 5 days; €27.50/€33.50/€38/€45) gives unlimited transport, discounts from 20% to 50% or free entry for dozens of museums, shows, shops, transportation and restaurants. On sale at the city's tourist offices. For further information: *℘932 853 832; www.barcelonaturisme.com.*

Articket: Valid six months, cost 25€, for entry to CCCB, Fundació Antoni Tàpies, La Pedrera, Fundació Joan Miró, MNAC, MACBA and the Museu Picasso: *℘932 853 832; www.barcelonaturisme.com.*

Arqueoticket: Valid one year, €14, for entry to: Museu d'Arqueologia de Catalunya, Museu Barbier-Mueller d'Art Precolombí, Museu Egipci de Barcelona and Museu d'Història de la Ciutat de Barcelona.
For information: *℘932 853 832; www.barcelonaturisme.com.*

Ruta del Modernisme: A Route pack including a guidebook and discount booklet offering discounts of up to 50% to the Modernist buildings in Barcelona, exploring the works of

Gaudí, Domènech i Montaner and Puig i Cadafalch. ✏18 *(available from the tourist office in Plaça Catalunya. ☎933 17 76 52. www.rutadelmodernisme.com).*

DISTRICTS

Barri Gòtic – Following an intense restoration programme undertaken during the 1920s, the area containing the city's major historical buildings was renamed the Gothic quarter.

Ciutat Vella – The old city includes districts as diverse as Santa Anna, La Mercè, Sant Pere and El Raval. The last, which used to be known as the Barri Xino (Chinatown), now contains Barcelona's leading cultural centres and is a fine example of urban renovation.

Eixample – Eixample (Ensanche) developed following the destruction of the city's medieval walls. The district personifies the bourgeois, elegant Barcelona of the end of the 19C, with its prestigious boutiques, smart avenues and some of the best examples of Modernist architecture.

Gràcia – This *barrio*, situated at the end of the Passeig de Gràcia, is one of the city's most characterful areas. Gràcia developed from its early agricultural origins into an urban area as a result of the influx of shopkeepers, artisans and factory workers. During the 19C, Gràcia was renowned for its Republican sympathies. Today, it still hosts a number of popular fiestas.

Ribera – With its narrow alleyways and Gothic architecture, this former mercantile quarter still retains an un-questionable charm, paticularly in the EL Born district near the port. Its main attractions are the Carrer Montcada (location of the Picasso Museum) and the Església de Santa Maria del Mar.

Barceloneta – Barceloneta is famous for its outdoor stalls, restaurants and nautical atmosphere.

Vila Olímpica – The Olympic Village was built to accommodate sportsmen and sportswomen participating in the 1992 games. Nowadays, it is a modern district with wide avenues, landscaped areas and direct access to some of Barcelona's restored beaches.

Les Corts – This district is located at the upper end of Diagonal and includes the **Ciudad Universitaria** and the **Camp Nou**, the home of Barcelona Football Club and its football-orientated **Museu FC Barcelona** *(www.fcbarcelona.com)*.

Sarrià – Sarrià nestles at the foot of the Serra de Collserola and has managed to retain its traditional, tranquil character. The neighbouring districts of **Pedralbes** and **Sant Gervasi de Cassoles**, at the foot of Tibidabo, have become a favourite hangout for the city's well-heeled inhabitants.

Sants – One of the city's main working-class districts close to the railway station of the same name.

Horta-Guinardó – This *barrio* at the foot of Collserola was first populated by peasants and then by factory workers. It is home to the **Laberinto de Horta** (to the north), an 18C property with attractive gardens, and the **Velódromo**, a venue for sporting events and major music events.

Poble Sec – Nestled at the foot of Montjuïc – the city's garden and museum belt – Poble Sec is a cozy neighbourhood of pretty 19C apartment buildings and outdoor cafés.

⊘ *Beware of pickpockets at all times and never let your belongings out of your sight.*

Castilian vs Catalan: Common Spelling Differences

Ayuntamiento	Ajuntament
Avenida	Avinguda
Calle	Carrer
Capella	Capella
Iglesia	Església
Paseo	Passeig
Plaza	Plaça

🐾 WALKING TOUR

BARRI GÒTIC★★

The Gothic quarter, named for the many buildings constructed between the 13C and 15C, holds traces of Roman settlement and massive 4C walls.

Plaça Nova

This is the heart of the quarter, where the Romans built an enclosure with walls 9m/29.5ft high. Two watchtowers that flanked the West Gate (converted to a house in the Middle Ages) remain. Opposite the Cathedral, the **Col.legi d'Arquitectes** (College of Architects; *Pl. Nova amb carrer del Bisbe*) is a contemporary building with a facade etched with a mural designed by d by Picasso.

▷ *To the left of the Architect's College, take a fews steps along Carrer Arcs.*

Dalí Barcelona

Arcs 5. ○Open daily 10am–10pm. ⊗€8 ☏933 181 774. www.dalibarcelona.com
The headquarters of the city's Real Círculo Artístico is the impressive Palacio Pignatelli excecuted in a faux-Gothic style (it was actually built in 1968). Two floors take up this permanent exhibition that goes under the name of Dalí Barcelona. Don't expect any paintings, but rather some 40 sculptures Salvador Dalí rendered in the 1970s, including the *Cosmic Elephant* (1974). The show is accompanied by preparatory drawings and watercolours, ceramics, photographs of the artist and models.

▷ *Return to Plaça Nova.*

Catedral Santa Eulàlia★

Pl. de la Seu. ○Open Summer Mon–Fri 8am–12.45pm, 5.15–7.30pm; rest of the year Mon–Sat 1pm–5pm, Sun 2–5pm ⊗€5. ☏933 42 82 60. www.catedralbcn.org.
The cathedral is on **Plaça de la Seu**, marked on one side by the **Casa de l'Ardiaca★** (👆 *see p315*), and on the other by the **Casa de la Canonja** (16C) and **pia Almoina**, which house the

Museu Diocesà de Barcelona (*Av. de la Catedral 4; ○open Tue–Sat 10am–2pm, 5–8pm, Sun and public holidays 11am–2pm; ○closed 1 Jan, 25–26 Dec; ⊗€6; ☏933 15 22 13*).

The cathedral was built on the site of a Romanesque church, from the late 13C to 1450. The façade and spire are 19C, based on old French designs.

The Catalan Gothic **interior★** has an outstanding elevation with slender pillars. The nave is lit by a fine lantern-tower; the perspective is broken by the **coro★★**, with double rows of beautifully carved **stalls**. Note the humorous scenes adorning the misericords. In the early 16C, the backs were painted with the coats of arms of knights of the Order of the Golden Fleece by Juan de Borgoña, in one of the most impressive achievements of European heraldry.

The side chapels hold exquisite retables and marble tombs. The white marble **choir screen★** was sculpted in the 16C after drawings by Bartolomé Ordóñez. Statues illustrate the martyrdom of St Eulàlia, patron of Barcelona. Her relics lie in the **crypt★** in a 14C Pisan-style alabaster sarcophagus.

The Capella del Santísimo (*right of the entry*) contains the 15C *Christ of Lepanto*, said to have been on the prow of the galley of Don Juan of Austria in the Battle of Lepanto (1571). In the next chapel is a Gothic retable by Bernat Martorell, also the artist of the **retable of the Transfiguration★** in the ambulatory.

Cathedral roof visit – *by lift from an ambulatory chapel*. Metal walkways under the imposing silhouettes of the cathedral towers and cupola allow exceptional **views★★** of the city.

The **cloisters★** are an oasis, and are home to a flock of geese. In the chapter house, a museum houses a *Pietà* by Bermejo (1490), altarpiece panels by the 15C artist Jaime Huguet and the missal of St Eulàlia, enhanced by delicate miniatures.

▷ *Facing the façade of the Cathedral, turn right into Carrer Sant Llúcia.*

Casa de l'Ardiaca★

Santa Llúcia 1. ⏰Open Sept–Jun Mon–
Fri 9am–8.45pm, Sat 9am–1pm; Jul–Aug
Mon–Fri 9am–7.30pm. ☎933 18 11 95.
Constructed in the 12C and altered in
the 15C, the Archdeacon's House (now
housing Arxiu Històric de la Ciutat or Historical City Archives) combines Gothic
and Renaissance elements.

▷ *Turn left into the Carrer del Bisbe*
and take the first right.

Plaça de Sant Felip Neri

Pl. de Sant Felip Neri 5.
The Renaissance houses on this square
were moved here when via Laietana was
built. The **Museu del Calçat** (footwear
museum) includes Columbus' shoes.
(⏰ *open Tue–Sun and public holidays*
11am–2pm; ⬤€2.50; ☎933 01 45 33).

▷ *Return to Carrer del Bisbe.*

Carrer del Bisbe

To the left is the side wall of the Palau de
la Generalitat (Provincial Council).
Above a door is a fine early 15C medallion of St George by Pere Johan. On the
right side is the **Casa dels Canonges**
(Canons' Residence), residence of the
President of the Generalitat.
A neo-Gothic covered gallery (1929),
over a star-vaulted arch, links the two.

▷ *Continue along Carrer del Bisbe.*

Plaça Sant Jaume

This handsome square, once the main-
crossroads of the old Roman city, is the
hub of Catalan political life and major
celebrations (and protests) take place
here.

Palau de la Generalitat

Pl. de Sant Jaume 4. ⏰Open to the
public 23 Apr, 24 Sept, 11 Sept.
⟿Guided tours (50min) 2nd and 4th
Sat–Sun of each month, 10.30am–
1.30pm. ⬤No charge; email booking
required. http://www.gencat.cat/
generalitat/cas/guia/palau/visites.htm.

This vast 15C–17C edifice is the seat
of the Autonomous Government of
Catalunya. It has a Renaissance-style
façade on Plaça de Sant Jaume (c. 1600).

Ajuntament (Town Hall)

Pl. de Sant Jaume 1. ⟿Guided
tours Sun 10am–1.30pm, 23 Apr
10am–6.30pm. ⬤No charge. ☎934 02
70 00. www.bcn.cat.
The town hall façade on Plaça Sant
Jaume is Neoclassical; that on Carrer de
la Ciutat is an outstanding 14C Gothic
construction.

▷ *Cross Plaça St. Jaume, turn left.*

Carrer del Paradis

At no. 10 stand four Roman **columns**★,
remains of the Temple of Augustus
(same hours as MUHBA, see below; ⬤ no
charge). Carrer Paradis leads into Carrer
de la Pietat, bordered on the left by the
Gothic façade of the Casa dels Canonges. The Cathedral cloister doorway
opposite is adorned with a wooden 16C
sculpture of a *Pietà*.

▷ *Turn right into the Baixada de*
Sant Clara.

Plaça del Rei★★

On this splendid square stand the Palau
Reial Major (at the back), the **Capella de
Santa Àgata** (right) and the **Palau del
Lloctinent**. In the right corner, the Casa
Clariana-Padellàs, housing the **Museu
d'Història de Barcelona (MUHBA)★★**,
is a 15C Gothic mansion moved stone by
stone when the via Laietana was built
in 1931.

Museu d'Història de Barcelona (MUHBA)★★

Pl. del Rei s/n. ⏰Open April–end Oct
Tue–Sat 10am–7pm, Sun 10am–8pm;
Nov–end March Tue–Sat 10am–5pm,
Sun 10am–8pm. ⏰Closed 1 Jan, 1 May,
24 Jun & 25 Dec. ⬤€7. ☎932 56 21 00.
www.museuhistoria.bcn.es.
The visit includes Roman remains, and
outbuildings of the Palau Reial Major.

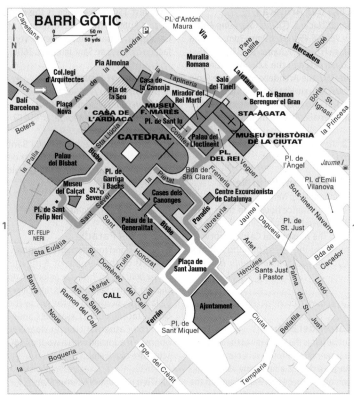

The Roman city★★★

Under the museum and Plaça del Rei are Roman foundations, drainage, and reservoirs. In adjoining vaulted rooms are sculptures from the 1C–4C (busts of Agrippina, Faustina and Antoninus Pius). Two 13C Gothic frescoes were uncovered in the Sala Jaime I in 1998.

Palau Reial Major

Built in the 11C and 12C, the palace acquired its present appearance in the 14C. It was the seat of the counts of Barcelona and the kings of Aragón.

Arches link huge buttresses in the façade; the original façade has rose windows.

The lofty 14C **Saló del Tinell**, 17m/56ft high, is topped with a double-sloped ceiling set on six monumental arches. It is said that the Catholic Monarchs welcomed Columbus here after his first voyage.

Capella de Santa Àgata★★

This 14C palatine chapel is covered by intricate polychrome woodwork pan-elling.

The **Altarpiece of the Constable**★★ by Jaime Huguet (1465) depicts the life of Jesus and the Virgin Mary.

In the centre, the *Adoration of the Three Wise Men* is a Catalan masterpiece.

A staircase leads to the **Mirador del Rei Martí**, a five-storey tower with a lovely **view**★★ of the old city (*currently closed for renovations*).

▷ *Return to the Baixada de Sant Clara and turn right into the Carrer Comtes.*

Palau del Lloctinent

This 16C late-Gothic palace was the resi-dence of the viceroys of Catalunya.

▷ *Continue on the Carrer Comtes.*

Museu Frederic Marès★

Pl. de Sant Lu 5–6. ⏰*Open Tue–Sat 10am–7pm, Sun 11am–8pm, public holidays 10am–3pm.* ⬡*€4.20; no charge first Sun in month, every Sun from 3pm.* 📞*923 56 35 00. www.museumares.bcn.cat.*

The threshold to this wonderfully eccentric museum is on the tiny **Plaça de Sant Lu**, which is always full of mime artists and street musicians. The collections were left to the city by sculptor Frederic Marès (1893–1991).

Sculpture Section – The works on two floors and in the crypt are in chronological order from the Iberian period to the 19C. Note the **Christs and Calvaries**★ in polychrome wood (12C–14C), Romanesque and Gothic **Virgins with Child**★; a 16C **Holy Entombment**★ and **The Vocation of St Peter**★, an expressive 12C relief attributed to the master Cabestany.

Gabinete del Coleccionista – Everyday objects, mainly 19C, include items from recreational rooms, the smoking parlour and the women's boudoir (spectacles, fans, clothes, etc.).

▷*Return to Plaça de la Seu. Turn right into Carrer Tapinera and follow it to the end.*

Plaça de Ramon Berenguer el Gran

From the Plaça, Roman walls are visible, incorporated into the Palau Reial.

🐾 WALKING TOUR

LA RAMBLA★★

The most famous promenade in Barcelona, La Rambla's five sections follow an old riverbed bordering the Gothic quarter.

La Rambla separates the Eixample district from the old quarter, and is alive at all hours with locals, tourists and down-and-outs and vendors.

The upper section, by Plaça de Catalunya, is Rambla de Canaletes, followed by Rambla dels Estudis or Rambla dels Ocells (Avenue of the Birds).

▷ *Walk S (towards the port) and stop at the corner of Carrer Portaferrisa.*

Palau Moja

The former home of poet Jacinto Verdaguer (1845–1902), is a Baroque palace dating from the late 18C. It houses a great bookshop specialising in Catalan history and culture on the ground floor.

▷ *Continue walking southwards.*

Església de Betlem

La Rambla 107. ⬡*No charge.*

This Baroque church – the interior was razed by a fire in 1936 – has retained its imposing façade, facing Carrer Carme.

▷ *Walk in the same direction to the corner of Carrer Carme and turn right.*

Antic Hospital de la Santa Creu

Hospital 56.

These Gothic, Baroque and Neoclassical buildings are a haven in this district. An ex-hospital is the Library of Catalunya. A charming planted **Gothic patio**★ (Jardines de Rubio y Lluch) can be reached through a hall decorated with *azulejos*.

▷ *Return to La Rambla.*

Rambla de les Flors

This stretch of La Ramblas is so-named for the abundance of flower stalls here, a scene that has been immortalised by many local painters, particularly from the *Modernisme* period.

Palau de la Virreina★

La Rambla 99. 📞*933 16 10 00. www.bcn.cat/virreinacentredelaimatge.*

The elegant 1778 palace of the Vicereine of Peru, with Baroque and Rococo decorations, hosts major exhibitions. Alongside is the traditional Mercat (market) de Sant Josep (La Boqueria). Down La Rambla on the right side stands the city's opera house, the **Gran Teatre del Liceu**★ (*La Rambla 51–59;* 📞*934 85 99 00; www.liceubarcelona.com*), rebuilt after a 1994 fire. Opposite lies **Plaça de**

317

la Boqueria, a charming esplanade whose pavement was decorated by the artist Joan Miró.

▷ *Turn left into Carrer Cardenal Casañes.*

Església de Santa Maria del Pi★

Pl. del Pi 7. ⏰*Open daily 9.30am–1pm, 5–7.30pm.* ☏*933 18 47 43. www.parroquiadelpi.com.*

This 14C Catalan Gothic church on a square is striking for its simplicity and the size of its single nave.

Palau Güell★★

Nou de la Rambla 3. ⏰*Open Apr–end Sept Tue–Sun 10am–8pm; rest of the year Tue–Sun 10am–5.30pm.* ⏰*Closed Dec 25, 26, Jan 1, 6–13.* ☞€10. ☏*934 725 775. www.palauguell.cat.*

Gaudí designed the Güell residence (1886–90). Note the parabolic entry arches and the extravagant bars typical of the Modernist movement. The most striking interior features are the **grand hall** and the innovative use of materials and the treatment of light as a design element of each space.

La Rambla meets the sea at **La Rambla de Santa Mònica**. The former **Convent de Santa Mònica** *(no. 7;* ⏰*open Tue –Fri 2–9pm, Sat, Sun and public holidays 11am–7pm;* ☞ *no charge;* ☏ *935 67 11 10; www.artssantamonica.cat)* is a modern arts centre that hosts exhibitions. The wax museum **(Museu de Cera)** is here *(Pas. de la Banca 7;* ⏰*open Mon–Fri 10am–1.30pm, 4–7.30pm, Sat-Sun and public holidays 11am–2pm, 4.30–7.30pm; summer daily 10am–10pm;* ☞€15, children €9; ☏*933 17 26 49; ww.museocerabcn.com).*

Plaça Reial★★

This vast pedestrian square shaded by palms and lined with cafés is surrounded by Neoclassical buildings. Gaudí designed the lampposts by the fountain. A stamp and coin market is held on Sunday mornings.

Monument a Colom

Pl. Portal de la Pau. ⏰*Open daily 8.30am–8.30pm.* ⏰*Closed 1 Jan, 25 Dec.* ☞€4. ☏ *933 02 52 24.*

This 1886 monument commemorates the return of the great navigator. A lift to the top gives a fantastic view over the city.

ADDITIONAL SIGHTS

Museu d'Art Contemporàni de Barcelona (MACBA)★★

Pl. dels Àngels 1. ⏰*Open 25 Sept–23 Jun Mon, Wed–Fri 11am–7.30pm, Sat 10am–8pm, Sun and public holidays 10am–3pm; 24 Jun–24 Sept Mon and Wed 11am–8pm, Thu–Fri 11am–8pm, Sat 10am–8pm, Sun and public holidays 10am–3pm.* ⏰*Closed 1 Jan, 25 Dec.* ☞€7.50. ☏ *934 12 08 10. www.macba.es.*

The monumental **building**★★, designed by American architect Richard Meyer, fuses the rationalist Mediterranean tradition with contemporary architecture. Two significant works can be found outside: *La Ola* by Jorge Oteiza and Eduardo Chillida's mural, *Barcelona* (☞*see Sights)*. The **standing collections**★ in pristine white halls cover major artistic movements of the past 50 years. Exhibits include works influenced by Constructivism and Abstract art (Klee, Oteiza, Miró, Calder, Fontana), as well as creations by experimental artists (Kiefer, Boltanski, Solano) and names of the 1980s (Hernández, Pijuán, Barceló, Tàpies, Ràfols Casamada, Sicilia).

Centre de Cultura Contemporània de Barcelona (CCCB)

Montalegre 5. ⏰*Open Tue–Wed, Fri–Sun 11am–8pm, Thu 11am–10pm. Ticket desks close 30min before museum.* ⏰*Closed 1 Jan, 25 Dec.* ☞€5. *www.cccb.org.*

This centre of art exhibitions, near MACBA, is in restored premises. Its **patio**★ combines original mosaics and silk-screen floral motifs with striking modern elements, such as a soaring wall of mirrored glass.

WALKING TOUR★★

L'EIXAMPLE AND MODERNIST ARCHITECTURE

Barcelona's Eixample (or enlargement) grew in the 19C. In Ildefons Cerdà's 1859 grid plan, streets circumscribe blocks of houses (*mançanes* in Catalan or *manzanas* in Castilian) octagonal in shape with trimmed corners. Wide avinguda Diagonal and La Meridiana cross the grid to meet on Plaça de les Glòries Catalanes. In this ordered new section, architects transformed L'Eixample into the centre of Modernism in Barcelona.

Plaça de Catalunya

This vast square is considered the centre of the city and acts as a link between the old town and Eixample. Always lively, it is Barcelona's principal transport hub and is lined with well-known department stores, the city's main tourist office and the octogenarian Café Zurich – a popular people watching spot.

▷ *Head N along the Passeig de Gràcia to Carrer Aragó and turn left.*

Fundació Antoni Tàpies★★

Aragó 255. ⏱*Open Tue–Sun 10am–7pm.* ⏱*Closed 1, 6 Jan, 25 Dec.* 👁€7. 📞*934 87 03 15. www.fundaciotapies.org.*
Tàpies established his foundation in an ex-publishing house designed by Domènech i Montaner. The brick building is crowned by a sculpture by Tàpies, *Núvol i Cadira* (cloud and chair), the emblem of the museum.
The newly renovated interior, where white walls are contrasted with original wooden detailing, is lit by skylights (a cupola and a pyramid). Paintings and sculptures trace the development of Tàpies' work since 1948.

▷ *Continue N along the Passeig de Gràcia to Carrer Valencia and turn left.*

Museu Egipci de Barcelona – Fundació Arqueològic Clos

Valencia, 284. ⏱*Open Mon–Sat 10am–2pm, Sun and hols 10am–2pm.*

⏱*Closed 1 Jan, 25-26 Dec.* 👁€11. 📞*934 88 01 88. www.museuegipci.com.*
This interesting private museum has about 600 pieces representing various periods of Egyptian civilization, in addition to some pieces from the Roman period.

▷*Return to Passeig de Gràcia.*

Passeig de Gràcia★★

Along this boulevard, with elegant wrought-iron **street lamps**★ by Pere Falqués (1900), lies some of Barcelona's finest Modernist architecture, in the **Manzana de la Discordia**★★ (Block of Discord): no. 35 **Casa Lleó Morera**★ (1905) by Domènech i Montaner, no. 41 **Casa Amatller**★ (1900) by Puig i Cadafalch (now the Instituto Amatller; *guided tours only, Mon–Fri hourly from 10am–6pm;* 👁€10; 📞*934 96 12 45; www.amatller.org*), and no. 43 **Casa Batlló**★★ (1904–06) by Gaudí, with its extraordinary mosaic façade and undulating roof (⏱*open daily 9am–8pm;* 👁€18.15; 📞*932 16 03 06; www.casabatllo.es*).

▷ *Continue in the same direction until you reach the corner of Carrer Provença.*

La Pedrera or Casa Milà★★★

Provença 261–265. ⏱*Open daily Nov–Feb 9am–6.30pm (last admission 6pm); Mar–Oct 9am–8pm.* ⏱*Closed 1, 6 Jan, 25–26 Dec.* 👁€14. 📞*902 40 09 73. www.lapedreraeducacio.org.*
With its undulating lines, this magnificent Gaudí building resembles a submarine cliff. Visit the **roof and attic**★ and a **residential floor**★.
The **Espai Gaudí** exhibits drawings and models by the artist. The roof, with its forest of chimneys, provides fine **views**★.
El Piso★ is a re-created apartment of an early 20C upper-class family.

▷ *Continue along the Passeig de Gràcia to the busy Avinguda Diagonal and turn right.*

Avinguda Diagonal

Palau Baró de Quadras (1904; ○*open Tue–Sat 10am–8pm, Sun and public holidays 10am–2pm; ⊛no charge; www. casaasia.es*), a Modernist building on the right (no. 373), was designed by Puig i Cadafalch and now houses a foundation for Asian art and culture.

Along on the left (no. 416), his **Casa de les Punxes (Casa Terrades★)** bears the stamp of Flemish influence.

▷ *Continue along the Diagonal to the intersection of Carrer Mallorca. Continue along Carrer Mallorca in the same direction.*

La Sagrada Família★★★ (Church of the Holy Family)

Mallorca 401. ○Open daily Oct–Mar 9am–6pm; Apr–Sept 9am–8pm; 25–26 Dec, 1, 6 Jan 9am–2pm. ⊛€12.50, €14.50 (combined with Casa-Museu Gaudí). ⬥Guided tours in Eng. (50min) daily Nov–May 11am, 1pm; June–Oct 11am, noon, 1pm, €16.50. ℘932 08 04 14. www.sagradafamilia.cat.

The project, begun in 1882, was taken over by Gaudí in 1883. He planned a Latin Cross church with five aisles and a transept with three aisles. Three façades were each to be dominated by four spires representing the Apostles with a central spire to represent Christ and the Evangelists. The nave was to be a forest of columns. In his lifetime, only the crypt, the apsidal walls, one of the towers and the **Nativity façade★★** were finished. The Nativity façade comprises three doorways, Faith, Hope and Charity. Work resumed in 1940. The Passion façade was completed in 1981.

The top of the east spire affords a good **view★★** of the work on the church, and of Barcelona. Domènech i Montaner's **Hospital Sant Pau★** (*Sant Antoni Maria Claret 167; ○info office open daily 10am–1.30pm; ℘ 933 17 76 52*), with its remarkable glazed tile roofs, may be seen at the end of Avinguda de Gaudí.

ADDITIONAL SIGHTS

L' Auditori

Lepant 150. ℘93 247 93 00. www.auditori.cat.

This state-of-the-art concert hall was designed by the Pritzker prize-winning architect Rafael Moneo in 1999 and hosts classical and jazz performances. The Museu de la Música – a wonderful collection of period instruments – is located inside (*○ open Mon, Wed–Sat 10am*

Modernist Architecture

Modernism developed between 1890 and 1920 alongside similar movements in other parts of Europe, such as Art Nouveau in both France and Great Britain, and Jugendstil in Germany. Modernist architecture sprang from artistic exploration that combined new industrial materials with modern techniques, using decorative motifs like curve and counter-curve and asymmetrical shapes in stained glass, ceramics and metal. The Catalan cultural movement of *modernsime* was an expression of the region's striving for independence at a time when large fortunes were being made as a result of industrialisation, with designs frequently containing hints and symbols of Catalan identity. The most representative architects of the style were Antoni Gaudí, Domènech i Montaner, Puig i Cadafalch and Jujol. A parallel movement in Catalan literature known as Renaixença also flourished during this period. The mixture of regional and foreign architectural tradition in the work of **Josep Puig i Cadafalch** (1867–1956) reflects the Plateresque and Flemish styles. His main works are the Casa de les Punxes, the Casa Macaya (1901) and the Palau Baró de Quadras (1904). **Lluís Domènech i Montaner** (1850–1923) attained his highly decorative style through extensive use of mosaics, stained glass and glazed tiles. His main works include the Palau de la Música Catalana and Castell dels Tres Dragons.

Parc Güell

Ph. Robic/MICHELIN

−6pm, Sun 10.30am–2.30pm; €4; 932 65 01 02; www.museumusica.bcn.cat).

Teatre Nacional de Catalunya
Plaça de les Arts 1. 933 06 57 00. www.tnc.cat.
Built by local architect Ricardo Bofill, Catalunya's National Theatre is a synthesis of modern and classical architecture. Inside all shows are performed exclusively in the Catalan language, ranging from the classics to more experimental pieces.

Torre Agbar
Plaça de les Glòries Catalans s/n.
Designed in 2005 by the French architect Jean Nouvel for the local water company, the Torre Agbar towers over its neighbours and has become a new city landmark. A sophisticated LED system lights up the building's cigar-shaped form in hues of red, blue and green.

Parc Güell★★
Olot 1–13. Open daily May–Sept 10am–9pm; Oct–Apr 10am–8pm. No charge. 934 13 24 00.
Gaudí's imagination shines in the most famous of his commissions by Güell. In this enchanted forest are mushroom-shaped pavilions, a mosaic dragon, the **Chamber of the Columns**, whose undulating mosaic roof covers a forest of sloping columns, and the remarkable **rolling bench**★★. **Casa-Museu Gaudí**

(Ctra del Carmel entrance; open daily Oct–Mar 10am–6pm; Apr–Sept 10am–8pm; last admission 15min before closing; closed 1 Jan, 6 Jan (afternoon), 25–26 Dec (afternoon); €5.50; 932 19 38 11; www.casamuseugaudi.org) is the architect's house.

WALKING TOUR★

LA RIBERA
During the 13C and 14C, the Catalan fleet exercised unquestionable supremacy over the western basin of the Mediterranean. Important merchant families acquired considerable social status and the **Carrer de Montcada** became a showcase for their high expectations and new standards of living. This street, named after the Montcada, an influential family of noble descent, is a unique ensemble of merchants' palaces and aristocratic mansions, most of which date back to the late Middle Ages. Behind the austere façades are quaint little patios with galleries and porches typical of Catalan Gothic architecture.

Mercat de Santa Caterina
Av. Francesc Cámbo 16. www.mercatsantacaterina.net.
Originally opened in 1848, this is Barcelona's oldest market. In 2004 it was given a stunning makeover by the late Catalan architect Enric Miralles and his wife Benedetta Tagliabue. The pair

modernised the interior and added an undulating roof scattered with colourful mosaic patterns of fruit and vegetables. Inside, the Espai Santa Caterina (⏱*open Jul–Sept Mon– Sat 10am–2pm, rest of the year until 3pm, and 8pm Thur–Fri;* ✆*no charge*) highlights the remains of the former Dominican Convent of Santa Catarina that stood on this site.

▶ *Facing the market's entrance, take the street on the right (Carrer Giralt el Pellisser) and follow it to the end.*

Carrer de Montcada★★

Maritime trade played a fundamental role in the history of the city when in the 13C and 14C Barcelona dominated the marine traffic in the western Mediterranean. The dynasties of merchants formed a strong oligarchy that ruled the city and the Carrer Montcada was the best "showcase" of this powerful social class. Here they built grand mansions and palaces, many of which are now occupied by museums and galleries.

Palau Berenguer d'Aiguilar★

This magnificent residence (*Montcada 15, part of the Picasso Museum*) which was modified in the 15C and again in the 18C has retained many architectural elements typical in the noble houses of medieval Barcelona. The sober façade features decorative windows on the lower floor, whilst a central patio (now the entrance to the museum) is enlivened by open arches and decorative mouldings.

Museu Picasso

Montcada 15–23. ⏱*Open Tue–Sun and public holidays 10am–8pm.* ⏱*Closed 1 Jan, 1 May, 24 Jun, 25–26 Dec.* ✆*€10; free first Sun of month and every Sun from 3pm.* ✆*932 56 30 00. www.museupicasso.bcn.es.*

The Gothic palaces of Berenguer de Aguilar and Baron de Castellet and the Baroque Palau Meca are the setting for the museum. The works here are dedicated, in most cases, to Picasso's friend Sabartès, shown in several portraits.

Picasso's early genius is evident in portraits of his family, *First Communion* and *Science and Charity* (1896). Among examples of his early Paris work are *La Nana* and *La Espera; Los Desemparados* (1903) is from his Blue Period, *Señora Casals* from his Rose Period. His **Las Meninas series**★ consists of variations on the famous picture by Velázquez. Picasso's skill as an engraver is seen in his outstanding etchings of bullfighting and his talent as a ceramist in vases, dishes and plates made in the 1950s.

Museu Barbier-Mueller d'Art Precolombí

Montcada 12–14. ⏱*Open Tue–Fri 11am–7pm, Sat 10am–7pm, Sun and public holidays 10am–3pm.* ⏱*Closed 1 Jan, Good Fri, 1 May, 24 Jun, 25–26 Dec.* ✆*€3.50; free first Sun of month (10am–7pm).* ✆*933 10 45 16. www.barbier-mueller.ch.*

The beautifully restored 12C Palau Nadal houses this interesting collection of pre-Columbian art.

▶ *Continue to the end of Carrer de Montcada.*

Església de Santa Maria del Mar★★

Pl. de Santa Maria 1. ⏱*Open daily 9am –1.30pm, 4.30–8pm.* ✆*No charge.* ✆*933 10 23 90.*

This church is one of the most beautiful in the Catalan Gothic style, built in the 14C by humble sailors to compete with the cathedrals of the wealthy. The result is a graceful church of outstanding simplicity.

The west front is adorned only by a portal gable and the buttresses flanking the superb Flamboyant **rose window**★. The **interior**★★★ gives the impression of spaciousness due to the elevation of the nave, and side aisles divided only by slender pillars.

Fossar de les Morenes (Mulberry Graveyard)

Opposite the Santa Maria del Mar, this little square is surrounded by pink-hued façades of apartment buildings. An eternal flame has been burning here since 1999, in memory of the victims of the 1714 siege on the city.

▷ *From the rear entrance of the Santa Maria del Mar, stroll along the Passeig del Born to the end.*

Mercat del Born

A work of Josep Fontseré (1874), this steel structure, once the city's principal wholesale market, is one of the first examples of Spanish industrial architecture.

It is currently begin converted into a library and cultural centre, a process made complicated by the fact that substantial remains of the medieval city were found when work started.

▷ *Standing with your back to the Mercat del Born, take the Carrer del Comerç to your right.*

Museu del Xocolata (Chocolate Museum)

Comerç, 36. ⏲*Open Mon and Wed–Sat 10am–7pm, Sun 10am–3pm.* ⊛*€4.30.* ℘*932 68 78 78. www.pastisseria.com.*
This fun museum presents both the discovery of cocoa and history of commercial chocolate making as well as *monas,* elaborate chocolate sculptures that are a Catalan Easter tradition.

▷ *With your back to the Chocolate Museum, turn left and walk a few steps to the Passeig Picasso.*

Parc de la Ciutadella★

⏲*Open daily 10am–dusk.*
Built by Philip V to control rebellious Barcelona, the citadel was demolished in 1868 and replaced by gardens. It hosted the 1888 World Fair.
Castell dels Tres Dragons★★ *(Parc de la Ciutadella;* ⊶ *currently closed for renovations; www.bcn.cat/museuciencies).* Domènech i Montaner built this pavilion for the World Fair in neo-Gothic style, using unadorned brick and iron. It houses the Laboratori de Natura, part of the Barcelona's group of Natural Science Museums. Gaudí collaborated on

the design of the waterfall while still a student.
The ⛫ **zoo**★ covers much of Parc de la Ciutadella (⏲ *open Jan–early Mar and late Oct–Dec 10am–5.30pm; late Mar–May and early Oct 10am–7pm; Jun–Sept 10am–8pm; ticket office closes 1hr before zoo;*⏲ *closed 25 Dec;* ⊛ *€16; child €9.60;* ℘ *902 45 75 45; www.zoobarcelona.com).* Animals from all over the world are kept in settings ranging from natural habitat to quite antiquated cages. The zoo has strong primate community and a dolphin show is held in the Aquarama.

ADDITIONAL SIGHTS
Palau de la Música Catalana★★
Palau de la Música 4–6. ⛫*Guided tours (50min) daily 10am–3.30pm; Aug and Holy Week 10am–6pm.* ⊛*€12; advanced purchase recommended.* ℘*902 47 54 85. www.palaumusica.org.*
This concert hall (1905–08) is Domènech i Montaner's most famous work.
The **exterior**★ displays lavish mosaics. The interior, dominated by an **inverted cupola**★★ of polychrome glass, is decorated with sculpted groups and mosaic figurines. A concert in this remarkable venue is a memorable occasion.

⛫ WALKING TOUR

SEAFRONT★
Allow half a day. 🚌 *Bus 157, 57 follows the seafront to Vila Olímpica.*
The seafront, from Montjuïc to the Besòs river, was completely redesigned for the 1992 Olympic Games, turning Barcelona once again towards the sea.

Drassanes (Shipyards)★★ and Museu Marítim★★
Av. de les Drassanes. ⊶*Closed for renovations until 2012.* ℘*93 342 99 20. www.museumaritimbarcelona.org.*
The **ropeworks** are among the best examples of civil Gothic architecture in Catalunya. Ten sections remain from the shipyard, under a timber roof supported by sturdy stone arches. This is an ideal setting for a **Maritime Museum** with

BARCELONA

Tibidabo

C 33 GIRONA/GERONA
C 17 PUIGCERDA

A   B

500 m
500 yds

Temple del
Sagrat Cor
Torre de Collserola

Parc
d'Atraccions

Vall d'Hebron

Parc de
Collserola

Penitents
Parc de la
Creueta del Coll

PARC GÜ

Casa-
Museu
Gaudí

VALLVIDRERA

Peu del Funicular

Cosmocaixa

Vallcarca

Carrer
de Levent

SANT
GERVASI
DE
CASSOLES

GRÀC

TÚNEL DE VALLVIDRERA

Av. del Tibidabo

Balmes

SARRIÀ

Pl. Lesseps

Josep V Foix

Pl.
de Borràs

El Putxet
Mitre

Lesseps

144

Pàdua

Muntaner

Ganduxer

Copèrnic

St Gervasi

Pl. Molina

Reina Elisenda

Augusta

Calatrava

Ronda
del
General

La Bonanova

Augusta

Gràcia

Josep V Foix

Sarrià

Les Tres
Torres

Via

Muntaner

MONESTIR
SANTA MARIA
DE PEDRALBES

PEDRALBES

Pl. de Prat
de la Riba

Pl. de
F. Macià

PAVELLONS
GÜELL

Av. de Pedralbes

Pas. de
Manuel Girona

Av.   Av.

Diagonal

de
Entença

Sarrià

Comte

Hospital
Clinic

Maria Cristina

Palau Reial
Jardins de
Pedralbes
Ciutat

Pl.
de la Reina
Maria Cristina

Corts

Numància

d'Urgell

Zona
Universitària

Palau Reial

Diagonal

TORRES
TRADE

les

Entença

Roma

Universitària

LES
CORTS

les Corts

Plaça
del Centre

Av. del Doctor
Marañón

Camp
Nou

Madrid

Sants
Estació

Pl. dels
Països Catalans

Av.

Tarragona

Rocafort

Museu
F.C. Barcelona

de

Traves. de

SANTS

Rbla del
Brasil

SANTS

Parc Joan Miró

Av.

Badal

Pl. de Sants

Parc de l'Espanya
Industrial
Hostafrancs

Pl.
d'Espanya

Collblanc

Collblanc

Sants

Creu Coberta

Espanya

COLLBLANC

Riera

Blanca

Mercat Nou

Gavà

CaixaForum

Pavelló Mies
van der Rohe

Font
Màgica

POBLE
ESPANYOL

Museu Etn

Torrassa

Magòria
La Campana

MUSEU
NACIONAL D'A
DE CATALUNY

Florida

Santa Eulàlia

Sta Eulàlia

Badal

Via de les Corts Catalanes

Pl. de
Sant Jordi

ESTADI OLÍMPIC
LL. COMPANYS

Enric Prat
de la Riba

del

Carrilet

Torre de
Comunicacions

PALAU
SANT JORDI

Amadeu
Torner

Aprestadora

Av.

Gran

en obras

Segura

Museu Oli
Juan Ant
Samaran

Ildefons
Cerda

Pg. de la Zona Franca

AUDITORI
SOT DEL MIGDIA

CASTELLDEFELS
SITGES

C 31

RONDA LITORAL

A   B

TERRASSA / TARRASA
AP 7- E 15

Tibidabo

B 23 - C 32

Parc Cervantès \ L'HOSPITALET

TARRAGONA
VILAFRANCA DEL PENEDÈS

RONDA DE DALT

C 33 GIRONA/GERONA
C 17 PUIGCERDA
C 58 SABADELL

N II GIRONA / GERONA / MATARÓ
C 33 GIRONA/GERONA
C 31 MATARÓ

HORTA

Maragall

Congrés

TÚNEL DE LA RO VIRA

PARC DEL GUINARDÓ

Pg. de Maragall

Sagrera

Menorca

Cantàbria

Sant Martí

Mare de Déu de Montserrat

Claret

Meridiana

Felip II

HOSPITAL DE SANT PAU

Guinardó

Maria
Camp de l'Arpa

Navas

Guipúscoa

Bac de Roda

Alfons X

Antoni

Indústria

Navas

Tolosa

de

les

Corts

Catalanes

Ronda

Padilla

Sant

Escorial

Pl. i Margall

Sardenya

Lepant

Hospital de Sant Pau

Mallorca

Av.

Clot

Aragó

Gran Via

de

Roda

Encarnació

Pl. de Gràcia

Joanic

Sagrada Família

Pl. de les Glòries Catalanes

Av. Diagonal

Pere

Bilbao

Travessera de

Passeig

Rosselló

SAGRADA FAMÍLIA

Diagonal

Torre Agbar

Glòries

Tànger

Re de Poblenou

Poblenou

de l'Olla

Verdaguer

Marina

Teatre Nacional de Catalunya

EL POBLENOU

Re del Poblenou

Pl. de Carles I

Casa Terrades (Les Punxes)

Plaça de Braus Monumental

Badajoz

Pallars

L'EIXAMPLE

Av.

Aragó

Auditori

Almogàvers

Llacuna

Casa Quadras

Girona

Sant

Catalanes

Sardenya

Marina

Zamora

Pamplona

Trueta

CASA MILÀ (LA PEDRERA)

Passeig de Gràcia

Corts

Joan

Parc
Estació del Nord

Bogatell

Doctor

FUNDACIÓ A. TÀPIES

les

Ronda de Sant Pere

Pas. de Pujades

Joan d'Àustria

Av. d'Icària

C 31

Balmes

GRÀCIA

Arc de Triomf

PARC DE LA CIUTADELLA

Ciutadella
Vila Olímpica

VILA OLÍMPICA

Torre Mapfre

Aribau

CATALUNYA

Urquinaona

Pl. Armes

PARC ZOOLÒGIC

Hotel Arts

Port Olímpic

Pl. de la Universitat

PALAU DE LA MÚSICA CATALANA

Via Laietana

Duana Nova

FRANÇA

SEBASTIÀ

Pl. de Catalunya

Universitat

CATEDRAL

STA MARIA

Barceloneta

Urgell

Museu d'Art Contemporani

LA RAMBLA

BARRI GÒTIC

LA LLOTJA

Jaume I

Pl. Pau Vila

Museu d'Història de Catalunya

Sant Antoni

LA MERCÈ

Porxos d'en Xifré

St Miquel del Port

d'Urgell

St A. Abat

Drassanes

Pl. Portal de la Pau

Moll de la Fusta

LA BARCELONETA

del Paral·lel

Monument a Colom

Imax

Poble Sec

Paral·lel

DRASSANES I MUSEU MARÍTIM

Rambla de Mar

Aquàrium

PLATJA DE

Rda de St Pau

Nou de la Rambla

Pl. de les Drassanes

Maremagnum

POBLE SEC

Pas. de Exposició

PORT VELL

Torre Sant Sebastià

useu Arqueològia

Miramar

ESTACIÓ MARÍTIMA

World Trade Center

TEATRE GREC

Av.

UTORAL

FUNDACIÓ JOAN MIRÓ

Jardí de Costa i Llobera

B 10

MONTJUÏC

RONDA

Castell de Montjuïc

rdí
ànic

L'HOSPITALET
C 32 TARRAGONA

BALEARES , GENOVA

C

D

Casas : Lleó i Morera, Amatller, Batlló	Y
Centre de Cultura Contemporània de Barcelona (Centre d'Estudis i de Recursos Culturals)	R
Museu Egipci de Barcelona	M¹

Casas : Lleó i Morera, Amatller, Batlló..............**Y**
Centre de Cultura Contemporània de Barcelona
(Centre d'Estudis i de Recursos Culturals)..........**R**
Museu Egipci de Barcelona...............................**M**¹

Gaudí (1852–1926)

Antoni Gaudí, born in Reus, studied architecture in Barcelona. His style was influenced first by Catalan Gothic architecture with its emphasis on large areas of space (wide naves, the effect of airy spaciousness) and subsequently by the Islamic and Mudéjar styles. He also studied nature, observing plants and animals, which inspired his shapes, colours and textures. He gave full rein to these images – liana-like curves, the rising and breaking of waves, rugged rocks and the serrations on leaves and flowers – when designing his fabulous buildings. Part of his great originality lay in his use of parabolic arches and spirals (as can be seen in the chimneys of Casa Milà). An intensely religious man, Gaudí drew upon a great many religious symbols for his buildings, especially for the Sagrada Família (Church of the Holy Family) on which he worked for over 40 years. He spent his last years here, hidden away in a small room in the middle of the site, until his tragic death when he was run over by a tram. Gaudí worked a great deal for the banker **Eusebi Güell**, his patron and admirer, who asked him to design his private houses. Gaudí's main works are the Sagrada Família, Casa Batlló, La Pedrera, Casa Vicens, Palau Güell, Pavellons Güell and the Parc Güell.

its interactive displays and priceless artefacts. Among many models is a lifesize replica of the **Royal Galley of Don Juan of Austria**★★, Christian flagship at the Battle of Lepanto (1571). The **Portulan of Gabriel de Vallseca** (1439) belonged to Amerigo Vespucci.

The area around the port includes the Moll de Bosch i Alsina (or **Moll de la Fusta**), a palm-lined promenade.

Monument a Colom

See La Rambla.

Port Vell★

The old harbour is a lively leisure area featuring bars, the **Maremàgnum** shopping and leisure centre *(www.mare magnum.es)*, an **aquarium** and the **IMAX** cinema *(www.imaxportvell.com)*.

From the Passeig Isabel II, cross the "Rambla del Mar" footbridge in front of the Columbus Monument.

Aquàrium★

Moll d'Espanya del Port Vell.
Open daily 9.30am–9pm (9.30pm Jun, Sept, weekends and public holidays; 11pm Jul–Aug); last admission one hour before closing. €17.75; child €12.75. 932 21 74 74. www.aquariumbcn.com.

One of Europe's most impressive sub-aquatic zoos, it includes a spectacular viewing tunnel, 80m/262ft long.

Return to the Passeig del Colom and turn right, following the water's edge to the intersection of Via Laitana.

La Llotja★

Pas. Isabel II 1. 933 19 24 12. www.casallotja.com.
The building housing the Chamber of Commerce and Industry was completely rebuilt in the 18C. The **Gothic hall**★★, a lofty chamber with three naves separated by triple round arches, remains from the medieval building.

Porxos de Xifré

After the discovery of America, many Catalans went there to seek their fortune. When they returned, these *indianos* (as they were called) built beautiful homes to show off their wealth. Josep Xifré Cases (1777–1856) amassed such a large fortune in Cuba that he became the richest man in Barcelona.

This block of Neoclassical buildings – all with arcades – now rather ironically houses a maze of cheap electrical goods stores.

Head S to the marina.

Museu d'Història de Catalunya★

Palau de Mar, Pl. de Pau Vila 3.
Open Tue, Thu–Sat 10am–7pm, Wed 10am–8pm, Sun and public holidays 10am–2.30pm. Closed 1, 6 Jan, 25–26 Dec. €4; no charge 23 Apr, 18 May, 11, 24 Sept, first Sun of month. 932 25 47 00. www.mhcat.net.

This museum in an ex-warehouse details Catalunya from prehistory to now.

Continue walking S along the Passeig Joan de Borbó, either following the marina or venturing into the maze of streets on the opposite side of the road.

La Barceloneta★

The "Iberian Naples" has quaint narrow streets, and restaurants and stalls offering seafood dishes.

At the end of Passeig Joan de Borbó, your will hit the beach. Now take the boardwalk in the opposite direction.

Vila Olímpica★

Built for the 1992 Olympics, this is one of Barcelona's most modern areas. Gardens and avenues of the Olympic Village are dotted with sculptures.

The **marina**★★, designed by JR de Clascà has bars, restaurants and pavement cafés.

Most striking are two 153m/502ft **towers** (Hotel Arts and the Torre Mapfre). The **view**★★★ from the top takes in Mallorca on a clear day.

ADDITIONAL SIGHTS

Basílica de la Mercè★

Pl. de la Mercè 1. Open daily 10am–1pm, 6–8pm. No charge. 933 15 27 56.

The entry of this 1760 church has the only curved Baroque façade in Barcelona. The façade on Carrer Ample is Renaissance and was moved from elsewhere.

A Gothic statue in the interior, the **Mare de Déu de la Mercè**★, is by Pere Moragues (1361).

WALKING TOUR

MONTJUÏC★

Alllow 1 day, including museum visits.

The fort built on this 173m/568ft mountain during the 1640 rebellion is being converted into a Centre of Peace but the exterior and ramparts can be visited. (*open Apr–Oct daily 9am–9pm; rest of the year 9am–7pm; 932 56 44 45; www.castillomontjuic.com*).

The castle commands city and harbour **views**★. The **Plaça d'Espanya** remains from the 1929 exhibition, along with the illuminated **fountain** *(Font Magica)* by Carles Buïgas, the **reception pavilion**★★ by Mies van der Rohe, a structure of outstanding simplicity, and the Spanish Village (Poble Espanyol, or Pueblo Español in Castilian).

Poble Espanyol★ (Spanish Village)

Av. Francesc Ferrer i Guàrdia 13.
Open Mon 9am–8pm, Tue–Thu 9am–2am, Fri 9am–4am, Sat 9am–5am, Sun 9am–midnight; 24 Dec 9am–8pm, 25 Dec 9pm–2am, 1 Jan 1am–8pm. €9.50; child €5.60. 935 08 63 30. www.poble-espanyol.com.

This "village", reflecting life in various parts of Spain, was built for the 1929 exhibition. Walk through a small Castilian square, a street in an Andalucían village with white houses set off by flowering geraniums, or by a Mudéjar tower from Aragón.

There are restaurants, bars and shops, and craftsmen making traditional Spanish wares. The **Collection of Contemporary Art** has works of Picasso, Miró, Dalí and Spanish artists from the 1950s to the present.

Walk down Av. Francesc Ferrer i Guàrdia.

CaixaForum

Av. Francesc Ferrer i Guàrdia 6–8.
Open Mon–Fri and Sun 10am–8pm, Sat 10am–10pm (Wed Jul–Aug until 11pm). Closed 1, 6 Jan, 25 Dec. No charge. 934 76 86 00. http://obrasocial.lacaixa.es.

A magnificent Modernist early 20C textile factory, built by Puig i Cadafalch, now houses a cultural centre with exhibits from a splendid Modern art collection of more than 800 works and exciting temporary shows.

▷ *Climb the stairs to the MNAC.*

Museu Nacional d'Art de Catalunya (MNAC)★★★

Palau Nacional, Parc de Montjuïc.
🕐*Open Tue–Sat 10am–7pm; Sun and public holidays 10am–2.30pm.*
🕐*Closed 1 Jan, 1 May, 25 Dec.* ⊜€8.50; *no charge 18 May, 11, 24 Sept and first Sun of month.* ✆ *936 22 03 76.*
www.mnac.cat.

This museum of Catalan art in the Palau Nacional built for the 1929 fair includes remarkable **Romanesque and Gothic collections★★★**.

Romanesque art – The display evokes contemporary churches. Note 12C frescoes by Sant Joan de Boí *(Room 2)*, the late 11C lateral apses by Sant Quirze de Pedret *(Room 3)*, the Santa Maria de Taüll ensemble (12C), dominated by a fine *Epiphany* and Sant Climent de Taüll *(Room 5)* with the remarkable *Christ in Majesty:* the apse is a Renaissance masterpiece. Note the anti-naturalism and geometry.

Altar frontals are painted on a panel or carved. In the magnificent sculpture galleries is the polychrome *Majestad de Batlló* (13C). The museum also presents superb **capitals★** *(Room 6)*, silverware and enamels. Paintings from the chapter house of **Sigena** (1200) evidence a great stylistic shift.

Gothic art – Exhibits of 13C–14C Catalan Gothic art include stone retables attributed to **Jaime Cascalls** *(Rooms 15 and 16)*; the collection of Catalan Gothic art *(Room 30)*, with works by **Guerau Gener, Juan Mates, Ramon de Mur, Juan Antigó, Bernardo Despuig** and **Jaime Cirera**; a room dedicated to **Bernardo Martorell** *(Room 32)*, for whom detail and shading were paramount; the famous *Virgin of the Councillors* by **Luis Dalmau**; works by the **Master of La Seu d'Urgell** *(Room 34)*; and, lastly,

14C–15C funerary sculpture *(Room 50)*.
Other Collections – The **Cambó Collection** includes painters of the rank of Zurbarán, Tintoretto, El Greco, Rubens, Cranach the Elder and Goya. The **Thyssen-Bornemisza Collection**, selected from the Museu Thyssen, comprises works from the Middle Ages to the 18C, notably paintings of the Virgin and Child. Portraits represent several schools of the 15C–18C.

In the **Renaissance and Baroque** section are Flemish and Italian masters along with works of Ayne Bru, Pere Nunyes and Pedro Berruguete. Other **19C–20C** artworks include paintings by Fortuny, Modernist furniture, sculpture, and posters by Gaudí, Domènech i Montaner, Casas, Rusiñol and others.

▷ *Go to the rear of the MNAC and take the escalator to the Av. l' Estadi.*

Anella Olímpica★

This complex high on the mountain consists of the **Olympic Stadium★**, with its 1929 façade *(now a football venue; www.rcdespanyol.cat)*, and the nearby **Palau Sant Jordi★★**, a sports centre designed by Arata Isozaki. The **telecommunications tower** is the work of Santiago Calatrava.

▷ *Continue along Av. l' Estadi, following the signs to the Fundació Joan Miró.*

Fundació Joan Miró★★★

Parc de Montjuïc. 🕐*Open Tue–Wed, Fri–Sat 10am–7pm (8pm Jul–Sept), Thu 10am–9.30pm, Sun and public holidays 10am–2.30pm; last entry 15min before closing.* ⊜€9. ✆ *934 43 94 70.*
www.fundaciomiro-bcn.org.

Joan Miró (1893–1983), a leading figure in Avant-Garde art, is linked to Barcelona: a mural at the airport, pavement mosaics on La Rambla, the famous logo of the savings bank La Caixa.

Born in Barcelona, Miró spent 1921 and 1922 in Paris, where he painted **La Masía**, signalling his departure from figurative art. Between 1939 and 1941

Fundació Joan Miró

©Turespaña

he executed **Constellations**, 23 panels expressing the horror of World War II. Miró's Foundation is housed in a modern building of harmonious proportions designed by Josep Lluís Sert, a close friend. The 10 000 items were largely executed during the last 20 years of his life. A small exhibition of contemporary art includes Alexander Calder's **Fountain of Mercury**.

ADDITIONAL SIGHTS
Museu d'Arqueologia de Catalunya (MAC)★
Pg. de Santa Madrona 39–41. ⊙*Open Tue–Sat 9.30am–7pm, Sun and public holidays 10am–2.30pm.* ⊛*€3; no charge last Sun in month, 23 Apr, 18 May and 11 Sept.* ℘*934 23 21 49. www.mac.es.*
Household effects, ceramics and votive figures trace the history of Catalunya from Palaeolithic times through to the Visigothic. The collection is housed in the former Palace of Graphic Arts on Montjuïc, which was built for the 1929 International Exhibition.

Monestir de Santa Maria de Pedralbes★★
Bajada Monestir 9. ⊙*Open Apr–end Oct Tue–Fri 10am–5pm, Sat 10am–7pm, Sun 10am–8pm; rest of the year Tue–Sat 10am–2pm, Sun 10am–5pm.* ⊙*Closed 1 Jan, 1 May, Good Fri, 24 Jun, 25 Dec.* ⊛*€7.* ℘*932 56 34 34.*
Founded in the 14C by King James II of Aragón and his fourth wife, the monas-

tery has a fine Catalan Gothic **church**★ with the tomb of the foundress.

The three-storey **cloisters**★ surrounded by cells and oratories are sober and elegant. The Sant Miquel Chapel is adorned with beautiful **frescoes**★★★ by Ferrer Bassá (1346), whose works combine the attention to detail of the Siena School with the acute sense of volume and perspective of Tuscan masters.

Museus Disseny Hub (DHUB)
Palau Reial, Av. Diagonal 686. ⊙*Open Tue–Sun 10am–6pm, 10am–3pm public holidays.* ⊙*Closed Jan. 1, Good Friday, Dec 25.* ⊛*€4.20 (free Sun after 3pm).* ℘*932 56 34 65. www.dhub-bcn.cat.*
Until a new purpose-built museum is finished near the Plaça de les Glóries (slated for late 2012), the city's collection of ceramics, textiles and clothing and decorative arts are here, in a palace originally built for King Alfonso XII.
Situated on the first level, the **Museu de les Arts Decoratives** is a rich collection that spans domestic objects from the medieval to *modernista* and onto contemporary industrial design, all movements Catalans have excelled at. Exhibits ranging from chests and desks, lamps, chairs and even bottles illustrate the changing face of design and technological breakthroughs through mass production.
The **Museu Tèxtil i d'Indumentaria** has a permanent exhibition entitled "El Cos Vestit" (The Clothed Body), which

takes the visitor on a journey from 16C fashion to today with the work of Spanish designers (such as Balenciaga and Paco Rabanne), to the haute couture of Dior and Karl Lagerfeld .

The **Museu de Ceràmica** has a rotating collection of Catalan and Valencian pieces, focusing on 18 and 19C and in particular Alcora, a Valencian town that excels in the medium. Do not miss the works of the famous Catalan ceramicist **Josep Llorens Artigas**, alongside those of Picasso and Miró.

Camp Nou

Av. Aristides Maillol. ⏰*Open Mon–Sat 10am–2pm, Sun and public holidays 10am–2.30pm.* ⏰*Closed Jan 1 and 6, Dec 25.*⊛€*8.50 (under 13 €6.80).* ✆*934 963 600. www.fcbarcelona.cat.* The FC Barcelona stadium has a capacity of nearly 100 000 and its extensive facilities include the **Museu FC Barcelona**, where fans can contemplate trophies won by the famous Barça team.

👥 Cosmo Caixa

Isaac Newton s/n. ⏰*Open Tue–Sun 10am–8pm.* ⏰*Closed 1, 6 Jan, Dec 25 and 26.* ⊛€*3 (under 16 €2).* ✆*932 12 60 50. www.cosmocaixa.com.* The city's Science Museum combines scientific fact with fun through a diverse range of exhibits such as a Foucault pendulum or a rainforest floor. You'll also find a Planetarium, a great gift shop selling books, toys and other knick-knacks, and a large outdoor area with a café.

ADDRESSES

🏠 STAY

The Barri Gòtic has the highest concentration of cheap accommodation. Crossing La Rambla, the Raval district should be approached with caution as it can get edgy by night. For the most chic and generally safest accommodation, the Eixample has a wide range of luxury and design hotels.

⊜⊜ **Hotel Condal** – *Boquería 23 (Barri Gòtic).* 🚇 *Liceu.* ✆*933 18 18 82. www.hotel condal.es. 53 rooms.* ⊠ €*3.* Situated between La Rambla and the Barri Gótic, this hotel is a fine base for visiting the old city. Request a quieter rear room.

⊜⊜⊜ **Hotel Gaudí** – *Nou de la Rambla 12 (Ciutat Vella).* 🚇 *Liceu.* ✆*933 17 90 32. www.hotelgaudi.es. 73 rooms.* ⊠ €*11.* Its location opposite the Palau Güell and Modernist décor evoke the namesake artist. Try for a room with balcony on an upper floor for superb views of the city and the Palau Güell.

⊜⊜⊜ **Hotel Granvía** – *Gran Via de les Corts Catalanes 642 (Eixample).* 🚇 *Catalunya.* ✆*933 18 19 00. www.nnhotels.es. 53 rooms.* ⊠ €*11.45.* This impressive banker's residence from the late 19C was converted into a hotel in 1936. The room rates here are very reasonable given the charming setting.

⊜⊜⊜ **Hotel Hesperia Metropol** – *Ample 31 (Barri Gòtic).* 🚇 *Jaume I.* ✆*933 10 51 00. www.hesperia-metropol.com. 71 rooms.* ⊠ €*11.50.* This pleasant hotel close to the waterfront is situated in a narrow street in the old quarter, between the post office and the Basílica de La Mercè. An attractive feature here is the lobby in a covered patio. The guest rooms are comfortable, with the usual creature comforts.

🍴/EAT

⊜⊜ **Senyor Parellada** – *L'Argentaria 37 (Ribera).* 🚇 *Jaume I.* ✆*933 10 50 94. www.senyorparellada.com.* Located in a 19C building, this restaurant has various dining rooms adorned with chandeliers and wooden furniture along with a delightful patio, topped with a glass roof. Regional cuisine with good value prices.

⊜⊜⊜ **La Provença** – *Provença 242 (Eixample).* 🚇 *Diagonal.* ✆*933 23 23 67. www.laprovenza.com.* In the Eixample district, just a stone's throw from the Passeig de Gràcia, this pleasant restaurant with cheerful, tasteful, décor, serves a range of regional cuisine. Good for the price.

⊜⊜⊜ **Los Caracoles** – *Escudellers 14 (Ciutat Vella).* 🚇 *Liceu.* ✆*933 01 20 41. www.loscaracoles.es.* Founded in 1835, this famous restaurant, one of the gastronomic emblems of Barcelona, is located on the corner of carrers Escudellers and Nou de Sant Franc. The décor here consists of tiled floors, wine barrels, murals and photos. Regional and traditional cuisine.

⊜⊜⊜ **El Tragaluz** – *Pas. de la Concepció 5 (Eixample).* 🚇 *Diagonal.* ✆*934 87 01 96. www.grupotragaluz.com/tragaluz.* One of

Barcelona's most charismatic and dynamic restaurants takes up three storeys, with a unique sliding greenhouse roof. It serves Mediterranean and avant-garde fare.

◔◔◔◔ **Casa Calvet** – *Casp 48 (Eixample).* ◔ *Urquinaona.* ☎*934 12 40 12. www.casacalvet.es. Closed Sun and public holidays.* The former offices of a textile company, in a magnificent Modernist building designed by Gaudí, are dominated by iron beams and wood floors. Traditional Mediterranean dishes.

◔◔◔◔ **Casa Leopoldo** – *Sant Rafael 24 (Ciutat Vella).* ◔ *Liceu.* ☎*934 41 30 14. www.casaleopoldo.com. Closed Sun and public holidays for dinner, Mon, Holy Week, a week in Jan, Aug.* This classic Barcelona restaurant is decorated with bullfighting mementos, signed photos of famous customers and a superb bottle collection.

TAPAS

Euskal Etxea – *Placeta Montcada 1–3 (Ribera).* ◔ *Jaume I.* ☎*933 10 21 85. http://euskaletxeak.org. Closed Christmas week and a fortnight in Aug.* By the church of Santa Maria del Mar, a bar and cosy dining room, this is the perfect setting for a glass of *txacolí* (a Basque white wine) and Basque pork chops and fried fish.

Irati Taverna Basca – *Cardenal Casañas 17 (Barri Gòtic).* ◔ *Liceu.* ☎*933 02 30 84. www. sagardi.com.* Near the Plaça de la Boqueria, in one of the busiest districts, this is a typical tapas bar with a counter full of Basque skewers along with a grill room.

Tickets – *Paral·lel 164 (Poble Sec).* ◔*Poble Sec.* Reserve online, www.ticketsbar.es. Closed weekends.* Tapas and cocktail bar from Ferran Adrià and brother Albert.

El Xampanyet – *Montcada 22 (Ribera).* ◔*Jaume I.* ☎*933 19 70 03. Closed Sun, Holy Week and Aug.* In an alleyway close to the Picasso Museum, this bar is famous for anchovies and sparkling wine.

⧓ BARS / ⧓ CAFÉS

Café de la Opera – *Rambla dels Caputxins 74 (Ciutat Vella).* ◔ *Liceu.* ☎*933 17 75 85. www.cafeoperabcn.com.* Because of its history, Modernist façade and 19C atmosphere, this café is one of the most famous in the city. Not to be missed!

La Fira – *Provença 171 (Eixample).* ◔ *Diagonal.* ☎*933 23 72 71.* Bar decorated with robots and fairground amusements.

Jamboree – *Pl. Reial 17 (Ciutat Vella).* ◔ *Liceu.* ☎*933 01 75 64. www.masimas.com.*

The meeting point in Barcelona for jazz musicians and aficionados.

Luz de Gas-Port Vell – *Moll del Dipòsit (Port Vell in front of Palau de Mar).* ◔ *Barceloneta.* ☎*932 09 77 11. www.luzdegas.com.* Busy, atmospheric bar on a boat with tables spilling onto the pier, plus a dance floor.

Margarita Blue – *Josep Anselm Clavé 6 (Ciutat Vella).* ◔ *Drassanes.* ☎*934 12 54 89. margaritablue.com.* Unusual decoration (mirrors of all shapes and sizes, weird objects and antique lamps) helps make this one of the city's most popular bars, hosting weekly shows and concerts. The cuisine is Tex-Mex.

Quatre Gats – *Montsió 3 bis (Ciutat Vella).* ◔ *Catalunya.* ☎*933 02 41 40. www.4gats. com.* The symbol of Modernist and bohemian Barcelona. This landmark café was a meeting place for artists such as Picasso, Casas and Utrillo. Reasonable lunchtime menu.

⧓ SHOPPING

ANTIQUES

Bulevard dels Antiquaris – *Pas. de Gràcia 55 (Eixample).* ◔ *Diagonal.* ☎*932 15 44 99. www.bulevarddelsantiquaris.com.* An area containing over 70 shops selling a range of artwork and antiques.

Plaça de la Catedra – *Ciutat Vella.* ◔ *Jaume I.* A small market with stalls selling antiques is held here on public holidays.

Plaça Sant Josep Oriol – *Ciutat Vella.* ◔ *Liceu.* Mirrors, furniture, and paintings are sold at this popular weekend market.

La Palla and Banys Nous – *Ciutat Vella.* ◔ *Liceu.* These two streets are well known for their reputable antique shops.

HOMEWARE

Vinçon – *Pas. de Gràcia 96 (Eixample).* ◔ *Diagonal.* ☎*932 156 050. www.vincon.com* Along from the Casa Milà, Vinçon has been offering a well-edited selection of stylish homeware since the 1960s.

FASHION

Custo Barcelona – *Plaça de les Olles 7 (La Ribera).* ☎*933 42 66 98. www.custo-barcelona.com.* Colourful casualwear for men, women and children. Six other stores throughout the city.

ART GALLERIES

Barcelona's most prestigious galleries can mainly be found in Carrer Consell de Cent along the Rambla de Catalunya and the Carrer Montcada in La Ribera.

Terrassa/Tarrasa

Located in the great industrial belt of Barcelona, Terrassa is most well-known for its textile production, an industry that has made the township prosperous. It is surrounded by the mountains of the Sant Llorenç del Munt i l'Obac natural park. Along its streets, various examples of industrial architecture and modernista buildings reflect the economic growth of the city in the early 20C. The Masía Freixa in the Plaça de Josep Freixa i Argemi is well worth seeking out.

▶ **Population:** 212 724
Michelin Map: 576 H 36.
Info: Montserrat, 14. ℰ937 39 70 19. www. terrassa.org.
Location: 31km/19mi NW of Barcelona along the C 58.
Kids: Museu de la Ciència y la Tècnica de Catalunya.
Timing: Terrassa makes a good day trip out from Barcelona.

SIGHTS

Conjunto Monumental de Esglésias de Sant Pere★★

Open Tue–Sat 10am–1.30pm, 4–7pm, Sun 11am–2pm. *Closed 1 Jan, 1 May, 25, 26 Dec.* €3. ℰ937 83 37 02.

The **Antiguo baptisterio de Sant Miquel**★ was built in the 9C using late Roman remains. The dome rests on eight pillars; four have Roman capitals, four are Visigothic.

Alabaster windows in the apse filter light onto 9C–10C pre-Romanesque wall paintings. The crypt's three apses have horseshoe arches.

The magnificent Romanesque Lombard church of **Santa Maria**★ has an octago-nal cupola and a *cimborrio* (lantern); a 5C mosaic survives in front. A 13C wall fresco in the south transept, of the martyrdom of Thomas à Becket, retains bright colours. Note the 15C north transept altarpiece by Jaime Huguet of **St Abdon and St Sennen**★★.

Sant Pere is a rustic church begun in the 6C on a trapezoid plan with a Roman-esque transept crossing. In the apse is a curious **stone altarpiece**★.

Museu de la Ciència y la Tècnica de Catalunya★

Rambla d'Ègara 270. *Open Sept–Jun Tue–Fri 10am–7pm, Sat–Sun 10am–2.30pm; Jul–Aug Tue–Sun 10am–2.30pm.* *Closed 1, 6 Jan, 25–26 Dec.* €3.50; no charge first Sun of the month. ℰ937 36 89 66. www.mnactec.cat.

This excellent modern National Museum of Science and Technology is housed in a 1909 woollen mill.

Museu Textil

Salmeron 25. *Closed Mon and public holidays.* €3. ℰ937 31 52 02. www.cdmt.es.

This museum presents a comprehensive overview of the development of textile and fashion throughout the 19C. Beauti-ful oriental fabrics are highlights of the collection.

Masía Freixa★

Parc de San Jordi.

This 1907 modernist building houses the music conservatory. The repetition of parabolic arches is stunning.

Masía Freixa

L. Campion/MICHELIN

Serra de Monserrat★★

The grand site★★★ of the Macizo de Montserrat (Montserrat Massif) was the setting for Wagner's *Parsifal*. where hard Eocene conglomerates rise above eroded formations. It is the main site of devotion to the Virgin in Catalunya. Views★★ from the road are impressive. The Montserrat cable car runs from near Monistrol de Montserrat.

- ⓖ **Michelin Map:** 574 H 35.
- **Info:** Pl. de la Creu, opposite the funicular 1. ☎938 77 77 77. www.montserratvisita.com
- ▷ **Location:** 49km/31mi NW of Barcelona along the C 58, 19km/12mi E of Terrassa.
- ⓞ **Timing:** You'll get the most out of a day spent here if you come out of season, or during the week.

A BIT OF GEOGRAPHY

With its bulbous peaks and troughs sculptured by erosion, Montserrat is a mountain of impressive beauty. In some places formations evoke human form, in others, inanimate objects and animals. Source of inspiration for musicians, poets (Verdaguer wrote the famous poem "Virolaia bout Montserrat" here), geographers and travellers, Montserrat is considered Catalunya's spiritual heart and remains an important place of devotion.

VISIT

Monastery and Basilica

ⓞ *Open daily 7.30am–8pm.*
€6.50 (museum). ☎938 77 77 66.
www.abadiamontserrat.net.
The Benedictines arrived in the 9C and every century since then has seen additions to the monastery. In 1812, it was sacked by the French.
The present buildings are 19C and 20C. At the end of the dark, ornate **basilica** (15C) is **La Moreneta ★★**, the shrine of the Black Madonna. According to legend, this 12C polychrome statue of the Black Madonna, now above the high altar, was discovered in a cave by shepherds.
The Basilica is famous for its **Gregorian chant**, particularly during Mass at 11am and Vespers at 6.45pm.
The **Escolanía**, *(Mon–Thu 1pm and 6.45pm, Fri 1pm, Sun and festivals noon and 6.45pm; ☎938 77 77 67; www. escolania.cat)* one of the world's oldest boys' choirs, is another fantastic aural experience.

Hermitages and viewpoints

Access via the ▮mountain trails, ⓚcable cars or funiculars. Sant Joan: Jan–Mar and Nov–Dec Mon–Fri 11am–4pm; Sat–Sun and public holidays 10am–4pm; Apr–Jun and Sept–Oct daily 10am–5.40pm; Jul–Aug daily 10am–7pm. €7.45 round-trip (every 20min). ☎93 205 15 15. Santa Cova: daily 10am–1pm, 2–5pm (4pm Nov–Feb).€3 (every 20min). www.cremallerademontserrat.com
The 13 hermitages, abandoned since the arrival of Napoleon's troops, offer historical interest and fine views.
Ermita de la Trinitat *(▮45min on foot),* charmingly nestled in a bucolic plain, is sheltered by three mountains: El Elefante (The Elephant), La Preñada (Pregnant Woman) and La Momia (The Mummy). On a clear day, **Sant Jeroni★** *(▮ 1hr30min on foot or ⇌by car)* at 1 238m/4 062ft, offers a **panorama** from the Pyrenees to the Balearic Islands.
Ermita de Santa Cecilia features an attractive 11C **Romanesque church★**. Its east end is circled by Lombard bands. The statue of the Virgin was found in **Santa Cova** (holy cave), *▮ 1hr walk*, which has views of the Llobregat Valley. **Sant Miquel★** *(▮ 30min from the monastery; 1hr from the upper terminal of the Sant Miquel funicular)* has a general view of the monastery. **Sant Joan** *(▮30min from upper terminal of the Sant Joan funicular)* offers a beautiful panorama; the Ermita de San Onofre may be seen clinging to the rock face.

Sitges★★

Sitges is a resort famous for its lovely beaches, exemplary Modernist architecture and exuberant Carnival. The seafront promenade, Passeig Marítim, is dotted with hotels and luxury residences.

SIGHTS
OLD TOWN★★
1hr30min

The parish church dominates the breakwater of La Punta. Balconies of white houses are brilliant with flowers. Museums in neo-Gothic mansions display canvases from the late 19C, when Rusiñol and Miguel Utrillo (father of the French painter) painted here.

Museu Cau Ferrat★★
Davallada 12. ⚬⚊*Closed for rennovations until 2012.*

Santiago Rusiñol (1861–1931) added Gothic features to two 16C fishermen's houses, which he left to the town, along with ceramics, paintings and sculptures.

Among the **paintings**, note two remarkable works by El Greco: *Penitent Mary Magdalene* and *The Repentance of St Peter*. The gallery also contains canvases by Picasso, Casas and Rusiñol himself (*Poetry, Music and Painting*).

The museum takes its name from the **wrought-iron** collection (*cau ferrat*). There is also a **ceramics** section.

Museu Maricel★
Fonollar s/n. ⚬⚊*Closed for rennovations until 2012.*

This museum in a 14C hospital displays medieval and Baroque art. A footbridge links it to an adjacent mansion.

Casa Llopis-Museu Romàntic★
Sant Gaudenci 1. ⏱*Open 15 Jun–30 Sept Tue–Sat 9.30am–2pm, 4–7pm, Sun and public holidays 10am–3pm; 1 Oct–14 Jun Tue–Sat 9.30am–2pm, 3.30–6.30pm, Sun and public holidays 10am–3pm.* ⏱*Closed 1 Jan, 24 Aug, 23 Sept, 25–26 Dec.* ⌾€3.50. ☏*938 94 29 69.*

- ▶ **Population:** 27 070.
- ⚲ **Michelin Map:** 574 I 35 – Catalunya (Barcelona)
- ℹ **Info:** Sinia Morera 1. ☏938 94 50 04. www.sitgestour.com.
- ⊚ **Location:** Sitges is a coastal resort between Barcelona and Tarragona.
- 👪 **Kids:** The Museu del Ferrocarril is the place to admire steam engines.
- 🕐 **Timing:** While away a few days at the beach.

This late-18C bourgeois house gives a good idea of middle- and upper-class life during the Romantic period with frescoes on the walls, English furniture, mechanical devices and musical boxes. Dioramas show scenes of daily life.

The **Lola Anglada collection** is an outstanding display of 17C, 18C and 19C dolls from all over Europe.

EXCURSIONS
Vilanova i la Geltrú★
⏵*7km/4.3mi SW.*

Situated in a small bay, this is an important fishing harbour and a holiday resort.

Museu Romàntic Can Papiol★
Major 32. ⏱*Open Fri-Sat 10am–1pm, 6–8pm, Sun 10am–2pm.* ⌾€3. ☏*938 93 03 82.*

This mansion, built 1780–1801 by the Papiol family, evokes the life of the devout, well-to-do industrial middle class. Austerity reigns in the library with its 5 000 or so volumes, in the chapel with its strange relic of St Constance and in the reception rooms with their biblical scenes in grey monochrome. However, the opulence of the house is evident in the furnishings and ballroom.

Biblioteca-Museu Balaguer★
Av. Víctor Balaguer. ⏱*Open Tue–Fri 10am–2pm, 5–7pm (Thur 9pm), Sat 11am–2pm, 5–7pm, Sun 10am–2pm.* ⌾€3; no charge Thu afternoon and first

Sun of month. ☏*938 15 42 02.*
www.victorbalaguer.cat.
This library-museum in a curious Egyptian-Greek building was an initiative of poet-historian-politician **Víctor Balaguer** (1824–1901). The **contemporary art collection** includes Catalan works from the 1950s and 1960s (*Legado 56*). Small works outline the evolution of painting since the end of the 14C. There are also **16C and 17C paintings** (El Greco, Murillo, Carducho, Maino, Carreño, etc.) and Egyptian and Asian art.

♛♛ Museu del Ferrocarril★

Pl. d'Eduard Maristany. ◷*Open Aug daily 10.30am–2.30pm, 5–8pm; Sept–Jul Tue–Sun 10.30am–2.30pm (Sat afternoons 4–6.30pm).* ⬤*€5; child €4.* ☏*938 15 84 91. www.museudel ferrocarril.org.*
This is one of the most impressive collections of railway engines in Spain.

Vilafranca del Penedès★

◷ *29km/18mi NW by the C 158 and C 15.*
Situated in the centre of the Penedés wine-growing region, Vilafranca proudly wears the badge of "Catalunya's Wine Capital". The Penedés is most famous for producing cava. The most famous wineries in the region include the premium cava makers Cordoníu (whose cellars are a glorious modernista affair), Torres and Jean León. There are over 60 *bodegas* dotted around the

countryside and many can be visited (*see www.enoturismepenedes.cat*).

Vinseum – Museu del Vi de les Cultures de Catalunya ★★

Pl. Jaume I5. ◷*Open Tue–Sat 10am–2pm, 4–7pm, Sun 10am–2pm.* ◷*Closed Mon, 1 May, 25–26 December, 1 and 6 Jan.* ⬤*€5.* ☏*938 900 582.*
www.vinseum.cat.
More than a museum, this centre celebrates the culture of wine. Through attractive exhibits, it tells of the evolution of the region through wine production and shows interesting examples of bottling techniques, the Penedés varietals and how to appreciate them, and even of the local music and folklore inspired by wine.

ADDRESSES

🏠 STAY

⊟⊟⊟ **Hotel Romàntic y la Renaixença** – *Sant Isidre 33.* ☏*938 94 83 75. www.hotel romantic.com. 69 rooms. Closed Nov–Feb.* This establishment takes up two 19C buildings, each with period décor and a certain decadent charm. Lovely interior courtyard with trees.

⊟/EAT

⊟ **La Oca** – *Parellades 41.* ☏*938 94 79 36. Closed Nov.* This inexpensive, modern restaurant, well located in the centre of Sitges, is known for its grilled meats, roast chicken and fast service. A cheap menu is also available at lunchtime.

Festivals in Sitges

Sitges is known for its Corpus Christi flowers, for the Catalunya International Cinema Festival (*early October; www.cinemasitges.com*), vintage car rally (*Mar*) and international theatre festival (*Jun*). Its major fiesta is on 24 August, the feast day of Sant Bartomeu, celebrated with a huge firework display and a traditional parade of giant figures. The town is also renowned for its exuberant Carnival. But perhaps it's most famous for being an international gay resort. The rainbow flag is a common sight on the streets here and many bars and clubs cater to a gay clientle. That said, the overall atmosphere of Sitges is mixed and laid back.

Festival of Sant Bartomeu

© Jordi Camí/age fotostock

Geographically, Catalunya is a triangle of varied landscapes, from snow-topped peaks to sun-kissed beaches, set between the French border, Aragón and the Mediterranean. Culturally, Catalunya is a nation unto itself. It has its own language, its own flag, its own proud history. Barcelona has been the shop window and public face of Catalunya since the hugely successful Olympics of 1992. However, as early as the 1950s north European visitors were flocking to the deep blue water and pine-fringed coves of the Costa Brava. The Pyrenees and the Principality of Andorra welcome mostly domestic and cross-border visitors, skiers and walkers.

Highlights

1. **Girona** in early May during the flower festival (p339)
2. The archetypal and art-filled village of **Cadaqués** (p344)
3. The coastal scenery of the **Cap de Begur** on the Costa Brava (p346)
4. Lose yourself at the Teatre-Museu Dalí in **Figueres** (p353)
5. Romanesque art and architecture in the **Vall de Boí** (p363)

The Mountains

The Pyrenees, between Andorra and the Cap de Creus headland, is a green wooded area with peaks over 3 100m/ 10 170ft high.

This is wonderful walking territory, dotted with delightful villages and a smattering of ski resorts and other adventure sports opportunities. Andorra is famous for its shopping but excels in its skiing and walking opportunities; the spectacular Port d'Envalira pass, the highest in the Pyrenees, is well worth the trip. The Pyrenees also contain one of Spain's richest cultural legacies.

During the 10C and 12C, Romanesque art and architecture became prolific throughout the Pyrenees as Catalunya emerged as a nation. Particularly in the Vall de Boí, a UNESCO World Heritage site, stout, slate-roof Romanesque churches are dotted everywhere over the bucolic landscape.

Art of the period was manifested in highly expressive religious frescoes featuring vivid colour and elongated, doe-eyed creatures. Most of the originals have been moved to Barcelona's MNAC but sensitive reproductions evoke a sense of time and place.

Costa Brava and Inland

The Costa Brava was "discovered" and made fashionable by artists such as Dalí, Picasso and Marc Chagall, and was in the vanguard of Spain's plunge into mass-market tourism. Fortunately, it has, with a few ugly exceptions (most notably Lloret de Mar), remained true to its name, meaning "wild" or "rugged coast", and is still the most beautiful of Spain's holiday costas. Beaches range from rocky coves to long soft golden sands, while the rugged coastlines softened by greenery are rarely less than interesting.

The international gateway to the coast is Girona, a typical Catalan city with real character and history and many of the features of a "mini-Barcelona". Figueres, the spiritual home of Salvador Dalí, is likely to delight even the most doubtful art sceptics.

Crique de Sa Riera, Cap de Begur, Costa Brava

D. Chapuis/MICHELIN

Vic★★

This important commercial centre and thriving industrial town (leather goods, food processing and textiles) lies in the foothills of the Pyrenees. Monumental buildings testify to its history as a Roman centre. Vic makes a good base for exploring the mountains while also being within striking distance of Barcelona.

THE CITY TODAY

Vic sees few overnighting north European visitors. It is known locally for its wide choice of good quality restaurants, so if you wish to escape fellow tourists and fill up on authentic Catalan cooking, before walking it off in the mountains, this is the place to come.

SIGHTS

Old Quarter★

Wide avenues *(ramblas)* follow the old walls, of which a few remnants remain.

Museu Episcopal★★★

Pl. Bisbe Oliba 3. Open Apr–Sept Tue–Sat 10am–7pm, Sun and public holidays 10am–2pm; Oct–Mar Tue–Fri 10am–1pm, 3–6pm, Sat 10am–7pm, Sun and public holidays 10am–2pm. Closed 1, 6 Jan, Easter Sunday, 25–26 Dec. €5. 938 86 93 60. www.museuepiscopalvic.com.
This magnificent museum displays Romanesque and Gothic works, along with fabrics and costumes, jewellery, ceramics and other arts.
Sala del Románico★★★ (Romanesque Gallery) – On exhibit are the *Descent of Erill la Vall*, a sculptural ensemble; the painting *Canopy of Ribes de Freser;* and outstanding **altar fronts**. The *Lluça Altar* marks the transition to the Gothic style.
Salas del Gótico★★★ (Gothic Galleries) – Among items from the early Gothic period (after 1275) are a magnificent marble altarpiece by **Bernat Saulet**, a *Virgin of Boixadors*, the altar front of Bellver de Cerdanya and parts of an altarpiece by **Pere Serra**. The impressive collection of international Gothic

- **Population:** 35 550
- **Michelin Map:** 574 G 36 – Catalunya (Barcelona).
- **Info:** Ciutat 4. 938 86 20 91. www.victurisme.cat.
- **Location:** Vic is in NE Spain, 70km/43mi N of Barcelona.
- **Don't Miss:** Museu Episcopal.
- **Timing:** A famous farmer's market is held in Vic's main square (Plaça Major) every Saturday.

altarpieces (15C) includes the **Santa Clara** and *Sant Antoni i Santa Margarida* altars, both by Borrasà, the *de Guimerà* altar, the work of Ramon de Mur, and the *Verdú* altarpiece of Jaume Ferrer II. The paintings of Jaume Huguet mark the transition to the Renaissance.
Tejido e Indumentari★★★ (Textiles and Costumes) – A magnificent display of liturgical wear and 13C–18C textiles.

Catedral★

Pl. de la Catedral. Open daily 10am–1pm, 4–5pm. €2 for the crypt. 938 86 44 49.
An elegant 11C Romanesque belfry and crypt remain from earlier churches.
The Neoclassical Cathedral was built between 1781 and 1803. In 1930 the famous Catalan artist **Josep Maria Sert** decorated the **interior**★ with wall paintings. These were burned during the Civil War, and repainted by Sert before his death in 1945.
The **paintings**★★ have a power reminiscent of Michelangelo. They evoke the mystery of the Redemption *(chancel)* from the time of Adam's original sin *(transept)* to the Passion *(apse)*, the Evangelists and the Martyrs *(nave)*.
Scenes on the back of the west door illustrate the triumph of human injustice in the Life of Christ and in the history of Catalunya: Jesus chasing the money-lenders *(right)*; Jesus condemned *(centre)* and the road to Calvary *(left)*. The monochrome golds and browns in the murals lend the effect of a relief.

The former high altar **retable**★★ *(end of the ambulatory)* is a 15C alabaster work in 12 panels. The Gothic tomb is of the canon who commissioned the retable, by the same sculptor.

Tracery-filled 14C arches surround the small **clasustro**★. In a cloister gallery is the tomb of the painter JM Sert, surmounted by his unfinished *Crucifixion*.

Palau Episcopal

Santa Maria. ℘*938 86 15 55.*
The 12C episcopal palace has been modified significantly. The **Sala dels Sínodes**, decorated in 1845, and the patio are the main features.

Plaça Major★

Note façades with Modernist, Gothic and Baroque details on this busy arcaded square. A popular market is held in the square every Saturday.

EXCURSIONS
Monestir de Sant Pere de Casserres★

▶ *17km/11.6mi NE of Vic. Take the C 153 NE from Vic, then turn right towards Tavernoles and Parador. At Parador take a paved lane to the left (3.5km/2.2mi).*
🕐*Phone for opening times.* ◉€*3.*
℘*937 44 71 18. www.santperede casserres.com.*

Stop just before Parador for a fine **view**★★ *(right)* of the marsh of Sau, between high banks.

The small Romanesque monastery enjoys a privileged **location**★★ at the end of a long and narrow peninsula in the marsh.

For many centuries, Sant Pere de Casseres was the only working Benedictine Monastery in the Osona region.

Monastic life ended at the hands of King Carlos III in 1797, but the complex's medieval structures have been well preserved for posterity.

Monestir de Santa Maria de L'Estany★

▶ *24km/15mi SW of Vic. Leave Vic along the C 25 towards Manresa. Turn right at Exit 164 and follow the BP 4313. Pl. del Monestir, L'Estany.*

🕐*Open Tue–Sun and public holidays 10am–2pm.* 🕐*Closed 20 Dec–20 Jan.* ◉€*3.* ℘*938 30 30 40. www.monestirestany.cat.*

The village of **L'Estany**★ grew up around this medieval Augustinian monastery. The bell tower of the 12C Romanesque church was rebuilt in the 15C. The arcades of the beautiful **cloisters**★ are supported by matching columns and decorated with 72 remarkable **capitals**★★.

The north gallery is Romanesque and narrative; the west, decorative with palm fronds and gaunt griffons; the south, geometrical and interlaced; the east features wedding scenes and musicians.

🚗 DRIVING TOURS

Through the Serra de Montseny★

The Serra de Montseny, an extension of the Pyrenees, is a granite massif covered in beeches and cork oaks. To the southeast, the **Parque Natural de Montseny** covers 17 372ha/42 925 acres; its highest peaks are Matagalls (1 695m/5 560ft) and **Turó de l'Home** (1 707m/5 601ft).

From Vic to Sant Celoni via the Northern Road

▶ *60km/37.3mi. Leave Vic to the S; turn left after 6km/3.7mi.*

The road goes through pine and beechwoods past delightful **Viladrau**. After **Arbùcies**, it runs beside the river then turns for **Breda**, with the Romanesque tower of the **Monestir de Sant Salvador**★, and Sant Celoni (🚌*Plaça de l´Estació*).

Beyond Campins, the road rises with **views**, to the lake *(embalse)* of Santa Fè (1 130m/3 707ft). The Ermita de Sant Marçal★★ hermitage is 7km/4.3mi ahead on Matagalls ridge.

There are good **views** of the serra from the road between Sant Celoni and Tona via Montseny★.

Beyond Montseny, the road rises to a wild area, then descends to Tona past the Romanesque church in **El Brull** and the tower of **Santa Maria de Seva**.

Girona/Gerona★★

Girona, with its heritage quarter, stands on a strategic site that has made it the target of repeated sieges. Its ramparts were built and rebuilt by Iberians, Romans and Catalans. Charlemagne's troops assaulted the city, and in 1809, Girona resisted Napoleon's troops for more than seven months.

THE CITY TODAY

Once seen as merely the international gateway to the region, Girona is now welcoming curious foreign visitors who have "done" Barcelona and are seeking similarly historic characterful Catalan cities to explore. With a mix of atmospheric streets and historic sights which reflect the city's rich multicultural heritage, all in a compact centre with a river running through its heart, Girona makes for a very satisfying day away from the coast.

➤ WALKING TOUR

BARRI VELL (OLD TOWN)
Allow 3hr
Narrow alleys lead up to the Cathedral, with its monumental stairway, the **Escaleras de la Pera**.
The 14C **Pia Almoina** building (*right*) is a fine example of Gothic architecture.

Hospital Santa Caterina
Joan Maragall 2. ○*Open Mon–Sat 9am –8pm, Sun 9am–2pm.* ✆*972 22 72 67.*
Facing the Plaça Pompey Fabra, this baroque building was modernised with a glass annex when it became the home of the Generalitat (local government) in

- ▶ **Population:** 96 188
- ✆ **Michelin Map:** 574 G 38 (town plan) – map 122 Costa Brava – Catalunya (Girona).
- **Info:** Joan Maragall 2. ✆872 975 975. www.girona.cat.
- ▷ **Location:** Girona connects with Barcelona (97km/60.2mi SW) and France via the N II and AP 7. The C 255 leads to Palafrugell (39km/24mi SW) and the C 250 to Sant Feliu de Guíxols (36km/22mi SW), both on the coast. ▭Plaça de Espanya.
- **P** **Parking:** Park along one of the wider streets and walk into the old city.
- **Don't Miss:** A walk through the old Jewish quarter is essential.
- ○ **Timing:** Walk around the old town, to the main sites, and also just to wander among the orange-and-ochre heritage buildings.

April 2010. But you can still admire its elegant Neoclassical façade and austere lines. As well as administrative offices, the building houses the tourist office, a great Catalan library and an auditorium, the latter in the old chapel.

▷ *After Plaça Pompeu Fabra, diagonally cross Plaça de Catalunya, over the river.*

Girona and Judaism

Girona's Jewish community, which settled on both sides of **Carrer de la Força** in the city's old quarter, was the second largest in Catalunya after Barcelona, and became famous in the Middle Ages for its prestigious Kabbalistic School, which existed for over 600 years from the 9C until the expulsions of 1492. This past can be felt in atmospheric narrow alleyways such as Carrer Cúndaro and Carrer Sant Llorenç, the latter home to the **Centro Bonastruc ça Porta**, dedicated to the town's Jewish history.

Rambla de Llibertat

Following the Onyar River and lined with cafés and shops, the lively Rambla de la Llibertat is the main route of entry into the old town. Beyond the stone bridge, medieval arcades once housed a large market. La Rambla flows onto the Carrer Argenteria, which is much narrower but just as colourful, and then leads to the bridge of Sant Agustí.

▶ *At the bridge, turn right into Plaça Lucerne then turn right again into Carrer Bonaventura Carreras Peralta.*

Fontana d'Or

Known by this name since the 18C, this Romanesque building has had various functions over the centuries. It now hosts art exhibitions.

▶ *Retrace your steps to Plaça Lucerne.*

El Call

Parallel to the Carrer Bonaventura Carreras Peralta, the Carrer de la Força winds through the "Call", the former Jewish quarter of Girona. This ensemble of tall buildings is crisscrossed with alleyways and steep staircases winding around the site of the ancient synagogue.

This road leads directly to the cathedral, but rather than heading straight on, meander around the looped side streets. Although the current layout no longer corresponds entirely to that of medieval times, and buildings have undergone various transformations, the evocative power of El Call is strong and its atmosphere charged with intensity and mystery.

Museu d'Histoia dels Jueus

Carrer Força, 8. ⊙Open Sept–May Tue–Sat 10am–6pm, Sun, Mon and long weekends 10am–2pm; Jul–Aug: Mon–Sat 10am–8pm, Sun 10am–2pm long weekends. ⊙Closed Jan 1 and 6, 25–26 Dec. ⊛€2 (under 16 years free). ℘972 216 761.

This museum reveals a moving history and tells the daily life of the Jewish community of 10C Girona through documents, text panels and engravings.

They narrate the Jews' economic and cultural significance, which was protected by both the Church and by the Catalan-Aragonese state, then of the circumstances leading to their tragic banishment.

Further along the same street, the Centre Ca Porta Bonastruc is located at the site of the ancient synagogue.

It now houses the Nahmanides Institute of Jewish Studies, named after the physician, philosopher and Rabbi Moshe ben Nahman (1194–1270), a leading member of Girona's Jewish community.

▶ *Continue along Carrer de la Força.*

Catedral★

Pl. de la Catedral. ⊙Open daily Apr–Oct 10am–8pm; Nov–Mar 10am–7pm. ⊛€5 (including nave, cloisters and museum); during Mass €3; no charge Sun. ℘972 21 58 14. www.catedraldegirona.org.

The Baroque façade is like an altarpiece with a single huge oculus. The rest of the building is Gothic: the chancel (1312) is surrounded by chapels; the single Gothic **nave**★★ is the largest in the world, and largely unadorned.

A silver-gilt embossed 14C **altarpiece**★ traces the Life of Christ. The Sant Honorat chapel has the outstanding tomb, in a Gothic niche, of Bishop Bernard de Pau.

Museu-Tresor de la Catedral★★

The treasury houses one of the most beautiful copies of the **Beatus**★★, or *St John's Commentary on the Apocalypse* (8C). The 10C embossed silver **Hixem Casket** is a fine example of Caliphate art, and there is Gothic silver and plate of the 14C and 15C. The end room contains the **Tapís de la Creació**★★★ (Tapestry of Creation), dating from about 1100, showing Christ in Majesty surrounded by the stages of creation.

The 12C–13C **cloisters**★, remain – like the 11C Torre de Carlomagno (Charlemagne Tower) – from an earlier Romanesque cathedral.

Colourful buildings by the Onyar

© Patrick Escudero/hemis.fr

Museu d'Art de Girona★★

Pujada de la Catedral 12. ⏰*Open Apr–Sept Tue–Sat 10am–7pm, Sun 10am–2pm; Nov–Mar Tue–Sat 10am–7pm, Sun 10am–2pm.* ⏰*Closed 1, 6 Jan, 25–26 Dec.* ⏰*€2.* ☎*972 20 38 34. www.museuart.com.*

The museum, in the Palau Episcopal, exhibits art from the Romanesque to the present. Holdings include a 10C portable altar from Sant Pere de Rodes of embossed silver, the 12C–13C **beam from Cruïlles**★, and apse paintings from Pyrenean churches. Among altarpieces in the Throne Room is one from **Sant Miquel de Cruïlles**★★ by Luis Borrassá (15C), Catalunya's greatest Gothic artist. Note the splendid **Púbol altarpiece**★, by Bernat Martorell (1437). The panels of the **Sant Feliu altarpiece** by Juan de Borgoña mark the transition from Gothic to Renaissance style.

▷ *Return to Carrer de la Força and take the first stairs on the left.*

Colegiata de Sant Feliu★

Pujada Sant Feliu 29. ⏰ *Open Mon–Sat 10am–1pm, 4–6pm, Sun 4–6pm.* ⏰*No charge.* ☎*972 20 14 07.*

This church outside the walls must originally have been a martyry over the tombs of St Narcissus, Bishop of Girona, and St Felix. The later Gothic church holds eight **early Christian sarcophagi**★, two with outstanding carvings, including a spirited **lion hunt**★.

▷ *Return to Carrer de la Força, cross it and veer to the left.*

Banys àrabs★ (Arab Baths)

Ferran el Católic. ⏰ *Open Apr–Sept Mon–Sat 10am–7pm, Sun and public holidays 10am–2pm; Oct–Mar Mon–Sat 10am–2pm.* ⏰*Closed 1, 6 Jan, 27 Mar, 25–26 Dec.* ⏰*€2.* ☎*972 21 32 62. www.banysarabs.org.*

These late-12C baths were built in accordance with Muslim tradition. They consist of four rooms in a row. Steps opposite lead to the **Passeig Arqueològic** (Archaeological Promenade) from which you can view the Ter Valley.

Monestir de Sant Pere de Galligants★

Santa Lucía 8. ⏰*Open Oct–May Tue–Sat 10am–2pm, 4–6pm, Sun and public holidays 10am–2pm; Jun–Sept Tue–Sat 10.30am–1.30pm, 4–7pm, Sun and public holidays 10am–2.30pm.* ⏰*Closed 1 Jan, 25–26 Dec;* ⏰*€2.30.* ☎*972 20 26 32. www.mac.cat.*

Not far from Sant Nicolau stands the fortified Romanesque church of Sant Pere, set into the town walls, housing the **Museu Arqueològic**. Shown are

Medieval memorial plaques and the magnificent 4C Roman **tomb of Las Estaciones**★.

ADDITIONAL SIGHTS
Museu del Cinema
Sèquia 1. ⊙*Open Oct–Apr Tues–Fri 10am–6pm, Sat 10am–8pm, Sun and Mon holidays 11am–3pm; May–Jun and Sept Tue–Sat 10am–8pm, Sun and Mon holidays 11am–3pm; Jul–Aug Tue–Sun 10am–8pm.* ⊙*Closed Mon, Jan 1 and 6, 25–26 Dec.* ⊙*€5 (under 16 free).* ℘*972 412 777. www.museudelcinema.cat.*
This unique museum brings to life the early days of cinema through screenings and varied exhibits. From silhouette montages to the delightful magic lanterns, visitors will discover the wonders of an age where a lack of technology was offset by an exuberant imagination.

Plaça de la Independencia
Designed by architect Martí Sureda Deulovol in 1855 (yet only completed in 1993 more or less according to his original design), this beautiful square is surrounded by Neoclassical buildings and affords some glimpses of the colourful facades along the Onya River.

Parc de la Devesa★
This park contains the largest grove of plane trees in Catalunya.

EXCURSION
Casa-Museu Castell Gala Dalí★
◯ *In Púbol. 16km/10mi E along the C 66 towards La Bisbal d'Empordà.*
⊙*Open 15 Mar–14 Jun and 16 Sept–1 Nov Tue–Sun 10am–6pm; 15 Jun–15 Sept daily 10am–8pm; 2 Nov–31 Dec Tue–Sun Dec 10am–5pm.* ⊙*Closed 1 Jan, 25 Dec.* ⊙*€7.* ℘*972 48 86 55, www.salvador-dali.org.*
In 1970, Salvador Dalí gave this 14C castle to his wife Gala. It now displays objects in a Surrealist atmosphere.

🚗 DRIVING TOUR

FROM GIRONA TO SANTA PAU
64.5km/40mi. Allow one day.

◯ *Head N from Girona along the C 66.*

Banyoles
◯ *20km/12.4mi NW of Girona.*
Banyoles is set by a **lake**★. The **Museu Arqueològic Comarcal**★ in a Gothic building shows the Palaeolithic Jaw of Banyoles *(Placeta de la Font 11;* ⊙*open Tue–Sat 10.30am–1.30pm, 4–6.30pm (7.30am in summer), Sun 10.30am–2pm;* ⊙*€6 (combined ticket with Cova dels Encantats, Serinya);* ℘*972 57 23 61).*
A 8km/5mi road around the lake passes the 13C **Església de Santa Maria de Porqueres**★, its columns sculpted with odd figures *(Ctra Circumval·lació de l'Estany;* ⊙*open by arrangement; enquire at the Museu Arqueològic Comarcal).*

👥 Estany de Banyoles
Lake Banyoles, over 2km long and 235m wide (1.2mi by 770ft), is flanked to the west by the Serra de Rocacorba and overlooks planes of oak trees alternating with green fields.
Besides the beauty of its landscape, it presents ecological significance because many protected species dwell here. Fishing and rowing are popular and the lake served as a gorgeous setting for the 1992 Olympic regatta events.

◯ *Take the C-66 7kms/4.3mi northwards.*

Serinya
In this little village, the church of Sant Andreu is a remarkable example of 13C Romanesque architecture with a gate adorned with archivolts.
Archaeological remains in the area include some splendid Middle and Upper Paleolithic remains in two caves: the Cova dels Encantats and Cova del Mollet *(℘972 593 310).*

◯ *Continue northwards on the C-66 for 7kms/4.3mi.*

Besalù★★

The first view of Besalú, across the river, with its Roman **fortified bridge**★, rebuilt in the medieval period, is extremely picturesque.

The **ancient city**★★ retains ramparts and many medieval buildings, including the Romanesque **Església de Sant Pere**★ with an unusual lion-flanked window *(Pl. de Sant Pere; guided tour by arrangement with the Tourist Office). 972 59 12 40)* and traditional **ritual baths** (12C) in the Jewish quarter *(guided tours arranged through the Tourist Office; €1.30; 972 59 12 40).*

▷ *Head 14km/8.7mi W along the N 260.*

Castellfollit de la Roca★

The village, in **Parc Natural de la Garrotxa**★, includes a medieval centre around the church of Sant Salvador.

▷ *Continue 8km/5mi along the N 260.*

Olot★

The 18C Neoclassical and Baroque **Església de Sant Estève**★, houses an unusual painting by El Greco – **Christ Bearing the Cross**★.

The **Museu Comarcal de la Garrotxa**★ displays a fine **collection of paintings and drawings**★★ by 19C and 20C Catalan artists *(Hospici 8; Tue–Fri 10am–1pm, 3–6pm (summer 11am–2pm, 4–7pm), Sat 11am–2pm, 4–7pm, Sun and public holidays 11am–2pm; €3; no charge first Sun of month; 972 27 11 66; www.mnac.cat).*

Note also the splendid **Modernist façade**★ of the **Casa Solà-Morales**★, by Domènech i Montaner.

▷ *Take the GI 524 E 9.5km/6mi.*

Zona Volcánica de la Garrotxa

Casal dels Volcans, Av. Sta Coloma de Farners. 972 268 112. www.parcsdecatalunya.net.
Declared a national park in 1982, the Zona Volcanica de la Garrotxa covers 11 300ha (27 923 acres) through the upper Fluvià valley. Thirty Strombolian-type volcanic cones, craters and more than 20 basaltic lava flows have created a lunaresque landscape of extreme beauty. This variation offers a mix of valleys and escarpments where it is not uncommon to see wild cats and boars. The park has also become a sanctuary for birds: nearly 150 different species have found refuge here.

On the road from Olot to Santa Pau, the Fageda D'en Jordà is an ancient beech forest standing on lava flow. Here there are easy walks to El Croscat (the youngest volcano in the park) and the Santa Margarida volcano, the largest in Garrotxa. Measuring 110m/360ft high and 1 200 m/3 930 ft wide, it is now covered in abundant vegetation.

Four signed routes starting from the information point of Can Serra allow you to discover the natural beauty of the park.

Santa Pau★

The Castillo de Santa Pau and the 15C–16C parish church both stand on the arcaded square of this village.

ADDRESSES

🏨 STAY

⊜ **Hostal Coll** – *Hortes 24, Girona. 972 203 086. www.hostalcoll.es. 8 rooms €2.* Simple, clean rooms, balconies and functional bathrooms on a quiet street.

⊜ **Pensió Viladomat** – *Ciutadans 5, Girona. 972 203 176. www.pensio viladomat.com. 8 rooms (4 with private bathroom).* Handy for the old town with simple, spacious rooms. Book ahead at Easter and in the summer.

🍽 EAT

⊜⊜ **Lloret** – *Pl. de la Independència 14, Girona. 972 213 671. Closed Sat evening and Sun.* Traditional cusisine served under the arcades of the square.

⊜⊜⊜ **Mimolet** – *Pou Rodó 12, Girona. 972 202 124. Closed Sun, Mon and Christmas–8 Jan.* Modern Catalan dishes served in stylish surrounds. Good value lunchtime set menus and superb wine list.

Cadaqués★★

This beautiful fishing village between mountains and sea is one of the most charming in Catalunya. It is located on the southern coast of Cape Creus, a peninsula that marks the meeting point between the Pyrenees and the Mediterranean. Its picturesque streets and bohemian atmosphere fascinated many famous artists in the first half of the 20C, including Picasso, Man Ray, Buñuel and Thomas Mann. Salvador Dalí spent much of his life in nearby Port Ligat. Cap de Creus became a recurring theme in his work.

THE TOWN TODAY

In high summer, Cadaqués has remained a fashionable retreat for Catalans and a large number of French visitors, so at times it can feel more like a resort on the French Riviera than a remote village in Northern Spain. Chic galleries and cafés line the waterfront and the local fleet of fishing boats is joined by pleasure yachts.

Such is the town's cachet that a seaside development in China will reproduce the whitewashed and bougainvillea-covered houses in a project that aims to replicate this archetypal Catalan seaside resort.

View of Cadaqués

© Fantuz Olimpio/Sime/Photononstop

▶ **Population:** 3 000
⏱ **Michelin Map:** 574 F 39.
🏢 **Info:** Des Cotxe 2-A. ☎972 258 315. www.cadaques.cat.
▶ **Location:** 36km/21mi S of the French border and 39km/24mi E of Figueres.
👪 **Kids:** The lighthouse at Cap de Creus.
🕐 **Timing:** July/August can be very crowded.

SIGHTS
Església de Santa Maria
Pl. Dr Callis 15. ◷*Open Mass only: Sat 7pm, Sun 11am (altarpiece can be viewed from the exterior via window).*
Overlooking the *casco antiguo* and indeed the focal point of the village, white-washed houses with picturesque porticoes cluster around the Església de Santa Maria, whose sober exterior contrasts with its interior: note the lovely **Baroque altarpiece**★★ in gilded wood by Joan Torres. The town hosts an annual international music festival *(late Jul–early Aug; www.festivalcadaques.cat).*

EXCURSIONS
Portlligat★
The **Casa-Museu Salvador Dalí**★ (◷*open 15 Jun–15 Sept daily 9.30am–9pm; rest of the year Tue–Sun 10.30am–6pm;* ◷*closed 25 Dec, Jan 1– Feb 11;* ☞€11; ☎972 25 10 15; www.salvador-dali.org*) is a cluster of fishermen's houses.
Dalí's workshop, library, rooms and garden are all open to the public.

Parque Natural de Cap de Creus★★
Steep roads and paths wind between cliffs and hidden bays to Cap de Creus, Spain's most easterly point. Many people come to enjoy a spectacular **view at sunset**, ★★★ which can be experienced from the terrace of the Restaurant Cap de Creus, next to the lighthouse at the highest point (☎972 19 90 05).

Costa Brava★★★

Spain's Costa Brava (literally "Wild Coast") is a twisted, rocky shoreline where the Catalan mountains fall away into the sea. Beautiful inlets, clear waters, picturesque harbours, and leisure and sporting activities draw tourists to these shores. Inland there are delightful medieval towns and villages.

DRIVING TOURS

1 FROM BLANES TO PALAMÓS
51km/31mi. Allow one day.

The circuit through two narrow coastal roads (GI 682 from Blanes to Sant Feliu) and C 253 from Sant Feliu to Palamós) provides excellent views of the coast.

Blanes★

The **Passeig Marítim**★ offers a lovely panorama of Blanes and its beach. The remains of the Castillo de Sant Joan are to the east, above the 14C Gothic Església de Santa Maria.

To the southeast is the **Jardí Botànic de Marimurtra**★ *(Pg. Karl Faust; ○open daily Mar-Apr and Oct 9am–6pm; Jun–Sept 9am–8pm; Nov–Mar 10am–5pm; €6; 972 33 08 26, www.marimurtra. cat)*, a botanical park with 5 000 plant species including many rare exotic varieties. At each bend the twisting paths reveal wonderful **views**★ of Cala Forcadera and the coast.

Jardí Botànic Pinya de Rosa★ *(Platja Santa Cristina (above the Marimurtra Jardí Botànic); ○open 9am–6pm; ○closed Jan 1 and 6, 24–26 Dec; €4; 972 355 290)*. Created in 1945, Pinya de Rosa has became the largest cactus garden in the world, with over 7 000 varieties.

Its founder, Fernando Riviere de Caralt, was an engineer who spent several decades on its development. Trails through the garden meander over the side of a steep cove, leading to a small pool surrounded by palm trees.

The foothills of the Serra de l'Albera form huge enclosed bays, like those of Portbou and El Port de la Selva. The clifftop

Michelin Map / Info box

- **Michelin Map:** 574 E 39, F 39, G 38-39 – Catalunya (Girona).
- **Info:** Girona: Joan Maragall 2. 872 975 975; Blanes: Plaça Catalunya 21. 972 33 03 48; Cadaqués: Des Cotxe 2 A. 972 25 83 15. www.costabrava.org.
- **Location:** The Costa Brava is the coastline from Blanes up to Portbou on the border with France. Lloret de Mar, Tossa de Mar and Platja d'Aro are major tourist centres; towns to the north are more low key.
- **Kids:** Beaches are the main attractions for younger tourists.

road section★★ from Portbou to Colera offers fine views of one of the most craggy coastlines in Catalunya.

▷ *Take the GI 682 NE for 7km/4.3mi.*

Lloret de Mar

Lloret de Mar has become the epicentre of bucket and spade tourism on the Costa Brava, replacing its original maritime ambiance with one of highrise hotels, outdoor discos, water parks and pleasure beaches.

Jardins de Santa Clothilde★★

▷ *Leave Lloret de Mar in the direction of Blanes. ○Open Apr–Sept 10am–8pm; Oct–Mar Tue–Sun 10am–5pm. €4. 972 370 471.*

This rare oasis of tranquility in Lloret de Mar was created in 1919 by architect and landscape designer Nicolau Maria Rubió i Tuduri (1891–1981).

The proprietor asked him to draw inspiration from the Italian Renaissance; terraced gardens are crossed by paths and stairs lined with ivy. Pines and cypresses abound and jazz concerts are held here in summer.

▷ *Take the GI 682 NE for 11km/6.8mi.*

Tossa de Mar★

This sandy beach curves around to Punta del Faro, the promontory on which stand the lighthouse and the 13C walls of the **Vila Vella**★ (old town). The **Museu Municipal**★ *(Roig i Soler;* open Tue–Sat 10am–2pm, 4–6pm, Sun 10am–2pm; €3; 972 34 07 09) contains artefacts from an ancient Roman villa nearby, and works by artists who stayed in the 1930s including Chagall, Masson and Benet.

Between Tossa and **Lloret de Mar**, the road follows a spectacular **clifftop route**★★.

Take the G1 682 N for 22km/13.6mi.

Sant Feliu de Guíxols★

Sheltered from the last spurs of the Serra de les Gavarres, this is one of the most popular locations of this coast. Its seaside boulevard, Passeig de la Mar, is lined with pavement cafés.

The **Església-Monastir de Sant Feliu**★ (open for Mass; 972 82 15 75) is part of a former Benedictine monastery. Its remains tower over the small municipality. It has retained its Romanesque façade, known as the **Porta Ferrada**★★, with horseshoe arches dating to pre-Romanesque times. The interior (14C) is Gothic in style.

The lookout by the chapel of Sant Elm commands beautiful **views**★★.

By the end of 2013, Sant Feliu de Guixol will have an exciting new venue; the **Centre d'art de Pintura Catalana Carmen Tyssen-Bornmesiza**. An immense 19C cork factory, situated in front of the monastery, is being converted for the museum, which will house over 350 works from 19C and 20C Catalan painters, as well as an auditorium.

Located on the edge of the town of Vila d'Aro, the **Roca de Pedralta**★, one of the largest rocking or "logan" stones in Europe, is a wonderful vantage point on the bay.

Head up the coast 4km/2.5mi.

S'Agaro★

An elegant resort with chalets and luxury villas surrounded by tidy gardens and pine forests. The Camino de Ronda offers fine views★ of the sheer cliffs.

Take the C 253 5.5km/3.5mi N.

Platja d'Aro

This coastal resort was built for the sole purpose of holidays. It comes alive during the summer when the streets become cosmopolitan and noisy and its fine stretch of sand packed with holiday makers.

Cova d'en Daina★

Access the C 31 to Calonge then Cabanyes Road.

The quiet winding road to Gavarres leads to this interesting megalithic tomb. A little further along, the medieval village of La Selva Romanyà is worth a look.

Take the C 253 5.5km/3.5mi N.

Palamós

This small fishing village has a vibrant marina offering range of leisure and services, making Palamós one of the busiest areas of the Costa Brava.

Museu de la Pesca

Open mid-Jun–mid-Sept 10am–9pm; rest of the year Tue–Sat 10am–1.30pm, 3–7pm; Sun 10am–2pm. €3. 972 600 424. www.museudelapesca.org.

This museum takes you on a journey into the world of fishing and its traditions, particularly those inherent to the Costa Brava. The traditional boats are a highlight.

② FROM PALAFRUGELL TO THE ILLES MEDES

59km/36.5mi. Allow half a day.

This northern swathe of the Costa Brava is where the scenery is at its most spectacular, particularly around the Cap de Begur.

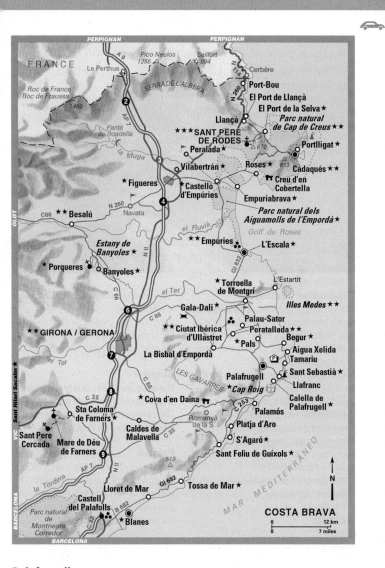

COSTA BRAVA

0	12 km
0	7 miles

Palafrugell

Located a few miles from the coast, the town of Palafrugell has a thriving cultural scene. In the early 20C, the production of cork made it extremely prosperous.

It is also the birthplace of the prolific writer Josep Pla (1897–1981). Palafrugell is very popular with visitors, especially in summer when they come for its festive atmosphere. *Suquet* – a fish stew – is a local speciality.

Museu del Suro (Cork Museum)

Calle Tarongeta 31. ⏰*Open mid-Sept–mid-Jun Mon–Sat 10am–1.30pm, 5–8.30pm, Sun 10am–1pm; rest of the year Tue–Sat 5–8pm, Sun and public hols 10.30am–1.30pm.* ⊚€3. ☎972 307 825. www.museudelsuro.cat.

This museum explains the different processes involved in the manufacture of cork. Most interesting are the old utensils used for to wash and cut the substance.

▷ *4.5 km/2.7 mi S on the GIV 6546.*

347

Golfet beach, Calella de Palafrugell

© Ingolf Pompe/hemis.fr

Calella de Palafrugell★

This fishing port is known for its **Festival de Habaneras** on the first Saturday in July. Visitors enjoy Afro-Cuban songs and dances while sipping *cremat*, flambéed coffee with rum.

A road southward leads to the **Jardin Botánic del Cap Roiga** (◷*open Apr–Sept daily 9am–8pm; rest of the year daily 9am–6pm;* ☞€6; ♪972 61 45 82).

A terraced park carved out of the rock, overlooking the Mediterranean, presents more than 1 200 plant species laid out along shaded avenues.

These gardens offer some wonderful **views**★★ of the coast.

Llafranc

▷ *2km/1.2 mi from Calella de Palafrugell by the small coastal road leading to Cap de Sant Sebastià or walk by the GR 12 that runs along the coast (15min).*

As is the case of Calella de Palafrugell, traditional fishermen's houses are juxtaposed with modern summer residences in Llafranc. The marina, which has 140 moorings, is the main attraction along with a small beach offering a host of summer activities.

Far de Sant Sebastià★

▷ *2km/1.2mi from Llafranc.*

Built in 1857, the lighthouse stands on a tiny isthmus surrounded by steep cliffs.

The nearby hermitage commands a lovely **view**★.

▷ *From Calella de Palafrugell, take the GIV 6591 and GIV 6542 11km/6.8mi NE.*

Begur★

The town overlooks pretty creeks from an altitude of 200m/656ft above the sea. The castle ruins (16C–17C) offer a nice view of the Cap de Begur.

Pals★★

At the mouth of the Ter river, Pals has an attractive old quarter, **El Pedró**. The vestiges of fortified ramparts enclose ancient houses and winding alleyways, some with covered stairways.

▷ *12km/7.5mi N of Pals on the C 66.*

La Bisbal d'Emporda

The capital of the Baix Empordá region has been famous for its ceramics and pottery for centuries and around this a vibrant crafts community has evolved. Along its main streets you will find dozens of shops selling the distinctive yellow, green and clay-coloured pots, vases and cookware of the Costa Brava.

Castell★

Pl. del Castell. ◷*Winter: open daily except Mon 10am–1pm; summer 11am–2pm, 5–8pm.* ☞€2. ♪ 972 645 166.

The former residence of the Bishops of Girona is the most remarkable building in La Bisbal, combining Romanesque and Gothic elements. Part of the building houses the historical archives of the region.

> *Back on the C 66, turn left on the C 252, then right on the IM 651.*

Peratallada★★

This fortified village is considered one of the finest medieval ensembles in the Empordà.

Winding old streets lead to the Plaça Major (main square) where a grand castle-fortress sits, now a luxury hotel. Also seek out the Plaça de les Voltes, with charming porticoes and ancient dwellings, one of the most characteristic snapshots of the village.

The church of Sant Esteve, an austere 13C building situated outside the village, has a bell perforated with a pattern common to the region.

> *Continue on the IM 651*

Ullastret★

This is one of the most picturesque villages in Empordà's hinterland. Its old medieval streets exude bags of character and it's a great place to buy regional products. The Church of Sant Pere – located in the centre of the village – is a fine example of Romanesque architecture. Notice the curious Gothic ossuary with its carvings of characters and animals.

Ciutat Ibérica

1km E of Ullastret. ⏱*Open Oct–May daily except Mon 10am–2pm, 3–6pm, Jun–Sept daily except Tues 10am–8pm.* ⏱*Closed 25, 26 Dec and 1 Jan.* ⬤€*2.30 (no charge under 16 years).* ✆*972 179 058. www.mac.es.*

One of Catalunya's most extensive Iberian discoveries is situated near Ullastret on the crest of Mont de Sant Andreu. Here you can see the remains of a settlement built by the Indiket tribe in the 5C, who constructed canals, a reservoir and a main square.

Artefacts such as scripts can be viewed in the Archaeological Museum on the same site.

> *Continue on the IM 644 and then turn right on the IM 643.*

Torroella de Montgrí★

Despite a Baroque front, the 14C **Església de Sant Genís** *(Pas. de l'Església)* is a fine example of Gothic Catalan art.

The **castle** on Montaña de Montgrì (🚶 *1hr on a signposted path among the rocks*) is an extraordinary **belvedere**★★ with a view to the sea and the Gavarres mountain range.

> *Take the GI 641 towards the coast.*

👥 Illes Medes★★

Boat trips around the islands are offered from l'Estartit. ℹ*For information contact the tourist office.* ✆*972 75 17 49 (Tourist Office of L' Estartit). www.visitestartit.com.*

These seven islets and coral reefs are the extension of the calcareous massif of Montgrí. It is interesting to ecologists for its marine species and ecosystems. The islets are popular for diving.

3 THE GOLF OF ROSES

36km/22mi.

The vast majority of this stretch of coastline forms part of the Parc Natural dels Aiguamolls de l'Empordà.

L'Escala★

This resort has sandy beaches and a long fishing tradition (anchovies are salted). Two inlets protect its harbour.
The Empúries ruins are located to the N.

Empúries/Ampurias★★

Puig i Cadafalch. ⏱*Open daily Oct–May 10am–6pm; Jun–Sept 10am–8pm.* ⏱*Closed 25, 26 Dec and 1 Jan.* ⬤€*3; no charge last Sun in month, 23 Apr, 18 May and 11 Sept.* ✆*972 77 02 08. www.mac.cat.*

Greco-Roman Ampurias (*Emporion* to the Greeks, meaning market) was built on a striking seaside **site**★★. It is still possible to make out the old town, or **Paliápolis**, the new town or **Neápolis**, and the Roman town.

In the mid-6C BC, the Phoenicians founded Paliápolis, on an offshore island, now joined to the mainland and occupied by the village of Sant Marti d'Empúries. A town began to develop on the shore opposite: Neápolis.

As a Roman ally during the Punic Wars, it saw the arrival of an expedition led by Scipio Africanus Major in 218 BC. In 100 BC the Roman town was established to the west. The two centres coexisted until Augustus bestowed Roman citizenship upon the Greeks. The colony suffered from barbarian invasions in the 3C AD. At one time it was a bishopric, as basilica ruins show.

Neápolis

The **Templo de Asclepio** (Aesculapius – god of healing) and a sacred precinct contained altars and statues of the gods. Nearby stood a **watchtower** and drinking water cisterns. The **Templo de Zeus Serapis** (a god associated with the weather and with healing) was surrounded by a colonnade. The **Agora** was the centre of town life; three statues remain. A street from the agora to the sea was bordered on one side by the **stoa** or covered market. Behind it are the ruins of a 6C **palaeo-Christian basilica** with a rounded apse.

Museu Arqueológic d'Empúries

A section of Neápolis is displayed along with models of temples and finds from the excavations.

The Roman Town

Unlike Neápolis, this is a vast, geometrically laid out town, partially excavated, with some restored walls. **House no. 1** (entrance at the back) has an atrium (inner courtyard) with six columns. Around this are residential apartments, the peristyle, or colonnaded court, and the impluvium, or rainwater catchment. The reception rooms are paved in geometric black-and-white mosaic.

House no. 2B has rooms paved with their original mosaic. One has been reconstituted in clay with its walls resting on stone foundations.

The **forum**, a large square lined by porticoes and, to the north and south respectively, by temples and shops, was the centre of civic life. A porticoed street led through the city gate to the oval **amphitheatre** which is still visible.

Castelló d'Empúries★

Situated a short walk from the archaeological site, the former capital of the principality of Empúries (11C–14C) is on a promontory near the coast.

The 14C–15C **Basílica de Santa Maria**★ is flanked by a typical Catalan belfry. The **portal**★★ is a unique example of Gothic art in Catalunya: the tympanum illustrates the Adoration of the Magi while the Apostles are shown on the jambs. The large central nave is lined by fine cylindrical pillars.

The alabaster **retable**★ in the high altar (15C), with conical pinnacles, depicts the Passion. (◷*open daily noon–2pm, 4–8pm; ☎972 25 05 19*).

The village retains buildings from its golden age: the **Ajuntament** (Maritime Commodities Exchange), combining Romanesque and Gothic elements, and the **Casa Gran**, of Gothic inspiration.

◗ *Take the C 68 towards the coast.*

Empuriabrava★

The luxury marina-residential development allows backyard docking.

◗ *9.5km/6mi N on the C 68.*

Roses

Sailors of Rhodes founded a colony in a splendid natural harbour overlooking the Golfo de Roses. Its 16C Renaissance **citadel**★ (*Av. de Roses; ◷open Tue–Sun Apr–Sept, 10m–8pm, Jul–Aug 10am–9pm, 10am–8pm; Oct–Mar 10am–6pm; ◷closed 25 Dec, 1, 6 Jan; ⊛€3; ☎972 15 14 66; www.rosesfhn.org*), a pentagon with many bastions, was commissioned by Charles V.

The Benedictine monastery inside was destroyed by the French during the War of Independence. The town is both resort and fishing port.

4 FROM CADAQUÉS TO PORT-BOU

52km/32mi - allow half a day.

This route traverses the northernmost stretch of the Catalan coast, from the beautiful peninsula of Cap de Creus (⚓ *see p344*) reaching Port-Bou at the French border. Begin the drive at Cadaqués (⚓ *CADAQUÉS*).

El Port de la Selva★

This bay is bathed in golden sunlight at dusk. Traditional white houses stand beside numerous flats and hotels. Fishing is still one of the main activities.

🚗 *7km/4.3mi inland from El Port de la Selva on the GI 612.*

Monestir de Sant Pere de Rodes★★★

🅿️*Leave your car in the car park and proceed on foot for 10min.* 🕐*Open Tue–Sun Oct–May 10am–5pm; Jun–Sept 10am–8pm.* 🕐*Closed 25 Dec, 1 Jan.* 🎫*€4; no charge Tue.* 📞*972 38 75 59.*

This imposing Benedictine monastery stands in a beautiful **setting**★★ that dominates the Gulf of León and the Cap de Creus peninsula. Begun in the 10C, it was pillaged, and abandoned in the 18C. The remarkable **church**★★★, showing pre-Romanesque influence, is an unusual example of architectural harmony. The central nave has barrel vaulting, the two lateral ones have surbased vaulting.

They are separated by huge pillars, reinforced with columns on raised bases. Splendid **capitals**★, intricate tracery and acanthus leaves evoke the tradition of Córdoba and Byzantium. The left arm of the transept leads to an upper ambulatory offering a sweeping view of the central nave.

The 12C **bell tower**★★ is a magnificent example of Lombardy Gothic.

The coast between El Port de la Selva and Cadaqués features many irregular creeks with crystal-clear waters, accessible only by sea. The road inland offers lovely views of the region.

🚗 *20km/12.5mi N on the GIP 6041, then the N 260 motorway.*

El Port de Llançà

🚉*Plaça de la Estación.*

A pleasant tourist resort sited on a bay sheltered from winds like the *tramontana* and sudden Mediterranean storms. The shallow waters are ideal for swimming.

🚗 *10km/6mi N via the N 260.*

Port-Bou★

Bordering French Roussillon, this popular holiday spot is also one of Catalunya's main border crossings, especially for rail traffic. The nucleus of Port-Bou is in fact situated next to the railway station, Nevertheless, Port-Bou does offer some amazing coastal scenery. Whether you come in via the N 260 or by the magnificent M 612 coastal route, you can admire some of the steepest cliffs on the Catalan coast and countless pristine coves.

ADDRESSES

🛏️ STAY

Accommodation on the **Costa Brava** can be expensive, and it is often difficult to find a room during high season without having booked well in advance. For more reasonable prices and better availability search the hinterland as well.

😊😊 **Hotel La Goleta** – *Pintor Terruella 22, El Port de LLançà.* 📞*972 38 01 25. www.hotel lagoleta.com. 30 rooms. Restaurant* 😊😊. Close to the port, the La Goleta offers comfort and an interesting décor of paintings and other furnishings. A friendly atmosphere and good value for money.

😊😊 **Hotel Rosa** – *Pi i Rallo 19, Begur.* 📞*972 62 30 15. www.hotel-rosa.com. 21 rooms. Restaurant*😊😊. This small hotel in a restored stone house by the church is popular with younger travellers for its modern décor, functional furniture and well-planned lighting. The restaurant serves traditional cuisine.

😊😊😊 **Hotel Diana** – *Plaça de Espanya 6, Tossa de Mar.* 📞*972 34 18 86. www.hotelesdante.com. 21 rooms.* The interior of this splendid Modernist building by the sea is exquisite, with high ceilings, cool rooms and a patio adorned with a marble fountain. The rooms are comfortable and furnished in style.

⊜⊜🍶🍶 **Hotel Plaça** – *Pl. Mercat 22, Sant Feliu de Guíxols.* ☎*972 32 51 55. www.hotelplaza.org. 19 rooms.* ⊑ *€8.* A practical choice for location and functional character. Pleasant, bright rooms – some overlook a square that's lively on market days. Outdoor jacuzzi and solarium on the top floor.

⊜⊜🍶🍶 **Hotel Port Lligat** – *Avenida Salvador Dalí 1, Port Lligat.* ☎*972 25 81 62. www.port-lligat.net/hotel. 30 rooms.* ⊑ *€10* The creature comforts in this attractive blue and white building in a cove full of fishing boats near Dalí's house are particularly popular with guests. Every room is different, and if you don't mind paying a bit extra, ask for one with a sea view.

⊜⊜🍶🍶 **Hotel Sant Roc** – *Pl. Atlàntic 2 (Sant Roc district), Calella de Palafrugell.* ☎*972 61 42 50. www.santroc.com. 45 rooms. Restaurant. Closed mid-Nov–late Mar.* This charming building crowned by a small tower enjoys a peaceful, relaxing setting amid pine groves overlooking the Mediterranean. The rooms are spacious and elegant, while the restaurant terrace enjoys fine views of neighbouring coves. Half-board compulsory in summer.

⊽/EAT

⊜⊜🍶🍶 **Snackmar Las Golondrinas** – *Sant Sebastià 63, Roses.* ☎*972 153 705. Closed Mon and Nov–Dec.* This small tapas bar, run by a former alumnus of El Bulli (Ferran Adrià's restaurant), is where many of the chefs who worked there ate in their down time. Well above the average tourist haunts in Roses.

⊜⊜🍶🍶 **Portal de la Gallarda** – *Pere Estany, 14, Mollet de Peralada. Castelló d'Empúries.* ☎*972 250 152. Closed Tue out of season.* The restaurant specialises in grilled fish and is set in a lovely 12C building with a beautiful terrace embracing part of the Natural Park.

⊜⊜🍶🍶 **Victoria** – *Passeig del Mar 23, Tossa de Mar.* ☎*972 34 01 66. www.hrvictoriatossa. com. Closed 15 Nov–31 Jan, Tue (Sept–Jun).* A pleasant restaurant specialising in seafood and fish dishes, with a terrace overlooking the beach. There are also hotel rooms available with sea views (⊜⊜).

⊜⊜🍶🍶 **La Brasa** – *Pl. de Catalunya, 6 El Port de Llançà.* ☎*972 38 02 02. Closed summer, mid-Dec–late Feb.* Low-key restaurant serving excellent grilled meat and fish on its shady terrace.

⊜⊜🍶🍶 **L Ca l'Herminda** – *L'Illa, 7, El Port de la Selva.* ☎*972 38 02 02. Closed Mon and Tue eves Apr–Jun.* Housed in a former fisherman's cottage this is a perfect restaurant for eating fresh fish at reasonable prices. Rustic in décor, the dining rooms are spread over several levels.

🎷 NIGHTLIFE

Moxo – *Empuriabrava.* The Moxo is the focal point for nightlife in this modern tourist resort, which has about 20 bars, nightclubs and restaurants. The Saloon specialises in country music and the Glass in techno.

Café Latino – *Rbla Roma, 10, Lloret de Mar.* ☎*972 366 153.* A lively dance bar where Latin music and cocktails are king.

Cala Banys – *Cami Cala Banys, Lloret de Mar* ☎*972 366 515 3.* One of the most romantic bars in the Costa Brava. This little paradise is as enchanting by day as it is by night with a shady terrace overlooking the water.

🎭 ENTERTAINMENT

Nautilus – *Pg Marítim 23, L'Estartit.* ☎*972 751 489. www.nautilus.es.* Tours of the Medes Islands on board glass-bottom boats (90min, €17.50 per person), Sant Martí to Empúries (2.30hr, €20.50 p.p.), and Cadaqués to Cap de Creus (5hr, €25.50 p.p.).

International Diving Center – *At the far end of the port, L'Escala.* ☎*972 770 077 and 610 015 920. www.internationaldiving.com.* Authorised dives around the Cap de Creus. (€56 p.p.)

Creuers Mare Nostrum – *Maranges 3, L'Escala.* ☎*972 773 797. www.creuers-marenostrum.com.* A fleet of 10 glass-bottom boats (including 2 catamarans) that tour the Medes Islands.

🚶🚶 **Parc Aquàtic Aqua Brava** – *Ctra de Cadaqués. 1km/0.5mi from Roses. Jun–mid-Sept 10am–7pm.* ☎*972 254 344. www.aqua brava.com.* Water park known for its huge wave pool, sandy beach and tropical vegetation. €23 day (children up to 1.20m/3ft6 €13) or €18 half a day (€10).

Hípica dels Aiguamolls – *Rte de Palau Savardera, Castelló d'Empúries.* ☎*639 787 732. www.haiguamolls.com.* Horseriding, from 30min to a whole day.

🛍 SHOPPING

Carrer de l'Aigüeta – *La Bisbal d'Empordà.* Ceramics are a centuries-old tradition, and you'll find all sorts of objects in the shops on this street. Try El Risser.

Figueres★

Figueres, capital of Alt Empordà, the birthplace of Surrealist artist **Salvador Dalí** (1904–89), is one of Catalunya's premier destinations. Dalí spent his last years here, building his extravagant museum.

A BIT OF HISTORY

The end of the Spanish Civil War – The last meeting of the Republican Cortes was held here on 1 February 1939. Three days later, Girona fell to the Nationalists. Two days after, the Republican leaders crossed into France.

SIGHTS

Teatre-Museu Dalí★★

Pl. de Dalí i Gala. ○*Open Mar–June and Oct Tue–Sun 9.30am–5.15pm; Jul–Sept daily 9am–7.15pm; Nov–Feb Tue–Sun 10.30am–5.15pm.* ○*Closed 25 Dec, 1 Jan.* ∞€11. ℘*972 67 75 24. www.salvador-dali.org.*

The theatre-museum, a world of folly and caprice, may charm or exasperate but never fails to impress. The artist himself said: "The museum cannot be considered as such; it is a gigantic surrealist object, where everything is coherent, where nothing has eluded my design." To a restored 1850 theatre Dalí added an immense glass dome (beneath which he is buried) and patio, and decorated everything with fantasy objects: giant eggs, bread rolls, basins and gilt dummies. He gave his eccentricity full rein in the squares around the museum where figures perch on columns of tyres, as well as inside. Some of his canvases are exhibited as well as works by Pitxot and Duchamp.

Torre Galatea★

The decoration of this tower by Dalí used vivid colours and fantasy objects.

CIUTAT VELLA (OLD TOWN)

Figueres also has a pleasant historical centre with attractive squares and alleys. The Rambla is a pleasant street full of outdoor bars and restaurants.

▶ **Population:** 44 255
⚲ **Michelin Map:** 574 F 38 – map 122 Costa Brava. See local map under Costa Brava p347.
▤ **Info:** Plaça del Sol. ℘972 50 31 55. www.figueresciutat.com
◐ **Location:** Figueres is located 20km/12.4mi inland, at the heart of the area known as the Ampurdán, at the crossroads of routes leading to the Costa Brava and the French city of Perpignan, 58km/36mi N. ▭Plaça de La Estació.
◉ **Don't Miss:** Everything Dalí: the Museum and Tower.
◔ **Timing:** Take a half-day at least, or longer if Dalí is your thing.

Museu de Joguets★

Hotel París, Sant Pere 1. ○*Open Jun–Sept Mon–Sat 10am–7pm, Sun and public holidays 11am–6pm; Oct–May Tue–Sat 10am–6pm, Sun and public holidays 11am–2pm.* ○*Closed 25 Dec, 1 Jan.* ∞€5. ℘*972 50 45 85. www.mjc.cat.*

The museum displays toys and stuffed animals from different countries.

Museu de l'Empordà

Rambla 2. ○*Open Tue–Sat 11am–7pm, Sun and public holidays 11am–2pm.* ○*Closed 1, 6 Jan and 25–26 Dec.* ∞€2; no charge with Museu Dalí ticket. ℘*972 50 23 05. www.museuemporda.org.*

This building houses collections devoted to the art, history and archaeology of the region. Of note is the exhibition of works by 19C and 20C painters (Nonell, Sorolla, Dalí and Tàpies).

Església de Sant Pere

Pl. de l'Església. ○*Open Tue–Fri 9am–1pm, 4.30–8pm (9pm Sat); Sun 8.30am–1pm, 6–9pm.* ○*Closed 25–26 Dec, 1, 6*

Teatre-Museu Dalí, Figueres

©Turespaña

The World of Dalí

Born in 1904, Dalí was to become one of the most famous Surrealist artists. His "paranoid-critical" method, based on an ironic vision of reality, resulted in his expulsion from the Surrealist ranks by its founder, André Breton. In his most famous paintings, *The Great Masturbator*, *The Persistence of Memory*, *Atomic Leda and Premonition of the Civil War*, Dalí expresses his personal world through bland forms loaded with sensuality and sexual connotations.

The Dalian attractions in Figueres are both located around the lively Plaça de Dalí i Gala. Further examples of Dalí's creativity can be seen in two museums within a short distance of Figueres: the first, the **Casa-Museu Salvador Dalí**, is situated in the charming fishing village of **Portlligat**★★ (see p344), 31km/19.2mi E of Figueres on the C 260 and GI 614; the second, the **Casa-Museu Castell Gala Dalí** (*GIRONA/GERONA*), in Púbol, 16km/10mi E of Girona on the C 66, is housed in the castle that Dalí gave to his wife, Gala, as a gift in 1970. Together they are known the Dalían Triangle.

Jan. €2; no charge 18 May.
972 50 03 25.
Built in the late 13C, this church has a single nave of Gothic influence. Most of the church was rebuilt after the Spanish Civil War.

EXCURSION
Castell de Sant Ferran★

Guided tours (2hr) daily Jul–mid-Sept and Holy Week 10.30am–8pm; Oct–Jun 10.30am–3pm. Closed 25 Dec, 1 Jan. €3. 972 51 45 85. www.castillosanfernando.org.
This mid-18C fortress, with star-shaped perimeter, defended the border with France. The castle was the second largest of its kind in Europe, with a parade ground alone that covered 12 000sq m/14 340sq yd.
The **stables**★ are worthy of particular note. The **views**★ from the walls take in the Empordà plain.

ADDRESSES

STAY

Hotel Duràn – *Lasauca 5.* 972 50 12 50. www.hotelduran.com. *65 rooms.* €9. Restaurant . This hotel is in the town centre near the Dalí Museum, with large, comfortable rooms. The restaurant, specialising in Catalan dishes, is where Dalí himself used to dine.

Hotel Rural Mas Falgarona – *Avinyonet de Puigventós. 5.4km/3.3mi SW of Figueres on the N 260.* 972 54 66 28. www.masfalgarona.com. *11 rooms.* Restaurant . This luxury hotel is housed in an old farmhouse. The minimalist décor, enhanced by various works of modern art, brings out the natural beauty of the stone, brick and wood. Delightful garden with pool.

Mas Pau Hotel and Restaurant – *Avinyonet de Puigventós. 5km/3mi SW of Figueres on the N 260.* 972 54 61 54. www.maspau.com. *20 rooms.* Restaurant *(closed Sun eve, Tue lunch).* This 16C farmstead has been sympathetically restored and decorated in exquisite taste. The restaurant, run by an ex-alumnus of Ferran Adrià, is superb.

Solsona★★

Solsona is a tranquil town with a noble air and attractive squares. Elegant medieval residences line its gently sloping streets.

SIGHTS

Museu Diocesà i Comarcal★★ (Diocesan and Regional Museum)

Pl. del Palau 1. Open Oct–Apr Tue–Sun 10am–1pm, 4–6pm, public holidays 10am–2pm; May–Sept Tue–Sun 10am–1pm, 4.30–7pm, public holidays 10am–2pm. €3. ℘973 48 21 01.

Romanesque and Gothic **paintings**★★ in the Palau Episcopal (Episcopal Palace, an 18C Baroque building), are excellent examples of Catalan art.

The frescoes include a painting from the **Sant Quirze de Pedret church**★★, discovered beneath an overpainting. Executed in an archaic style, it shows God, with arms outstretched, in a circle which represents Heaven, surmounted by a phoenix symbolising immortality. Totally different are the thinly outlined 13C paintings from **Sant Pau de Caserres**★ – in particular, wonderful **angels**★★ of the Last Judgement.

Known for its **altar fronts**, another highlight of the museum is **La Cena de Santa Constanza**★, a realistic Last Supper, by Jaime Ferrer (15C).

In the **Museu de la Sal** (Salt Museum), everything is carved out of rock salt from Cardona.

Catedral★

Pl. de la Catedral. Open Mon–Sat 9am–1pm, 4–9pm, Sun 10am–1pm, 4–6pm. No charge. ℘973 48 23 10.

Only the belfry and the apse remain of the Romanesque church; the rest is Gothic with Baroque additions such as the portals and the sumptuous 18C Capella de la Virgen (Lady Chapel) off the south transept. This chapel houses the **Mare de Déu del Claustro**★, a beautifully carved Romanesque figure of the Virgin Mary in black stone.

After visiting the Cathedral, stroll around the rest of the old city, particularly the Plaça Major, which is framed by medieval houses and porches, the Carrer del Castell (home of the 16C *ajuntament*, or town hall, and the Plaça de Sant Joan.

▶ **Population:** 9 233
⌖ **Michelin Map:** 574 G 3 – Catalunya (Lleida).
ℹ **Info:** Carretera Bassella 1. ℘973 48 23 10. www.tourisemsolsones.com.
▷ **Location:** The capital of the Solsonès region is on the C 1410 road linking Manresa with the C 1313 heading into the Pyrenees.
⏲ **Timing:** Avoid Mondays, when musuems are shut.

EXCURSION

Cardona★

▷ *20km/12.4mi SE along the C 55.*

Cardona sits at the foot of an imposing castle.

Castillo de Cardona★

This spectacular hilltop fortress, at 589m/1 933ft, dates back to the 8C. Of the 11C buildings there remain only a truncated tower, the **Torre de la Minyona**, and the collegiate church, surrounded by Vauban-style walls and bulwarks built in the 17C and 18C. The castle is a parador, commanding a marvellous **view**★ of the **muntanya de sal**★★ (Tue–Fri 10am–3pm (descent to mine 11.30am and 1.30pm), Sat–Sun every 30min 10am–6pm (August daily 10am–7pm); €11; ℘938 69 24 75; www.salcardona.com), a salt mine worked since Roman times.

Colegiata de Sant Vicenç★★

Open Tue–Sun Oct–end May 10am–1pm, 3–5pm; Jun–Sept 10am–1pm, 3–7pm. Closed 1, 6 Jan, 25–26 Dec. €3; no charge Tue. ℘938 68 41 69. www.mhcat.net.

The collegiate church built in 1040 has Lombard features. The groined vaulting in the **crypt**★ rests on six graceful columns. The Gothic cloisters date from the 15C.

Pirineos Catalanes★★★

The Catalan Pyrenees form a barrier of 230km/143mi long and 100km/62mi wide, stretching from the Vall d'Aran to the Mediterranean, with altitudes above 2500m/8202ft. These mountains are deeply cut by isolated valleys, with their own personality and traditions.
All offer delicious regional cuisine and opportunities for skiing, hunting, fishing, mountain climbing and adventure sports. The area is great for driving around and the following tours can be followed on the map in this section.

ART AND ARCHITECTURE

The Pyrenean villages and valleys of Catalunya denote a unique Romanesque style of art and architecture.
In the 11C, as the local population was fighting against the Arabs, small village churches were built and painted with entrancing murals graphically depicting Christian doctrine for a largely illiterate population. The movement reached its climax in the Vall de Boí (see p363), which has been listed as a World Heritage Site by UNESCO.

🚗 DRIVING TOURS

1 VALL DE CAMPRODON
30km/18.6mi. Allow half a day.

Two large valleys lie in the Ripollès area under mountains towering to 3 000m/10 000ft.

Camprodon★
Camprodon is at the confluence of the Ritort and Ter rivers, crossed by a 12C humpbacked bridge, **Pont Nou**★.
The community developed around the **Monesteri de Sant Pere**. Only the 12C **Romanesque church**★ remains.
The cloisters of **Monasterio de Sant Pere de Camprodon**★ *(Pl. de Santa Maria; no charge)* are simple and ele-

- **Michelin Map:** 574 D 32, E 32–37 and F 32–37 – Catalunya (Girona, Lleida)
- **Info:** Camprodon: Plaça d'Espanya 1. 972 74 00 10; Carretera Comarcal 151, km 23,5. 972 74 09 36. www.valldecamprodon.org; Puigcerdà: Querol 1. 972 88 05 42; La Seu d'Urgell: Avinguda Valls d'Andorra 33. 973 35 15 11. www.laseu.org; Pas. Joan Brudieu 15. 973 35 31 12; Tremp: Plaça de la Creu 1. 973 65 00 09. www.ayuntamentdetremp.com; Vielha: Sarriulera 10. 973 64 01 10. www.turisme.aran.org. www.visitpirineos.com.
- **Location:** The Pyrenees extend almost unbroken for 230km/143mi from the Mediterranean to the high Aran Valley (2 500m/8 202ft). The last range, the Montes Alberes, plunges into the Mediterranean from 700m/2 297ft.
- **Timing:** Geography will oblige you to select one or two valleys to explore from the south access.

gant, with sweeping arches and slender columns with capitals decorated with plant motifs. The **museum** houses a collection of embroidered fabric.
Opposite the church on the square stands the 14C former Abbatial Palace. The **medieval bridge**★ spans the Ter river on the way towards Ripoll.

> *Leave N via the C 38 and after 3.5km/2mi take the winding Carretera Camprodón-Baget mountain road.*

Beget★★
This attractive mountain village with stone houses enjoys a pleasant **setting**★ deep in a peaceful valley.

The **San Cristófol church**★★ (10C–12C) with Lombard arcatures and slender lantern-tower, houses the **Majestad de Beget**★, a magnificent figure of Christ carved in the 12C (⏱*open daily 9am–7pm; ask for the keys from Joan Coma, Carrer Bellaire;* ✆€1; ☎972 74 01 36).

▷ *Continue on the Carretera Camp-rodon-Baget before taking the C 38 to Molló.*

Molló

The 12C Romanesque church has a lovely Catalan belfry. Further along the C 38 and at 1 513m/5 000ft, the Col d'Ares marks the Spanish-French border.

② **VALL DE RIBES**
22km/13.6mi from Ripoll to Vall de Núria. Allow a couple of hours.

The Vall de Ribes is popular with Barceloneses as an easily-reached skiing and hiking spot, particularly the Vall de Núria.

Ripoll★

☎972 70 23 51. www.ripoll.cat.
Nestled in a valley deep in the first Pyrenean cliffs, this small industrial city and commercial centre is considered the "cradle of Catalonia." It derives its fame from the great Benedictine monastery of Santa Maria, founded in the 9C by Count Wilfred the Hairy, which, until the 12C, served as a necropolis for the Counts of Barcelona, Besalú, Girona, Ausona and Cerdanya.
Ripollès's capital is also a former small core at the confluence of two rivers and a few modernist houses (Can Codina, Can Dou and Casa Bonada).

Monasterio de Santa Maria★

Pl. de l'Abat Oliba. ⏱*Open daily Oct–Mar 9am–1pm, 3–6pm; Apr–end Sept 9am–1pm, 3–7pm.* ✆€3. ☎972 70 02 43.
All that remains of the original monastery are the church portal and the cloisters.
In 1032, Abbot Oliba consecrated an enlarged **church**★, a jewel of early Romanesque art that was damaged over

the years. It was rebuilt at the end of the 19C to the original plan.
The **portada**★★★, or portal design, is composed of a series of horizontal registers illustrating the glory of God victorious over His enemies (Passage of the Red Sea). The **Claustro**★ (cloisters) abutting the church dates to the 12C; others were added in the 14C.

Museu Etnografic

Opposite the monastery, ⚠*closed for renovations; temporary exhibitions in the town hall.*
The Ethnographic Museum traces the history of the area. Inaugurated in 1920, it contains more than 5 000 pieces: from clothing and ceramics and rooms devoted to the iron industry, showing ancient forges and firearms from the 16 to 19C.

▷ *Take the C 26 NW.*

Monasterio de Sant Joan de les Abadesses★★

⏱*Open Mar–Apr and Oct 10am–2pm, 4–7pm; May–June and Sept 10am–2pm, 4–6pm; Jul–Aug 10am–7pm; Nov–Feb Tue–Sat 10am–2pm, 4–7pm, Sun 10am –2pm 4–6pm.* ✆€3. ☎972 72 23 53.
www.santjoandelesabadesses.cat.
The monastery was founded in the 9C under the rule of a Benedictine abbess, though it soon shut out women.
With its arches and columns with carved capitals the church recalls those of southwest France.
A magnificent 1251 **Descent from the Cross**★★ in polychrome wood is in the central apse. In 1426 an unbroken host was discovered on the Christ figure's head; it is venerated to this day.

▷ *Head N along the N 152 for 17km/10.5mi.*

Ribes de Freser

www.vallderibes.cat.
This famous spa stands at the confluence of three rivers and is known for the healing properties of its waters. A rack railway runs to the Vall de Núria.

▶ *Continue 7km/4.3mi N along N 152 to the Vall de Núria, passing through the mountain village of Queralbs, which offers good views of the valley and is a stop on the* 🚠*rack railway.*

Vall de Núria★

The valley is surrounded by a rocky amphitheatre stretching from Puigmal to the Sierra de Torreneules. The Virgin of Núria, the patron saint of Pyrenean shepherds, is venerated in a sanctuary located in the upper part of the valley.

3 LA CERDANYA★★

145km/90mi from La Seu d'Urgell to La Molina. Allow about 5hr.

The fertile Cerdanya Basin, watered by the River Segre, was formed by subsidence. The northern section, La Cerdagne, was ceded to France under the Treaty of the Pyrenees in 1659.

The **Túnel del Cadí**, opened in 1984, facilitates access from Manresa.

From Ribes de Freser to Puigcerdà, the road cut into the cliff face up to the Collado de Toses commands impressive **views**★ of the Segre and its slopes.

▶ *66 km/41mi W on the N 116 then N 152, passing Pugicerdá.*

La Seu d'Urgell – Past and Present

Relics from Bronze-age settlements have been discovered at the nearby mount of Castellciutat, but Romans preferred to settle on the plain at the confluence of the Segre and Valira rivers. In the 5C, the bishops of Urgell established their Episcopal (or Seu), making way for expansion of the city. Thus, La Seu d'Urgell became the capital of this region, which by the 10C was the most powerful in Catalunya.

Today, this lively township – gateway to Andorra, capital of the Alt Urgell region and unofficial capital of the Catalan Pyrenees – has important agriculture, livestock and tourism industries, as well as a significant industrial sector. Its dairy products, particularly cheese, are renowned and protected by their own DOC (designation of origin label).

Due to an historical twist of fate, the Bishop of Urgell (along with the President of France) is bestowed with the title of Co-Prince of Andorra.

View of Cerdanya at Lles de Cerdanya

© M & M Valledor/age fotostock

La Seu d'Urgell/ Seo de Urgell★

This city of prince-archbishops stands where the Valira, which rises in Andorra, joins the Segre river.

Catedral de Santa Maria★★

Santa Maria. ⏱*Open Oct–May Mon– Sat 10am–1pm, 4–6pm; Jun–Sept Mon– Sat 10am–1pm, 4–7pm; Sun and public holidays 10am–1pm.* ✆€3 *(with museum).* 𝄐*973 35 32 42.*

The cathedral, started in the 12C, shows strong Lombard influence. The central section of the west face, crowned by a small campanile, is typically Italian.

Inside, the nave rises on cruciform pillars, surrounded in French style by engaged columns. A most effective twin-arched gallery on the east transept wall reappears outside.

The **cloisters**★ are 13C; the east gallery was rebuilt in 1603 and features granite capitals illustrating humans and animals carved by masons from the Roussillon.

The Santa Maria door (southeast corner) opens into the 11C **Església de Sant Miquel**★, the only remaining building of those constructed by St Ermangol.

The cathedral houses the **Museu Diocesano**★, which has works of art dating from the 10C to the 18C.

The most precious is a beautifully illuminated 11C **Beatus**★★, one of the best-preserved copies of St John's Commentary on the Apocalypse written in the 8C by the priest Beatus of Liébana.

Of note also is an interesting **papyrus**★ belonging to Pope Sylvester II. The crypt contains the 18C funerary urn of St Ermangol.

▷ *Follow the N 260 W for 31km/19mi.*

Bellver de Cerdanya★

Poised on a rocky crag dominating the Vall del Segre, Bellver de Cerdanya has a fine main square with beautiful balconied stone houses and wooden porches.

▷ *18km/11mi NW on the N 260.*

Puigcerdà

The capital of Cerdanya, which developed on a terrace overlooking the River Segre, is one of the most popular holiday resorts of the Pyrenees, with old-fashioned shops, ancient streets and balconied buildings.

▷ *Follow signs to Llívia along the D 68.*

Llívia

This 12sq km/5sq mi Spanish enclave in France, 6km/3.7mi from Puigcerdà, results from an administrative subtlety. Under the Treaty of the Pyrenees, France was to be granted the Roussillon area as well as 33 villages from Cerdanya. But, since Llívia was considered to be a town, it remained part of Spain.

Llívia features Europe's oldest chemist's shop, the **Farmacia de Llívia** (⊶*closed for renovation*).

Take the Ca. Barcelona-Puigcerdà N 152 SE.

La Molina
www.lamolina.com.
This is one of Catalunya's most important ski resorts. The village of Alp is popular in winter and in summer.

From here it is possible to continue your visit on the E 9 to the Parc Naturel del Cadí-Moixeró.

Parc Natural del Cadí-Moixeró
Information Centres in Bellver de Cerdanya, Casa del Bosc, ℰ 973 51 00 16 and Bagà (approx. 20 km/12.5mi N of Berga), Centro del Parque, ℰ 93 824 41 51; www.parcsdecatalunya.net
The 41,342 ha park is located between the Cadí and Moixeró mountain ranges, which form an imposing 30km/18.6mi-long barrier of altitudes of between 900m/2 952ft and 2 647m/8 684ft. Vertical cliffs enclose the deep valleys and canyons and the vegetation is exceptional; low temperatures and high humidity favour the proliferation of unusual Mediterranean flora.
More than 400km/248.5mi of trails for all levels wind throughout the park.

4 **VALL DEL SEGRE★**
73km/45mi. Allow 3hr.

The River Segre forms a huge basin where it flows into the Valira.

Congost de Tresponts★★
The Segre winds through dark rocks *(puzolana)* and pastures. Downstream, the limestone of Ares and Montsec de Tost offers a typically Pyrenean landscape dropping to a cultivated basin, where the river disappears.

Organyà
This picturesque village has a small medieval centre, with the old streets lined with arcades, porches and Gothic mansions. Organyà is renowned for the *Homilies*, the oldest text written in Catalan, from the late 12C.

Pantà d'Oliana★
The dam is surrounded by grey rocks with lively waterfalls in spring. From the road the sight is quite spectacular.

6km/3.7mi S on the C 14.

Coll de Nargó
http://collnargo.ddl.net.
This hamlet has one of the most splendid Romanesque churches in Catalunya, dating back to the 11C: **Sant Climent**★ has a single nave and a pretty apse adorned with Lombard bands. Its sober **bell tower**★ is pre-Romanesque.

Collado de Bòixols Road★★
Between the Coll de Nargó and Tremp, the L 511 follows canyons on slopes clad in pine and holm oak, or barren hillsides. Further on, the road proceeds up the slope, under yellow and pink crests, offering lovely **landscapes**, especially from the Collado de Bòixols.
Then the road enters a wide U-shaped valley, where terraced cultivation extends to the foot of the glacial ridge of Bòixols, to which cling the church and nearby houses. The road descends the valley until it eventually merges into the Conca de Tremp.

Abella de la Conca
This tiny, don't-blink-or you'll-miss-it village is tucked behind the rocky Sarsús summit. Do not miss the Romanesque church of Sant Esteve (11C).

Head back to the L 511 and continue to Isona.

Isona
This ancient Roman city was founded around 100 BC. Isona hosts an interesting museum, mainly devoted to Roman times and paleontological sites in the area where the remains of dinosaurs have been found (it also organises tours). Its parish church was restored after the civil war of 1936.

Head out of Isona via the C- 1412 in the direction of Lleida and turn right for Covet.

Covet

Covet's Esglesia de Santa Maria boasts a beautiful interior. The vaulted nave, is reinforced by supporting arches and columns topped with carved capitals yet the **doorway**★★ is the most remarkable. It features a beautiful carved tympanum and skillfully sculptured arch-based columns. Notice the figurines of angels, musicians, beasts, the characters of the Holy Family and scenes from the book of Genesis.

▷ *Continue on the C 1412 towards Tremp.*

Figuerola d'Orcau

This small medieval town has interesting streets lined with arcaded houses.

▷ *Continue to Tremp.*

⑤ VALL DEL NOGUERA PALLARESA

143km/89mi. Allow 1 day, from Tremp to Llavorsí.

Pallars is in the uppermost region of the Catalan Pyrenees. The highest summit is Pica d'Estats (3 145m/10 318ft). To the north is **Pallars Sobirà**, at the heart of the Pyrenees; to the south, **Pallars Jussà** incorporates the vast pre-Pyrenean zone formed by Conca de Tremp. The road follows the bed of the Noguera Pallaresa, and after La Pobla de Segur, cuts across a limestone landscape of remarkable uniformity.

Tremp

In the centre of the Conca de Tremp – a huge basin with lush crops – the village retains its old quarter and three towers from its walls. The **Església de Santa María**★ houses an astonishing 2m/6.5ft high Gothic statue in polychrome wood: **Santa Maria de Valldeflors**★ (14C). The municipality has a reservoir, the ▲♨ **pantano de Sant Antoni**★, an ideal spot to fish, canoe/kayak, windsurf, sail and water ski.

▷ *13km/8mi N on the C 13.*

La Pobla de Segur

☏ *973 68 02 57. www.pobladesegur.cat.* This popular resort is the only means of access to the Valle de Arán, Alta Ribagorça and Pallars Sobirà.

▷ *The C 147 follows the course of the river and along the lake of Sant Antoni.*

Vall Fosca★

Hemmed in by peaks, this valley is dotted with delightful hamlets, each with its Romanesque church: **Torre de Capdella** (*www.torredecapdella.org*), **Espui** and **Capdella**. In the upper valley, in a large lake area, the main attraction is **Lago Gento**.

▷ *Return to La Pobla de Segur and proceed upwards along the N 260.*

Congost de Collegats★★

Eroded by torrents, the red, grey and ochre limestone rocks take on the appearance of spectacular cliffs. Note the **Roca de l'Argenteria**★, stalactite-shaped rocks near the Gerri de la Sal.

Sort

☏ *973 62 10 02.*
The resort is famous throughout Europe because of its wild waters and kayaking and rafting events held on the Noguera Pallaresa. The village – whose name means "luck" in Catalan – is also a favourite place to buy lottery tickets and has actually won the big draws more times than most.

▷ *At Rialp, bear left towards Lessui.*

Vall de Llessui★★

The road winds way up to the north-west, through a steep granite landscape featuring numerous ravines.

▷ *Take the C 13 N to Llavorsí.*

⑥ UPPER VALLEY OF THE NOGUERA PALLARESA★

105km/65mi. Allow half a day, from Llavorsí to Port de la Bonaigua. On this drive through three valleys, mountains dominate a wild landscape.

Llavorsí

http://llavorsi.ddl.net.

This peaceful village sits at the conflu-ence of the Aneu, Cardós and Ferrera basins.

▷ *Take the L 504 then turn right on to the L 510 in a NE direction.*

Val Ferrera

http://vallferrera.com.

The easternmost and closest of the three valleys is wedged between high mountains including the Pica d'Estats (3 145m/10 318ft), the highest mountain in Catalunya. From here, some beautiful hikes can be taken to Andorra.

▷ *Rejoin the L 504 and continue N.*

Vall de Cardós★

www.valldecardos.org

The Noguera de Cardós River forms the axis of this valley which is studded with over 20 pretty hamlets.

▷ *Return to Llavorsí and take the C 13 towards Baqueira.*

Vall d'Aneu★★

www.vallsdaneu.org.

Below is the valley of **Espot**, a pictur-esque village beside a mountain stream, gateway to the Pallars section of a

national park★★ (*see Parc Nacional d'AIGÜESTORTES I ESTANY DE SANT MAURICI*).

Beyond Esterri d'Aneu the road crosses a breathtaking landscape, dotted with Romanesque churches such as the **Església de Sant Joan d'Isil**★, glimpsed between summits, and twists up to **Port de la Bonaigua** (2 072m/6 799ft), circled by many peaks.

Esterri d'Àneu

The Ecomuseu Àneu Valls, situated inside an 18C homestead, explains the traditional lifestyles of the region. (*973 626 436; www.ecomuseu.com*). After Esterri Àneu, the road rises to an imposing landscape where Romanesque churches are hidden among the peaks.

9 LA VALL DE BOÍ★★ AND LA VALL DE LA NOGUERA RIBAGOCANA

58km/36mi. Allow half a day, from Caldes de Boí to Vielha.

Watered by the Noguera de Tor and the Sant Nicolau rivers, this valley is renowned for its cluster of Lombard **Romanesque churches** (11C–12C), the finest in the Pyrenees and a UNESCO world heritage site. With their slate roofs and irregular masonry, they stand out for their pure, sober lines and for the fine wall frescoes (*several reproductions*

Església de Sant Climent, Taüll, La Vall de Boí

© Jean-Paul Azam/hemis.fr

remain) now in the **Museu d'Art de Catalunya** (👁 *see BARCELONA)*. Note the distinctive high silhouette of the belfries, separate but resting against the nave, and ornamentation of Lombard bands.

Caldes de Boí★
℘973 69 62 10. www.caldesdeboi.com. At an altitude of 1 550m/5 084ft, Caldes de Boí is a thermal spa with 37 springs at temperatures between 240ºC and 560ºC (750ºF to 1330ºF). Nearby is the ski resort of **Boí-Taüll**.

Taüll★
Taüll is famous for the frescoes of its two early 12C churches. Considered to be masterpieces of Romanesque art, they are exhibited in Barcelona's Museu d'Art de Catalunya.

The village of labyrinthine streets, stone houses and wooden balconies clusters around the **Església de Santa Maria**★ *(🕐open daily 10am–8pm; ℘973 69 40 00)* a Romanesque church with three naves separated by cylindrical pillars. Just outside the village is the **Església de Sant Climent**★★ *(🕐open daily 10am–2pm, 4–7pm; ◉€1.50; ℘973 69 40 00)* with its slender six-storey belfry. A replica of the famous Pantocrator of Taüll is in the apse.

▷ *Return to the L 500.*

Erill la Vall
As well as the beautiful Romanesque church of Santa Eulália, the village has an information centre on Romanesque art, the Centre del Romànic.

Vall D'Erill to the Pont de Suert
Continuing on the L 500, your discovery of Romanesque heritage continues with visits to the churches of Sant Felíu de Berruera, and La Nativitat in Durro (2km/1.2mi on the left). Shortly after the pretty village of Castelló de Tor marks the entrance of the Vall de Boí.

▷ *Take the N 230 on the left to El Pont de Suert.*

El Pont de Suert
This area, dotted with attractive hamlets – **Castelló de Tor, Casòs, Malpàs** – retains its rusticity and charm.

▷ *Take the N 230 9km/6mi N to Vilaller.*

Vilaller
Perched on a rocky outcrop, the village has retained the steep and narrow streets of his ancient heart. In medieval times, the village was surrounded by walls and some remains are still visible.

▷ *Continue on the N 230 and take the the tunnel to Vielha.*

7 LA VALL D'ARAN★★
45km/28mi. Allow half a day, from Vielha to Baqueira Beret.

The **Aran Valley**, in the northwest tip of the Catalan Pyrenees, occupies the upper valley of the Garonne river. Its isolation has helped it to preserve its local traditions and language *(aranés* is a variation of the *langue d'oc* of southern France). The Vielha Tunnel ended the valley's seclusion in 1948. In recent years the region has seen the creation of several ski resorts.

Vielha
At an altitude of 971m/3 186ft, the capital of the Arán Valley is a holiday resort. Don't miss the 16C and 17C homes in the old town as well as the **Església Parroquial de Sant Miquèu**★ with its 14C octagonal tower and 13C Gothic doorway. Inside lies the **Cristo de Mijaran**★, a fragment dating from a 12C Descent from the Cross.

Museu dera Val d'Aran
Major, 28. 🕐Open daily except Mon. ◉€2 (under 16 years €1). ℘973 641 815. www.aran.org. Housed in an elegant 16C manor house, this museum introduces visitors to the geology, glaciology, history and language of the Vall de Aran.

▷ *Leave Vielha to the E on the C 28.*

Betren

The **Església de San Esteve**★, built during the transition from Romanesque to Gothic, boasts archivolts on the **portal**★★, decorated with human faces, alluding to the Last Judgement and the Resurrection.

⊙ *Continue along the C 28 1.3km/1mi to Escunha.*

Escunhau

The **Església de San Pedro**★ has a fine 12C **portal**★★ bearing an expressive Christ and unusual capitals decorated with human faces.

⊙ *Continue along the C 28 3km/2mi to Arties.*

Arties★

The Romanesque church has an apse decorated with scenes illustrating the Last Judgement, Heaven and Hell.

⊙ *Continue along the C 28 3km/2mi to Salardú.*

Salardú★

𝄐 *973 64 51 97. www.torismearan.org.* Salardú is a charming village with granite and slate houses gathered around the **Església de Sant Andreu**★ (12C–13C), whose interior contains some interesting 16C **Gothic paintings**★★ and a fine 12C **Christ in Majesty**★★, a stylised 65cm/25in wooden statue of remarkable anatomical precision. Note the slender octagonal belfry (15C).

⊙ *Leave the town to the N and drive for 1.5km/1mi.*

Unha

This tiny hamlet is home to the 12C Romanesque church of Santa Eulàlia. From the exterior, note the corbels supporting the roof while inside there are vestiges of Romanesque paintings. In the village itself, the fortified, late 16C residence Çò de Brastet, features Renaissance windows and doors.

⊙ *Return to the C 28 and follow the road W for 9km/5mi.*

Baqueira Beret

𝄐 *973 63 90 10. www.baqueira.es.* This ski resort, rising from 1 500m/ 4 900ft to 2 510m/8 230ft, offers excellent lodging and services.

8️⃣ VIELHA TO BOSSOST
52km/32mi. Allow half a day.

Vall de Varrados

The most famous natural site in this valley is the Sauth deth Pish waterfall, which descends through a gorge.

⊙ *From Vielha, take the N230 12km/7.5mi NW.*

Vilamòs

This ancient village, suspended on a natural platform 400m/1 300ft above the valley, has retained its traditional architecture and affords magnificent, unobstructed views.
At the far end of the village, a traditional home has been restored, illustrating traditional Aranese life. (*Çò de Joanchiquet;* ⏱ *open Tue–Sun 11am–2pm 4–7pm, mornings only in winter;* 𝄐*973 64 07 39).*

⊙ *Back on the N 230, head towards Bossòst.*

Vall de la Artiga de Lin

The Joeu River crosses this valley, which is resplendent with magnificent pine and beech trees.

Bossòst

The **Església de la Purificació de Maria**★★ is the area's best example of Romanesque architecture (12C). Its three naves are separated by sturdy columns. Its three apses are adorned with Lombard bands and the pretty, colourful north **doorway** features archaic relief work in its tympanum, depicting the Creator surrounded by the Sun, the Moon and symbols of the Evangelists.

ADDRESSES

🏨 STAY

Casa La Vall del Cadí – *Ctra Cerc-Tuixent, 1km/.06mi from La Seu d'Urgell, near the Parc Olímpic.* ℘973 350 390. www.valldel cadi.com. ▣ 7 rooms. ⌧€7.50. This period building has beautifully renovated rustic rooms featuring wood with wrought-iron and stone elements.

Hostal del Ripollès – *Pl. Nova 11, Ripoll* ℘972 700 215. www.hostaldelripolles.com. 8 rooms. ⌧. Clean rooms with a pleasant restaurant on the ground floor with an outdoor terrace serving pizza, Italian and Catalan dishes.

Catalunya Park Hotel – *Pg. Mauri 9, Ribes de Freser.* ℘972 727 198. www.catalunyaparkhotels.com. Open Easter and Jul–Sept. 55 rooms. ⌧€6. Restaurant. This hotel in the mountains is comfortable without being luxurious, and the pool is a wonderful asset. Good base for exploring the beautiful sites nearby and the Vall de Núria.

Hotel Estel – *Sant Fruitós 39, Berga.* ℘938 213 463. www.hotelestel.com. ▣ 37 rooms. ⌧€6. This friendly hotel in one of the main avenues into the city is simple and functional.

Hotel Segle XX – *Pl. de la Creu 8, Tremp.* ℘973 650 000. www.hotelseglexx. info. 🛏 48 rooms. ⌧. Restaurant. Founded in 1880, this hotel has comfortable rooms that have been renovated over the years. Its classic restaurant has a warm, slightly old-fashioned atmosphere.

Hotel Vall d'Àssua – *Altron in the Vall de la Noguera Pallaresa, 4km/2.5mi NE of Sort via the C 13 then left.* ℘973 621 738. Closed Nov. ⯐ ▣ 9 rooms. ⌧. This small hotel has comfortable rooms with en suite bathrooms. The restaurant's specialty is chargrilled meat.

Hotel Vall de Núria – *Vall de Núria ski resort, Queralbs.* ℘972 732 020. www.hotelserhsvalldenuria.com. Closed Nov. 65 rooms. This hotel has a wonderful natural setting, attentive service and a good restaurant serving local dishes. Minimum stay of two nights.

Mas la Casanova – *Ctra de Ribes de Freser, 3km/1.87mi from the Queralbs in the Vall de Ribes.* ℘972 198 077. ⯐ 6 rooms. ⌧ €6. Pretty little cottages set around a homestead in the heart of the Vall de Ribes. It provides home-cooked meals on request and a warm welcome.

Ribaeta – *Pl. Coto Març, Vielha.* ℘973 642 036. www.grupohg.com. 24 rooms ⌧ €3.90. Restaurant (evenings only). Central establishment with simple rooms.

Edelweis – *Ctra de Sant Joan 28, Camprodon.* ℘972 740 614. ▣ 21 rooms. ⌧. Classical hotel with very nice common areas and comfortable rooms.

Hotel Calitxó – *Passatge El Serrat, Molló.* ℘972 740 386. www.hotelcalitxo.com. ▣ 25 rooms. ⌧. Restaurant. An elegant building surrounded by gardens and meadows. Functional rooms with all round comfort. This is the ideal place for mountain and sports enthusiasts.

Hotel La Coma – *Setcases, 10km/6mi N of Comprodon.* ℘972 136 074. www.hotellacoma.com. ▣ 🛏 22 rooms. ⌧ Restaurant. This high-mountain hotel, popular with skiers, is situated in an old stone building. Facilities include a welcoming rustic style restaurant.

Hotel Fonda Bianya – *Sant Roc 11, Bellver de Cerdanya.* ℘973 510 475. Closed 25 Dec. 17 rooms. ⌧. Restaurant. This noble and attractive edifice is wedged between stone houses. The comfortable rooms have retained their original features, including tiny bathrooms.

Hotel del Lago – *Av. Dr. Piguillem 7, Puigcerdà, Cerdanya.* ℘972 881 000. www.hotellago.com. ▣ 23 rooms. ⌧€8.50. This small family hotel near the lake is surrounded by a large landscaped area with a pool. The classically styled rooms have functional bathrooms.

Hotel Can Boix – *on the outskirts of Peramola, 17km/10.5mi SW of Coll de Nargó in the Vall del Segre.* ℘973 470 281. www.canboix.cat. Closed mid-Jan–mid-Feb and 2 weeks in Nov. ▣ 🛏 ♿ 41 rooms. ⌧€12. Restaurant. Nestled in natural surroundings, attention to detail is evident throughout this hotel. The rooms combine the warmth of wood with soft-toned furnishings and more modern touches, especially in bathrooms.

Parador de La Seu d'Urgell – *Sant Domènec 6, La Seu d'Urgell.* ℘973 352 000. www.parador.es. ▣ 78 rooms. ⌧€15. Restaurant. Set around a former Renaissance cloister, this hotel offers modern amenities and minimalist design. The large restaurant serves traditional regional dishes of varying quality.

○⊖🗄 **Riberies** – *Camí de Riberies, Llavorsí.* ☏*973 622 051. www.riberies.com.* 🅿 🛏 🖕 *€15.* 🖵*Restaurant.* This pleasant, relaxing hotel offers both contemporary rooms and a more traditional feel in the attic rooms. The restaurant has some daring dishes on the menu.

○⊖🗄🗄 **Parador de Vielha** – *2.5km/ 1.5mi S of Vielfa on the N 230.* ☏*973 641 100. www.parador.es.* 🅿 🛏 *116 rooms.* 🖕*€17.* ○⊖🖵*Restaurant.* This *parador* offers splendid views over the valley, especially from the circular living area. Spacious rooms with outstanding comfort.

🍴 EAT

🎩 In Puigcerdà, typical dishes include tiró amb naps (goose with turnips) and rabbit cooked with the famous pears of the region.

○⊖ **Boixetes de Cal Manel** – *on Ctra N 230 at Pont d'Arròs.* ☏*973 641 168. Closed May, Nov and Mon.* In a traditional homestead located just outside the village, this restaurant specializes in local cuisine.

○⊖ **Can Dachs** – *on Ctra de Ripoll at Berga (C 26), 7.5km/4.5mi SW of Ripoll.* ☏*972 714 425.* 🖵 *Thur–Sun for lunch; Fri–Sat for dinner; daily in Aug.* Excellent cuisine based on regional products. Specialties include meats grilled over a wood fire.

○⊖ **Can Jan Restaurant** – *Sant Roc 9, Camprodon.* ☏*972 130 407. Closed first two weeks Nov.* A cheerful and friendly atmosphere reigns in this central restaurant decorated with wooden furniture painted in different colours and the work of local artists. It serves typical dishes from the valley.

○⊖ **Cal Teo** – *Av. Pau Claris 38, La Seu d'Urgell.* ☏*973 353 393. Closed Sun eve and Mon.* Small, personable restaurant in the heart of La Seu, which offers a personalised greeting and rustic specialties including grilled meats. Its the place to go after visiting the cathedral.

○⊖ **Dolcet** – *Zulueta 1, Alàs i Cerc, 7km/6mi E of La Seu d'Urgell.* ☏*973 352 016. Closed Fri, Nov and 15 days in Jun–Jul.* In the centre of the village, this family-run restaurant serves traditional Catalan cuisine based on market products. Its strategic location on the road to Cadí-Moixeró natural park makes it a popular destination, but absolutely worth the wait.

○⊖ **Llacs de Cardós** – *Vall de Cardós on Ctra Tavascan, Tavascan in the Vall de l'Alt.* ☏*973 623 178 179. www.llacscardos.com.* This restaurant serves hearty mountain fare; trout a specialty. A few comfortable rooms are also on offer. (○⊖).

○⊖ **Miscela** – *Av. Pau Claris 24, La Seu d'Urgell.* ☏*973 350 104.* A contemporary backdrop in shades of orange and purple sets the scene for pizzas, salads, pasta and a daily lunch menu for €12.

○⊖🗄 **La Fonda Xesc** – *Pl. Roser 1, Gombrèn, 12.5km/7.5mi NW of Ripoll via the N 152 (towards Puigcerdà) then left on the GI 401.* ☏*972 730 404. Closed Sun eve, Mon, Tue eve, Wed eve, 15 days in Jan and 10 days in Jul.* Restaurant with a spacious vaulted dining room where you can enjoy creative Catalan cuisine prepared with quality products. Comfortable rooms available (○⊖ 🖵).

○⊖🗄 **Casa Irene** – *Major 4, Arties, in the Vall de l'Alt.* ☏*973 644 364. Phone for opening times.* One of the best restaurants in the valley serving local specialties with a big smile.

○⊖🗄 **Sala** – *Passeig de la Pau 27, Berga.* ☏*938 211 185. www.restaurantsala.com. Closed Sun eve and Mon.* Modern restaurant serving regional dishes located on a shady path near the centre of Berga. The dining room is spread over two floors and has stucco walls embellished with Venetian touches.

○⊖🗄 **La Taverna dels Noguères** – *El Pont de Bar, 15km/9mi E of La Seu on the N 260.* ☏*973 384 020. Phone for opening times.* Friendly, rustic place with a fireplace, wooden-beamed ceilings and checkered tablecloths. Great value home cooking.

○⊖🗄🗄 **Fogony** – *Av. Generalitat 45, Sort.* ☏*973 621 225. www.fogony.com. Closed Sun eve, Mon and 2 weeks in Jan.* Innovative Catalan dishes that will delight and surprise you. The small dining room features quality crockery, classical furniture and faultless waiters. An excellent restaurant.

🏃 SPORTS AND RECREATION

Hiking and skiing are the most popular sports in the Pirineos Catalanes. The region has numerous ski resorts, some with large hotels. The best known include **La Molina** (☏*972 89 20 31; www.lamolina. com*), in Girona province, and **Baqueira-Beret** (☏*973 63 90 10; www.baqueira.es*) popular with the Spanish royal family, in the Val d'Aran (Lleida). For general information visit *www.acem-cat.com.*

Parc Nacional d'Aigüestortes i Estany de Sant Maurici★★

This national park in the Catalan Pyrenees abounds in falls and rushing streams. Twisting waterways – *aigües tortes* – wind between mossy meadows and wooded slopes. Glaciers created the harsh beauty of U-shaped valleys, high mountain lakes and snow-covered peaks. Vegetation includes firs and Scots pines. Birch and beech trees provide a stunning splash of colour in autumn.

SIGHTS

The park's 14 119ha/34 888 acres, between altitudes of 1 500m/4 921ft and 3 000m/9 842.5ft, are mainly granite and slate, formed in the Paleozoic era when they emerged from the depths of the sea, drawing steep cliffs and deep valleys. Cows graze in the meadows and the grouse and partridge inhabit the woods. Wild deer inhabit the higher, less accessible peaks.

P Both entries (Espot, to the east, and Boí, to the west) have parking areas.

Take an organised excursion by four-wheel drive (private vehicles are prohibited). Paths are well signposted.

Head first for the **Casa del Parc del Boí** or the **Casa del Parc del Espot**. Both open Jun–Sept Mon–Sat 9am–1pm, 3.30–7pm; Oct–May Mon–Sat 9am–2pm, 3.30–6pm, Closed 1, 6 Jan, 25–26 Dec. Tours €7.20 (half-day); €14.20 (full-day); min. 5 people. 973 69 61 89. www.visitpirineus.com.

Lago de Sant Maurici (reached by a tarmac road from Espot) is the most accesble and therefore most visited of the 24 lakes in the park. It is surrounded by forest and reflects the peaks of the Sierra dels Encantats.

- ▶ **Population:** 52 224
- **Michelin Map:** 574 E 32–33. Local map, see PIRINEOS CATALANES – Catalunya (Lleida)
- **Info:** Centro del Parque de Boí: Graieres 2. 973 69 61 89; Centro del Parque de Espot: Prat del Guarda 4. 973 62 40 36. http://mediambient.gencat.net/eng.
- **Location:** The park is just west of Andorra and south of France.
- **Don't Miss:** A forest walk up to grand panoramas.
- **Timing:** Allow a day for the park, with hikes.

Hikes

Portarró d'Espot – *3hr there and back on foot from the Estany de Sant Maurici.* The path crosses the Sant Nicolau Valley. At Redó lake, admire the splendid **panoramas★★**.

Estany Gran d' Amitges – *3hr there and back on foot from Sant Maurici lake.* Beside the lake, mountain streams form impressive waterfalls. The snow-capped Bassiero (2 887m/9 472 ft) and peak Saboredo (2 814m/9 232ft) dominate this unique area of high mountains.

Estany Negre – *5hr there and back on foot from Espot; 4hr from Sant Maurici lake.* Cross the stunning Peguera Valley to Estany Negre (Black Lake), hemmed in by awesome summits.

Aigüestortes

Western section. *3hr there and back.* The entry road leads to Aigüestortes where a stream winds through rich pastures. Hike to Estany Llong.

Accommodation

Camping is prohibited but there are 14 mountain refuges. Most are open from June to September and during Holy Week.

Principat d'Andorra★★

Principality of Andorra

The seven parishes that make up the principality of Andorra occupy high plateaux and valleys cut by charming mountain roads. In recent years Andorra has seen urbanisation, hydroelectric schemes and a tourism boom. But tradition remains in the terraced slopes planted with tobacco and in religious pilgrimages (the famous Catalan *aplec*).

ANDORRA TODAY

Andorra is well known for the duty-free shopping opportunities it offers, primarily in the tiny capital of Andorra la Vella. In fact an astonishing 10 million visitors a year descend upon the principality, many clutching their credit card.

The main skiing valleys are also very busy in season, with some €50 million recently invested in their infrastructure. By contrast the outlying villages remain largely uncommercialised.

A BIT OF HISTORY

Until 1993 Andorra was a co-principality subject to an unusual political regime dating back to the days of feudalism. The neighbouring rulers, the Bishop of Urgell and the President of the French Republic, enjoyed rights and exercised powers over this small territory, which was jointly governed by them.

At present Andorra is a sovereign state – a full member of the United Nations.

🚗 DRIVING TOURS

VALL DEU VALIRA D'ORIENT

30km/18.6mi from Pas de la Casa to Andorra la Vella. Allow half a day.

This drive will lead you around Andorra's stunning countryside, slowly easing into the shopping, spa and hotel frenzy of Andorra La Vella.

▶ **Population:** 85 168
⚙ **Michelin Map:** 574 E 34-35.
ℹ **Info:** Andorra la Vella: Plaça de la Rotonda. ℘00 376 82 71 17. www.tourisme-andorre.net.
▷ **Location:** Between Spain and France, 20km/12.4mi from La Seu d'Urgell.
Kids: Museu Nacional de l'Automòbil.
🕐 **Timing:** Spend a day driving through the valleys.
🅿 **Parking:** Forget about parking on the crowded streets of Andorra la Vella.
Customs and Formalities: Visitors need a valid passport and, for those driving a car, a Green Card and current driving licence. There are customs checkpoints on the borders.

Pas de la Casa★

Alt 2 091m/6 861ft. Once only a frontier post, the highest village in Andorra is the main ski resort of the region.

▷ *The road snakes through the mountains before reaching Port d'Envalira, offering great views of Font Negre.*

Port d'Envalira★★

Roads may be snow-blocked but usually reopen within 24hr.
Alt 2 407m/7 897ft. Envalira boasts the highest altitude of major Pyrenean passes. On the Atlantic-Mediterranean divide, it commands a lovely mountain panorama.

▷ *Take the CG-2 in the direction of Canillo, stopping just outside the town.*

Església de Sant Joan de Caselles

Av. Sant Joan de Caselles, Canillo.
🕐 *Open Jul-Aug daily 10am–3pm, 5–9pm; otherwise prior booking required.*
No charge. ℘00 376 84 41 41.

Below an openwork tower and rows of ornamental windows, this church is one of the best examples of Romanesque architecture in Andorra. Behind the wrought-iron grid of the presbytery stands a painted altarpiece by the master **Canillo** (1525), representing the life and visions of the Apostle St John. The Romanesque **Crucifixion**★ was restored in 1963: a Christ in stucco was placed atop a fresco illustrating the Calvary.

▷ *Continue to Canillo.*

Canillo
The bell tower of the church set against rocks is the highest in Andorra. At its side is an ossuary, characteristic of early Iberian occupation.

Santuari de Meritxell
Beyond Los Bons pass lies a lovely **site**★ of houses gathered under a ruined castle and the Capella de Sant Romà. Nearby stands the church of Nuestra Señora de Meritxell (*open Mon–Sat 9am–1pm, 3–6pm, Sun 9am–1pm; no charge*), national sanctuary of the principality since 1976.

▷ *Continue on the same road to Encamp.*

Encamp
This village has two interesting churches: Santa Eulàlia, which has the highest steeple in Andorra (23 m/75.5ft), a 14C porch and Baroque altarpieces. Sant Romà de les Bons contains reproductions of Gothic paintings.

Casa Cristo - Museu Etnografic★
(*Cavallers 2; Jul–Aug Mon–Sat 9.30am – 1.30pm, 3.30–7.30pm, Sun 10am– 3pm; rest of the year to 6.30pm and closed Sun; €3; 00 376 833 551*).
Set in a 19C homestead, this museum aims to illustrate what everyday life was like in the period for a modest agrarian family.

▲ Museu Nacional de l'Automòbil★
(*Av. Coprincep Episcopal 64; open 9.30am–1.30 pm, 3–6.30pm, Sun 10am –2pm; €3, under 18 €1.50; 00 376 83 97 60*).
Spread over five floors of a former garage, this collection offers over a century of automotive history, with 88 cars, 105 bicycles and 68 motorcycles from vintage breeds such as Bugatti, Rolls-Royce, Ferrari and Cadillac.

Estany d'Engolasters (Engolasters Lake)
The Engolasters plateau is a pastured extension of Andorra la Vella used for sports and recreation. The fine Romanesque tower of the church of Sant Miquel rises above the rolling plains.
Climb over the crest among the pine trees at the end of the road and descend on foot to an impressive hydroelectric dam, surrounded by trees, which has raised the waters of the lake (alt 1 616m/ 5 301ft) by a total of 10m/33ft.

▷ *Continue S on the CS 200.*

Andorra la Vella
Houses in the capital cluster onto a terrace overlooking the Gran Valira. Streets in the old quarter remain almost intact, as has the **Casa de la Vall** (Parliament House; *Vall; guided tours (30min, must be booked in advance) May–Oct Tue–Sat 10am–2pm, 3–6pm, Jul–Aug until 7pm; closed Mon morning rest of the year; 00 376 82 91 29*).
This ancient stone building houses the Consell General de les Valls, both Parliament and courthouse to the small nation. To the east, Andorra la Vella joins the lively municipality of Les Escaldes, dominated by **Caldaea** (*www.caldea. com*), a thermal spa with futuristic lines featuring Turkish baths, jacuzzis, bubble beds, hot marble slabs, etc.

VALLS DE GRAN VALIRA AND VALIRA DEL NORD
9km/5.5mi from Sant Julia de Loria to La Cortinada to Andorra la Vella. Allow half a day.

This drives takes you through the valleys of Andorra's ski country, but is beautiful out of season too.

Sant Julia de Loria

Museu del tabac★ (*Dr. Palau, 17;* 🕐 *open Tue–Sat 10am–8pm, Sun 10am–2.30pm;* ⊛€5; 📞*00 376 74 15 45; www. museudeltabac.com*). This museum occupies the former tobacco factory in the Reig family. It takes you on a journey of the tabacco-making process, from the way the leaves were dried, to cigarette rolling and packaging, all accompanied by a video narrated by former workers.

▷ *Continue N on the CS 100, then take the CG 3 towards La Massana.*

Gargantas de Sant Antoni

From the bridge over the Vall de Valira de Nord you can see the old bridge used by medieval shepherds on your right. It was restored in the 19C.

▷ *Go through the Túnel de Sant Antoni on the CG 3.*

La Massana

Casa Rull de Sispony★(*Carrer Major;* 🕐*open Tue–Sat 9.30am–1.30pm, 3–6pm;* ⊛€3; 📞*00 376 83 97 60*). This 17C homestead reconstructs everyday life of the area at the time. The home supposedly belonged to one of the richest families in La Massana, and there are many

details to ponder over, particularly in the kitchen and other work areas.

▷ *Continue N on the CG 3.*

Ordino

🅿*Park by the church in the upper town.* Ordino is a quaint village with a maze of charming alleyways. Admire the wrought-iron grilles of the church, and nearby, the 18m/60ft balcony adorning the Casa de Don Guillem, built for a master blacksmith.

Casa Areny-Plandolit★ (🕐*Tue–Sat 9.30am–1.30pm, 3–6.30pm, Sun 10am–2pm;* ⊛€3; 📞*00 376 83 97 60*). This home dating from 1676 belonged to the Areny-Plandolit family, a clan that included the master ironworker Baron Guillem. Highlights include the metal work on the balconies, the Art Nouveau dining room and the ceramic-tiled kitchen. Nearby sites include the **Museu Postal d'Andorra** (*postal museum in Camí de Segudet;* 📞*376 839 760*) and the **Museu de la Microminiatura** (*Edifici Maragda;* 📞*376 838 338; phone for opening times and prices*).

▷ *From here continue to La Cortinada to visit its Nature Centre and working sawmill.*

With the exception of tourist resorts on the coast and Port Aventura, Spain's largest theme park, Southern Catalunya (comprised of the Tarragona and Llerida provinces) is often overlooked by visitors. This seems unfair. The capitals of both regions (and particularly Tarragona) offer a wealth of cultural interest, from expansive Roman remains to soaring Gothic cathedrals, while many inland towns are every bit as atmospheric as the prettied-up Medieval hamlets of the north – and restaurants and hotels are cheaper, too. The landscape is diverse, with blankets of vineyards and licorella terraces around Montsant – one of Spain's most promising new wine-growing regions – to the wide plains of orchards around Lleida and the wetlands of the Ebro Delta.

Highlights

1 Tarragona's atmospheric **Medieval Quarter** and **Cathedral** (p375)

2 The moving **Monastery of Poblet** (p379)

3 Soaking up the sun on the **Costa Daurada** (p383)

4 A day out out with the kids at **Port Aventura** (p383)

5 Getting away from it all in the **Ebro Delta** wetlands (p384)

Tarragona and the Coast

Easily accessible by both car and train, the Costa Daurada takes its name from the long golden beaches that begin south at the Ebro Delta and stretch north almost as far as Sitges. With the exception of Salou, the resorts here are mostly low-key and (again, aside from Salou) geared to Spanish holidaymakers. Tarragona also has good beaches but this fine old historic town is best known for its UNESCO World Heritage recognised Roman archeological ensemble and a magnificent cathedral.

When Barcelona was a mere trading post, Tarragona (or Tárraco, as it was called) was the Roman capital of Hispania. The Romans built a forum, amphitheatre, sophisticated aqueduct and many other infrastructures in this bustling port, many of which today form part of Tarragona's multilayered cityscape. By contrast just 10km/6.2mi away is Spain's best theme park, Port Aventura.

Inland and Lleida

Lleida on the other hand had its golden age during the 11 and 12C, when nobles and knights set about making a stronghold of the Catalan plains. The small town of Montblanc also boasts many surviving medieval features, while Poblet and Santes Creus are two of the finest monasteries in Spain.

The Delta Ebro and Tortosa

Spain's most voluminous river meets the sea at the Delta Ebro, scene of one of the bloodiest battles of the Spanish Civil War.

Today people come to watch its abundant bird life, to fish or simply laze around alongside the marshy waters. Well beyond the cities and resorts, the town of Tortosa has a fine cathedral and makes an ideal base from which to explore the delta wetlands.

Little Egret in the Ebro Delta

© Jean-Claude Carton/Biosphoto/Photoshot

Tarragona★★

Tarragona, with its ancient and medieval heritage, is also a modern town with wide avenues and a lively commercial centre. Its gardened seafront promenade skirts the cliffside and surrounds the old city and Palace of Augustus, following the city walls in the shadow of the Cathedral. Long a major port, Tarragona also has 15km/9.3mi of beaches that attract summer visitors.

▶ **Population:** 140 323
⚬ **Michelin Map:** 574 I 33 – Catalunya (Tarragona)
▯ **Info:** Major 39. ℘977 25 07 95. www.tarragona turisme.cat.
▶ **Location:** Tarragona is in Cataluña in NE Spain, SW along the coast from Barcelona. ▭Passeig de Espanya
▲▪ **Kids:** The city's beaches.

SIGHTS

ROMAN TARRAGONA★★
Passeig Arqueològic★
(Archaeological Promenade)

Av. Catalunya. ◷*Open Jan–end Mar, Oct–end Dec Tue–Sat 9am–7pm, Sun and public holidays 10am–3pm; rest of the year Tue–Sat 9am–9pm, Sun and public holidays 9am–3pm.* ◷*Closed 1, 6 Jan, 1 May and 25–26 Dec.* ◉*€3 (€10 combined with other Museu d'Història sites).* ℘*977 24 57 96. www.museutgn.com.*

Scipios built Tarragona's walls in the 3C BC on existing Cyclopean bases. They were so massive that they were long thought to have been barbarian or pre-Roman. Medieval inhabitants rebuilt the ramparts; 18C citizens remodelled them but still left us with walls bearing the marks of 2 000 years of history. A garden walk follows the walls. Part of the walls can be inaccessible due to renovation.

Museu Nacional Arqueològic de Tarragona★★
(Archaeological Museum)

Pl. del Rey 5. ◷*Open Jun–Sept Tue–Sun 9.30am–8.30pm, Sun and public holidays 10am–2pm; rest of the year Tue–Sat 9.30am–6pm; Sun and public holidays 10am–2pm.* ◉*€2.40 (includes entry to Necrópolis).* ℘*977 23 62 09. www.mnat.es.*

The exhibits, mostly from Roman times, are from Tarragona or its environs.

The **Roman architecture** (*Room II, ground floor*) section gathers vestiges of the most imposing buildings in Tarraconensis. The **Roman mosaics★★** collection is the finest in Catalunya. Exhibits in Rooms III (*first floor*) and VIII (*second*

Capital of Tarraconensis

The history of Tarragona dates back many centuries. The imposing ramparts built of enormous Cyclopean blocks of stone indicate that it was founded by peoples from the eastern Mediterranean early in the first millennium BC. In due course it suffered occupation by the Iberians. The Romans, who by 218 BC had control of the larger part of the peninsula, developed Tarraconensis into a major city and overseas capital. Although it could never equal Rome, it enjoyed many of the same privileges as the imperial capital and Augustus, Galba and Hadrian did not disdain to live in it.

Conversion to Christianity, often attributed to the work of St Paul, brought it appointment as a metropolitan seat, and its dignitaries the primacy of Spain. This honour was retained throughout the barbarian invasions of the 5C and the destruction of the Moors in the 8C but lost finally to the ambition of Toledo in the 11C. The city was then abandoned until the 12C, when it reverted to the Christians.

Amfiteatre

© Rustam Shigapov/Fotolia.com

floor) testify to the high craftsmanship of the Romans.

The most extraordinary piece is the **Mosaic of the Medusa**★★ (late 2C), with its penetrating gaze.

Roman sculpture★ *(Rooms VI to X, second floor)* is exemplified by superb **funerary sculptures** *(Room IX)*.

Note *(Room VI)* the bust of Lucius Verusa, executed in the 2C, a perfect example of the art, and the small **votive sculpture of Venus**★.

Recinte Monumental del Pretori i del Circ Romà★ (Praetorium and Roman Circus)

Pl. del Rey 5. ○*Open mid-Apr–end Sept Tue–Sat 9am–9pm, Sun 9am–3pm; Rest of the year Tue–Sat 9am–7pm, Sun 10am–3pm.* ○*Closed 1, 6 Jan, 1 May, 25–26 Dec.* ⊚€3 *(€10 combined with other Museu d'Història sites).* ℘977 24 19 52. www.museutgn.com.

Visit the **vaulted underground galleries**★ of a restored 1C BC square tower, or enjoy the sweeping **view**★★ from the top. **Hippolyte's sarcophagus**★★, found virtually intact on the bed of the Mediterranean, bears fine and lively sculptured ornamentation.

The vast **Roman Circus** (325m x 115m/1 066ft x 378ft) was designed for chariot races. Only a few terraces, vaults and sections of the façade remain.

Amfiteatre★★

Parque del Miracle. ○*Open mid Apr– Sept Tue–Sat 9am–9pm, Sun 9am–3pm; rest of the year Tue–Sat 9am–7pm, Sun 10am–3pm.* ○*Closed 1, 6 Jan, 1 May, 25–26 Dec.* ⊚€3 *(€10 combined with other Museu d'Història sites).* ℘977 24 19 52. www.museutgn.com.

The seaside elliptical amphitheatre is in a naturally sloped **site**★. Bishop Fructuosus and his deacons, Augurius and Eulogius, were martyred here in 259. The Església de Santa Maria del Miracle (church) replaced a Visigothic basilica in the 12C and is itself now in ruins.

Forum Romà

○*Open mid Apr–Sept Tue–Sat 9am– 9pm, Sun 9am–3pm; rest of the year Tue–Sat 9am–7pm, Sun 10am–3pm.* ○*Closed 1, 6 Jan, 1 May, 25–26 Dec.* ⊚€3 *(€10 combined with other Museu d'Història sites).* ℘977 24 19 52.

The Forum was the core of the Roman city. A few reliefs, pieces of frieze and sections of a street remain.

Museu i Necrópolis Paleocristianas

Av. Ramon y Cajal 80. ○*Open Jun–Sept Tue–Sun 9.30am–8.30pm, Sun and public holidays 10am–2pm; rest of the year Tue–Sat 9.30am–6pm; Sun and public holidays 10am–2pm.* ⊚€2.40

(includes entry to Museu Arqueològic). 📞 *977 211 175. www.mnat.es.*
A 3C–7C burial site, including over 2 000 tombs, were uncovered at this location in 1923. A section has been restored for viewing, with many of the remains now in the Archaeological Museum.

🐾 WALKING TOUR

CIUDAD MEDIEVAL
In the Middle Ages, the higly visible remains of the Roman City were integrated into the medieval fabric of Tarragona.

Plaça de la Font
Dominated by the façade of the **Ajunta-ment** (city hall) and adorned with fountains, this pedestrianised square is Tarragona's main meeting point and is a great place to relax at one of its many café terraces.

▷ *Turn right on Carrer de l'Ajuntament Sant Domènec, then right again on Carrer Roser.*

Plaça del Pallol
Roman remains are hidden under the Medieval buildings in this peaceful square. Next to the Antiga Audiència building (an old courthouse) porches and large Gothic windows survive, as well as the remains of the Roman gate to the provincial forum.

▷ *From the plaça, take the exit onto Carrer dels Cavallers.*

Carrer dels Cavallers
As is the case of Barcelona's Carrer Montcada (💺 *see p321*), the Carrer dels Chevaliers, was the main artery of medieval Tarragona. It is still lined with a few mansions that belonged to the wealthiest families in the city.

Casa-Museu Castellarnau★
Cavallers 14. ⏰*Open Mid Apr–end Sept Tue–Sat 9am–9pm, Sun 9am–3pm; rest of the year Tue–Sat 9am–7pm, Sun 10am–3pm.* ⏰*Closed 1, 6 Jan, 1 May, 25–26 Dec.* ⬤*€3 (€10 combined with*

other Museu d'Història sites). 📞 *977 24 22 20. www.museutgn.com.*
The Emperor Charles V is said to have stayed in this wealthy 14C–15C residence. It features a pretty Gothic patio and fine 18C furniture.

▷ *Turn left into the Carrer Major.*

Carrer Major
The "Main Street" of Tarragaona leades directly to the cathedral's main portal. Arcades and shops, sometimes beautifully historic, at times with a distinct retro feel, lend an attrative amabiance.
Arcades on Carrer Merceria *(on the right before you reach Plaça del Seu).*
These are the only remnants of the old medieval market. In summer, the arcades provide repsite frome the heat.

▷ *Continue to the Plaça de la Seu.*

Catedral★★
Pl. de la Seu. ⏰*Open Tue–Sat Jun–mid-Oct Mon–Sat 10am–6pm (Mon 3–6pm); rest of the year 10am–2pm.* ⏰*Closed public holidays.* ⬤*€3.80 (includes Museu Diocesá).* 📞 *977 21 10 80.*
Construction began in 1174 on the site of Jupiter's Temple, in transitional Gothic style, although the side chapels are both Plateresque and Baroque.

Façade★
A Gothic central section with rose window is flanked by Romanesque sections. The **main doorway** displays the Last Judgement, with expressive relief work. The archivolts are carved with Apostles and Prophets. On the pier, the Virgin (13C) receives the Faithful.

Interior★★
Following a Latin cross plan, there are three naves and a transept. The Romanesque apse has semicircular arches. At each end of the transept are 14C rose windows with stained glass.
The three naves are mostly Gothic. The finest work of art is undoubtedly the **altarpiece of Santa Tecla★★★** *(Capella Mayor,* 1430), closing off the central apse, which is reached by two Gothic door-

ways. Santa Tecla (St Thecla) is the city's patron saint.

This work by Pere Joan shows a talent for detail, ornamentation and the picturesque. To the right of the altar lies the 14C **Tomb of the Infante Don Juan de Aragón**★★, attributed to an Italian master.

The **Capella de la Virgen de Montserrat** (*second chapel, left*) houses a **retable**★ by Luis Borrassà (15C). **Reliefs**★ in the Capella de Santa Tecla (third chapel in the right-hand aisle) recount the saint's life.

The **Capella de los Sastres**★★ (*to the left of the Capella Major*) features intricate ribbed vaulting, a lovely altarpiece and paintings. Sumptuous tapestries are decorated with allegorical motifs.

Claustro★★

The 12C–13C cloisters are unusually large – each gallery is 45m/148ft long. The arches and geometric decoration are Romanesque, but the vaulting is Gothic, as are the supporting arches.

Moorish influence is evident in the *claustra* of geometrically patterned and pierced panels filling the oculi below the arches, the line of multifoil arches at the base of the Cathedral roof and the belfry in one corner, rising 70m/230ft. Inlaid in the west gallery is a *mihrab*-like stone niche, dated 960.

A remarkable **Romanesque doorway**★, with a Christ in Majesty, links the cathedral to the cloisters.

Museu Diocesá★★

Pl. de la Seu. 🕐*Open same hours as Cathedral.*

The capitular outbuildings contain religious vestments, paintings, altarpieces and reliefs. Tapestries in Room III include the 15C Flemish **La Buena Vida**★. In the Capella del Corpus Christi are a richly ornate **monstrance**★ (n°105) and a polychrome alabaster relief work depicting St Jerome (16C).

▷ *Retrace your steps to the Carrer Major, then turn left into the Carrer Sant Lorenç.*

Antic Hospital★

Coques.

This 12C–14C hospital, now used by the local council, is a surprising mix of styles, including the original Romanesque façade and doorway.

▷ *Backtrack along Carrer de Sant Lorenç.*

Museu d'Art Modern

Carrer Santa Anna 8. 🕐*Open Tue–Fri 10am–8pm, Sat 10am–3pm, 5–8pm, Sun and hols 11am–2pm.* 🕐*Closed 1, 6 Jan, 1 May, 11 Sept, 25–26 Dec.* 🎫*No charge.* 📞*977 235 032.* *www.altanet.org.*

Inaugurated in 1991, this museum presents a harmonious collection of *modernisme*, the Catalan equivalent to Art Nouveau. The local sculptor Julio Antonio (1889–1919), author of the monument to the heroes of 1811 on La Rambla, is well represented.

MODERNIST HERITAGE

Tarragona's *modernista* buildings, include a clutch of residential houses along the Rambla Nova, the Mercat Central (1905), southwest of the Rambla Nova and El Escorxador, the old abattoir (1902).

El Serrallo

▷ *Southwest of the centre, beyond the railway tracks. Access by bus #2 or # 5 or a 20-minute walk.*

This old fishermen's district, created in the mid 19C, hosts some of the best restaurants in town, and a famous fish market is held here every day. Consisting of a handful of narrow alleys around the church of Sant Pere, El Serrallo comes alive at night and is very popular with locals.

Museu del port de Tarragona

Moll de Costa. 🕐*Open Mon–Sat 10am–2pm, 4–7pm, Sun and hols 11am–2pm.* 🎫*€2.*

Housed in an outbuilding of the old ferry terminal, this museum traces the history of the Port of Tarragona from Roman times.

EXCURSIONS

Acueducto de Les Ferreres★★

▷ *Leave the city along rambla Nova.*
4km/2.5mi from Tarragona you will see the well-preserved two-tier Roman aqueduct on your right, 217m/712ft long. ⚑ *You can walk (30min) through the pines to the base.*

Mausoleo de Centcelles★★

▷ *4km/2.5mi NW. Exit the city along avinguda Ramon i Cajal. Take the Reus road; bear right after crossing the Francolí. Turn right in Constantí into Centcelles; continue 450m/492yd on an unsurfaced road; turn left just before the village.* ⊙*Open Tue–Sat 10am–1.30pm, 3–6pm, Sun 10am–2pm.* ⊙*Closed 1 Jan, 1 May, 25–26 Dec.* ⊛€1.80. ☏977 52 33 74. www.mnat.es.

Two monumental buildings in a vineyard are faced in pink tiles. They were built in the 4C by a wealthy Roman near his vast summer residence. The first chamber is covered by an immense cupola (diameter: 11m/36ft), decorated with **mosaics**★★ on themes such as hunting, Daniel in the lion's den, etc. The adjoining chamber has an apse on either side.

Torre de los Escipiones★

▷ *Leave Tarragona along via Augusta. After 5km/3mi turn left.*
The upper and central parts of this square funerary tower (1C) bear reliefs portraying Atis, a Phrygian divinity associated with death rituals (not the Escipion brothers as once thought).

Villa Romana de Els Munts★

▷ *12km/7.4mi E along the N 340. Leave Tarragona along via Augusta.*
⊙*Open Jun–Sept Tue–Sat 10am–1.30pm, 4–8pm; Oct–Feb Tue–Sat 10am–1.30pm, 3–5.30pm, Mar–end May Tue–Sat 10am–1.30pm, 3–6.30pm. Sun and public holidays (all year) 10am–1.30pm.* ⊙*Closed 1, 6 Jan, 25–26 Dec.* ⊛€1.80. ☏977 23 62 09. www.mnat.es.
This Roman villa nestles in Altafulla, in a privileged **site**★★ gently sloping towards the sea. The L-shaped arcaded passage was flanked by gardens and **baths**★ with a complex plan.

Arco de Berà★

▷ *Follow the via Augusta. The arch is situated in the locality of Roda de Berà, 20km/12.4mi along the N 340.*
The Vía Augusta once passed under this imposing, well-proportioned arch (1C). Its eight grooved pilasters are crowned by Corinthian capitals.

ADDRESSES

⌂ STAY

⊜⊜ **Hotel Urbis Centre** – Pl. Corsini 10. ☏977 24 01 16. www.hotelurbiscentre.com. 44 rooms. ⊠€7.50. Restaurant⊜⊜.
Situated near the convention centre and the old city, this modest family hotel offers functional rooms with modernised bathrooms.

⊜⊜⊜ **Hotel Imperial Tarraco** – Pas. Palmeres. ☏977 23 30 40. www.hotel husaimperialtarraco.com. 145 rooms. ⊠€14.Restaurant ⊜⊜. Despite its luxury tag, the rates here are not extortionate. The hotel is housed in a half-moon-shaped modern building near the city's Roman ruins, overlooking the amphitheatre. Many of the international-style rooms enjoy views of the Mediterranean.

⍾/EAT

⊜⊜⊜ **Merlot** – Caballers 6. ☏977 22 06 52. Closed Sun, Mon lunchtime, first fortnight in Feb, last week in Dec. The vaulted ceiling, subtle lighting and high-quality rustic furniture create a refined, intimate ambience. The menu covers a range of Catalan dishes (rice dishes in particular) as well as an excellent selection of home-made desserts.

⍾/ CAFÉS

Pla de la Seu – Pl. de la Seu 5–7. ☏977 23 04 07. The best feature of this establishment is its terrace facing the cathedral. Perfect for a refreshment before or after your visit. Live music on weekends.

Rest. Rovira – Vinatería – Av. Prat de la Riba 34. ☏977 22 61 58. The impressive choice at this prestigious wine bar includes a huge selection of sparkling wines from Catalunya. The Sumpta also has its own restaurant.

Montblanc★★

Montblanc lies in an impressive setting★ amid vineyards and almond orchards. Within its ancient walls lie narrow, cobbled streets, stone buildings, and legends and deep secrets from a golden age in the 14C.

▶ **Population:** 7 456

Michelin Map: 574 H 33 – Catalunya (Tarragona)

Info: Antigua Església de Sant Francesc. ℰ977 86 17 33. www.montblanc.cat.

Location: Montblanc is in Catalunya at the crossroads of the N 240 (Tarragona-Lleida) and the C 240 from Reus (29km/18mi S).
Roberto Aguilo 12.

SIGHTS

The Ramparts★★

The ramparts were commissioned by Peter IV of Aragón in the mid-14C. Two thirds of the original walls (1 500m/5 000ft) remain, along with 32 square towers and two of four gates: that of Sant Jordi (S) and Bover (NE).

Església de Santa Maria★★

Pl. de l'Església. Open daily 11am–1pm, 4–6pm. ℰ977 86 17 33 (tourist office).

This beautiful Gothic church overlooking the city has a single nave and radiating chapel. The unfinished façade is Baroque. The interior features a sumptuous 17C **organ**★★, a Gothic altarpiece in polychrome stone (14C) and an elegant silver monstrance.

Museu d'Historia Natural de la Conca de Barbera – CIAR – Museu d'Art Frederic Marès

Pedrera, 2. Open Tue–Sat 10am–2pm, 4–7pm, Sun and hols 10am–2pm. Closed 1 Jan, 25–26 Dec. €2.90. ℰ977 860 349. www.mccb.cat.

This two-in-one museum presents the physical environment of the region and reconstructions of the type of rock art that was practiced by its first inhabitants.

On the first floor, the magnificent Marès collection (*see Museu Frederic Marès, Barcelona, p317*) was bequeathed to the city in 1975 from the sculptor and collector who between 1945 and 1952 stayed in Montblanc in order to restore the Royal Tombs of the Poblet Monastery (*see p379*). The religious paintings and sculptures from the 14C to 19C are remarkable, particularly the early Gothic wooden figurines.

Part of the museum is situated 1km/0.6mi out of town towards Prenafeta where you can visit the Molins de la Vila; two ancient flour mills in their original setting.

Plaça Mayor

Among the arcades of shops and cafés around the main square, note the town hall *(ayuntamiento)* and the Gothic-style Casa dels Desclergue.

Església de Sant Miquel★

Pl. de Sant Miquel. Guided tours by prior arrangement. ℰ977 86 17 33 (tourist office).

Fronted by a Romanesque façade, this small 13C Gothic church has pure, sober lines. It hosted the Estates General of Catalunya several times in the 14C and 15C. Next to the church stands the **Palau del Castlà**, formerly the residence of the king's representative. A 15C prison is on its ground floor.

Call Judío (Jewish Quarter)

Until 1489, Montblanc was a thriving town with a prosperous Jewish community *(Jueus)*. Its golden age was the 14C, when its economic supremacy was reflected in the political arena with several Estates General being held in the town at the instigation of Catalan-Aragonese monarchs. Only the Carrer dels Jueus (Street of Jews) and part of a Gothic house in Plaça dels Àngels remain of the former Jewish district. Another interesting building is the 14C **Casa Alenyà**, a slender Gothic house.

OUTSIDE THE WALLS
Convent i Santuari de la Serra★

⏱Open 11am–1pm, 4–6pm. ✆€4.
℘977 86 17 33 (tourist office).
This ex-convent of the Order of St Clare stands on a small hill. It houses the venerated **Mare de Déu de la Serra**, an alabaster statue made in the 14C.

Hospital de Santa Magdalena★

⏱Open Aug–mid-Sept daily 11am–3pm; rest of the year 8pm–7pm.
The remarkable though small 15C **cloisters** illustrate the transition between Gothic and Renaissance. The vertical perspective on the ground floor, featuring fluted columns and pointed arches, is broken in the upper section.

EXCURSION
Valls

The prosperous city of Valls is wedged between two tributaries and its small historic center has kept its medieval character.
The city is still known for its famous *castellers* and especially for its *calçots*, tender, over-sized spring onions that are considered a Catalan delicacy.
In season in early winter, they are fire-grilled over vines and served on curved tiles, together with a romesco sauce that combines almonds, tomatoes, garlic, peppers and other ingredients. But beware! They are eaten whole with your hands – a messy, if not delicious experience.

🚗 DRIVING TOUR

CISTERCIAN ROUTE
90km/56mi. Allow one day.

Along this route, visit the most important Cistercian monasteries in Catalunya, founded in the 12C after the reconquest of Catalunya by Ramon Berenguer IV.

▷ *Exit Montblanc on the N 240 to l'Espluga de Francolí. From here, follow the T 700 for 4km/2.5mi.*

Monestir de Poblet★★★

Zona del Monasterio, Vimbodí.
🍃Guided tours (45min) Mon–Sat 10am–12.40pm, 3–5.25pm (5.55pm 15 Mar–15 Oct), Sun and public holidays 10am–12.25pm, 3–5.25pm ⏱Closed 1 Jan, Easter Thur and Fri, 26 Dec. ✆€6 (€9 with Santes Creus and Vallbona). ℘977 87 02 54. www.poblet.cat.
The splendid **site**★ of one of the largest and best-preserved Cistercian monasteries is sheltered by the Prades mountains. Founded in the 12C, it enjoyed the protection of the crown of Aragón. A 2km/1.2mi-perimeter protected the monastery and its vegetable gardens.

Capella de Sant Jordi★★
The Late Gothic interior of this tiny 15C chapel features splendid broken barrel vaulting. An inner wall with polygonal towers enclosed annexes where visitors were received. The 15C **Porta Daurada** (Golden Door), named after the gilded bronze sheets that form its covering, was commissioned by Philip II.

Plaça Major★
On this irregular main square stand the 12C **Capella de Santa Caterina**, shops, a hospital for pilgrims and a carpentry workshop. On the right are the ruins of the 16C Abbatial Palace and the **stone cross** erected by Abbey Guimerà, also 16C. A third wall (608m/1 995ft long, 11m/36ft high and 2m/6.5ft thick), built by Peter the Ceremonious, surrounds the monastery proper, fortified by 13 towers. On the right stands the **Baroque façade of the church**, built around 1670 and flanked, 50 years later, by heavily ornate windows. Pleasing in itself, it breaks with the overall austerity.

Porta Reial★
This is the gateway to the conventual buildings, appearing somewhat like the entrance to a fortress.

Palau del Rei Martí★
Beyond the door, to the right, a narrow staircase rises to this 14C Gothic palace. Its splendid rooms are wonderfully light thanks to pointed bay windows.

Monestir de Poblet

© Patrick Escudero/hemis.fr

Locutorio

Originally a dormitory for converts, this room became a wine press. The 14C vaulting rests directly on the walls.
The magnificent Gothic **cellar** is used as a concert hall.

Claustro★★

The size of these cloisters (40 x 35m/ 131 x 115ft) and their sober lines indicate the monastery's importance. The south gallery (c. 1200) and huge lavabo or **templete**★ with its marble fountain and 30 taps are in pure Romanesque style; the other galleries, built a century later, have floral motif tracery; beautiful scrollwork adorns the **capitals**★.

The **kitchen** *(cocina)* and the huge **monk's refectory** *(refectorio de los monjes)*, both built around 1200 and still in use, open onto the cloisters.

The **library** *(biblioteca)* – the former scriptorium – is crowned by ogival vaulting on 13C columns. The 13C **chapter house**★★ *(sala capitular)*, through a Romanesque doorway, has four slender octagonal columns and palm-shaped vaulting.

Església★★

The light, spacious church is typically Cistercian. It has pure lines, broken barrel vaulting and unadorned capitals. The windows and wide arches dividing the nave join in a large eave. The church incorporated numerous altars for its growing community; the apse

was ringed by an ambulatory and radiating chapels, a feature more commonly found in Benedictine churches.

The **royal pantheon**★★ *(panteó reial)*, the church's most original feature, has immense shallow arches spanning the transepts, surmounted by the royal tombs. These were constructed of alabaster in about 1350.

The **retable**★★ *(retablo)* at the **high altar** *(altar mayor)* is a monumental marble Renaissance altarpiece carved by Damián Forment in 1527. Figures in four superimposed registers can be seen glorifying Christ and the Virgin.

In the narthex, an opening to the outside world added in 1275, is the Renaissance **altar of the Holy Sepulchre**.

A wide flight of stairs leads from the north transept to the monks' dormitory. Massive central arches support the ridge roof above the vast, 87m/285ft long gallery of the **Dormitorio**.

▷ *Leave Poblet on the T 232 towards Maldà. From here, take the road to Vallbona.*

Monestir de Vallbona de les Monges★★

Mayor. ⬛⬛Guided tours (45min), Tue–Sat 10.30am–1.30pm, 4.30–6.45pm, Sun and public holidays noon–1.30pm, 4.30–6.45pm (6pm in winter). ○Closed 1,6 Jan, Good Friday, 25 Dec. ✑€4 (€9 with Poblet and Santes Creus Monasteries). ℘973 33 02 66. www.vallbona.com.

The Cistercian **Monestir de Santa Maria** completes the Cistercian Trinity. The convent was founded in 1157 by the hermit Ramon de Vallbona and became a Cistercian community for women.

Església★★

Built chiefly in the 13C and the 14C, this church is a fine example of transitional Gothic. The interior is simple and surprisingly light thanks to two octagonal lantern towers: one (13C) lies above the transept crossing while the other (14C) overlooks the centre of the nave. The church contains the beautiful tombs of Queen Violante of Hungary, wife of James I the Conqueror of Aragón, and her daughter, as well as a huge polychrome Virgin from the 15C.

Cloisters★

The east and west galleries are Romanesque (12C–13C). The 14C Gothic north wing features attractive capitals with plant motifs. In the south gallery (15C) note the 12C statue of Nuestra Señora del Claustro (of the Cloisters).

Head towards Rocallaura then towards Montblanc along the C 240 to link up with the AP 2. Turn off onto the TP 2002 at exit 11.

Monestir de Santes Creus★★★

Pl. Jaume el Just, Aiguamurcia. 46km/ 29mi SE of Vallbona. Guided tours (2hr). Open Tue–Sat 10am-5pm (6pm June-Sept). €4.50, no charge Tue. 977 63 83 29. www.larutadelcister.info.
The monastery was founded in the 12C by monks from Toulouse and its plan is similar to that of Poblet, with three perimeter walls. A Baroque gateway leads to the courtyard where the monastic buildings, enhanced with fine *sgraffiti*, now serve as shops and private residences. To the right is the abbatial palace, with its attractive patio, now the town hall; at the end stands the 12C–13C church.

Gran Claustro★★★

Construction began in 1313 on the site of earlier ("great") cloisters. The ornamentation on capitals and bands illustrates Gothic motifs: plants and flowers, animals, biblical, mythological and satirical themes. The Puerta Real or Royal Gate on the south side opens onto cloisters with Gothic bays with lively carvings – note Eve shown emerging out of Adam's rib, and the fine tracery of the arches (1350–1430). In contrast, the transitional style of the **lavabo** appears almost clumsy. Carved noble tombs fill the niches.

The **chapter house**★★ *(sala capitular)* is an elegant hall with arches on four pillars. Stairs next to the chapter house lead to the 12C **dormitory** *(dormitorio)*, a gallery divided by diaphragm arches supporting a timber roof, now used as a concert hall.

Església★★

The church (1174) closely follows the Cistercian pattern of a flat east end and overall austerity. The lantern (14C), stained glass, and the superb apsidal **rose window** relieve the bareness. Ribbed vaults rest on pillars which extend back along the walls and end in unusual consoles. Gothic canopies at the transept openings shelter the **royal tombs**★★: on the north side (c. 1295) that of **Pere the Great** (III of Aragón, II of Barcelona) and on the south (14C), that of his son, **Jaime II**, the Just, and his queen, **Blanche d'Anjou**. The Plateresque decoration below the crowned recumbent figures in Cistercian habits, was added in the 16C.

Claustro Viejo

Although they were built during the 17C, these "old cloisters" occupy the site of former cloisters dating back to the 12C. The design is simple with a small central fountain and eight cypresses in the close. Leading off are the kitchens, refectory and the **royal palace** (note a splendid 14C **patio**★).

ADDRESSES

STAY

Fonda dels Àngels – *Pl. Els Àngels 1. 977 86 01 73. Closed first two weeks Sep, Christmas holidays. 9 rooms. €5.* Simple rooms in a bay-windowed Gothic house. Homemade food is served on site in the small dining room ( ).

Lleida/Lérida★

Lleida, an ancient citadel, was stormed by the legions of Caesar, and occupied by the Moors from the 8C to the 12C. The Arab fortress, the Zuda, sited like an acropolis, was savaged by artillery fire in 1812 and 1936. The glacis has been converted into gardens. Lleida is an important fruit-growing centre.

SIGHTS
LA SEU★★★
(OLD CATHEDRAL)

To reach the Cathedral, take the lift from Plaça de Sant Joan. Turó la Seu Vella. ○*Closed 1, 6 Jan, 25–26 Dec*◔○€3; *no charge Tue.* ◔973 23 06 53.

The Cathedral **site**★ dominates the city from inside the walls. It was built between 1203 and 1278 over a mosque; the octagonal belfry was added in the 14C. Philip V converted it into a garrison fortress in 1707.

Església★★

The **capitals**★ of this transitional-style church are outstanding for their variety and detail. Those in the apses and transept illustrate the Old Testament, those in the nave and aisles, the New Testament. Moorish influences show in the exterior decoration, particularly the Puerta de Els Fillols (Godchildren's Doorway) and Puerta de la Anunciata (Annunciation Doorway). The extremely delicate carving, reminiscent of Moorish stuccowork, has come to be known as the Romanesque School of Lleida. It is seen throughout the region, in particular on the superb **portal**★★ of the Església de **Agramunt** *(52km/32.3mi NE)*.

Claustro★★

The cloisters have an unusual position in front of the church. Their 14C galleries are remarkable for the size of the bays and the beautiful stone tracery. The Gothic style shows Moorish influence in the plant motifs on the **capitals**★. There is a fine view from the south gallery.

In the southwest corner stands the Gothic **bell tower**★★, 60m/197ft high.

▶ **Population:** 137 387

◔ **Michelin Map:** 574 H 31 – Catalunya (Lleida)

▣ **Info:** Major 31 bis. ◔902 25 00 50. www.turismedel leida.com.

◗ **Location:** Lleida is linked to Barcelona by the AP 2 motorway, the Pyrenees by the C 1313 and N 240, and Huesca via the N 240. ▬▬Plaça Berenguer IV

ⓟ **Parking:** Space is limited in the old quarter.

◉ **Don't Miss:** A walk up to the Zuda for commanding views of city and plain.

Along Carrer Major are the 13C **Palau de la Paeria**, now the town hall *(ajunta-ment;* ○ *open Mon–Sat 11am–2pm, 5–8pm, Sun 11am–2pm;* ◌*no charge;* ◔*973 70 03 00 or 973 70 03 94)*, with its fine **façade**★; the **Hospital de Santa Maria** *(*◔*973 27 15 00; www.fpiei.es)*, with a **patio**★ showing Renaissance influence; and the 18C **Seu Nova** (New Cathedral; ○*open daily 9.30am–1pm, 5.30–8.15pm;* ◔*973 26 94 70)*.

Museu de Lleida i Diocesà Comarcal

Jaume I el Conqueridor 1. ○*Open Tue–Sat 10am–2pm, 4–7pm (8pm during summer), Sun and public holidays 10am–2pm .* ○*Closed 1, 6 Jan, Good Fri, Easter Mon, and 25–26 Dec.* ◌○€4; *no charge first Sun in month, 11, 18 May, 11, 29 Sept.* ◔*973 28 30 75. www.museudelleida.cat.*

Opened in late 2007, this exciting museum spread out over several levels of a purpose-built edifice tells a chronological history of the region, from the Bronze Age to Muslim occupation, the Christian reconquest and beyond. Among the outstanding ancient exhibits, note the remains of the Roman Villa del Romeral, the Visigothic baptistery and 5C chess pieces. Flemish tapestries, Gothic paintings and various religious works complete this notable collection.

La Costa Daurada★★

The Golden Coast unfolds along the shores of the province of Tarragona with beautiful beaches offering calm, shallow waters. Its benign climate has fostered the development of many tourist resorts, which overall cater to more low-key, family holidaymakers than the upmarket Costa Brava. Admittedly, high-rise hotels have caused a blip in the landscape, yet there are still plenty of opportunities to escape the crowds.

- **Michelin Map:** 574 I-K31-34.
- **Info:** Xalet Torremar, Pg. Jaume I, Salou. ℘977 350 102. www.costadaurada.info.
- **Location:** A 150km/ 93mi stretch of coast in Tarragona province.
- **Kids:** Days on the beach, at a water park, or at Port Aventura.
- **Timing:** If doing a day trip, be warned that last trains back to Barcelona can get very crowded.

SIGHTS
Coastal Towns

Easily reached via the train line between Barcelona and Tarragona, the towns and villages of the Costa Daurada make ideal day or overnight beach destinations. The best include **Altafulla**, with its long stretch of unspoilt sand and impressive Roman Villa, **Els Munts** and **Cambrils**, which has retained the atmosphere of an authentic fishing village. Towns such as Calafell, Torrdembarra and Coma-Ruga are popular with Spanish holiday-makers. For more cultural pursuits, the town of **El Vendrell** was the birthplace of the famed cellist Pau Casals and you can visit his former home (Casa-Natal Pau Casals, Santa Ana 2; ℘ 977 684276). Reus's most famous son is Gaudí, and has a new "experience centre" on the famous architect (Gaudí Centre, Plaça Mercadal 3; ℘977 010 670).

Port Aventura★★

- 10km/6.2mi SW towards Salou.
- Open daily from 10am, phone for closing times. ⊜€44; child €36 (different rates available for mulitple day tickets). ℘902 20 22 20. www.portaventura.es. Tickets can be purchased in advance through the website ℗ €7 per day.

The huge Universal Studios Port Aventura amusement park is divided into five geographical zones, each with characteristic rides, performances, shops etc.

Mediterrània at the park entrance is a coastal town. In **Polynesia★**, a path winds through tropical vegetation. **China★★** is the heart of the park, symbolising the magic and mystery of a millenary civilisation. The star attraction is **Dragon Khan★★★**, one of the world's most spectacular roller coasters, with eight gigantic loops. **Mexico★★** spans Mayan ruins, colonial Mexico, Mariachi music and traditional Mexican cuisine. In the **Far West★★** town of **Penitence**, visitors play the lead in a western or dance in the saloon. Adjacent is the **Caribe Aquatic Park** (⊜€24; child €19), with a Caribbean island theme.

Salou★

- 10km/6.2mi SW. ▦Carles Roig.

This is the principal resort on the Costa Dorada, very popular with British and German tourists. Aside from Port Aventura (℘see above) the most popular day off the beach is at **Aquopolis** a very popular water park and dolphinarium (La Pineda; Open 16 May–30 Jun, 1–18 Sept 11am–6pm; Jul–Aug 10.30am–7pm; 21 Sept–9 Oct 11.30am–5pm; ⊜€25.50; child €19.40; ℘902 34 50 11; www.aquopolis.es/costa-daurada).

Salou merges into the attractive little fishing port of **Cambrils** (8km/5mi W; ▦Avinguda Virgen de Montserrat). Renowned for the quality of its fish restaurants.

Tortosa★

Tortosa, for centuries the last town before the sea, once guarded the region's only bridge. From the Castillo de la Suda, a castle (now a parador), enjoy a fine view of the Ebro and the valley. Tortosa's artistic endowment ranges from Gothic monuments to fine examples of Modernism.

▶ **Population:** 36 574
◉ **Michelin Map:** 574 J 31.
ℹ **Info:** Plaça del Carrilet 1. ℘977 44 96 48. www.turismetortosa.com.
◐ **Location:** Tortosa is 14km/8.7mi off the coastal motorway in Catalunya 90km/56mi south of Tarragona.
👥 **Kids:** Sampling *pastissets*, a sweet delicacy from the town's bakeries.

SIGHTS
Catedral★★

Croera. ◐*Open Tue–Sat 10am–1pm, 4–6pm, Sun 12–2pm.* 🎫*3€.* ℘*977 44 6 1 10*

The Cathedral was built in pure Gothic style even though construction, begun in 1347, continued for 200 years. The 18C Baroque **façade**★ is lavishly decorated: capitals with plant motifs, curved columns and outstanding reliefs.

In Catalan tradition the lines of the **interior**★★ are plain, the high arches divided into two tiers only in the nave. The retable at the high altar has a large 14C wood **polyptych**★ illustrating the Life of Christ and the Virgin Mary. Another interesting work is the 15C **altarpiece of the Transfiguration**★. Two stone 15C **pulpits**★ in the nave are carved with low reliefs: those on the left illustrate the Evangelists, those on the right, Saints Gregory, Jerome, Ambrose and Augustine.

Capella de Nuestra Señora de la Cinta★

Built in Baroque style between 1642 and 1725, the Chapel of Our Lady of the Sash is decorated with paintings and local jasper and marble; at its centre is the sash of Our Lady *(services of special veneration: first week in September)*. The stone **font** is said to have stood in the garden of the antipope Benedict XIII, Pedro de Luna, and bears his arms.

Palau Episcopal★

Croera 9. ◐*Open Mon–Fri 10am–1pm.* ◐*Closed public holidays.* 🎫*No charge.* ℘*977 44 07 00.*

The 14C Catalan patio of this Bishop's Palace, built in the 13C–14C, is known for its straight flight of steps which occupies one side, and the arcaded gallery. On the upper floor, the **Gothic chapel**★, has ogive vaulting in which the ribs descend to figured bosses.

Reials Col·legis de Tortosa★

Sant Domènec. 12. ◐*Open Tue–Sat 10am–1.30pm, 3.30–6pm, Sun 11am–1.30pm.* 🎫*No charge.* ℘*977 44 95 648.*

In 1564 Emperor Charles V sponsored this lovely Renaissance ensemble.

The **Colegio de Sant Lluís**★ at one time educated newly converted Muslims. The fine oblong **patio**★★ is curiously decorated with characters in a wide range of expressions and attitudes.

The Renaissance façade of the **Colegio de Sant Jordi y de Sant Domingo** bears a Latin inscription (*Domus Sapientiae*, House of Knowledge).

The adjacent **Església de Sant Domènec** was built in the 16C and once formed part of the Reales Colegios.

EXCURSION
Parque Natural del Delta del Ebro★★ (Ebro Delta Nature Reserve)

◐ *25km/15.5mi E.*

This vast delta (*www.deltebre.net*) is a swampy stretch of alluvium deposits collected by the Ebro and now acts as a bird reserve.

👥 **Boat trips** between Deltebre and the river mouth can be taken (℘*977 480 128; www.creuers-delta-ebre.com*).

One of Spain's least known and least visited regions, Aragón is over twice the size of Wales or New Jersey, but is a sparsely populated wild land with more than half its 1.2 million population huddled into its only city, Zaragoza. The very name Aragón evokes images of a romantic, medieval Spain and is well known in European history as its kingdom once held sway across Barcelona, Valencia and as far afield as Sardinia. The Crown of Aragón was disbanded after its union with Castile, however, and, by the early 18C, had reverted to its sleepy provincial role. Today it is largely a destination for lovers of the great outdoors.

Zaragoza and Central Aragón

The tongue-twisting capital of Aragón – its present name supposedly derives from the Roman colony of Caesar Augusta – is a vibrant city.

At first sight it is unprepossessing with traffic-laden streets and numerous unattractive modern buildings, many designed to accommodate the steady influx from the countryside over the last 50-or-so years, but at its heart is the historical old town *(casco viejo)* so typical of many Spanish cities.

Outside the capital, much of central Aragón is flat and featureless. The main source of livelihood is farming around Huesca and stock-raising in the valleys. Huesca, the quiet capital of Upper Aragón, has an appealing historic centre. Nearby Barbastro boasts fine 16C architecture and makes a good base for exploring the Central Pyrenees and picturesque historic villages such as Roda de Isábena.

Northern Aragón

The northernmost part of Aragón butts right up to the French border and is known as the Aragonese Pyrenees (Pirineos Aragoneses). The highlight of this spectacular region is the Parque Nacional de Ordesa y Monte Perdido, while the Ordesa Canyon is one of Spain's natural wonders and Europe's riposte to the Grand Canyon in the US. Near here, the Monasterio de San Juan de la Peña occupies a spectacular location beneath overhanging rock.

Southern Aragón

The clay hills bordering the Ebro Basin in Bajo Aragón (Lower Aragón) around Daroca and Alcañiz are planted with vineyards and olive groves. Brick villages

Highlights

1. The sheer size and various styles of La Seo, **Zaragoza** (p387)

2. Magnificent Mudéjar towers and other architecture in **Teruel** (p390)

3. The location of **Monasterio de San Juan de la Peña** (p396)

4. Trekking in the breathtaking **Parque Nacional Ordesa** (p398)

5. Traversing the **Valle de Pineta** in the Aragonese Pyrenees (p203)

and ochre-coloured houses merge with the tawny-hued and deeply scored hillsides. The jewel of Bajo (Lower) Aragón is Teruel, declared a UNESCO World Heritage Site on account of its rich Mudéjar (Christian-Moorish) architecture.

Parque Nacional de Ordesa y Monte Perdido

© Chad Ehlers/Tips/Photononstop

Zaragoza★★

The domes of the Basílica del Pilar dominate Zaragoza, on the right bank of the River Ebro. The city, rebuilt after the 19C War of Independence, combines historic monuments with bustling modern boulevards. Zaragoza is a university and religious centre. The Virgen del Pilar (Virgin of the Pillar) makes it the leading Marian shrine in Spain. Expo 2008 brought a facelift to Zaragoza.

▶ **Population:** 699 127
🕭 **Michelin Map:** 54 H 27 (town plan).
ℹ **Info:** Ntra. Sra. del Pilar, s/n. 𝄡976 20 12 00. www.zaragoza.es.
▷ **Location:** Zaragoza is in NE Spain in a fertile pocket watered by the Aragón canal and the Ebro, Gállego, Jalón and Huerva rivers. 🚆Zaragoza-Delicias, Rioja 33.

THE CITY TODAY

Like major events in other Spanish cities, the legacy of Zaragoza's successful Expo 2008 (🕭 see sidebar) is a much more visitor-friendly city. The most notable addition is the Parque del Agua, a development along the Ebro of outdoor bars and restaurants, urban beaches and bike lanes. New hotels, better infrastructure (within the city and with the rest of Spain) and improvements in tourist facilities are also evident. The only downside, of course, is an inevitable hike in prices.

A BIT OF HISTORY

Caesaraugusta-Sarakusta – Salduba, at the confluence of the Ebro and its tributaries, became Roman Caesaraugusta in 25 BC. On 2 January in AD 40, according to tradition, the Virgin appeared to St James, leaving the pillar around which the **Basílica de Nuestra Señora del Pilar** was later built. The

Uncounted Martyrs of the 3C, persecuted by Diocletian, are interred in the crypt of **Santa Engracia**.

To learn more of the Roman city, visit the **Caesaraugusta theatre museum** (San Jorge 12; 🕑open Tue–Sat 10am–9pm, Sun and public holidays 10am–2pm; ⬤€4, €7 combined ticket for all Ceasaragusta sites; 𝄡976 20 50 88); the **Caesaraugusta public baths museum** (San Juan y San Pedro 3–7; 🕑open Tue–Sat 10am–2pm, 5–9pm, Sun and public holidays 10am–2pm; ⬤€3; 𝄡976 29 72 79); the **Caesaraugusta Forum Museum** (pl. la Seo 2; 🕑open Tue–Sat 10am–2pm, 5–9pm, Sun and public holidays 10am–2pm; ⬤€3; 𝄡976 39 97 52) and the **Caesaraugusta River Port Museum** (pl. San Bruno 8; 🕑open same hours as Forum Museum; ⬤€3; 𝄡976 39 31 57). Muslim occupation of the city renamed Sarakusta lasted four centuries.

The **Aljafería** (🕭 see Sights), a palace built by the first Benihud monarch of an 11C taifa kingdom, is a unique example of Hispano-Muslim art.

Capital of Aragón – The Aragón kings freed Zaragoza from the Moors and proclaimed it capital. The city retained its autonomy and prospered. It protected its Muslim masons, who embellished the apse of **La Seo** (Cathedral, 🕭see Sights), and the **San Pablo** (San Pablo 42) and **Magdalena** (pl. Magdalena) churches in Mudéjar style. Houses with elegant patios and artesonado ceilings reflect prosperity in the 16C.

Water, Water...

The theme of **Expo 2008** was Water and Sustainable Development. The most iconic structures from the Expo are located in Avenida de Ranillas: the **Water Tower**, a 76m/249ft high skyscraper in the shape of a water droplet, and the **Bridge Pavilion**, a 270m/295yd long bridge shaped in a curving line over the River Ebro.

Two heroic sieges – Zaragoza resisted a siege by Napoleon's army from June to 14 August 1808. Exultant Zaragozans sang "The Virgin of Pilar will never be French." Alas! General Lannes laid siege from 21 December until 20 February, 1809. By its end, 54 000, half of the city, had died. The shrapnel-pitted **Puerta del Carmen** (Carmen Gate; *av. César Augusto*) still bears witness.

SIGHTS

La Seo★★

Pl. de la Seo. ⏱*Open summer Tue–Sun 10am–9; winter Tue–Fri 10am–1.30pm, 4–5.30pm, Sat 10am–noon, 4–5.30pm, Sun 10–11.20am, 4–5.30pm.* ✆€4 (inc. Tapestry Museum). ☏976 29 12 31. www.cabildodezaragoza.org.

The Cathedral of Zaragoza, La Seo, of remarkable size, includes all styles from Mudéjar to Churrigueresque, although it is basically Gothic. The tall belfry was added in the 17C, the Baroque façade in the 18C. View the Mudéjar **east end** from calle del Sepulcro.

The interior has five aisles of equal height. Above the high altar is a Gothic **retable**★ with a predella carved by the Catalan Pere Johan, and three central panels of the Ascension, Epiphany and the Transfiguration sculpted by Hans of Swabia (the stance and modelling of the faces and robes strike a German note).

The **surrounding wall of the chancel** (*trascoro*) and some of the side chapels were adorned in the 16C with carved figures, evidence of the vitality of Renaissance Spanish sculpture. Other chapels, ornamented in the 18C, show Churrigueresque exuberance. One exception is the **Parroquieta**, a Gothic chapel with a Burgundian-influenced 14C tomb and a Moorish **cupola**★ in polychrome wood with stalactites and strapwork (15C).

Museo Capitular★

In the sacristy. Exhibited are paintings, an enamel triptych and church plate including silver reliquaries, chalices and an enormous processional monstrance made of 24 000 pieces.

Museo de Tapices★★

An outstanding collection of Gothic hangings, woven in Arras and Brussels.

La Lonja★

Pl. del Pilar. ⏱*Open during exhibitions Tue–Sat 10am–2pm, 5–9pm, Sun and public holidays 10am–2pm.* ☏976 39 72 39.

Zaragoza, like other trading towns, founded a commercial exchange as early as the 16C. These buildings, in a style between Gothic and Plateresque, include some of the finest civil architecture in Spain. The vast hall is divided in three by tall columns, their shafts ornamented with a band of grotesques. Coats of arms supported by cherubim mark the start of the ribs which open into star **vaulting**.

The **ayuntamiento** (town hall; *pl. del Pilar 18*) has been rebuilt in traditional Aragón style with ornate eaves. Two modern bronzes stand at the entrance.

Basílica de Nuestra Señora del Pilar★

⏱*Open daily 5.45am–8.30pm (9.30pm in summer and on public holidays).* ✆*No charge.* ☏976 29 95 64.

Successive sanctuaries on this site have enshrined the miraculous pillar *(pilar)* above which the Virgin appeared. The present building, Zaragoza's second cathedral, was designed by Francisco Herrera the Younger in about 1677.

A buttressed quadrilateral, it is lit by a central dome. The cupolas, with small lantern towers, whose ornamental tiles reflect in the Ebro, were added by Ventura Rodríguez in the 18C.

Inside, some of the frescoes decorating the cupolas were painted by Goya as a young man.

The **Capilla de la Virgen** (Lady Chapel) by Ventura Rodríguez is virtually a miniature church. It contains, in a niche on the right, the pillar and a Gothic wood statue of the Virgin. The Virgin's mantle is changed every day except on the 2nd of the month (the Apparition was on 2 January), and the 12th of the month (for the celebration of the Hispanidad, 12 October). Pilgrims kiss the pillar through an opening at the rear.

The **high altar** is surmounted by a **retable**★ by Damián Forment of which the predella is outstanding. The **coro** is closed by a high grille and adorned with Plateresque stalls.

Museo Pilarista★

Inside the Basilica. ⏱*Open Tue–Sun and public holidays 9am–1.30pm, 4–7.30pm.* ✆€2. ✆976 39 74 97.
Displayed are sketches made by Goya, González, Velázquez and Bayeu for the cupolas of Our Lady of the Pillar, a model by Ventura Rodríguez, and some of the jewels which adorn the Virgin during the Pilar festivals. Among old ivory pieces are an 11C hunting horn and a Moorish jewellery box.

Aljafería★

Av. de Madrid. Access by Conde de Aranda. ⏱*Open Apr–Oct daily 10am– 2pm, 4.30–8pm; Nov–Mar Fri–Wed 10am–2pm, 4–6.30pm. Last admission 30min before closing.* ✆€3; no charge Sun. ✆976 28 96 32.
www.cortesaragon.es.
It is unusual to find such magnificent Moorish architecture in this part of Spain. Built in the 11C by the Benihud family, it was modified by the Aragonese kings (14C) and Catholic Monarchs (15C) before being taken over by the Inquisition and later converted into a barracks. The Moorish palace centres on a rectangular patio bordered by porticoes with delicate tracery and carved capitals.
The **musallah**, the mosque of the emirs, is restored with *mihrab* and multifoil arches and floral decoration.
The first floor and the staircase are in the Flamboyant Gothic of the Catholic Monarchs. Only the ornate **ceiling★**, its cells divided by geometric interlacing and decorated with fir cones, remains of the throne room.

Museo Ibercaja Camón Aznar★

Calle Espoz y Mina 23. ⏱*Open Tue–Sat 10am–2.30pm, 5–9pm, Sun and public hols 10am–2.30pm.* ✆No charge. ✆976 39 73 28. www.ibercaja.es.
This museum, fruit of a collection gathered by the historian Jose Camón Aznar *(1898–1979)* and his wife, consists of a plethora of paintings from the 15–20C exhibited in, the Casa Alguilar, a sumptuous Renaissance palace. An entire section is devoted to drawings and prints by Goya, from the famous *Los Caprichos* to *The Disasters of War* and the *Tauromaquia* (Bullfighting) series.
Executed at the turn of the 18–19C, these works were a creative breakaway for Goya as he embarked upon controversial subjects – such as the sheer violence of war, the educated poor and prostitution – in a dynamic and realistic way.

Museo Pablo Gargallo★

San Felipe Pl 3. ⏱*Open daily except Mon 10am–2pm, 5–9pm, Sun and hols 10am–2pm.* ✆€3.50. ✆976 39 25 24.
The beautiful Condes de Argillo palace plays host to this delightful and surprising museum dedicated to the great Aragonese sculptor Pablo Gargallo *(1881–1934)*. A good friend of Picasso and Juan Gris, Gargallo divided his time between Barcelona and Paris and worked mainly in metals (copper, iron, lead etc.), mainly focusing on the human body in a figurative style marked by a gradual reversal of volumes. The museum also includes drawings, documents, his working tools and a timeline, all which help place this little known artist in context amongst his contemporaries.

EXCURSIONS
Fuendetodos

▶*45km/28mi SW along the N 330; after 21km/13mi bear left onto the Z 100.* ✆976 14 38 67. www.fuendetodos.org.
It was in a modest house, now the **Casa Natal de Goya y Museo del Grabado** (⏱ *open Tue–Sun and public holidays 11am–2pm, 4–7pm;* ⏱ *closed 1 Jan, 24, 25, 31 Dec;* ✆€3; ✆976 14 38 30; www. fundacionfuendetodosgoya.org) in this village that the great painter Francisco Goya y Lucientes was born in 1746. There is a display of his etchings next door.

Tarazona

▶*21km/13mi SW on the N 121.*
Tarazona was once the residence of the kings of Aragón. The royal mansion, now the **Palacio Episcopal** (Episcopal Palace; *Rúa Alta de Bécquer;* ⏱*open Sat–Sun*

and public holidays 11am–2pm, 5–8pm; ☎976 64 28 61), is in a quarter with narrow streets overlooking the quays of the River Queiles.

Catedral

Juicio. ◯Open Mon–Sat 10am–1.30pm, 4–7pm, Sat, Sun 10am–1.30pm. (Sun access to cloisters only). ◉€3.10 (includes musuem). ☎948 40 21 61.

The Cathedral was largely rebuilt in the 15C and 16C. Its mix of styles includes Aragón Mudéjar in the belfry tower and lantern, Renaissance in the portal and, in the **second chapel**★ as you walk left round the ambulatory, delicately carved Gothic **tombs** of the two Calvillos cardinals from Avignon.

The **Mudéjar cloisters** have bays filled with 16C Moorish plasterwork tracery.

Monasterio de Veruela★★

▷ *39km/24mi S from Tudela. From Tarazona (17km/10.5mi), take the N 122 towards Zaragoza then bear right onto the Z 373. ◯Open Apr–Sept Wed–Mon 10.30am–8.30pm; Oct–Mar 10.30am–6.30pm. ☎976 64 90 25.*

Cistercian monks from France founded a fortified monastery in the mid-12C. The 19C Sevillian poet **Bécquer** stayed here while writing *Letters from My Cell*, in which he described the Aragón countryside much in the manner of later guidebooks!

Iglesia★★

The church, built in the transitional period between Romanesque and Gothic, has a sober façade with a single oculus, a band of blind arcades lacking a baseline, and a doorway decorated with friezes, billets and capitals.

In the large interior, the vault groins are pointed over the nave, and horseshoe-shaped elsewhere. A 16C Plateresque chapel is built onto the north transept. The sacristy door opposite is in a surprising Rococo style.

Claustro★

The cloisters are ornate Gothic. At ground level the brackets are carved with the heads of men and beasts; above

are three Plateresque galleries. In the **Sala Capitular**★ (chapter house), in pure Cistercian style, are the tombs of the first 15 abbots.

Daroca★

▷ *At the crossroads of the N 234 and N330, close to Calatayud (40km/25mi N); Zaragoza (85km/53mi NE); Teruel (96km/59.6mi S).*

Daroca's battlemented walls★, originally with 100 towers and gateways, lie between two ridges. **Puerta Baja** (Lower Gate) is flanked by square towers.

Colegiata de Santa María

Pl. de España 8. ◯Open Tue–Sun 8am–1pm, 5.30–6.30pm. ◉€3. ☎976 80 07 32.

This Romanesque collegiate church, a repository for the holy cloths, was modified in the 15C and 16C. Beside the belfry is a Flamboyant Gothic portal.The late Gothic nave includes a Renaissance cupola above the transept crossing.

The **south chapels** are partly faced with 16C *azulejos*. To the right of the entrance is a 15C **altarpiece**★ in multicoloured alabaster believed to have been carved in England. The 15C **Capilla de los Corporales**★ (Chapel of the Holy Relics) is on the site of the original Romanesque apse. The altar includes a shrine enclosing the holy altar cloths. Statues in delightful poses are carved of multicoloured alabaster. The painted Gothic **retable**★ is dedicated to St Michael.

Museo Parroquial★

Pl. de España. ◯Open Tue–Sun 11am–1pm, 6–8pm. ◉€3. ☎976 80 07 61.

Holdings include two rare though damaged 13C panels and **altarpieces** to St Peter (14C) and St Martin (15C), and gold and silver plate mostly of local manufacture, as well as **chasubles**.

Iglesia de San Miguel

Pl. Colegial.

This fine church, outstanding for the purity of its Romanesque east end and its 12C portal, is restored to its original design. A short distance below is the restored Mudéjar-style belfry of the **Iglesia de Santo Domingo**.

Monasterio de Piedra★★

Hidden in a fold of this arid plateau is an oasis fed by the River Piedra. Approach the monastery via Ateca, across a parched landscape above the Tranquera Reservoir and past the village of Nuévalos. The site was discovered by Cistercian monks, who generally chose pleasant surroundings. Monks from the Abbey of Poblet in Tarragona established a monastery in 1194. It was rebuilt several times. The buildings have been reconstructed as a hotel.

Park and Waterfalls★★

🕐 *Open daily Apr–Nov 9am–8pm; Dec–Mar 9am–6pm.* ⊷*€12.* 🕿*902 19 60 52.* *www.monasteriopiedra.com.*

Waterfalls and cascades are everywhere along the footpath through the forest *(follow red signposts to go, blue to return).* The paths, steps and tunnels laid out last century by **Juan Federico Muntadas** have transformed an impenetrable forest into a popular park.

The first fall is the **Cola de Caballo** (Horse's Tail), a cascade of 53m/174ft. You come on it again at the end of your walk if you descend steep and slippery steps into the beautiful **Cueva Iris** (Iris Grotto).

Baño de Diana (Diana's Bath) and **Lago del Espejo** (Mirror Lake), between tall cliffs, are both worth a halt.

Teruel★

Isolated amid rugged hills and deep ravines, Teruel has retained the charm of its narrow streets and splendid buildings which transport visitors back through the centuries. The smallest provincial capital, of Bajo (Lower) Aragón, it is a UNESCO World Heritage Site for its magnificent Mudéjar architecture.

▸ **Population:** 35 241
🕭 **Michelin Map:** 574 K 26.
🯄 **Info:** Plaza Amantes 6.
    🕿978 61 99 03.
    http://turismo.teruel.net.
▸ **Location:** Teruel is at 916m /3 005ft directly east of Madrid on the Turia river. 🚃Camino de la Estación

SIGHTS

Plaza del Torico, the heart of the town, is lined with Rococo-style houses. It is named for a small statue of a bull calf.

Torre de San Martín★

Plaza del Perá Prado.

The most central of the four Mudéjar towers in Teruel actually consists of two; one embedded within the other. Observe the lovely green and white ceramic embellishment.

Casa de la Comunidad-Museo Provincial★

Pl. Fray Anselmo Polanco 3.
🕐*Open Tue–Fri and public holidays 10am–2pm, 4–7pm, Sat–Sun 10am–2pm.* 🕐*Closed 1 Jan, 1 May, 24, 25, 31 Dec.* ⊷*No charge.* 🕿*978 60 01 50.* http://museo.deteruel.es.

The museum, in a mansion with an elegant Renaissance façade crowned by a gallery, displays ethnological and archaeological collections, including tools and everyday objects. Note the reconstitution of a forge and the 15C Gothic door knocker.

The first floor is given over to ceramics, for which Teruel has been renowned since the 13C. The upper floors contain prehistoric (an Iron Age sword from Alcorisa), Iberian, Roman (a catapult) and Arab (an 11C censer) objects.

Catedral de Santa María de Mediavilla

Pl. de la Catedral. 🕐*Open Jun–end Oct Mon–Sat 11am–2pm, 4–8pm, Sun 4–8pm; Nov–May Mon–Sat 11am–2pm, 4–7pm, Sun 4–7pm.* ⊷*€3.* 🕿*978 61 80 16.*

The cathedral, originating in the 13C (tower), was enlarged in the 16C and again in the 17C. The late 13C **artesonado ceiling**★, once hidden beneath star vaulting, is a precious example of Mudéjar art. Its beams and consoles are painted with decorative motifs, people at court and hunting scenes.

In the north transept is a 15C **altarpiece** of the Coronation of the Virgin. Scenes shown in perspective along the second band suggest Flemish influence. The 16C **high altar retable** is by **Gabriel Joli**, known for powerful portraits and skill in illustrating movement.

Iglesia de San Pedro

Matías Abad. Open daily Sept–Jul 10am–2pm, 4–8pm; Aug 10am–8pm. €8 (includes Mausoleum). 978 62 41 05. www.amantesdeteruel.es.

In spite of 18C alterations, the church retains a Mudéjar tower and east end. The adjoining **Mausoleo de los Amantes** (The Mausoleum of the Lovers) shows the deceased in an alabaster relief by Juan de Ávalos (20C).

EXCURSIONS
Albarracín★

38km/23.6mi W along the N 234 and A 1512.

Hidden in the Sierra de Albarracín, this medieval city tinged with pinkish hues has an exceptional **situation**★, on a cliff above the Guadalaviar river. The ramparts rising behind the town were built by the Moors in the 10C and restored by the Christians in the 14C.

Caves in the surrounding sierra contain **rock engravings** from the Upper Palaeolithic era, such as the sites at Callejón del Plou and Cueva del Navaza *(5km/3mi SE towards Bezas and Valdecuenca).*

Alcañiz

49km/92mi NE of Teruel along the N 420 and N 211.

Alcañiz, set in olive groves, is the capital of Lower Aragón. The region is famous for Holy Week ceremonies.

Two memorable façades meet on the **Plaza de España**★: the tall Catalan Gothic arcade of the **Lonja**, once a market, and the Renaissance town hall *(ayuntamiento)*. Both are crowned by an Aragón gallery with overhanging eaves. Vertical lines and curves and a Baroque **portal**★ mark the collegiate **Colegiata de Santa María la Mayor** (open daily 9am–1pm, 4–7pm; no charge), rebuilt in the 18C. Massive columns with composite capitals rise to a projecting cornice. The hilltop **Castillo de los Calatravos** (open Sept–Jul Wed–Sun 10am–1.30pm, Aug daily 10am–1.30pm, 4–7pm; €4.70) was the local seat of the Order of Calatrava in the 12C. The part used as a parador largely dates from the 18C. Note the Gothic chapel, with its aisle of equilateral arches, and in the keep, 14C wall paintings.

View of Albarracín

© Kaos03/Sime/Photononstop

Huesca★

The tranquillity of Huesca, capital of Alto Aragón (Upper Aragón), belies its turbulent past. The old town huddles around the top of a promontory crowned by an imposing cathedral.

A BIT OF HISTORY

Historical notes – Huesca was the capital of a Roman state, a Moorish stronghold until its reconquest by **Pedro I of Aragón** in 1096, and capital of Aragón until 1118. **The origins of a well-known Spanish saying** – "Ringing like the bell of Huesca" – is a Spanish way to describe a dire event. In the 12C, King **Ramiro II** summoned his truculent nobles to watch the casting of a bell – and promptly had them beheaded.

SIGHTS
OLD QUARTER
Catedral★
Pl. de La Catedral 4 ○*Open Mon–Fri 10.30am–2pm, 4–7.30pm (mornings only Nov–Mar), Sat 10.30am–1.30pm* ◉€3 *(including Cathedral museum).* ℘974 23 10 99.

The 13C Gothic façade is divided unusually by a gallery and an Aragonese carved wood overhang. A gable encloses a rose window and the portal covings with weathered statues.

On the tympanum are the Magi and Christ before Mary Magdalene. The alabaster **altarpiece★★** dates from 1533. In this masterpiece by Damián Forment, three scenes of the Crucifixion appear in high relief in the middle of Flamboyant canopy and frieze decoration.

Facing the Cathedral, the *ayuntamiento* (town hall) is a tastefully decorated Renaissance town house.

Museo de Huesca★
Pl. Universidad 1. ○*Open Tue–Sat 10am–2pm, 5–8pm, Sun and public holidays 10am–2pm.* ○*Closed 1, 6 Jan, 24, 25, 31 Dec.* ◉*No charge.* ℘974 22 05 86.

The museum is in the old university, built in 1690 around a fine octagonal

- **Population:** 52 347
- **Michelin Map:** 574 F 28.
- **Info:** Plaza Luis López Allué. ℘974 29 21 70. www.huescaturismo.com.
- **Location:** Huesca is 72km/ 44.7mi N of Zaragoza, 91km/56.5mi S of Jaca and 123km/76.4mi NW of Lleida/Lérida, along the E 7 motorway. It is a good base for excursions into the Pyrenees. ▬José Gil Cávez 10.
- **Timing:** 2hr for the town.

patio incorporating parts of the royal palace (and notorious massacre site). The collection includes prehistoric artefacts and **Aragonese primitive paintings★**, several by the Maestro de Sigena (16C).

Iglesia de San Pedro el Viejo★
Pl. de San Pedro. ○*Open Mon–Sat 10am–1.30pm, Sun 11am–12.15pm, 1–1.45 pm* ☞*Guided tour* ◉€2.50. ℘974 22 23 87.

The 11C monastery's **cloisters★**, with their historiated capitals, are a jewel of Romanesque sculpture in Aragón. The tympanum of the cloister doorway has an unusual Adoration of the Magi with all the emphasis on movement.

A Romanesque chapel holds the tombs of kings Ramiro II and Alfonso I, the Battler.

CDAN – Fundación Bealas
Av. Doctor Artero (access by bus from the Coso Bajo and Alto, or drive towards Zaragoza and Pamplona). ○*Open Tue–Sat 11am–2pm, 5–8pm, Sun and hols 10am–2pm.* ◉*No charge.* ℘974 23 98 93. www.cdan.es.

Huesca's Centro de Arte y Naturaleza, which opened in 2006, was founded by local artist José Beulas in order to create a space dedicated to contemporary art in a serene, purpose-built setting.

Rock formations of Los Mallos de Riglos

© Fantuz Olimpio/Sime/Photononstop

EXCURSION
Monasterio de Monte Aragón
▷ *5km/3mi E along the N 240.*
The monastery was originally a fortress built by Sancho I Ramírez.

 DRIVING TOUR

Tour through Sierra de Loarre – Los Mallos de Riglos
100km/62mi NW. Allow half a day.
⎈ *See Pirineos Aragoneses map p402.*

▷ *Leave Huesca on the A 132 towards Pamplona. After 12.5km/7.5mi just beyond Esquedas, take the A 1206 right.*

Bolea
The main church **altarpiece** is a superb example of 15C Hispano-Flemish art.

▷ *Follow the road to Loarre. before the village, follow signs to the castle.*

Castillo de Loarre★★
🕐*Open daily Nov–end Feb 11am–5.30pm; 16 Jun–15 Sept 10am–2pm, 4–8pm; rest of the year 10am–2pm, 4–7pm.* 🕐*Closed 1 Jan, 25 Dec.* ⊛*€3.30.* ⟿*Guided tours* ⊛*€1.50.* 📞*974 34 21 66. www.castillodeloarre.org.* In the 11C, Sancho Ramírez, King of Aragón and Navarra, had this castle-fortress built at an altitude of 1 100m/3 609ft. The walls, flanked by round towers, command a vast **panorama**★★ of the Ebro Basin. After the massive keep and fine covered stairway, view the 12C church. The capitals are very beautiful.

▷ *Take the A 206 9.5km/6mi to Ayerbe.*

Los Mallos de Riglos★★
The Río Gállego is banked by tall crumbling cliffs, red ochre in colour. **Los Mallos** are a formation of rose puddingstone, eroded into sugar loaf forms. The most dramatic group *(to the right)* dominates the village of **Riglos**.

▷ *Return to the A 132 and after 1.5km/1mi bear left towards Agüero.*

Agüero
The village is set against a spectacular background of *Mallos*. Before Agüero, a road leads *(right)* to the Romanesque **Iglesia de Santiago**. Three aisles of the church are covered by three separate stone roofs.

ADDRESSES

🏠 STAY

⊜⊜⊜⊜ **La Posada de la Luna** – *Joaquín Costa 10, Huesca.* 📞 *974 24 08 57. www.posadadelaluna.com, 8 rooms.* ⊆*€15.* Adjacent to the city's ancient wall this hotel has an eclectic yet warm atmosphere with each of the rooms named after a planet. Extras include WiFi and hyrdromassage baths.

Barbastro

Barbastro's interesting architecture bears witness to its 16C importance. It is a base for excursions into the central Pyrenees and capital of the Somontano wine region.

SIGHTS
Catedral★
San José de Calasanz.

The cathedral is a standard hall-church with three elegant aisles beneath richly ornamented vaulting with gilded decoration, borne by slender columns.

The predella on the high altar **retable** is an important work by Damián Forment. Several side chapels are Churrigueresque; the first on the left-hand side holds a fine early 16C retable.

The **Museo Diocesano** (◷*open July and Aug; Mon–Sat 10am–1.30pm, 4.30–7.30pm, Sun 4.30–5.30 pm rest of the year; daily 11.30am–1.30pm, 6–7.30pm ⊚suggested donation €2; ☎974 30 83 50*) is open to the public.

Complejo de San Julián y Santa Lucía
Av. de la Merced.

The former Hospital de San Julián houses the tourist office, a wine shop, and a **museum** dedicated to the excellent Somontano appellation.

Vaults of the cathedral

M. Lemaire/MICHELIN

▶ **Population:** 16 802
⏱ **Michelin Map:** 574 F 30 – Aragón (Huesca).
🛈 **Info:** Avenida de la Merced 64. ☎974 30 83 50. www.barbastro.org.
▶ **Location:** Barbastro is at the end of two Pyrenean valleys, one leading to Parque de Ordesa, the other to the Maladeta range, via the Congosto de Ventamillo canyon.

The 16C Renaissance church of San Julián opposite houses the **Centro de Interpretación del Somontano**★ (◷*open July and Aug Mon–Sat 10am–8pm, Sun 10am–2pm, 4.30–7.30pm. Rest of the year Mon–Sat 10am–2pm, 4.30–7.30pm; ◷closed 25 Dec; ⊚€2*), highlighting the area and its tourist sites via a short film.

EXCURSIONS
Alquézar★
▶ *23km/14mi NW on the A 1232, following the Río Vero.*

Alquézar enjoys a magnificent isolated **setting**★★ amid red earth, appearing to cling to a rocky promontory in a loop of the river.

Old quarter
The medieval old quarter is a maze of uneven streets lined by houses adorned with rounded stone doorways and coats of arms. The arcaded main square is enchanting.

Colegiata★ A Moorish **alcázar** on the site fell to Sancho Ramírez, King of Aragón. In the late 11C and early 12C, the walls were constructed, along with a church (rebuilt in 1530). A beautiful Romanesque Christ dates from the 12C.

Cañón de Río Vero★ – 🔲 Allow a day to walk up and in some places wade or swim this spectacular canyon. Or hike only to the Roman bridge at Villacantal (*2hr round trip*) for an overview and to see impressive ochre and grey walls.

DRIVING TOUR

Through the Ribagorza

85km/53mi. Allow one day.
See Pirineos Aragoneses map p402.

Follows the Esera and Isábena rivers, through the historic county of Ribagorza, in the pre-Pyrenees of Aragón.

Leave Barbastro on the N 123; after 16km/10mi go right onto the A 2211.

Santuario de Torreciudad

Open July–mid-Sept daily 10am–2pm, 4–7.30pm, (Sun until 8.30pm), slightly reduced hours rest of the year (check website). 974 30 40 25. www.torreciudad.org.

In 1804, an 11C Romanesque statue of Our Lady of Torreciudad was placed in a small shrine and locally venerated. In 1975 a pilgrimage church was built under the auspices of Monsignor José María Escrivá de Balaguer (now canonised), founder of Opus Dei (1928).

Before the brick buildings, a vast esplanade affords beautiful **views**★ of the Pyrenees and the El Grado dam. The statue of Our Lady of Torreciudad is in the lower part of the altarpiece.

From Torreciudad, return to the A 2211, heading towards La Puebla de Castro, then take the N 123ª.

Graus

The village huddles around the irregular **Plaza de España**, lined by old houses decorated with frescoes, carved beams and brick galleries. The 16C **Santuario de la Virgen de la Peña**★★ has a Renaissance doorway and single aisle crowned by pointed vaulting.

The A 1605 crosses the Esera river.

Roda de Isábena★

26.5km/16.5mi from Graus.
This picturesque village perches on a promontory in a beautiful mountain **setting**★. Construction of the impressive **cathedral**★ (guided tours (30min); €2.50; reserve in advance 974 54 45

35) began in the 11C. Most of the interior, basilical in plan with three aisles, was built in the 12C.

In the central **crypt** is the **tomb of San Ramón**★★, with interesting polychrome low reliefs. A 13C fresco adorns a chapel off the cloisters.

Continue 16km/10mi N on A 1605.

Monasterio de Santa María de Obarra

Only the 10C–11C church, built by Lombard masters, remains of this monastery. A 12C hermitage, the Ermita de San Pablo, stands to one side.

ADDRESSES

STAY

⊜ **Hospedería de Roda de Isábena** – *Pl de la Catedral, Roda de Isábena. 974 54 45 54. Closed November, 20–26 December. 10 rooms. €6.60.* This Medieval building, which overlooks the cathedral, has clean rooms at competitive prices. The rear balconies offer magnificent views.

⊜ **Hospedería el Seminario** – *Pl Pérez Prado 2, Teruel 978 61 99 70. 57 rooms.* Situated next to the Torre San Martín in the centre of Teruel, this 18C building offers simple and clean accommodation as well as decent meals. Popular with students, academics and (as the name suggests) visiting clergy, it's wise to book ahead.

EAT

⊜⊜ **Hospedería La Catedral** – *Pl Pons Sorolla, Roda de Isábena. 974 54 45 45. Closed Sunday evening, Nov, 20–26 December.* This restaurant occupies the former refectory of the monastery. It is decorated with reproductions of paintings by Velázquez and furniture from the same period as well as original 14C frescoes on one wall. It serves simple yet original cuisine and a set-lunch menu for 15 € .

⊜⊜⊜ **Flor** – *Goya 3, Barbastro. 974 31 13 18.* A famous restaurant in the area serving dishes based on local produce accompanied by wines from the Somontano region.

Jaca★

Jaca, the "pearl of the Pyrenees" stands strategically at the foot of the Pyrenees, under the Peña de Oroel. It was an important stop along the Camino de Santiago, and became the capital of Aragón in the 9C.

SIGHTS

Catedral★

◷Open daily 11.30am–1.30pm, 4–8pm. ☎974 35 62 41.

Spain's oldest Romanesque cathedral, from the 11C, influenced craftsmen who worked on churches along the pilgrim route to Santiago de Compostela. Note the **historiated capitals**★ of the south porch and great detail in the south doorway figures.

Gothic vaulting covers unusually wide aisles. The apse and side chapels are decorated with sculpture but the cupola on squinches over the transept crossing has retained its simplicity.

Museo Diocesano (Diocesan Museum)

Pl. de San Pedro.◷Open Tue–Sat 10am–1.30 pm, 4–7pm (Sat till 8pm), Sun 10am–1.30 pm. ☞€6. ☎974 35 63 78.

The cloisters and adjoining halls contain Romanesque and Gothic **wall paintings**★ from village churches in the area, and Romanesque paintings.

Castillo de San Pedro

Av. del Primer Viernes de Mayo. ◷Open Aug Tue–Sun 10am–2pm, 5–9pm. Slightly reduced hours rest of the year: check website. ☞€10 (includes toy soldier museum). ☎974 35 71 57.

Built in 1595 during the reign of Philip II as part of a network of castles and towers to guard the French border, this citadel is an outstanding example of 16C military architecture and has been declared a National Monument. Surrounded by a moat, the fortress has a perfect pentagonal plan, with defensive bulwarks at each vertex. Inside is the **Museo de Miniaturas Militares** (www.museominiaturasjaca.es), which contains over 32 000 military figurines.

▸ **Population:** 13 374
◉ **Michelin Map:** 574 E 28.
▯ **Info:** Plaza de San Pedro nº 11–13. ☎974 36 00 98. www.jaca.es.
◉ **Location:** Jaca is along the A 23, from Huesca to El Puerto de Somport, and the N 240, to Pamplona (111km/69mi NW).

🚗 DRIVING TOURS

1 MONASTERIO DE SAN JUAN DE LA PEÑA★★

25km/15.5mi. Allow half a day.

▷ Take the N 240 from Jaca. After 11km/6.8mi, turn off towards Santa Cruz de la Serós.

Santa Cruz de la Serós★

Pl. Mayor. ◷Same hours as Monasterio de San Juan de la Peña. ◷Closed 1 Jan, 25 Dec. ☞€4.50. ☎974 35 51 19.

This 10C convent, endowed by nobles and princesses, was abandoned in the 16C. Only the **Romanesque church**★, surrounded by small Aragonese houses, remains. The stout belfry, crowned by an octagonal turret, abuts the lantern. The portal recalls Jaca Cathedral.

▷ Beyond Santa Cruz de la Serós the road winds through the sierra.

Monasterio de San Juan de la Peña★★

◷Open daily Nov–early Mar 10.30am–2pm, 3.30–5.30pm; Jun–early Jul 10am–2pm, 3–8pm, late Jul–Aug 10am–8pm; early Mar–May and Sept–Oct 10am–2pm, 3.30–7pm. ◷22 Nov–3 Dec. ☞€6.50 (€13 including New Monastery, Monastery Interpretation Centres and Santa Cruz de los Serós). ☎974 35 51 19. www.monasteriosanjuan.com.

The most spectacular feature of this monastery is its **setting**★★ in a hollow beneath overhanging rocks. The monastery was chosen as a pantheon for the kings and nobles of Aragón and Navarra, and expanded in the 12C.

The oldest features can be seen on the lower storey, where the Lower Church dates from the early Mozarabic monastery. The **Sala de Concilios** (Council Chamber) was built by King Sancho Garcés around the year 922.

The 11C–14C **Panteón de Nobles Aragoneses** are niches with coats of arms, sacred monograms and in many cases a cross with four roses, the emblem of Iñigo Arista, founder of the Kingdom of Navarra.

The late 11C **Iglesia Alta** (Upper Church) comprises a single aisle, while the three apsidal chapels with blind arcades are hollowed out of the cliff. The **Panteón de Reyes** (Royal Pantheon) opens off the north wall.

The 12C **cloisters**★★, between precipice and cliff, are accessed by a Mozarabic door. Only two galleries and fragments of another remain. The **capitals**★★ exhibit a personal style and use of symbolism which influenced sculpture in the region for years.

2 VALLE DE HECHO AND VALLE DE ANSÓ★

114km/71mi (146km/91mi with the detour to Zuriza). Allow one day.

The bucolic twin valleys of Hecho and Ansó played an important role during the Spanish Reconquest. Self-sustaining for centuries, they have retained an almost archaic economic structure based on sheep farming and agrarian activities and a lost-in-time landscape; grey stone mountain homes with distinctive, conical chimneys are clustered together in pretty hamlets in order to provide protection against the harsh winters.

The inhabitants of both valleys speak a distinct dialect and their ancient culture and traditional dress is celebrated in a string of charming festivals, which attract more locals than tourists.

Leave Jaca on the N 240. In Puente la Reina de Jaca, turn right on the A 176.

The road follows the Aragón Subordán. The traditional houses of **Hecho**★ *(www.hecho.es)* have stone doorways, many with coats of arms.

The **Museo de Escultura al Aire Libre**, by the tourist office, shows sculpture in the open. There is also a **Museo Etnológico** (○*open Jul–mid-Sept 10.30am–1.30pm, 6–9pm;* ◎*€1;* ℘*974 37 55 02).*

2km/1.2mi to the north in Siresa is the **Iglesia de San Pedro**★★, once part of a monastery. It was visited by **St Eulogus of Córdoba**, martyred in 859.

The 11C **church** has a fine elevation and walls with blind arcades and buttresses. The **altarpieces**★ are principally 15C. (○*open daily 11am–1pm, 3–5pm; summer 11am–1pm, 5–8pm;* ◎*€1.50).*

▷ *The road continues through a narrow valley towards Selva de Oza. Return to Hecho and go right on the A 17 and right again to Ansó.*

Surrounded by spectacular landscape, the sleepy village of Ansó consists of traditional mountain homes clustered around the village church. Inside is an interesting Ethnological Museum, which focuses on traditional costumes of the area *(by appointment;* ℘*974 37 00 22;* ◎*€2).*

After taking a stroll around the village, head to Zuriza (16km/10mi away) at the bottom of the valley which opens out on to a large field dominated by mountains. By following the course of the Veral River via the 1602 you'll come across the 500m/1640ft-long Foz de Biniés (Biniés Gorge) enclosed by two natural stone overhanging arches.

▷ *Take the N 240 back to Jaca.*

3 TOUR THROUGH SERRABLO

20km/19.5mi. Allow half a day.

This excursion follows the rio Gállego and includes extraordinary 10C and 11C Mozarabic churches.

▷ *Leave Jaca on the A 23 E towards Sabiñánigo.*

Museo de Dibujo

In Larrés, 18km/11mi E of Jaca along the A 23. Open Nov–Mar Tue–Sat 11am–1pm, 3–6pm, Sun and public holidays 11am–1pm, 4–6pm; Apr–Jun Sept–Oct Tue–Sun and public holidays 11am–1pm, 4–7pm; Jul–Aug daily 10am–2.30pm, 4.30–9pm. €3. 974 48 29 81. www.serrablo.org/museodibujo.

This museum, in the 14C Castillo de Larrés, displays sketches by Martín Chirino, Salvador Dalí and others. A section covers graphic humour.

Mozarabic churches

The churches of the Serrablo region are small and rectangular, with a semicircular apse. Walls are generally devoid of bays, while the arches are either horseshoe or semicircular; occasionally, doors are framed by an alfiz surround. The most impressive churches are in Orós Bajo, San Martín de Olivián, **San Juan de Busa**★ (with unfinished apse), **San Pedro de Lárrede**★ and Satué.

Museo Ángel Oresanz y Artes de Serrablo★

San Nicolás 1, Sabiñánigo. In Puente de Sabiñánigo S of the town centre. Open Oct–May Tue–Sun 10am–1pm,

3.30–6.30pm; Jun–Sept Tue–Sun 11am–2pm, 4–8pm (Jul–Aug daily). €2. 974 48 42 61. www.serrablo.org/museoartespopulares.

The major ethnographic collection in the Huescan Pyrenees is in a wonderful traditional Serrablan house.

▶ *From here you can continue to the Graganta del Escalar and Puerto del Portalet (see p402).*

EXCURSION
Parque Nacional de Ordesa y Monte Perdido★★★

▶ *This national park is 61km/38mi E of Jaca in the central Pyrenees (with its twin on the French side) and can be approached from Torla to the W or Ainsa from the SE.*

The Ordesa canyon cuts through vast, layered limestone folds. Escarpments rise nearly 1 000m/3 280ft in grey and ochre strata, streaked in spring with cascades of snowmelt. Growing up the lower slopes are pines, larches, firs – some 25m/82ft tall – and a carpet of box, hawthorn and service trees.

The park's valleys lie under such impressive peaks as Monte Perdido (3 355m/11 004ft).

🐾 Walking Tours in the park

Valle de Ordesa★★★

A viewpoint on the entry road offers a general panorama. A second point, near the road's end, overlooks 60m/197ft-high **cascada de Tamborrotera** (waterfall). 🚶The rest of the park may only be visited on foot. The best route for inexperienced walkers or families with young children is the shaded path along the bottom of the canyon. *Allow a day from the car park to the end of the canyon and back.*
🚶The following walks are feasible for experienced, well-equipped hikers.

Circuito del Circo de Soaso (Soaso Cirque Route)

🚶 *Start from the Cadiera hut beyond the car park; 7hr. The walk to the valley floor is easy. The second part, via the Cola de Caballo (Horse's Tail), is only recommended to those who are well equipped and in good physical condition (steep climbs).*
This walk provides the best and most complete tour of the Ordesa Valley. From the Circo de Soaso path several waterfalls can be seen including the **Gradas de Soaso**, or Soaso Steps, followed by the impressive, 70m/230ft high **Cola de Caballo**. The path continues along the **Faja de Pelay** overlooking the canyon to a depth of 2 000m/6 550ft at the foot of the Sierra de Cutas.
Continue on the **Senda de los Cazadores** (Huntsman's Path) for a wonderful view of the canyon. The best panorama is from the **Mirador de Calcilarruego** 🚴. The path back to the hut drops almost 1 000m/3 281ft.

Circo de Cotatuero (Cotatuero Cirque)

🚶 *Start from the restaurant; 4hr.*
On the park's northern border are the **Cotatuero** and the **Copos de Lana** (Tufts of Wool) *cascadas* (waterfalls) with a drop of 250m/820ft.

Circo de Carriata

🚶 *From the Centro de Información; 4hr.*
The walk is worth doing although the *clavijas* (mountaineering peg track) is

not for those who suffer from vertigo. A long hike is possible to Monte Perdido via the Goriz refuge; or to the Cirque de Gavarnie in France via the Brecha de Rolando (Roland Gap) *(ask at the Centro de Información).*

Cañón de Añisclo★★★

Access from Escalona village on the Bielsa-Ainsa road – a 13km/8mi drive.
In the cool and lovely Añisclo Canyon, narrower than Ordesa, pine trees cling to the limestone walls.

Walk to Ripareta

🚶 *Start from the San Urbez bridge. 5hr there and back.*
A wide, well-defined path follows the enclosed Río Vellos down to its confluence with the Pardina.

ADDRESSES

Pirineos Aragoneses★★

The central Pyrenees, in the north of Huesca province, include the highest peaks: Aneto (3 404m/11 165ft), Posets (3 371m/11 060ft) and Monte Perdido (3 355m/11 004ft). The foothills are often ravined with sparse vegetation; at the heart of the massif, accessible up the river courses, valleys lead to mountain cirques well worth exploring.

A BIT OF HISTORY

Structure and relief – Vast longitudinal bands are clear in this region. The **axis of Palaeozoic terrain** comprises the Maladeta, Posets, Vignemale and Balaïtous massifs, where there are remains of Quaternary glaciers. In the **Pre-Pyrenees** (Monte Perdido), deep **Mesozoic limestone** is eroded into the canyons, gorges and cirques of the upper valleys. The limestone area, which extends in broken mountain chains to the Ebro Basin, is divided at Jaca by the long depression of the River Aragón. Tertiary sediment has accumulated into hills; some are bare of vegetation, in an unusual blue marl landscape like that around the **Yesa Reservoir**.

Life in the valleys – The upper valleys of the Kingdom of Aragón developed self-contained communities. Folk traditions are still followed and native costume is worn in certain valleys. Emigration has led to the abandonment of a number of villages. Tourism is a major economic activity. Winter resorts include Candanchú, Astún, Canfranc, Panticosa, El Formigal and Benasque.

🚗 DRIVING TOURS

1 FROM AINSA TO BENASQUE

121km/75mi. Allow half a day.

Ainsa★

Ainsa, one of the prettiest towns in the Pyrenees, stands on a promontory still

- 🕯 **Michelin Map:** 574 D 28-32, E 29-32 and F 30-31 – Aragón (Huesca)
- 🔲 **Info:** Avenida Pirenaica 1, Ainsa. ℘974 50 07 67. www.pirineo.com.
- ⬤ **Location:** From Pamplona/Iruña follow the N 240 to Jaca (111km/69mi SE); from Huesca the N 330 to Jaca (91km/57mi N); from Barbastro the N 123 and the A 138 to Ainsa (52km/32.5mi N).
- ⬤ **Don't Miss:** A hike in a spectacular canyon, and a hearty meal of local game.

girded by a wall, commanding the juncture of the River Cinca and River Ara. In the 11C it was the capital of the kingdom of Sobrarbe.

Its arcaded **Plaza Mayor**★★ in the upper town, under the tower of a Romanesque church, is a gem of Aragonese architecture. The contemporary-style **Museo de Oficios y Artes Tradicionales**★ *(pl. San Salvador 10;* 🕐*open Thur–Mon 10am–12pm, 4–7pm.* ☞*€2.50;* ℘*974 51 00 75)* is a museum devoted to traditional arts and crafts.

⬤ *Take the N 260. At Morillo de Liena, head N.*

Campo

Museo de los Juegos Tradicionales *(park near the tourist office, on the N 260 and walk up.* 🕐*Open Tue–Sat 11am–2pm, 5–8pm, Sun 1am–2pm.* ℘*974 55 01 36).* This site aims to keep the memories of games played in the region, mainly in rural areas.

⬤ *11km/7mi further on is Siera.*

Siera

Museo de le electricidad *(in the tourist office;* 🕐*Tue–Fri noon–2pm.* ℘*974 55 31 31)* Known for its power plant, the municipality has opened a museum

Aínsa

M. Lemaire/MICHELIN

which shows the construction of the plant between 1913 and 1918, and production equipment (turbines, transformers, ammeters, etc).

Congosto de Ventamillo★★

This 3km/1.8mi defile has sheer limestone rock walls.

▷ *Take the N 260 to Castejón de Sos, a paragliding centre, then the A 139. The road goes through Villanova, which has two 11C churches*

Valle de Benasque★

Benasque (1 138m/3 734ft) lies in an open valley, lush and green, overshadowed by the Maladeta massif, a base for walkers, climbers (ascending the Aneto) and skiers (Cerler, 5km/3mi). Streets are lined with old mansions.

Anciles, 1.6km/1mi away, is known for its attractive houses. 15km/9.3mi further north, just before the road ends, a turn-off leads to the Hospital de Benasque *(www.llanosdelhospital.com)*, departure point for excursions into Parque Natural Posets-Maladeta.

2 NORTH OF AINSA
50km/31mi to Gistaín.

▷ *From Ainsa take the A 138 towards Escalona and Bielsa. At Labuerda, take the turning to San Vicente de Labuerda.*

San Vincente de Labuerda
3km/1.2mi from Labuerda.

⏰*Open every day in summer, the rest of the year, get the key from a villager.*
By a narrow and sometimes steep road, you arrive at this small 12C church, set apart from the village. You enter through an *esconjuradero* (a small stone shelter). Inside, is a beautiful late 15C Gothic altarpiece. From the church, a walk of 40 mins leads to the hermitage of San Visorio, a French saint whose relics are preserved in the church. From there, the view extends over the valley of the Cinca.

▷ *Take the A 138 towards Bielsa.*

In **Escalona**, you can turn left into the **Cañón de Añisclo★★★** (⏰*see p399*) or continue on the A 138 through dramatic landscape up to the **Desfiladero de las Devotas★★**.

▷ *Take the A 138 and bear right at Salinas de Sin.*

Valle de Gistaín★

In this valley, also known as the Valle de Chistau, are some of the most picturesque villages in the Pyrenees, including **Plan**, **San Juan de Plan** and **Gistaín**.

▷ *Following the A 138 N will take you to Biesla and the Vall de Pineta.*

Bielsa and Valle de Pineta

19km/11.8mi NW of Plan, along A 138.

From the pleasant village of Bielsa, a narrow road climbs the valley of the Cinca River, traversing the impressive landscapes of the **Valle de Pineta★★** to the Parador de Bielsa, nestled in a spectacular glacial cirque.

③ FROM AINSA TO BIESCAS

81km/51mi
Allow about 3hr.

Between **Boltaña** (16C church; *www. boltana.es*) and **Fiscal** (medieval tower; *www.aytofiscal.es*), the river course reveals underlying strata. The church of **Broto** *(www.broto.es)* has an interesting Renaissance doorway. Beyond Broto, the great mass of the Mondarruego (alt 2 848m/9 341ft), closing the Ordesa Valley, backdrops the spectacular **landscape★★** where the village of **Torla★** lies on the western slope of the Ara Valley.

The church, the Iglesia de San Salvador, houses noteworthy 18C altarpieces. The castle-abbey in Torla has an **ethnographic museum** *(for information, call town hall; ∞€1; ℘974 48 63 78).*

Broto, Torla and Fiscal are good bases from which to explore the **Parque Nacional de Ordesa y Monte Perdido★★★** (⌖*see p398*).

④ THE PORTALET ROAD

52km/32.3mi – allow about 2hr.
The **Tena** Valley beyond Biescas widens out into the vast Búbal reservoir.

▷ *A short distance before Escarilla, bear right onto HU 610 for Panticosa.*

Garganta del Escalar★★ (Escalar Gorge)

The sun rarely penetrates this gorge. The road cuts down the west slope by ramps and hairpin bends to an austere mountain cirque, the setting for the **Balneario de Panticosa★** (℘902 25 25 22; *www.panticosa.com*), a spa with six sulphurous and radioactive springs, and a charming 19C air.

▷ *Return to Escarilla and continue to the Portalet Pass.*

The mountain town of **Sallent de Gállego**, at 1 305m/4 281ft, hosts a summer music festival and is renowned for trout fishing and mountaineering. **El Formigal** (alt 1 480m/4 856ft), further on, is a ski resort.

Carretera del Portalet

Alt 1 794m/5 886ft.
The pass lies between Portalet peak and Aneu summit to the west. The view extends to the Aneu cirque and Pic du Midi d'Ossau in France (alt 2 884m/9 462ft).

⑤ FROM BIESCAS TO THE PUERTO DE SOMPORT

58km/36mi. Allow about 2hr.

▷ *Continue S on the N 260 to Sabiñánigo – from here it is possible to follow the tour through the Serrablo (⌖see JACA – Excursions) – then take the N330 to Jaca (⌖see JACA). From Jaca, the N 330 continues northwards.*

The **Cueva de las Güixas**, a cave in Villanúa, has some 300m/330yd of galleries (⬥€4.80; ☎974 37 81 39; www.sargantana.info). Beyond Canfranc is the abandoned early 20C **Canfranc international resort**★★ (www.canfranc.es), an extraordinary example of early 20C architecture.

The **Puerto de Somport**★★ (alt 1 632m/5 354ft), beside the Somport tunnel (opened in 2003), is the only pass in the Central Pyrenees which generally remains snow-free all year.

Candanchú (www.candanchu.com), the best-known ski resort in Aragón, is less than 1km/0.6mi away. Climb the mound to the right of the monument commemorating the building of the road for an extensive **panorama**★★ of the Spanish Pyrenees.

ADDRESSES

🏨 STAY

🛏 **Hostal Dos Ríos** – Av Central 2, Aínsa. ☎974 50 01 06. www.hoteldosrios.com. Closed Nov–Mar. 18 rooms. Located in the lower part of the resort beside the road, this hostel is a good bet given its moderate prices, and offers well-kept rooms.

🛏🛏 **Los Arcos** – Plaza Mayor 23, Aínsa. ☎974 50 00 16. www.hotellosarcosainsa.com 7 rooms. This is one of the most romantic getaways in upper Aragón. Its tasteful

rooms feature natural stone walls and wooden beams and are fitted out with modern bathrooms and comfortable furniture.

🛏🛏🛏 **Peña Montañesa** – 2km/0.75mi S of Labuerda on the 138 road. ☎974 51 00 51. www.hotelpenamontanesa.com. 49 rooms. ⬚€15. Mountain hotel offering high levels of comfort.

🛏🛏🛏 **Monastario de Boltaña-Spa** – 6km/4mi NE from Aínsa on the N 260. ☎974 50 80 00. www.monasteriodeboltana.es. 96 rooms. ⬚€15. A 17C monastery makes for an austere hotel that is surprisingly welcoming and remarkably furnished and decorated. Rooms are large and comfortable and there is a great pool.

🍴/EAT

🍽 **El Portal** – Calle Portal Bajo 5, Aínsa. ☎974 50 03 53. This restaurant is located in the upper part of town, opposite the Plaza Mayor. It has a pretty terrace that affords a view of the river and serves simple food from a friendly staff.

🍽 **Tasca Lansac** – Plaza Mayor, Aínsa. Raciones (small plates) €4–8. This small, unpretentious bar with a terrace under the arcades serves tasty *raciones* and generous salads.

🍽🍽 **Bodgeas del Sobrarbe** – Plaza Mayor, Aínsa. ☎974 50 02 37. www.bodegas delsobrarbe.com. Closed Jan–Feb. This atmospheric restaurant has vaulted medieval rooms and pretty tables decorated with florid tiles as well as a beautiful garden where you can dine in summer. Its specialises in game including the famous *jabalí* (wild boar) and goat.

The eastern coastal strip of Valencia, Alicante and Murcia includes (from north to south) comprises the lesser-known Costa del Azahar (Orange Blossom Coast), the hugely popular Costa Blanca (White Coast) and the Costa Cálida (Warm Coast). Their beaches and dunes are mostly low-lying with offshore sandbars, pools and lagoons. The climate is Mediterranean but drier than average; little rain falls except during the autumn months when the rivers sometimes flood. The natural vegetation, of olives, almond and carob trees and vines, has been gradually replaced, and the countryside transformed into *huertas* (irrigated areas), lush citrus orchards and market gardens. There are palm groves around Elche/Elx and Orihuela in the south and rice is grown in swampy areas. The region's economy is based increasingly around the booming tourist industry.

Highlights

1 Valencia's stunning **Ciudad de las Artes y las Ciencias** (p413)

2 Enjoying a plate of paella in Valencia's **Old Town** (p405)

3 Exploring the old quarter of picture-postcard **Peñíscola** (p416)

4 Sheltering from the heat in Elche's remarkable **Palm Grove** (p422)

5 The view from the Castillo de Santa Bárbara, **Alicante** (p422)

Alicante and Costa Blanca

Alicante province is expat and cheap holiday territory, and the coastal landscape is sadly scarred by huge swathes of building projects. The most famous resort is Benidorm, an evergreen with package tourists since the 1960s. Its two beautiful (man-made) beaches, excel-

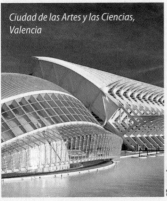
Ciudad de las Artes y las Ciencias, Valencia

lent theme parks, cheap accommodation amid ugly high-rise hotel canyons have come to be a stereotype of tourism in Spain. Alicante/Alacant town on the other hand has remained very Spanish, while inland destinations such as Elche/Elx and the beautiful Sierra Serella provide a different perspective.

Murcia

In the hot, flat region of Murcia, visitors tend to flock around the tourist beach developments of the Costa Cálida and particularly the Mar Menor, both the largest natural lake in the country and the largest salty lagoon in Mediterranean Europe. In the midst of the tourist development, the city of Murcia remains an unspoiled oasis with a beautiful Cathedral.

Valencia and Costa del Azahar

Valencia City has always had a fascinating Old Town, fine beaches and excellent food (it is famous as the home of paella). More recently La Ciudad de las Artes y las Ciencias – a high-profile museum-arts complex – has put it on the international tourist radar. The city's image was also boosted when it played host to the America's Cup in 2007 and the port area was converted into a pleasure ground. Much less built up than the southern costas, the Costa del Azahar is a favourite with Spanish holidaymakers who like their resorts low-key. The jewel here is Peñíscola (Spain's Mont St-Michel) while inland, the mountain region of El Maestrazgo boasts wonderful scenery and some charming villages. Xátiva/Játiva also makes a pleasant inland excursion.

Valencia★★

Spain's third-largest city, Valencia is unprepossessing at first glance with anonymous high-rise suburbs at its outer limits. However, wide palm-lined avenues encircle the old quarter with its fortified gateways, quaint shops and Gothic houses. This is a city reborn, thanks to works by Santiago Calatrava and **Sir Norman Foster** and by its hosting the America's Cup in 2007. To top it off, superb beaches are easily reached by tram.

THE CITY TODAY

Over the last five years Valencia has become a popular city break to rank alongside Barcelona, and like its Catalan cousin, it too has turned its face back to the sea with its beach and particularly its port area revitalised since 2007. The eating, drinking and nightlife, both here and in the Old Town are excellent.

A BIT OF HISTORY

2 000 years of history – The city founded by the Greeks in 138 BC passed into the hands of Carthaginians, Romans, Visigoths and Arabs, was briefly reconquered in 1094 by **El Cid**, and taken definitively in 1238 by James the Conqueror. Valencia prospered until the discovery of America, and again with a silk renaissance in the 17C.

Valencia sided with Charles of Austria in the War of the Spanish Succession, and lost its privileges. In 1808, it rose against the French. In 1939 it was the last Republican redoubt.

Art in Valencia – Valencia flourished economically in the 15C, and artistically as well, as seen in the Gothic architecture of palaces, the Cathedral and the Lonja (Exchange). Among painters were **Luis Dalmau**, who developed a Hispano-Flemish style; **Jaime Baço (Jacomart)**, **Juan Reixach** and the **Osonas**, father and son.

Notable 15C decorative arts were wrought ironwork, gold- and silver-smithing, and ceramics (*see the Museo Nacional de Cerámica in Sights*).

▶ **Population:** 815 440

Michelin Map: 577 N 28 (town plan) or 574 N 28.

Info: Pl. de la Reina 19. *963 15 39 31. www.turisvalencia.es.

Location: Valencia is the main city of the Levante region. Avenida Blasco Ibáñez (Cabanyal); Xàtiva 24 (Estaciò Nord).

Parking: Don't try to find a space in the old quarter.

Don't Miss: A walk in the old quarter and the Ciudad de las Artes y las Ciencias.

Timing: Start with unmissable modern architecture (Santiago Calatrava's City of Arts and Sciences and the convention centre) and Sir Norman Foster's Turia bridge; or with the heritage section of the city.

Kids: L'Oceanogràfic is one of the world's great aquariums.

The Valencia huerta and Albufera – The Roman irrigation system around Valencia was improved by the Moors. Orchards and market gardens produce fruit and early vegetables for Europe. South of Valencia lies a vast lagoon, the **Parque Natural de La Albufera** (*see COSTA DEL AZAHAR*).

WALKING TOUR

1 CIUDAD VIEJA★ (OLD TOWN)

Allow 3hr. Follow route on town plan.

The best starting point is El Miguelete, the bell tower of the Cathedral.

Catedral★

Pl. de la Reina. Open mid-Mar–end Oct daily Mon 8.30am–8.30pm, Sun and public holidays 2–5.30pm. Rest of the year closed Sun. €4.50 (including

*museum). 𝄐963 91 81 27.
www.catedraldevalencia.es.*

Work began in 1262; most of the building is Gothic from the 14C and 15C. The elegant and slender early 18C west face imitates Italian Baroque style. The Assumption on the pediment is by Ignacio Vergara and Esteve.

The south door is Romanesque; the north, the **Portada de los Apóstoles** (Apostles' Door), is Gothic, decorated with time-worn sculptures. A statue of the Virgin and Child on the tympanum is surrounded by angel musicians.

Inside, light filters through the alabaster windows in the beautiful Flamboyant Gothic **lantern**. The **retable** in the capilla mayor (chancel), the work of Fernando de Llanos and Yáñez de la Almedina (early 16C), influenced by Leonardo, illustrates the Lives of Christ and the Virgin.

In the ambulatory, a Renaissance portico protects an alabaster relief of the Resurrection (1510). Opposite is the 15C late Gothic Virgen del Coro (Chancel Virgin) in polychrome alabaster. In a chapel is a Baroque Cristo de la Buena Muerte (Christ of Good Death).

Capilla del Santo Cáliz or Sala Capitular★ (Chapel of the Holy Grail or Chapter House)

Last chapel along the north aisle.

This chapel has elegant star vaulting and, behind the altar, 12 alabaster low reliefs. In the centre, a magnificent 1C carnelian agate cup is said to be the Holy Grail, brought to Spain in the 3C. The **museum** beyond contains a sizable body of work from the Valencian painter Juan de Juanes (1523–79) (🕓*same hours as cathedral).*

▷ *From in front of the cathedral's main entrance cross C. de la Correjería to the plaza de la Reina.*

El Miguelete★

Pl. de la Reina. 🕓*Open mid-Mar–end-Oct daily 10am–7pm. Rest of the year morning only.* ≋€2. 𝄐963 91 81 27.

"Little Michael" (Micalet in Valencian) is the main bell of this octagonal Gothic tower, consecrated on St Michael's day in 1418. Climb up for a view of the cathedral and the town's glazed roofs.

At the left are ruins dating from the Roman era up to medieval times.

L'Almoina

Pl Décimo Junio Bruto. 🕓*Open Tue–Sat 10am–2pm, 4.30–8.30pm, Sun 11am–3pm.* 𝄐962 08 41 73. ≋€2.

Archaeological excavations have uncovered Roman and Visigothic remains. An underground tour lets you discover the substructure of ancient Valencia including remains of the Visigothic cathedral.

▷ *Cross C. de la Correjería again and follow C. de la Bachilla to Plaza de la Amoina.*

Casa del Punt de Gantxo

Plaza de la Almoina.

The façade of this building built by Manuel Peris Ferrando is distinguished by the use of original decorative elements.

Against a background of coloured ceramic decorated with foliage stand pilasters whose capitals are made with plant motifs (branches and flowers). These ornaments are reminiscent of those that were used in the 15C to decorate the Lonja (🕭*see p 410).*

▷ *Return to C. de la Bachilla and turn left.*

Museo de la Ciudad

Pl del Arzobispo, 3. 🕓*Open Tue–Sat 10am–2pm, 4.30–8.30pm, Sun and hols 10am–3pm.* ≋€2; no charge weekends. 𝄐963 52 54 78.

Situated inside the palace of the Marquis de Campo (18C–19C), this museum displays the municipal art collections. Exhibits are varied, from beautiful 14C and 15C ivory carvings to a large collection of old weights and measures.

Cripta Arqueológica de la Cárcel de San Vicente

Pl. del Arzobispo 1. 🕓*Open Tue–Sat 9.30am–2pm, 5.30–8pm, Sun and*

The World's Largest Food Fight

The town of **Buñol** (40km/25mi W of Valencia off the A 3), numbering some 10 000 inhabitants, lies in the tranquil setting of the Sierra de Las Cabrillas. At the end of every August, the town swells beyond all proportion for the celebration of one of the most famous festivals in Spain, **La Tomatina** (www.tomatina.es). A week-long festival of parades honour the town's patron, San Luis Bertràn. This culminates on the Wednesday, when at 10am, the crowds are challenged to snatch a ham placed on a greasy pole. The feat achieved, the firing of water cannons mark the release of over a hundred metric tons of tomatoes and one hour of chaotic tomato throwing. Legend has it that this helter-skelter celebration has its roots from when a food fight among the town's youths broke out in 1945. It has now become one of the defining images of the Spanish lust for life.

public holidays 9.30am–2pm. ☞€2; free Sun and hols. ℘963 94 14 17.
The remains of a Visigothic funerary chapel with four finely worked screens and a 6C burial, and two Visigothic stone sarcophagi.

▷ Cross C. Almudín.

Almudín

Pl. San Luis Bertrán. ⏱Open Tue–Sat 10am–2pm, 4.30–8.30pm, Sun and public holidays 10am–3pm. ☞€2; no charge weekends. ℘963 52 54 78.
This is a 14C–16C granary with primitive frescoes and two 19C azulejos altars.

▷ Head in the direction of the cathedral to P. de la Virgen.

Plaza de la Virgen★

The Basilica of the Virgen de los Desamparados and the Apostle Doorway of the Cathedral face this pleasant plaza.

Real Basílica de Nuestra Señora la Virgen de los Desamparados

Pl. de la Virgen, s/n.
⏱Open daily 7.30am–2pm, 4.30–9pm. ☞No charge. ℘963 91 86 11.
www.basilicadesamparados.org.
This late 17C church is linked to the apse of the Cathedral by a Renaissance arch. The floor plan is oval.
Beneath the painted cupola is the venerated statue of the patron of Valencia, the Virgin of the Abandoned (desamparados), which receives a steady flow of devotees.

▷ Go to c. Caballeros, on the west of the Plaza.

Palacio de la Generalitat★

Caballeros 2. ⏱Open Mon–Fri 10am–2pm, bookings required. ☞No charge. ℘963 86 34 61.
A tower was added to this fine 15C Gothic palace in the 17C and an identical one in the 20C. It was, until 1707, the meeting place of the Valencia Cortes. In the Gothic patio is Benlliure's sculpture of Dante's Inferno (1900).
A golden salon has a wonderful gilt and multicoloured **artesonado ceiling**★ and a large painting of the Tribunal de las Aguas (Water Tribunal, see entry). On the first floor are the Sala de los Reyes (Royal Hall) with portraits of the Valencian kings, and the Gran Salón de las Cortes Valencianas (Grand Council Chamber).
The azulejos frieze and the coffered ceiling are 16C. The rear façade and the Palau de la Batlia (the provincial administration) give onto the pleasant **plaza de Manises**.

▷ From P. Manises take C. Serranos and walk to the end.

Torres de Serranos★

Pl. Fueros. ⏱Open Tue–Sat 10.30am–2pm, 4.30–8.30pm, Sun and public holidays 10am–3pm. ☞€2; free Sat–Sun and public holidays. ℘963 91 90 70.
The towers are a good example of late 14C military architecture; they guarded one of the city entrances. Note theflow-

VALENCIA

Museo de Historia de Valencia

0   200 m
0   200 yds

ing lines of the battlements and the delicate tracery above the gateway.

▷ *Return to P. de Manises.*

Calle Caballeros

The most important street of the old city heads from Plaza de la Virgen into the colourful Carmen district.

Some of the houses have preserved their Gothic patios (seek out nos. 22, 26 and 33).

Iglesia de San Nicolás de Bari

Caballeros 35. ⏰*Open Tue–Sat 9.30am–11am, 6.30–8pm. Sun and public holidays 10am–1pm.* ☎*963 91 33 17.*

This is one of Valencia's oldest churches, built Churrigueresque style, with an altarpiece by Juan de Juanes *(to the left)* and, by the baptismal font, *Calvary* by Osona the Elder.

▷ *Continue to P. del Esparto, then follow C. de Quart to the end.*

Torres de Quart
Av. Guillem de Castro.
These 15C towers were damaged in the 19C by Napoleon's cannons.

▷ *From P. del Esparto, take C. Bolsería.*

La Lonja★★
(Silk Exchange)
Pl. del Mercado. ⏱ *Open Tue–Sat 10am –2pm, 4.30–8.30pm, Sun and public holidays 10am–3pm.* ◉ *€2; free Sat– Sun and public holidays.* ☏ *963 52 54 75.*
This 15C Flamboyant Gothic building replaced an earlier exchange outgrown by prosperous merchants. The left wing, separated from the entrance by a tower, is crowned by a gallery with a medallion frieze. The old commercial **silk hall**★★ is lofty, with ogival arches supported on slender, elegantly cabled columns; the bays are filled with delicate tracery.

Iglesia de los Santos Juanes
Pl. del Mercado. ⏱ *Open Mon–Tue, Thu–Fri 7.30am–10am, 7–8pm, Wed 7.30am–1pm, 7–8pm, Sat 6–8pm, Sun and public holidays 8am–1pm, 6–8pm.* ◉ *No charge.* ☏ *963 91 63 54.*
This is a vast church with a Baroque façade. The single aisle, originally Gothic, was modified in the 17C and 18C with exuberant Baroque stuccowork.

Iglesia de Santa Catalina
Pl. de Santa Catalina. ⏱ *Open daily 10.30am–1.30pm, 5.30–7.30pm.* ◉ *No charge.* ☏ *963 91 77 13.*
The church is notable for its magnificent 17C **Baroque belfry**★. The interior is soberly Gothic.

Plaza Redonda
A passage on the right leads to this curious little 19C circular plaza; a sort of urban patio surrounded by shops that sell laces and trimmings.

▷ *Out on C. Pere Compte, cross C. San Vicente Martyr then immediately turn right into C. Abadía San Martín.*

Palacio del Marqués de Dos Aguas★★
Poeta Querol 2.
This magnificent Baroque building houses the Museo Nacional de Cerámica y de las Artes Suntuarias González Martí The 18C marble portal was once covered by paintings.

Las Fallas

The origins of this festival date back to the Middle Ages when on St Joseph's Day, the carpenters' brotherhood burned their accumulated wood shavings in bonfires known as *Fallas* (from the Latin *fax*: torch). The name became synonymous with a festival for which, in time, objects were made solely for burning – particularly effigies of less popular members of the community. In the 17C single effigies were replaced by pasteboard groups or floats produced by neighbourhoods: rivalry is such that the figures today are fantastic in size, artistry and satirical implication. Prizes are awarded during the general festivities, which include fireworks, processions, bullfights, etc., before everything goes up in the *cremà* (fires) on the evening of 19 March. Figures (*ninots*) dating from 1934 to the present day, which have been spared from the bonfires, are on display in the **Museo Fallero** (pl. Monteolivete 4; open Tue–Sat 10am–3pm, 4.30–8.30pm, Sun and public holidays 10am–3pm; closed 1 Jan, 1 May, 25 Dec; ◉€2; no charge Sat–Sun; ☏963 52 54 78; www.fallas.com).

Museo Nacional de Cerámica y de las Artes Suntuarias González Martí★★
(National Museum of Ceramics and Decorative Art)

Poeta Querol 2. ◔*Open Tue–Sat 10am–2pm, 4–8pm, Sun and public holidays 10am–2pm.* ◔*Closed 1, 6 Jan, 1 May, 25, 26, 31 Dec.* ✆*€2.40; free Sat afternoon, Sun.* ✆*963 51 63 92. http://mnceramica.mcu.es.*

This museum occupies the lovely Baroque **Palacio del Marqués de Dos Aguas★★**. On the **ground floor** is the richly decorated **carriage**★ of the Marquis of Dos Aguas (1753). Rooms on the **first floor** include the Chinese salon, the *fumoir*, and the chapel.

The **ceramic collection** on the **second floor** includes Moorish ceramics (the basis of the craft in Spain), green and black porcelain, and later pieces from Málaga, Murcia and Manises. Christian ceramics of the 13C and 14C evidence continuity from the Moorish. Outstanding are green and manganese ceramics from **Paterna** *(6km/3.7mi N of Valencia).* The golden age of ceramics in **Manises** *(8km/5mi N of Valencia)* is represented by lovely pieces.

Also on display are Chinese porcelain and European imitations, and an impressive Toledo urn.

The **Real Fábrica de Alcora**, established in 1727, became the centre of innovation in Spain, spreading the Louis XIV, Classic and Baroque styles. Pieces from 19C **Manises** evidence later styles that spread through southern and eastern Spain. There is also a Valencian kitchen with 18C and 19C tiles.

▷ *Go down C. Poeta Querol and turn left into C. Salva.*

Colegio del Patriarca o del Corpus Christi★
(Patriarch or Corpus Christi College)

Nave 1. ◔*Open daily 11am–1.30pm.* ◔*Closed Good Fri.* ✆*€2.* ✆*963 51 41 76.*

This ex-seminary dates back to the 16C. The **church** (*enter by left door*) is one of the few Renaissance churches in Spain with frescoes; on the lower wall sections are Manises tiles. The seminary is built around a harmonious patio decorated with Talavera *azulejo* friezes.

The small **museum** of 15C–17C art includes paintings by Juan de Juanes, a **triptych of the Passion**★ by Dirk Bouts, a 14C Byzantine crucifix from the Monastery of Athos, a 13C Romanesque *Christ* and a portrait of the founder, Ribera, by Ribalta, and paintings by Ribalta, Morales and El Greco.

In the same plaza is the **Universidad** (University; *www.uv.es*).

▷ *Return to C. Juan de la Ribera, cross C. de la Paz, turn right into C. Medines.*

Iglesia de San Juan del Hospital (Church of St John of the Hospital)★

Trinquete de Caballeros 5 (access through courtyard). ◔*Open Mon–Sat, 9.30am–1.30pm, 5–7pm, Sun 11am–2pm, 5–9pm.* ✆*No charge.* ✆*963 92 29 65. www.sanjuandelhospital.es.*

This early 13C Gothic church consists of a single nave with pointed barrel vault. In the first chapel are beautiful 13C murals.

☙WALKING TOUR

2 MODERNIST VALENCIA★

Allow 1.5hr from the Mercado Central to Plaza de la Reina. ☙*Follow the route on town plan.*

Valencia's important economic development at the end of the 19C created the need for new neighbourhoods and a partial remodelling of the historic district.

The bourgeoisie, the local administrative powers and financial movers and shakers, including banks, seized the opportunity to show off their wealth by building spectacular edifices.

This architectural movement adopted the *modernista* style in the early years of the 20C, before returning to a more conformist approach.

Mercado Central

Pl. del Mercado. ⏰*Open Mon–Sat 8am–3pm.* 𝄞*963 82 91 00. www.mercado centralvalencia.es.*

Dating from 1928, the enormous metal and glass Central Market is fine example of *modernista* architecture. It is busiest in the mornings when the stalls are bursting with fish and local produce.

▷ *Head S to the P. del Ayuntamiento.*

Plaza del Ayuntamiento

This vast square is Valencia's meeting point and a flower market makes it more colourful than most. The building that holds the town hall (*ayuntamiento*), was built in 1915 and has a colossal façade with two corner towers topped with domes, and a grandiose entrance with a portico and campanile.

Inside the **Museo Histórico Municipal** (⏰*open Mon–Fri 9am–2pm;* 🎟€2; 𝄞*963 525 478)* exhibits the sword of Jaume I the Conqueror.

The main post office (**Correos** at the corner of Calle Correos) sits opposite. Inaugurated in 1923, its is distinguished by a dome decorated with neoclassical garlands of flowers and ribbons. North of this stand two **neo-Gothic buildings** with colourful façades.

Avenida Marqués de Sotelo

Many buildings along this avenue feature detailed façades and a wide range of decorative elements including monumental gates, towers, terraces, steeples and pediments.

▷ *Walk down to C. de Xativa.*

Estación del Norte★★

This landmark *modernista* railway station was built by Demetrio Ribes between 1909 and 1917.

Very strongly influenced by the architecture of the Austrian Secession (note its geometric structure), it also pays homage to local culture and imagery; ceramic relief friezes depict orange trees and mosaic murals scenes of Valencian agrarian life. The lobby has a riot of decorative details: columns, lamp posts,

signs of gold mosaic with phrase *buen viaje* in several languages and carved wooden windows. Next to the station, **Plaza de Toros** (bullring), built in the mid-19C, is one of the most beautiful and important in Spain.

▷ *Pass the P. de Toros, then turn right on C. Ruzafa and left into C. Cirilo Amorós.*

Calle de Cirilio Amorós

This road passes through the El Pla del Remei residential neighbourhood which developed in the late 19C–20C. It now hosts chic designer and fashion boutiques, clustered around the Mercado Colón. At no. 26, notice the beautiful bay windows incorporating elements of Gothic architecture, including a rosette, and at no. 27, a door and balcony in Art Nouveau style.

At no. 29 the **Casa Ferrer** was built in 1908 by Vicente Ferrer Pérez in an Art Deco style. It features stylised rose motifs and ceramic disk-like elements on a chequerboard background raised above a triglyph.

▷ *Continue along C. de Cirilo Amorós.*

Mercado Colón★

Calle Cirilo Amorós, on the left, between Calle Jorge Juan and Calle Conde Salvatierra de Alava.

The beautiful building from 1913 is the work of Francisco Mora y Belenguer. The two brick façades are joined by a supporting structure and a metal frame covered in glass. The main façade features a rich decor that is rooted in Valencia's artistic traditions including aged stone, colourful mosaics depicting harvest scenes, shiny ceramics and stained glass. It houses an upmarket selection of shops, bars and trendy restaurants.

▷ *Turn left on C. Conde Salvatierra de Álava then left into C. de Sorni.*

Casa de los Dragónes

Located at the corner of Calle de Sorni and Calle Jorge Juan, the Casa del Dragón owes its name to the sculptures that adorn the façade. Built in 1901 by Jose Manuel Cortina, it incorporates Gothic-inspired elements.

▷ *Cross C. Colon and continue to C. Don Juan de Austria.*

Banco de Valencia

At the intersection of Calle Pintor Sorolla, this building features a pretty neo-Baroque style in hues of pink and yellow, with curved balconies, ornate, framed windows and a host of mouldings and decorative details.

▷ *From C. Poeta Querol turn right at the Teatro Reial. Continue on C. Marqués de Dos Aguas and then turn left into C. de la Paz.*

Calle de la Paz

This street has lots of buildings of historic interest.

At the far end, in the Plaza de la Reina, La Isla de Cuba, a former retail complex, was designed by the architect Lucas García Cardona in 1896. He successfully blended classicist vocabulary with new techniques (note the use of cast iron columns). The decoration is heaviest on the upper frieze, where you can see ceramic panels of ancient Greek dancers in blue and pink.

AVANT GARDE VALENCIA

Ciudad de las Artes y las Ciencias★★★

The City of Arts and Sciences is a 350 000sq m/420 000sq yd cultural and recreational complex consisting of a series of spectacular avant-garde white buildings that reflect onto pools of water, mostly designed by the world-renowned, Valencian-born architect Santiago Calatrava. The following sights are based here.

👥 L'Oceanogràfic★★

Autopista del Saler 1. ◔*Open Jan–mid-Jun and mid-Oct–end Dec Mon–Fri 10am–6pm, Sat 10am–8pm; mid-Jun–mid-July Mon–Sat 10am–8pm; Aug–mid-Oct Mon–Fri 10am–7pm, Sat 10am –8pm; mid-Jul–Aug daily 10am–*

midnight. ⊜*€24.50 (€32.40 with L'Hemisfèric and Museu de les Ciències Príncipe Felipe); child €18.50.* ✆*902 10 00 31. www.cac.es.*

The largest aquarium in Europe is set around a lake and joined by gardens and tunnels. The exhibits focus on marine life in the Mediterranean, the Arctic and the Antarctic (with plenty of penguins) and the oceans, the highlight here being a 30m/100ft aquarium-tunnel with sharks and rays. The dolphin enclosure hosts performances all day.

L'Umbracle★ – White parabolic arches shelter this pleasant palm garden on a terrace facing the Museu de las Ciencias.

Museu de les Ciencies Príncipe Felipe★★

Av. Autopista del Saler 1–7. ◔*Open daily mid-Sept–Jun 10am–7pm; Jul–mid-Sept 10am–9pm.* ◔*Closed 1 Jan, 31 Dec.* ⊜*€7.70.* ✆*902 10 00 31. www.cac.es.*

The largest interactive Science Museum in Europe is set in a spectacular building that resembles the skeleton of a giant sea creature. Inside is a hands-on encounter with the human genome, space travel, astronomy and more.

L'Hemisfèric★

Autopista del Saler.
⊙*Check programmes and prices by calling* ✆*902 10 00 31. www.cac.es.*
Also the work of Calatrava, this building – at Valencia's City of Arts and Sciences – symbolises a human eye open to the world. Set in a huge pool, it houses a planetarium and Omnimax cinema.

Palau de les Arts Reina Sofía *(Autopista del Saler 1.* ✆*961 97 58 00. www.lesarts.com)* – The four halls here host classical and modern opera, music, theatre and dance.

ADDITIONAL SIGHTS

Museo de Bellas Artes★

San Pío V 9. ◔*Open Tue–Sun 10am–8pm.* ◔*Closed 1 Jan, Good Friday, 25 Dec.* ⊜*No charge.* ✆*963 87 03 00, http://museobellasartesvalencia.gva.es.*
This fine arts museum is in an 18C–19C collegiate church and seminary, and a

THE AMERICA'S CUP

Like Barcelona, Valencia latched upon an international event as a catalyst for change. Valencia won the bid to host the 32nd America's Cup – a prestigious boat challenge – against Barcelona and like its northern sister city the shoreline was a major beneficiary. British architect David Chipperfield set about creating an arresting headquarters for the event and a number of chic bars, restaurants and hotels were opened in its immediate vicinity. Transport to the port area also improved, and the port is now served by metro, tram and wide avenues with bike lanes. Progress comes at a price and as gentrification continues, many are worried that the traditional charm of El Cabayal – Valencia's old maritime neighbourhood – will be lost forever.

contemporary extension, near the Jardines del Real (Royal Gardens).
The collection is notable for its **Valencian Primitives**★★ with altarpieces by the likes of Jacomart, Reixac and others, whilst the Renaissance period is represen by Macip and Juan de Juanes. On the upper floor outstanding works include *St Bartholomew* by Luca Giordanom *St John the Baptist*by El Greco, an impressive *St Sebastian* by Ribera and a self-portrait by Velázquez. The portrait mastery of Goya is shown in his paintings of Francisco Bayeu and Joaquina Candado.

Jardines del Real (Royal Gardens)
San Pío V. Open daily 7.30am–sunset
The city's biggest park is close to the pleasant **Jardín de Monforte**. The **Puente del Real** (Royal Bridge) across the **Jardín del Turia** is 16C.

Instituto Valenciano de Arte Moderno (IVAM)
Guillem de Castro 118. Open Tue–Sun 10am–8pm. €2; free Sun.
963 86 30 00. www.ivam.es.

This modern building houses more than 7 000 works of contemporary art on rotating display. It also owns the largest collection of the works of **Julio González** (1876–1942), a major 20C sculptor.

Jardín Botánico de la Universidad (Botanical Garden)
Calle Quart, 80. Open Tue–Sun 10am–sunset. €0.50. 963 15 68 18.
Valencia was one of the first Spanish cities to embrace the trend for public gardens. The current location of this one dates from 1802 and, despite a turbulent history it now has a research centre and an informative, pleasant ambience.

Convento de Santo Domingo
Pl. de Tetuán 22
Highlights of this building include a beautiful courtyard, the Capilla de los Reyes chapel and a front gate designed by Rey Philipe II himself.

Museo Valenciano de la Ilustración y la Modernidad (Museum of Illustration and Modernity)
Calle Guillen de Castro, 8. Open Tue–Sat 10am–2pm, 4–8pm, Sun and hols 10am–8pm. Guided tour, reserve at the tourist office. No charge.
963 883 730.
The beautiful contemporary building by the architect Guillermo Vázquez Consuegra provides the backdrop for numerous art exhibitions. One titled "The Adventure of Thought' traces five centuries of social and intellectual history in Europe.

Museo de la Historia★
Valencia 42. Open Tue–Sat 10am–2pm, 4.30–8.30pm, Sun and public holidays 10am–3pm. €2; free Sat–Sun and public holidays. 963 70 11 05 www.valencia.es/mhv.
Located in a 19C water works, this museum tells the story of Valencia from its beginnings to the end of the 20C. Most evocative are the dramatised audiovisual presentations of each era.

ADDRESSES

🏨 STAY

🛏🍽 **Hostal Antigua Morellana** – *En Bou 2.* ☎*963 91 57 73. www.hostalam.com. 18 rooms.* A stone's throw from the Lonja and main market, this family-run hotel offers excellent value for money. The comfortable and bright rooms provide the best views of the picturesque narrow streets in the Carmen district.

🛏🍽 **Hotel Reina Victoria** – *Barcas 4–6.* ☎*963 52 04 87. www.husa.es. 95 rooms.* 🍽*€13. Restaurant*🛏🍽. Behind an immaculate Baroque façade, the interior lives up to expectations, with marble and mirrors, an elegant English bar, and classic rooms with modern comforts.

🛏🍽 **Hostal Residencia Venecia** – *Pl. Ayuntamiento (enter through Llop 5).* ☎*963 52 42 67. www.hotelvenecia.com. 62 rooms.* 🍽*€7.* The building is outstanding, with balconies facing the plaza del Ayuntamiento. Rooms are well furnished and the breakfast room enjoys fine views.

🛏🍽 **Hotel Alkazar** – *Mosén Fernandes 1.* ☎*963 91 55 51. www.hotel alkazar.es. 18 rooms.* 🍽*€5.* Simple, comfortable rooms in a no-fuss establishment.

🍽 EAT

🍽 **Tasca Ángel** – *Púrísima 1 (adjacent to Plaza Ibáñez).* ☎*963 91 78 35.* Founded in 1946, this is a legendary place where fans of simply seasoned, grilled sardines come in droves.

🍽 **Asador del Carme** – *Pl. del Carme 6.* ☎*963 92 24 48. www.asadordelcarme.com. Closed Sun evening.* Customers are attracted by the pleasant covered terrace and extensive menu of grilled meats and copious salads.

🍽 **Montes** – *Pl. Obispo Amigó 5.* ☎*963 85 50 25. Sun–Tue for dinner.* Great value and good service for a budget restaurant.

🍽 **Sagardi** – *San Vicente Mártir.* ☎*963 91 06 68. www.sagardi.com.* This top class Basque restaurant and tapas bar attracts gourmands from all over the city.

TAPAS

Bar Pilar – *Moro Zeit 13.* ☎*963 91 04 97. Open daily noon–midnight.* Founded in 1917, Pilar is one of the best tapas bars in the city. The house speciality is tiny mussels called *clochinas*.

Las Cuevas – *Samaniego 9.* ☎*963 91 71 96. Closed Sun and Aug.* Nothing but tapas is served here, prepared in the Valencian way from mussels to stuffed red peppers, and sardines.

🍸 CAFÉS

El Siglo – *Pl. Santa Catalina 11.* ☎*963 91 84 66.* Founded in 1836, El Siglo (The Century) is a chocolate maker, ice-cream producer and *horchata* specialist rolled into one.

🌙 NIGHTLIFE

Calle Caballeros – This street is the hub of Valencia's nightlife. Especially between the Plaza de la Virgen and Plaza Tossal, a popular square for tapas,

Café de las Horas – *Conde de Almodóvar 1.* ☎*963 91 73 36. Open from 4pm.* This sumptuous café with a 19C atmosphere is just steps from the Plaza de la Virgen.

Café del Negrito – *Pl. Negrito 1.* ☎*963 91 42 33. Open from 4pm.* This artists' café, on a small square in the old town, is a popular meeting-place for friends who come here to enjoy orange juice and cava cocktails.

La Marxa – *Cocinas 5.* ☎*963 91 70 65.* At the heart of the Carmen district, La Marxa is the emblem of Valencian nightlife.

🛒 SHOPPING

Lladró – *Poeta Querol 9.* ☎*963 51 16 25. www.lladro.com. Open Mon–Sat 10am–2pm, 4–8pm.* This famous porcelain manufacturer has boutiques around the world selling stunning works across a broad price range.

Mercadillo de la Plaza Redonda – *Open daily 9am–1pm, 4–9pm.* This open-air flea market is the place to buy a whole range of clothes and bric-a-brac.

Turrones Ramos – *Sombrerería 11 (next to pl. Redonda).* ☎*963 92 33 98. Closed Sat–Sun and in Aug.* This shop has sold hand-made *turrón* since 1890.

🎆 FESTIVALS

During the week of 12 to 19 March, the city celebrates the famous **Las Fallas** (*www. fallasfromvalencia.com;* 🔖 *see sidebar p410*). The 9th October commemorates the end of Moorish rule in 1238 and is celebrated as a national day for the region. Among religious festivals, the solemn **Corpus Christi** procession and the festival of the **Virgen de los Desamparados**, patroness of the city (second Sunday in May; *www. basilicadesamparados.org*) are notable.

Costa del Azahar

The mountain-sheltered Orange Blossom Coast is one of Spain's major tourist centres, marked by high-rise blocks and hotels along sandy beaches and orange groves. A number of small towns and villages preserve old quarters redolent of history.

- **Michelin Map:** 577 K 31, L 30, M 29, N 28–29, O 28–29.
- **Info:** Castellón de la Plana: Plaza María Agustina 5. ☎964 35 86 88; Gandía: Paseo Marítimo Neptuno, s/n. ☎962 84 24 07; Peñíscola: Paseo Marítimo, s/n. ☎964 48 02 08. www.castellon-costaazahar.com.
- **Location:** Costa del Azahar stretches along the Mediterranean coast in eastern Spain, from Valencia. The AP 7 Autopista connects the beaches.
- **Kids:** Sand, surf and kids go together; apply the sunblock.

🚗 DRIVING TOUR

From Vinaròs to Castellón
72km/45mi.

▶ *Follow either the N 340 or the AP 7 toll motorway.*

The northern coast of the province of Castellón is separated from the interior by the Maestrazgo mountains, recalling knights from the Templar and Montesa orders who controlled this area during the Middle Ages. Large resorts include Peñíscola and Benicàssim.

Vinaròs
🚂*Plaza de la Estación.*
Vinaròs has the 16C **Iglesia de Nuestra Señora de la Asunción** *(pl. Parroquial; ☎964 45 19 33)*, and a pleasant promenade close to the fishing port.

Peñíscola★★
🚂*Plaza de la Estación, Benicarló. 10km/6.2mi N.*
The **old quarter**★, surrounded by walls, sits on a small rocky peninsula in the shadow of an imposing fortress, while its sandy beaches extend to either side. A small **fishing port** is still active.

Castillo★
Castillo. ⊙Open daily Holy Week–15 Oct 9.30am–9.30pm; 16 Oct–Holy Week 10.30am–5.30pm. ⌖€3. 50. ☎964 48 00 21.
Built by Templars in the early 14C, the castle was subsequently modified by Pope Luna, whose coat of arms, featuring a crescent moon in allusion to his

name, can be seen on a gate. Grouped around the parade ground are the vast church, with pointed vaulting and a free-standing tower containing the conclave room and the study of the learned antipope who confirmed the foundation in 1411 of the University of St Andrews in Scotland (⌖*see The Michelin Green Guide Scotland).*
The terrace offers a **panorama**★ of the village and coastline. The castle is the setting for events such as the Festival of Baroque and Ancient Music, in the first fortnight of August.
The coastal road passes through an arid landscape. The resort of Alcossebre, popular with Spanish families, stands between Peñíscola and Benicàssim.

Benicàssim
🚂*Plaza Estación.*
The other major tourist centre in the province of Castellón is separated from the interior by the **Desierto de las Palmas** (Palm Desert), which has suffered badly from fire in the past few years. Benicàssim has excellent beaches, lined by villas and apartments. The quieter town of Oropesa is located to the north. It also hosts an internationally renowned rock music festival every July *(www.fiberfib.com).*

Castelló/Castellón de la Plana
Pintor Oliet 2.

Just a couple of miles separate Benicàs-sim from the port of Castellón, whose origins date back to the 13C. The capital of the province is situated in La Plana, an extensive fertile area irrigated by the River Mijares. On the main square is the **Catedral de Santa María** (*Arcipreste Balaguer 1;* ○*open Mon–Fri 10–11am, 6–8pm;* ◎*no charge;* ☏*964 22 34 63*), rebuilt after the Spanish Civil War; the octagonal bell tower is from the late 16C. The town hall (*ayuntamiento*) is from the late 17C.

Other sights include paintings attrib-uted to Zurbarán in the Convento de las Madres Capuchinas, and the Museo Pro-vincial de Bellas Artes (*av. Hermanos Bou 28;* ○*open Tue–Sat 10am–8pm, Sun and public holidays 10am–2pm;* ◎*no charge;* ☏*964 72 75 00*), with prehistoric objects and local canvases and ceramics.

From Castellón to Valencia
69km/43mi. 22km/14mi NW on the CV 10 and CV 160.

Vilafamés★★
Vilafamés is an attractive town of Moor-ish origin with whitewashed houses and artists' workshops extending below the ruins of a castle.

Museo Popular de Arte Contemporáneo★
Diputación 20. ○*Open Tue–Fri 10am–1pm, 5–8pm, Sat–Sun 11am–2pm, 5–8pm;* ◎*€1.80.* ☏*964 32 91 52.*
The museum, in a 15C palace, displays works by Miró, Barjola, Serrano, Gen-ovés, Chillida and Grupo Crónica.

▷ *Return to Castellón; continue along the A 7 for 25km/15mi to Vall d'Uxo.*

Cuevas de San José
In Vall d'Uxo, follow signs to the caves (grutas). ◁*Guided tours (35min) daily Oct–May 11am–1.15pm, 3.30–5.45pm; Jun–Jul and Sept 11am–1.15pm, 3.30–6.30pm; Aug 11am–1.15pm, 3.30–7.15pm.* ○*Closed 1, 6 Jan, 25 Dec.* ◎*€9.50.* ☏*964 69 67 61. www.riosubterraneo.com.*

An underground river hollowed out these caves at the foot of the Parque Natural de la Sierra de Espadán. Tours by boat cover a distance of around 1.2km/0.75mi.

▷ *Continue for 20km/12.4mi along the CV 230, then follow the N 234.*

Segorb/Segorbe
Explanada Estación 2.
The **cathedral** (*pl. de San Cristóbal*) is chiefly important for its **museum** (*museo;* ○*open Tue–Sun 11am–1.30pm, 5–7pm;* ○*closed 1 Jan, Good Friday, 25 Dec;* ◎*€2.40;* ☏*964 71 10 14*), which con-tains a large **collection of altarpieces** painted by the **Valencia School★**.
There are several paintings by **Vicente Macip** (d. 1545), who was influenced by the Italian Renaissance style. An Ecce Homo by his son **Juan de Juanes** bears the gentle touch favoured by Leonardo da Vinci. There are also works by Rodrigo de Osona and Jacomart and a 15C marble low relief of a Madonna by Donatello.

▷ *Continue along the N 234, towards the coast.*

Sagunt/Sagunto★
Vía Férrea.
Historic Sagunto sits at the foot of a hill occupied by the ruins of a castle and Roman theatre. The port is 5km/3mi to the east.

Ruins
Castillo. ○*Open Apr–Oct Tue–Sat 10am–8pm, Sun and public holidays 10am–2pm; Nov–Mar Tue–Sat 10am–6pm, Sun and public holidays 10am–2pm.* ○*Closed 1 Jan, Good Friday, 25 Dec.* ◎*No charge.* ☏*962 66 55 81.* *Access the ruins by the alleyways of the old Jewish quarter.*
The 1C **theatre**, restored and still in use, with fine acoustics, was built into the hillside by the Romans. The **Acro-polis** consists of the ruins and remains of ramparts, temples and houses built by Iberians, Phoenicians, Carthaginians, Romans, Visigoths and Moors. Buildings

A Legendary Siege

Sagunto has a place in Spain's heroic history. In 218 BC the Carthaginian general **Hannibal** besieged Sagunto, then a small seaport allied to Rome, for a period of eight months. Seeing only one alternative to surrender, the local inhabitants lit a huge fire and women, children, the sick and the old then proceeded to throw themselves into the furnace while soldiers and menfolk made a suicidal sortie against the enemy. The event marked the beginning of the Second Punic War. Five years later, Scipio Africanus Major rebuilt the city, which became an important Roman town.

to the west date from the War of Independence, when the French general Suchet besieged the town. The **view**★ encompasses the town, countryside and sea.

Valencia
⚲See VALENCIA

From Valencia to Játiva/Xàtiva
122km/76mi.

▷ Leave Valencia along the coast road S.

Parque Natural de La Albufera

This vast body of water (albufera, "small sea" in Arabic) south of Valencia is the largest freshwater lagoon in Spain, separated from the sea by an offshore bar, the Dehesa, that has been planted with rice since the 13C. Its eels appear on typical menus in restaurants in **El Palmar** (to the S) which also serve Valencia's famous dish, **paella**.

🛈For further details on the park, contact the **Centro de Interpretación del Racó de l'Olla** (⨀open daily 9am–2pm, Tue 4–5.30pm (mid-Oct–mid-May only); ⨀closed 1, 6 Jan, 25 Dec; ℘961 62 73 45). The novel Cañas y Barro, by **Vicente Blasco Ibáñez** (1867–1928), was set in the Albufera.

▷ Continue along the CV 500.

Cullera

This resort is at the mouth of the River Júcar; its bay is demarcated to the north by a lighthouse, the Faro de Cullera (www.culleraturismo.com). In the town are remains of a 13C castle.

▷ Head 27km/17mi S along the N 332.

Gandia
🚃Parc de L'estacio.

Gandia is at the centre of a huerta which produces large quantities of oranges. A resort has developed near the harbour along a 3km/1.8mi-long sandy **beach**.

Palacio Ducal

Duc Alfons El Vell 1. ⨀Open Apr–Sept Tue–Sat 10am–2pm, 4–8pm, Sun 10am–2pm; Oct–May Tue–Sat 10am–2pm, 3–7pm, Sun 10am–2pm. ⨀Closed public holidays in afternoon. ⊛€6. ℘962 87 14 65. www.palauducal.com.

The mansion in which St Francis Borja was born, now a Jesuit college, underwent considerable modification between the 16C and 18C. Only the patio remains Gothic in appearance and typical of those along this coast.

Colegiata de Santa María (⨀6–8pm; ⊛no charge; ℘962 87 19 51), a collegiate church in nearby Plaza Mayor, built in the 14C–15C and expanded in the 16C, is one of the finest Gothic structures in Valencia province.

▷ Head inland along the CV 60. Before Palomar, bear right on the A 7.

Xàtiva/Játiva
🚃Plaza de la Estación.

Known as "the town of the thousand fountains", Xàtiva stands in a plain covered with a Mediterranean landscape of vineyards, orchards and cypress trees. The town was the birthplace of two members of the Borja family who became popes, Calixtus III (1455–58) and Alexander VI, and, in 1591, of the painter **José Ribera**. The 16C **colegiata** (collegiate church; pl. Calixto III; ⨀open daily 10.30am–1pm; ℘962 27 38 36), modified in the 18C, faces the former **Hospital Royal**, which has an ornate Gothic-Plateresque façade.

Museo de l'Almodí

Corretgeria 46. 🕐*Open 16 Sept–14 Jun Tue–Fri 10am–2pm, 4–6pm, Sat–Sun 10am–1.30pm; 15 Jun–15 Sept Tue–Fri 9.30am–2.30pm, Sat–Sun 10am–1.30pm* ⌨*€2.40; free Sun.* 🖋*962 27 65 97. www.xativa.es/museu/cas/museo.htm.* The Almudin, a Renaissance-style former granary with a Gothic façade, houses fine Moorish-era artefacts, along with gold and silverwork and paintings. An 11C **Moorish fountain** *(pila)* of pink marble is exceptional for its depiction of human figures, extremely rare in Islamic art.

Ermita de Sant Feliu

▶*On the castle road.* 🕐*Open Nov– Mar Mon–Sat 10am–1pm, 3–6pm, Sun and public holidays 10am–1pm; Apr–Oct Mon–Sat 10am–1pm, 4–7pm, Sun and public holidays 10am–1pm.* 🖋*962 27 33 46.* Built on the flank of the hill, this chapel contains a group of 15C–16C Valencian primitives. At the entrance is a white marble **stoup**★ hollowed out of a former capital.

Castillo

Subida al Castillo. 🕐*Open Tue–Sun Apr–Sept 10am–7pm; Oct–Mar 10am– 6pm.* 🕐*Closed 1 Jan, 25 Dec.* ⌨*€2.40.* 🖋*962 27 42 74.*

ADDRESSES

🛏 STAY

⬮ **Hotel Mare Nostrum** – *Molino 4, Peñíscola.* 🖋*964 48 16 26. 24 rooms.* At the foot of the citadel near the beach, this small hotel has rooms with magnificent views. Breakfast is served on the rooftop terrace, facing the old city.

⬮⬮ **Albatros** – *Clot de la Mota 11 (near beach), Gandia.* 🖋*982 84 56 00. www.hotel-albatros.com. 44 rooms.* ⌨*€6.* This hotel's sharp style and amenities are rare in the beach area. Limited menu served in the evening.

⬮⬮ **Hostal Simó** – *Portet 5, Peñíscola.* 🖋*964 48 06 20. www.restaurantesimo.es. Closed Nov–Feb. 10 rooms.* This hostelry is very well located by the seaside at the foot of the wall. The rooms have small bathrooms but offer beautiful views.

⬮⬮⬮⬮ **Hostería del Mar** – *Av. Papa Luna 18, Peñíscola.* 🖋*902 48 06 00. www.hosteriadelmar.net. 85 rooms.* ⌨*€8.* This smart modern hotel maintains a traditional Castillan atmosphere. The restaurant specialises in fish and rice dishes as well as grilled meats.

⬮⬮⬮⬮ **Hotel Mont Sant** – *Ctra de Castillo, Xàtiva.* 🖋*962 27 50 81. www.mont-sant.com. 16 rooms.* ⌨*€12.* Situated on the road that leads uphill to the castle and set amidst a lush garden, this lovely boutique hotel has both rooms decorated with antiques (in the main building) and a more contemporary vibe in a chalet-style annexe. The smallish pool is surrounded by orange trees and protected by the old Arab city wall.

⬮⬮⬮⬮ **El Jardin Vertical** – *Nou 15, Vilafamés.* 🖋*964 32 99 38. www.eljardin vertical.com. 7 rooms.* Perched high up in the village, this *casa rural* occupies a 17C mansion built over five levels. Rooms are nice and cosy and some feature a fireplace. Breakfast is served on a terrace overlooking the horizon.

🍴 EAT

⬮ **Casa La Abuela** – *Reina 17, Xàtiva.* 🖋*962 27 05 25. Closed Sun.* Not far from the tourist office, this acclaimed restaurant has been specialising in rice dishes for over 60 years.

⬮ **Luna Gansa** – *Plaza del Mercat, Xàtiva.* 🖋*962 28 09 23.* This restaurant has a large dining room with stone walls and modern decor, with picture windows overlooking the square. It serves excellent, slightly sophisticated regional cuisine.

⬮⬮ **El Peñón** – *Santos Mártires 22, Peñíscola. On the way up to the castle, next to the Ermita de la Virgen.* 🖋*964 48 07 16. Closed Christmas–Feb and Wed.* Half-hidden in one of the narrow streets of the old town, the Peñón is a friendly restaurant with attractive decor and a pleasant small terrace, where you can enjoy excellent fish dishes.

⬮⬮⬮⬮ **Salvia** – *Ctra Subida al Castillo, Cullera.* 🖋*961 72 03 98. www.salvia restaurant.com. Closed Mon for dinner, Tue and a fortnight in Nov.* Enjoy traditional cuisine along with the panoramic views of the sea and the town.

Morella

Morella has an amazing **site**★: 14C ramparts, punctuated by towers, form a mile-long girdle round a 1 004m/3 294ft hill which the town ascends in tiers to castle ruins.

SIGHTS

A stroll around Morella's concentric streets reveals a number of mansions and religious buildings. The Puerta de San Miguel, houses a small **museum** dedicated to the age of dinosaurs (◯open Tue–Sun 11am–2pm, 4–6pm (7pm in summer); ◯closed public holidays; ◠€2; ✆964 17 31 17).

Iglesia de Santa María la Mayor★

Placeta de la Iglesia. ◯*Open daily Jul–Aug 11am–2pm, 4–7pm; Sept–Jun Tue–Sat 11–2pm, 4–7pm.* ◯*Closed 1, 6 Jan, 25, 31 Dec.* ◠*No charge. Museum €1.50.* ✆*964 16 07 93.*

One of the most interesting Gothic churches in the Levante has two fine portals and a raised Renaissance *coro* which has a spiral staircase carved with biblical scenes. The small **museum** has a beautiful Valencian *Descent from the Cross* and a 14C Madonna by Sassoferrato.

Castillo

Pl. San Francisco. ◯*Open daily Apr–Oct 10am–7.30pm; Nov–Mar 9am–6.30pm.* ◯*Closed 1 Jan, 24–26 Dec.* ◠€1.50. ✆964 17 31 28.

On the way up there are good **views**★ of the town, the 13C–14C ruins of the Convento de San Francisco with its Gothic cloisters, the 14C–15C aqueduct and the reddish heights of the surrounding sierras.

EXCURSIONS
Santuario de la Balma

▶*25km/15.5mi NW along the CV 14.*

This unusual Marian sanctuary is built into a rock wall overlooking the River Bergantes. The cave in which the Virgin appeared is enclosed by a 13C side wall and a 17C façade. Access is via a narrow gallery excavated into the rock.

▶ **Population:** 2 834
⚙ **Michelin Map:** 577 K 29.
▤ **Info:** Pl. de San Miguel, s/n. ✆964 17 30 32. www.morella.net.
▶ **Location:** Morella is in the Maestrazgo of Valenciana, linked to the coast by the N 232 to Peñíscola (78km/49mi) and Castellón de la Plana (98km/61mi).

Mirambel

▶*30km/19mi W on the CS 840. Bear left after 11km/7mi.*

This small, well-preserved mountain village retains its medieval character.

Vallivana

▶*24km/15mi SE via the N 232.*

On the road down to Vinaròs, Morella and the Costa del Azahar, a few houses and a chapel make up this small village. The shrine houses a statue of the Virgin who, according to legend, is the one who stopped the plague in Morella in 1672.

Sant Mateu★

▶*40km/25mi SE on the N 232 then right on the CV 132i.*

In the historic capital of the Maestrazgo region, Sant Mateu's **Church**★ (◯*Open Tue–Sun 10am–2pm, 4–7pm,* ◠€1.50) is one of the most remarkable Gothic sanctuaries in Valencia. It is reached by a 13C Romanesque portal though the rest of the building dates from the 14C. Only the **chapel of San Clemente** was rebuilt in the 18C. The octagonal Gothic bell tower had a defensive function for the city. The **Museo del Palacio Borrull** narrates the history of the city.

ADDRESSES

STAY

⬭ **Del Pastor** – *San Julián 12, Morella.* ✆*964 16 10 16. www.hoteldelpastor.com. 12 rooms. Closed 17–26 Dec. Restaurant⬭⬭.* A small, family-run establishment, with a lovely stone façade and well maintained rooms. The restaurant serves local cuisine.

Alicante/ Alacant★

The Greeks called Alicante *Akra Leuka* (white citadel), the Romans *Lucentum* (city of light). It combines provincial calm with the bustle of tourism.

 WALKING TOUR

OLD TOWN

▷ *Follow the route marked on the town plan.*

Explanada de España★

The most pleasant promenade in the region, running past the marina, is shaded by magnificent palms. Sunday concerts are held on the bandstand.

Catedral de San Nicolás

Pl. Abad Penalva. ◯*Open Mon–Fri 7.30am–noon, 5.30–8pm, Sat–Sun 8.30am–noon, 6–8pm* ⊕*No charge.* ✆*965 21 26 62.*

The 17C building on the site of a mosque – the city was only reconquered in 1296 – has a well-proportioned cupola, 45m/148ft high, over a Herreran nave. On calle Labradores, with its terraces, are the 18C Palacio Maisonnave, no. 9 (now the Municipal Archives; ◯*open Mon–Fri Sept–Jun 9am–2pm; Jul–Aug 9am–1.30pm*); and an 18C mansion, no. 14, now a cultural centre.

Ayuntamiento (Town Hall)

Pl. del Ayuntamiento 1. ◯*Open Mon–Fri 9am–2pm.* ✆*965 14 91 10. www.alicante-ayto.es.*

This imposing 18C palace of golden stone, with two tiers of balconies, is flanked by two towers. Visit the Rococo **capilla** (chapel) with *azulejos* from Manises, and reception rooms with blue silk hangings.

Museo de Bellas Artes Gravina – MUBAG★

Gravina, 13. ◯*Open Tue–Sat 10am–2pm, 5pm–9pm (4pm–8pm in winter), Sun 10am–2pm.* ⊕*No charge.* ✆*965 14 67 80. www.mubag.org.*

▶ **Population:** 339 947
⚲ **Michelin Map:** 577 Q 28 (town plan) – map 123 COSTA BLANCA.
▣ **Info:** Rambla Mendez Nuñez 23. ✆*965 20 00 00.* www.alicanteturismo.com.
▷ **Location:** Alicante is the mid-point of Spain's Mediterranean coast, 110km/69mi from Cartagena. ▭Avenida de Salamanca 1
⊛ **Don't Miss:** A stroll along the Explanada by the harbour.
◯ **Timing:** Start with a view from the Castillo de Santa Bárbara.
▲▲ **Kids:** They will love the castles; the Castillo de Santa Bárbara is a must.

Situated over two 17C and 18C mansions, the permanent collection of this museum occupies the first level. A visit begins with a few decorative art objects, including three intricate sideboards from the 16C–17C. In the painting section, notice the beautiful *Calvary* by Rodrigo de Osona (late 15C) which reflects a strong Flemish influence and *Saint John, Saint Joseph and Child* by **Cristobal Llorens** (16C). More topically, a view of Alicante by Vincente Suarez Ordoñez gives a good idea of what the city was like in the early 19C.

Iglesia de Santa María

Pl. de Santa María. ◯*Open daily noon–1pm, 6–7.30pm.* ⊕*No charge.* ✆*965 21 60 26.*

The church is in a square below Santa Bárbara Castle. The 18C Baroque **façade**★ has wreathed columns, pillars and breaks in its cornices. Once a mosque, it altered in the 17C when Churrigueresque decoration was added. Note the graceful Renaissance marble fonts and a painting of John the Baptist and John the Apostle by Rodrigo de Osuna the Younger.

Museo de la Asegurada★

Pl. de Santa María 3. Open Tue–Sat 10am–8pm, Sun 10am–2pm. 965 21 31 56. No charge.

On the same plaza, in a 17C granary, this museum exhibits 20C painting and sculpture donated by sculptor Eugenio Sempere. There are works by artists both Spanish (Miró, Picasso, Gargallo, Tàpies and Dalí) and foreign (Vasarely, Braque, Chagall and Kandinsky).

Castillo de Santa Bárbara

Frente Playa Postiguet. Ascend by lift and walk down, either all the way (good views) or to the halfway stop. Open daily 10am–2.30pm, 4–8pm. Closed 25 Dec, 1 Jan. No charge. 965 16 21 28.

This fortress atop Benacantil hill dates from the 9C in Muslim times, though outbuildings were raised in the 16C. The Revellín del Bon Repós rampart was built in the 18C. The Philip II hall is a worthy highlight.

The Plaza de la Torreta is surrounded by the oldest buildings. A platform commands a fine **view**★ of the harbour and town. The 16C section is at the halfway stop on the lift; the 17C perimeter is lower down. A footpath leads into the medieval streets and tiny squares of the working-class Santa Cruz quarter.

El Palmeral

©Turespaña

SIGHTS

MARQ (Museo Arqueológico Provincial de Alicante)★★

Pl. Doctor Gómez Ulla. Open Tue–Sat 10am–7pm, Sun and public holidays 10am–2pm. €3. 965 14 90 00. www.marqalicante.com.

MARQ opens archaeology to all, with a magnificent presentation focused on the ancients of this area.

The museum is organised into large halls (Prehistory, Iberian, Roman, Middle Ages and Modern) around a space devoted to archaeology itself. Here you can get right into excavations in a cave, a church and an underwater site.

EXCURSIONS
ELCHE/ELX★

24km/15mi SW. Pl. del Parc 3. 966 65 81 95. www.turismedelx.com. Avenida del Ferrocarril Este.

Elche (Valencian: Elx) lies along the Vinalopó river. The **Dama de Elche** (4C BC), a masterpiece of Iberian art now in the Museo Arqueológico de Madrid, was discovered in **La Alcudia** (2km/1.2mi S). **El Misteri** is a medieval verse drama with an all-male cast. It recounts the Dormition, Assumption and Coronation of the Virgin. It is on UNESCO's Oral and Intangible Heritage of Humanity list *(played in the Basílica de Santa María; Aug, Oct and Nov; www.misteridelx.com).*

El Palmeral (Palm Grove)★★ *(Porta de la Morera 49; open daily 10am–sunset)* – The groves, planted by the Phoenicians and expanded by the Arabs, are the largest in Europe with more than 200 000 trees, and are a UNESCO World Heritage Site. The palms flourish with the aid of a remarkable irrigation system. Female trees produce dates, and the fronds from the male trees are used in Palm Sunday processions and handicrafts.

Huerta del Cura★★ *(open daily from 10am; check tourist office for closing times which vary throughout the year)* – This delightful garden of Mediterranean and subtropical plants lies under magnificent palm trees; one, with seven trunks, is said to be 160 years old.

Parque Municipal★ *(pas. de l'Estació)* – A well-tended garden covered with palm trees.

Museo Arqueológico y de Historia de Elche (MAHE) *(Diagonal del Palau;* ⓘ*open Tue–Sat 10am–1.30pm, 4–8pm, Sun 10am–1.30pm;* ✆*€3;* ✆ *966 65 82 03)* – The museum is in the Moorish Palacio de Altamira. The archaeological section traces Elche from its origins to the Visigoth era. Notable are sculpture and ceramics from the Iberian period and the *Venus of Illicis*, a delicately carved white marble Roman sculpture.

Basílica de Santa María *(pl. del Congreso Eucarístico;* ⓘ*open daily 11am–7pm, 6pm in winter;* ✆*€2)* – This monumental 17C–18C Baroque basilica with a beautiful portal by Nicolás de Bussi is the setting for the annual mystery play. View the palm groves from the tower. Nearby are the 17C–18C Almohad tower, **La Calahorra** *(Uberna 14)*, and the Baños árabes.

Baños árabes *(pas. de Santa Llucía 13; access by a side door of the Convento de la Merced;* ⓘ*open Tue–Sat 10am–1.30pm, 4.30–8pm, Sun and public holidays 10.30am–1.30pm;* ✆*€1;* ✆ *965 45 28 87)* – A well-prepared exhibition details the culture of the bath in the 12C.

La Alcudia: archaeological site and museum *(ctra Dolores; 2km/1.2mi S;* ⓘ*open Apr–Sept Tue–Sat 10am–8pm, Sun 10am–3pm;* ⓘ*closed afternoons rest of the year;* ✆*€3;* ✆ *966 61 15 06)* – The remains and museum reveal the story of a city from the Neolithic period to its decline in Visigoth times.

🚗 DRIVING TOUR

Inland from Alicante/Alacant
176km/110mi N.

▷ *Take the N 340 in San Juan, then the Alcoi road and then turn right.*

Cuevas de Canalobre

🎧*Guided tours (40min) mid-Sept–Jun Mon–Fri 10.30am–4.50pm, Sat–Sun and public holidays 10.30am–5.50pm; Jul–mid-Sept and Holy Week daily 10.30am–7.30pm.* ⓘ*Closed 1 Jan, Mon after Easter Monday, 25 Dec.* ✆*€5.* ✆ *965 69 92 50. www.cuevasde canelobre.com.*

The caves are at 700m/2 296.5ft up Mount Cabezón de Oro, with candelabra *(canalobre)* formations.

▷ *Return to the N 340.*

Cross dry country of figs and carobs.

Jijona/Xixona

The speciality of this town is *turrón*, an almond-honey sweet. Visit a **museum** (El Lobo; *ctra Jijona-Busot;* ⓘ*open Jan–Jun Mon–Fri 10am–1.30pm, 4–7.30pm, Jul–Sept Mon–Fri 10am–7.30pm, all year Sat–Sun 10am–1pm, 5–7pm;* ✆*€1;* ✆ *965 61 02 25; www.museodelturron.com)* and factories. Beyond Jijona (Valencian: Xixona) the road twists up through almond terraces to the **Puerto de la Carrasqueta**★ (1 024m/3 360ft), a pass with a view towards Alicante.

Alcoy/Alcoi

🚉*Plaza Estación.*
Alcoy is an industrial town in a mountain setting. Every year, between 22 and 24 April, **Moors and Christians**★ (Moros y Cristianos) **festival** *(www.ajualcoi.org)* celebrates a Christian victory in 1276. It is the biggest, most colourful and noisiest of Spain's many Moors and Christians events.

▷ *Take the CV 795 to Barxell, then follow the CV 794.*

Bocairent

🚉*Camino de la Estación, Ontiyent 10km/7mi N.*
The church in this hilltop market village has an interesting **Museo Parroquial** (Parish Museum; *Abadía 36;* 🎧*guided tours (45min) by appointment only;* ✆*€1.80;* ✆ *962 35 00 62)* with works by **Juan de Juanes** (1523–79) – who died

here – and his school, and a 14C Last Supper by Marcial de Sax.

▷ *Take the CV 81.*

Villena

🚌 *Ronda de la Estación.*

Castillo de la Atalaya (👁️◀*guided tours every hour Tue–Fri 10.30am–1.30pm, Sat–Sun and public holidays 11am–2pm; 🖉965 80 38 04*) – This castle of Arabic origin dominates its former feudal domain. Among its owners have been famed men of letters: **Don Juan Manuel** in the 14C and **Prince Henry of Aragon** (**Marqués de Villena,** 1384–1434), poet and magic fan. Its keep survives, with circular towers in the corners, and large Homenaje (homage) tower (upper section 15C). Fine views from the walls.

Iglesia de Santiago (*pl. de Santiago;* 🕐*open Tue–Sat 10am–1pm, Sun and public holidays 10am–noon; 🖉965 81 39 19*) – This Gothic-Renaissance church (14C–17C) with notable bell tower stands near the town hall. Note unusual **spiral pillars**★ supporting Gothic vaults, and a Renaissance-style baptismal font.

Museo Arqueológico (Archaeological Museum) – (*pl. de Santiago 1;* 🕐*open Tue–Fri 10am–2pm (and 5–7pm Tue and Thur), Sat–Sun and public holidays 11am–2pm;* 🕐*closed 1 Jan, 25 Dec;* ⊖*no charge;* 🖉*965 80 11 50; www.museovillena.com*) – The museum, in the town hall (*Palacio Municipal,* fine Renaissance façade and patio), displays solid gold from the Bronze Age (1500–1000 BC). The outstanding **Villena Treasure**★★ includes jewellery and gourds decorated with sea urchin shell patterns.

ADDRESSES

🛏️ STAY

🛏️ **Residencia La Milagrosa** – *Villavieja 8.* 🖉*965 21 69 18. 29 rooms.* This young and cosmopolitan *pensión* has bright rooms with some overlooking the Plaza de Santa María. There is a huge garden-terrace upstairs.

🛏️ **Hostal Les Monges Palace** – *San Agustín 4.* 🖉*965 21 50 46. www.lesmonges.net. 23 rooms.* ⊠*€6.* An excellent location in the heart of old Alicante, with a standard not normally found in a *pensión*. Features of this charming 18C building include a marble staircase and large mirrors and windows.

🛏️🛏️ **Mediterránea Plaza** – *Pl. de Ayuntamiento 6.* 🖉*965 21 01 88. www.eurostarshotels.com. 50 rooms.* ⊠*€10.* Located in the historical centre by the town hall, the ample facilities provided here make this a good place to explore the city.

🍴 EAT

🍴🍴🍴 **La Goleta** – *Explanada de España 8, bajos.* 🖉*965 21 43 92.* On a busy street near the marina, this restaurant has a pleasant covered terrace and marine decor inside. It offers regional sausages, fried seafood, faultless paella, and good home-made desserts.

🍴🍴🍴 **Nou Manolín** – *Villegas 3.* 🖉*965 20 03 68. www.noumanolin.com.* A classic restaurant with a rustic feel. The lovely banqueting room is the highlight of this three floor establishment.

🍴🍴🍴🍴 **La Ereta** – *Parque de a Ereta.* 🖉*965 14 32 50. Reservations essential.* Situated on a hillside between the castle and city, this restaurant has large windows that afford exceptional views of Alicante. It serves exceptional gourmet cuisine and fine tasting menus.

Horchateria Azul – *Calderón de la Barca 38* 🖉*965 21 63 10. Closed Sun.* A tiny shop without pretension, specialising in *horchata*, a drink made from *chufas*, or tiger nuts. Friendly staff.

TAPAS

El Canto – *Alemania 26.* 🖉*965 92 56 50.* A delicious menu of *pinchos* and *raciones* offered in a bar atmosphere.

🌙 NIGHTLIFE

Barrio del Carmen – Alicante's old quarter is pleasant by day, and after 11pm, the whole district is transformed into one huge disco.

Puerto de Alicante – One of the liveliest areas on summer nights. On one side are locales with Latin and Spanish rhythms, on the other the shops and cafés and terraces of the Panoramis complex.

Costa Blanca★

The White Coast stretches south from Valencia to Murcia. It is flat and sandy, with occasional highlands where the sierras drop to the sea. A hot climate, low rainfall, dazzling light, long beaches and turquoise water attract vast numbers of tourists.

 DRIVING TOUR

From Denia to Guadalest
115km/71mi. Allow 2 days.

Denia (Dénia)

The former Greek colony became Roman *Dianium*. Denia today is a fishing harbour, toy manufacturing centre and seaside resort. In the fortress (🎫€2.50, *including museum;* 📞966 42 06 56) above town is an archaeological museum. The coast south of Denia becomes steep and rocky with pine forests.

Cap de Sant Antoni★

Near the lighthouse on this headland, a last foothill of the Sierra del Mongó, is a good **view**★ towards Xàbia and the Cabo de la Nao headland.

Xàbia/Jávea★

The old quarter is on high ground around a fortified 14C Gothic church. The modern quarter is near the harbour, beach and parador.

Cap de la Nau/Cabo de la Nao★

The climb affords views over Jávea at the foot of the Sierra del Mongó; then enter thick pinewoods where villas stand in clearings.

Cabo de la Nao is an eastern extension of the Sierras Béticas (Baetic Cordillera) that continues under the sea to reappear as the island of Ibiza.

There is a beautiful **view**★ south from the point down the coast to the Penyal d'Ifac. Sea caves (approached by boat) and charming creeks such as **La Granadella** (south) and **Cala Blanca** (north) are excellent for diving.

Michelin Map: 577
P 29–30, Q 29–30 – Communidad Valenciana (Alicante/Alacant), Murcia.

Info: Altea: San Pere 9. 📞965 84 41 14; Denia: Plaza Oculista Buigues 9. 📞966 42 23 67. www.costablanca.org.

Location: Costa Blanca towns are linked by the N 332 and the AP 7 toll motorway.

Don't Miss: Beaches, sun, villages.

Kids: Tierra Mítica amusement park.

Calp/Calpe

The **Penyal d'Ifac**★, a rocky outcrop 332m/1 089ft high, is the setting of Calp. A path leads to the top of the Penyal (🥾*about 1hr walk*) with views along the coast of Calp and its salt pans, of the dark mountain chains, and northwards of the coast as far as Cabo de la Nao. The Sierra de Bernia road twists and turns before crossing the spectacular Barranco de Mascarat (Mascarat Ravine) in the hinterland to Cabo de la Nao.

Altea

Altea's white walls, rose-coloured roofs and glazed blue tile domes rise in tiers up a hillside overlooking the sea – a symphony of colour and reflected light below the Sierra de Bernia. A walk through the alleys to the church and then the view from the square over the village and beyond to the Penyal d'Ifac will reveal the attraction of so many painters towards Altea.

Benidorm

The excellent climate, cheap packaged holidays from Britain and Germany, and two immense beaches (the Levante and the Poniente), curving away on either side of a small rock promontory, are the elements of Benidorm's incredible growth from a modest fishing village in the 1950s to a Mediterranean

Manhattan. From the lookout on **El Castillo** point, there are **views**★ of the beaches and sea. The old quarter stands behind the point, close to the blue-domed church.

🏃🏃 Terra Mítica

3km/2mi from Benidorm. Exit 65 A of the AP 7. ⏰Open daily 10am–8pm (check website before travelling). ☞€35; child €26.50 (2-day and eve tickets available). ☎902 02 02 20. www.terramiticapark.com.

This vast theme park is based upon ancient Egypt, Greece, Rome and Iberia. Terra Mítica has attractions for visitors of all ages and tastes, as well as shows and a choice of shops and restaurants.

Main attractions – In Ancient Egypt, enter the Pyramid of Terror, or descend the Cataracts of the Nile on an exciting white-water roller-coaster ride. In Greece, emulate Theseus in the Labyrinth of the Minotaur, or experience the sensation of falling down a waterfall in the Fury of Triton. The Magnus Colossus in Rome is a spectacular wooden roller coaster. In the Flight of the Phoenix, enjoy the excitement of a free fall from 54m/177ft, or battle against currents and whirlpools in the Rapids of Argos, in the Islands section.

▷ *Take the CV 70 to Callosa d'En Sarrià then head along the CV 755 to Alcoi.*

On the drive inland, you pass through small valleys cloaked in all sorts of fruit trees, including citrus and medlars. The village of **Polop** stretches up a hillside in a picturesque mountain setting. Beyond, the landscape becomes more arid but the views more extensive, the mountains more magnificent.

Guadalest★

Guadalest stands out from the terraced valleys of olive and almond trees to face the harsh limestone escarpments of the Sierra de Aitana. The **site**★ is impressive. The village, forced halfway up a ridge of rock, is a stronghold accessible only through an archway cut into stone. Walk round the **Castillo de San José**

(now a cemetery; *Iglesia 2; ⏰open daily Holy Week–Oct 10.15am–1.45pm, 3.15–8pm; Nov–Holy Week 10.15am–1.45pm, 3.15–6pm; ⏰closed 1 Jan, 25 Dec; ☞€3; ☎965 88 53 93*) where ruins remain of fortifications wrecked by an earthquake in 1744. The splendid view takes in the Guadalest reservoir with its reflections of surrounding mountain crests, the amazing site of the old village, and, in the distance, the sea.

ADDRESSES

🛏 STAY

😋 **Hostal L'Ánfora** – *Expl. Cervantes 8, Denia. ☎966 43 01 01. www.hostallanfora.com. 20 rooms.* This small building with its distinctive green façade is located at the fishing port in Denia. Although small and basic, the rooms here are bright and clean. In the mornings, guests can also enjoy the sight of local fishing boats from their windows.

😋😋😋 **Hostal Triskel** – *Sor María Gallart 3. ☎966 46 21 91. www.hostal-triskel. com. 5 rooms.* In the heart of the historic district in a beautiful edifice, this hotel welcomes you with a bottle of cava and a fruit basket. Each room is unique yet all are furnished with antiques, terracotta floor tiles, porcelain switches and retro phones.

🍴 EAT

😋 **El Racó Gallego** – *Plaza de la Villa 17, Calp. ☎965 83 86 31.* Located in an old home with a nice terrace and a rustic dining room, this restaurant serves excellent seafood and fish, and delicious tapas – try the home-made croquetas.

😋😋 **La Maga de Altea** – *Pg Marítim/ carrer Conde d'Altea, Altea. ☎966 88 55 46.* This refined eatery on the waterfront serves local specialties including fish and several kinds of rice.

TAPAS

La Cava Aragonesa – *Pl. de la Constitución (also entry on Callejón Santo Domingo), Benidorm Old Town. ☎966 80 12 06. www. lacavaaragonesa.es.* This typical bar makes a refreshing change from the dozens of neighbouring tower blocks, with its cured hams hanging from the ceiling, and its good choice of tapas. Also on the attractive alleyway of Callejón de Santo Domingo, try the tapas at **Bar Aurrerá**.

Murcia★

Murcia, an historic but also booming university town, lies along the Segura in a fertile market-gardening area *(huerta)*.

A BIT OF HISTORY

The city, founded in the reign of Abd ar-Rahman II in 825 as Madina Mursiya, was reconquered in 1266. Up to the 18C, Murcia prospered from agriculture and silk weaving.

SIGHTS
Catedral★

Pl. Cardenal Belluga. ⏰Open daily 10am–1pm, 6–8pm. ⊘No charge. ⏰Closed during the Virgen de la Fuensanta pilgrimage (twice per year in Lent and Sept). ℘968 21 63 44.

The original 14C cathedral is camouflaged beneath Renaissance and Baroque additions. The **façade★**, with an arrangement of columns and curves, is a brilliant example of Baroque. The impressive belfry, 95m/311ft in height, was completed by Ventura Rodríguez in the 18C. The interior, beyond the entry cupola, is preponderantly Gothic, apart from the 16C **Capilla de los Junterones** *(fourth south chapel)*, which has rich Renaissance decoration.

The **Capilla de los Vélez★** *(off the ambulatory)* is sumptuous Late Gothic with splendid star vaulting, and wall decoration with Renaissance and Mudéjar motifs. The sacristy, approached through two successive Plateresque doors (beautiful panels on the first), is covered by an unusual radiating dome. The walls are richly panelled with Plateresque carving below and Baroque above.

Museo Salzillo★

Pl. San Agustín 3. ⏰Open Tue–Sat 10am–2pm, 5–7pm, Sun and public holidays 11am–2pm. ⏰Closed 1, 6 Jan, Holy Week, 1 May, 9 Jun, 6, 25 Dec. ⊘€5. ℘968 29 18 93. www.museosalzillo.es.

The museum possesses Salzillo's masterpieces including the eight polychrome wood sculptures of **pasos** carried in

the Good Friday procession during Holy Week, kept in side chapels off the nave of the Church of Jesus. The deep emotion on the faces is impressive. The museum also contains vivid terracotta pieces used to create scenes from the life of Jesus.

Palacio Episcopal★

Plaza del Cardenal Belluga.

Built between 1748 and 1768, this palace shows a clear influence of Italian Baroque. The two-level patio has medallions embossed with figures of bishops in the pediments of the windows and the courtyard is decorated with many carved coats of arms. This leads to the grand staircase which is topped with a cupola. Don't miss the circular chapel.

Museo de Bellas Artes – MuBAM★

Calle Obispo Frutos 8–12. ⏰Open May–Sept Mon–Fri 10am–9pm, Oct–Apr Mon–Sat 10am–8.30pm, Sun 10am–2pm. ℘968 23 93 46. www.museobellasartes murcia.com. ⊘No charge.

This museum contains some fine exhibits. On the ground floor is an altarpiece by Juan de Vitoria (16C) representing Calvary and the Martyrdom of Santiago. On the first floor, which is devoted to the Golden Age, is *St Jerome* (1613), attributed to José de Ribera. In the same room is a beautiful Crucifixion by Murillo (1670) and by the same artist, a moving **Ecce Homo★**.

Museo Santa Clara★★

Paseo Alfonso X El Sabio 1. ⏰Open May–Sept daily except Mon 10am–1pm, 5–7.30pm, Sun and holidays 10am–1pm;

▶ **Population:** 441 345
⚅ **Michelin Map:** 123.
　Costa Blanca.
🅷 **Info:** Plaza Cardenal Belluga. ℘968 36 61 00. www.murciaturistica.es.
▣ **Location:** 50km/31mi from the coast. ▭Plaza de la Industria.

Oct–Apr daily except Mon 10am–1pm, 4–6.30pm, Sun and holidays 10am–1pm. 📞*Free guided tour; reservation required.* ☎*699 39 65 44. www.museo santaclara.com.*

This monastery was founded in the 14C on the site of an Almohad palace which had not been completely destroyed. The Gothic cloister was built around the central basin of the Arabian palace. The beds have been replanted with plant species in accordance with the original flora. Behind the magnificent arcades of the cloister stands a **portico★** with three richky decorated arches, which gave access to one of the main halls of the palace.

Excavations have unearthed the oldest remains, including traces of a courtyard belonging to a 12C Almoravid palace. In the centre stand the remains of a colonnaded pavilion, in which is preserved a fragment of 12C painting representing a **flutist★**.

The **museum★** maintains a collection of paintings, sculptures and liturgical objects held by the community of the convent of Santa Clara. Note a Christ on the Cross★★ (1770), by Francisco Salzillo. Carved life-size, the piece shows exceptional balance and features a serene face.

EXCURSIONS
Orihuela★

▶ *24km/15mi NE on the A 7.*
🚌*Avenida Teodomiro 68.*

This peaceful town, with its many churches, lies along the Segura, which provides water for market gardens *(huertas)* and for the local **palm grove**. For centuries, Orihuela was a university town.

The house of poet and dramatist Miguel Hernández is now a museum *(Miguel Hernández 73;* 🕐*open Jun–Sept Tue–Sat 10am–2pm, 5–8pm, Sun and public holidays 10am–2pm; Oct–May 10am–2pm, 4–7pm, Sun and public holidays 4–7pm;* 🕐*closed 1, 6 Jan, 25 Dec;* 💳*no charge;* ☎*965 30 63 27).*

Catedral del Salvador★

Mayor. 🕐*Open Mon–Fri 10.30am–1pm, 4–6.30pm, Sat 10.30am–1pm.*
💳*No charge.* ☎*965 30 06 38.*

Constructed in the 14C–16C, the cathedral has a Renaissance north doorway. The interior has three cruciform Gothic naves, ambulatory, and unusual vaulting with spiral ribs.

The stalls of the choir are carved in Baroque style. There are notable Renaissance **grilles** around the choir and presbytery. The **Museo de la Catedral** houses a *Temptation of St Thomas Aquinas* by Velázquez, a *Christ* by Morales and a *Mary Magdalene* by Ribera.

The **Palacio del Obispo** on calle Ramón y Cajal behind the cathedral has a magnificent 18C patio.

Convento de Santo Domingo

Adolfo Clavarana (north of the city).
🕐*Open Tue–Fri 10am–1.30pm, 5–8pm, Sat 10am–2pm, 5–7pm, Sun 10am–2pm.* 🕐*Closed 1, 6 Jan, 17 Jul, 25 Dec.*
💳*No charge.* ☎*965 30 02 40.*

This monumental building (16C–18C), formerly the university, started out in Renaissance style and transformed into Baroque. The long college façade conceals two sober cloisters (17C–18C). The 18C **church★** is covered with murals and exuberant stucco mouldings.

Museo de la Muralla

Río. 🕐*Open Tue–Sat 10am–2pm, 4–5pm, Sun and public holidays 10am–2pm.* 💳*No charge.* ☎*965 30 46 98.*

Descend below street level to the remains of the city wall, dwellings and baths from the Moorish era, and a Gothic palace and a Baroque building.

The **Iglesia de Santiago** *(pl. de Santiago 7;* 🕐*open daily Jul–Sept 10am–2pm, 5–8pm; Oct–Jun 10am–2pm, 4.30–7pm;* 💳*€1;* ☎*965 30 13 60),* near the town hall, is Gothic in style, with Renaissance transept and apse. It was founded by the Catholic Monarchs whose yoke and arrow emblems, together with a statue of St James, are on the Gothic portal; the doorway on the right is Baroque. In the interior, note statues attributed to Salzillo in the side chapels.

Santuario de la Fuensanta (La Fuensanta Shrine)
7km/4.3mi S.

▶ *Follow the signs from Puente Viejo.*

From the shrine of the Virgen de la Fuensanta, patron saint of Murcia, enjoy fine **views** of the town and the *huerta*.

Cartagena
▶ *62km/39mi SE along the N 301.*

🚌 *Plaza de México 2.*

In 223 BC this bay settlement was captured by the Carthaginians; it was subsequently colonised by the Romans, as *Cartago Nova*. Philip II fortified the surrounding hilltops, and Charles III built the Arsenal. The city is known for its dramatic Holy Week processions.

Near plaza del Ayuntamiento is the early **submarine** invented by native son Isaac Peral, in 1888. From the top of the **Castillo de la Concepción** (*Gisbert*), there is a good general **view** of the harbour and the ruins of the former Romanesque cathedral of Santa María la Vieja.

Museo Nacional de Arqueología Subacuática★★
Pas. del Muelle Alfonso XII 22. 🕐 *Phone/check website for opening times.* €3; no charge Sat (from 3pm), Sun. 📞 968 12 11 66. http://museoarqua.mcu.es.

This museum displays underwater finds, notably Phoenician, Punic and Roman amphorae. Maps and models of vessels (galleys, biremes and triremes) illustrate seafaring in times past.

Mar Menor
▶ *At La Manga: 81km/51mi SE via the N 301 and MU 312 and 33km/21mi from Cartagena.*

Mar Menor, or Little Sea, is a lagoon separated from the open Mediterranean by **La Manga**, a sand bar 500m/1 640ft wide which extends from the eastern end of the Cabo de Palos headland. Gilthead, mullet and king prawns are fished from its shallow salt water.

La Manga del Mar Menor is a large, elongated seaside resort with surrealistic tower blocks stretching for miles. In **Santiago de la Ribera**, where there is no natural beach, pontoons with changing cabins line the seafront. **San Javier**, nearby, is the seat of the Academia General del Aire (Air Academy).

Alcantarilla
▶ *9km/5.6mi W on the N 340.*

The **Museo de la Huerta** (*av. Príncipe;* 🕐 *open 1 Apr–26 Oct Tue–Fri 1am–8pm, Sat–Sun 10am–1.30pm, 4–6pm; 27 Oct–30 Mar Tue–Fri 10am–6.30pm, Sat–Sun 10am–1pm;* 🕐 *closed public holidays;* 🚌 *no charge;* 📞 *968 89 25 86)* is dedicated to local **agriculture and irrigation**. Among the orange trees are white rustic dwellings *(barracas)* and a **noria**, a giant waterwheel devised for irrigation by the Moors.

Lorca★
▶ *67km/42mi SW along the N 340-E 12.*

🚌 *Alameda de Menchirón.*

Lorca lies in an irrigated valley at the foot of a hill crowned by a **castle**, the 👥 **Fortaleza del Sol** (🕐 *open Mar–Dec daily 10.30am–6.30pm;* 🚌 *€10; child €7;* 📞 *902 40 00 47)*, where visitors may spend the day back in the Middle Ages. The main sights are the **plaza de España**, surrounded by the Baroque façades of the **ayuntamiento** (town hall), the **Juzgado** (Law Courts), embellished with a corner sculpture, and the **Colegiata de San Patricio** (📞 *968 46 99 66)*, a collegiate church built in the 16C and 18C, and the **Palacio de Guevara★★**. Its doorway, although in poor condition, is a fine example of Baroque sculpture (1694; *now the tourist office;* 📞 *968 44 19 14; http://lorcatallerdeltiempo.es)*.

Caravaca de la Cruz★
▶ *70km/44mi W along the C 415. Tourist Office, calle de Las Monjas, 17.* 📞 *968 70 10 03. www.turismocaravaca.org.*

This attractive town is topped by its castle of Muslim origin, which was extended in the 15C by the Knights Templars. Within the compound the **Santuario de la Santa Cruz** is an impressive Baroque monument. Below, the town also retains many fine examples of superb Renaissance architecture, the jewel in the crown being the **Iglesia de San Salvador**, which has been declared a Historic-Artistic Site.

THE BALEARIC ISLANDS

The Balearics evoke summer sunshine and frenetic nightlife, yet their history and beauty are as impressive as those of any island in the Mediterranean. Although the archipelago is one of the most popular destinations in the world, over 40 per cent of its verdant landscapes are protected by law.

Highlights

1 A leisurely morning spent wandering **Palma's Historic Centre** (p433)

2 Exploring the coves and caves of Mallorca's **Costa Rocosa** (p438)

3 The traditional architecture of tranquil **Menorca** (p442)

4 Sunset or sunrise gazing on **Ibiza** (p446)

5 Laid-back and low-key **Formentera** (p449)

The **Balearic archipelago** lies off Spain's Levante, in the Mediterranean, and covers 5 000sq km/1 900sq mi. It includes three large islands – **Mallorca**, **Menorca** and **Ibiza** – each with a distinctive character, two smaller inhabited isles – Formentera and Cabrera – and many uninhabited islets. All three larger islands have airports and inter-island ferries link them together.

Palma, capital of Mallorca, and the only real city in the archipelago, is also administrative capital of the Comunidad Autónoma Balear (Balearic Autonomous Community). The language, Balearic, is derived from Catalan and runs alongside Castilian.

The Balearics took off as **holiday islands** in the 1950s and Mallorca in particular was in the vanguard of mass tourism. Initially a fashionable "jet-set" destination, **Majorca** (as it is known in English) had by the 1980s become synonymous with the worst excesses of holiday commercialisation and badly behaved tourists. In order to reverse this trend, during the late 1990s the island was rebranded by the local authorities both from a marketing perspective and also physically, as the island infrastructure was moved upmarket. Old hotels were demolished with great ceremony, and new policies to encourage visitors to discover inland **Mallorca** were put in place. Today, mass tourism is still very much alive but the island also now attracts fashionable visitors and consequently a whole new range of designer-chic hotels, rural retreats, and restaurants, bars and nightclubs have sprung up to grace the island, particularly in and around the capital of Palma which has become virtually a city break destination in its own right.

The situation is similar in **Ibiza**. It, too, has long suffered from charmless mass-market tourist centres, like San António, but these contrast with its charming hippy-chic **Eivissa** (Ibiza Town) and, away from the noisy centres, much of the island is undisturbed and surprisingly rural. The music scene remains of prime importance and ensures an annual "pilgrimage" of young tourists from all over the world.

Menorca meanwhile is the quietest of the developed islands, relying on its beautiful sandy beaches, prehistoric sites and natural attractions to bring a constant stream of UK and German visitors to its low-key family-orientated resorts.

Eivissa

M. Lemaire/MICHELIN

Mallorca★★★

Mallorca, the largest and by far the most popular of the Balearic Islands, is a holiday paradise for north Europeans, particularly popular with British and German visitors. The dramatic, steep cliff landscapes of the north coast, indented with coves, contrast with the beaches of the gentle south coast with their crystalline turquoise waters. Concrete seaside developments are offset by Mallorca's picturesque inland towns and villages.

LANDSCAPE AND TRADITION

The **Serra de Tramuntana** in the north-west rises in limestone crests – the highest is **Puig Major** (1 445m/4 740ft) – parallel to the coast.

Spectacular cliffs plunging into the sea are high enough to block winds from the mainland. Pines, junipers and holm oaks cover the slopes, interspersed with Mallorca's famous olive trees. Terraces of vegetables and fruit trees surround hillside villages.

The central plain, **Es Pla**, is divided by low walls into fields and fig and almond orchards; market towns, with outlying windmills to pump water, retain the regular medieval fortress plan.

The **Serra de Levant** to the east is hollowed out into wonderful caves. The

▶ **Population:** 862 397
◔ **Michelin Map:**
   579 –Baleares.
▯ **Info:** Palma: Pg. del
   Born 27. ✆ 902 10 23
   65. www.illesbalears.es/
   ing/majorca/home.jsp.
   Airport: ✆ 971 78 90 00.
♟ **Kids:** Marineland;
   Palma Aquarium.

GETTING THERE

BY AIR – From the mainland, the Balearic Islands are best served by the Spanish airlines Vueling *(www.vueling.com)* and Spanair *(www.spaniar.com)*.
BY SEA – Trasmediterranea *(www.trasmediterranea.es)* and Baleària *(www.balearia.com)* run regular ferries from the mainland and between the islands.

rocky coast is indented with sheltered, sand-carpeted coves.

A BIT OF HISTORY

A Short-lived kingdom (1262–1349) – James I (Jaume I) of Aragón recaptured Mallorca from the Muslims in 1229. Thirty years later James united Mallorca-Baleares, Roussillon and Montpellier in a kingdom which he presented to his son,

View from the Mirador des Colomer, La Costa Rocosa

© Bildagentur/Tips/Photoshot

James II. He and his successor, Sancho, founded new Catalan towns. Pedro IV seized the archipelago in 1343 to reunite it with Aragón. A merchant navy was established which brought prosperity, and a school of cartography rapidly became famous.

The Mallorcan Primitives (14C–15C) – Gothic Mallorcan painting, characterised by a gentleness of expression, was open to external influences: the so-called **Master of Privileges** (Maestro de los Privilegios) showed a Sienese preference for miniaturisation and warm colours; later, **Joan Daurer** and the **Maestro de Obispo Galiana** were inspired by Catalan painting.

Artists of the 15C included **Gabriel Moger**, **Miguel de Alcanyis** and **Martí Torner**, who had studied in Valencia. The **Maestro de Predelas** is distinguishable by his attention to detail, **Rafael Moger** by his realism. **Pedro (Pere) Nisart** and **Alonso de Sedano** introduced the Flemish style (see Museo de Mallorca).

Famous Mallorcans and visitors – **Ramón Llull** (1232–1315) personifies the cosmopolitan 13C outlook of Mallorca. He learned languages and studied philosophy, theology and alchemy, and was beatified. **Fray Junípero Serra** (1713–84) founded missions in California. He was beatified in 1988.

Among the foreign artists to visit in the 19C were **Frédéric Chopin** and **George Sand**. **Robert Graves** (1895–1985), the English poet and author, lived here from 1929. The Austrian archduke **Ludwig Salvator** (1847–1915) compiled the most detailed study of the archipelago. He was patron to the French speleologist E A Martel.

ADDRESSES

🛏 STAY

🛏 **Hostal Ritzi** – Apuntadors 6, Palma. ℘971 71 46 10. www.hostalritzi.com. 17 rooms. This guesthouse offers small, simple rooms and a warm welcome.

🛏🛏 **Hotel Born** – Sant Jaume 3, Palma. ℘971 71 29 42. www.hotelborn.com. 25 rooms. This hotel occupies a former 16C

palace with a delightful Ibizan-style patio. The rooms are quiet with tasteful decor.

🛏🛏 **Ca Sa Padrina** – Teresa 3, Palma. ℘971 42 53 00. www.hotelcasapadrina.com. 6 rooms. This 19C mansion has been transformed into a comfortable hotel where furniture and decor evoke the era of the building.

🛏🛏🛏 **Santa Clara Urban Hotel & Spa** – Sant Alonso 16, Palma. ℘971 72 92 31. www.santaclarahotel.es. 20 rooms. This nobleman's townhouse has been converted to a boutique hotel and spa with stylish rooms. The rooftop terrace has a superb view.

🛏🛏🛏 **Hotel San Lorenzo** – San Lorenzo 14, Palma. ℘971 72 82 00. www.hotelsanlorenzo.com. 9 rooms. 🖵€13. An attractive 17C stately mansion with an inviting atmosphere. Beautifully decorated rooms are complemented by the swimming pool and garden.

🍴 EAT

🍴 **Bar Boschi** – Pl. del Rei Joan Carles I, 6, Palma. ℘971 72 11 31. One of the most famous bars in Palma, the Boschi has existed since 1936. It offers a wide range of tapas, a lively atmosphere and a terrace overlooking the Passeig del Born.

🍴 **Cafe Es Pes de Sa Palla** –Pl. of Pes Her Palla, Palma. ℘971 72 25 05. Managed by a local association for people with learning difficulties, this modern café is outside the touristy old city. Mediterranean cuisine at moderate prices served on a very nice terrace overlooking the square. The perfect lunch spot.

🍴🍴 **S'Eixerit** – Vicari Joaquím Fuster, Palma. ℘971 27 37 81. http://seixerit.es/. Facing the sea and with a lush indoor garden, this restaurant offers a variety of rice dishes and excellent grilled fish.

🍴🍴 **El Xop Blanc** – Av Joan Miró, 117,Palma. ℘971 91 91 57. This arrosseria near the Castell de Bellver offers no fewer than 23 different rice dishes from paella valenciana to arros negro with bogavante (black rice with lobster).

🍴🍴🍴 **La Bodeguilla** – Sant Jaume 1, Palma. ℘971 71 82 74. www.la-bodeguilla. com. Closed a week in Jul, Sun. A restaurant spread over two floors with an adjoining wine shop. Large barrels are used as dining tables to enjoy dinner or tapas.

🍴🍴 **Forn de San Joan** – S. Joan 4, Palma. ℘971 71 16 15. www.forndesantjoan.com. Stylish, multi-tasking place serving tapas, cocktails, contemporary Mediterranean cuisine and a good-value menu del día.

Palma de Mallorca★★

Palma spreads along a wide bay. Residential quarters with hotels stretch on either side of the historic centre, and along avinguda Gabriel Roca, shaded by palms. The old harbour, bordered by passeig Sagrera, serves passenger and merchant ships; the new harbour at the southern tip of El Terreno accommodates the largest liners. Bahía de Palma – the bay, protected from north and west winds by the highest peak on Mallorca – Puig Major – has a mild climate all year. To the west, hotels stand along the indented Bendinat coastline where there is little sand, except at **Palmanova** and **Magaluf**. The coast to the east is less sheltered, but has mile upon mile of fine sand with a series of resorts – **Can Pastilla, Ses Meravelles** and **S'Arenal**.

The "Ciutat de Mallorca"

Palma was known by this name after its liberation on 31 December 1229. Trade links were forged with the mainland, Africa and northern Europe; Jews and Genoese established themselves. James II (Jaume II) and his successors endowed the city with beautiful Gothic buildings. Aragonese expansion to Naples and Sicily enabled Palma to extend her commerce.

Palma's old mansions

In the 15C and 16C, the great families of Palma favoured the Italian style. They built elegant residences with stone façades, relieved by windows with Renaissance decoration. In the 18C a characteristic Mallorcan *casa* (house) appeared, with an inner court of massive marble columns, wide shallow arches and a high and graceful loggia.

Modern Palma

Palma is home to a large proportion of the population of the island and is one of the most popular cities in Spain to visit.

▶ **Population:** 401 270.
⊙ **Michelin Map:** pp438–9.
▮ **Info:** Pg. del Born 27 and Pl. Espanya, s/n. ☎902 10 23 65, Airport Office: ☎971 78 95 56. www.palmademallorca.es. ▭Estació Intermodal (Palma to Sa Pobla). ☎971 75 22 45.
◐ **Location:** Palma is located on the southwest coast of of the island of Mallorca.
▲▲ **Kids:** The Spanish Village (Poble Espanyol).
◕ **Timing:** Allow a good half day to see the main sites of the city.

Tourists congregate in and around **El Terreno** – especially in plaza Gomila – and **Cala Major** quarters in the west of town. The native heart of the city remains the **passeig des Born**. Shops sell pearls, glassware and leather in the old town east of El Born, in pedestrian streets around Plaça Major and in avinguda Jaume III.

BARRIO DE LA CATEDRAL★ (HISTORIC CENTRE)
Catedral★★
Pl. Almoina. ⊙Open Apr–May and Oct Mon–Fri 10am–5.15pm, Sat 10am–2.15pm; Jun–Sept Mon–Fri 10am–6.15pm, Sat 10am–2.15pm; rest of the year Mon–Fri 10am–3.15pm, Sat 10am–2.15pm. ⊚€4. ☎902 02 24 55. www.catedraldemallorca.info.

The bold yet elegant Cathedral, its buttresses surmounted by pinnacles, rises above the sea. The Santanyí limestone of its walls changes colour according to the time of day: ochre, golden or pink. Begun in the early 14C, it is one of the great late-Gothic constructions.

The west face was rebuilt in neo-Gothic style in the 19C after an earthquake; its 16C Renaissance portal remains intact. The south door, the **Portada del Mirador** (Viewpoint Doorway), overlooks the sea, the delicate Gothic decoration

Catedral viewed from the port

© Michel Gotin/hemis.fr

dating from the 15C. Statues of St Peter and St Paul on either side prove that Sagrera, architect of the Llotja (Exchange), was a talented sculptor.

The **interior** is large and light, measuring 121m x 55m (397ft x 180ft) and 44m/144ft to the top of the vaulting. Slender octagonal pillars divide the nave from the aisles.

The Capilla Mayor or Real (Royal Chapel) contains an enormous wrought-iron baldaquin by Gaudí (1912) with Renaissance choir stalls on either side. Tombs of the kings of Mallorca, James II and Jaume III, lie in the Capilla de la Trinidad (Trinity Chapel).

Museo de la Seu

Almoina house, next to the cathedral bell tower. ○*Open same hours as cathedral.* ℘*902 02 24 45. www.catedraldemallorca.info.*

In the Gothic chapter house is the Santa Eulàlia altarpiece by the Maestro de los Privilegios (1335). In the oval Baroque chapter house are reliquaries including one of the True Cross.

L'Almudaina

Palau Reial. ○*Open Apr–Sept Mon–Fri 10am–5.45pm, Sat and public holidays 10am–1.15pm; Oct–Mar Mon–Fri 10am–1.15pm, 4–5.45pm, Sat and public holidays 10am–1.15pm.* ∞€*3.20.* ℘*971 71 91 45.*

This fortress of the Córdoba caliphate was converted in the 14C and 15C into a royal palace. Today, as a residence of the King of Spain, several rooms have been restored and furnished with Flemish tapestries and paintings. In the courtyard, note the carved eaves and the doorway of the Iglesia de Santa Ana (St Anne's Church), a rare Romanesque structure in the Balearics.

Ayuntamiento

Pl. Cort 1.
Carved wooden eaves overhang the 17C façade of the town hall.

Iglesia de Santa Eulàlia

Pl. Santa Eulàlia 2. ○*Open Mon–Sat 9am–10.30am, 5–8pm.* ∞*No charge.* ℘*971 71 46 25.*

13C–15C. The tall nave is unusually bare for a Gothic church. In the first chapel off the south aisle is a 15C altarpiece. Between the churches of Santa Eulàlia and Sant Francesc, at no. 2 Carrer Savellà, is the 18C **Can Vivot**, its beautiful patio decorated with marble columns.

Iglesia de Sant Francesc

Pl. Sant Francesc 7. ○*Open Mon–Sat 9.30am–12.30pm, 3.30–6pm; Sun and public holidays 9am–12.30pm.* ∞€*1.50.* ℘*971 71 26 95.*

13C–14C. The church façade, rebuilt in the late 17C, has an immense Plateresque rose window and a Baroque portal with a beautifully carved tympanum by Francisco Herrera. The first apsidal chapel on the left contains the tomb of Ramón Llull.

The **cloisters**★ *(claustro)*, begun in 1286, are elegant. Apart from one side of trefoil openings, the architect divided the remaining galleries into multifoil bays on slender columns in varied diameters. The ceiling is painted.

Casa Marqués del Palmer
Sol 7.

In Carrer del Sol stands Casa Marqués del Palmer (Can Catlar), a mansion built in 1556 in stone now blackened by age. Renaissance decoration around the upper-floor windows mellows the austerity of Gothic walls.

The upper gallery, under deep eaves, is a replica of that on the Llotja.

The old Jewish quarter, **La Portella**, lies close against the town wall.

Museo de Mallorca
Portella 5. ○*Open Tue–Sat 10am–2pm, 5–7pm (8–9pm in Jun), Sun 10am–2pm.* ○*No charge.* ℘*971 71 75 40.*

The ground floor displays Muslim capitals, *artesonado* ceilings and ceramics. The **Fine Arts**★ section displays Mallorcan Gothic paintings. Works from the early 14C show clear Italian influence. Catalan works begin to appear after 1349 when Mallorca was annexed by Aragón: the *Crucifixion* by Ramón Destorrents, interesting for its composition and expression, was to influence other paintings.

Francesch Comes, one of the most prestigious of the early 15C painters, is represented here by his **St George**★ *(room 3)*, remarkable for the depth and detail of the landscape.

Baños Árabes
Can Serra 7. ○*Open daily Apr–Nov 9am–7pm; Dec–Mar 9am–6pm.* ○*€1.50.* ℘*971 72 15 49.*

The Moorish baths, the only relic from the caliphate, are beneath small circular windows and a classical dome on 12 columns with rudimentary capitals.

Museo Diocesano (Diocesan Museum)
Mirador 5. ○*Open daily 10am–2pm.* ○*€3.* ℘*971 72 38 60.*

Among the many Gothic works is Pere Nisart's outstanding **St George**★ (1568) which shows the saint slaying the dragon against a backdrop of 16C Palma.

TO THE WEST OF EL BORN
Museu d'Art Espanyol Contemporani – Colecció March★
Sant Miguel 11 . ○*Open Mon–Fri 10am–6.30 pm, Sat 10.30am–2pm.* ○*Closed 25 Dec, I Jan.* ○*No charge.* ℘*971 71 35 15. www.esbaluard.org.*

In this 18C mansion is a **permanent collection**★ of contemporary Spanish artists, from the Avant-Garde (Picasso, Miró, Dalí and J González) to recent figures.

Palau Solleric
Pg. des Born 27. ○*Open Tue–Sat 10am–2pm, 5–9pm, Sun and public holidays 10am–1.30pm.* ○*No charge.* ℘*971 72 20 92.*

This 18C palace overlooking the Born is completed by an elegant loggia; follow the narrow covered way to the most perfect **patio**★ in Palma, along with a double staircase with delicate ironwork.

Casa Berga
Pl. Mercat 12.

This 1712 mansion is the Palacio de Justicia (Law Courts). The façade is encumbered with stone balconies but the vast inner courtyard is typically Mallorcan.

Sa Llotja (La Lonja)★
Pas. Sagrera. ○*Open for exhibitions only: Tue–Sat 11am–2pm, 5–9pm, Sun 11am–1.30pm.* ℘*971 71 17 05.*

Guillermo Sagrera designed this 15C commodities exchange. The Llotja's military features are only for appearances, to distract the eye from the buttresses and austerity of the walls. The interior, with pointed arches on spirally fluted columns, is quite elegant.

Antiguo Consulado del Mar (Former Maritime Consulate)

Pas. Sagrera. ℘ *971 71 60 92.*
The early 17C building with a Renaissance balcony was the meeting-place of the Tribunal de Comercio Marítimo (Merchant Shipping Tribunal). Today it houses the regional administration.

Es Baluard Museu d'Art Modern i Contemporani de Palma (Museum of Modern and Contemporary Art of Palma)

Pl. Porta Santa Catalina 10. ⏰*Open Oct –mid-Jun Tue–Sun 10am–8pm; mid-Jun–Sept Tue–Sun 10am–10pm.* ⏰*Closed 1 Jan, 25 Dec.* €6, Fri by donation (minimum €0.10). ℘ *971 90 82 00. www.esbaluard.org.*
Occupying part of a medieval fortress this gallery occupies a stunning angular white concrete-and-glass building. The permanent collection includes: Mediterranean landscapes by the likes of Joaquín Sorolla, Santiago Rusiñol and Joan Miró; ceramics by Picasso; drawings by Chagall, Toulouse-Lautrec, and Barceló; a Miró gallery. High-quality temporary exhibitions feature international artists.

OUTSIDE THE CENTRE
Poble Español★ (Spanish Village)

Off the town plan, Pueblo Espanyol 55. ⏰*9pm–8pm onwards (closing times vary)* €8.90. ℘ *971 73 70 75. www.congress-palace-palma.com.*
The buildings are exact reproductions of famous houses or monuments: the Myrtle Court from the Alhambra in Granada, the Casa de El Greco in Toledo, etc. Craftsmen and folk troupes bring the village to life. Features of all major Roman sites in Spain have been incorporated in the monumental **Palacio de Congresos** (Convention Centre) facing the village.

Castillo de Bellver★

Camilo José Cela 17. ⏰*Open Apr–Sept Mon–Sat 8.30am–8.30pm, Sun and public holidays 10am–6.30pm; Oct–Mar Mon–Sat 8.30am–7pm, Sun and public holidays 10am–6.30pm.* €2.50. ℘ *971 73 06 57.*
The castle, built by the Mallorcan kings of the 14C as a summer residence, served as a prison until 1915.
The round buildings and circular perimeter and court are highly original; a freestanding keep dominates all. The Roman statues belong to the **Museo Municipal de Historia** (City History Museum; €2.50). Also displayed are finds from excavations in Pollença. View a **panorama★★** of the bay from the terrace.

Fundació Pilar i Joan Miró (Pilar and Joan Miró Foundation).

Joan de Saridakis 29. ⏰*Open mid-May –mid-Sept Tue–Sat 10am–7pm, Sun and public holidays 10am–3pm; mid-Sept–mid-May Tue–Sat 10am–6pm, Sun and public holidays 10am–3pm.* ⏰*Closed 1 Sept & 25 Dec.* €5. ℘ *971 70 14 20. http://miro.palmademallorca.es.*
The museum is the legacy of Joan Miró (1893–1983) and his wife. In the shadow of Son Abrines, Miró's residence from 1956, works donated by the artist are displayed in a part of the building called the Espacio Estrella.

EXCURSIONS
Palma Aquarium

Manuela De Los Herreros i Sora 21. ⏰*Open Daily 10am–6. 30pm (4.30pm Nov–end Mar) Ticket office closes 1.5hr before park.* €20.50; child €16. ℘ *971 26 42 75. www.palmaaquarium.com.*
Located near the airport, but in lovely grounds, this spectacular new aquarium is one of the finest in Europe. It comprises over 50 different viewing areas with 8 000 specimens from 700 species – from seahorses to sharks – plucked from the Mediterranean and more exotic waters.

Marineland

Calle Garcilaso de la Vega 9, Costa d'en Blanes. ⏰*Open Spring onwards (check website for details) daily 9.30am–6pm (ticket office closes 4.30pm).* €22.50; child €16.50. ℘ *971 67 51 25. www.marineland.es.*

This huge dolphinarium is rated among the best in Europe and also includes Californian Sea Lions. There are many other attractions on site including an exotic birds show, an aquarium with penguins and sharks, a tropical bird house and aviary, and a children's water park.

🚗 DRIVING TOUR

3 SOUTH SIDE OF THE TRAMUNTANA RANGE
75km/46.5 mi. Allow 3hr.

▶ *Leave Palma on the Ma 13 heading NE towards Alcúdia.*
🕭 *See map pp438-39.*

Inca
31km/19mi from Palma.
This sizeable market town prospered during the wine making boom, but was virtually abandoned during the phylloxera epidemic of the late 19C – hence today many *bodegas* (cellars), have been converted into cafés and restaurants. The present prosperity of Inca due to the leather industry in general and footwear in particular – and many famous Spanish brands are based here. As you stroll around seek out the Església de Santa Maria la Major and the Església de Sant Domingo – both Baroque buildings.

Coves de Campanet
15km/9mi along the Ma 13 and 4km/2mi along a secondary, signposted road.
🎫 *Guided tours (45min) daily Oct–end Mar 10am–5.30pm; Apr–end Sept 10am –6.30pm. ≈€9. ℘971 51 61 30. www.covesdecampanet.com.*
About half of these caves along the 1.3km/0.8mi-long path have ceased formation. In the waterlogged area, the most common features are straight and delicate stalactites.

▶ *The road crosses countryside bristling with windmills.*

Muro
The **ethnological section** of the **Museo de Mallorca** (*Major 15;* 🕭 *open Tue–Wed*

Fundació Pilar i Joan Miró

and Fri–Sat 10am–3pm, Thur 5–8pm, Sun 10am–2pm; ≈€2.40; ℘971 86 06 47), in a large 17C noble residence, displays exhibits on traditional furniture, dress, farming and many island trades.

▶ *Return to the Ma 13 and follow it to Alcúdia.*

Alcúdia
Alcúdia, encircled by 14C ramparts, guards the promontory which divides the bays of Pollença and Alcúdia. Two gates (**Puerta del Muelle** to the harbour, and the **Puerta de San Sebastián** across town) from early walls were incorporated into 14C ramparts. The streets in the shadow of the walls have a distinctive medieval air.

About 2km/1.2mi south is the site of Roman **Pollentia** founded in the 2C BC. Only the theatre ruins remain.

Museo Monográfico de Pollentia
Sant Jaume 30, Alcúdia. 🕭*Open Oct –end Jun Tue–Fri 10am–4pm, Sat–Sun 10am–1.30pm; rest of the year Tue–Sun 10am–3pm.* 🕭*Closed holidays. ≈€3. ℘971 54 70 04.*
A chapel in Alcúdia's old quarter houses statues, oil lamps, bronzes and jewellery from the ancient city of Pollentia.

Port d'Alcúdia
2km/1.2mi E.
The port of Alcúdia overlooks a vast bay built up with hotels. A beach stretches to the south as far as Can Picafort. The marsh of La Albufera is a nature reserve.

La Costa Rocosa★★★

The western rocky coast of Mallorca is one of the island's highlights. Here, mountains drop steeply into deep turquoise waters. This sharp contrast is tempered by the presence of abundant Mediterranean vegetation in some places and acres of orchards in others. The beaches are a delight, especially north of Pollensa and Alcúdia and east of the beautiful Cap de Formentor, known locally as the "meeting point of the winds".

- **Michelin Map:** 579 I-M 4-6.
- **Info:** Major 17, Alcúdia. 971 89 71 13. www.alcudiamallorca.com.
- **Location:** The Costa Rocosa stretches west of the island from Palma and Alcúdia, along the coast 157km/ 98mi (55km/34mi inland).
- **Kids:** Discovering the coast's many *calas* (coves) and beaches.
- **Timing:** At least two days to explore the coast.

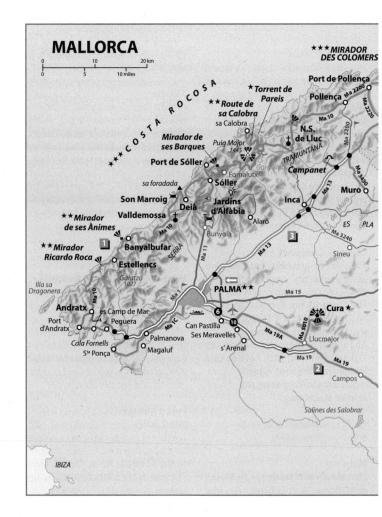

🚗 DRIVING TOUR

1 FROM PALMA TO ALCÚDIA
264km/165mi. Allow 2 days.

Mallorca's west coast is dominated by the limestone Serra de Tramuntana, rising to 1 445m/4 740ft at Puig Major. In the south, around Estellencs and Banyalbufar, slopes are terraced into *marjades* of olives, almonds and vines.

▷ *Leave Palma along passeig Sagrera.*

Port d'Andratx★
32km/18.6mi W of Palma.

The small fishing port is now also used by pleasure craft.
The C 710 from Andratx to Sóller is a very **scenic road**★★★, mostly along a cliff.

Mirador Ricardo Roca★★
18km/11.2mi NE of Port d'Andratx.
The **view** from this lookout drops sheer to tiny coves lapped by the limpid sea.

▷ *Follow the M 10.*

Estellencs
This pretty little village is surrounded by stone terraces covered with almond and apricot trees.

▷ *Continue along the M 10.*

Mirador de Ses Ànimes★★
The **panorama** from the watchtower stretches south from the Isla de Dragonera and north to Port de Sóller.

Cartuja de Valldemossa (Valldemossa Carthusian Monastery)
Pl. de la Cartuja, Valldemossa.
45km/28mi NE of Port d'Andratx.
🕐*Open daily from 10am (check the website for closing times)* €8. 𝄞971 61 21 06. www.museochopin.com.
The monastery was made famous by the visit George Sand and Chopin paid in the winter of 1838–39. Sand invoked the countryside in *A Winter in Majorca*. **Valldemossa** is one of the prettiest villages on Mallorca but do arrive either early or late to avoid the coach parties.

Son Marroig
Ctra de Valldemossa-Deià.
7km/4.3mi N of Valldemossa.
🕐*Open Mon–Sat from 10am (check ahead for closing times).*
€3. 𝄞971 63 91 58. www.sonmarroig.com.
The former residence of Archduke Ludwig Salvator includes an exhibition of archaeological

- Cap de Formentor ★
- Cabo de Formentor Road ★★
- Platja de Formentor
- Alcúdia ★
- Pollentia
- Port d'Alcúdia
- Parque Natural de s'Albufera
- Can Picafort
- Ma 3410
- Ma 12
- Cala Agulla
- Capdepera
- Cala Ratjada
- Artà   Ma 15
- Ses Païses
- Ma 4040
- ARTÀ ★★★
- San Llorenç des Cardassar
- Son Servera
- Petra
- Ma 320
- Ma 15
- 2
- Ma 4023
- Manacor   Ma 4020
- Hams   Porto Cristo
- DRACH ★★★
- LLEVANT
- Ma 14
- Felanitx
- Ma 4010
- Ma 4014
- LA COSTA DE LAS CALAS
- ★ Sant Salvador
- SERRA   DE
- Ma 14
- Ma 19
- Cala d'Or ★
- Parque Natural de Mondragó
- Santanyí
- ★ Cala Santanyí
- Cala Figuera ★
- Cap de ses Salines
- N

finds and Mallorcan furniture. A belvedere in the garden affords a view of the **Fora-dada**, a pierced rock rising out of the sea.

Deiá

4km/2.5mi E of Son Marroig.
Another typical Mallorcan village, enjoying a beautiful setting in the Tramuntana, Deiá has maintained its character despite the hordes of visitors it receives. Writer and poet Robert Graves lived here from 1929, on and off, until his death in 1985, and is buried in Deià Cemetery.

Sóller

11km/6.8mi NE of Deiá.
The delightful 19C houses of Sóller spread in a quiet valley.
The charming vintage narrow-gauge **Tren de Sóller** *(tickets payable on board; €10; ℘971 63 01 30; www.trendesoller. com)* has been running the 27km/17 miles from Palma direct to Sóller since 1913.

Port de Sóller

5km/3mi N of Sóller.
Port de Sóller, on an almost circular bay which shelters pleasure boats, is the major seaside resort of the west coast.

> *Take the C 711 from Sóller to Alfàbia.*

Jardines de Alfàbia

Open Apr–Oct Mon–Sat 9.30am–6.30pm; Nov–Mar Mon–Fri 9.30am–5.30pm, Sat 9.30am–1pm. €4.50. ℘971 61 31 23. www.jardinesde alfabia.com.
Only the *artesonado* ceiling over the porch remains from a 14C Moorish residence. Follow the path through the gardens to the **library** for a taste of a traditional seigniorial residence.

> *Return to Sóller. Take the narrow mountain road via the picturesque villages of Biniaraix and Fornalutx, then follow the C 710.*

Mirador de Ses Barques

From this viewpoint there is a **panorama** of Port de Sóller. The road heads through a long tunnel before following the upper valley of the Pareis.

> *After skirting the Gorg Blau reservoir, take the Sa Calobra road.*

Sa Calobra road★★★

The magnificently planned road plunges 900m/2 953ft in 14km/8.7mi through steep, jagged rocks.

Sa Calobra★

Near the village is the mouth of the **Pareis river**★, its clear water pouring over round white shingle.

> *Return to the C 710.*

About 1km/0.6mi north of the Sa Calobra fork, a small **mirador**★ *(lookout, alt 664m/2 178ft)* gives a good view over the cleft hollowed out by the Pareis.

Monasterio de Nuestra Señora de Lluc

Open daily 10am–1.30pm, 2.30–5pm. €4 (museum). ℘971 87 15 25. www.lluc.net.
The monastery dates from the 13C when a young shepherd found a statue of the Virgin. *La Moreneta*, the dark stone statue, is patron of Mallorca.

Port de Pollença

This large resort has a perfect **setting**★ in a sheltered bay between the Cabo Formentor headland to the north and Cabo del Pinar to the south, and provides a vast expanse of calm water for water sports.

Cabo de Formentor road★

The road commands spectacular views as it twists upward. The **Mirador des Colomer viewpoint**★★★ *(access along a stepped path)* overlooks great rock promontories. The **Platja de Formentor** is a sheltered beach. The grand Hotel Formentor was once famous for its casino and millionaire guests.
The road continues through a tunnel and a steep and arid landscape. **Cabo de Formentor**★, with its lighthouse, is the most northerly point of the island.

> *Return to Port de Pollença, then skirt the bay until you reach Alcúdia (see p437).*

La Costa de las Calas★★

The east coast of Mallorca is renowned for its string of *calas* – or coves and caves (*cuevas*). Formed through thousands of years of erosion and of varying sizes, they provided sheltered swimming spots and fascinating natural formations.

🚗 DRIVING TOUR

② EAST COAST COVES AND CAVES★★
From Artà to Palma
165km/102.5mi. Allow 1 day.
⚙ See map pp438–39.

Artà
The high rock site is crowned by the Iglesia de Sant Salvador and the ruins of an ancient fortress.

▷ *Continue along the C 715.*

Capdepera
Access to the fortress: by car, along narrow streets; on foot, up steps.
The remains of a 14C fortress give Capdepera an angular silhouette of crenellated walls and square towers.

Cala Rajada
3km/1.8mi NE of Capdepera.
Cala Rajada is a delightful fishing village and pleasure boat harbour.

▷ *Return to Capdepera and follow the signs to the Coves d'Artà.*

Coves d'Artà★★★
🕐*Daily Mar–Oct 10am–8pm; rest of the year 10am–6pm.* ⊛€10. ☏971 84 12 93. www.cuevasdearta.com.
Largely hollowed out by the sea, inside these caves are the Dantesque **Reina de las Columnas** (Queen of Columns), the **Sala del Infierno** (Chamber of Hell) and a fantastical **Sala de las Banderas** (Hall of Flags).

👁 **Michelin Map:** 579. O5-8 and pp438–39.
ℹ **Info:** Passeig de Manacor Cales de Mallorca, Manacor. ☏971 83 41 44.
👪 **Kids:** Cave exploring!

▷ *Return to the PM 404 and bear left. At Portocristo, take the Manacor road; turn shortly for the Coves dels Hams.*

Coves dels Hams
🐚*Guided tours (45min) Mar–Oct 10am–6pm; rest of the year 10am–5.30pm.* ⊛€16. ☏971 82 09 88. www.cuevas-hams.com.
As these caves meet the sea the water level in several pools rises and falls with the Mediterranean tide.

▷ *Return to Portocristo and bear right.*

Coves del Drach★★★
🐚*Guided tours (1hr) daily Apr–Oct 10am–5pm; rest of the year 10am–3.30pm.* ⊛€11.50. ☏971 82 07 53. www.cuevasdrach.com.
Four chambers succeed one another over a distance of 2km/1.2mi. The cave **roofs**, are amazing, glittering with countless sharply pointed icicles.

▷ *Continue along the road towards Santanyí then right onto the PM 401.*

Monasterio de Sant Salvador★
🕐*Open daily 8am–9pm.* ⊛*No charge.* ☏971 93 61 36.
The monastery, on a rise 500m/1 640ft above the plain (⚙*tight hairpin bends*), commands a wide **panorama**★★.
It was founded in the 14C. In the church, behind the Baroque high altar, is a venerated **Virgin and Child**, in the south chapels are three **Nativities** set in dioramas and a multicoloured 14C stone **altarpiece** carved with the Passion.

▷ *Return to the Santanyí road.*

Secondary roads lead to resorts built up in the creeks along the coast, namely

Cala d'Or★, **Cala Figuera★**, which is still a delightful little fishing village, and **Cala Santanyí★**.

▷ *From Santanyí follow the C 717 towards Palma. In Llucmajor, bear right onto the PM 501.*

Santuario de Cura★
◷ *Open daily 10am–1pm, 3.30–6pm.*
℘971 12 02 60. www.santuariode cura.com.

The road climbs to the monastery. The buildings have been restored and modernised by the Franciscans and include the 17C **church**, Sala de Gramática (Grammar Room) and a small **museum**. From the terrace on the west side there is a **panorama★★** of Palma, the bay, the Puig Major and, in the northeast, Cabo de Formentor headland.

▷ *Return to Llucmajor and continue W along the C 717 to Palma.*

Menorca★★

Menorca, with an area of 669sq km/258sq mi, has managed to avoid the rampant development that has blighted its neighbours, and its coastline is dotted with sandy coves of crystal-clear water, excellent for diving. The island is also famous for its prehistoric monuments.

▶ **Population:** 92 434
◔ **Michelin Map:** 579.
▯ **Info:** Mahón: Plaça Colon 5. Cuitadella: Plaça Catedrál 5. ℘902 92 90 15. www.menorca.es.
▷ **Location:** Menorca is the second-largest of the Balearic Islands and the furthest from the mainland.

LANDSCAPE AND TRADITION

Menorca's highest point, Monte Toro, 358m/1 175ft, is in the north of the island, known as the Tramuntana, where there are outcrops of dark slate rock. Along the coast, these ancient, eroded cliffs have been cut into a saw's edge of *rías* (inlets) and deep coves. South of the Maó-Ciutadella line, the Migjorn limestone platform forms cliffs along the coast.

Vegetation is typically Mediterranean: pinewoods, gnarled and twisted wild olives, heather and aromatic herbs such as rosemary, camomile and thyme. Dry-stone walls divide fields, punctuated by gates of twisted olive branches.

Megalithic monuments – In the second millennium BC, the cavernous nature of the Menorcan countryside offered shelter for both the living and the dead; some of the caves, such as **Calascoves**, are even decorated.

At the same time, **talayots** began to appear (over 200 have been identified), great cones of stones, possibly covering a funeral chamber and form-ing the base for a wooden house. Other monuments of the civilisation include **taulas**, consisting of two huge stone blocks placed one on top of the other in the shape of a T, possibly serving as altars, and **navetas**, which take the form of upturned boats and contain funeral chambers.

⊛ *A locally available map shows the monument sites: Mapa Arqueológico de Menorca, by J Mascaró Pasarius.*

Architecture – The walls and even the roofs of Menorcan houses are brightly whitewashed; low dividing walls have a white band along the top. Tiles are used for roofing, chimneys and guttering. Houses face south, their fronts charac-terised by wide, open bays. Northern walls, exposed to fierce *tramontana* winds, have small windows.

English influence on architecture is evi-dent. Many houses in towns have sash windows and some mansions are in the Palladian style of 18C Britain.

The fields around Ciutadella are scattered with *barracas*, curious stone constructions with false ceilings, which served as shelters for shepherds.

A BIT OF HISTORY

Prehistoric peoples have left monuments throughout the island. Menorca was colonised by the Romans, conquered by Vandals in 427, and came under Muslim control in 903. In the 13C, Alfonso III of Aragón invaded, made Ciutadella capital and encouraged settlers from Catalunya and Aragón.

In the 16C, Barbary pirates left Maó and Ciutadella in virtual ruin.

In 1713, Menorca, which had begun to prosper through trade in the late 17C, was ceded to the English crown by the Treaty of Utrecht. Maó became England's stronghold in the Mediterranean. Apart from a short period of French rule from 1756 to 1763, the island remained throughout the 18C under the British. The first road, between Maó and Ciutadella, still exists (north of the C 721), known as camino Kane for a British governor. At the beginning of the 19C, Menorca was restored to Spain.

The island's economy has gradually been orientated towards the leather industry and jewellery-making while cattle raising provides the island with its well-known cheeses.

SIGHTS
CIUTADELLA/CIUDADELA★

In the Middle Ages, Ciutadella, citadel and capital of Menorca, was ringed with walls. The fortified aspect of the city becomes evident when viewed from the harbour. Sacked by Turkish pirates in the 16C, Ciutadella was partly rebuilt in the late 17C and 18C.

The **Midsummer's Day festivities**, or **Fiestas de San Juan** *(24 Jun)*, are celebrated in traditional fashion. On the preceding Sunday, a man representing John the Baptist, dressed in skins and carrying a lamb, runs to the sound of *fabiols* (flutes) and *tambourins*. On 24 and 25 June, over 100 horsemen take part in jousting tournaments and processions.

Barrio Antiguo (Old Quarter)

Plaza del Born, the ex-parade ground, is flanked by the eclectic 19C **ayuntamiento** (town hall) and the early 19C **Palacio de Torre-Saura**, a palace with side loggias. An obelisk commemorates resistance against the Turks in the 16C.

Castell de Sant Nicolau

Pl of Almirall Farragut. ◷*Summer 10am–1pm, 5–9pm. Winter: check at Tourist Office.* ⊙*No charge.*

This castle was built in the late 17C, before the British occupation, to defend the port. Its entrance is adorned with the emblem of the Crown of Aragón and the ground floor was used for storing food, weapons and ammunition.

A spiral staircase near the front door provides access to the upper floor and the top of the tower.

Catedral

Plaça de la Catedral. ◷*Open Mon–Sat 10.30am–1.30pm, 4–7pm.* ℘*971 38 26 93.* ⊙*€2.*

The late-14C fortified church retains a minaret from Islamic days. The single aisle is ogival and the apse pentagonal. View the Baroque doorway from calle del Rosario. At the end of the street, turn left into calle del Santísimo. **Palacio Saura** has a Baroque façade with a cornice. **Palacio Martorell** across the street is more sober.

Take calle del Obispo Vila, passing the Claustro de Socorro (Socorro Cloisters) and the Iglesia de Santo Cristo (Church of the Holy Christ) to the main street which leads to **plaza de España** and the arcaded **carrer de Ses Voltes**.

Puerto (Harbour)

The ramp approach to the harbour, which serves pleasure craft, is along a former counterscarp. Quayside cafés and restaurants bustle with life. The esplanade, plaça de Sant Joan, the centre for Midsummer's Day festivities, is bordered by boat shelters hollowed out of rock. The area comes alive at night.

A British Town

Menorca was ceded to Britain by the Treaty of Utrecht in 1713 and the British subsequently made Maó their Mediterranean economic base for the next 70 years.

The city is built on a cliff at the edge of a deep harbour. This combination facilitated the protection of both harbour and city for centuries from the greed of European powers. Situated at the crossroads of maritime routes between Southern Europe and North Africa, Menorca held a strategic position. Maó can be conveniently discovered by boat. Several companies offer a tour of the harbour with possible stops at various points along the way. Departures generally leave between 10am and 3.30pm and head south towards the Costa de Ses Voltes.

EXCURSIONS
Pedreres de s'Hostal

◗ *1km/0.8mi from Ciutadella on the Me 1. Camí Vell 1* ◷*Open Jul–Aug 9.30am–2.30pm, 4.30pm–sunset, Sun 9.30am–2.30pm; rest of the year 9:30am–sunset, Sun 9.30am–2.30pm.* ◉*€24.* ✆*971 48 15 78, www.lithica.es.*

This surprising venue is situated in sandstone quarries that ceased to operate in 1994, after over 200 years of loyal service. Through the action of a local association, it is now open to visitors. Plants and greenery have been placed between the labyrinthine formations of the mined sandstone, lending the quarries the appearance of land art.

Nau or Naveta des Tudons

◗ *5km/3mi E of Ciutadella.*

This funerary monument, shaped like an upturned ship, is notable for the vast stones in the walls and lining the floor.

Cala Santandria

◗ *3km/1.8mi S of Citadella.*

This is a small sheltered beach in a creek, a local resort popular with locals.

Arenal de Son Saura, Cala en Turqueta, Cala Macarella

◗ *SE of Ciutadella. Son Saura: 12km/7.4mi via Torre Saura; Turqueta: 12km/7.4mi via Sant Joanet; Macarella: 14km/8.7mi via Sant Joan Gran.*

The three beaches are set in small, beautifully unspoilt creeks fringed by pines.

Maó/Mahón★★

◗ *45km/28mi E of Ciutadella along Me 1.* Maó's **site**★ is most striking when approached from the sea, atop a cliff in the curve of a deep, 5km/3mi-long natural harbour. Maó was endowed with Palladian-style mansions during English occupation. On the north side of the harbour is the Finca de San Antonio – the Golden Farm – where Admiral Nelson put the finishing touches to his book, *Sketches of My Life* (October 1799). Maó gave its name to mayonnaise.

Most of Maó's shops are between **plaza del Ejército**, a large, lively square lined with cafés and restaurants, and the quieter **plaza de España** with its two churches: **Santa María**, with a beautiful Baroque organ, and **Carmen**, the Carmelite church, whose cloisters now hold the municipal market.

Museo de Menorca

Av. de Guardia. ◷*Open Tue–Sun 10am–2pm, 6–8pm.* ◷*Closed public holidays.* ◉*€2.40.* ✆*971 35 09 55.*

The museum is a former Franciscan monastery. Rooms around a sober 18C cloister display prehistoric and other objects relating to Menorcan history. A room is dedicated to *talayot* culture.

Puerto (Harbour)

Walk down the steep ramp from carrer de Ses Voltes, cut by a majestic flight of steps, and follow the quay to the north side. From here is the classic view of the town lining the top of the cliff.

La Rada★ (Roadstead)

On the south side are coves and villages, among them Cala Figuera with its fishing harbour and restaurants. **Es Castell** was an English garrison named Georgetown. It has a grid plan, with a parade ground at its centre. The islands in the harbour include Lazareto and Cuarentena, which was a quarantine hospital for sailors. A road follows the northern shore to the lighthouse affording views of Maó.

Talayot de Trepucó

▷ *1km/0.6mi S of Maó.*

This megalithic site is famous for its 4.80m/16ft *taula.*

Sant Lluís

▷ *4km/2.5mi S.*

This town with narrow streets was founded by the French. Small resorts have grown up nearby at **Alcaufar** and **Binibèquer**, a new village made to look like a fishing hamlet.

Es Grau

▷ *8km/5mi N.*

Beside the attractive white village with its long beach is a vast lagoon, **Albufera de es Grau,** 2km/1.2mi long and 400m/437yd wide. It is an ideal spot to watch migrant birds (rails, ducks and herons).

Cala en Porter

▷ *12km/7.4mi W.*

Promontories protect a narrow estuary, lined by a sandy beach. Houses perch upon the left cliff. Ancient troglodyte dwellings, the **Coves d'en Xoroi** (*www.covadenxoroi.com*), overlook the sea.

Mercadal

▷ *19km/11.8mi NW of Cala en Porter.*

Mercadal, a village of brilliantly whitewashed houses halfway between Maó and Ciutadella, is where roads to the coast meet on the north–south axis.

Monte Toro

▷ *3.5km/2mi along a narrow road.*

On a clear day, the **view**★★ from the church-crowned summit (358m/1 175ft) is of the entire island.

Fornells

▷ *8.5km/5.3mi N on the C 723.*

Fornells, a fishing village of whitewashed houses with green shutters,

Puerto, Maó
©Turespaña

lies at the mouth of a deep inlet, surrounded on all sides by bare moorland. The village lives off crayfish. The local speciality, crayfish soup or *caldereta*, is a delight.

Cap de Cavalleria

▷ *12km/7.4mi N along the PM 722.*

The drive to the cape, northernmost point on the island, is through windswept moorland, battered by the *tramontana*, with large, elegant country houses, like that at Finca Santa Teresa. The **view** from the lighthouse is of a rocky, indented coast, more Atlantic than Mediterranean.

Cala (Santa) Galdana

▷ *16km/10mi SW via Ferreries.*

This cove set in a limpid bay flanked by tall cliffs has been marred by large hotels.

🚶 It is possible to walk to the cove from **the Algendar ravine** (*on leaving Ferreries, take the track left towards Ciutadella; 3hr there and back*).

Within walking distance of Cala Galdana are the idyllic Caribbean-like **white-sand coves** of Cala Mitjana, Cala Turqueta, Cala Macarella and Cala Trébaluger. Beware that they get very busy in peak season. Small boats also service these beaches, running from Cala Galdana and Cala n'Bosch.

Ibiza★

Ibiza, with an area of 572sq km/221sq mi, is renowned for nightlife and visiting hedonists, yet parts of the island remain a natural paradise. There are stunning beaches, hidden coves and delightful villages with narrow streets lined by whitewashed houses, all of which forge a personality that is unique in the Balearics.

LANDSCAPE AND TRADITION

Ibiza, the **Isla Blanca** (White Island), 72.4km/45mi southwest of Mallorca, is 41km/25mi in length.

Dazzling whitewashed walls, flat roof terraces, tortuous alleys and an atmosphere similar to that of a Greek island give Ibiza its unique character. It is mountainous, with little space for cultivation. Among pines and junipers on the hillsides stand the cube-shaped houses of many small villages.

The shore appears wild and indented; promontories are marked by rocks out to sea, some as high as the limestone needle known as **Vedrá**★ (almost 400m/ 1 300ft).

Traditional architecture – The typical Ibizan cottage, or **casament**, now largely found inland, is made up of several white cubes with few windows. Arcaded porches provide shade and a sheltered area for storing crops.

Country churches are equally plain with gleaming white exteriors and dark interiors. Façades are square, surmounted by narrow bell gables, pierced by wide porches. Fortified churches once provided shelter from pirates in Sant Carles, Sant Joan, Sant Jordi and Sant Miquel.

Folklore and traditional costume – Ibiza's uncomplicated folklore lives on. Women still wear the traditional long gathered skirt and dark shawl. At festivals the costume is brightened with fine gold filigree necklaces or **emprendades**. Dances are performed to the accompaniment of flute, tambourine and castanets.

▶ **Population:** 129 562
⏱ **Michelin Map:** 579.
▯ **Info:** Eivissa: Passeig Vara de Rey 1. ℘971 30 17 40. www.illesbalears.es/esp/ ibiza/home.jsp.
◯ **Location:** Ibiza is the closest island to the Spanish mainland (83km/52mi).

A BIT OF HISTORY

In the 10C BC, Phoenicians made the island a staging-post for ships loaded with Spanish ores; in the 7C BC, Carthage founded a colony; under the Romans the capital grew in size and prosperity.

SIGHTS
EIVISSA★

Eivissa's colourful beauty and impressive **site**★★ are best appreciated from the sea; alternatively, take the **Talamanca** road and look back (3km/1.8mi NE). The town, built on a hill, consists of an old quarter ringed by walls, the lively Marina district near the harbour, and, further out, residential and shopping areas. Along the shore are large hotels.

UPPER TOWN★ (DALT VILA)
Allow 1hr30min.
The Dalt Vila, enclosed by the 16C walls built under Emperor Charles V, is the heart of the old city and retains a rustic, medieval character. There remain many noble houses worth looking at particularly for their vast patios and Gothic windows.

Enter the quarter through the **Porta de Taules**, a gateway surmounted by Philip II's crest. Continue by car up a steep slope to the Cathedral square or stroll the quiet meandering streets with their shops and art galleries.

Catedral
Pl. de la Catedral. ◯*Open May–Sept Mon–Sat 9.30am–1.30pm, 5–8pm; Oct–Apr Mon–Sat 9.30am–1.30pm, 4–7pm.* ◉*No charge.* ℘*971 39 92 32.*
The Cathedral's massive 13C belfry, which resembles a keep but for its two storeys of Gothic bays, dominates the

town. The nave was rebuilt in the 17C. An ancient bastion behind the east end affords a **panoramic view**★.

Museo Arqueológico de Ibiza y Formentera★

Pl. de la Catedral 3. ⏰*Open Apr–Sept Tue–Sat 10am–2pm, 6–8pm, Sun 10am–2pm; Oct–Mar Tue–Sat 9am–3pm, Sun 10am–2pm.* ⏰*Closed public holidays.* €2.40. ☎971 30 12 31. *www.aamaef.org.*

The most impressive exhibits are its Punic art, which developed around the Mediterranean from the 7C BC to the AD 3C. Particularly impressive are the ex-votos discovered on Ibiza and Formentera, predominantly from excavations at Illa Plana and the Es Cuiram cave. The cave is believed to have been a temple to the goddess **Tanit**, who was venerated from the 5C BC to the 2C BC. Also worthy of note are the polychrome moulded glass and Punic, Roman and Moorish ceramics.

Museo Puget

Carrer Sant Ciriac 18. ⏰*May–Sept Tue–Fri 10am–1.30pm, 5–8pm Sat–Sun 10am–1.30pm; Oct–Apr Tue–Fri 10am–1.30pm, 4–8pm, Sat–Sun 10am–1.30pm* No charge. ☎971 39 21 37.

Situated in Can Comasema, a nobleman's house, this museum exhibits 130 watercolours, drawings and paintings by **Narcís Puget Viñas** (1874–1960) and his son, Narcís Puget Riquer (1916–83). They are an interesting testimony to the customs and habits of Ibizans in the last century and the landscapes of the island.

LOWER TOWN
Necrópolis Puig des Molins★

Vía Romana 31. ⏰*Open Mar–Oct Tue–Sat 10am–2pm, 5–8pm, Sun 10am–2pm; Oct–Mar Tue–Sat 9am–3pm, Sun 10am–2pm.* ⏰*Closed public holidays.* No charge. ☎971 30 17 71.

The Puig des Molins hillside necropolis was a burial ground for the Phoenicians from the 7C BC and for the Romans until the AD 1C. There is a model of the site; some of the hypogea, or funerary chambers, of which over 3 000 have been discovered, may be visited. The objects displayed were found in the tombs and include everyday and ritual articles.

The outstanding, partly coloured, 5C BC **bust of the goddess Tanit**★, a Punic version of the Phoenician Astarte, exemplifies Greek beauty. A second bust is more Carthaginian.

La Marina

The Marina district near the market and harbour, with its restaurants, bars and shops, stands in lively contrast to the quieter Dalt Vila.

Sa Penya★

The former fishermen's quarter, now the centre of Ibiza's nightlife, is built on a narrow rock promontory at the harbour mouth. White cubic houses overlap in picturesque chaos, completely blocking streets forcing bypasses via steps cut out of the rock.

SANT ANTONI DE PORTMANY/ SAN ANTONIO ABA

Sant Antoni with its vast, curved bay has been extensively developed. The old quarter, hidden behind modern apartment blocks, centres on a fortified 14C church rebuilt in the 16C. There is a large pleasure boat harbour. Several coves and creeks are within easy reach.

EXCURSIONS
Cala Gració
▶ *2km/1.2mi N.*
A lovely, accessible, sheltered creek.

Cala Salada
▶ *5km/3mi N.*
The road descends through pines to a sheltered beach in a cove.

Port des Torrent & Cala Bassa
▶ *5km/3mi SW.*
Port des Torrent is all rocks; Cala Bassa a long, pine-fringed beach. Rocks are smooth and separate and just above or just below the water line, providing perfect underwater swimming conditions.

Cala Vedella

▶ *15km/9.3mi S.*

A road skirts the shoreline through pine trees between the beaches of Cala Tarida (rather built-up), Es Molí (unspoiled) and Cala Vedella in its enclosed creek. You can return to Sant Antoni along a mountain road cut into the cliffs as far as Sant Josep.

SANTA EULÀRIA DES RIU/ SANTA EULÀLIA DEL RÍO

Santa Eulària des Riu, in a fertile plain watered by Ibiza's only river, is a large seaside resort. Nearby beaches such as **Es Canar** have also been developed.

Puig de Missa★

▶ *Bear right off the Eivissa/Ibiza road 50m/55yd after the petrol station (on the left).*

This minute, fortified town crowning the hilltop provides a remarkable overview of the island's traditional peasant architecture; in times of danger, the church (16C) served as a refuge.

Portinatx★

▶ *27km/17mi N on the PM 810, PM 811 and C 733.*

The road passes through **Sant Carles**, which has a fine church and is a departure point for quiet local beaches. It descends to the vast **Sant Vicent** creek *(cala)* with its sandy beach and opposite, the Isla de Togomago, then crosses a landscape covered in pines. The last section threads between holm oaks and almond trees looking down on **Cala Xarraca**.

Creeks sheltered by cliffs and pine-fringed beaches make **Cala de Portinatx** one of the island's most attractive areas.

ADDRESSES

🛏 STAY

🛏🛏 **Hostal La Marina** – *Barcelona 7.* 🕻*971 31 01 72. www.hostal-lamarina.com. 30 rooms.* 🛏*€2.50. Restaurant*🛏🛏🛏*. A friendly and colourful hostel established in the 19C and centrally located by the*

port. The rooms have been recently renovated with the best have sea views. The restaurant has a neo-rustic decor with a very agreeable terrace.

🛏🛏🛏 **Hotel Montesol** – *Pg. Vara de Rei 2.* 🕻*971 31 01 61. www.hotelmontesol.com. 55 rooms.* 🛏*€5.* Nothing in the town can compare with this large, mustard-coloured building, with its comfortable rooms overlooking the streets of the old quarter. Make sure you enjoy a drink on the terrace café, which continues to be one of Ibiza's famous locations.

🛏🛏🛏🛏 **La Colina** – *Sangha Colina, ctra Ibiza a Santa Eulària. 5.5km/3.5mi SW of Santa Eulària des Ríu.* 🕻*971 33 27 67. www.lacolina-ibiza.com. Closed Nov–Jan. 13 rooms.* 🛏. This traditional, Ibizan-style country house stands on the side of a small hill. Now a quiet, family-run hotel, it is increasingly popular with foreign visitors. Pleasant outdoor areas, including a swimming pool.

🛏🛏🛏🛏 **Hotel Rural Es Cucons** – *Santa Agnès de Corona. 1km/0.6mi along Corona, Camí des Plà de Corona.* 🕻*971 80 55 01. www.escucons.com. 14 rooms. Restaurant*🛏🛏🛏*. Closed Nov–Mar.* The family who own this hotel have succeeded in converting a former Ibizan farm into an architectural jewel which has been magnificently decorated in keeping with its origins. A superb combination of luxury and simplicity at the heart of an expansive valley.

ℙ/EAT

Typical Ibizan desserts include *flaó*, a tart made of sheep or goat's cheese with mint and (sometimes) anise and *greixonera*, a sort of pudding made from leftover *ensaimadas* (a regional pastry) to which milk, eggs and cinnamon are added.

🍽 **Croissant Show** – *Plaza de la Constitució 2, Eivissa.* 🕻*971 31 76 65.* An ideal place to enjoy coffee and good croissants and pastries (the owner is French) before embarking on the climb to the old city.

🍽 **Peixet** – *Plaza de Sa Tertúlia4, Eivissa.* 🕻*971 31 10 25.* This bar with designer decor is located in the Sa Penya district. *Greixonera* is a speciality.

🍽 **El Rincón de Pepe** – *Sant Vincent 53, Closed Wed.* 🕻*971 31 96 68.* Authentic tapas bar on a busy street in the centre of town.

Formentera

Formentera, the Roman Island of Wheat (from *frumentum*), smallest in the archipelago (area 84sq km/32sq mi), is ideal for those in search of peace and quiet, impressive scenery and beautiful beaches lapped by crystal-clear water.

LANDSCAPE AND TRADITION

Formentera is two islets and a sandy isthmus, 14km/8.7mi long. The capital, Sant Francesc de Formentera, the passenger port, Cala Savina, the salt pans, Cabo de Barbaria and the dry open expanse where cereals, figs, almonds and a few vines grow, are on the western islet; the island's 192m/630ft mountain rises from the **Mola** promontory on the eastern islet.

Rock cliffs and sand dunes alternate along the shore. Access to the island is exclusively by sea, and the best way of exploring Formentera is by bicycle.

A BIT OF HISTORY

Formentera's inhabitants arrived comparatively recently, the island having been abandoned in the Middle Ages in the face of marauding Barbary pirates and only repopulated at the end of the 17C. Most of the present population consists of fishermen and farmers, shipping figs and fish to Ibiza and salt to Barcelona.

SIGHTS

The Beaches (Playas or Platjas)

White sandy beaches with clear water are the main attraction. Long beaches stretch along either side of the isthmus, the rocky Tramuntana to the north and the sheltered, sandy Migjorn to the south. Smaller beaches include Es Pujòls (the most developed), Illetas and Cala Saona.

▶ **Population:** 9 147
🕭 **Michelin Map:** 579.
🔲 **Info:** Sant Francesc: Port de Savina (Obras del Puerto building). ℘971 32 20 57. www.turismoformentera.com.
◐ **Location:** Formentera lies just 7km/4.3mi S of Ibiza.

Island of the Sargantana

The symbol of Formentera is the Sargantana – a kind of lizard that is found almost exclusively on the "Pine Islands" (Ibiza, Formentera their islets). Larger than their reptilian cousins on the peninsula, they eat insects and pollen. Divided into thirty sub-species, their skins are shaded in whites, blues and greens of varying intensity.

Cala Savina

Your landing point is in the main harbour: a few white houses stand between two big lagoons, salt marshes glisten in the distance on the left.

Sant Francesc (San Francisco Javier)

3km/1.8mi SE of Savina.
Chief town on the island. Its houses are clustered around the 18C church-fortress.

El Pilar de la Mola

14km/8.7mi SE of Sant Francesc.
The hamlet at the centre of the Mola promontory has this geometrically designed church which is similar to those on Ibiza, only smaller.

Far de la Mola

2km/1.2mi SE of Pilar de la Mola.
The lighthouse overlooks an impressive cliff. There is a monument to Jules Verne who mentioned this spot in *Off on a Comet* (1877).

PORTUGAL

EXTREMADURA

CÓRDOBA

HUELVA

Sierra de Aracena y Picos de Aroche

GRUTA DE LAS MARAVILLAS

Sierra Norte

Arecena

Minas de Río Tinto

Medina Azahara

Almodóvar del Río

CORDO

Itálica

Carmona

SEVILLA

La Palma del Condado

Huelva

Moguer

Paraje Natural de las Marismas del Odiel

Palos de la Frontera

Almonte

Osuna

Ayamonte

La Rábida

El Rocío

Estepa

Matalascañas

Costa de la Luz

PARQUE NACIONAL DE DONANA

Trabujen

Utrera

Desfiladero de los Gaitanes

El To

Sanlúcar de Barrameda

Jerez de la Frontera

Arcos de la F.

Zahara de la Sierra

Grazalema

MÁLAG

Ronda

Alc

La Cartuja

Ubrique

Cueva de la Pileta

OCÉANO ATLÁNTICO

El Puerto de Sta María

CÁDIZ

Medina-Sidonia

Puerto Banus

Mijas

San Fernando

MARBELLA

CÁDIZ

Los Alcornocales

Estepona

Vejer de la Frontera

COSTA

DE

Cabo de Trafalgar

Barbate

Los Caños de Meca

Baelo Claudia

Algeciras

Gibraltar

Tarifa

ESTRECHO DE GIBRALTAR

TANGER

Ceuta

AL MAGHRIB (MAROC)

TETOUAN

SEVILLA	★★★ Highly recommended
Baeza	★★ Recommended
Gibraltar	★ Interesting
Ubrique	Other sight described in this guide

Andalucía

40 km
20 miles

CASTILLA-LA-MANCHA

RÍO GUADIANA

Ciudad Real

N 430

N 401

A 43

CM 412

N 420

R. Azuer

Valdepeñas

CM 412

R. Jabalón

N 322

A 31

A 30

A 4

Río Guadalmena

CM 412

R. Segura

C 415

JAÉN

Sª de Cardeña

Sª de Andújar

Despeñaperros

A 317

Segura de la Sierra

PARQUE

Andújar

Linares

N 322

R. Guadalimar

C 330

NATURAL

N 420

A 4

A 32

Baeza

Úbeda

A 315

A 319

DE CAZORLA,

A 311

A 44

Cazorla

Río

A 315

SEGURA Y LAS VILLAS

Guadajoz

A 316

Jaén

Sierra Mágina

Guadalquivir

MURCIA

Priego de Córdoba

Alcalá la Real

Sierra Subbética

GRANADA

A 330

A 7

Lorca

R. Genil

N 432

432

R. Cubillas

A 44

A 92

Baza

Río Almanzora

A 92 N

ALMERÍA

Mojácar

A 92

GRANADA

Alhama de Granada

La Calahorra

A 7

Comares

SIERRA

Trevélez

Yegen

N 340

A 92

La Axarquía

Pampaneira

NEVADA

Tabernas

Parque Natural de Cabo de Gata

Montes de Malaga

Lanjarón

Las Alpujarras

A 348

Los Millares

Rodalquilar

Cueva de Nerja

Motril

N 340

A 7

ALMERÍA

Isleta del Moro

MÁLAGA

Nerja

Salobreña

San José

Faro de Gata

Playa de Monsul

MAR

MEDITERRÁNEO

Canary Islands

LANZAROTE

La Palma

Santa Cruz de Tenerife

Santa Cruz de la Palma

Fuerteventura

TENERIFE

Las Palmas de Gran Canaria

La Gomera

Gran Canaria

El Hierro

100 km

50 miles

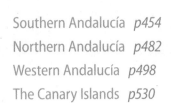

Andalucía and the Canary Islands

Village of Olvera surrouded by olive trees, Cádiz province, Southern Andalucía

SOUTHERN ANDALUCÍA

Andalucía is picture-postcard Spain. Inland, set among the olive groves are dazzling white villages, their red-roofed houses decked with geraniums and black iron-grilles. But southern Andalucía is much more than the Spain romanticized by Washington Irving, natural habitat for flamenco, fighting bulls, sherry, gazpacho and all things quintessentially Spanish: surprisingly maritime, five of Andalucía's eight provinces – each named for its capital city– are coastal and of those five four are on Spain's southern coast, popular with holidaymakers since the 1950s for sun, sea, sand and tanning. This is both quintessential Spain and a pastiche of itself. Holidaymakers can do and see most things here, from an African wildife safari to skiing the snowy slopes of the Sierra Nevada.

Highlights

1 A stroll in the shady gardens of Granada's **Generalife** (p457)

2 Stunning scenery of the **Alpujarras** (p464)

3 **Málaga**'s unexpected cultural riches in its museums (p468)

5 Extraordinary rock formations in the **Sierra del Torcal** (p472)

4 Contemplating *Death in the Afternoon* in the Bullring of **Ronda** (p474)

Southern Andalucía

The recently revitalised and thoroughly Spanish city of Málaga is the gateway to Málaga Province and the Costa del Sol, Spain's frenetic holiday playground. A few miles inland lie some of Spain's prettiest *pueblos blancos* (white villages) and quintessentially Andalucían towns, such as Antequera and Ronda, the home of bullfighting.

Southeast Andalucía

Granada is the glistening focus of this region with a fabulous natural setting and, in the Alhambra, one of the greatest Moorish palaces ever built. Despite its appeal to tourism the city has an earthy atmosphere and more than its share of attractions.

Literally just beyond (actually above) the city is the snow-capped Sierra Nevada range. It is quite possible to ski here in the morning and sunbathe on the beach in the afternoon, perhaps on the sands of the Almería coastline, the latest of Spain's costas to be fashionably developed for sun-starved north Europeans. Although this is the driest part of Spain, it grows huge amounts of fruit and vegetables, mostly under giant swathes of plastic sheeting, which deface the landscape.

Capileira in the Alpujarras, Sierra Nevada in the background

Granada★★★

Granada enjoys a glorious setting★★★ on a fertile plain overlooked by three hills and the majestic peaks of the Sierra Nevada. Watching over the modern Christian city stands the breathtaking Alhambra, one of the most magnificent monuments ever created by man and, for many, the highlight of Spain.

THE CITY TODAY

Granada has an undoubtedly glorious past and a bright present too. The vast majority of visitors take in more than just the Alhambra and the picturesque cobbled labyrinth that is the Albaicín district. The city beyond is young and vibrant, from the earthy Gypsy clubs of Sacromonte to its crammed tapas bars and hip nightclubs driven by a high student population.

A BIT OF HISTORY

Granada gained importance in the 11C as Córdoba declined. It became capital of the Almoravids, who were ousted a century later by the Almohads. In the 13C, Muslims from Córdoba, fleeing the Christians in 1236, sought refuge, enriching the city. In 1238, the new **Nasrid** ruler, Mohammed ibn Nasr, submitted to the authority of Ferdinand III, thus ensuring peace, and the kingdom flourished.

The fall of Granada – In the 15C, the Catholic Monarchs turned their attention to Granada. By 2 January 1492, after a six-month siege, the city fell. Boabdil, the last Nasrid king, delivered the keys of the city and went into exile. As he looked back, his mother is said to have scolded him: "You weep like a woman for what you could not hold as a man."

Granada flourished again in the Renaissance, but its fortunes suffered during the ruthless suppression of the Las Alpujarras revolt in 1570.

Modern Granada – The old quarters east of **plaza Nueva**, havens of peace and greenery on the Alhambra and Albaicín hills, contrast with the noisy,

▶ **Population:** 234 325
⚲ **Michelin Map:** 578 U 19 (town plan) map 124 Costa del Sol.
🛈 **Info:** Central Tourist Reception Centre: Virgen Blanca 9. ℘902 40 50 45. Info points: Plaza Bib-Rambla; Plazade Mariana Pineda 10; Avenida Generalife; Plaça de Santa Ana. www.granadatur.com.
▷ **Location:** Granada is in southern Andalucía, separated from the sea by the Sierra Nevada. The A 44 and other highways link with major cities in the region. ▭▭ Avenida de los Andaluces.
🅿 **Parking:** Space is limited in the Albaicín; there is visitor parking at the Alhambra.
⊛ **Don't Miss:** The Alhambra.
🕓 **Timing:** Organise your stay around your visit to the Alhambra, fitting other sights as time allows.
👪 **Kids:** Parque de las Ciencias or a flamenco performance in the caves of Sacromonte.

bustling lower town and the pedestrian quarter around the Cathedral between the **Gran Vía de Colón** and **Calle de los Reyes Católicos**.

SIGHTS

The Alhambra and the Generalife★★★

Real de la Alhambra. 🕓*Open daily mid-Mar–mid-Oct 8.30am–8pm; mid-Oct–mid-Mar 8.30am–6pm. Night-time visits mid-Mar–mid-Oct Tue–Sat 10–11.30pm; mid-Oct–mid-Mar Fri–Sat 8–9.30pm.* 🕓*Closed 1 Jan, 25 Dec.* *€13; advance purchase from la Caixa banks, using ATMs. One ticket covers the entire Alhambra and Generalife gardens and specifies entry time to the Nasrid Palace. €7 for gardens only.* ℘*902 44 12 21. www.alhambra-patronato.es.*

Nasrid architecture was the last desperate expression of a civilisation in decline. Nasrid princes built for the moment: beneath fabulous decoration lie ill-assorted bricks and rubble, so it is surprising how little time has diminished this masterpiece.

Decoration was the main concern. Walls and ceilings everywhere reveal an art without equal. **Stuccowork** is worked in patterns in a low relief of flat planes to catch the light; another type of decoration was made by cutting away layers of plaster to form stalactites *(mocárabes)*. This type of ornament, painted and even gilded, covered capitals, cornice mouldings, arches, pendentives and entire cupolas.

Ceramic tiles provided geometric decoration for walls: *alicatados* formed a colourful marquetry, with lines of arabesque motifs making star designs; *azulejos* gave colour, different hues separated by a thin raised fillet or a black line *(cuerda seca)*. **Calligraphy** employed elegant Andalucían cursive; the more decorative Cufic was reserved for religious aphorisms in scrollwork.

The Alhambra★★★
See map p461.
The Calat Alhambra (Red Castle) must be one of the most remarkable fortresses ever built. It commands views of the town, the Sacromonte heights, hillsides and the gardens of the Albaicín. Enter through the Puerta de Las Granadas (Pomegranate Gateway) built by Emperor Charles V; a paved footpath then leads through to the **shrubbery**★.

Palacios Nazaríes★★★ (Nasrid Palace)
The 14C Nasrid Palace was built around the Patio de los Arrayanes and Patio de los Leones. Its richness and the originality of its decoration defy description. In the **Mexuar**, used for government and judicial administration, a frieze of *azulejos* and an epigraphic border cover the walls. An oratory stands at one end. Cross the **Patio del Cuarto Dorado**. The south wall, protected by a remarkable carved wood cornice, exemplifies Granada art: windows are surrounded by panels covered with every variety of stucco and tile decoration. The **Cuarto Dorado** (Golden Room) has tiled panelling, fine stuccowork and a beautiful wooden ceiling. The delightful **view**★ extends over the Albaicín.

Adjoining is the beautiful oblong **Patio de los Arrayanes** (Myrtle Courtyard). A pool banked by myrtles reflects the **Torre de Comares** (Comares Tower), which contrasts with slender porticoes that give onto the **Sala de la Barca** (from *barakha*, benediction) and the **Salón de Embajadores** (Hall of Ambassadors), an audience chamber with a magnificent domed cedar ceiling.

Alhambra

At the heart of a second palace stands the **Patio de los Leones** (Lion Courtyard) built by Mohammed V. Twelve rough stone lions support a low fountain. Arcades of slender columns lead to the main state apartments. The **Sala de los Abencerrajes** (named for the family massacred here) has a splendid star-shaped *mocárabe* cupola.

The vaulting of alcoves at the end of the **Sala de los Reyes** (Kings' Chamber) is atypically painted to illustrate pastimes of Moorish and Christian princes – possibly done after the Reconquest.

The **Sala de las Dos Hermanas** (Hall of the Two Sisters), named for two marble slabs in the pavement, is renowned for honeycomb cupola vaulting.

Beyond are the resplendent **Sala de los Ajimeces** and the **Mirador de Lindaraja**. Past a room once occupied by Washington Irving is a gallery with views of the Albaicín. *Descend to the Patio de la Reja.*

▶ *Cross the Patio de Lindaraja to the Partal Gardens.*

Gardens and perimeter towers★★

The terraced Jardines del Partal descend to the 14C porticoed **Torre de las Damas** (Ladies' Tower). The Torre de Mihrab (*right*) is a former oratory. The Torre de la Cautiva and Torre de las Infantas (Captive's and Infantas' towers) are sumptuously decorated inside.

▶ *Enter the Palacio de Carlos V.*

Palacio de Carlos V★★ (Emperor Charles V's Palace)

In 1526, Pedro Machuca was commissioned to design a palace to be financed by a tax on the Moors. The 1568 uprising delayed construction. It is one of the most successful Renaissance creations in Spain. Although in comparison with the Nasrid Palaces the building may at first appear lacking, its grandeur becomes apparent, in its perfect lines, its dignity, and its simple plan of a circle within a square.

Museo de la Alhambra★

Palacio de Carlos V. ○*Open Tue–Sun 8.30am–2pm.* ○*Closed 1 Jan, 25 Dec.* ⊗*No charge.*

This museum is devoted to Hispano-Moorish art: ceramics, woodcarvings, panels and more. Outstanding are the famous 14C **blue** (or **gazelle**) **amphora**★ and the Pila de Almanzor, decorated with lions and deer.

Museo de Bellas Artes (Fine Arts Museum)

Palacio de Carlos V. ○*Open Tue 2.30–6pm, Wed–Thurs 9am–6pm, Fri–Sat 9am–8pm, Sun and public holidays 9am–2.30pm.* ○*Closed 1, 6 Jan, 1 May, 24–25, 31 Dec.* ⊗*€1.50; free for EU citizens.* ✆*958 57 54 50.*

Religious sculpture and paintings of the 16C to the 18C predominate: works by Diego de Siloé, Pedro de Mena, Vicente Carducho and Alonso Cano, and a magnificent still life, *Thistle and Carrots*★★, by Brother Juan Sánchez Cotán.

Alcazaba★

The two towers of this austere fortress on the Plaza de los Aljibes (Cistern Court) date to the 13C. The Torre de la Vela (Watchtower) commands a fine **panorama**★★ of the palace, gardens, Sacromonte and the Sierra Nevada.

Puerta de la Justicia★

The massive Justice Gateway is built into a tower in the outer walls. On the façade, a strip of delightful 16C *azulejos* bears an image of the Virgin and Child.

The Generalife★★

The **water gardens** are one of the most enjoyable parts of the 14C Generalife, the summer palace. The Patio de los Cipreses (Cypress Alley) and Patio de las Adelfas (Oleander) lead in. The nucleus is the **Patio de la Acequia** (Canal Court), a pool with fountains, a pavilion at either end, and a *mirador* in the middle. The pavilion to the rear contains the Sala Regia, with fine stuccowork.

The upper gardens contain the famous **escalera del agua**, or water staircase.

CATHEDRAL QUARTER
Capilla Real★★ (Chapel Royal)

Oficios 3. ⏰*Open Apr–Oct Mon–Sat 10.30am–1.30pm, 4–7.30pm, Sun 11am –1pm, 4–7pm; Nov–Mar Mon–Sat 10.30am–1.15pm, 3.30–6.15pm, Sun 11am–1pm, 3.30–6.30pm.* ⏰*Closed 1, 2 Jan, Good Friday, 12 Oct (morning), 25 Dec.* ♿*€3.50.* ☏*958 22 78 48. www.capillarealgranada.com.*

The **Catholic Monarchs** commissioned this Isabelline Gothic chapel by Enrique Egas. To enter *(by the south door)*, cross the courtyard of the old **Lonja** (Exchange), also by Egas. The south front has an elegant Renaissance

Mirador de San Cristóbal

Pl. Larga · Pl. Aliatar

Museo Cuevas del Sacromonte

Panaderos

Arco de las Pesas · El Salvador · Pl. San Salvador

Cta de los Chinos

Horno de la Charca

Cuesta de San Nicolás

SAN NICOLÁS

Casa-Museo Max Moreau

Carril de San Agustín

Camino

Casa del Chapiz

Sacromonte

Cam. nuevo de S. Nicolás

MIRADOR DE SAN NICOLÁS

ALBAYZÍN

Placeta Toqueros

Pianista García Carrillo

del

Chapiz

Palacio de los Córdova

de Trillo

de

los

Reyes

Juan

Candil

Cuesta de la Victoria

Convento de Sta Catalina de Zafra

Museo Arqueológico

Darro

Paseo del Padre Manjón

Palacio de los Córdova

El Bañuelo

BAÑUELO

San Pedro y San Pablo

Paseo de los Tristes

Darro

GENERALIFE

MIRADOR

Puente del Cadí

Santa Inés

voir plan de l'Alhambra

Cta del Rey Chico

ALHAMBRA

TORRE DE LAS DAMAS

TORRE DEL MIHRAB

Paseo de las Adelfas

ALCAZABA

PALACIOS NAZARÍES

PALACIO DE CARLOS V

TORRE DE LA VELA

Puerta del Vino

JARDINES

DEL

PARTAL

TORRE DE LA CAUTIVA

Cta de los Chinos

Gomérez

PTA DE LA JUSTICIA

PUERTA DE LAS GRANADAS

Pilar de Carlos V

Real

PARADOR

TORRE DE LAS INFANTAS

Paseo de los Cipreses

TORRES BERMEJAS

Fundación Rodríguez-Acosta

Pl. Arquitecto García de Paredes

Cuesta del Aire

REALEJO

Antequeruela Baja

Paseo de los Mártires

Av. del Generalife

Campo del Príncipe

Carril de San Cecilio

Cuesta del

Auditorio Manuel de Falla

Billetterie, entrée au Generalife et à l'Alhambra

Cuesta del Realejo

Belén

Molinos

Santiago

del

Caldero

Casa-museo Manuel de Falla

Camino Nuevo del Cementerio

Carmen de los Mártires

Seco de Lucena

Solares

Cuesta del Pescado

Vistillas de los Ángeles

GRANADA

N

Salón

Paseo de la Bomba

Escoriaza

Genil

0   200 m

0   200 yds

SIERRA NEVADA

façade of superimposed arcades with turned columns. Every conceivable decoration of the Isabelline style is seen inside: ribbed vaulting, coats of arms, the yoke and fasces (revived in 1934 by the Falange), monograms, and the eagle of St John. In the chancel, closed by a gilded **screen**★★★ by Master Bar-

tolomé, are the **mausoleums**★★★ of the Catholic Monarchs on the right, and of Philip the Handsome and Juana the Mad, the parents of Charles V, on the left. The first was carved by Fancelli in Genoa in 1517, the second, magnificent in scale and workmanship, by Bartolomé Ordóñez (the sarcophagi are in the

459

Mausoleums, Capilla Real

© Markus Bassler/age fotostock

crypt). The high altar **retable**★ (1520) by Felipe Vigarny shows great movement and expression.

The lower register of the predella depicts the siege of Granada and the baptism of the Moriscos.

Sacristía-Museo

Among objects on display are **Queen Isabel's sceptre and crown**, **King Ferdinand's sword**, and outstanding **paintings**★★ by Flemish (Rogier Van der Weyden), Italian (Perugino, Botticelli) and Spanish (Bartolomé Bermejo, Pedro Berruguete) artists.

The central section of the *Triptych of the Passion* was painted by the Fleming Dirk Bouts. Two sculptures of the Catholic Monarchs at prayer are by Felipe Vigarny.

Opposite are the 18C Baroque-style former **town hall** (*ayuntamiento*), and just below, the **Centro de Arte José Guerrero**, dedicated to modern art, especially Granada's José Guerrero (1914–91) (*Oficios 8;* ◷ *open mid-Sept–May Tue–Sat and public holidays 10.30am–2pm, 4–9pm, Sun 10.30am–2pm; Jun–mid-Sept Tue–Sat and public holidays 11am–2pm, 5–9pm, Sun 10.30am–2pm;* ◷ *closed 1 Jan, 24–25, 31 Dec;* ☞ *no charge;* ✆ *958 22 01 09; www.centroguerrero.org).*

Catedral★

Gran Vía de Colón 5. ◷ *Open Apr–Oct Mon–Sat 10.45am–1.30pm, 4–8pm, Sun and public holidays 4–8pm; Nov–Mar Mon–Sat 10.45am–1.30pm, 4–7pm, Sun and public holidays 4–7pm.* ☞ *€3.50.* ✆ *958 22 29 59.*

Construction started in 1518. Diego de Siloé introduced the Renaissance style to the design of Enrique Egas. The façade (1667) is by Alonso Cano.

The **Capilla Mayor**★ is surprising. Siloé designed a rotunda circled by an ambulatory, cleverly linked to the basilica. The rotunda combines superimposed orders, the uppermost with paintings by Alonso Cano of the Life of the Virgin and beautiful 16C stained glass. Marking the rotunda entrance are figures of the Catholic Monarchs by Pedro de Mena and, in a medallion by Alonso Cano, Adam and Eve.

The **organ**★ from about 1750 is by Leonardo of Ávila. The finely carved Isabelline doorway in the south transept is the original **north portal**★ of the older Capilla Real.

Alcaicería

The area, with craft and souvenir shops, was a silk market in Moorish times.

Corral del Carbón

Mariana Pineda. ◷ *Open Mon–Fri 9am–7pm, Sat–Sun 10am–2pm.* ☞ *No charge.*

This 14C former Moorish storehouse has an arched doorway with *alfiz* surround and panels of *sebka* decoration.

ALBAICÍN★★

This quarter covers a slope facing the Alhambra. It was here that the Moors lived after the Reconquest.

Alleys are lined by white-walled houses. Walls enclose luxuriant gardens of *cármenes* (town houses). Go to the **Iglesia de San Nicolás** (*Plaza de San Nicolás*) at sunset, for a **view**★★★ of the Alhambra and the Generalife. The Sierra Nevada beyond is spectacular under snow in winter.

ALHAMBRA

Torre del Homenaje

Cubo

Torre Quebrada

Torre del Adarguero

ALCAZABA★

Jardín de los Adarves

Plaza de los Aljibes

Puerta del Vino

Puerta de la Justicia

★★★ PALACIOS NAZARÍES

Torre de Comares

Torre de los Puñales

Torre de las Gallinas

Galería del Peinador

Habitaciones de Washington Irving

Mirador de Lindaraja

Baños Árabes

Patio de Lindaraja

Sala de las Dos Hermanas

Sala de los Reyes

Patio de los Leones

Sala de los Abencerrajes

SANTA MARÍA

Calle Real

Sala de la Barca

Salón de Comares

Patio de los Arrayanes

Cuarto Dorado

Oratorio

Mexuar

Machuca

Patio de Machuca

★ MUSEO DE LA ALHAMBRA

Museo de Bellas Artes ★

PALACIO DE CARLOS V ★★

JARDINES DEL PARTAL

40 m
40 yds
20

Baños Árabes★ (El Bañuelo)

Car. del Darro 31. ⓞOpen Tue–Sat 10am –2pm. ⓞClosed public holidays. ⊜No charge. ℘958 22 97 38.
These 11C baths with star-pierced vaulting are the best preserved in Spain.

Monasterio de San Jerónimo★

Rector López Argüeta. ⓞOpen daily Oct–Mar 10am–1.30pm, 3–7.30pm; Apr–Sept 10am–1.30pm, 4–7.30pm. ⊜€3.50. ℘958 27 93 37.
This 16C monastery was principally designed by Diego de Siloé. Plateresque and Renaissance doorways lead

461

View of Albaicín district from the Alhambra

to harmonious cloisters. The **church**★★, with the tomb of Gonzalo Fernández de Córdoba, the Gran Capitán, has a rich Renaissance apse, and superb coffers and vaulting adorned with saints, angels and animals. The **retable**★★ is a jewel of the Granadine School. The paintings are from the 18C.

Basílica de San Juan de Dios★

San Juan de Dios 23. Guided tours (50min) Sept–Jul Mon–Sat 10am–1pm; open afternoons by prior arrangement. Closed public holidays. 958 27 57 00.

The Baroque Church of St John of God is noted for its richness and stylistic uniformity. Behind a massive Churrigueresque altarpiece of gilded wood is a lavish *camarín* with the funerary urn of **San Juan de Dios**, founder of the Order of Knights Hospitallers.

Monasterio de la Cartuja★

Pas. de la Cartuja. Open Apr–Oct 10am–1pm, 4–8pm; Nov–Mar daily 10am–1pm, 3.30–6pm. €3.50. 958 16 19 32.

Go in through the cloisters. The church is exuberantly decorated with Baroque stucco. At the back of the apse is the early 18C Sancta Sanctorum, a *camarín* decorated with multi-hued marble; beneath the cupola, painted in false relief, a marble Sagrario contains the Tabernacle.

The outstanding Late Baroque **sacristy**★★ (1727–64) is called the Christian Alhambra for its intricate stuccowork. The door and cedarwood furnishings, inlaid with tortoiseshell, mother-of-pearl and silver, are by a Carthusian monk, José Manuel Vásquez.

Parque de las Ciencias★

Av. de la Ciencia. Open Tue–Sat 10am–7pm; Sun and public holidays 10am–3pm. Closed 1 Jan, 1 May, 25 Dec. €6 (child €4.50), €2.50 planetarium (child €2). 958 13 19 00. www.parqueciencias.com.

This science park comprises an interactive museum, planetarium, observatory and tropical butterfly collection.

Museo Arqueológico

Carrera del Darro 43. Currently closed for renovations. 958 57 54 08. www.museosdeandalucia.es.

The archaeological museum is in Casa Castril, a Renaissance palace with a fine **Plateresque doorway**★. It exhibits Egyptian alabaster vases found in a necropolis in Almuñecar, a bull figure from Arjona and Roman and Moorish decorative art.

Sacromonte

The hillside opposite the Generalife is the Gypsy quarter where flamenco performances are given in caves. At the end of Camino del Sacromonte is the 17C–

18C abbey for which the hill is named (*Barranco de los Negros;* ⏱museum open *Apr–Oct Tue–Sun 10am–2pm, 5–9pm; Nov–Mar Tue–Sun 10am–2pm, 4–7pm;* ⏱€5; 𝄢958 21 51 20; www.sacromontegranada.com).

Hospital Real
Cuesta del Hospicio.
The royal hospital, now the university rectorate, was founded by the Catholic Monarchs. The plan, similar to those in Toledo and Santiago de Compostela, is of a cross within a square. Four Plater-esque windows adorn the façade.

Fundación Rodríguez-Acosta★
Callejón Niños del Rollo 8. ⏱*Open Wed –Fri 6.30–8.30pm, Sat–Sun 11am–2pm.* ⏱*Closed public holidays.* ⏱€4; €6 *with cave, library tour.* 𝄢958 22 74 97. www.fundacionrodriguezacosta.com.
This foundation houses the legacies of painter José María Rodríguez-Acosta (1886–1941) and archaeologist Manuel Gómez-Moreno (1870–1970), in a fine *carmen* built between 1914 and 1928. Gómez-Moreno's personal collection includes Romanesque and Gothic pieces, and canvases by Zurbarán, Ribera, Alonso Cano and others, as well as Aztec and Chinese items.

Carmen de los Mártires
Pas. de los Mártires. ⏱*Open Nov–Mar Mon–Fri 10am–2pm, 4–6pm, Sat–Sun and public holidays 10am–6pm; Apr–Jul Sept–Oct Mon–Sat 10am–2pm, 6–8pm, Sun and public holidays 10am–8pm.* ⏱*No charge.* 𝄢958 22 79 53.
The romantic terraced **gardens**★ of this Carmelite monastery on the Alhambra hill are embellished with fountains and sculptures.

EXCURSIONS
Fuente Vaqueros
Federico García Lorca, poet and dramatist, was born 20km/12.4mi from Granada in this village in 1898.
The house museum **Huerta de San Vicente** (⏱open Tue–Sun Oct–Mar 10am–1pm, 4–6pm; Apr–Jun and Sept 10am–1pm, 5–7pm; Jul–Aug 10am–

2pm; ⏱€1.80; 𝄢958 51 69 62; www.museogarcialorca.org) offers admirers an insight into his life.

SIERRA NEVADA★★
The Sierra Nevada between the Costa del Sol and Granada is massive, beautiful, and often snow-capped. There is ⛷**skiing** at **Solynieve**★★, with over 60km/37mi of slopes, 45 runs and 20 ski lifts. Lodging is at **Pradollano**.
Vehicular access to the **national park** is restricted; the best way to tour is on foot. The most interesting routes are the ascents to the Laguna de la Yeguas, **Mulhacén** (3 482m/11 424ft) and **Veleta** (3 394m/11 132ft). Contact **El Dornajo Visitor Centre** (⏱*open 9am–2pm (2.30pm in summer), 4.30–6pm (7pm in summer);* 𝄢958 34 06 25).

Alhama de Granada★
▶ *60km/37mi SW on the A 92 and A 335.*
Alhama de Granada is a village of white-washed houses and narrow streets above a deep gorge, dominated by the **Iglesia de la Encarnación**★, a well-pro-portioned church built of golden stone. The stunning **view**★ from the belvedere behind the Iglesia del Carmen encom-passes the canyon of the Alhama River. Baths on the outskirts date from the Roman period. A Moorish **cistern**★ survives.

🚗 DRIVING TOUR

THE ALPUJARRAS★★
90km/56mi. Allow one day.

This isolated region stretches across the southern slopes of the Sierra Nevada.

From Lanjarón to Valor
The High Alpujarras encompass the valley of the Guadalfeo river. Houses typically have a flat roof terrace, a *terrao.*

Lanjarón
This resort is famous for its medicinal mineral water and spa. The 16C castle affords fine valley views.

The Alpujarran Uprising

In 1499 the Arabs who did not wish to leave Spain were forced to renounce their religion and to convert to Christianity. They were known as Moriscos. In 1566 Philip II forbade them their language and traditional dress, which sparked off a serious uprising, especially in Las Alpujarras where the Moriscos proclaimed as king Fernando de Córdoba under the name Abén Humeya. In 1571 Philip II sent in the army under Don Juan of Austria, who crushed the rebellion. However, a tense feeling of unrest remained, and in 1609 Philip III ordered the expulsion of all the Moriscos (who numbered about 275 000) from Spain.

▷ *9km/5.6mi from Lanjarón, before Órgiva, take the GR 421, a narrow mountain road.*

Pampaneira★★

Of all the villages in the **Poqueira Valley**★★ Pampaneira best preserves its traditional architecture, including the 17C Iglesia de Santa Cruz.
Bubión, a centre of Morisco resistance in 1569, is 5km/3mi further along. In **Capileira** is the **Museo de Artes y Costumbres Populares**, a museum re-creating 19C Alpujarran life through its popular arts and customs (*Casa de la Cultura;* ⏰*open Mon–Fri 11.30am–2.30pm, Sat 4–7pm (8pm in summer);* ℘*958 76 30 51*).

▷ *Return to the GR 421. The road enters the Trevélez Valleya.*

Trevélez★

Trevélez, the highest municipality in Spain (1 600m/5,248ft), is famous for cured hams and dried sausages. Behind the village rises **Mulhacén**, Spain's highest peak (3 482m/11 424ft). Beyond Trevélez, the valley opens and the verdant landscape gives way to drier terrain planted with the occasional vineyard. **Yegen** owes it fame to the Englishman Gerald Brenan, the author of *South from Granada*.
Abén Humeya (⏰*see The Alpujarran Uprising above*) was born and lived in Válor, the next village after Yegen. Its 16C church, like many in the region, is built in Mudéjar style.

ADDRESSES

🛏 STAY

⊜ **Hotel Los Tilos** – *Pl. Bib Rambla 4.* ℘*958 26 67 12. www.hotellostilos.com. 30 rooms.* ⌑*€8.* This no-frills hotel fronts a charming square filled with flower stalls, adjacent to the Cathedral. Rooms are basic but comfortable, some with views over the plaza.

⊜ **Hotel Maciá Plaza** – *Pl. Nueva 5.* ℘*958 22 75 36. www.maciahoteles.com. 44 rooms.* ⌑*€8.* Attractive façade on a central square at the foot of the Alhambra. Standard-quality rooms.

⊜⊜ **Hotel América** – *Real de la Alhambra 53.* ℘*958 22 74 71. www.hotel americagranada.com. 16 rooms.* ⌑*€9. Restaurant* ⊜⊜. *Closed Dec–Feb.* Small, family-run hotel superbly located within the confines of the Alhambra. A warm welcome and friendly service are the trademarks of the América which also has a pleasant patio.

🍽 EAT

⊜⊜ **La Ermita en la Plaza de Toros** – *Av. Doctor Olóriz 25 (at the bullring).* ℘*958 29 02 57. www.ermitaplazadetoros.com. Closed 24, 31 Dec for dinner.* In an unusual location within the confines of the city's bullring with tasteful decoration of exposed brickwork, wooden tables, bullfighting memorabilia and Andalucían cuisine: restaurant upstairs, tapas bar downstairs.

⊜⊜⊜ **Chikito** – *Pl. Campillo 9.* ℘*958 22 33 64. www.restaurantechikito.com. Closed Wed. Reservations recommended.* A hugely popular restaurant and bar with locals and visitors alike, and renowned for serving local specialities and superb cured hams. It was here that artists and intellectuals such as García Lorca used to meet in the 1930s.

⊖⊜🍽 **Mirador de Morayma** – *Pianista García Carrillo 2. ☎958 22 48 12. www.alqueriamorayma.com. Closed Sun July–Aug, Sun eve rest of year.* This restaurant in the Albaicín district has one of the best settings of any in the city. Rustic décor, a plant-filled terrace and magnificent views of the Alhambra. Private-label wines; flamenco show Tue evening.

TAPAS

Bodegas Castañeda – *Almireceros 1. ☎958 22 32 22. Closed Sun.* The bar and tables in this typical bodega, its décor enhanced by the myriad bottles on display, are often full with customers enjoying the delicious hot and cold tapas and regional specialities.

Casa Enrique – *Acera del Darro 8. ☎958 25 50 08. Closed Sun and fortnight in Aug.* This tavern dates from 1870 and has become a symbol of the city. Its small size and careful decoration make it a good meeting-point. Outstanding wine cellar, Iberian ham and local cheeses.

Los Diamantes – *Navas 28. ☎958 22 70 70. Closed Aug.* One of the most popular seafood tapas brawls in town.

La Trastienda – *Pl. Cuchilleros 11. ☎958 76 33 29. Closed Aug.* Founded in 1836. Once through the small entrance door, head down some steps to the former grocery store, which has retained its original counter, where you can enjoy excellent chorizo and tapas, either at the bar or in the small room to the rear.

🍷 BARS / 🍸 CAFÉS

Teterías – *Calle Calderería Nueva.* Calle Calderería Nueva, between the city centre and the Albaicín, is a typical example of a street found in the Moorish quarter of any city. The small and cosy *teterías* are typical cafés which give a welcoming feel to this particular street. Two are worth mentioning: the quiet and pleasant **Pervane** *(no 24)*, with its huge selection of teas, coffees, milkshakes and cakes; and **Kasbah** *(no 4)*, decorated with cushions and rugs on the floor in true Moorish coffee shop style.

🌙 NIGHTLIFE

El Camborio – *Camino de Sacromonte 47. ☎958 22 12 15.* One of Granada's oldest and most established nocturnal haunts, El Camborio has been open for the past 30 years. Best approached by car or taxi as it is located in one of the city's least salubrious districts. The venue itself is quite unique with four interconnected caves and with good dance music. Popular with an eclectic crowd, though predominantly frequented by students. A good place to end the night.

Fondo Reservado – *Calle Santa Inés 4. ☎958 22 23 75.* Dance music of all kinds until all hours in a chilled-out space in the lower Albaicín for the young and not so young.

La Fontana – *Carrera del Darro 19. ☎958 22 77 59.* Housed in an old residence at the foot of the Alhambra and Albaicín hills, this inviting antique-adorned café is an ideal place for a quiet drink in an atmosphere dominated by lively conversation. An excellent choice of coffees, herbal teas and cocktails.

Sala Príncipe – *Campo del Príncipe 7. ☎958 22 80 08.* This large venue is the place to be seen for the city's in-crowd, hosting regular concerts by leading Spanish groups. It is always crowded with a mix of ages.

El Tercer Aviso – *Real Maestranza 1, Pl. de Toros. ☎958 20 60 42. Open Sun–Wed.* A surprising location inside the bullring, where its spacious design combines with modern, tasteful décor. The café is located on several floors, and from each floor it is possible to look down onto the floors below. Good chart music popular with the 25–45 crowd, and also quiet areas for those wanting to enjoy a chat.

FIESTAS

The city's religious festivals are lively, colourful events, especially those held in Holy Week and at Corpus Christi. The city also holds an annual **music and dance festival** *(www.granadafestival.org)* in June and July in the delightful surroundings of the Generalife gardens.

Almería

Almería is a swathe of white between the Mediterranean and a fortress-crowned hill. Its magnificent climate – hills shelter it from winds – has made it a tourist hotspot. Life bustles in the city centre on the tree-lined Paseo de Almería. Another oasis, the parque de Nicolás Salmerón, stretches along the harbour. Houses in La Chanca, the fishermen's quarter, are built into rock.

A BIT OF HISTORY

The city was founded by Emir and Caliph of Córdoba Abd ar-Rahman III in 955, and played an important role in the 11C when it was the capital of a taifa kingdom. It was captured by Alfonso VII in 1147; however, upon his death ten years later, it fell into Moorish hands once more. Almería formed part of the Nasrid kingdom of Granada until 1489, the year in which it was reconquered by the Catholic Monarchs.

In the last third of the 20C, the development of advanced agricultural techniques and the opening-up of modern infrastructures placed this provincial capital at the forefront of Span's year-round fruit and vegetable cultivation.

SIGHTS

⚫⚫ Alcazaba★

⏱ *Open Tue–Sun Nov–Apr 9am–6.30pm; May–Oct 9am–8.30pm.* ✆*No charge.* ✆*950 17 50 00.* *www.juntadeandalucia.es/cultura/museos/CMAAL.*

Abd ar-Rahman III ordered this fortress built in the 10C. Almotacín built a splendid palace, enlarged by the Catholic Monarchs. Its crenellated ochre walls dominate Almería. A section of old ramparts links the fort to San Cristóbal hill, once crowned by a castle.

Attractive **gardens** are laid out in the first walled enclosure where rivulets spring from fountains. The bell in the Muro de la Vela, a wall separating the enclosures, once warned of pirates. In the third enclosure, the keep *(torre del*

- **Population:** 18 810
- **Michelin Map:** 124 Costa del Sol.
- **Info:** Plaza del Bendicho. ✆950 88 11 70. www.almeria-turismo.org.
- **Location:** Almería lies on the southern coast on the Mediterranean. 🚉Plaza de la Estación.
- **Don't Miss:** The Alcazaba of Almería, the Moorish castle that overlooks the city.
- **Timing:** Take a half day for the fortress and a stroll.
- **Kids:** Kids always love castles and wild-west movie sets.

homenaje), with incredibly thick walls, looks down on the Christian *alcázar.* The **view★** from the battlements takes in the town, surrounding hills and sea.

Catedral★

Pl. de la Catedral. 👥Guided tours *Mon–Fri 10am–2pm, 4–5pm; Sat 10am–1pm.* ⏱*Closed festive holidays.* ✆€3. ✆*690 02 49 57.*

The cathedral was built in 1524, fortified against raids by Barbary pirates. It has two well-designed **portals★** and, at the east end, a **delicately carved sunburst★**. The high altar and pulpits of inlaid marble and jasper are 18C, the choir stalls are from 1560 and the jasper *trascoro* with three alabaster statues is 18C. A chapel in the ambulatory houses a statue of the Cristo de la Escucha.

Aljibes de Jayrán

Tenor Iribarne. ⏱*Open Mon–Fri 11am–1pm, 6–8pm.* ✆*950 27 30 39.*
The Moorish cisterns that once supplied the city.

Iglesia de Santiago

Tiendas. ⏱*Open Mon–Fri 9.30–11.30am, 6.30–7pm.* ✆*950 23 71 20.*
This 16C church on one of the city's main shopping streets (Calle de las Tiendas) has a fine **Renaissance doorway★** similar to the cathedral's.

Museo Arqueológico de Almería

Ctra de Ronda 91. ⏰*Open Tue 2.30–8.30pm, Wed–Sat 9am–8.30pm, Sun and public holidays 9am–2.30pm.* 🎫*No charge.* 📞*950 17 55 10.*
Museum exhibits cover prehistory through the Islamic era, with pieces from sites in the province, notably the El Argar and Los Millares cultures.

🚗 DRIVING TOUR

The East Coast★
Approx. 240km/150mi.

▷ *Take the airport road and turn right after 14.5km/9mi.*

Parque Natural de Cabo de Gata-Níjar★★

📞*950 16 04 35.*
http://.cabodegata-nijar.com.
South of the volcanic Cabo de Gata mountains, past the Acosta salt flats, this park is a haven of wild, unspoiled beaches. The lighthouse faces Mermaid Reef, popular for underwater fishing. On the other side of the mountain is the small summer resort of San José with two beautiful beaches; los **Genoveses**★ and **Monsul**★ *(nudist)* (about 2km/1.2mi from the centre of the town). Ask locally for directions to Cala Rajá and Cala de Entremedio, two quieter beaches.

▷ *Take the AL 12; turn at Venta del Probe.*

Agua Amarga
Agua Amarga is a pleasant seaside village with an attractive beach and a good café at Bar La Plaza.

▷ *Follow the coast road to Mojácar (32km/20mi). The road twists upwards, offering views of the coast, a 17C fortified tower and a 13–14C Moorish watchtower.*

Mojácar★
The village stands on a splendid **site**★ on an outcrop with **views** of the coast (2km/1.2mi away) and a plain broken by

odd rock formations. The steep, narrow village streets are clearly Moorish.

▷ *Follow the AL 12 back towards Almería, turning off at Níjar.*

Níjar
This one-time Arab village carries on the craft of weaving *jarapas* (blankets), using strips of material *(trapos)*.

The Road Northeast
55km/34mi along the N 370.
Sand dunes stretching from Benahadux to Tabernas were used as a desert film location for such films as *Lawrence of Arabia*. Film sets are open to the public at **Oasys**, a desert theme park *(*⏰*open Apr–Oct daily 10am–8pm; Nov–Mar Sat–Sun and public holidays 10am–7pm.* 📞*950 36 52 36).*

Cinema Studios Fort Bravo *(www.fort-bravo.com)* is a wild-west village used as a location for spaghetti westerns, compete with saloon, jail, general store and all the general components of an American cow town, interesting for children and grownups alike.
Beyond Tabernas, the land is red and barren; pottery-making is the main occupation. **Sorbas** has a singular and vertiginous **setting**★. Its houses cling to a cliff, circled below by a river loop.

ADDRESSES

🏨 STAY

🛏️🍽️🛏️ **Hotel Costasol** – *Pas. de Almería 58.* 📞*950 23 40 11. www.hotelcostasol.com.* *55 rooms.* 🚯*€7.* The Costasol is housed in a 1960s-style building on Almería's busiest shopping street, although the rooms are spacious and comfortable, some with a balcony.

🛏️🍽️🛏️🛏️ **Las Salinas de Cabo de Gata** – *Barriada La Almadraba de Monteleva, Las Salinas, 04150 El Cabo de Gata.* 📞*950 37 01 03. www.lasalinascabodegata.com. 20 rooms.* 🚯*€6. Closed Oct.* The hotel's tranquil location in Parque Natural de Cabo de Gata makes this an ideal base from which to enjoy a number of excursions. All the rooms offer views of the bright-white salt pans or the beach.

Málaga★

Founded by Phoenicians, Málaga became a Roman colony and later, the main port of Moorish Granada. Today, it is the capital of the Costa del Sol, but it retains characteristic old houses and gardens that reflect its importance as a 19C port. Beaches stretch eastwards from La Malagueta, at one end of the Paseo Marítimo, to El Palo *(5km/ 3mi E)*, a former fishermen's quarter.

THE CITY TODAY

Málaga may be the gateway to the Costa del Sol but, unlike its resort neighbours, it has retained its authentic Spanish character and is well worth a visit of at least two days before hitting the beaches. Revitalised over the last decade by the Museo Picasso, the Carmen Thyssen Museum, the Centro de Arte Contemporáneo and major seaport and airport infrastructure, Málaga, a candidate for 2016 European Cultural Capital, has finally taken its place as one of Andalucía's most vibrant cities. Plaza de la Merced is the in-town hub, while in spring and summer the action shifts to the beaches, particularly to the Pedregalejo northeast of town.

SIGHTS

Fundación Museo Picasso (Picasso Museum)★★

San Agustín 8. ◷*Open Tue–Thu, Sun and public holidays 10am–8pm, Fri–Sat 10am–9pm.* ◷*Closed 1 Jan, 25 Dec.* ◒*€6; free last Sun of month 3–8pm.* ℘*902 44 33 77. www.museopicasso malaga.org.*

The 16C Palacio de Buenavista houses oils, sketches, engravings, sculptures and ceramics from the collections of Christine and Bernard Ruiz-Picasso, the artist's daughter-in-law and grandson. Among paintings are *Bust of Woman with Arms Crossed Behind Head* (1939), *Woman in an Armchair* (1946) and *Jacqueline Seated* (1954). There is also a library and archive. Temporary exhibitions *(additional charge)* of other artists' work are held.

▸ **Population:** 568 305
◔ **Michelin Map:** 578 and 124.
🖼 **Info:** Pasaje de Chinitas 4. ℘951 30 89 11. www.malagaturismo.com.
◗ **Location:** Málaga is 59km/ 37mi E of Marbella and 124km/77mi SW of Granada. Whitewashed Málaga is at the mouth of the Guadalmedina along the Mediterranean. 🚃 Explanada de la Estación.
🅿 **Parking:** Park outside old quarter and walk.
◉ **Don't Miss:** Museo Picasso; Alcazaba; Museo Carmen Thyssen Málaga.

Alcazaba★

Alcazabilla 2. ◷*Open daily 30 Mar–26 Oct 9.30am–8pm; 27 Oct–29 Mar 8.30am–7pm.* ◷*Closed last day in Feb.* ◒*€2.* ℘*952 12 20 20.*

The ruins of a **Roman theatre** line the approach to this 11C Moorish fortress. Inside the final gateway are Moorish gardens. There is a **view**★ of the harbour and city from the ramparts. The former Nasrid palace is within.

Catedral★

Molina Lario. ◷*Open Mon–Fri 10am–6pm, Sat 10am–5pm.* ◷*Closed Sun and public holidays.* ◒*€3.50.* ℘*952 22 84 91.*

Construction spanned three centuries (16C–18C); the south tower still lacks its full elevation. **Oven vaulting**★ covers the aisles. Classically ordered Corinthian columns, entablatures and cornices add a monumental appearance. **Choir stalls**★ bear figures by Pedro de Mena. There is an impressive early 15C carved and painted **Gothic retable**★ in the ambulatory.

The 18C **Palacio Episcopal** (Episcopal Palace) on the square, in Baroque style, has a lovely marble façade.

El Sagrario, an unusual 16C rectangular church in the cathedral gardens, features a fine **north portal**★ in Isabelline

Gothic style. The 18C interior is Baroque; a beautiful **Mannerist altarpiece**★★ is crowned by a well-preserved Calvary.

Casa-Museo Pablo Ruiz Picasso

Pl. de la Merced 15. ◷*Open daily 9.30am–8pm.* ◷*Closed public holidays.* ◎€1. ℘952 06 02 15. *www.fundacionpicasso.es.*

The mid-15C building on the **Plaza de la Merced** shows a number of Picasso's drawings as well as photos and ceramics.

Museo de Artes y Costumbres Populares (Museum of Popular Arts and Customs)

Pasillo de Santa Isabel 10. ◷*Open Oct –mid-Jun Mon–Fri 10am–1.30pm, 4–7pm, Sat 10am–1.30pm; mid-Jun– Sept Mon–Fri 10am–1.30pm, 5–8pm, Sat 10am–1.30pm.* ◷*Closed public holidays.* ◎€2. ℘952 21 71 37. *www.museoartespopulares.com.*

The museum, housed in a 17C inn, displays objects once used for work on land or sea, as well as 18C and 19C folklore and costumes.

Santuario de la Virgen de la Victoria★

Pl. del Santuario. ◝◟*Guided tours (45min) Tue–Fri, Sun 10am–noon, 4.30– 7pm, Sat 10am–noon.* ℘952 25 26 47. The sanctuary was founded by the Catholic Monarchs. The church is dominated by a large 17C altarpiece at the centre of which stands the **camarín**★★, a Baroque masterpiece covered by stuccowork and presided over by a fine 15C German *Virgin and Child.*

Centro de Arte Contemporáneo de Málaga

Alemania s/n. ◷*Open Tue–Sun 25 Sept–Jun 10am–8pm; Jul–24 Sept 10am–2pm, 5–9pm.* ◷*Closed 1 Jan, 25 Dec.* ◎*No charge.* ℘952 12 00 55. *www.cacmalaga.org.*

The old wholesale market, a Rationalist building by Luis Gutiérrez Soto (1939), houses a modern art centre.

Museo Carmen Thyssen Málaga

Compañía 10. ◷*Open Tue–Thur 10am –8pm, Fri–Sat 10am–9pm, Sun 10am– 8pm.* ◷*Closed 1 Jan, 25 Dec.* ◎€6. ℘902 303 131. *www.carmenthyssen malaga.org.*

The stately 16C Palacio de Villalón is the setting for 230 works of art from the collection of Baroness Carmen von Thyssen-Bornemisza. The paintings concentrate on 19C Spanish artists with works by Julio Romero de Torres, Joaquim Sorolla and Ignacio Zuloaga among the most famous.

Mercado de Atarazanas

Atarazanas 10. ◷*Open Mon–Sat 7am–4pm.* ◷*Closed 1 Jan, 25 Dec.* ◎*No charge.* ℘952 12 00 55. *www.mercadodeatarazanas.com.*

The recently restored and refurbished central food market, just one street in from the Alameda Principal, is a colourful, sensorial brouhaha.

Beaches

Málaga's favourite strand is the Pedregalejo beach northeast of the city, where nightlife rages and the famous Malagueño sardine roasts are an attraction any time of the year. *Espetas de sardinas* are sardines cooked on stakes inclined over coals so the juice runs down into the sand instead of dripping into the fire and creating a conflagration. The beaches west of Málaga proceed from La Malagueta through San Andrés, La Misericordia, Guadalmar, Los Álamos, Playamar and La Carihuela to Torremolinos, each with lifeguards, rentable lounge chairs and blue flag ratings.

EXCURSION

Jardín Botánico Histórico Finca de la Concepción★

◯*Ctra de las Pedrizas, 7km/4.3mi N.* ◷*Open Tue–Sun Oct–May 9.30am– 7pm; Jun–Sept 9.30am–4pm.* ◎€4.20. ℘952 25 07 87. *http://laconcepcion. malaga.eu.*

Visitors will enjoy strolling through this delightful jungle, planted with more than 300 tropical and subtropical species and dotted with streams, ponds, waterfalls and Roman ruins.

🚗 DRIVING TOURS

Axarquía★

This pocket-sized and little-known region is filled with hillsides covered with almond and olive trees with waves of grain spreading out at their feet. Bordered on the west side by the Sierra de Málaga and on the east by the Sierras de Tejeda and Almijara, the Axarquía falls south to the Costa del Sol.

Pretty Mudéjar bell towers rise over narrow alleyways as most of the villages are marked by the nearly 800-year Moorish sojourn here, while others were built by villagers attempting to escape the attacks of the Barbary pirates along the coast. The Axarquía was also the base for the Moorish uprising that followed the 1492 completion of the Christian Reconquest.

Comares

About 40km/25mi from Rincón de la Victoria toward Benagalbón (approx. 45min).

1 bus daily to and from Málaga Mon–Sat. (Calle Alsa; ☏ 902 422 242; www.alsa.es).

Comares, accessible via a serpentine but scenic road, is know as "the balcony of the Axarquía". Perched on a hilltop, the town overlooks the entire region and has magical sunsets. A marked route has been set up to guide you through the tiny streets of this village of Moorish origins: just follow the ceramic tiles set into the pavement. Several long-range hiking trails also originate in the main square. During the walk, you'll come across the Mudéjar **Iglesia de Nuestra Señora de la Encarnación**, built on the footprint of the former mosque. **Plaza de los Verdiales**, named for the typical regional dances of Málaga, leads into a street through two exposed-brick Moorish arches.

From the ruins of the **Moorish castle**, the view over the rooftops and the mountains is memorable. Comares

was a strategic military prize. Omar ibn Hafsun was based here during his revolt against the Ummayyads. Don't miss the **cemetery★** for a look at a typical burial technique: as the earth was too rocky, superimposed tombs were constructed into which caskets were introduced. The oldest tombs are at the entrance, to the right.

Northen Axarquía

Allow half a day.

The small roads leading to **Alfarnate** (via Riogordo) cross though fruit and olive orchards. More than the village itself, the countryside around Alfarnate is what merits the detour: the rough terrain as a result of the proximity of the mountains and the vegetation of Mediterranean scrub and oak trees. Three marked GR circuits depart from the village.

The most spectacular leads to the summit of the **Pico de Vilo** (1 415m/4 600ft), from which a 360° view looks over the Sierra Nevada, the Maroma peak, Viñuela lake and the sea (*moderately difficult 4hr round trip*). After resting up at the Venta, you can descend to the south through olive-oil producing **Periana** and **Viñuela** (a large dammed lake). En route, to the east is the impressive **Ventas de Zafarraya**, a breach carved through the Sierra de Almijara back to Alhama de Granada.

The Nerja Road

South of Viñuela, the superb MA 4106 and MA 4105 connect several adorable villages.

Salares, built next to a roaring brook spanned by a Roman bridge, is filled with sleepy little streets with the sweet perfume of Al-Andalus. Don't miss the beautiful brick and tile bell tower-**minaret** from the Almohade era. On the far side of the bridge follow the marked path (*an easy 3hr, 6km/4mi loop*) that winds along the flank of the mountain, after having crosssed an irrigated zone planted with orange, lemon, walnut and cherry trees.

The bell tower-minaret of **Archez** is a gem of Mudéjar art, with motifs in brick *sekba* in its main body.

The largest village of the Axarquía, Competa *(23km/14mi from Nerja and 60km/37mi from Málaga, served by 2 or 3 daily buses calling at Calle Ruiz y Ávila; ℘ 952 54 11 13)* has a lovely old nucleus as well as real tourist infrastructure. The excellent **Málaga wine**, for sale everywhere, celebrates its popular fiesta on 15 August.

Another example of the white villages perched over the coast, beautifully restored but very tourist-frequented, **Frigiliana** has pretty streets, the ruins of a castle, and a sugar cane manufacturerer installed in a former palace. Frigiliana is connected to Nerja *(6km/4mi)* by bus about 8 times a day Mon–Sat.

ADDRESSES

🏨 STAY

🍷🍴 **Hotel Castilla y Guerrero** – *Córdoba 7.* ℘*952 21 86 35. www.hotel castillaguerrero.com. 40 rooms.* Plain but comfortable and well located, with everything needed for a good rest, and adequate bathrooms. Go up the stairs to check in. Good for the price.

🍷🍴🍴 **Hotel Don Curro** – *Sancha de Lara 7* ℘*952 22 72 00. www.hoteldoncurro.com. 118 rooms.* 🍽*€10. Restaurant*🍴🍴. This slim tower is right downtown, with cosy, comfortable rooms and a games room that's always full.

🍴 EAT

🍷🍴 **El Chinitas** – *Moreno Monroy 4–6.* ℘*952 21 09 72. www.elchinitas.com.* Ceramic murals, photos and pictures of popular personalities and artists make this one of the most characteristic restaurants of Málaga. The terrace on a pedestrian street is pleasant, and there are dining areas on three floors.

🍷🍴🍴 **Restaurante-Museo La Casa del Ángel** – *Madre de Dios 29 (facing Teatro Cervantes).* ℘*952 60 87 50. Closed Mon.* Ángel Garó captures the senses by conjuring up the best of Andalucían gastronomy in a unique artistic setting. Enjoy delicious cuisine while surrounded by paintings by the likes of Picasso, Dalí, Miró, Sebastiano del Piombo and Julio Romero de Torres, master of "La España cañí": flamenco, bullfighters, and Andalucían beauties.

TAPAS

Bar La Mesonera – *Gómez Pallete 11.* ℘*952 22 59 65.* This small bar fills up with stars and the rich and famous before and after flamenco performances at the Teatro Cervantes opposite (and for shows right here on Mon and Wed evenings, €10). Delicious tapas and a colourful, typically Andalucían atmosphere.

Bar Lo Güeno – *Marín García 9.* ℘*952 22 30 48. www.logueno.es.* Over 75 choices from wild mushrooms to venison stew to quail and partridge fill the endless tapas menu in this quintessentially Malagueño favourite.

Antigua Casa de Guardia – *Alameda 18.* ℘*952 21 46 80.* With a back door leading out to the Mercado de Atarazanas, this low wooden counter where they chalk up your tally in chalk is Málaga's oldest bar, dating from 1840.

🍴 CAFÉS

Café Central – *Pl. de la Constitución 11.* ℘*952 22 49 72. www.cafecentralmalaga.com* One of Málaga's most typical and long-standing coffee houses. Although the terrace on the square is particularly pleasant, the large tea room stands out as the café's most impressive feature.

Casa Aránda – *Herrería del Rey 3.* ℘*952 22 28 12.* This lively, atmospheric café has taken over every building on this narrow street. A great place for a chat with friends over *chocolate con churros*.

🌙 NIGHTLIFE

El Pimpi – *Granada 62.* ℘*952 22 89 90.* One of Málaga's most traditional locales, in the old city next to the Museo Picasso, its old-time tavern décor is perfect for enjoying sweet wine and tapas. Leading luminaries have signed its casks and the walls display old bullfighting posters.

Puerta Oscura – *Molina Lario 5.* ℘*952 22 19 00. www.malaganet.com/ puertaoscura.* Excellent for a cup of coffee or something stronger, while you listen to chamber music. The setting is classically elegant, intimate and distinguished. During Málaga's fiesta, the decorations of religious imagery transform the space.

Liceo – *Beatas 21.* ℘*952 60 24 40.* This disco with a lively upstairs bar, in one of Málaga's old town houses, is popular with an international crowd, particularly those in their thirties. This old mansion with its 19C feel really comes to life at the weekend.

Antequera★

Backed up against the Sierra del Torcal, home of an extraordinary park with phantasmagorical rock formations, whitewashed Antequera overlooks a fertile plain with the silhouette of the Peña de los Enamorados in the distance. This "lovers' cliff" was the birthplace of a legend: an Arab princess and a young Christian threw themselves off the cliff to escape the soldiers sent after them by the young woman's father. The town's cobblestone alleys, grilled windows, churches and the fine brick Mudéjar belfry of San Sebastián are the essence of Andalucía.

A BIT OF HISTORY

Geographical centre of Andalucía, Antequera, the Roman Antikaria or "old city", has always been prized as a natural crossroads between Málaga, Córdoba, Granada and Sevilla. For this reason, the town has always been a busy front with battles between Castilian and Nasrid troops. The same strategic position after the Reconquest by Ferdinand of Castile in 1410, brought artistic and religious treasure of the first order that has left its imprint in the town's thousand monuments.

SIGHTS
Alcazaba

◷ *Open Tue–Sat 10am–2pm, 3.30–6pm, Sun and public holidays 10am–2pm. Contact tourist office for further details.*
This was the first fortress taken by the Christians during the reconquest of the kingdom of Granada (1410), but it was soon lost again. Today, its walls shelter a pleasant garden and its towers offer a fine **view**★ over Antequera.

Real Colegiata de Santa María★

Pl. de Santa María. ◷*Open Tue–Sat 10.30am–1.30pm, 4.30–8.30pm, Sun and public holidays 10.30am–1.30pm.* ⬦€6 (also valid for the Real Colegiata de Santa María). ℘952 84 61 43.

▶ **Population:** 45 168
◷ **Michelin Map:** 578 U 16.
🗐 **Info:** Plaza de San Sebastián 7. ℘952 70 25 05 www.antequera.es.
◐ **Location:** Antequera lies in southern Andalucía, inland from the Costa del Sol. 🚆 Plaza de la Estación.
🏛 **Don't Miss:** Ancient dolmens (burial chambers).
👥 **Kids:** Unusual rock formations in the Parque Natural de El Torcal.

Access this church, at the foot of the castle gardens, by the 16C **Arco de los Gigantes** (Arch of Giants). Built in 1514, it has one of the earliest Renaissance façades in Andalucía. The adjacent observation point looks out on 1C Roman baths.

Iglesia del Carmen★

Pl. del Carmen. ◷*Open Tue–Fri 10.30am–1.30pm, 4.30–5.45pm, Sat–Sun and public holidays 10.30am–1.30pm.* ⬦€2.
The central nave of the church boasts a Mudéjar artesonado ceiling and a magnificent Churrigueresque altarpiece.

Museo Municipal

Palacio de Nájera, Pl. del Coso Viejo. ◷*Open Tue–Fri 10am–1.30pm, 4.30–6.30pm, Sat 10am–1.30pm, Sun 11am–1.30pm.* ◷*Closed public holidays.* ⬦€3. ℘95 270 40 21.
The museum in this 17C palace exhibits archaeological pieces. The most outstanding item is the **Ephebus of Antequera**★, a 1C bronze Roman sculpture.

Dolmen de Menga y Viera★

Avenida de Málaga 1. To the left of the Antequera exit on the A 354, towards Granada. ◷*Open Tue–Wed, Sat and public holidays 9am–6pm, Sun 9.30am–2.30pm.* ℘952 71 22 06.
Dating from 2 500 to 2 200 BC, these are enormous funerary chambers beneath great stone slabs. Menga, the older and

larger, is oblong, divided by pillars supporting stone slabs.

▶ *Continue along the A 354 and turn left onto the N 331.*

Dolmen de El Romeral★

Cerro Romeral. Antigua CN 232 towards Córdoba. ⊙*Open same hours as dolmens Menga y Viera.*
This is the most recent chamber (1800 BC), consisting of small flat stones laid to create a trapezoidal section.

EXCURSIONS
Parque Natural de El Torcal★

▶ *14km/8.7mi SE. Take the C 3310 towards Villanueva de la Concepción; go right at the Centro de Recepción "El Torcal" signpost.* ⊙*Open daily 10am–5pm.* ☏ *952 70 25 05.*
The park, spread over 12ha/30 acres, has some of Spain's most unusual eroded karst scenery. Two signposted paths *(1hr and 3hr)* lead to strangely shaped limestone rocks.

TOUR TO THE DESFILADERO DE LOS GAITANES★★

50km/31mi SW.
This protected area in the Subbética mountain range includes a gorge through which the River Guadalhorce flows. Golden eagles nest in the peaks.

> 😊 **A Bit of Advice** 😊

Given the dangerous nature of the defile and to ensure the safety of visitors, we recommend that you go no further than the metal bridge suspended high above the El Chorro defile.

▶ *Take the A 343 to Álora.*

After the Abdajalís Valley, the road zigzags through superb mountain scenery up to **Álora**★, an attractive village of twisting alleyways overlooking the Guadalhorce river.

▶ *Take the MA 444 from Álora. Leave your car at the El Chorro campsite. Continue on foot along a tarmac track (30min there and back) up to a metal bridge with magnificent canyon views.*

FROM ANTEQUERA TO MÁLAGA★

62km/39mi S by the A 45, C 356 and C 345.
These pleasant roads, within sight of majestic hills, afford splendid **views**★★ beyond the Puerto del León (Lion Pass, 960m/3 150ft) to Málaga and the sea.

Desfiladero de Los Gaitanes

© Sami Sarkis/age fotostock

Ronda★★

Ronda stands above a deep ravine. Its isolation and legends of local highwaymen made it a place of pilgrimage for writers and poets during the 19C Romantic period and afterwards. Erich Maria Remarque and Ernest Hemingway were 20C Ronda regulars, each seduced by the cobbled streets, whitewashed houses and impressive mansions that still combine to make the town an enchanted mountain getaway.

SIGHTS
Museo de la Ciudad★★
Pl. Mondragón. ◷*Open Mon–Fri 10am–7pm, Sat–Sun and public holidays 10am–3pm.* ◷*Closed 1 Jan, Good Friday, 25 Dec.* ☞€3. ✆952 87 84 50.

The charming **Mudéjar patio**★★ has the remains of *azulejos* and stucco work between its arches. The collection includes an exhibition on the natural habitats of the Serranía de Ronda, and historical and ethnological sections.

Plaza de Toros: Museo Taurino★
Virgen de la Paz. ◷*Open daily 10am–8pm.* ☞€6. ✆952 87 41 32. *www.rmcr.org.*

Dating from 1785 and with a capacity for 6 000, this is one of Spain's oldest and most beautiful bullrings. Enter through an elegant gateway. Traditional *Corridas Goyescas*, fights in period costumes, are held annually. The museum contains sumptuous costumes and mementoes of Ronda matadors.

Casa del Rey Moro
Cuesta de Santo Domingo. ◷*Open daily 10.45am–7.30pm.* ☞€3.50. ✆952 18 72 00. *www.museobandolero.com.*

Inside are impressive Moorish steps, known as **La Mina**, which descend to the river. The **gardens**★ were laid out in 1912 by French landscapist **Jean-Claude Forestier**, who also designed María Luisa Park in Sevilla.

▶ **Population:** 36 827
◔ **Michelin Map:** 578 V 14.
▤ **Info:** Plaza de España 9. ✆952 87 12 72. www.turismoderonda.es.
◑ **Location:** Ronda lies in SE Spain, 60km/37mi inland and over the mountains from Marbella. ▰Avenida de la Victoria 31.

Museo del Bandolero
Armiñán 65. ◷*Open daily 10.30am–7pm.* ☞€3. ✆952 87 77 85.

The Serranía de Ronda range was once frequented by bandits, brigands and outlaws. This museum provides insight into these legendary figures.

⚘ WALKING TOUR
The River Guadalevín divides Ronda into two parts, connected by the 18C Puente Nuevo, offering a **view**★ of the El Tajo ravine: to the south, the **Ciudad**, the old quarter; and, to the north, the **Mercadillo**, the old market area. The Camino de los Molinos road provides views of cliffs and the **Tajo**★.

LA CIUDAD★★
⚘*Guided tours (2hr).*
Depart from Puente Nuevo.
The old walled town, a vestige of Moorish occupation until 1485, is a picturesque quarter of alleys and whitewashed houses with wrought-iron balconies.

▷ *Cross the bridge and follow Santo Domingo, passing the 18C neo-Mudéjar Casa del Rey Moro.*

Palacio del Marqués de Salvatierra
This small mansion is graced with an exceptional Renaissance **portal**★★ and a wrought-iron balcony decorated with pre-Columbian-inspired statues.

▷ *From the Arco de Felipe V, by the Puente Viejo, a stone path leads to the Baños Árabes.*

Baños Árabes★

San Miguel. ⏱*Open Mon–Fri 10am–6pm, Sat–Sun and public holidays 10am–3pm.* ⏱*Closed 1 Jan, 24 Dec.* ☞*€2.* ☎*952 87 08 18.*

Built at the end of the 13C in the artisans' and tanners' district, the Moorish baths comprise three rooms topped with barrel vaults and illuminated by star-shaped skylights or *lunettes*.

▶ *Follow a stone staircase parallel to the walls, then pass through a 13C gateway, the Puerta de la Acijara.*

Minarete de San Sebastián★

This graceful minaret is the only one remaining from a 14C Nasrid mosque. A horseshoe arch frames the door.

Iglesia de Santa María la Mayor★

Pl. de la Duquesa de Parcent. ⏱*Open daily 15 Jun–15 Sept 10am–8pm; 16 Sept–14 Jun 10am–7pm.* ☞*€3.* ☎*952 87 22 46.*

The Collegiate Church of St Mary was built over the town's main mosque. Today, only a 13C horseshoe arch, decorated with *atauriques* and calligraphic motifs, and a minaret remain from the original building. The interior is divided into three distinct architectural styles: Gothic (aisles), Plateresque (high altar); and Baroque (choir stalls). On the exterior, note the double balcony used as a tribune by local dignitaries.

▶ *Continue along Manuel Montero.*

Palacio de Mondragón

Two Mudéjar towers crown the Renaissance façade of the palace, now the **Museo de la Ciudad** (🔗 *see p474*).

EXCURSIONS
Iglesia Rupestre de la Virgen de la Cabeza★

▶ *2.7km/1.7mi along the A 369 towards Algeciras.* ⏱*Open Mon–Sat 10.30am–2pm.* ⏱*Closed 1 Jan, 24 Dec.* ☞*€3.* ☎*952 87 12 72.*

This 9C Mozarabic monastery was excavated out of rock. The frescoes in the church were painted in the 18C. The **views**★★ of Ronda are impressive.

Ruinas de Acinipo

▶ *19km/11.8mi along the A 376 towards Sevilla.* ⏱*Open Tue–Sun 10am–5pm. Call to confirm hours.* ☞*No charge.* ☎*951 04 14 00.*

Known as Ronda la Vieja, the ruins of Acinipo retain a 1C AD theatre, with part of the stage and terraces.

Cueva de la Pileta★

▶ *20km/12.4mi SW. Take the A 376 towards Sevilla, then the MA 555 towards Benaoján. Bear onto the MA 561.* 🔗*Guided tours (1hr) daily 10am–1pm, 4–5pm (till 6pm 16 Apr–31 Oct).* ⏱*Closed 1 Jan, 24 Dec.* ☞*€8.* ☎*952 16 73 43. www.cuevadelapileta.org.*

The cave has over 2km/1.2mi of galleries. Red and black wall paintings predate those of Altamira, with figurative motifs from the Palaeolithic era (20 000 BC) and symbolic art and Neolithic animal drawings (goats, panthers, etc. 4 000 BC).

Cradle of Bullfighting

Ronda is indelibly linked with the world of bullfighting. Francisco Romero, who was born here in 1700, laid down the rules of bullfighting, which until then had been only a display of audacity and agility. He became the father of modern bullfighting by his introduction of the artistic work with the small cape, or *muleta*. His son Juan introduced the *cuadrilla*, or supporting cast, and his grandson, Pedro Romero (1754–1839), became one of Spain's greatest bullfighters. He founded the Ronda School, known for artistic classicism, strict observance of the rules, and for the *estocada recibiendo*, in which the matador holds his ground and allows the charging bull to impale himself on the sword, considered the most dangerous and beautiful kill.

Ronda to San Pedro de Alcántara by road★★

▶ *49km/30mi SE on the C 339. About 1hr.*

For 20km/12.4mi the road crosses a bare mountain landscape; it then climbs steeply into a **corniche**★★ above the Guadalmedina valley. The route is deserted; there's not a single village.

 DRIVING TOURS

Ronda to Algeciras★
118km/71mi SW on the C 341, C 3331 and A 7. About 3hr.

The road climbs to overlook the Genal Valley, then winds around the foot of **Jimena de la Frontera** (🚃 *Juan de Dios 17*) perched on a hill, and crosses the **Parque Natural de los Alcornocales★**, one of the largest forests of cork oaks in Spain.

After 22km/13mi, a narrow road leads *(right)* to **Castellar de la Frontera**★, a village of flower-filled alleyways huddled within the castle grounds.

Pueblos Blancos★★
To the west of Ronda, in often curiously shaped mountains, are the remains of the *pinsapos* forest of pines dating from the beginning of the Quaternary era.

The beauty of the countryside is set off by delightful white towns *(pueblos blancos)*, often perched on rocky crags or stretched along escarpments, their whitewashed houses dominated by a ruined castle or a church.

From Ronda to Arcos de la Frontera
By the northern route; 130km/81mi. About 4hr.

▶ *Take the MA 428 towards Arriate, then continue on the CA 4211.*

Setenil de las Bodegas★
In this unique village, in the gorge of the Guadalporcún river, are a number of troglodyte dwellings built into the rock. Also of interest are the **tourist office** *(Villa 2; ℘956 13 42 61; www.setenil.com),*

in an impressive building with a handsome 16C **artesonado ceiling**, the keep *(torre del homenaje)*, and the Iglesia de la Encarnación.

▶ *Travel 16km/10mi NW.*

Olvera
Olvera enjoys an impressive hillside **site**★★ amid olive groves, crowned by the keep of its triangular-shaped **castle** and the Iglesia de la Encarnación.

Olvera is renowned for its superb olive oil *(Pl. de la Iglesia; ◷ open Tue–Sun 10.30am–2pm, 4–6.30pm; ⊜€3 with museum; ℘956 12 08 16).*

▶ *Take the A 384 towards Algodonales; turn off to the right onto the CA 531.*

Zahara de la Sierra★
The village enjoys an extraordinary hilltop **setting**★★. Zahara was a defensive enclave for the Nasrids, and later for Christians. The outlines of the 12C **castle** and the 18C Baroque **Iglesia de Santa María de Mesa** stand out.

▶ *Return to the A 382 and continue towards Villamartín.*

Villamartín
The **Alberite dolmen** *(℘956 73 35 55)*, dating from around 4 000 BC, can be visited 4km/2.4mi to the south. A 20m/65ft gallery is formed by large stone slabs.

Bornos
The Plaza del Ayuntamiento is fronted by the **Castillo-Palacio de los Ribera**★ *(Pl. Alcalde José González; ℘956 72 82 64; www.bornos.es),* now the tourist office. Inside are a Renaissance-style **patio** and a 16C garden. Also on the square is the **Iglesia de Santo Domingo**, a Gothic church built in the late 15C.

Espera
▶ *10km/6.2mi NW of Bornos via CA 402*
This village on a small outcrop is dominated by the ruins of a Moorish castle, the **Castillo de Fatetar** *(⊜no charge; ℘956 72 00 11).*

The Adoration of Orson and Papa

Ronda's romantic landscape and link to bullfighting inspired both Ernest "Papa" Hemingway and Orson Welles, who now have *paseos* named in their honour. In *Death in the Afternoon* (1932), Hemingway states that Ronda "is where you should go if you ever go to Spain on a honeymoon". The ashes of Orson Welles are interred in the nearby farm of El Recreo (on the estate of Antonio Ordóñez, whom Hemingway wrote about in *The Dangerous Summer*). In Welles' own words "A man is not from where he is born, but where he chooses to die".

Arcos de la Frontera★★

Arcos has a remarkable **site**★★ atop a crag enclosed by a loop in the Guadalete river. The old town huddles against formidable crenellated castle walls and those of the two churches.

Park below the village in Plaza de Andalucía. Ascend the Cuesta de Belén, a hill which connects modern Arcos with the medieval town.

Note the 15C Gothic-Mudéjar **façade**★ of the **Palacio del Conde del Águila**.

Continue to the right along Calle Nueva to Plaza del Cabildo.

Plaza del Cabildo

Overhanging the precipice, one side of the plaza boasts a **view**★ that extends to a meander of the Guadalete. On the plaza are the town hall *(ayuntamiento)*, parador (a former palace), and the castle (closed to visitors).

Basilica de Santa María★

Pl. del Cabildo. Open daily 10am–1pm, 4pm–7pm. Closed 1, 6 Jan, 25 Dec. €2. 956 70 00 06.
This church was built around 1530. The **west façade**★ is Plateresque. Don't miss the 17C **altarpiece** of the Ascension of the Virgin.
A charming maze of alleys leads to the other side of the cliff, where the Capilla de la Misericordia, the Palacio del Mayorazgo (now a music conservatory) and the **Iglesia de San Pedro** can be seen.

Iglesia de San Pedro

San Pedro. Open Mon–Sat 10am–1pm, 4–7pm, Sun 10am–1.30pm.

This church dates from the early 15C and boasts a façade crowned by an impressive Neoclassical bell tower.

Arcos de la Frontera to Ronda

102km/61mi – about 3hr.
Leave Arcos along the A 372 towards **El Bosque**. The Parque Natural Sierra de Grazalema visitor centre is here *(Av. de la Diputación; 956 71 60 63).*

Leave El Bosque on the A 373.

Ubrique

The **road**★ enters the heart of the Sierra de Grazalema. Beyond the **Plaza del Ayuntamiento**, is the 18C parish church of **Nuestra Señora de la O**.

From Ubrique, continue 10km/6.2mi E along the A 374.

Villaluenga del Rosario

This village is the highest in Cádiz province. Its irregularly shaped **bullring** *(Plaza de toros; Calle Real 19; 956 46 00 01)* is built on top of a rock.

Head 15km/9.3mi NE on the A 374.

Grazalema★★

Grazalema, one of Andalucía's most charming villages, is the wettest place in the whole of Spain. It retains its Moorish layout, as well as the tower of the **Iglesia de San Juan** *(José M Jiménez; 956 13 20 10)*. The 18C **Iglesia de la Aurora** *(Pl. de España 8)* is adorned with an unusual fountain. Grazalema is famous for its white and brown woollen blankets; a traditional **hand loom** operates at the entrance to the town.

Return to Ronda on the A 372.

Costa del Sol★

Sheltered by the Sierra Nevada, Spain's Sun Coast enjoys mild winters and hot summers. Millions of visitors are attracted by sandy beaches, whitewashed towns and villages and a variety of leisure activities. In summer, the beaches are packed, and the nightlife continues until dawn.

🚗 DRIVING TOURS

Tour of the Western Coastline★★

From Estepona to Málaga
139km/86mi. Allow one day.

Estepona★

The **old quarter**★ retains its Andalucían charm. Its attractions are the **Plaza de las Flores**, the ruins of the castle and the 18C **Iglesia de los Remedios** *(Pl. San Francisco).*

In the hills above is 👪**Selwo Aventura Park** *(🕐open mid-Feb–Oct daily; Nov Fri–Sun, 4–8 Dec from 10am; see website for closing times; ⬤€24.50, child €17; 🖉902 19 04 82; www.selwo.es)* where open-sided lorries take visitors on safari, spotting rhinos, giraffes, zebras, lions and tigers roaming freely in large enclosures which give the illusion of natural surroundings.

Casares★, 24km/15mi inland along the A 377 and MA 539, is a charming much photographed whitewashed town of Moorish origin with a maze of narrow streets, clinging to a rock in the Sierra de Crestenilla.

San Pedro de Alcántara

22km/14mi E of Estepona, off E 15.
Archaeological sites close to the beach include **Las Bóvedas** *(thermal baths dating from the 3C AD)* and the palaeo-Christian basilica of Vega del Mar *(💬guided tours (1hr45min); ⬤no charge; 🖉it is advisable to reserve a day ahead; 🖉952 78 13 60). For a description of the road from Ronda, 🕐see RONDA.*

🚲 **Michelin Map:** 578 V16-22, W 14-15.16.

📋 **Info:** Estepona: Av. San Lorenzo 1. 🖉952 80 20 02; Marbella: Glorieta de la Fontanilla. 🖉952 77 14 42; Nerja: Carmen 1. 🖉952 52 15 31; Salobreña: Plaza de Goya. 🖉958 61 03 14. www.visitcostadelsol.com.

🔵 **Location:** The Costa del Sol stretches along the Mediterranean from the Straits of Gibraltar to east of Almería.

🅿 **Parking:** You'll have to search in beach towns, so get there early.

👪 **Kids:** Selwo Aventura Park.

Puerto Banús★★

4km/2.5mi E of San Pedro along A 7.
This magnificent marina attracts some of the world's most luxurious sailing craft. Its many restaurants, bars and boutiques are hugely popular on summer evenings.

Marbella★★

8km/5mi E of Puerto Banús along N 340.
The long-established capital of the Costa del Sol is still an international jet-set destination. Whitewashed old buildings stand beside shops, bars and restaurants along a maze of streets and lanes in the **old quarter**★.

The enchanting **Plaza de los Naranjos**★, named for its orange trees, is lined by the 16C town hall, the 17C Casa del Corregidor, and a small 15C chapel, the Ermita de Nuestro Señor Santiago.

Other sights in the old quarter are the 17C Iglesia de Santa María de la Encarnación and the **Museo del Grabado Español Contemporáneo**★ *(🕐open 22 Sept–15 Jun Mon and Sat 9am–2pm, Tue–Fri 9am–9pm; 16 Jun–21 Sept Mon and Sat 9am–2pm, Tue–Fri 9am–2pm, 6–9pm; ⬤€3; free on Sat; 🖉952 76 57 41; www.museodelgrabado.es)* devoted to contemporary prints, in a 16C former hospital.

Marbella also has a marina, luxury accommodations, excellent beaches, a long promenade, designer boutiques, health spas and golf courses.

Fuengirola
35km/22mi E of Marbella off E 15.
The Castillo de Sohail, a castle of Moorish origin, dominates this large resort. The remains of some Roman baths and villas are in the Santa Fe district.

▷ *Head N for 9km/5.6mi towards Mijas.*

Mijas★
Views★ from this picturesque whitewashed town in the sierra encompass much of the coast. It is well worth strolling narrow, winding streets dotted with tiny squares and charming nooks and crannies.

Highlights are sections of the old Moorish wall, and the 16C Iglesia de la Inmaculada Concepción, crowned by a Mudéjar tower.

Shops display Andalucían arts and crafts (pottery, basketwork and textiles). Mijas also has an unusual miniatures museum, known as the **Carromato de Max** *(Avenida del Compás; ⏲open daily 10am–7pm (10pm in summer); ⚲€3; Tourist Office ✆952 58 90 34).*

Benalmádena
8km/5mi E of Mijas along A 7.
Benalmádena stands several kilometres inland from the resort of Benalmádena Costa. Its main historical sights include several 16C watchtowers and a small **archaeological museum** *(⏲open late-Sept–Jun Tue–Sat 9.30am–1.30pm; Jul–early Sept Tue–Sat 9.30am–1.30pm, 5–7pm; Sun and public holidays 10am–2pm; ⏲closed 1, 6 Jan, Good Fri, 1 May, 24, 25, 31 Dec; ⚲no charge; ✆952 44 85 93).*

Torremolinos
12km/7.4mi NE of Benalmádena, off E 15 www.ayto-torremolinos.org.
The promenade and the long beach are the main attractions of this onetime fishing village, now a huge resort.

Málaga★ *(⚲See MÁLAGA)*
17km/10.5mi NE from Torremolinos off A 7. ▦Explanada de la Estación.

Tour of the Eastern Coastline★
From Málaga to Almería
204km/127mi – allow one day.
This beautiful coast is punctuated by the ruins of *torres de vigía*, fortified watchtowers built after the Reconquest against attacks by Barbary pirates.

Nerja★
53km/33mi E of Málaga along E 15.
Nerja, a large resort, overlooks the Mediterranean from the top of a promontory. The **Balcón de Europa**★ is a magnificent mirador offering views of this dramatic coastline and occasional glimpses of North Africa.

View from the Balcón de Europa, Nerja

Y. Duhamel/MICHELIN

Cueva de Nerja★★
4.5km/2.7mi E along the Motril road. ⏲Open daily 10am–2pm, 4–6.30pm. ⚲€8.50. ✆952 52 95 20. www.cuevasdenerja.es.
In this cave were found paintings, weapons, jewels and bones, indicating habitation in the Palaeolithic era. Its size and stalactites and stalagmites are impressive. An annual festival of music and dance is held in the Sala de la Cascada (Cascade Chamber) the second and third weeks of July.

The Road from Nerja to La Herradura★

The scenic road snakes along a mountainside with delightful **views**★★.

Almuñécar

23km/14mi E of Nerja along N 340.
Bananas, medlars, pomegranates and mangoes are grown on the small alluvial plain *(hoya)* behind this resort. The **Cueva de los Siete Palacios** houses an archaeological museum *(○ open Tue–Sat 10.30am–1.30pm, 6.30–9pm, Sun 10.30am–1.30pm; ○ €2.35, also valid for Castillo de San Miguel; ℘958 63 11 25).* The **Castillo de San Miguel** is also open to the public *(San Miguel; ○ open Tue–Sat 10.30am–1.30pm, 5–7.30pm, Sun 10.30am–2pm; ○ €2.35).*

Salobreña★

13km/8mi E of Almuñécar along E 15.
Salobreña, prettiest town on this coast, spreads across a hill, a white blanket punctuated by purple splashes of bougainvillea. An imposing Moorish **fortress** converted into a palatial residence by Nasrid kings in the 14C stands above *(○ open daily 9.30am–2pm, 4–6.30pm; ○ €1.50; ℘958 61 03 14).*

The Road from Calahonda to Castell de Ferro★

The road hugs the rocky coast, offering mountain and sea views. After Balanegra the N 340 turns inland through an immense sweep of greenhouses around El Ejido, where flowers, vegetables and tropical fruit are grown.

Almería

○ *See ALMERÍA*

ADDRESSES

 STAY

ALMUÑÉCAR

○○ **Hotel Casablanca** – *Pl. San Cristóbal 4.* ℘958 63 55 75. wwwhotelcasablanca almunecar.com. 35 rooms. ○€4.50. *Restaurant* ○○. With its cupola, raspberry-coloured façade and arches that imitate the architecture of Moroccan palaces, the Casablanca is a visual experience not to be missed! Once inside your room, the crystal chandeliers and marble décor add a decidedly Oriental touch. Book in advance.

BENALMÁDENA

○○○ **Hotel La Fonda** – *Santo Domingo 7* ℘952 56 83 24. 26 rooms. ○€4.50. A charming hotel in the Sierra de Castillejos, overlooking the sea. Spacious rooms, indoor pool, flower-filled patios and terraces with views of the hills and sea. Very reasonably priced given the standard.

ESTEPONA

○○ **Hostal El Pilar** – *Pl. de las Flores 10.* ℘952 80 00 18. www.hostalelpilar.es. 17 rooms. Time would appear to have stopped in this charming *hostal* on the main square. The interior, decorated with black and white family photos, has an impressive staircase leading up to the basic but pleasant rooms.

MARBELLA

○○○○ **Hotel La Morada Más Hermosa** – *Montenebros 16.* ℘952 92 44 67. www.la moradamashermosa.com. 9 rooms. ○€8. Find this hotel on a plant-bedecked alley right in the old part of town. The charming rooms have been decorated with care by the owner in a country Andalucían style with colonial details. Ask for room 2 with its terrace or wood-panelled room 5.

○○○○ **Marbella Club** – *Bulevar Príncipe Alfonso von Hohenlohe.* ℘952 82 22 11. www.marbellaclub.com. 137 rooms. ○€35. Three restaurants ○○○○. One of the best hotels along the coast, built in the middle of a superb garden planted with palm trees. The bungalow accommodation here frequently hosts the rich and famous. The Marbella Club is the perfect place to unwind and enjoy the magnificent sports facilities available.

NERJA

○○○ **Hostal San Miguel** – *San Miguel 36.* ℘952 52 18 86. www.hostalsanmiguel.com. 12 rooms, 1 appartment. ○€5. This hotel is in a recently restored town house near the centre, with modest but comfortable rooms. There's a bar-coffee shop, and a special feature is the top-floor terrace with small pool and sea and mountain views.

○○○ **Hostal Marissal** – *Pas. Balcón de Europa 3.* ℘952 52 01 99. www.hostal marissal.com. 22 rooms. ○€3. *Restaurant* ○○. In a privileged location, at the entry to the famed Balcony of Europe, with fine views to the passage from some rooms. Coffee shop and restaurant.

OJÉN

😊😊🍽 **Refugio de Juanar** – *Sierra Blanca s/n.* ☎*952 88 10 00. www.juanar.com. 23 rooms, 3 suites.* ⬛€8. This charming hotel located in the middle of a game preserve is a peaceful getaway from the beach madness along the coast. Rooms are spacious, with country furnishings. The restaurant specialises in game dishes.

⍩ EAT

MARBELLA

😊🍽 **El Balcón de la Virgen** – *Remedios 2.* ☎*952 77 60 92. www.elbalcondelavirgen.com. Closed Jan, 1–15 Feb.* In an attractive street lined by an endless succession of restaurant terraces. The restaurant, recognisable by the image of the Virgin Mary on its attractive façade, is mainly popular with tourists. Andalucían cuisine.

😊😊🍽 **Casa de la Era** – *Finca El Chorrearo. 1km/0.6mi N.* ☎*952 77 06 25. www.casade laera.com. Closed Mon–Thu (except Aug) for dinner, Aug for lunch, Sun.* In a typical chalet house, this restaurant affords superb mountain views to go with the Andalucían and Morrocan cuisine.

MIJAS

😊😊🍽 **La Alcazaba de Mijas** – *Pl. de la Constitución.* ☎*952 59 02 53. www.restaurantemesonelolivar.com. Closed Sat and Feb. Reservations recommended.* Perched on the Arab walls of Mijas with fine vistas and careful decoration, La Alcazaba's best feature is its timeless *Mozarabic* dining room, with flowing detailing and two venerable horseshoe arches framing an endless landscape.

😊😊🍽 **El Olivar** – *Av. Virgen de la Peña, edificio El Rosario.* ☎*952 48 61 96. Closed Feb, Sat.* This country restaurant offers fine sierra views through its large windows and finer views from its terrace.

NERJA

😊😊🍽 **Marisquería La Marea** – *Pl. Cantarero s/n.* ☎*952 52 57 78. www.marisquerias.com. Reservations recommended.* A good address for fish and seafood. The scallops and clams on display at the bar are grilled fresh when you order them and served either in the bar itself or in the nautically decorated restaurant.

😊😊😊🍽 **Pepe Rico** – *Almirante Ferrándiz 28.* ☎*952 52 02 47. www.peperico.info. Closed 3 weeks in Jan, Sun.* On a pedestrianised street, this cosy, Swedish-run eatery serves dishes such as duck cooked in wine and suckling pig. Holiday flats are available around a patio (😊😊🍽).

😊😊🍽 **Udo Heimer** – *Pueblo Andaluz 27.* ☎*952 52 00 32. www.udoheimer.net. Closed Jan, Mon–Wed and Sun for dinner. Reservations required.* An arresting variety of textures and flavours epitomises the cuisine of this establishment, made with locally sourced produce.

OJÉN

😊😊🍽 **Mesón Lorente** – *Junquillo 32.* ☎*952 88 11 74. Closed 2nd half of Jan and Jul, Thu. Reservations recommended.* Many Andalucíans and tourists looking for a breather from the coast head for this restaurant, which is well known for its home cooking. The greenhouse looks onto the liveliest street in the town.

TAPAS

The pedestrianised district of **La Carihuela**, alongside the beach, is the most attractive part of Torremolinos, with dozens of bars, restaurants, hotels and shops. Two of the best restaurants are **Casa Juan** *(pas. Marítimo 28;* ☎*952 38 56 56)*, which has been specialising in seafood for more than 30 years, and **La Jábega** *(Mar 17;* ☎*952 38 63 75)*, overlooking the promenade.

🛍 SHOPPING

Marbella is one of the best places for shopping on the Costa del Sol with all the top names in international fashion represented here.

Most of these stores are concentrated in Puerto Banús where there is an impressive nucleus of modern, designer boutiques, and in the centre of Marbella, particularly along **Avenida Ricardo Soriano** and **Calle Ramón y Cajal**. The best indoor shopping centre on the Costa del Sol is also found in Puerto Banús.

Markets are an important feature of life on the Costa del Sol. The one in Marbella takes place on **Saturday mornings** next to the Nueva Andalucía bullring *(Pl. de Toros)* near Puerto Banús.

Northern Andalucía begins south of the spectacular Despeñaperros Pass, the natural barrier separating the *meseta* or tableland of Castilla and the Guadalquivir Valley. The Guadalquivir river is the thread that connects much of Andalucía, from its headwaters in the Sierra de Cazorla to the estuary at Sanlúcar de Barrameda. The river that launched ships to the New World in the late 15C passes through the olive groves of Jaén and Úbeda and then the urban hubs of Córdoba and Sevilla, two of the "three sisters" (including Granada) that developed into the most important cities in southern Spain.

Highlights

1 Walking between the 856 columns of the Mezquita in **Cordóba** (p483)

2 Baroque and Moorish jewls in **Priego de Córdoba** (p491)

3 Exploring Rennaissance **Baeza**, capital of olive oil (p492)

4 Driving through the dramatic **Parque Natural de las Sierras de Cazorla, Segura y Las Villas** (p496)

Córdoba

Córdoba was the Manhattan of the 9C, the city where the three cultures that defined the Iberian Peninsula – Christian, Muslim and Jewish – lived in harmony for a brief but fruitful interlude during the reign of King Abderraman III. Seneca, Averroës, Lucan and Maimónides all called Córdoba home at one time or another and the city still celebrates their thinking with monuments and museums such as the Torre de Calahorra where a facsimile of Alfonso X El Sabio – the great Christian warrior, king, musician and poet – debates the Muslim and Judaic philosophies of Maimónides and Averroës. The painter Julio Romero de Torres is modern Córdoba's favourite son, a multi-talented artist known for his dashing figure and his flamenco *cante hondo* performances as well as for his sensual and symbolic canvases.

Northern Andalucía today

Jaén province is the most overlooked part of Andalucía which is possibly a bonus for independent travellers as its majestic scenery, magnificent castles and historic paradors make it perfect unspoiled touring country, with little in the way of tourist fripperies.

Baeza and Úbeda are two of Andalucía's architectural treasures and either make a good touring base. Jaén is famous for its cathedral and Moorish Baths. Away from the monumental buildings, a driving excursion and walk in the hills of the Sierras de Cazorla, Spain's largest nature reserve, is highly recommended.

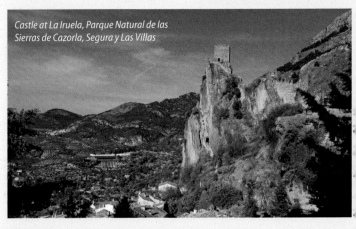

Castle at La Iruela, Parque Natural de las Sierras de Cazorla, Segura y Las Villas

Córdoba★★★

Córdoba owes its fame to the brilliance of the Roman, Moorish, Jewish and Christian civilisations that have endowed its rich and varied history. The Mezquita, the city's most precious jewel, dominates the old section whose narrow, whitewashed streets and charming small squares are embellished with wrought-iron grilles and flower-filled patios.

THE CITY TODAY

The city is on the same well-trodden "Moorish Treasures" sightseeing trail as Seville and Granada, though due to its distance from the coast it receives fewer visitors. However, Córdoba is not just a preserved tourist theme park: beyond the medieval core lies a lively modern sophisticated centre with buzzing bars and nightlife.

A BIT OF HISTORY

The Roman city – Córdoba was the birthplace of **Seneca the Rhetorician** (55 BC–AD 39), and his son **Seneca the Philosopher** (4 BC–AD 65). A noted early bishop was **Hossius** (257–359), counsellor to Emperor Constantine.

Of Roman Córdoba only the mausoleum in the Jardines de la Victoria, the ruins of a 1C temple, and the bridge linking the old section with the Torre de la Calahorra remain.

The Córdoba Caliphate – Emirs from Damascus established themselves in Córdoba as early as 719. In 756 **Abd ar-Rahman I**, sole survivor of the **Umayyads**, founded the dynasty which was to rule Muslim Spain for three centuries. In 929 **Abd ar-Rahman III** proclaimed himself Caliph of Córdoba. In the 10C a university was founded. Christians, Jews and Muslims lived side by side and enriched each other intellectually and culturally.

On the accession, in 976, of the feeble **Hisham II**, power fell into the hands of the ruthless **Al-Mansur** (the Victorious). Al-Andalus fragmented into warring kingdoms, the **reinos de taifas**.

▶ **Population:** 328 428
◔ **Michelin Map:** 578 S 15.
🛈 **Info:** Estación Ave Renfe. ℘902 20 17 74. www.turismodecordoba.org.
▶ **Location:** Córdoba lies along the Guadalquivir river in Andalucía, between ranchland and olive country. The A4 highway runs to Écija (52km/32mi SW) and Sevilla (143km/89mi SW). ▭Glorieta de las Tres Culturas.
🄿 **Parking:** Park outside the old city and walk Córdoba's lanes and alleys.
👁 **Don't Miss:** The Mezquita.
🕓 **Timing:** See the Mezquita, followed by the Jewish quarter.

Córdoba became part of the Kingdom of Sevilla in 1070. However, intellectual life flourished. **Averroës**, physicist, astrologer, mathematician and doctor, brought the learning of Aristotle to the West. The Jew **Maimónides** (1135–1204) was famed in medicine, theology and philosophy, but fled in order to escape persecution.

Reconquered in 1236, Córdoba declined until the 16C and 17C, when its tooled leatherwork became fashionable.

SIGHTS

THE MEZQUITA AND THE JUDERÍA★★★
Mezquita-Catedral★★★ (Mosque-Cathedral)

Torrijos. ◔🕓*Open Mon–Sat 8.30am–7pm, Sun and public holidays 8.30–10am, 2–7pm.* ☞€8. ℘957 47 05 12.

The Mezquita

The traditional Muslim crenellated square encloses the Patio de los Naranjos (Orange Tree Court) with a **Basin of Al-Mansur (1)** for ritual ablution, a hall for prayer and a minaret.

The first Muslims in Córdoba shared the Visigothic church of St Vincent with the Christians. Soon Abd ar-Rahman I (731–788) purchased part of the site. He razed the church and around the year 780 began the construction of a splendid mosque with 11 aisles each opening onto the Patio de los Naranjos. Marble pillars and Roman and Visigothic stone were re-used. The mosque became famous for an innovation: the superimposition of two tiers of arches to add height and spaciousness. After the reconquest, Christians built chapels in the west nave, including the 17C **Capilla de la Purísima Concepción (2)**, completely covered with marble.

In 848 Abd ar-Rahman II had the mosque extended to the present-day Capilla de Villaviciosa (Villaviciosa Chapel). In 961 El Hakam II built the *mihrab*, and in 987, Al-Mansur added eight aisles (with red-brick floors).

Interior

Enter by the Puerta de las Palmas. The interior is a forest of columns (about 850) and the horseshoe-shaped arches. The wide main aisle off the doorway has a beautiful *artesonado* ceiling. It leads

to the **kiblah** wall, where the faithful prayed, and the **mihrab**★★★, normally a simple niche, but here a sumptuous room preceded by a triple **maksourah** (3) (enclosure) reserved for the caliph. Its three ribbed domes rest on unusual apparently interweaving multifoil arches. Alabaster plaques and ornate stucco arabesques and palm-leaf motifs sometimes framed by Cufic script enhance the architecture.

In the 13C, Christians walled off the aisles from the court. A few columns were removed and pointed arches substituted for Moorish ones when the first **cathedral (4)** was built. Alfonso X was responsible for the chancel in the **Capilla de Villaviciosa** or **Lucernario (5)**, and built the **Capilla Real**★ (6) decorated in the 13C with Mudéjar stucco. Chapels were built in the western nave, including the fine marble-faced 17C **Purísima Concepción (2)**.

Catedral

In the 16C the canons cut away the centre of the mosque to erect loftier vaulting. Emperor Charles V was far from pleased: "You have destroyed something unique," he said, "to build

484

The Sephardic Jews

No history of Spain is complete without a mention of the *Sefardíes* whose presence may still be felt in *juderías* (old Jewish quarters) and synagogues. The main Jewish towns in the past were Córdoba, Toledo and Granada.

The Sephardic Jews (*Sepharad* is the Hebrew word for Spain) came to the Iberian Peninsula in Antiquity at the same time as the Greeks and Phoenicians. In the 8C, during the Arab occupation, they welcomed the Muslims, who regarded them as sympathetic allies. The Muslims put them in charge of negotiating with the Christian community. As merchants, bankers, craftsmen, doctors and scholars, Jews played an important economic role and influenced the domains of culture and science. Some became famous, like the Torah scholar Maimónides of Córdoba (1135–1204).

Maimónides

© neftali/Fotolia.com

The Jews were particularly prosperous under the Caliphate of Córdoba (929–1031). However, at the end of the 11C, Jews from Andalucía moved to Toledo and Catalunya, especially Girona, as a result of intolerance and persecution under the Almohads. They were often persecuted by Christians during the Reconquest: a royal decree forced them to wear a piece of red or yellow cloth. The Alhambra Decree expelling all non-Catholics from Spain was proclaimed in 1492 by the Catholic Monarchs. Some chose to convert, others (known as *Marranos*), though having publicly converted, continued practising their Jewish faith in hiding. The Inquisition was established In 1478 for the purpose of identifying and punishing so-called crypto-Jews. Most of Spain's Jewish community emigrated to other parts of the Mediterranean. Today, Sephardic Jews account for up to 20 per cent of the total Jewish population in the world. Most of them have kept their language, Ladino, derived from 15C Castilian.

something commonplace." The roof is a mix of 16C and 17C styles (Hispano-Flemish, Renaissance and Baroque). Additional enrichments are the Baroque **choir stalls**★★ (8) by Pedro Duque Cornejo (c. 1750) and two **pulpits**★★ (7) of marble, jasper and mahogany.

Tesoro

The treasury, built by the Baroque architect Francisco Hurtado Izquierdo, in the **Capilla del Cardenal** (Cardinal's Chapel) (9), includes a large 16C **monstrance**★ by E Arfe and an exceptional Baroque figure of Christ in ivory.

Exterior features include the **minaret**, enveloped by a 17C Baroque tower. Giving onto the street is the 14C Mudéjar **Puerta del Perdón** (Pardon Doorway) faced with bronze. Further on is the small chapel of the **Virgen de los Faroles** (Virgin of the Lanterns) (10).

The Alcázar of the Umayyads stood in magnificent gardens facing the mosque where the Palacio Episcopal (Bishop's Palace) now houses the **Museo Bellas Artes** (*Plaza del Potro;* ⏰*open Tue 2.30–8.30pm, Wed–Sat 9am–8.30pm, Sun and public holidays 9am–2.30pm.* ✆€1.50; free for EU citizens; ☎957 35 55 50).

Judería★★
(Old Jewish Quarter)

NW of the Mezquita. Narrow streets, flower-draped walls, cool patios, and lively nightlife characterise the quarter from which Jews were expelled.

Sinagoga

Judíos. ♿⏰*Open Tue–Sun 9.30am–2pm, 3.30–5.30pm.* ✆€0.30; free for EU citizens. ☎957 20 29 28.

Built in the early 14C, this synagogue is a small square room with a balcony for

Patio, Palacio de Viana

the women. The upper walls are covered in Mudéjar stucco.

Casa de Sefarad★

Calle Judíos. Guided tours Mon–Sat and holidays 10am–6pm, Sun 11am–2pm. €5. 957 421 404. www.casadesefarad.es.
Opened in 2006, this cultural centre has become a key venue devoted to Spain's Sephardic jews. Five rooms spread around a central patio show the daily life of the medieval Jewish community; other rooms evoke the history of the Cordoban Jewish quarter, the Hebrew fiestas and and traditions, and Sephardic music. Concerts are held in the patio *(€10; inquire at the centre for programme).*
Nearby is the **Zoco Municipal** (souk) where craftsmen work around a large patio, a setting for flamenco dancing in summer. In the 16C Casa de las Bulas is the **Museo Taurino** with a collection of *trajes de luces*, posters, documents and engravings on tauromachy and tributes to the most famous Cordoban matadors such as El Cordobés, Machaquito and Lagartijo. On the first floor a room is dedicated to Manolete, who died in the bullring in 1947, an iconic martyr for all Spanish aficionados of the sport. In one of the showcases are the two ears and tail of the bull that killed him.

Palacio de Viana★★

Pl. de Don Gome 2. Guided tours (1hr) Tue–Fri 10am–7pm, Sat–Sun 10am–3pm. Closed public holidays. €6 (€3 patios only, no tour). 957 49 67 41.
This fine example of 14C–19C Córdoban civil architecture has 12 patios and an attractive garden, outstanding in a city famous for its beautiful patios.
On the ground floor are collections of porcelain, 17C–19C side-arms and tapestries. The staircase to the first floor has a beautiful Mudéjar *artesonado* ceiling of cedar. The most interesting areas are the Córdoban leather room; tapestries made in the royal workshops from cartoons by Goya; the library; and the main room with a rich *artesonado* ceiling and tapestries illustrating the Trojan War and Spanish tales.

Museo Arqueológico★★

Pl. Jerónimo Páez. Open Tue 2.30–8.30pm, Wed–Sat 9am–8.30pm, Sun 9am–2.30pm. €1.50; free for EU citizens. 957 35 55 31.
The archaeological museum is in the 16C Palacio de los Páez, a palace designed by Hernán Ruiz. Displayed here are prehistoric Iberian objects, Visigothic remains and, in particular, the **Roman collection**★ (reliefs, capitals, sarcophagi and mosaics). There are also Muslim

ceramics, capitals, and the outstanding 10C **stag**★ *(cervatillo)* from Medina Azahara.

Alcázar de los Reyes Cristianos★

Caballerizas Reales. ◔Open Tue–Fri 8.30am–7.30pm, Sat 9.30am–4.30pm, Sun 9.30am–2.30pm. ◉€4 *(includes Museo Julio Romero)*, €2 for the baths; free on Wed. ☏957 42 01 51.

This 14C complex, later expanded, retains attractive Moorish patios with ornamental basins and pools, baths, rooms with Roman **mosaics**★ and a fine 3C **sarcophagus**★.

The towers afford garden and city **views**. The **gardens**★, in Arabic style, are terraced and refreshed with pools and fountains.

Iglesias Fernandinas★

The beauty of the 14 parish churches built soon after the reconquest by Ferdinand in 1236 can still be seen today, particularly in **Santa Marina** *(Pl. del Conde de Priego)*, **San Miguel** *(Pl. de San Miguel)* and **San Lorenzo** *(Pl. de San Lorenzo)*. Built in a primitive Gothic style, they show a sober beauty in purely structural elements. The single trumpet-shaped doorways are the only lighter aspect of the architecture.

Palacio de la Merced★

Pl. de Colón.

The provincial Parliament building is the former Convento de la Merced, built in the 18C. The façade is graced by a white marble Baroque doorway. Inside are a patio, staircase and church.

Museo Torre de la Calahorra

Puente Romano. ◔Open daily 10am– 6pm. ◉€4.50. ☏957 29 39 29.

In the 14C Moorish fortress a museum traces the caliphate using audio and video. There is also a fine **model**★ of the mosque as it was in the 13C.

El Cristo de los Faroles

The Calvary surrounded by lanterns *(faroles)* in **Plaza de Capuchinos**★ is known throughout Spain.

EXCURSIONS

Medina Azahara★★

▶ *Leave Córdoba on the A 431 (W of plan). After 8km/5mi bear right.*
◔*Open Tue–Sat mid-Sept–Apr Tue– Sat 10am–6.30pm; May–mid-Sept 10am–8.30pm, Sun and public holidays 10am–2pm.* ◉€1.50; free for EU citizens. ☏957 35 28 70.

This sumptuous city, built by Abd ar-Rahman III from 936, was sacked by Berbers in 1013. The city rose in three tiers – mosque below, gardens and public areas, and an *alcázar* above. The jewel is the **Abd ar-Rahman III room**, featuring magnificent carved stone.

Castillo de Almodóvar del Río★★

▶ *25km/15mi W along the A 431.*
◔*Open Mon–Fri 11am–2.30pm, 4–7pm (8pm in summer); Sat–Sun 11am–7pm (8pm in summer).* ◔*Closed 25 Dec, 1 Jan.* ◉€5. ☏957 32 82 17. *www.castillodealmodovar.com.*

This imposing 14C eight-towered Gothic **castle** dominates town and countryside. Stroll the path behind the parapet, parade ground and towers.

Andújar★

▶ *76km/47mi E along the A 4.*

Andújar retains many 15–16C houses and churches. On the last Sunday of April, a popular *romería* (pilgrimage) is held to the Santuario de la Virgen de la Cabeza *(32km/20mi N on the J 5010)*, set in the **Parque Natural de la Sierra de Andújar**★, with pasture and ravines.

Iglesia de Santa María

▶ *Pl. Santa María.* ☏953 50 01 39.

The 15C–17C Church of St Mary holds El Greco's *Christ in the Garden of Olives*★★, set in a chapel enclosed by a fine **grille**★ by Master Bartolomé.
An *Assumption of the Virgin* by Pacheco is in the north apsidal chapel.

Iglesia de San Bartolomé

▶ *Corredera San Bartolomé.*
☏953 50 01 11.

This church, dating from the end of the 15C, has three **Gothic portals**★.

ADDRESSES

🛏 STAY

📧 **Hostal La Milagrosa** – *Rey Heredia 12.* 📞*957 47 33 17. 8 rooms (doubles only).* Good central location near the Mezquita. Attractive features are the plant-filled typically Córdoban patio and well-kept large, cool guest rooms with full bathrooms.

📧🍽 **Hostal El Triunfo** – *Corregidor Luis de la Cerda 79.* 📞*957 49 84 84. www.hostal triunfo.com. 58 rooms.* ⌨*€5. Restaurant*📧. *Closed 24–25 Dec.* Most of the rooms look onto the Mezquita, just across a narrow street. Stay on the top floor if you can to make use of the huge terrace. All rooms have a TV.

📧🍽 **Hostal Séneca** – *Conde y Luque 7.* 📞*957 47 32 34. 12 rooms. Closed fortnight in Aug.* The Seneca is a quiet *hostal* near the Mezquita with typical Andalucían décor and a flower-filled patio. Despite the rooms being fairly basic (some without a bathroom), the hotel is often full, so advance booking is recommended.

📧🍽🍽 **Hotel González** – *Manríquez 3.* 📞*957 47 98 19. www.hotel-gonzalez.com. 20 rooms.* ⌨*€3.80. Restaurant*📧🍽🍽. The rooms in this 16C palace, in the triangle of the Mezquita, the Judería and the gardens of the Alcázar, are spacious and well appointed. The Moorish-inspired patio doubles as the hotel restaurant.

📧🍽🍽🍽 **Hotel Casa de los Azulejos** – *Fernando Colón 5.* 📞*957 47 00 00. www.casadelosazulejos.com. 8 rooms. Closed 24–25 Dec.* This charming hotel is a traditional Andalucían house with a colonial flavour. Outstanding features include a lovely interior garden with plants, and magnificent large rooms with period furnishings, iron headboards, original floors and colourful designer baths.

📧🍽🍽🍽 **Hotel Posada de Vallina** – *C. del Corregidor Luis de la Cerda 83.* 📞*957 49 87 50. www.hhposadavallina.es. 24 rooms.* ⌨*€6.* Elegance and comfort are the main features of this small hotel in a tastefully restored Córdoban house, whose windows open out onto the Mezquita. The pleasant restaurant on the ground floor is particularly popular.

🍽/EAT

📧 **Taberna los Faroles** – *Velázquez Bosco 1.* 📞*957 486 876. Closed Sat–Sun.* This tavern is named for the lanterns

that illuminate its attractive patio. Specialities here include local dishes such as *salmorejo* (a variant of gazpacho), aubergine with honey and *rabo de toro* (braised oxtail). A cool, pleasant atmosphere is enhanced by the *azulejos* on the walls.

📧🍽 **Paseo de la Ribera** – *Pl. Cruz del Rastro 3.* 📞*957 47 15 30. www.paseo ribera.com.* One of the best places for Córdoban cuisine. The dining room, between stone arches, brings to mind a Romanesque church. The terrace, on Pas. de la Ribera, overlooks the Guadalquivir river. Specialities are rice dishes and oxtail.

📧🍽 **El Rincón de Carmen** – *Romero 4.* 📞*957 29 10 55. Closed Mon in low season and Sun in high season.* The patio provides an escape from the frenzied tourist activity in the Judería. Plenty of alternatives to the traditional gazpacho and an interesting wine list.

📧🍽🍽 **Almudaina** – *Pl. Campo Santo de los Mártires 1.* 📞*957 47 43 42. www.restaurantealmudaina.com. Closed Sun eve.* An attractive restaurant in a plaza, near the Alcázar. High point is the painstaking regional décor, with dining on two levels around a pleasant covered patio. The excellent food is a good introduction to Córdoban cuisine.

📧🍽 **Casa Palacio Bandolero** – *Torrijos 6.* 📞*957 47 64 91. www.restaurante bandolero.com.* The Bandolero is superbly located opposite the Mezquita and is popular with locals. Home-made tapas are served in the bar, in addition to local cuisine and a long wine list in the medieval-style dining room and on the flower-decked patio.

TAPAS

Córdoba does full justice to Andalucía's great tapas tradition with a wide range of bars offering a huge selection of local specialities such as *salmorejo* (a type of local gazpacho), *rabo de toro* (braised oxtail), *embutidos* (sausage) and sherries *(finos, amontillados, olorosos)*.

Bodega Guzman – *Calle de los Judíos 6.* Local Moriles-Montilla sherries served straight from the barrel in a taurine ambience.

Taberna Casa Pepe de la Judería – *Romero 1.* 📞*957 20 07 44. Reservations recommended.* This bar opened in 1928 and the counter dates from this period. Several rooms around an attractive patio offer tapas, and there is an Andalucían restaurant upstairs.

Taberna Salinas – *Tundidores 3.* ✆*957 48 01 35. www.tabernasalinas.com. Closed Aug, Sun.* Open for more than a century, this welcoming bar consists of a counter, two rooms decorated with *azulejos* and photos of celebrities, and a small patio.

Taberna San Miguel-Casa El Pisto – *Pl. San Miguel 1.* ✆*957 47 01 66. Closed Sun and Aug.* Founded in 1886, the Taberna San Miguel, opposite the church of the same name, is popular choice for tapas. The traditional décor is enhanced by the bullfight posters and photos on the walls.

♀ BARS/ ♀/CAFÉS

Cafetería Siena – *Pl. de las Tendillas.* ✆*957 47 30 05. Closed Sun.* A long-established café in Córdoba's main square, with one of the city's most popular outdoor terraces. A perfect venue for a morning coffee or an evening drink.

Málaga Café – *Málaga 3.* ✆*957 47 62 98.* A quiet café with classical décor and comfortable sofas and armchairs near the Plaza de las Tendillas in the centre of the city. Highly recommended for evening drinks with friends.

Sojo – *Benito Pérez Galdós 3.* ✆*957 48 39 98. Closed Sun.* Popular with the over-25s, this avant-garde bar is open from breakfast time to late at night. The Sojo also organises concerts by soloists, as well as art, photography and video exhibitions. Highly recommended, whatever the hour.

⌚NIGHTLIFE

El Puentecillo – *Poeta Emilio Prados. Closed Fri in low season.* A small venue on the way to the El Brillante district. Warm and inviting décor inside and on the small patio. Tends to be frequented by an older, quieter crowd. Popular for drinks early in the evening.

Tablao Cardenal – *Calle Torrijos 10. t957 48 33 20. www.tablaocardenal.com.* Popular flamenco club in a lovely 16C courtyard.

🛒 SHOPPING

The city's traditional craftwork includes embossed leather and cordovans, in addition to gold and silver filigree. Another good buy is the local wine, **Montilla-Moriles** *(www.montilla-moriles. org),* produced to the south of Córdoba in the area around Montilla, Puente Genil, Lucena and Baena. The excellent wines and brandies from Montilla-Moriles are similar in style to those of Jerez.

🎭FESTIVALS

Festival of the Crosses (Cruces de Mayo) – At the beginning of **May**, the central squares of the city (San Basilio, Santa Marina and San Augustín) are adorned with over 80 large crosses made of flowers with a prize for the best. Also in early May Córdoba is famous for its glorious **patios**, with many of these opened up to the public for a close look. As with the Crosses, many compete in the Concurso de Patios Córdobes for the title of town's best patio. Ask at the *turismo* for a map, or simply browse the Old Town, particularly on and around Calle San Basilio, looking out for *Patio* signs. The ever-popular **Feria** is held at the end of the month with the usual Andalucían equestrian events, fireworks, flamenco and revelries.

Córdoban patio

©Turespaña

Jaén

Jaén is known for its imposing fortress, and is famous for the oil produced from its olive trees. The name derives from *geen* (on the caravan route). Its heritage includes Moorish remains and Renaissance buildings, many designed by Andrés de Vandelvira.

SIGHTS

Catedral★★

Pl. Santa María. ⊙*Open Mon–Sat 10am –2pm, 4–7pm, Sun 10am–2pm, 4–7pm (Sept–May).* ✎€5 (sacristry and museum). ℘953 23 42 33. www.catedraldejaen.org.

The Cathedral looms over the historical quarter. It was built in the 16C and 17C by **Andrés de Vandelvira**, master of Andulcían Baroque. The façade with statues, balconies and pilasters resembles that of a palace.

The triple-nave **interior**★★ is crowned by fine ribbed vaulting and an imposing cupola above the transept. Behind the Renaissance altarpiece with its Gothic image of the **Virgen de la Antigua**★, a chapel holds the **Reliquía del Santo Rostro**★ – believed to be the cloth used by St Veronica to wipe Christ's face. The **choir stalls**★★ are carved in the Ber-

ruguete style. The sacristy, also by Van-delvira, houses the **museum** *(museo)*, which includes two canvases by Ribera, a Flemish *Virgin and Child*, a large bronze candelabra by Master Bartolomé, and miniature choir books.

Baños Árabes★★

These Moorish baths are the largest in Spain (470sq m/5 059sq ft). They lie beneath the 16C **Palacio de Villar-dompardo** and have been restored to their 11C appearance *(Pl. de Santa Luisa de Marillac;* ⊙*open Tue–Fri 9am–8pm, Sat–Sun 9.30am–2.30pm;* ⊙*closed public holidays;* ℘953 24 80 00).

Castillo de Santa Catalina★

Carretera del Neveral 5.○━*Closed for renovation. Check with Tourist Office for re-opening date and further information.* ✎€5. ℘953 12 07 33.

On a ridge to the west of Jaén stands the Castillo de Santa Catalina (Castillo de Jaén), built during a period of Arab rule in the early 13C.

It was captured in 1246 by Ferdinand III and extended to hold out against the repeated attacks by the Moors over the next two hundred years.

The castle was rebuilt and extended to form the parador, which opened in 1968, though you can visit the castle and parador wing quite separately. There is a magnificent 360° panorama from here.

- **Population:** 116 557
- **Michelin Map:** 578 S 18.
- **Info:** Calle Ramón y Cajal 4. ℘953 31 32 81. www.turjaen.org.
- **Location:** Jaen is at the base of the Sierra de Jabalcuz. The A 44 heads south to Granada (94km/59mi S) past the Parque Natural de la Sierra Mágina.
- **Tip:** If you suffer from hay fever, beware the high levels of pollen from the olive trees in May.
- **Timing:** 1 or 2 days .

Catedral

Y. Duhamel/MICHELIN

Priego de Córdoba★★

This capital of Córdoban Baroque flourished with the silk industry in the 18C. Its fountains, churches and delightful old Moorish quarter are a pleasant surprise in this isolated part of Andalucía.

SIGHTS

Fuentes del Rey y de la Salud★★ (Fountains of the King and of Health)

At the end of calle del Río.

These fountains surprise the visitor. The older, the **Fuente de la Salud**, is a 16C Mannerist frontispiece. The lavish **Fuente del Rey** was completed at the beginning of the 19C.

Its dimensions and rich design evoke Baroque palace gardens; 139 jets spout water from masks. The central display represents Neptune's chariot.

Barrio de la Villa★★

This charming quarter, dating back to Moorish times, has narrow, winding streets and flower-decked houses.

El Adarve★

This delightful viewpoint looks onto the Subbética range to the north.

Parroquia de la Asunción★ (Parish Church of the Assumption)

Abad Palomino. Open for Mass Mon–Tue and Thu–Sat 7.15–8pm, Sun 11.15am–noon.

This 16C church was remodelled in Baroque style in the 18C. The presbytery is dominated by a carved and painted 16C Mannerist **altarpiece**.

El Sagrario★★

The chapel, which opens on to the Nave del Evangelio, is a masterpiece of Andalucían Baroque. An antechamber leads into an octagonal space. Light plays on the scene; intensified by white walls and ceiling, it shimmers over the extensive

---

- ▶ **Population:** 23 513
- ⛭ **Michelin Map:** 578 T 17.
- ▮ **Info:** Carrera de las Monjas 1. ✆957 70 06 25. www.turismodepriego.com
- ◗ **Location:** Priego is on a plain in the Subbética Cordobesa range, away from major road and rail links.

---

and lavish **yeserías**★★★ (plasterwork decoration), creating a magical atmosphere. In spite of excessive adornment, the effect is one of delicacy.

From the paseo del Abad Palomino view the remains of a Moorish **fortress** (⏱ *open Tue–Sat 11.30am–1.30pm, 4–6pm;* ⊜*no charge*), modified in the 13C and 14C. Priego has numerous churches: the charming Rococo-style **Iglesia de las Angustias**; the **Aurora**, with a fine portal; and **San Pedro**, adorned with interesting statues.

Also noteworthy amid this Baroque splendour is the 16C **royal abattoir** (*Carnicerías Reales, San Luis;* ⏱ *open Tue–Sat 11.30am–1.30pm, 4–6pm, Sun 11.30am–1.30pm;* ⊜*no charge*), now an exhibition centre.

Richly decorated interior of El Sagrario

© J.D. Dallet/age fotostock

Baeza★★

This Renaissance gem with golden stonework overlooking the fertile valleys of the Guadalquivir and its tributary, the Guadalimar, stands over an undulating landscape. Along with Úbeda, 9km/5mi away, Baeza is an exceptional urban architectural complex, today a UNESCO World Heritage Site. These two towns are at the heart of a region in which olive oil, elevated nearly to the status of a religion, occupies centre stage of social and economic life. The historical centre of Baeza, a peaceful refuge, is an open invitation to leisurely strolls.

▶ **Population:** 16 253
◔ **Michelin Map:** 578 S 19.
🛈 **Info:** Plaza del Pópulo.
   𝒫953 74 04 44.
   www.andalucia.org.
▷ **Location:** With nearby Úbeda, Baeza is in the green centre of Jaén province, near Parque Natural de Cazorla (to the east). 🚆Linares Baeza (17km/10.5mi).
◉ **Don't Miss:** The heritage plazas.
◔ **Timing:** Take half a day for the old quarter.

SIGHTS
MONUMENTAL CENTRE★★★
Plaza del Pópulo★

In the small, irregular square is the **Fuente de los Leones** (Lion Fountain), built with fragments from Cástulo. The Renaissance building to the left, bearing the coat of arms of Charles V, was, surprisingly, the **carnicería** (abattoir). The **Casa del Pópulo** (now the tourist office), at the end of the square, has Plateresque windows and medallions. Six doors once opened on six notaries' offices; court hearings were held upstairs.

A balcony projects onto the **Puerta de Jaén**, which, along with the Villalar arch, honoured Charles V. The Jaén gate marked the emperor's visit on his way to Sevilla to marry Isabel of Portugal in 1526. The **Arco de Villalar** was erected in submission to the king after his victory, in 1521, over the Comuneros, whom the town had supported.

Plaza de Santa María★

The walls of the 17C **Seminario de San Felipe Neri** bear inscriptions – traditionally done in bull's blood upon graduation. Behind the **Fuente de Santa María**, an arch adorned with atlantes, is the Gothic façade of the **Casas Consistoriales Altas**, with the coats of arms of Juana the Mad and Philip the Fair.

Also in the plaza is the **Iglesia de San Andrés**, notable for the **Gothic paintings**★ in the sacristy.

Catedral★

Pl. de Santa María. ◔*Museum open Mon–Fri 10.30am–2pm, 4–7pm, Sat–Sun 10am–7pm.* 👓€4.
   𝒫953 74 41 57.

The **interior**★★ was remodelled by Vandelvira and his followers in the 16C. The outstanding Capilla Dorada (Gold Chapel) bears Italianate relief; St James' chapel has a fine Antique setting and St Joseph's is flanked by caryatids. The sacristy door has scrollwork and angels' heads. A monumental iron grille by Bartolomé closes the first bay in the nave; a pulpit of painted metal (1580) is in the transept. In the **Capilla del Sagrario**, to one end on the right, is a Baroque silver monstrance carried in procession on the feast of Corpus Christi.

In the cloisters are four Mudéjar chapels with *atauriques,* inscribed in Arabic.

Palacio de Jabalquinto★

Pl. de Santa Cruz. ◔*Open Mon–Fri 9am–2pm.* ◔*Closed public holidays.*
   𝒫953 74 27 75.

The palace **façade**★★, in perfect Flamboyant-Gothic style, is best seen in the morning when the sun accentuates the decoration of windows and pinnacles. The **patio** (c. 1600) is more sober, with a monumental Baroque stairway guarded by two lions. Opposite is the Romanesque **church of Santa Cruz**, built immediately after the town's reconquest, with a Gothic chapel and wall paintings in the apse.

Antigua Universidad
Conde de Romanones.
Now a secondary school, the seat of the university was built between 1568 and 1593 and functioned until the 19C. Past the plain façade is an elegant Renaissance patio.

Plaza del Mercado Viejo (or Plaza de la Constitución)
This busy square is lined by bars and cafés. Fronting it are the **Antigua Alhóndiga** (former grain and cereals market), with porticoed façade (1554), and the **Casas Consistoriales Bajas** (1703) whose gallery is used by officials to view celebrations.

Ayuntamiento★ (Town Hall)
Pj Cardenal Benavides. www.baeza.es.
The old law courts and prison has a Plateresque façade and ornate balconies.

Ruinas de San Francisco
San Francisco.
Only the vast transept, apse and majestic stone altarpieces remain of the beautiful 16C church that once stood here. It is now an auditorium.

Palacio de Los Salcedo (Palace of the Counts of Garcíez)
San Pedro 18. ℘953 74 72 00. *www.palaciodelossalcedo.com.*
Beautiful Gothic windows and a Plateresque patio adorn this early-16C palace, now a hotel. Along the street is the **Iglesia de San Pablo**, with its Renaissance façade.

EXCURSION
Museo de la Cultura del Olivio★
◯ *On the Jaén road 9km/5.5mi SW of Baeza, turn right toward Complejo la Laguna (1km/.06mi).*
Puente del Obispo. ◷*Open mid-Jun–mid-Sept 10.30am–1.30pm, 5.30–8pm;*

Capital of Olive Oil
"An olive grove opens and closes like a fan," wrote Federico García Lorca. Olive plantations stretch as far as the eye can see across the undulating expanse around Jaén, Spain's leading producer of olives with 60 000 trees and an annual harvest of 370 000 tonnes (about 45% of national production). The principal olive varietal cultivated is the slightly acidic *picual*. The province of Jaén has three *Denominación de Origen* zones: Sierras de Segura, de Cazorla and Mágina.

mid-Sept–mid-Dec 10.30am–1.30pm, 4.30–7pm; mid-Dec–mid-Mar 10.30am–1.30pm, 4–6.30pm. ◉€3.60.
◖*Guided tours in English, French, German.* ℘953 76 51 42. *www.museo delaculturadelolivo.com.*
This excellent museum on olive culture occupies the premises of a former olive manufactuer. From the botanical garden, which displays different kinds of olives, to the magnificent *bodega*, where deep barrels stand in rows under vaulted ceilings, to the powerful wooden olive presses, the secrets of Jaén's green gold are revealed, with detailed explanations in English, French and German.
Just 2.5km/1.5mi away, **Laguna Grande** is a protected natural area reached by crossing several beautiful olive groves, a perfect ending to this excursion.

ADDRESSES

▨ STAY
◍◍▤ **Puerta de la Luna –** *Canónigo Melgares Raya 7.* ℘953 74 70 19. *www.hotelpuertadelaluna.com.* 44 rooms. ⬒€13. *Restaurant*◍◍▤. This 16C palace by the cathedral perfectly melds contemporary service with the tranquillity of another era.

❙ EAT
◍◍▤ **Vandelvira –** *San Francisco 14.* ℘953 74 81 72. *www.vandelvira.es. Closed Jan; Sun eve, Mon.* Elegant restaurant in part of the 16C Monasterio San Francisco.

Úbeda★★

Úbeda, set amid olive groves, is one of Andalucía's architectural treasures. It flourished in the 16C, when palaces, churches and fine squares were built.

SIGHTS
BARRIO ANTIGUO★★ (OLD QUARTER)
Allow one day.
Plaza Vázquez de Molina★★
The square is lined with historic buildings, such as the **Palacio del Deán Ortega** (*953 75 03 45*), which serves as a parador.

Plaza Vázquez de Molina

Y. Duhamel/MICHELIN

Palacio de las Cadenas★ (House of Chains)
Pl. Vázquez de Molina.
Now the *ayuntamiento* (town hall), this mansion is named for the chains round the forecourt. It was designed in 1562 by Vandelvira, also responsible for the Jaén Cathedral. The majestic **façade**★★, relieved by bays and pilasters, is decorated with caryatids and atlantes.
The Renaissance patio is delightful. On the upper floor is the Archivo Histórico Municipal, with pleasant views of the square.
In the **Centro Municipal de Interpretación Turística** (tourist centre; *open Mon–Fri 8am–10pm, Sat 10am–2pm*)

▶ **Population:** 35 649
Michelin Map: 578 R 19.
Info: Calle Bajo del Marqués 4 (Palacio Marqués de Contadero). *953 77 92 04. www.ubedainteresa.com.*
Location: Úbeda is south of Madrid, between the Guadalquivir and Guadalimar rivers.
Don't Miss: The summer music and dance festival.

downstairs, panels explain Úbeda's heritage, and craft items are displayed.

Colegiata de Santa María de los Reales Alcázares★
Pl. Vázquez de Molina.
Open daily 11am–noon.
The church was built in the 13C on the site of a mosque and damaged in the Civil War. Note the harmonious façade; the main door; the late 16C Puerta de la Consolada *(left side)*; and the 16C Renaissance cloisters.
Several delightful **chapels**★, are adorned with sculptures and profuse decoration and enclosed by impressive **grilles**★, most the work of Master Bartolomé.

Capilla de El Salvador★★
Pl. Vázquez de Molina. *Open Mon–Sat 10am–2pm, 4.30–7pm, Sun and public holidays 10.45am–2pm, 4.30–7.30pm.* €3. *953 75 81 50.*
Diego de Siloé designed this sumptuous church in 1536. Its façade is ornamented with Renaissance motifs.
The **interior**★★ is frankly theatrical: the single nave, closed by a monumental grille, has vaulting outlined in blue and gold. The Capilla Mayor (chancel) forms a kind of rotunda. A huge 16C altarpiece includes a baldaquin with a sculpture by Berruguete of the Transfiguration (only the Christ figure remains).
The **sacristy**★★, by Vandelvira, is ornamented with coffered decoration, caryatids and atlantes with all the splendour of the Italian Renaissance style.

Casa de los Salvajes (House of the Savages)

Ventaja.

On the façade, two odd savages in animal skins support a bishop's crest.

Iglesia de San Pablo★

Pl. Primero de Mayo. ◷*Open for Mass Mon–Sat 7.30–8.30pm, Sun and public holidays 11.30am–1pm.* ◉*No charge.*

The church mixes a Gothic west door and the Isabelline style, in the **south door** (1511). The Capilla de las Calaveras (Skull Chapel) was designed by Vandelvira. The Isabelline Capilla de las Mercedes is enclosed by an extraordinary **grille**★★ – note the highly imaginative depiction of Adam and Eve.

The Palladian-influenced 17C former town hall is on Plaza Primero de Mayo.

Convento de San Miguel

Carmen 13. ◷*Open Tue–Sun 11am–12.45pm, 5–6.45pm.* ◉€2.
✆*953 75 06 15.*

The **Museo de San Juan de la Cruz** (St John of the Cross Museum) in this ex-convent traces the final days of this great mystical poet who died in Úbeda.

Palacio del Torrente

Pl. Primero de Mayo.

This early Renaissance palace has a monumental gate flanked by twisted columns.

Casa Mudéjar

Cervantes 6. ◷*Open mid-Oct–mid-Jun Mon–Sat 9am–8.30pm, Sun 9am–2.30pm; mid-Jun–mid-Oct Tue–Sun 9am–2pm.* ◷*Closed public holidays.* ◉*No charge.* ✆*953 77 94 32.*

In this restored 14C Mudéjar house is the **Museo Arqueológico**, displaying objects discovered in Úbeda and nearby).

Palacio del Conde de Guadiana

Real.

The early 17C Palace of the Count of Guadiana is crowned by a fine **tower**★ with angular balconies.

Palacio de la Vela de los Cobos

Juan Montilla. ✆*953 75 00 34.*

The palace's façade is late 18C. A Renaissance appearance bears witness to the long survival of this style in Úbeda.

Palacio del Marqués del Contadero (Palace of the Marquis of Contadero)

Baja del Marqués 4. ◷*Open Mon–Fri 8am–3pm, 5–8pm, Sat–Sun 10am–2pm.* ✆*953 75 08 97.*

The late 18C façade, crowned by a gallery, is also Renaissance in style.

Iglesia de Santo Domingo

Calle Escuelas.

The church's delicate south door is decorated with Plateresque reliefs.

ADDITIONAL SIGHTS

Antiguo Hospital de Santiago – *(Av. Cristo Rey)*
Palacio de los Bussianos – *(Trinidad)*
Iglesia de la Trinidad – *(Corredera de San Fernando)*
Palacio de la Rambla – *(Pl. del Marques 1)*
Casa de las Torres and **Iglesia de San Lorenzo** – *(Pl. de San Lorenzo)*

ADDRESSES

🛏 STAY

⊖⊖ **La Paz** – *Andalucía 1.* ✆*953 75 08 48. www.hotel-lapaz.com. 39 rooms.* ⊑€6.
This is a small family-run hotel, with attentive service and impeccably clean rooms.

⊖⊖⊟ **Palacio de la Rambla** – *Pl. del Marqués 1.* ✆*953 75 01 96. www.palaciodel arambla.com. 8 rooms. Closed 16 Jul–10 Aug.*
This fine 16C palace treats you like a family guest in a refined yet relaxed atmosphere. It has a magnificent Renaissance patio; on the façade are life-size warriors bearing weapons.

🍴 EAT

⊖⊖ **Mesón Gabino** – *Fuente Seca.* ✆*953 75 75 53. www.mesongabino.com. Closed Sun*
Set in the fortress walls, this traditional restaurant specialises in grilled meats and regional specialities.

Parque Natural de las Sierras de
Cazorla, Segura y Las Villas★★★

Spain's largest nature reserve extends over 214 300ha/529 535 acres at an altitude of between 600m/1 968ft and 2 017m/6 616ft. Steep cliffs, deep gorges and a complex of rivers and streams, including the source of the Guadalquivir, make up this park. The dense montane vegetation is similar to that found in Mediterranean regions. Deer, mountain goats, wild boar, golden eagles, griffon vultures and osprey abound.

- **Michelin Map:** 578 S 20-21-22 R 20-21-22 Q 21-22.
- **Info:** Carretera del Tranco, Km 48.3, Torre del Vinagre. ℘953 71 30 40; Juan Domingo 2, Cazorla. ℘953 72 01 15. www.acazorla.com.
- **Location:** The park lies in southeastern Spain, east of Úbeda.
- **Timing:** Allow a full day at least for the park.

DRIVING TOURS

Before setting out, visit an **information point** at Torre del Vinagre, Cazorla, Segura de la Sierra or Siles. Mountain-bikers, horse-riders and hikers can follow the extensive network of forest tracks and marked footpaths.

From Tíscar to the Embalse del Tranco de Beas
92km/57mi. Allow one day.

Tíscar★
The **Santuario de Tíscar** (*open for worship daily Oct–May 11.30am–1pm, 4.30–6pm; Jun–Sept 11am–1pm, 5–7pm; ℘953 71 36 06*) enjoys a superb site enclosed by rocks. Below this place of pilgrimage is the impressive **Cueva del Agua**★, a cave formation where a torrent of water emerges from between the rocks.

Follow the C 323 as far as Quesada.

Quesada
Quesada sits on the Cerro de la Magdalena hill, amid olive groves. A **museum** is dedicated to painter Rafael Zabaleta (1907–60) *(Pl. Cesáreo Rodrí-*

guez Aguilera; open Wed–Sun and public holidays May–Sept 10am–2pm, 5–8pm; Oct–Apr 10am–2pm, 4–7pm; closed 1 Jan, 25 Dec; €6; ℘953 73 30 25; www.museozabaleta.org).

The Cañada de las Fuentes, a ravine on the outskirts, is the **source of the Guadalquivir river** *(access via a track off the A 315, to the N of Quesada).* Wall paintings from the Palaeolithic era can be viewed in Cerro Vitar and in the Cueva del Encajero, a short distance from the town.

Take the A 315 towards Peal de Becerro; bear right on the A 319.

Cazorla★
Cazorla occupies an outstanding **site**★ below the Peña de los Halcones, dominated by the **Castillo de la Yedra** *(Camino del Castillo; ℘953 72 00 00),* its whitewashed houses adorned with balconies. At the centre of the plaza de Santa María stands a Renaissance fountain; the ruins of the Iglesia de Santa María *(Pl. Santa María),* by Vandelvira, are now used as an auditorium.

Head 1.5km/1mi NE along the A 319; turn right at a signposted junction.

La Iruela
The remains of a Templar castle offer superb **views**★★ *(Camino del Castillo; no charge)* of the Guadalquivir Valley. The Iglesia (church) de Santo Domingo was designed by Vandelvira.

The road from La Iruela to the Tranco Reservoir★

The first 17km/10.5mi stretch provides **spectacular views★★**. The Parador de **El Adelantado** is 8km/5mi along a branch road up through pine forests.

▷ *Follow the A 319 along the river.*

Torre del Vinagre

Carretera del Tranco, A 319.
Open daily 10am–2pm, 4–6pm (7pm in spring, 8pm in summer). Closed 25 Dec. *953 71 30 40.*
This information centre contains a hunting museum as well as a botanical garden with species native to the park. Several routes start here.
A game reserve, **Parque Cinegético de Collado del Almendral**, 15km/9.3mi along the A 319, has lookouts for viewing deer, mouflons and mountain goats.
Information 953 71 01 25.

Embalse del Tranco de Beas

⚠ Several camping areas and hotels are close to this reservoir. Water sports are available. Islands in the reservoir are Isla de Cabeza la Viña; and **Isla de Bujaraiza**, with the ruins of a Moorish castle. Both are seen from the **Mirador Rodríguez de la Fuente** viewpoint.

Santiago-Pontones to Siles

80km/50mi. Allow half a day.

Santiago-Pontones

This municipality includes scattered mountain villages along with the **Cueva del Nacimiento**, a cave 9 000 years old, and the **Cuevas de Engalbo**, with their impressive wall art.

▷ *From Pontones, go NW on the A 317.*

Hornos

Fortress remains rise above a steep cliff from where there are some spectacular **views★** of the reservoir and the Guadalquivir Valley.

▷ *Take the A 317, then bear right to Segura de la Sierra at a junction.*

Segura de la Sierra★

This picturesque village, birthplace of the 15C poet Jorge Manrique, is at an altitude of 1 240m/4 067ft in the shelter of its Mudéjar **castle** *(paraje del Castillo)*, with its sweeping **panorama★★** of the Sierra de Segura. In the centre of the village are the **town hall** *(Regidor Juan de Isla 1; 953 48 02 80)* with its Plateresque doorway; the **parish church**, containing a delicate, polychrome statue of the Virgin Mary carved in Gothic style from alabaster, and a recumbent Christ attributed to Gregorio Hernández; and the **Moorish baths** *(baños árabes)*.

▷ *Follow the JV 7020 to Orcera.*

Orcera

The Iglesia de Nuestra Señora de la Asunción, with its sober Renaissance portal, and the Fuente de los Chorros, a 15C fountain, can be seen in the main square. Vestiges of the former Moorish fortress are on the outskirts of Orcera.

▷ *Continue along the JV 7020 beyond Benatae, then take the JV 7021.*

Siles

The village retains sections of its old walls. Nearby is the nature reserve of Las Acebeas.

ADDRESSES

🏠 STAY

🍽 **Molino La Fárraga** – *Cam. de la Hoz. 953 72 12 49. www.molinola farraga.com. 8 rooms. Closed 15 Dec–15 Feb.* In an 18C olive oil mill with basic rooms, a garden with a small stream and a swimming pool with views of the castle and mountains.

🍴 EAT

CAZORLA

🍽 **La Sarga** – *Pl. de Andalucía 13. 953 72 15 07. www.lasarga.com. Closed Mon dinner, second fortnights in Jan and Sept.* This well-run restaurant in the centre of town has impressive mountain views. Good-quality regional cuisine and attentive service.

WESTERN ANDALUCÍA

Cádiz and its province are acclaimed as the birthplace of no less a Spanish culinary institution than tapas, while Huelva's uplands are famous for the dehesa oak park and the Ibérico pig. Each province attracts Spanish holidaymakers, with most north European tourists found among the surfers who have colonised the windy beaches of the Costa de la Luz. Cádiz is a characterful very Spanish city which hosts relatively few visitors. Jerez de la Frontera, by contrast, is the home of sherry bodegas and Andalucían horsemanship, both of which deservedly attract coachloads of holidaymakers. Aracena's Cave of Marvels is a popular day trip, though only the most determined make it as far inland as the Aracena Mountains; their reward is stunning scenery and quiet picturesque villages.

Highlights

1 Dazzling white sand of the **Costa de la Luz** (p512)

2 Spotting flamingos in the **Parque Nacional de Doñana** (p513)

3 Enjoying a tipple in a sherry bodega in **Jerez** (p516)

4 **Cádiz** at carnival time, the most famous and lively in Spain (p524)

5 Cheeky Barbary apes on a tour of the Rock of **Gibraltar** (p526)

Cádiz: Birthplace of Tapas

The eternal debate about who invented tapas and whose are best can be settled quickly with a tour through Cádiz and its province. Sanlúcar de Barrameda, Puerto de Santa María, and Jerez de la Frontera, along with the city of Cádiz, itself, offer such a bewildering variety of top quality miniature cuisine that the mere sight of a northern Spanish tapas counter laden with puddings and pastes on bread pales by comparison. Cádiz's privileged location at the confluence of the Atlantic, the Mediterranean and the Guadalquivir river estuary creates such an abundance of seafood that tapas tend to be pure product, fresh and raw or quickly cooked.

Spain's caviar

La dehesa (from the word *defensa*) is the southwestern Spanish oak park, an ecosystem maintained primarily by and for the free-range Ibérico pig, a direct descendant of the *sus mediterraneus* boar that roamed the Mediterranean oak forests of antiquity. These strictly regulated black pigs eat only acorns for the final three months of their lives, giving their marbled meat an exceptionally nutty, grassy taste and aroma.

Sherry bodega and the cathedral, Jerez de la Frontera

©Turespaña

Sevilla★★★

Sevilla, set in the plain of the Guadalquivir, is capital of Andalucía and Spain's fourth largest city. To appreciate its many moods, take time to stroll the narrow streets of old quarters like Santa Cruz, or ride slowly through peaceful parks and gardens in a horse-drawn carriage. Sevilla is the centre of flamenco, famous for its bullfights, its 18C Maestranza bullring, and for its cafés and tapas bars.

THE CITY TODAY

If Spain had a beauty contest for its cities, or a contest for the most Spanish city in Spain, Sevilla would probably win both. It boasts more monumental set pieces and more pretty, unspoiled corners than any other Andalucían city. It also claims the best tapas, the best nightlife, the best *ferias*, and is a stronghold for bullfighting and flamenco. Come here in spring when the orange blossom is in full fragrance, but avoid the heat of high summer.

A BIT OF HISTORY

Sevilla is summed up on the Puerta de Jerez (Jerez Gate): "Hercules built me; Caesar surrounded me with walls and towers; the King Saint reconquered me." Sevilla was chief city of Roman Baetica and capital of the Visigothic kingdom before Toledo. In 712 the Moors arrived; in the 11C, it became capital of a king-

▶ **Population:** 703 206
◔ **Michelin Map:** 578 T 11-12 (town plan).
▤ **Info:** Av de la Constitución, 21B. ℘954 22 14 04. www.turismosevilla.org.
▶ **Location:** Sevilla, in southwestern Spain, is lined by motorways and dual carriageways to Huelva (92km/57mi W), Jerez de la Frontera (90km/56mi SW), Cádiz (123km/77mi SW) and Córdoba (143km/89mi NE). ▭Avenida Kansas City
🅿 **Parking:** Find a space in the centre, leave your car, and stroll the streets.
◉ **Don't Miss:** The Giralda and the Alcázar.
◔ **Timing:** Take at least a day for the marvels of central Sevilla, then enjoy quarters such as Santa Cruz, Triana and La Macarena and sites nearby.
👪 **Kids:** Isla Mágica beckons for at least a day.

dom which prospered under the Almohads. In 1195 **Sultan Yacoub al-Mansur** (1184–99), builder of the Giralda, defeated the Christians at Alarcos. On 19 November 1248, **King Ferdinand III of Castilla**, the Saint, delivered the city from the Moors.

A Tradition of Fiestas

The great festivals, when vast crowds flock to the city from all over Spain and overseas, reveal the provincial capital in many guises. During **Semana Santa**, or **Holy Week**, *pasos* processions are organised nightly in each city quarter by rival brotherhoods. *Pasos* are great litters sumptuously bejewelled and garlanded with flowers on which are mounted religious, polychrome wood statues; these constructions are borne through the crowd on the shoulders of between 25 and 60 men. Accompanying the statues are penitents, hidden beneath tall pointed hoods; from time to time a voice is raised in a *saeta*, an improvised religious lament. During the **April Fair or Feria**, which began life in the middle of the 19C as an animal fair, the city becomes a fairground with horse and carriage parades. The women in ruffled dresses and the men in full Andalucían costume ride up to specially erected canvas pavilions to dance *sevillanas*.

PRACTICAL INFORMATION
GETTING THERE
Airport – Aeropuerto de San Pablo, 8km/5mi towards Madrid on the N IV motorway, (*954 44 90 00; www. aena.es*). A bus service operates from the airport to the railway station and city centre.

Trains – Estación de Santa Justa. The high-speed AVE (Tren de Alta Velocidad) departs from this station, taking just 45min to Córdoba and 2hr 15min to Madrid. For information and bookings, call *902 24 02 02 or visit www.renfe.com*.

Inter-city buses – Sevilla has two bus stations: **Estación Plaza de Armas** *954 23 44 65*; and **Estación del Prado de San Sebastián** *954 17 11 18*.

Taxis – Radio Taxi. *954 67 55 55*. www.taxigiralda.es.

SIGHTSEEING
Publications – Two free bilingual publications (Spanish-English) are published for tourists every month. These brochures, **Welcome Olé** and **The Tourist**, can be obtained from major hotels and tourist sites around the city. Sevilla City Hall's Department of Culture **(NODO)** also publishes a monthly brochure listing all the city's cultural events. A monthly publication covering the whole of Andalucía, **El Giraldillo**, contains information on the region's fairs, exhibitions and theatres, as well as details on cinemas, restaurants and shops. *www.elgiraldillo.es*.

Horse-drawn carriages – It is well worth taking a trip in one of the numerous horse-drawn carriages operating in the city. They can normally be hired by the Cathedral, in front of the Torre del Oro and in the María Luisa park.

Boat trips on the Guadalquivir – Boat trips lasting 1hr during the day and 1hr 30min at night depart every half-hour from the Torre del Oro. *954 56 16 92*.

The discoveries brought new prosperity. By 1503, Isabel the Catholic created the *Casa de contratación* or Exchange to control trade with America. This monopoly lasted until 1717.

Art and architecture in Sevilla – The northern ramparts, the Alcázar walls, the **Torre del Oro** (Golden Tower) and the Giralda were all built by the Moors. The **Mudéjar style**, a mix of Moorish and Christian, is testimony to the lasting influence of Arab design in the Alcázar and other monuments after the city's reconquest.

Golden Age painters of the **Seville School** corresponded to three reigns: under Philip III (1598–1621) **Roelas** and **Pacheco**; under Philip IV (1621–65) **Herrera the Elder** and **Zurbarán** (1598–1664), who portrayed figures with spiritual intensity. Finally, under Charles II (1665–1700) **Murillo** (1617–82) created radiant Immaculate Conceptions and brilliant everyday scenes. The best work of **Valdés Leal** (1622–90) can be seen in the Hospital de la Caridad. **Diego Velázquez** (1599–1660) was born in Sevilla. Many statues are the work of 17C sculptor **Martínez Montañés**. Well known are the **Cristo del Gran Poder** (Christ of Great Power) by **Juan de Mesa** and the **Cachorro** by Francisco Antonio Gijón in the **Capilla del Patrocinio** (calle Castilla). The **Macarena Virgin** is the most popular figure in Sevilla.

SIGHTS
The Giralda and Cathedral★★★
Allow 1hr30min.
Open Mon–Sat 11am–5pm (Cathedral Jul–Aug 9.30am–4pm), Sun and public holidays 2.30–6pm.
Closed 1, 6 Jan, 20, 22 Mar, 26, 30 May, 15 Aug, 8, 25 Dec. Restricted opening times during Holy Week.
€8 including both sites. www.catedraldesevilla.es.

La Giralda★★★

Alemanes. ℰ *954 21 44 71.*

When built in the 12C, the 98m/322ft minaret resembled the Koutoubia in Marrakesh. The top storey and Renaissance lantern were added in the 16C. Typically Almohad, it creates grandeur in harmony with the ideal of simplicity. A gently sloping ramp *(accessible from inside the cathedral)* leads to the top (70m/230ft) for excellent **views**★★★.

CATHEDRAL★★★

Av. de la Constitución. ℰ *954 21 49 71.*

Sevilla's cathedral is the third largest in Europe after St Peter's in Rome and St Paul's in London. When its construction began in 1401, members of the cathedral chapter are said to have declared "Let us build a cathedral so immense that everyone, on beholding it, will take us for madmen".

The late Gothic cathedral shows Renaissance influence. The main portals are modern. However, the Puerta de la Natividad (Nativity Doorway) and the Puerta del Bautismo (Baptism Doorway), right and left of the west door, include beautiful sculptures by Mercadente de Bretaña (c. 1460). Miguel Perrin (1520) made full use of Renaissance perspective in the tympana of the Puerta de los Palos and Puerta de las Campanillas *(east end doorways)*.

▷ *Enter by the Puerta de San Cristóbal.*

The **interior** is striking. Massive columns appear slender because they are so tall. Flamboyant Gothic vaulting rises massively 56m/184ft above the transept crossing. A **mirror** on the floor affords a striking view.

Capilla Mayor (Chancel)

Splendid Plateresque **grilles**★★ (1518–33) precede an immense Flemish **altarpiece**★★★, profusely carved with scenes from the life of Christ and gleaming with gold leaf (1482–1525).

Tesoro (Treasury)

The **Sacristía de los Cálices** (Chalice Sacristy) contains canvases by Goya (*Santa Justa* and *Santa Rufina*), Valdés Leal, Murillo and Zurbarán, and a triptych by Alejo Fernández.

In the 16C **Sacristía Mayor** are a Renaissance **monstrance** by Juan de Arfe, 3.9m/13ft in height and weighing 475kg/1 045lb, and paintings by Zurbarán and Lucas Jordán.

Capilla Real★★ (Chapel Royal)

An elegant Renaissance dome is decorated with carved busts. On either side are the tombs of Alfonso X of Castilla (d. 1284) and his mother, Beatrice of

Catedral de Sevilla

G. Bludzin/MICHELIN

Museo de Bellas Artes

© Turespaña

Swabia. On the high altar is the robed **Virgen de los Reyes**, patron of Sevilla, given by St Louis of France to St Ferdinand of Spain, who is buried in a silver gilt shrine below.

Patio de los Naranjos (Orange Tree Court) – This patio served as the ablutions area in the mosque.

Exit by the **Puerta del Perdón**, an Almohad arch decorated with stucco and two statues by Miguel Perrin.

NORTH OF THE CATHEDRAL
Museo de Bellas Artes★★★ (Fine Arts Museum)

Pl. del Museo 9. ◷*Open Tue 2.30–8.30pm, Wed–Sat 9am–8.30pm, Sun and public holidays 9am–2.30pm.* ◷*Closed 1, 6 Jan, 1 May, 24, 25, 31 Dec.* ◉*€1.50; free for EU citizens.* ℘*954 78 65 00.*

The Convento de la Merced (Merced Friary) was built in the 17C by Juan de Oviedo around three beautiful patios. **Sala I** of the museum inside contains medieval art. **Room II** is dedicated to Renaissance art, in particular a fine sculpture of *St Jerome* by Pietro Torrigiani, a contemporary of Michelangelo. Two magnificent portraits of *A Lady and a Gentleman* by Pedro Pacheco are the highlight in **Room III**.

In **Room V★★★** walls decorated with paintings by the 18C artist Domingo Martínez are a stunning backdrop to outstanding work by Murillo and a Zurbarán masterpiece, *The Apotheosis of St Thomas Aquinas* (in the nave), with its skilful play of light and shade. **Murillo**'s monumental *Immaculate Conception*, with its energetic movement, is in the transept. On the right-hand side of the transept is a benevolent *Virgen de la Servilleta* (note the effect of the Child approaching).

Upper Floor: Room VI displays a fine collection of saints. **Room VIII** is devoted to Baroque artist Valdés Leal. European Baroque is represented in **Room IX**. **Room X★★** includes works of **Zurbarán**. In *Christ on the Cross*, the body of Christ appears as if sculpted. His *St Hugh and Carthusian Monks at Table* displays errors in perspective. The ceiling of the inner room should not be missed. In **Room XI** is Goya's *Portrait of Canon José Duato*.

Casa de Pilatos★★ (Pilate's House)

Pl. de Pilatos 1. ◷*Open daily Apr–Oct 9am–7pm; Nov–Mar 9am–6pm.* ◉*€8(€5 ground floor only; free Wed 10.30am–noon).* ℘*954 22 52 98.*

The large Mudéjar patio of this 15C–16C palace displays fine stuccowork and magnificent lustre **azulejos★★**. *Artesonado* ceilings, the chapel with Gothic vaulting and *azulejo* and stucco decoration, and a remarkable wood **dome★**

over the grand **staircase**★★ illustrate
the vitality of the Mudéjar style during
the Renaissance. The gardens are open
to the public.

Iglesia de San Luis de los Franceses★

San Luis 37. ⏰*Open Tue–Thu 9am–2pm,
Fri–Sat 9am–2pm, 5–8pm.* ✍*No charge*
☎*954 55 02 07.*
This church, by Leonardo de Figueroa, is
one of the best examples of the Sevillan
Baroque. The exuberant **interior**★★ is a
mix of outstanding murals, sumptuous
retables and fine azulejos.

Convento de Santa Paula★

Santa Paula 11. ⏰*Open Tue–Sun
10.30am–1pm.* ⏰*Closed for certain
religious ceremonies.* ✍*€3.*
☎*954 53 63 30.*
The church's breathtaking **portal**★
(1504) is adorned with ceramics. Despite
its mix of styles, the overall effect is harmonious. **Inside**★, the nave is covered
by a 17C roof and the chancel by a Gothic
vault with attractive frescoes.
The **museum**★ *(entrance through no. 11
on the plaza)* has works by Ribera, Pedro
de Mena, Alonso de Cana and others.
The gilded **Capilla de San José**★
(St Joseph's Chapel) gleams at night.

Palacio de la Condesa de Lebrija★

Cuna 8. ⏰*Open Mon–Fri 10am–
1.30pm, 5–8pm, Sat 10am–2pm.*
✍*€7.50 (€4.20 ground floor only).*
☎*954 21 81 83.*
This noble home is decorated with
Roman mosaics★ from Itálica, Mudéjar
artesonado ceilings, 16C–17C *azulejos*,
and a sumptuous **stairway**★.

Iglesia del Salvador★

Pl. del Salvador. ⏰*Open Sat–Sun
and public holidays May–Sept 10am–
1.30pm, 4–7.30pm; Oct–Apr 10am–
1.30pm, 5–8.30pm.* ✍*€3 suggested
donation.* ☎*954 59 54 05.*
www.colegialsalvador.org.
This 17C–18C church has some of the
city's most impressive 18C **Baroque
retables**★★.

The Cuarto Real Alto

An optional 30min guided tour
enables visitors to view the King
and Queen of Spain's official
residence in Sevilla. The various
rooms, with their fine *artesonado*
ceilings, contain an impressive
display of 19C furniture and clocks,
18C tapestries and French lamps. Of
particular note are the **Capilla de
los Reyes Católicos** (Chapel of the
Catholic Monarchs) – an exquisite
oratory with a ceramic font, by
Nicola Pisano – and the Mudéjar
Sala de Audiencias.

Ayuntamiento (Town Hall)

Pl. Nueva 1. ⏰*Open with prior booking
Sept–Jul Tue–Thu 5.30–6pm.*
☎*954 59 01 01.*
The attractive **east façade**★ (1527–34)
is Renaissance in style and adorned with
delicate scrollwork decoration.

AROUND THE CATHEDRAL
Iglesia de Santa María la Blanca★

Santa María la Blanca 5.
✍*No charge.* ☎*954 41 05 93.*
In the **interior**★ of this former synagogue, exuberant Baroque ceilings are
balanced by pink marble columns.

Hospital de la Caridad★ (Hospital of Charity)

Temprado 3. ⏰*Open Mon–Sat 9am–
1.30pm, 3.30–7.30pm, Sun and public
holidays 9am–1pm.* ✍*€5.* ☎*954 22
32 32. www.santa-caridad.org.*
The hospital was founded in 1625.
Great Sevillan artists decorated the
church★★. Valdés Leal illustrated Death
with a striking sense of the macabre.
Murillo showed Charity in *The Miracle
of the Loaves and Fishes, Moses Smiting
Water from the Rock, St John of God*
and *St Isabel of Hungary Caring for the
Sick.* Pedro Roldan's **Entombment**★★
adorns the high altar.

Archivo General de Indias (Archives of the Indies)

Av. de la Constitución 3. ○*Open Mon–Sat 10am–4pm, Sun and public holidays 10am–2pm.* ○*Closed 25, 31 Dec.* ⌦*No charge.* ✆*954 50 05 28. www.mcu.es.*
The building (1572), designed as an exchange *(lonja)* by Juan de Herrera, houses priceless documents on the Americas at the time of the Conquest, including maps and charts.

SOUTH OF THE CATHEDRAL
Parque de María Luisa★★

The vast **plaza de España**★ of this 19C park remains from the 1929 Ibero-American Exhibition. Each bench represents a province of Spain.

Museo Arqueológico★

Pl. de América. ○*Open Tue 2.30–8.30pm, Wed–Sat 9am–8.30pm, Sun and public holidays 9am–2.30pm.* ○*Closed 1, 6 Jan, 1 May, 24, 25, 31 Dec.* ⌦*€2; free for EU citizens.* ✆*954 78 64 74*
The archaeological museum is in a palace on plaza de América.
 The 7C–6C BC **Carambolo Treasure**★ includes a statue with a Phoenician inscription. In the **Roman section**★ are statues and mosaics from Itálica (○*see Excursions).*

Patio de las Doncellas, Real Alcázar

©Thomas Snaaijer/Dreamstime.com

REAL ALCÁZAR★★★

Patio de Banderas. ○*Open Oct–Mar Tue–Sat 9.30am–5pm, Sun and public holidays 9.30am–1.30pm; Apr–Sept Tue–Sat 9.30am–7pm, Sun and public holidays 9.30am–5pm.* ○*Closed for official ceremonies.* ⌦*€8.50; top floor €4.50.* ✆*954 50 23 24.*
All that remains of the 12C Almohad Alcázar are the **Patio de Yeso** and a courtyard wall. In the 13C, Alfonso X, the Wise, built a palace, known today as **Charles V's rooms**. Peter the Cruel (1350–69) erected the nucleus of the present building, known as **Peter the Cruel's Palace**, in 1362, using masons from Granada. It is one of the purest examples of the Mudéjar style.

Cuarto del Almirante (Admiral's Apartments)

Right side, the Patio de la Montería.
In the Sala de Audiencias (Audience Chamber) the **Virgin of the Navigators**★ altarpiece (1531–36) is by Alejo Fernández.

Palacio de Pedro el Cruel★★★ (Palace of Peter the Cruel)

A passage leads to the **Patio de las Doncellas** (Court of the Maidens), a Moorish arched patio; the upper storey was added in the 16C.
An elevated round arch leads to the **Dormitorio de los Reyes Moros** (Bedroom of the Moorish Kings), two rooms decorated with blue-toned stucco and a magnificent *artesonado* ceiling.
Through a small room is the **Patio de las Muñecas** (Dolls' Court) with Granada-type decoration. The gallery on the upper floor dates from the 19C. The Catholic Monarchs' bedroom leads to the **Salón de Felipe II** (Philip II Salon), the **Arco de los Pavones** (Peacock Arch) and the **Salón de Embajadores** (Ambassadors Hall), the most sumptuous room, with a remarkable 15C half-orange cedarwood **cupola**★★★.
The **Sala del Techo de Carlos V** (Charles V Room), the former chapel, has a magnificent ceiling.

▷ *Cross the Patio de la Montería and go down a vaulted passage (right).*

Palacio Gótico or Salones de Carlos V (Gothic Palace or Charles V's Rooms)

The palace, which was built in the reign of Alfonso X, houses magnificent **tapestries**★★ from the Real Fábrica de Tapices illustrating Charles V's conquest of Tunis in 1535.

Jardines★

Continue to the Mercurio pool and 17C **Galería del Grutesco**★ to view the magnificent Moorish gardens. The most enchanting parts are **Charles V's pavilion**, the maze and the English garden. The silhouette of the Giralda rises above the **Patio de Banderas** (Flag Court), bordered by elegant façades.

BARRIO DE SANTA CRUZ★★★ (SANTA CRUZ QUARTER)

The former Jewish quarter is replete with alleys, wrought-iron grilles and flower-filled patios. It is delightful in the evenings when cafés and restaurants overflow into the squares.

Hospital de los Venerables★

Pl. de los Venerables 8. ✎Guided tours (15min) daily 10am–2pm, 4–8pm. ◐Closed 1 Jan, 25 Mar, 25 Dec. ☞€5; free Sun afternoon. ℘954 56 26 96. www.focus.abengoa.es.

This building, in lively plaza de los Venerables, is one of the best examples of 17C Sevillan Baroque. Its fine **church**★ is covered with frescoes by Valdés Leal and his son Lucas Valdés.

⛪ ISLA DE LA CARTUJA (LA CARTUJA ISLAND)
Isla Mágica★(Magic Island)

◐Open Apr–Oct daily and Jun–Sept 11am–10pm (or midnight); check hours for rest of season and holidays. ☞€29, child €20 during high season; 26€/18€ low season; €23/€17 Christmas. ℘902 16 17 16. www.islamagica.es.

This amusement park focuses on the Century of Discovery, with such theme areas as **Amazonia** and **The Pirates' Den**, live performances and rides such as **Rapids of the Orinoco**.

Centro Andaluz de Arte Contemporáneo

Av. de Américo Vespucio 2. ◐Open Tue –Fri 10am–9pm (8pm Oct–Mar), Sat 11am–9pm, Sun and public holidays 10am–3pm. ◐Closed 1, 6 Jan, 1 May, 1 Nov, 24, 25, 31 Dec. ☞€3; free Tue for EU citizens and 7–9pm, Sat 11am–9pm. ℘955 03 70 70. Buses C1 and C 2. www.caac.es.

This modern art museum is in the former La Cartuja monastery; some **convent buildings**★ remain. The collection includes 20C artists Miró and Chillida.

ADDITIONAL SIGHTS
Barrio de Triana★

Sevilla's classic seafarer, gypsy, bullfighter and flamenco neighbourhood on the western bank of the Guadalquivir river.

Even though most gypsies and bullfighters have moved out to the edge of town, Triana remains a colourful Bohemian quarter with a flamenco vibe. The Santa Ana church, the food produce market, and the **Capilla de los Marineros** are important sights, along with the Capilla de la Estrella and the Iglesia de San Jacinto. Calle Alfarería is the **ceramics** centre of Sevilla, while Calle Betis along the edge of the Guaqalquivir is lined with taverns and restaurants. Casa Anselma on Calle Pagés del Corro is a popular flamenco jam session that starts up around midnight.

Basílica de la Macarena★

Puerta de la Macarena, Barrio de la Macarena. ◐Open Mon–Sun 9.30am –2pm, 5pm-9pm. ◐Closed 1, 6 Jan, 1 May, 24, 25, 31 Dec. ☞€5 museum, no charge for Basilica. ℘954 90 18 00.

Home to Sevilla's most beloved icon, La Virgen de la Esperanza Macarena, the basilica is the hub of a vibrant working-class neighbourhood.

Built in 1949 by Aurelio Gómez Millán, the neo-Baroque Basílica de la Macarena contains the most universally admired Marian image in Sevilla. Sculpted In the 17C by Luisa Roldán, La Macarena is named for the Puerta de la Macarena, an entrance through the city walls built by Roman centurion Macarius Ena in the 2C AD. Her face, glistening with glass tears, is acclaimed as the most beautiful of all. A favourite of gypsies and bullfighters, La Macarena's Easter Week procession through the streets is one of the celebration's most emotional moments.

Iglesia de la Magdalena★

Calle San Pablo 10. ⏰*Open Mon–Sat 8–11am, 6.30pm–9pm, Sun 8am–1pm.* ⏰*Closed 1, 6 Jan, 1 May, 24, 25, 31 Dec.* 🎫*No charge.* 📞*954 22 96 03.*

This immense monolith between Plaza Nueva and the Museo de Bellas Artes contains important artistic treasures. From the Mudéjar **Capilla de la Quinta Angustia** (Chapel of the fifth anguish) to the 1709 Baroque section by architect Leonardo de Figueroa, this rambling jumble of cupolas and domes is filled

with art. Zurbarán's *Santo Domingo de Soria* and the Lucas Valdés frescoes *Alegoría del triunfo de la fé (Allegory of the Triumph of Faith)* are the works to look out for.

Museo del Baile Flamenco

Calle Manuel Rojas Marcos 3. ⏰*Open Mon–Sun 9.30am–7pm.* ⏰*Closed 1 & 6 Jan, 1 May, 24, 25, 31 Dec.* 🎫*€10.* 📞*954 34 03 11. www.museoflamenco.com.*

For a look into the world of flamenco, this fascinating dance museum brings it all to life. **Cristina Hoyos**, one of the great *bailaoras* in the history of Andalucía's most important art form, founded and promoted this museum as an introduction for tourists and flamenco beginners as well as a repository of flamenco history for aficionados and profesionals.

EXCURSIONS

Ruinas de Itálica★

▶ *Av. de Extremadura 2, Santiponce. 9km/6mi NW on the N 630.* ⏰*Open Apr–Sept Tue–Sat 8.30am–8.30pm, Sun 9am–3pm; Oct–Mar Tue–Sat 9am–5.30pm, Sun 10am–4pm.* ⏰*Closed public holidays.* 🎫*€2; free for EU citizens.* 📞*955 99 73 76.*

This **Roman town** was the birthplace of emperors Hadrian and Trajan. Mosaics of birds and Neptune are in their original sites. The **Anfiteatro** (amphitheatre), seating 25 000, was one of the largest in the empire.

Carmona★★

▶ *40km/25mi W along the A 4.*

Carmona, with its heritage buildings, overlooks the River Corbones.
🅿*Park in the lower part of town.*

Old Town★

Note the **Baroque tower**★ of the **Iglesia de San Pedro**★ *(Arco de la Carne)*, a church with a sumptuous sacrarium chapel (Capilla del Sagrario), and, further along, the **Convento de la Concepción** with its fine cloisters and Mudéjar church. Through the **Puerta de Sevilla**★ is the 17C–18C **Iglesia de San Bartolomé** *(Prim 29)*. The *capilla mayor*

The Legendary *Jamón*

The free-range, Ibérico black pig stores monounsaturated fats from acorns in marbled layers in its muscle tissue. These fats are among the few animal fats proven to reduce the polyunsaturated fats, cholesterol and triglycerides that clog human arteries. Not only are these acorn-based oleic acids healthy, but their flavours and aromas, after two years of ageing, are so complex, nutty, buttery, earthy and floral that Japanese enthusiasts have declared Ibérico ham "umami". *Jamón ibérico de bellota* (Ibérico pig fattened up exclusively on acorns – up to 10kg/22lb a day) possesses the property of liquefying at room temperature, so it literally melts in your mouth. It can cost twice as much as normal *ibérico* ham.

---

in the Mudéjar church of **San Felipe**★ *(San Felipe)* is covered with 16C ceramics. The Baroque **town hall** *(ayuntamiento)*, facing **Plaza de San Fernando** (entrance on calle de El Salvador), has a Roman mosaic. Next door, the 17C–19C **Iglesia del Salvador** is adorned with a magnificent Churrigueresque altarpiece (◷open Mon, Thu, Fri 11am–2pm, 4–6pm, Sat–Sun 11am–2pm; ➿€1.20; ☏954 14 12 70). The 15C Gothic **Iglesia de Santa María la Mayor**★ is nearby. A monumental **Plateresque altarpiece**★ illustrates the Passion. The **Convento de las Descalzas**★ is a stunning example of 18C Sevillan Baroque. The Mudéjar church of the **Convento de Santa Clara** contains paintings by Valdés Leal. The **Alcázar de Arriba** (Upper Fortress), a Roman structure, offers superb **views**★. It is now a parador.

Necrópolis Romana★

Av. de Jorge Bonsor 9, Carmona. *☝Access to the Roman necropolis is indicated along the road to Sevilla.* *◷Open 15 Jun–15 Sept Tue–Fri 8.30am–2pm, Sat 10am–2pm; 16 Sept–14 Jun Tue–Fri 9am–5pm, Sat–Sun 10am–2pm. ◷Closed public holidays. ➿No charge. ☏954 14 08 11.* Of more than 300 1C tombs, mausoleums and crematoria, the most interesting are the large **Tumba del Elefante** and the huge **Tumba de Servilia**.

Aracena★

Aracena rises in tiers up a hillside, crowned by the remains of a Templars castle, its whitewashed houses adorned with ornate grilles.

No trip to Aracena is complete without trying the exquisite **pata negra cured ham** in one of the town's *mesones*

⚎ Gruta de las Maravillas (Cave of Marvels) ★★★

Pozo de la Nieve. ⚑*Guided tours (45min) daily 10am–1.30pm, 3–6pm.* ◷*Closed 24, 25, 31 Dec.* ➿*€8.50.* ☏*959 12 83 55 (⊙advance booking from tourist office recommended).* Rivers below the castle formed vast caves with limpid pools. Formations include draperies and pipes coloured by iron and copper oxide or brilliant white calcite crystal as in the **Salón de la Cristalería de Dios**★★ (God's Crystalware Chamber).

Here also is the **Museo Geológico Minero** (◷open daily 10am–1.30pm, 3–6pm; ➿no charge), a geological and mining museum.

Castillo e Iglesia del Mayor Dolor

◷*Open daily Sept–Jun 10am–5.30pm; Jul–Aug 10am–7pm.* ➿*No charge.* The castle was built in the 9C over an Almohad fortress. Note the decoration on the north side of the tower next to the church, similar to that of the Giralda in Sevilla.

Parque Natural de la Sierra de Aracena y Picos de Aroche★★

The cool forests of this park are punctuated by slender peaks and picturesque villages such as whitewashed **Alájar**★, and **Almonaster la Real**★ *(www.almonasterlareal.com)*, concealed amid chestnut, eucalyptus, cork and holm oak, which has a rare intact **mosque**★ (◷open Sat–Sun and public holidays 11am–7pm; www.sierradearacena.net). Nearby **Jabugo** *(www.jabugo.es)* is justifiably famous for its delicious cured hams.

Minas de Riotinto★★

▷ *35km/22mi S.* The mining tradition of this area dates back to Antiquity.

Parque Minero de Riotinto★★

☏*959 59 00 25.* *www.parquemineroderiotinto.com.* This mining theme park takes in the mining and railway museum, the **Museo Minero y Ferroviario**★ (◷open daily Oct–early Jul 10.30am–3pm, 4–7pm, late Jul–Sept 10.30am–3pm, 4–8pm; ➿€4), the spectacular open-cast mines of **Corta Atalaya**★★★ and **Cerro Colorado**★★, and a **tourist train** *(call for schedule ☏959 59 00 25; ➿€10)* along a 19C line built by the Río Tinto Company.

ADDRESSES

🛏 STAY

Sevilla has a huge range of accommodation for visitors, but beware that during Holy Week and the Feria, prices are likely to double or even triple. If you're planning to stay in the city for these events, make sure you check the room rate carefully beforehand.

🛏🛏 **Hotel Amadeus Sevilla** – *Farnesio 6.* ✆954 50 14 43. www.hotelamadeussevilla. com. 14 rooms. 🍽€9. A family of musicians converted this typically Sevillan house with courtyard in the heart of the Santa Cruz district into a delightful small hotel, in which the décor enhances the building's original architectural features.

🛏🛏 **Hotel Londres** – *San Pedro Mártir 1.* ✆954 50 27 45. www.londreshotel.com. 22 rooms. Near the Museo de Bellas Artes. This centrally located hotel has basic but clean rooms, some with balcony. The best rooms have balconies and overlook the street. The hotel is slowly upgrading, while maintaining its traditional charm.

🛏🛏🍽 **Hotel Las Casas de la Judería** – *Callejón Dos Hermanas 7, Pl. de Santa María La Blanca.* ✆954 41 51 50. www.casasy palacios.com. 175 rooms. 🍽€19. Restaurant🛏🛏🍽. A pleasant surprise in the city's old Jewish quarter. Elegant, traditional and full of colour, this charming, old hotel is housed in the former mansion of the Duke of Béjar.

🛏🛏🍽 **La Casa del Maestro** – *Niño Ricardo 5.* ✆954 50 00 07. www.lacasadel maestro.com. 11 rooms. A delightful hotel, the Maestro is located in the birthplace of the famous flamenco guitarist Niño Ricardo (1904–72). A pleasant patio area and rooms decorated in yellow and earth red.

🛏🛏🛏🍽 **Hotel Alfonso XIII** – *San Fernando 2.* ✆954 91 70 00. www.starwoodhotels.com. 147 rooms. 🍽€25. Built in 1928 in neo-Mudéjar style, the Alfonso XIII is Sevilla's most luxurious and famous hotel. An excellent location opposite the gardens of the Alcázar.

🛏🛏🛏🍽 **Reyes Catolicos** – *Gravina 57.* ✆954 21 12 00. www.hotelreyescatolicos. info. 29 rooms. 🍽€12. Restaurant🛏🛏🍽. Centrally located close to the Plaza de Armas and the Isla Mágica theme park. Well-equipped rooms complemented by the restaurant.

ARACENA

🛏🛏 **Hotel Los Castaños** – *Av. de Huelva 5.* ✆959 12 63 00. www.loscastanoshotel. com. 25 rooms. 🍽€6. This modern, three-storey Andalucían-style building is in the centre of town. Accommodation is functional, comfortable and well maintained. Some rooms face a large inner patio. The hotel also has a fine restaurant.

🍽 EAT

🛏🛏 **Corral del Agua** – *Callejón del Agua 6.* ✆954 22 48 41. www.corraldelagua.es. Closed Sun. A pleasant, refreshing surprise awaits you in this quiet, atmospheric alley. The terrace, with its abundant vegetation, is delightful in the heat of summer. Classic Andalucían cuisine.

🛏🛏🍽 **Bodegón La Universal** – *Betis 2 (Triana).* ✆954 33 47 46. Closed Wed. The terrace, cooled by the fresh air rising from the Guadalquivir, provides a great view of the city and bullring. Traditional cuisine and a pleasant place to eat either before or after exploring the Triana quarter.

🛏🛏🛏🍽 **Taberna del Alabardero** – *Zaragoza 20.* ✆954 50 27 21. www.taberna delalabardero.es. Closed Aug. This 19C mansion houses one of the best restaurants in Sevilla, a high-class hotel with a dozen or so rooms, a very pleasant tea room and the city's school of hotel management. One of the best tables in Sevilla.

ARACENA

🛏🛏🛏🍽 **José Vicente** – *Av. Andalucía 53.* ✆959 12 84 55. Closed eve except Fri & Sat during low season, mid-Jun–mid-Jul and Tue. One of the best restaurants in the province where, according to its owner, only fresh produce is served. The menu in this tastefully decorated restaurant includes local cep mushrooms and a range of cured ham and pork dishes.

TAPAS

Bar Europa – *Siete Revueltas 35 (Pl. del Pan)* ✆954 22 13 54. www.bareuropa.info. The Europa, in a street behind Plaza del Salvador, is a traditional bar that has retained its Belle Epoque feel. Popular with a young crowd who head here in the early evening for tapas and people-watching. Wines served at cellar temperature.

Bodeguita Romero – *Harinas 10.* ✆954 22 95 56. Closed Mon and fortnight in Aug. Held in high esteem by residents, its bar bursts with tapas and larger portions, all made with quality ingredients. The décor has a local flair.

Bodega San José – *Adriano 10.*
954 22 41 05. Given its location close to the Maestranza bullring, it's not surprising that this typical bodega is popular with aficionados of bullfighting and good fino sherry. The air of authenticity is enhanced by the dirt floor and the aromas emanating from the huge barrels.

La Giralda – *Mateos Gago 1. 954 22 74 35.* Built into what was once a Moorish bath, this little bar just up from the Giralda tower serves an ample selection of excellent tapas from *patatas importancia* (potato gratin) to *chocos* (cuttlefish).

El Rinconcillo – *Gerona 40 y Alhóndiga 2. 954 22 31 83. www.elrinconcillo1670.com. Closed 3 weeks Jul–Aug.* One of the oldest and most attractive bars in Sevilla. Although it dates back to 1670, the décor is from the 19C, including the attractive *azulejo* panelling and the wooden ceiling and counter. Complete meals too at a modest price.

♀ CAFÉS

Confitería La Campana – *Sierpes 1. 954 22 35 70. www.confiterialacampana.com.* One of Sevilla's classic cafeterias. The Modernist décor creates a pleasant atmosphere in which to enjoy La Campana's pastries, which are famous throughout the city. Varied clientele ranging from the district's senior citizens to tourists passing through the centre.

Horno San Buenaventura – *Av. de la Constitución 16. 954 45 87 11. www.hornosanbuenaventura.com.* Part of a network of old furnaces over six centuries old. Particularly popular because of its proximity to the Cathedral and its spacious lounge on the top floor. Its cakes are justifiably famous.

🎭 NIGHTLIFE

Café de la Prensa – *Betis 8. 954 33 34 20.* This modern café with a young and intellectual ambience is located alongside the riverbank. Its outdoor tables offer a magnificent view of both the Guadalquivir and the monumental heart of the city. Perfect for whiling away the late afternoon or for a few drinks to start the evening.

La Carbonería – *Leviés 18 (Pl. de las Mercaderías). 954 21 44 60.* One of Sevilla's institutions and the key to the culture of the city's alternative crowd. Housed in a former coal warehouse in the Jewish quarter (Judería), La Carbonería is split up into a number of different areas, where you can listen to a musical recital in intimate surroundings around a chimney or to authentic lively flamenco (live music every night). The venue also hosts art and photography exhibitions.

Paseo de las Delicias – This avenue is home to four venues *(Chile, 954 23 52 58; Líbano, 954 23 34 77; Alfonso, 954 23 37 35; and Bilindo, 954 62 61 51).* Although not open all year round, they become lively in summer, when they are perfect for bar hopping.

El Tamboril – *Pl. de Santa Cruz 1–12.* Tucked away in a corner of the Santa Cruz district, this taberna is always heaving with its faithful clientele, who occasionally burst into song with an impromptu *sevillana* or *rumba*. Always busy until the early hours of the morning. The Salve Rociera, a prayer to Our Lady of El Rocío, is sung at midnight every day.

🎭 ENTERTAINMENT

Casa Anselma – *Pagés del Corro 49. 954 27 41 63. Spontaneous flamenco 11.30pm–4am.* Anselma herself is the hostess, MC and occasional performer in this rollicking late-night flamenco refuge.

El Patio Sevillano – *Pas. de Cristóbal Colón 11 A. 954 21 41 20. www.elpatio sevillano.com. Daily flamenco shows 7–8.30pm and 9.30–11pm. €37.* A long-running flamenco club catering to aficionados of the art form in its many variations, in a good location by the La Maestranza bullring, with public parking opposite.

Tablao El Arenal – *Rodó 7 (Arenal). 954 21 64 92. www.tablaoelarenal.com. Daily flamenco shows 8.30pm, 10.30pm.* Rated by those in the know as a place to enjoy flamenco in its pure form.

🛒 SHOPPING

Antique lovers should wander the historic centre of the city, particularly the Santa Cruz district. The **Jueves** (Thursday) is a weekly small market held along Calle Feria. Sevilla has a rich **arts and crafts** tradition. Potters can still be found in the Santa Cruz and **Triana** districts (in the latter on calle Alfarería, literally Pottery Street). The La Cartuja factory is heir to this tradition, which dates back to Roman times and the period of Moorish occupation of the city. Other products from Sevilla include inlaid woodwork, shawls, fans, wrought iron, harnesses, guitars and castanets.

Osuna★★

This elegant town in the Sevillan countryside retains a beautiful **monumental centre**★ from its past as a ducal seat of the house of Osuna, one of the most powerful on the Iberian Peninsula.

SIGHTS
Zona Monumental★
Follow signs to Centro Ciudad (town centre) and Zona Monumental.

Colegiata★
Pl. de la Encarnación. Guided tours (45min) May–Sept Tue–Sat 10am–1pm, 4–7pm, Sun 10am–1pm; Oct–Apr Tue–Sun 10am–1.30pm, 3.30–6.30pm. Closed public holidays. €3. 954 81 04 44.
This 16C Renaissance-style collegiate church houses five **paintings**★★ by **José (Jusepe) de Ribera "El Españoleto"** (1591–1652), including *The Expiration of Christ*, in the side chapel off the Nave del Evangelio. The remainder are exhibited in the sacristy.

Panteón Ducal★★ (Ducal Pantheon)
The pantheon was built in Plateresque style in 1545 for the Dukes of Osuna. It is approached by a delightful patio. The chapel (1545) stands below the Colegiata's main altar and is crowned by a blue-and-gold polychrome coffered ceiling, now blackened by candle smoke. Another crypt, built in 1901, holds the tombs of the most important dukes.

Nearby stand the 16C **former university** (Antigua Universidad) and the 17C **Monasterio de la Encarnación**★ *(cuesta de San Antón 15; open same hours as Colegiata; €3; 954 71 04 44)*, in which the highlight is the magnificent **dado**★ of 17C Sevillan *azulejos* in the patio. The nuns here produce and sell several types of delicious biscuits and pastries.

On the descent into the town centre, note the 12C–13C Torre del Agua, a former defensive tower now a small

- **Population:** 17 813
- **Michelin Map:** 578 U 14.
- **Info:** Carrera 82. 954 81 57 32. www.andalucia.org.
- **Location:** Osuna rises to the south of the Guadalquivir Basin, near the A 92 highway linking Granada (160km/100mi E) with Sevilla. Avenida de la Estación.
- **Don't Miss:** The Ducal Pantheon and heritage buildings untouched by time.

archaeological museum *(Pl. de la Duquesa; open same hours as Colegiata; €3; 954 81 12 07)*.

THE TOWN CENTRE
Mainly around Pl. del Duque and Pl. España.

Osuna's streets are lined by numerous Baroque **mansion houses and palaces**★★, whose massive wooden doors, darkly shining and copper nailed, reveal fine wrought-iron grilles and cool green patios. Of particular note are the **calle San Pedro**★ (Cilla del Cabildo, Palacio de los Marqueses de la Gomera), the Antigua Audencia (former Law Courts), the Palacio de los Cepeda, the former Palacio de Puente Hermoso, several fine churches (Santo Domingo, la Compañía) and the **belfry of the Iglesia de la Merced**★, built by the same architect as the **Cilla del Cabildo**.

EXCURSIONS
Écija★
▶ *34km/21mi N along the A 351.*

The town lies in the Guadalquivir depression and is renowned for its lofty Baroque belfries decorated with ceramic tiles, such as the 18C **Torre de San Juan**★ *(Pl. de San Juan; open Mon–Sat 10am–1pm, 6–9pm, Sun 10am–1pm; no charge; www.turismoecija.com) park in plaza de España)*.

The **Ayuntamiento** (town hall) has two **Roman mosaic floors**★ and a *camera oscura* which offers lovely and surprising

Cilla del Cabildo, Osuna

© Juan José Pascual/age fotostock

perspectives of the city *(Pl. de España 1;* ◷*open daily 10am–1.30pm;* €*3;* ℘*955 90 02 40).*

Écija has several delightful small squares, and houses adorned with decorative columns, coats of arms and charming patios. Along the streets adjoining avenida Miguel de Cervantes are several old palaces with fine **façades**★: the 18C Baroque **Palacio de Benamejí** *(Pl. de la Constitución;* ◷*open Oct–May Tue–Fri 10am–1.30pm, 4.30–6.30pm, Sat 10am–2pm, 5.30–8pm, Sun and public holidays 10am–3pm; Jun–Sept Tue–Fri 10am–2.30pm, Sat 10am–2pm, 8–10pm, Sun and public holidays 10am–3pm;* ✆*no charge;* ℘*954 83 04 31);* the concave and fresco-adorned **Palacio de Peñaflor** *(Emilio Castelar 26),* its portal built on columns; and the Plateresque-style **Palacio de Valdehermoso** *(Emilio Castelar 37).* Several churches are noteworthy: **Los Descalzos**, renowned for the exuberant decoration of its **interior**★; **Santa María** *(Pl. de Santa María;* ◷*open May–Sept Mon–Sat 10am–1pm, 6–9pm, Sun 10am–1pm; Oct–Apr Mon–Sat 10am–1pm, 5.30–7pm, Sun 10am–1pm;* ✆*no charge;* ℘*954 83 04 30),* crowned by an impressive tower; the Convento de los Marroquíes, with its lofty **bell tower**★, where the delicious *marroquíes* biscuits are still produced and sold by the nuns; and the **Iglesia de Santiago**★, which

retains the Mudéjar windows of an earlier building and a Gothic **retable**★ at the high altar illustrating the Passion and the Resurrection.

The outbuildings of the Iglesia de Santa Cruz, following a restoration, house the **Museo de Arte Sacro** (sacred art museum) with 16C-19C works. *(Pl. Virgen del Valle.* ☛*guided tour (30min) daily Oct–May 10am–1.30pm, 4.30–8pm; Jun–Sept 9.30am–1pm, 5–9pm;* ✆*no charge;* ℘*954 83 06 13; www.museosanta cruz.com).*

Estepa★

▶ *25km/15mi E of Osuna.*

Famous for the collective suicide committed in 206 BC to avoid capture by the Roman army, and, later, for the *bandoleros,* both Spanish and Moorish, chronicled by Washington Irving in the 19C, Estepa today is a peaceful labyrinth of narrow streets and elegant mansions. The **Iglesia de Nuestra Señora del Carmen** is Estepa's best architectural site, while the Iglesia de San Sebastián and Palacio de los Marqueses de Cervales are also handsome examples of Andalucían rural architecture.

Cerro de San Cristóbal offers memorable panoramas of Estepa's towers, such as the **Torre de la Victoria**★ rising from the plaza of the same name, and rolling countryside, *la campiña,* beyond.

Costa de la Luz★

The southwestern coast in the provinces of Huelva and Cádiz is edged with beaches interrupted by the mouths of major rivers – the Guadiana, Tinto and Guadalquivir. Several resorts are being developed beside the dazzling white sand and translucent skies that make this the Coast of Light.

DRIVING TOURS

The Huelva Coast★
Ayamonte to the Parque Nacional de Doñana – 135km/84mi. Alow one day.

Ayamonte★
This fishing port at the mouth of the Guadiana is a lively border town of cobbled streets and whitewashed and brightly coloured houses. In the old quarter are the 16C colonial-style Iglesia de las Angustias, the Convento de San Francisco, with its elegant bell tower and magnificent *artesonado* work, and the 13C Iglesia del Salvador.
Boat service is available to Vila Real de Santo António in Portugal.
Coastal resorts between Ayamonte and Huelva include **Isla Canela, Isla Cristina** (*www.islacristina.es*), **La Antilla** (*www.lepe.es*) and **Punta Umbría** (*www.ayto-puntaumbria.es*). This area also includes the marshland of the **Marismas del Río Piedras y Flecha de El Rompido**★, the Portil lagoon, and the Enebrales de Punta Umbría, a landscape dominated by juniper trees.

Huelva★
Avenida de Italia 36.
In the 15C and 16C, the estuary formed by the Tinto and Odiel rivers saw the departure of numerous expeditions to the New World, notably those led by Columbus. A large monument to these explorers, the **Monumento a Colón** (1929), stands near the harbour at Punta del Sebo.
In Huelva, see the unusual **Barrio Reina Victoria**★, an English-style district

Michelin Map: 578 U 7-8-9-10, V 10, W 10-11, X 11-12-13 – *Andalucía (Huelva, Cádiz)*

Info: El Puerto de Santa María: Luna 22. ℘956 54 24 13; Huelva: Plaza Alcalde Coto Mora 2. ℘959 65 02 00; Sanlúcar de Barrameda: Avenida Calzada Del Ejército. ℘956 36 61 10; Tarifa: Paseo de la Alameda. ℘956 68 09 93. www.andalucia.org.

Location: The Costa de la Luz extends from Ayamonte, at the mouth of the Guadiana, to Tarifa, the most southerly town on mainland Spain.

named after Queen Victoria; the **Catedral de La Merced** (*Pl. de la Merced; ℘959 24 30 36*), with its Renaissance façade and sculpture of the Virgen de la Cinta, the town's patron saint, by Martínez Montañés; and paintings by Zurbarán in the **Iglesia de la Concepción** (*Concepción*) and the **Museo** (*Alameda Sundheim 13;* ⏰*open Tues 2.30–8.30pm, Wed–Sat 9am–8.30pm, Sun 9am–2.30pm;* €2; ℘959 25 93 00).

Paraje Natural de las Marismas del Odiel★★
2km/1.2mi SE. Exit Huelva along Avenida Tomás Domínguez (Cto de Recepción La Calatilla, Carretera del Dique Juan Carlos I; activities require advance booking, ℘954 50 90 11).
This marshland (*marisma*) of outstanding beauty, at the mouth of the Tinto and Odiel rivers, close to an industrial chemical facility, is a **World Biosphere Reserve**. It provides a habitat for over 200 bird species. Visited by **canoe** or small boat.

La Rábida★
10km/6.2mi SE of Huelva off N 442.
In 1484, the Prior of the **Monasterio de Santa María** (*Camino del Monasterio;* ⏰*open Sept–Jul Tue–Sat 10am–1pm, 4–*

6pm, Sun and public holidays 10.45am–
1pm, 4–7pm; Aug daily 10am–1pm, 4.45–
8pm; €2.50, audioguide €2; 959 35
04 11), Juan Pérez, believed in Columbus
and his claim that the world was round
and interceded to obtain the support of
the Catholic Monarchs.

The **church** preserves old frescoes,
wooden *artesonado* work and the delicate 14C alabaster statue of the **Virgen
de los Milagros** (Virgin of Miracles),
in front of which Columbus is said to
have prayed prior to setting sail. A small
room displays a **mapamundi**, by Juan
de la Cosa, which outlined the coast of
America for the first time.

Full-scale replicas of Columbus' three
caravels are moored at the **Muelle
de las Carabelas** (open Oct–May
Tue–Sun 10am–7pm, Jun–Sept Tue–Fri
10am–2pm, 5–9pm, Sat–Sun 11am–8pm;
€3.75; 959 53 03 12), a modern dock
and museum on the Tinto Estuary.

Palos de la Frontera★

13km/8mi SE of Huelva by A 5026.
This picturesque town on the left bank
of the Río Tinto was the birthplace of
the Pinzón brothers, who sailed with
Columbus. The **Casa-Museo de Martín
Alonso Pinzón** (open daily 10.30am–
1.30pm, 5–7.30pm; no charge; 959 35
01 99) and the *azulejos* dotted around
the town provide a reminder of the first
voyage. The 15C **Iglesia de San Jorge**
is fronted by an interesting Gothic-
Mudéjar doorway.

Moguer★

20km/12.4mi NE of Huelva off A 494.
Expeditions left this tranquil town with
its elegant houses for points unknown.
The verses of **Juan Ramón Jiménez**
(1881–1958), Moguer's most illustrious
son and winner of the Nobel Prize for
Literature in 1956, adorn *azulejo* panelling dotted around the town centre. His
home is a museum, the **Casa-Museo
Juan Ramón Jiménez** (Juán Ramón
Jimenez 10; open Tue–Sat 10.15am–
1pm, 5.15–7pm; €3; 959 37 21 48).
The **town hall** (ayuntamiento) has a
fine Renaissance **façade**. Head along
the pedestrianised **Calle Andalucía**,

lined by interesting buildings, including the Archivo Histórico Municipal and
Biblioteca Iberoamericana; and the 15C
Convento de San Francisco, with its Mannerist cloisters, Baroque altarpiece and
lofty belfry. The **tower** of the Iglesia de
Nuestra Señora de la Granada recalls
the Giralda in Sevilla.

Convento de Santa Clara★

Guided tours (40min) Tue–Sat 11am
–12.30pm and 5–7pm. Closed public
holidays. €3. 959 37 01 07.
The church of this Gothic-Mudéjar monastery houses the Renaissance-style
marble **tombs of the Portocarrero
family**, noteworthy **tombs** at the
high altar, and some quite exceptional
14C **Nasrid-Mudéjar choir stalls★★**.

▷ *Return to the C 442, which follows
the coast.*

Parque Nacional de Doñana★★★

This park, at the crossroads of continents
and of the Atlantic and the Mediterranean, acts as a rest stop for African and
European migratory birds. Doñana is
Spain's largest wildlife reserve with a
protected area (inner and outer park)
of 73 000ha/180 387 acres. The **salt
marshes** are the larger part of the park
and are the ideal habitat for birds which
migrate to Europe over the winter. **Sand
dunes** are grouped in formation parallel

*Aerial view of salt marshes
in Parque Nacional de Doñana*

©Turespaña

to the Atlantic and advance inland at a rate of 6m/19.6ft per year. The stabilised sands or **cotos** are dry, undulating areas covered with heather, rockrose, rosemary and thyme, and trees such as cork oak and pine.

The Doñana is home to lynx, wild boar, deer and a wide variety of birds, including Spanish imperial eagles, flamingos, herons, wild ducks and coots.

See p515 for sightseeing information.

El Rocío
65km/40.4mi E of Huelva, along A 483.
This small village is famous as the site of the **Santuario de Nuestra Señora del Rocío** *(Sanctuary of the Virgin of the Dew;* ✆ *959 44 24 25)*, to which Spain's most popular religious pilgrimage *(romería)* is made during Whitsun weekend every year.

The Cádiz Coast★
From Sanlúcar de Barrameda to Tarifa 160km/99.4mi – allow one day

Sanlúcar de Barrameda★
The fishing port of Sanlúcar, at the mouth of the Guadalquivir, is the home town of *manzanilla*, a sherry matured like Jerez *fino* but which has a special flavour thanks to the sea air. The bodegas (cellars) are in the old quarter on the hill around the massive **Castillo de Santiago** *(Cava de Castillo)*.

The **Iglesia de Nuestra Señora de la O** *(Pl. de la Paz)* close by has a fine Mudéjar **doorway★★** and a 16C **Mudéjar artesonado ceiling★**.

In the modern town, pass the **Palacio de Orleans y Borbón** *(Cuesta de Belén)*, a 19C palace built in neo-Moorish style, and now Sanlúcar's town hall, and the **covachas★**, a mysterious series of five ogee arches decorated with Gothic tracery. The lower town has two main churches: the **Iglesia de la Trinidad** *(Pl. de San Roque)*, with its magnificent 15C Mudéjar **artesonado★★**; and the **Iglesia de Santo Domingo** *(Santo Domingo)*, with the noble proportions of a Renaissance building. The **Centro de Visitantes Fábrica de Hielo** (open daily 9am–7pm (8 or 9pm in summer);

✆*956 38 65 77)*, a visitor centre in Bajo de Guía, near the mouth of the Guadalquivir, provides information on the Parque Nacional de Doñana across the river.

Park excursions also depart from here.

Rota
23km/14mi S of Sanlúcar off A 491.
The **old town★** inside the ramparts is laid out around the **Castillo de la Luna** *(Avenida Mancomunidad Bajo Guadalquivir 3;* ✆*956 84 62 88)* and the **Iglesia de Nuestra Señora de la O★** *(Luis Vázquez 2;* ✆*956 81 00 84)*. Rota is known for beaches such as the **Playa de la Costilla★**. A large naval base is on the outskirts of the town.

El Puerto de Santa María★
24km/15mi SE of Sanlúcar, off A 491.
The harbour, in Cádiz Bay, played an active role in trade with the New World. Today, fishing, the export of sherry and tourism (beaches and golf courses) are important. A palm-shaded promenade overlooking the quays along the north bank leads to the 12C **Castillo de San Marcos**, a castle which was the seat of the Dukes of Medinaceli. The late 15C **Iglesia Mayor Prioral** *(Pagador 8)* stands in the centre of the town. The **Portada del Sol★**, or Sun Gateway, in Plaza de España, is a mix of Plateresque and Baroque styles.

The **Fundación Rafael Alberti** *(Santo Domingo 25;* *open Tue–Sun 11am–2.30pm;* €4. ✆ *956 85 07 11; www. rafaelalberti.es)* nearby shows photos, letters and manuscripts by the poet. The **Casa-Museo de Pedro Muñoz-Seca** (1879–1936), author of tragi-comic play *La Venganza de Don Mendo*, is also here *(Nevería 48;* *open Tue–Sun 11am–2.30pm;* €1.50; ✆*956 85 17 31; www. fundacionpedromunozseca.org)*.

Cádiz★★ *See CÁDIZ*
52km/32mi S of Sanlúcar.
South of Cádiz, there are good beaches at **La Barrosa★★**, Chiclana de la Frontera and **Conil de la Frontera** (**Playa de la Fontanilla** and **Playa de los Bateles**).

Vejer de la Frontera★

57km/35mi SE of Cádiz along E 5.

Vejer, perched on a crag, is one of the prettiest white villages of Andalucía. The best approach is along the hillside road from the south. The **Iglesia del Divino Salvador** has a three-aisle **interior**★ a mix of Romanesque and Gothic features. The road on to Tarifa runs through the Baetic foothills. The **Parque Natural La Breña y Marismas de Barbate**★ (*℘956 27 48 42*), with spectacular cliffs and picturesque coves, such as the **Cala de los Caños de Meca**★★, is 10km/6mi from Vejer.

Ruinas Romanas de Baelo Claudia★

Open Sun 9am–2pm; Tue–Sat Jun–Sept 9am–8pm, Mar–May and Oct 9am–7pm, Nov–Feb 9am–6pm. Closed 24, 25, 31 Dec, 1, 6 Jan. €1.75; free for EU citizens. *℘956 10 67 97.*

The remains of the Roman city of Baelo Claudia date back to the 2C BC, when a salting factory specialising in the production of *garum* (a sauce made from the remains of fish) was established here. Vestiges of the basilica, forum and theatre are still visble.

Tarifa

105km/65mi S of Cádiz, along E 5.

Spain's southmost point, a major centre for windsurfing and kitesurfing. The **Castillo de Guzmán el Bueno**, taken by the Christians in 1292, was commanded by Guzmán el Bueno who accepted the execution of his sons by the Moors rather than surrender.

ADDRESSES

🏨 STAY

🛏🍴🛏 **Hotel Convento de San Francisco** – *La Plazuela, Vejer de la Frontera. ℘956 45 10 01. www.tugasa.com. 25 rooms. ☲€4.50. Restaurant🛏🍴🛏.* This former convent for Poor Clares dating from the 17C is situated in Vejer's old quarter. Although soberly decorated, the rooms are pleasant, with high ceilings and exposed beams. The hotel also has a good restaurant.

🛏🍴🛏 **Hotel Toruño** – *Pl. del Acebuchal 22, El Rocío. ℘959 44 23 23. www.toruno.es 30 rooms.* At the edge of Parque Nacional de Doñana, this traditional great house blends perfectly into the village of El Rocío. Some rooms have lovely marsh views. Prices soar for the pilgrimage.

🛏🍴🛏 **Posada de Palacio** – *Caballeros 11 (Barrio Alto), Sanlúcar de Barrameda. ℘956 36 48 40. www.posadadepalacio.com. 30 rooms. ☲€8. Closed 8 Jan–Feb.* This family-run hotel is in an 18C mansion opposite the town hall in the upper section of Sanlúcar. The rooms, laid out around an attractive patio, are simply yet tastefully decorated.

🍽 EAT

🛏🍴🛏 **Casa Bigote** – *Bajo de Guía 10, Sanlúcar de Barrameda. ℘956 36 26 96. www.restaurantecasabigote.com. Closed Nov, Sun.* This old tavern in the river district of Bajo Guía has become a gastronomic landmark. Run by the same family for the past 50 years, it is decorated with old photos, fishing mementos and antique objects. Pride of place on the extensive menu is given to local fish and prawns.

🛏🍴🛏 **Trafalgar** – *Pl. de España 31, Vejer de la Frontera. ℘956 44 76 38. Closed Jan, first two weeks Feb, Sun dinner, Mon (except Jun–Aug).* This welcome culinary surprise, on the attractive Plaza de los Pescaítos, specialises in delicious fresh fish. Tapas are also served at the entrance. Guests can dine on the terrace in summer.

SIGHTSEEING

Because of the park's fragile ecology, entry to the **Doñana** is rigorously controlled. The El Acebuche visitor centre *(Pl. Acebuchal, 22 El Rocío, Huelva; ℘959 448 711)* coordinates all park activities. **River trips** (4hr) are also available if booked in advance (*℘956 36 38 13*). Contact the administrative centre for more information: *℘959 448 640.*

GUIDED TOURS

Several types of excursions are possible within the park and leave from El Acebuche visitor centre in Huelva: **Jeep tours** should be booked in advance. Two visits per day Tue–Sun at 8.30am and 3pm (5pm in high season). Itineraries vary according to the time of year. **Walking tours** depart from the four information centres where details are available on the level of difficulty and duration of the walks. **Horseback** excursions are available by horseback or horse-drawn carriage.

Jerez de la Frontera★★

Jerez looks out at fertile countryside. A provincial capital, it springs into life at fiesta time, sharing its tradions of wine, horsemanship and flamenco.

THE CITY TODAY

Modern Jerez was built around 150 years ago on its Anglo-Spanish sherry wealth and retains its elegant, aristo-cratic, rather staid air. Relatively few visitors stay overnight but those that do can enjoy authentic flamenco (the town has a large *gitano* population) and may also like to seek out the lively bars just north of the Alcázar.

A BIT OF HISTORY

Jerez was one of the first towns to be founded by the Moors on the Iberian Peninsula. A number of vestiges remain from the Moorish "Sahrish", including sections of the old walls, the fortress (*alcazaba*) and a mosque. In 1264, Jerez was conquered by the troops of Alfonso X, and developed into a settlement of strategic importance as well as a lead-ing commercial centre. The economic resurgence experienced by the province of Cádiz in the 18C left its mark on Jerez, with the construction of fine Baroque buildings and its famous wine cellars, some of which can still be seen today.

SIGHTS

Bodegas Domecq

San Luis. Guided tours by arrangement Mon–Fri 11am–12.30pm, 12.30–2pm. €6 weekday mornings (€8 afternoons, Sat–Sun and public holidays). ℘956 33 96 34. www.alvarodomecq.com.
The visit to the oldest Jerez bodega includes storehouses where a host of celebrities have signed their names.

Bodegas González Byass

Manuel María González 12. Guided tours Oct–Jun Mon–Sat 11am, noon, 1pm, 2pm, 4pm, 5pm and 6pm, Sun at

▶ **Population:** 207 532
◉ **Michelin Map:** 578 V 11.
▯ **Info:** Alameda Cristina. ℘956 34 17 11. www.turismojerez.com.
◐ **Location:** Jerez is in the Andalucían countryside, just 35km/22mi from the provincial capital Cádiz and 90km/56mi from Sevilla. ▭Plaza de la Estación.
◉ **Don't Miss:** A bodega tour.
◑ **Timing:** Take several hours to stroll around the town's historic quarters, stopping off at at least one bodega.

11am, noon, 1pm and 2pm; Jul–Sept Mon–Sat 11.30am, 12.30pm, 1.30pm, 2pm, 4.30pm, 5.30pm, 6.30pm, Sun 11.30am, 12.30pm, 1.30pm, 2pm. €10. ℘902 44 00 77. www.gonzalezbyass.com.
The most famous storehouse is the spec-tacular La Concha bodega, designed by Gustave Eiffel in 1862.

Palacio del Tiempo★★

Cervantes 3. ◐Open Tue–Sat 10am–2pm, 5–7pm, Sun 10am–2pm. Guided tours on the hour and at quarter past. ◐Closed 24–25, 31 Dec. €7 (€10 with Misterio de Jerez). ℘956 18 21 00. www.elmisteriode jerez.org.
This clock museum in the 19C Palacete de la Atalaya exhibits 300 18–19C time-pieces in perfect working order. In the same gardens the **Misterio de Jerez** tells the story of Jerez wines (*guided tour, same hours as Palacio del Tiempo; €5*).

Real Escuela Andaluza del Arte Ecuestre★

Av. Duque de Abrantes. Guided tour (30min) including facilities and training sessions Mon, Tue (Nov–Feb), Wed and Fri 11am–1pm; horse show Tue (Mar–Dec), Thu, Fri (Aug) at noon. ◐Closed public holidays.

€10; show: €20 or €26. *956 31 96 35. www.realescuela.org.
The foundation in a 19C mansion by Charles Garnier, is dedicated to equestrian arts, including the training of horses. A **show**★★ in the main arena is not to be missed.

Museo Arqueológico de Jerez
Pl. del Mercado. Open Sept–mid-Jun Tue–Fri 10am–2pm, 4–7pm, Sat–Sun and public holidays 10am–2.30pm; mid-Jun–Aug daily 10am–2.30pm. €2. *956 33 33 16. www.museo arqueologico.webjerez.com.*
The outstanding exhibit in the archaeological museum is a **Greek helmet**★.

☛ WALKING TOUR

THE OLD TOWN
Plaza del Mercado
The medieval market is now a tranquil square bordered by the **Palacio Riquelme**, with imposing Renaissance façade, the 15C **Iglesia de San Mateo**, and the **Museo Arqueológico**.

◗ *Take Cabezas to the Iglesia de San Lucas, then Ánimas de Lucas, Plaza de Orbaneja and San Juan.*

Iglesia de San Juan de los Caballeros★
*Pl. de San Juan. *956 32 43 41.*
This medieval church has a magnificent 14C **polygonal apse**★, topped by a ribbed cupola with jagged decoration.

◗ *Take Francos, then Canto to Plaza de Ponce de León.*

Note the fine **Plateresque window**★★ on one of the corners.

◗ *Go along Juana de Dios Lacoste, cross Francos, then follow Compañía.*

Iglesia de San Marcos
*Pl. de San Marcos. *956 34 18 97.*
This late 15C church has a beautiful 16C **star vault**. The apse is hidden by a 16C polygonal **altarpiece**★ showing strong Flemish influence.

◗ *From the square, Tonería leads to Plaza de Plateros.*

Plaza de Plateros
The **Torre de Atalaya**, a 15C tower, is adorned with Gothic windows.

◗ *Head down José Luis Díez.*

Plaza de la Asunción★
The Renaissance façade of the **Casa del Cabildo**★★ (1575) is adorned with grotesque figures. The Gothic **Iglesia de San Dionisio** (*956 34 29 40) shows Mudéjar influence.

◗ *Continue along José Luis Díez.*

Plaza del Arroyo
The **Palacio del Marqués de Bertemati**★ has fine Baroque balconies.

◗ *Continue on José Luis Díez and on to Plaza del Arroyo, turn left at del Encarnación, then right at Manuel María González.*

Catedral★★
Pl. de la Encarnación. Open Mon–Fri 11am–1pm. No charge. *956 34 84 82.*
This monumental cathedral, with five aisles, combines Renaissance and Baroque features. The cupola bears bas-reliefs of the Evangelists. The annual wine harvest festival is held in front of the Cathedral.

◗ *Return to Manuel María González and head NE. Turn right at Plaza Monti, left at Armas and right at Plaza del Arenal.*

Alcázar★
Alameda Vieja. Open daily May–mid-Sept 10am–8pm; mid-Sept–Apr 10am–6pm. Closed 1, 6 Jan, 25 Dec. €3.35 (with camera obscura), €1.35 (baths, mosque and windmill). *956 14 99 55.*
From this 12C Almohad fortress, enjoy an excellent **view**★★ of the cathedral. Enter by the **Puerta de la Ciudad** (City Gateway). The prayer room in the **mosque**★★, located within the walls of the

JEREZ DE LA FRONTERA

0 — 200 m
0 — 200 yds

N

*Map labels:*
PALACIO DEL TIEMPO · Bodega Sandeman · REAL ESCUELA ANDALUZA DEL ARTE ECUESTRE · CENTRO TEMÁTICO DE LA ATALAYA · Museo de Enganches · Pl. de la Constitución · Atalaya · Pizarro · Cádiz · Av. Alcalde Álvaro Domecq · Av. Duque de Abrantes · Divina Pastora · Leales · Asta · Cervantes · Pozo del Olivar · Sevilla · Paúl · Domingo · Taxdirt · Barreras · Ponce · Guadalete · Pl. Mamelón · Santo · Nuño de Cañas · Circo · Pl. Santiago · Beato Juan Grande · Zaragoza · Santiago · Ancha · Porvera · Alameda Cristina · Pl. Aladro · Casa Domecq · Merced · Muro · Centro Andaluz de Flamenco · S. JUAN DE LOS CABALLEROS · Palacio de los Pérez Luna · Rosario · Santo Domingo · Clavel · Museo Arqueológico · S. Lucas · Sta María de Gracia · Cordobeses · Palacio Riquelme · Pl. del Mercado · Palacio de los Ponce de León · S. Marcos · Pl. Rafael Rivero · SAN PEDRO · S. Lucas · L. de Isasy · Pl. Peones · Bizcocheros · Morenos · Gaspar · Fernández · San Mateo · Pl. Belén · Cabezas · PALACIO DEL MARQUÉS DE BERTEMATI · POL · 7 · Pl. de la Asunción · S. Dionisio · Pl. Plateros · Sta Larga · Arcos · San Blas · San Ildefonso · 5 · 3 · Algarve · Teatro Villamarta · Bodega Domecq · Calzada del Arroyo · Cruces · J. L. Díez · CABILDO · H · Consistorio · Pl. Romero Martínez · Pl. de la Encarnación · Pozuelo · Pl. Monti · 4 · Lancería · Doña Blanca · PUERTA DEL ARROYO · CATEDRAL · Pl. del Arenal · Manuel María González · Armas · Corredera · ALCÁZAR · Alameda Vieja · S. Agustín · Caballeros · Pedro Alonso · Pl. de las Angustias · Bodega González Byass (Tío Pepe) · Puerto · Conde de Bayona · Sta Clara · SAN MIGUEL · Barja · Sol · Empedrada · Av. Torresoto · A 4 CÁDIZ · Bodega Williams & Humbert

Left margin: Zoo-Jardín Botánico · A 480 · SANLÚCAR DE BARRAMEDA · Cta de la Chaparra · Ronda del Caracol

Right margin: A 4 · RONDA, ARCOS DE LA FRONTERA · CIRCUITO · YEGUADA DE LA CARTUJA

Alcázar, is covered by a delightful **octagonal cupola**. A **camera obscura** in the **Palacio de Villavicencio** provides a unique view of Jerez via its mirrors and lenses.

◯ *Head NE along Plaza del Arenal towards Caballeros, turn right at San Miguel and bear left towards the church.*

Iglesia de San Miguel★★
Pl. de San Miguel. ℘*956 34 33 47.*
Construction began in Gothic style in the late 16C; the Baroque tower dates from two centuries later.
The older San José façade is a fine example of the Hispano-Flemish style. The Renaissance **altarpiece**★ is by Martínez Montañés.

La Cartuja

EXCURSIONS
La Cartuja★

▶ *Carrera de Jerez a Algeciras, 6km/ 3.5mi SE.* ⏱*Gardens and patio are open Mon–Sat 9.30am–11.15am, 12.45–6.30pm.* ⏱*Closed public holidays.* �441*No charge.* ℘*956 15 64 65.*

This Carthusian monastery, founded in 1477, has a Greco-Roman portal attributed to Andrés de Ribera. The Flamboyant Gothic church has a richly decorated Baroque **façade**★★★.

La Cartuja Stud Farm★ (Yeguada de la Cartuja)

At the Finca Fuente del Suero, 6.5km/ 4mi from Jerez on the Medina Sidonia road. ⟿*Guided tours (2hr) Sat, 11am– 1pm.* ⏱*Closed 15 Dec–15 Jan.* �441*€14–19.* ℘*956 16 28 09.*

Visitors to the stud farm get a close look at the famous Cartujana horses.

ADDRESSES

🏠 STAY

⟳⟳🛏 **Serit** – *Higueras 7.* ℘*956 34 07 00. www.hotelserit.com. 35 rooms.* ⟷*€7.* A central family-run hotel, functional and up-to-date. Best rooms, in the annex, have wood floors and wrought-iron furniture.

⟳⟳🛏🛏 **Hotel Doña Blanca** – *Bodegas 11.* ℘*956 34 87 61. www.hotel donablanca.com. 30 rooms.* ⟷*€8.* This unpretentious hotel in an attractive Andalucían-style building has the great advantage of a superb location between the market and post office in the centre of Jerez. The bedrooms here are on the spacious side with all the usual creature comforts.

🍽/EAT

⟳🛏 **Gaitán** – *Gaitán 3.* ℘*956 16 80 21. www.restaurantegaitan.es. Closed Sun.* This well-respected restaurant serves good-quality, innovative regional cuisine. The small whitewashed dining room is long and narrow and abundantly embellished with decorative objects.

⟳⟳🛏 **La Taberna Flamenca** – *Angostillo de Santiago 3.* ℘*956 32 36 93. www.latabernaflamenca.com. Closed Sun, Mon Nov–May. Reservations advised.* This restaurant in an ex-wine storehouse offers meals with a *tablao flamenco* performance.

TAPAS

Juanito – *Pescadería Vieja 8–10.* ℘*956 33 48 38. www.bar-juanito.com. Closed during Jerez fair.* This Jerez classic in a pedestrianised street lined with outdoor terraces, has been serving its huge choice of tapas in Jerez for the past 50 years or more. The décor could not be more Andalucían, with its ceramic tiles and bullfighting-inspired pictures.

🍸 NIGHTLIFE

Bereber – *Cabezas 10.* ℘*956 34 42 46. www.tablaodelbereber.com. Closed Sun. Reservations recommended.* Bereber, in a Moorish palace, is the obligatory night-time stopping-point. Its spaces (café, bar, patios, dance floors in wine cellars and restaurant with flamenco) are variously decorated in impeccable Arabian and Andalucían style.

🎭 ENTERTAINMENT

The **Teatro Villamarta** (*Pl. Romero Martínez;* ℘*956 14 96 85; www.villamarta. com*) offers opera, music, dance and theatre, including flamenco. The city's best-known flamenco clubs (*peñas flamencas*) are the **Peña Tío José de Paula** (*Merced 11;* ℘*956 32 01 96*), and the popular **Peña el Garbanzo** (*Santa Clara 9;* ℘*956 33 76 67*).

🏃 LEISURE

Baños Árabes Hammam Andalusí – *Salvador 6.* ℘*956 34 90 66. www.hammam andalusi.com. Baths 10am–10pm in 2hr sessions (reserve).* These re-created Moorish baths transport us to other times. The terrace and tea house look out to the Cathedral.

FIESTAS

Horses are as important as sherry in Jerez. In the 16C, the Carthusian monastery (Cartuja) crossed Andalucían, Neapolitan and German breeds, giving rise to the famous **Cartujana** horse. In **early May** there are racing, dressage and carriage competitions at the **Feria del Caballo** (Horse Fair).

In **September** the **Fiesta de la Vendimia** (Wine Harvest Festival) showcases a cavalcade and a flamenco festival; the *cante jondo* is particularly alive and popular in Jerez, a town which is home to such famous singers as **Antonio Chacón** (1869–1929) and **Manuel Torres**.

Cádiz★★

Surrounded by water on three sides, Cádiz has attracted mariners for over 3 000 years. It is also one of Andalucía's most delightful provincial capitals, with charming squares, narrow alleyways and a quiet air, broken only by the exuberant Carnival, the best on the Iberian Peninsula.

THE CITY TODAY

Despite its location and the fine beaches on either side of the town, Cádiz has never embraced costa-style tourism. In summer Spanish holidaymakers and, to a lesser degree, cruise ship day trippers make up most of its visitors.

At other times of year its fishing and shipbuilding ports make it a hive of activity with all nationalities passing through, adding a dash of colour to the cobbled streets, and custom to the many excellent fish restaurants of its old town.

A BIT OF HISTORY

Oldest city in Europe – Cádiz was founded by the Phoenicians in 1100 BC. It was conquered by the Romans in 206 BC, and in turn by the Visigoths and Moors. Alfonso X reconquered the city in 1262. During the 16C, Cádiz was attacked by English corsairs, and partially destroyed by the Earl of Essex in 1596. In the 18C, Cádiz became a great port.

Constitution of Cádiz – During the French siege of 1812, patriots convened the Cortes which promulgated Spain's first liberal constitution.

Watchtowers – Between the 16C and 18C, merchants in Cádiz built over 160 towers to watch over the arrival and departure of their ships.

SIGHTS

Museo Catedralicio★

Pl. Fray Félix. ◷*Open Tue–Fri 10am–1.30pm, 4.30–7pm, Sat 10.30am–1pm.* ◉€*3 (includes visit to the cathedral).* ℘*956 25 98 12.*

This medieval complex around a fine 16C **Mudéjar patio**★ holds liturgi-

cal objects and art, including the 16C **Custodia del Cogollo**★, a gold-plated monstrance attributed to Enrique Arfe, and the 18C **Custodia del Millón**.

Oratorio de la Santa Cueva★

Rosario. ◷*Open Tue–Fri 10am–1pm, 4.30–7.30pm, Sat–Sun 10am–1pm.* ◉€*5.* ℘*956 22 22 62.*

Three **canvases**★★ in this elliptical oratory were painted by Goya in 1795.

Museo de Cádiz★

Pl. de Mina. ◷*Open Tue 2.30–8.30pm, Wed–Sat 9am–8.30pm, Sun and public holidays 9am–2.30pm.* ◉€*3; free for EU citizens.* ℘*956 20 33 77.*

The city's museum is in a small mid-19C Neoclassical palace.

The collection includes vases, oil lamps and jewellery, including two 5C BC Greek **anthropoidal sarcophagi**★★ based on Egyptian models.

Paintings include nine **panels**★ by Zurbarán from the Carthusian monastery in Jerez.

Torre Tavira★

Marqués del Real Tesoro 10. ◷*Open daily Oct–May 10am–6pm; Jul–Sept 10am–8pm.* ◷*Closed 25 Dec, 1 Jan.* ◉€*4.50.* ℘*956 21 29 10.*

The first 18C watchtower houses the first **camera obscura** in Spain, a device capturing real-time images of the city.

▸ **Population:** 126 766
⚲ **Michelin Map:** 578 W 11.
▯ **Info:** Paseo de Canalejas. ℘956 24 10 01. www.cadizturismo.com.
◉ **Location:** This coastal city is positioned with the Atlantic to the south and west, the Bahía de Cádiz to the north and east. 🚌Plaza de Sevilla 1.
🅿 **Parking:** It's difficult in the old quarter.
◈ **Don't Miss:** A wander within the walls.

Oratorio de San Felipe Neri

Santa Inés. ⏰*Open Mon–Sat 10am–1.30pm.* 👁€3. 📞*956 21 16 12.*
In this elliptical Baroque church the Cortes proclaimed the liberal Constitution of Cádiz in 1812. The **Immaculate Conception** was painted by Murillo in 1680 shortly before his death.

Museo de las Cortes de Cádiz

⏰*Open Tue–Fri 9am–1pm, 4–7pm, Sat–Sun 9am–1pm.* ⏰*Closed public holidays.* 📞*956 22 17 88.*
The museum's main exhibit is a **model**★ of Cádiz in the reign of Charles III.

Playa de la Caleta★

Could this charming beach facing the open ocean have been the site of the first Phoenician landing in the 11C BC? In any case, this was Cádiz's natural port for many years. The location is very pleasant, with a small spa protected from Atlantic by the long breakwater leading out to the **Castillo de San Sebastián**. The other extremity of the beach ends in the **Castillo de Santa Catalina** where, in season, there are musical performances *(Paseo Antonio Burgos s/n;* ⏰*open Mar–Oct 10am–9pm; Nov–Feb 10am–9pm;* 👁*no charge;* 📞 *956 226 333).*

🦶 WALKING TOUR

AROUND SANTA MARÍA AND THE PÓPULO DISTRICT
Plaza de San Juan de Dios

This 16C square is the most popular in the city. On one side stands the Neoclassical façade of the 1799 **town hall** *(ayuntamiento),* by Torcuato Benjumeda, beside the Baroque tower of the Iglesia de San Juan de Dios. The tourist office is in an attractive Neoclassical building.

▷ *Take Sopranis, to the left of the Iglesia de San Juan de Dios.*

Calle Sopranis

The street contains some of the best Baroque civil architecture in Cádiz, particularly the houses at nos. 9, 10 and 17.
At the end of the street note the 19C iron-and-brick former **tobacco factory**, and the **Convento de Santo Domingo** (⏰*open Mon–Sat 8.45am–noon, 7–8.45pm, Sun 8am–noon, 7–8pm;* 👁*no charge).*

▷ *Continue along Plocia as far as Concepción Arenal.*

Cárcel Real★

Concepción Arenal.
The 1792 royal jail, by Torcuato Benjumeda, is one of the most important Baroque civil buildings in Andalucía. The façade with triumphal-arch entry bears the escutcheon of the monarchy. It houses the city's law courts.

Iglesia de Santa María

Santa María.
The spire on the belfry of this 17C Mannerist church is adorned with *azulejos.*

▷ *Continue along Santa María, past the 18C Casa Lasquetty to the left; cross Félix Soto towards the 13C Arco de los Blancos.*

Casa del Almirante

Pl. de San Martín.
🔒*Closed to the public.*
The outstanding feature of this 17C Baroque palace is the double-section Italian marble **doorway**★★, with Tuscan and Solomonic columns.

The Battle of Trafalgar

On 21 October 1805, Admiral de Villeneuve sailed out of Cádiz harbour with his Franco-Spanish fleet to confront the English under Nelson off the Cabo de Trafalgar headland. The ships were ill equipped and poorly manned; after some heroic combat Villeneuve's fleet was destroyed and he was taken prisoner. Nelson had been mortally wounded during the course of the battle but England's supremacy at sea was established.

The Order of Alcántara

The Knights of San Juan de Pereiro became the Order of Alcántara when entrusted with the defence of the town in 1218. Like the other great orders of chivalry in Spain its aim was to free the country from the Moors. Each order, founded as a military unit under the command of a master, lived in a community under Cistercian rule. These religious militias, always prepared for combat and capable of withstanding long sieges, played a major role in the Reconquest.

Iglesia de Santa Cruz★

Pl. Fray Féliz. ⏱*Open Tue–Sat 10am–2pm, 5–8pm, Sun 10am–2pm.* ⏱*Closed mornings in Aug.* ✆*No charge.* 📞*956 28 77 04.*

The old cathedral was rebuilt following the sacking by the Earl of Essex in 1596. Robust Tuscan columns define spaces. The church museum (**Museo Catedralicio**) is alongside in the Casa de la Contaduría (👣*see Sights*).

Catedral★★

Pl. de la Catedral. ⏱*Open Tue–Fri 10am –1.30pm, 4.30–7pm, Sat 10am–1pm.* ✆*€3.50 (includes museum).* 📞*956 25 98 12.*

Work on the new cathedral began in 1722 and lasted over a century. The result is Baroque in character with the occasional Neoclassical feature. The **façade**★ is flanked by two lofty towers. The triple-aisle interior is surprisingly light and spacious. The crypt holds the remains of the composer **Manuel de Falla** (1876–1946).

FROM PLAZA SAN JUAN DE DIOS TO THE CATHEDRAL

▷ *Follow Nueva to Pl. San Juan de Dios. Turn left into Cristóbal Colón.*

Casa de las Cadenas

This Baroque mansion has a Genoese marble **doorway**★ and Solomonic columns.

▷ *Continue along calles Cristóbal Colón and Cobos to Pl. de la Candelaria; return to Nueva. Past Pl. de San Agustín, take Rosario, to the Oratorio de la Santa Cueva (👣see Sights).*

Plaza de San Francisco

This charming plaza, under the Baroque tower of the Iglesia de San Francisco, is lined by lively bars and cafés.

Plaza de Mina★★

Once the kitchen garden of the Convento de San Francisco, this verdant square is imbued with a colonial feel. Fine examples of Isabelline buildings around the square include the **Museo de Cádiz** (👣*see Sights*).

▷ *Head down de San José to the Oratorio de San Felipe Neri. The oratory stands alongside the Museo de las Cortes de Cádiz (👣see Sights).*

Hospital de Mujeres★

Hospital de Mujeres. ⏱*Open Mon–Sat 10am–1.30pm.* ✆*€0.80.* 📞*956 22 36 47.*

This Baroque building is planned around two patios linked by an extraordinary Imperial-style **stairway**★★. The Vía Crucis in the patio is created from 18C Triana *azulejos*.

▷ *Continue to the Torre Tavira (👣see Sights) on Sacramento.*

Plaza de las Flores

Flower and plant stalls, cafés and shops contribute to the delightful atmosphere in one of the city's liveliest squares.

▷ *Take Compañía to return to Pl.de la Catedral.*

EXCURSIONS
El Puerto de Santa María

On the northern shore of the bay facing Cádiz (23km/14mi), El Puerto de Santa María is heavily frequented by tourists but pleasant in the off-season.

Christopher Columbus set sail twice from the docks of El Puerto de Santa María, and the town subsequently prospered with the commerce from the American colonies. One of Jerez's sherry capitals, it is also known for its bullfights. The old part of town is on the west bank of the Guadalete river, known as **La Ribera del Marisco** (seafood coast). Avenida de la Bejamar runs along the river and borders the old quarter.

On the waterfront, Plaza de las Galeras Reales (Square of the Royal Galleys) is the main square. Opposite, Calle Luna, a pedestrianized street filled with shops, crosses the old quarter and ends in Plaza de España.

Fiestas and festivals

The *corridas* (bullfights) held here are among the most important in Andalucía, staged in an arena dating from 1880 with a capacity for up to 15 000 spectators *(on the southwest edge of town)*. *Corridas* are usually held on Sundays, in summer, and during the spring festival in April (902 15 78 70; €25–60).

Plaza de las Galeras Reales

At the edge of the Guadalete on the spot where royal galleys used to dock, is this bustling square. Restaurant seating spills out around the square, and Calle Luna, the main shopping street, leads to the Tourist Office and Plaza de España.

Iglesia Mayor Prioral

Plaza de España. Mon–Fri 8.30am–12.45pm, 6–8.30pm, Sat 8.30am–noon, 6–8.30pm, Sun 8.30am– 1.45pm, 6.30–8.30pm. No charge. 956 85 17 51. Consecrated in 1493, completed a few years later and often rebuilt since then, this church stands next to Plaza de España. The **Portada del Sol** (17C), with both Plateresque and Baroque elements is the church's main treasure.

Fundación Rafael Albertia

Calle Santo Domingo, 25. Open mid-Jun–mid-Sept Mon–Fri 10.30am–2.30pm; mid-Sept–mid-Jun Tue–Sun 11am–2.30pm. €4. 956 85 07 11. www.rafaelalberti.es.

Painter and poet, communist and Franco opponent (1902–99), Rafael Alberti was born in this house. He was part of the literary "generation of 1927", a movement that included, among others, Federico García Lorca and the Machado brothers Antonio and Miguel. Alberti's alphabeta unifying poetry and calligraphy is on display here, demonstrating his commitment to the cause of social justice throughout Spain's turbulent 20C.

Castillo de San Marcosa

This castle was built by Alfonso X on the site of a mosque, of which the mihrab is still visible. The conquering Christians enlarged the building, converting it to a fortified church. The castle attained its full size in the 15C.

Las Bodegas

The *bodegas* (wineries) are almost all open to the public. Bodegas Terry *(Calle de los Toneleros;* guided tour (90min), closed Sun; 956 15 15 00/51/52; www.bodegasterry.com), takes in a visit to the cellars and the collection of winemaking artifacts.

Bodega Osborne *(Bodega de Mora;* 956 86 91 00; *Bodega El Tiro;* guided tour with prior reservation; 956 85 42 28; www.osborne.es) became famous for its black bull silhouette found along highways all over Spain, now classified as a national monument in order to elude a ban on roadside billboards.

San Fernando

9km/5.5mi SE along the CA 33. 956 94 42 26.

This town has been a naval base since the 18C. The main monuments are all have Royal *(Real)* grants: the town hall, Iglesia del Carmen, and the Museo Histórico Municipal. The main civil building is the Neoclassical **Observatorio Astronómico de la Marina** *(Cecilio*

Pujazón; ☛ guided tours (1hr); &956 59 93 67), from 1753.

Medina Sidonia★

▶ 44km/27mi E on CA 33, A 48 and A 390. &956 41 24 04. www.turismo medinasidonia.com.

The **Iglesia Mayor Santa María la Coronada**★ (Pl. de la Iglesia Mayor); a 15C Gothic church, holds an exquisite Plateresque **altarpiece**★ by Juan Bautista Vázquez el Viejo.

The **Torre de Doña Blanca**, a tower next to the church, provides access to the remains of the alcázar and the old quarter, with its 16C houses. The descent to the modern town passes under the Arco de la Pastora, to reach the **Conjunto Arqueológico Romano**, a Roman complex with 30m/98ft of underground galleries from the 1C AD. (Espíritu Santo 3; ⏰Open 10am–1.30pm, 4.30–6.30pm (Apr–Jun 8pm; Jul–Oct 5–9.30pm); ⚌€4; &956 41 24 04).

The cardo maximus was the main street in Roman days. On the Plaza de España lies the 18C Neoclassical **town hall**.

ADDRESSES

🏠 STAY

🛏🍽🏷 **Hostal Fantoni** – Flamenco 5. &956 28 27 04. www.hostalfantoni.net. 12 rooms. Closed Dec–mid-Feb. Why spend more when you can stay in this pleasant hostal? Try for a room with ensuite bathroom facing a pedestrian lane.

🛏🍽🏷 **Hospedería Las Cortes de Cádiz** – San Francisco 9. &956 22 04 89. www.hotellascortes.com. 36 rooms. Rooms in this 19C home in the old quarter are well equipped, set around a covered patio, individually decorated, and dedicated to a local event or personality. Attractive outside areas.

🛏🍽🏷 **Hotel de Francia y París** – Pl. de San Francisco 6. &956 21 23 19. www.hotelfrancia.com. 57 rooms. ⚌€8.50. An early 20C hotel with pleasant rooms fronting an attractive small square in the centre of the city.

🍽 EAT

🛏🍽🏷 **El Faro** – San Félix 15. &902 21 10 68. www.elfarodecadiz.com. This fine

restaurant-tapas bar offers a cosy interior and a menu that emphasises local fare.

🍽 TAPAS

Aurelio – Zorrilla 1. &956 22 10 31. Closed Mon in Aug–Jun. This popular seafood bar is one of the places for tapas in Cádiz. Its only drawback is its small size – it soon fills up. A good central location close to Plaza de Mina.

Casa Manteca – Corralón de los Carros 66. &956 21 36 03. Closed Mon. Cádiz's most rustic Andalucían tavern, serving Ibérico ham or sausage on wax paper where your tally is chalked up on the low wooden counters.

Joselito – San Francisco 38. &956 25 22 51. Closed Sun. There's a covered terrace providing welcome shade. Inside, the dining room serves fish, paella and stews.

🍷 BARS / ☕CAFÉS

El Café de Levante – Rosario 35. &956 22 02 27. www.cafelevante.com. A quiet café with tasteful modern décor on one of the old quarter's most typical streets. Its relaxed atmosphere attracts an eclectic crowd who come here to enjoy a quiet chat. Live music Thursday evenings.

La Cava – Antonio López 16. &956 21 18 66. www.flamencolacava.com. Closed Jan and Mon. ⚌Show and drink €25 from 9.30pm (low season shows are on Tue, Thu and Sat; high season Tue–Sat). This cosy tavern offers authentic flamenco interpreted by young artists.

🎭 FESTIVALS

Carnaval de Cádiz – www.carnavalde cadiz.com. Early Feb. This Carnival on the week before Ash Wednesday, is without doubt the most famous and lively in Spain. It is famed for uniformed chirigotas (comedy groups), and poet-dramatic comparsas.

🎬 ENTERTAINMENT

Gran Teatro Falla – Pl. Falla. &956 22 08 34. Named after the composer Manuel de Falla (1876–1946), this theatre organises a programme of events throughout the year. The city's **cultural centres** – **El Palillero** (Pl. Palillero; &956 22 65 16), **El Bidón** (Alcalde Juan de Dios Molina 23; &956 26 15 02), **La Viña** (Av. Campo Del Sur 38; &956 22 51 04), and **La Lechera** (Pl. Argüelles 2; &956 22 06 28) host a wide range of exhibitions, workshops etc, as well as flamenco concerts at the fifth venue, the **Baluarte de la Candelaria** (Alameda Marqués de Comillas; &956 22 14 42).

Gibraltar★

One of the last outposts of the British Empire and a self-governing British Overseas Territory, the towering bulk of Gibraltar is impressive and distinctive, visible for miles. For many visitors, the first contact with Gibraltar is likely to be the incredible landing strip, crossed by the main road into town.

GEOGRAPHY

The **Rock of Gibraltar**★ is a gigantic monolith of Jurassic limestone which forms a craggy promontory connected with mainland Spain to the north and stretching south into the Strait. It covers an area of about 6.5km/2.5sq mi (4.5km/3mi long and 1.4km/0.9mi at its widest), rising to 423m/1 388ft at its highest point, Mount Misery. The east face of the Rock drops sheer into the sea, while the less steep west face has been partially reclaimed at the water's edge and forms the site of the town.

A BIT OF HISTORY

Archaeological discoveries on Gibraltar testify to 100 000 years of human occupation, by Carthaginians, Phoenicians and even Neanderthal Man.

The Rock of Gibraltar, considered by the Ancient Greeks to be one of the **Pillars of Hercules**, was transformed into an Islamic citadel after the Moors invaded

▶ **Population:** 31 045
⏱ **Michelin Map:** 578 X 13.
🔲 **Info:** The Piazza, Main Street. ℘350 74982 (956 77 49 50 from Spain); www.gibraltar.com.
◐ **Location:** Gibraltar lies at the southwest tip of Spain only 24km/15mi from North Africa.
🅿 **Parking:** Can be tight in town.
◉ **Don't Miss:** The Top of the Rock.
🕐 **Timing:** Take a morning drive from Spain.
👥 **Kids:** The Apes' Den; dolphin spotting.

under **Tarik-ibn-Zeyad** in AD 711. Jebel Tarik (Tarik's Mountain, hence Gibraltar) was the site of a castle, now in ruins but still known as the Moorish Castle. Gibraltar was recaptured by Spain on 20 August 1462. During the War of Spanish Succession, Anglo-Dutch naval forces, under **Admiral Rooke**, captured the Rock in 1704. Gibraltar was ceded to Britain in the Treaty of Utrecht in 1713. The citadel guarding the Strait of Gibraltar has remained in British hands ever since. In the **Great Siege of 1779–83**, the garrison heroically resisted Spanish and French efforts to starve or

Upper Rock of Gibraltar

©Bernd Haak/Fotolia.com

bomb them into submission. The old city of Gibraltar was destroyed, but the Rock lived up to its reputation of being impregnable. Gibraltar became a British Crown Colony in 1830.

In 1967, Gibraltar's inhabitants voted resoundingly to retain their connection with Britain, by 12 138 votes to 44, in a referendum. In 1969, Spain closed the border and maintained a blockade until 1985. It is still not unusual for Spanish customs to delay vehicles. With its people descended from a variety of races, religions and cultures, their identity shaped by years of resisting sieges, Gibraltar is an excellent example of a harmonious, multicultural society.

Gibraltar's economy is based on financial services and tourism. The territory is a free port and trade is based on transit and refuelling.

The naval and commercial ports, as well as the town with its mixture of English- and Spanish-style houses, pubs and shops, lie against the west face of the Rock. Numerous examples of Moorish architecture are still to be found, notably in the cathedral which has the ground plan of a mosque.

SIGHTS
Tour of the Rock★

Open daily 10am–6pm. Cable car Mon–Sat 9.30am–5.45pm. Closed 1 Jan, 25 Dec. £8. 350 200 45957.

350 200 77826 (cable car). www.gibtaxi.com (private car).

The Top of the Rock can be reached on foot, by cable car and in official tour vehicles (*private cars are not allowed on the Upper Rock*). Go down Queensway and follow the signs to Upper Rock, a **nature reserve** and home to a number of Gibraltar's most interesting historical sites. The road leads first to **St Michael's Cave**, once inhabited by Neolithic man, which features some stalactites and stalagmites. From here, it is possible to walk to the Top of the Rock (*1hr there and back),* from where there are excellent **views**★★ of both sides of the rock and of the Spanish and North African coasts.

The road continues to the **Apes' Den**, home of the famous Barbary Apes.

Visitors interested in military history should not miss the **Great Siege Tunnels**, excavated in 1779 to mount guns on the north face of the Rock, creating a defence system still impressive for its ingenuity. A military heritage centre is housed in Princess Caroline's Battery. Finally there are the ancient ruins of the **Moorish Castle** and the northern defences dominating the hillside.

Gibraltar Museum

18/20 Bomb House Lane. Open Mon–Fri 10am–6pm, Sat 10am–2pm (last entry 30min before closing). £2. 350 200 74289. www.gib.gi/museum.

Barbary Apes

The origin of the apes, one of Gibraltar's best-known attractions, is unknown. Legend has it that British rule will last as long as the apes remain in residence on the Rock. When it looked as if they might become extinct in 1942, Churchill sent a signal ordering reinforcements. The ape colony has since flourished – there are currently some 230 of them. They are renowned for their charm and highly inquisitive natures. The apes, in reality tailless monkeys, are the protégés of the Gibraltar Regiment.

©David Stanley/iStockphoto.com

PRACTICALITIES

Customs and other formalities:
Gibraltar is a British Crown Colony.
The border is open 24hr a day. Visitors
must be in possession of a valid
passport. Holders of UK passports
and citizens of other EU countries do
not need a visa. Other nationalities
should check visa requirements with
a British consulate, high commission,
or embassy. Gibraltar is a VAT-free
shopping area.

Travel and accommodation: There
are daily scheduled flights from
London Heathrow, Gatwick and Luton
and a daily ferry service between
Gibraltar and Morocco (*350 78305).
Regular flights also operate to
and from North Africa. Hotel
accommodation is available. (*see
p529). There are no campsites.

Money matters: The currency is the
Gibraltar pound, on a par with sterling.
The Euro and credit cards are widely
accepted.

Language: The official language
spoken on the Rock is English, but
most people speak some Spanish.

Time: Gibraltar is on European time
(one hour ahead of GMT).

Motoring: Driving is on the right.
Drivers must have a current licence,
vehicle registration documents,
evidence of insurance and nationality
plates.

Telephoning: The international code
for Gibraltar is 350 (from Spain, omit
this and dial 9567 before the five-digit
local number).

Tourist information: Further tourist
information is available from: Gibraltar
Government Office, 150 Strand,
London WC2R 1JA. *(020) 7836 0777;
Gibraltar Information Bureau, 1156
15th St NW, Washington, DC 20005.
t202 452 1108. www.gibraltar.gov.gi.

This museum contains extensive collections on local military and natural history. It also houses the well-preserved
Moorish Baths.

The **Alameda Gardens** display interesting and exotic plants, including Canary
Islands dragon trees, cacti, succulents
and Mediterranean vegetation. Gibraltar
is home to some 600 species of flowering plant, which flourish in the subtropical climate, including a few unique to
the Rock, such as its national flower, the
Gibraltar Candytuft.

For those interested in seeing more
examples of Gibraltar's plant and bird
life, the **Mediterranean Steps**, leading from Jew's Gate (good view of the
other Pillar of Hercules, Jebel Musa in
Morocco) round the south of the Rock
and up the east face of the Rock to the
summit, make a rewarding walk (⏱3hr
walk from Jew's Gate, steep in parts; wear
good boots).

STRAITS OF GIBRALTAR

**Michelin map 578 X 1, *Gibraltar:
British Overseas Territory*.** *The A 7
motorway links the southernmost part
of Spain to the Costa del Sol.*

The Straits, the gateway to the Mediterranean and a mere 14km/9mi wide,
have always played a strategic role in
the region. The Bay of Algeciras is surrounded by Algeciras and La Línea de
la Concepción, and the British outpost
of Gibraltar.

TOURING THE STRAITS

Fourteen species of cetaceans – whales,
dolphins and porpoises – are to be found
in the Straits so **whale- and dolphin-
watching cruises** are consequently
very popular, sailing from Gibraltar,
Algeciras, La Línea and Tarifa. Reputable operators include Turmares Tarifa
(*956 68 07 41; www.turmares.com)
and Whale Watch (*956 62 70 13; www.
whalewatchtarifa.net). The probability of
seeing these beautiful creatures is very
high (90%–95%) and some operators

View of mountains in Morocco across the Straits of Gibraltar from near Tarifa

will refund your money in the unlikely event of a "no-show".

While boats for larger groups may provide underwater viewing areas, small fast boats provide more thrills as they race along with the dolphins swimming in their wake and criss-crossing the bows. The 21km/13mi of road linking Tarifa to Algeciras provides stunning **views**★★★ of the North African coast. The best viewpoint is at the Mirador del Estrecho, 8km/5mi from Tarifa.

Tarifa *See COSTA DE LA LUZ*

Algeciras

Arabs arrived in al-Yazirat-al-jadra (Green Island, now joined to the mainland) in 711 and remained until 1344. The Bahía de Algeciras is a safe anchorage and strategic vantage point overlooking the Straits.

Neanderthal Man or Gibraltar Woman?

Eight years before the discovery in 1856 of a 60 000-year-old skeleton in the Neander Valley, east of Düsseldorf, Germany, a skull of the same age, thought to be that of a woman, was discovered on Gibraltar. However, delays in publicising the Gibraltar findings meant that Gibraltar Woman didn't gain the fame of Neanderthal Man.

Algeciras is Spain's busiest passenger port with crossings to Tangier and **Ceuta** several times a day. The main sights of interest are the the plaza Alta, the hub of the town, fronted by two churches: the 18C **Iglesia de Nuestra Señora de la Palma**, and the Baroque Iglesia de Nuestra Señora de la Aurora, and the **Museo Municipal** *(Ortega y Gasset;* ○*open 27 Oct–30 Mar Mon–Fri 9am–2pm, 5–7pm; 1 Apr–26 Oct 9am–2pm;* ○*closed public holidays;* ℘*956 57 06 72; www.fmcjoseluiscano.com)*, displaying interesting exhibits on the **Siege of Algeciras** (1342–44).

ACROSS THE STRAITS
Ceuta

Michelin map 742 folds 5 and 10 – North Africa. Population 78 320.
Trasmediterránea *operates services between Algeciras and Ceuta. Journey time: 40min.* ℘*902 45 46 45. www.trasmediterranea.es.*

Ceuta occupies a strategic position, dominating the Straits of Gibraltar. With its European architecture, it is situated on a narrow isthmus on the coast of North Africa. The closest African port to Europe, Ceuta was conquered by the Portuguese in 1415, and passed to Spain in 1580, when Philip II annexed Portugal.

Museo Municipal

Pas. de Revellín 30. ○*Open Jun–Sept Tue–Sat 10am–2pm, 7–9pm, Sun and public holidays 11am–2pm; Oct–May*

Tue–Sat 10am–2pm, 5–8pm, Sun and public holidays 10am–2pm. ◑*Closed 1 Jan, 25 Dec.* ◉*No charge.* ☎*956 51 73 98.*

This museum houses a white marble Roman sarcophagus, Punic and Roman amphorae, a collection of coins and old weapons and ceramic ware.

Parque Marítimo del Mediterráneo

Compañía del Mar. ◑*Open Sept–May daily 11am–8pm; Jun–Aug Mon, Thu 10am–8pm, Tue–Wed 10am–1am, Fri–Sun and public holidays 10am–8pm.* ◉*€1.50–6, price varies by day and time.* ☎*956 51 77 42.*

Palm trees, exotic plants, swimming pools, lakes, waterfalls and sculptures have all been perfectly integrated by César Manrique to create this spectacular leisure park on 56ha/138 acres facing the sea. Several restaurants, a nightclub and a casino operate inside the fort which dominates the park. A cinema complex is in the Poblado Marinero.

Other places of interest are the **Iglesia de Nuestra Señora de África** (Church of Our Lady of Africa; *Pl. de África;* ☎*956 51 77 32*), housing the statue of the town's patron saint, the 18C **Catedral** (*Pl. de África;* ◑*open Tue–Sun 9am–1pm, 6.15–7.30pm;* ☎*956 51 77 71*) and **Foso de San Felipe** (◑*open daily 11am–7pm;* ☎*956 51 17 70*), a Portuguese fort where San Juan de Dios, the founder of the Orden de los Hospitalarios (Order of the Hospitallers of St John), worked in 1530.

Monte Hacho★

Best visited in the morning.

Calle Independencia and Calle Recintor Sur, parallel to the seafront, lead to the foot of Monte Hacho, which has a citadel at its summit. The corniche road encircling the peninsula offers beautiful **views** of the Western Rif coastline to the south and the Spanish coast and the Rock of Gibraltar to the north.

▷ *Before reaching the lighthouse (no entry), bear left.*

Ermita de San Antonio

◉ *Leave your car in the car park.*

The wide flight of steps leads to a charming square fronted by the 16C Capilla de San Antonio (Chapel of St Anthony). The imposing **Fortaleza de Hacho** (*ctra. de circunvalación del Monte Hacho; guided tours available by booking beforehand;* ☎*956 51 16 21*) stands atop a hill nearby.

From here there is a magnificent **view**★★ to the left, of the town spread out on its curving isthmus around the port, and to the right, the distant peninsula coastline.

ADDRESSES

🛏 STAY

🛏 **Emille Youth Hostel** – *25 Line Wall Road.* ☎*350 200 51106. www.emilehostel.net.* In the heart of Gibraltar 100m/110yd from Casemates Square, this 42-bed hostel arranged in single, double and triple rooms offers free breakfast and great value.

🛏 **Cannon Hotel** – *9 Cannon Lane.* ☎*350 200 51711. www.cannonhotel.gi. 18 rooms.* An excellent and central location in the centre of Gibraltar, this intimate hotel is a cosy hideaway on The Rock.

🛏 **Hotel Bristol** – *8 Cathedral Square.* ☎*350 200 76800. www.bristolhotel.gi. 60 rooms.* With a pool and a subtropical garden, the Bristol is breath of fresh air in this busy British enclave.

🍴 EAT

🍴 **Restaurant Al Andalus** – *Ctra. Sanamaro-Pinogordo s/n.* ☎*956 51 39 21.* For Moroccan cuisine and ambience and sea views, this restaurant near the centre of Ceuta is a excellent choice.

🍴 **The Venutre Inn** – *2 Lynch's Lane.* ☎*350 200 75776.* An Irish pub and sports bar with beer for every palate and hearty food from Irish stews to soups and fish and chips.

🍴 **Parador H La Muralla** – *Pl. Nuestra Señora de África 15.* ☎*956 51 49 40. www.parador.es.* A good place to pause during your visit, an attractive dining area with lush tropical plants and exposed beams. The cooking is Andaucían with Arab influences.

THE CANARY ISLANDS

The Canary Islands – seven in total with six smaller isles – lie between 100km/62mi and 300km/186.4mi off the northwest coast of North Africa. Ferries and inter-island flights connect the islands, though (unlike in Greece) there is no "island-hopping" culture. They provide visitors with many contrasts: from exuberant vegetation to desert landscapes; steep cliffs to endless beaches; picturesque villages to overcommercialised resorts. All this, coupled with a fantastic climate, has turned the Canaries into one of the world's leading holiday destinations, particularly during the European winter.

Highlights

Volcanic creation

The islands were thrust up from the Atlantic seabed by volcanic eruptions. La Gomera and Gran Canaria have a conic silhouette and most of the islands are hilly and end in steep cliffs. Crowning Tenerife, Pico del Teide at 3 718m/ 12 195ft is the highest point in Spain. La Palma rises to 2 426m/7 959ft and because of its relatively small area is said to be the steepest island in the world. It features the world's largest *caldera* (volcanic crater) too. Here, and elsewhere, lava, slag fields and cinder cones form what is known as *malpaís*, most extensive and most spectacular on Lanzarote where huge areas resemble a moonscape. The Spanish Conquista-

dores found a native Stone Age population known as the **Guanches**, who lived in caves, practised trepanning and mummified their dead. The Guanches had little answer to the invaders and were decimated, not least as a result of common illnesses introduced inadvertently by the Spaniards, to which they had no natural resistance. By the end of the century the islands were taken and most Guanches were either dead or had assimilated into the new order.

The Fortunate Islands

Ancient mariners nicknamed the archipelago The Fortunate Islands on account of their year-round mild climate. While El Teide is snow-capped for several months of the year, the coastal temperature rarely drops below 18°C/65°F. The climate varies, however, between the north and south of the larger islands, most notably on Tenerife and Gran Canaria. This has encouraged sun-and-fun resorts (such as Playa de las Américas and Playa del Inglés) to develop in the south, which remains sun-kissed almost all year round. By contrast, the northern coasts of Tenerife and Gran Canaria respectively can be (relatively) chilly and wet in winter and as a result have been less commercialised for the holiday trade.

Tenerife★★★

The snow-capped silhouette of El Teide, the highest peak in Spain, is the symbol of this beautiful island, literally "snow-covered mountain" in Guanche. The spectacular Las Cañadas crater is witness to Tenerife's volcanic past. Year-round sun draws package tourists and youngsters to the brash man-made resorts of the parched south, while natural beauty and a mild climate attracts others to the north.

PICO DEL TEIDE★★★

Clouds often enshroud Mount Teide and the superb panoramas from its viewpoints.

Ensure that you have comfortable footwear and a warm jacket. Temperature and weather can change dramatically in a short time.

La Esperanza Approach★

The road climbs to the crest which divides the island.

Pinar de la Esperanza★

The road runs for several miles through this extensive pinewood. In a clearing at **Las Raíces**, an obelisk commemorates the rebellion in July 1936 against the Republican government by Francisco Franco, who was stationed here.

▶ **Population:** 886 033

Info: Santa Cruz de Tenerife: Plaza de España. ℘922 23 98 11; Puerto de la Cruz: Las Lonjas. ℘922 28 12 87. www.webtenerifeuk.co.uk. www.todotenerife.es.

Location: Tenerife is the largest of the Canary Islands, with an area of 2 036sq km/786sq mi.

Kids: Loro Parque, Lago Martiánez, Siam Park, Parque Ecológico de las Aguilas del Teide, Aqualand.

Belvederes★★

When the cloud disperses, admire the stark contrast between the lush north coast and the aridity of the Güimar Valley from roadside belvederes. After La Crucita, the road enters a high-mountain landscape. The Astronomical Observatory at Izaña is visible *(left)*.

El Portillo

Alt 2 030m/6 660ft. This pass is the gateway to the extraordinary geological world of the Las Cañadas crater.

GETTING TO THE CANARY ISLANDS

BY PLANE – Each island has an airport (Tenerife has two), offering easy, rapid access to the Spanish mainland and the rest of Europe. A number of inter-island routes also operate throughout the year. The two major airports are Tenerife and Gran Canaria.
www.aena-aeropuertos.es.
Iberia ℘902 40 05 00. www.iberia.com.
Binter Canarias: Inter-island flights only. ℘902 39 13 92.
www.bintercanarias.com.
Spanair ℘902 13 14 15.
www.spanair.com.

easyJet *www.easyjet.com*
Air Europa ℘902 40 15 01.
www.air-europa.com (flights to Gran Canaria, Tenerife and Lanzarote).
Vueling ℘807 20 01 00.
www.vueling.com (flights to the four main islands from Spain and Europe).

BY FERRY – From mainland Spain, a two-day boat trip leaves from Cádiz and travels to Santa Cruz de Tenerife and Las Palmas de Gran Canaria. Ferry, jet-foil and hydrofoil services travel between islands.
Trasmediterránea ℘902 45 46 45.
www.trasmediterranea.es.

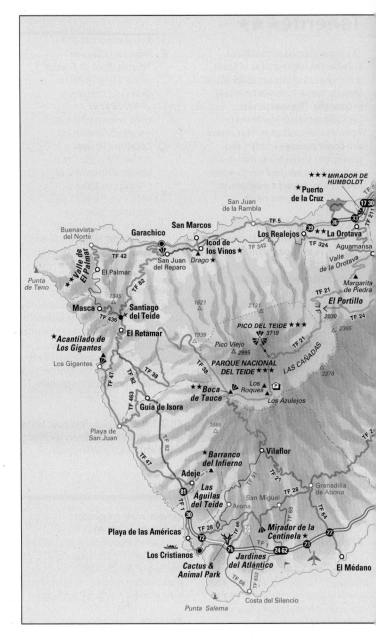

Parque Nacional del Teide★★★

There are two visitor centres (○both open daily 9am–4pm; ☎922 29 01 29). the El Portillo Centre has exhibits on volcanism, and trail information, the geological history of the park and its flora and fauna; the Cañada Blanca Visi-

tor Centre is next to the parador hotel. About 350m/1 150ft below the summit lies Las Cañadas plateau, a spectacular crater at over 2 000m/6 560ft which fell in on itself before El Teide was created. The peak rises from its northern side. In the centre of the park, opposite the

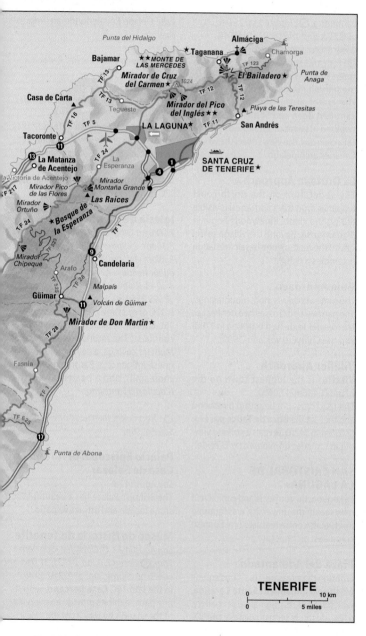

Punta del Hidalgo

Almáciga

Bajamar
★ Taganana
★★ MONTE DE
LAS MERCEDES
Chamorga

El Bailadero ★
TF 123

Mirador de Cruz
del Carmen ★
1024
Punta de
Anaga

Casa de Carta
TF 12

TF 16
TF 13
Tegueste
Mirador del Pico
del Inglés ★★
Playa de las Teresitas

Tacoronte
TF 5
LA LAGUNA ★
TF 11
San Andrés

La Matanza
de Acentejo
TF 24
La
Esperanza
SANTA CRUZ
DE TENERIFE ★

La Victoria de Acentejo
Mirador Pico
de las Flores
TF 217
Mirador
Montaña Grande

Mirador
Ortuño
Las Raíces

TF 24
★ Bosque de
la Esperanza

Mirador
Chipeque
TF 523
Arafo
Candelaria

Güímar
TF 28
Malpaís

Mirador de Don Martín ★
Volcán de Güímar

TF 28
TF 1

Fasnia

TF 1

TF 6-25

Punta de Abona

TENERIFE

0   10 km
0   5 miles

parador, are **Los Roques**, a spectacular
outcrop of lava boulders, laid bare by
erosion. Another geological feature is
Los Azulejos, boulders covered with
copper oxide, which glint blue-green
in the sun.

Pico del Teide★★★

🚡 *Ascent by* **cable car** *from La
Rambleta (2 356m/7 728ft); not
suitable for those with respiratory or
heart problems (the cable car climbs
1 199m/3 932ft in 10min).*
🕐 *Operates daily 9am–4pm, weather*

permitting. ⊙Closed 1 Jan, 25 Dec.
∞€25 round-trip. ☎922 01 04 45.
www.telefericoteide.com.

🔼From the top (3 555m/11 660ft), a
steep 30min walk across scree leads to
the summit (⊘the path is closed).
The crater at the summit is almost
25m/82ft deep and 50m/164ft across,
swathed in wisps of sulphurous smoke.
On a clear day, the view covers the whole
Canaries archipelago.

La Orotava Approach★

The vegetation on the north coast
(bananas, fruit trees and vines) is visible
during the climb. Pinewoods begin in
Aguamansa. Beyond the village at the
side of the road, a huge basalt formation
resembles a daisy.

Guía Approach

The climb via Guía is more mountainous.
The narrow road crosses two defiles, Las
Narices del Teide (last eruption in 1798)
and the Chinyero volcano (1909).

Vilaflor Approach

Vilaflor is the highest town on the
island (1 466m/4 806ft).
The road crosses a beautiful pinewood
and then, at the **Boca de Tauce pass**★★
(2 055m/ 6 742ft), reveals a striking view
of Las Cañadas dominated by El Teide.

SAN CRISTÓBAL DE LA LAGUNA★

La Laguna, the former island capital and
now seat of the university, was founded
in 1496. Its centre features fine Spanish
colonialist architecture.

Plaza del Adelantado

Fronting this pleasant, tree-lined square
are the old **Convent of Santa Catalina**,
which retains its original upper gallery,
a feature rarely seen nowadays; the 17C
Palacio de Nava with stone façade,
reminiscent of the Bishop's Palace,
and the town hall, or **ayuntamiento**,
with Neoclassical façade (Obispo Rey
Redondo 1; ⊙ open Mon–Fri 10am–
1.30pm; www.aytolalaguna.com).
The last is a combination of several
buildings. The 16C and 18C portals on

calle Obispo Rey Redondo are impressive.

▷ Follow calle Obispo Rey Redondo.

Catedral

Pl. Fray Albino. ⊙Call for opening times.
☎902 00 31 21.
The elegant Neoclassical façade was
erected in 1819; the nave and four aisles
were rebuilt in neo-Gothic style in 1905.
In the Capilla de los Remedios (right transept), note the retable, a 16C Virgin and
17C Flemish panels.

Iglesia de la Concepción★

Pl. Doctor Olivera. ⊙Open Mon–Fri
8.30am–1.45pm, 5.30–7.30pm, Sat
8.30am–1.45pm, 5–7.30pm, Sun and
public holidays 7.30am–1.45pm,
4.30–8.30pm. ∞No charge.
☎922 25 91 30.
A 17C grey stone tower rises over this
16C church, typical of the time of the
conquest. The interior retains several
Mudéjar ceilings, a ceiling with Portuguese influence, a Baroque pulpit and
choir stalls, and a beaten silver altar
(Capilla del Santísimo).

▷ Take Belén, then head down
San Agustín.

Palacio Episcopal or Antigua Casa de Salazar

San Agustín 28.
The Bishop's Palace has a beautiful 17C
stone façade and attractive patio.

Museo de Historia de Tenerife

San Agustín 22. ⊙Open Tue–Sun 9am–
7pm. ⊙Closed 1, 6 Jan, 24–25, 31 Dec.
∞€3; no charge Sun. ☎922 82 59 49.
In the late-16C **Casa Lercano**, with its
fine patio, exhibits provide an overview
of the island's history from the 15C.

SANTA CRUZ DE TENERIFE★

The capital began as a port serving La
Laguna. An oil refinery, tobacco factory
and other industries operate here.
From the harbour breakwater there is
a **view**★ of the stepped semicircle of
high-rise buildings against the back-

drop of the Pico del Teide. The Guimera Theatre – the oldest theatre in the Canaries inaugurated in 1851 – and the stunning, space-age Auditorio de Tenerife, designed by Santiago Calatrava, witness the city's strong cultural tradition.

Santa Cruz is also famous for its **Carnival** (*last week in Feb; ☎922 60 60 06*), arguably the most colourful and certainly the largest in all Spain.

Iglesia de la Concepción

Tomás Pérez. ◷*Open daily 9am–1pm, 4.30–8pm.* ☞*No charge.* ☎*922 33 01 87.*

A few houses with balconies around the 16C–18C church (fine Baroque retables) are all that remains of the old city.

Museo de la Naturaleza y el Hombre★ (Museum of Nature and Man)

Fuente Morales. ◷*Open Tue–Sun 9am–7pm.* ◷*Closed 1, 6 Jan, Carnival Tue, 24–25, 31 Dec.* ☞*€3; no charge Sun.* ☎*922 53 58 16. www.museos detenerife.org.*

In the ex-Hospital Civil, a large Neoclassical building, are archaeology and natural science collections.

Palacio de Carta

Pl. de la Candelaria. ⊶*Closed to the public.*

This 18C palace on Plaza de la Candelaria, now a bank, retains its delightful wooden arches, galleries and patio.

Iglesia de San Francisco

San Francisco 13. ◷*Open for Mass.* ☎*922 24 45 62. www.parroquia sanfrancisco.org.*

The 17C–18C church displays the characteristics of Canary Island churches from this period: naves with wooden roofs and cylindrical pillars.

Parque Municipal García Sanabria★

☎*922 60 60 99.*

This alluring tropical and Mediterranean garden is close to La Rambla General Franco, a landscaped boulevard.

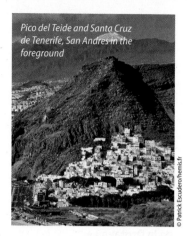
Pico del Teide and Santa Cruz de Tenerife, San Andres in the foreground

© Patrick Escudero/hemis.fr

Museo Militar

Castillo de Almeida, San Isidro 1. ◷*Open Tue–Sat 10am–2pm.* ☞*No charge.* ☎*922 84 35 00.*

Nelson lost both the battle and his right arm when attacking the castle on 24 July 1797.

Parque Marítimo César Manrique★

Avenida Constitución 5. ◷*Open daily 10am–6pm (7pm in summer). Last admission 1hr before closing.* ☞*€2.* ☎*922 20 32 44.*

This lido, designed by the great Lanzarote artist, César Manrique, combines water, volcanic rock and vegetation.

PUERTO DE LA CRUZ★

Puerto de la Cruz is the principal resort on the north coast with black beaches and several first-class visitor attractions. It attracts an older clientele than the resorts in the south but is still very lively, particularly at Carnival time.

The old town, between the Plaza de la Iglesia and Plaza del Charco, features many attractive 17C and 18C balconied houses and, unlike the other resorts on the island, retains a genuine Canarian atmosphere.

Just east of town the **Mirador de Humboldt**★★★offers a magnificent view of the town and the verdant sweep of the **Orotava Valley** running down to the sea from the slopes of mighty Mount Teide.

👥 Costa Martiánez★

Av. de Colon. 🕐*Open daily 10am–5pm.* 🕐*Closed fortnight in May.* ⊚€3.50; *child €1.20; parasols available €1.50.* 📞922 38 59 55.

This beautifully designed landmark lido (also known as the Lido or Lago Martiánez, famous for its fountains, is another example of the work of César Manrique, using vernacular architectures and local natural features to maximum visual effect.

The **Casino Taoro** is located within the Costa Martiánez complex.

Jardín de Aclimatación de la Orotava★★

Retama 2. 🕐*Open daily Apr–Sept 9am–7pm; Oct–Mar 9am–6pm.* 🕐*Closed 1 Jan, Good Fri, 25 Dec.* ⊚€3. 📞922 38 35 72.

This 2ha/5-acre botanical garden, created in the 18C, contains trees and flowers from the Canary Islands and elsewhere, some of which are over 200 years old.

Playa Jardín★ (Garden Beach)

This black-sand beach is surrounded by gardens designed by César Manrique. The **Castillo de San Felipe** (📞922 38 36 63), a watchtower now used for cultural functions, can be seen at its eastern end.

👥 Loro Parque (Parrot Park)

Avenida Loro Parque. 🕐*Open daily 8.30am–6.45pm; last admission at 4pm.* ⊚€33; child €22; combined ticket with Siam Park €53/€36.50. 📞922 37 38 41. www.loroparque.com.

Originally just a bird park, this is now one of the finest animal and marine theme parks in the world outside Florida, and is the island's most popular destination after Mount Teide. It features a world-class dolphinarium, killer whales, sea lions, a penguinarium, a large aquarium, tigers, gorillas, chimps and one of the world's finest collections of birds, all set in beautiful grounds. Kinderlandia is a mini-African theme park for little ones.

LA OROTAVA★★

This ancient town is arranged in terraces at the foot of Mount Teide. It boasts elegant balconied mansions and is famous for its Corpus Christi festival.

Plaza de la Constitución

The square is fronted by the 17C Baroque church of San Agustín and the Liceo Taoro cultural centre.

Iglesia de la Concepción

Tomás Pérez. 🕐*Open daily 9am–1pm, 4.30–8pm.* ⊚*No charge.* 📞922 33 01 87.

The 18C church has a graceful Baroque façade. Visit the treasury.

Calle Carrera

Pass the **Plaza del Ayuntamiento**, with its Neoclassical Palacio Municipal.

Behind here the lush **Jardín de Aclimatación** (*Retama 2;* 🕐 *open daily Apr–Sept 9am–7pm; Oct–Mar 9am–6pm;* 🕐*closed 1 Jan, Good Friday and 25 Dec;* ⊚€3; 📞922 38 35 72) began life as a nursery for the botanical gardens in Puerto de la Cruz

Calle de San Francisco★

This street is adorned with some of the town's most beautiful balconies.

La Casa de los Balcones y la Casa Molina

San Francisco 3 & 5. 🕐*Casa de los Balcones (no. 3): open Mon–Fri 8.30am –6.30pm, Sat 8.30am–4.30pm; Casa Molina (no. 5): open Mon–Fri 9.30am –6.30pm.* ⊚€2 (museum). 📞922 33 06 29. www.casa-balcones.com.

These two 17C houses feature delightful patios, a handicraft shop and a small museum which shows the inside of a local bourgeois house

Museo de Artesanía Iberoamericana

Tomás Zerolo 34. 🕐*Open Mon–Fri 9.30am–6pm, Sat 9.30am–2pm.* ⊚€2. 📞922 35 29 06.

Set in the ex-Convento de San Benito Abad (17C) this displays Spanish and Latin-American handicrafts.

DRIVING TOUR

TOUR OF THE ISLAND
310km/194mi. See pp532–33 for map.

Garachico
Set on a picturesque stretch of rocky coast with natural pools, Garachico was the finest harbour on the north coast until in 1706 when the lava slick, clearly visible today, destroyed the old town. Its elegant 16C Castillo de San Miguel *(Avenida de Tomé Cano; open for temporary exhibitions; €1; 922 83 00 00)* was the most notable survivor and is now home to a museum. The Iglesia de San Francisco also dates from the 16C, while the 17C Convento de Santo Domingo houses a museum of contemporary art.

Masca
This remote hamlet is well worth the detour, set in lovely **countryside**★ where the houses are set on narrow ridges which plunge down into a verdant valley of dramatic rock formations.

Los Gigantes★
The Teno mountain range ends in black cliffs called Los Gigantes, "the giants", for their 400m/1 300ft vertical drop.

Adeje
Close to the village lies the **Barranco del Infierno (Hell Canyon)**★ which is justifiably popular with walkers.

Playa de las Américas
This large sprawling man-made resort is the most popular destination on the island. It features beaches of black sand, several family attractions on its outskirts, and a raucous nightlife. Neighbouring **Los Cristianos** is a busy port (ferries depart to La Gomera; *www.fredolsen.es*), which has been subsumed into the tourist sprawl.

Follow the TF 28 in the Valle de San Lorenzo.

Mirador de la Centinela★
Like a sentinel, the viewpoint on a rocky projection commands a vast area.

Return to the inland road.

Mirador de Don Martín★
The belvedere provides a view of the Güimar rift valley and its plantations.

Güimar
A major town near the east coast.

Candelaria
This coastal town is a well-known place of pilgrimage. Its **basílica** *(Pl. de la Basílica; 922 50 01 00)* houses a statue of the Virgin to which islanders make a pilgrimage on 14 and 15 August.

EXCURSIONS
MONTE DE LAS MERCEDES★★
Round trip of 49km/30mi from La Laguna. Allow 3hr.
The Anaga headland traps clouds from the north; tree laurel, giant heather and *fayas*, a local species, flourish.

Mirador de Cruz del Carmen★
See the La Laguna Valley from this viewpoint in Parque Rural de Anaga. *(Visitor centre open daily 9.30am–3pm (4pm in winter); 922 82 20 56.)*

Mirador del Pico del Inglés★★
A marvellous panorama spreads from the 1 024m/3 360ft peak of the Anaga headland to distant Pico del Teide.

El Bailadero★
The road crossing this pass commands good views in both directions.

Taganana★
On the way down to this coastal village are magnificent **views**★★. Visit the **Iglesia parroquial de Nuestra Señora de Las Nieves** for its Hispano-Flemish altarpiece *(Pl. de la Virgen de las Nieves; open 10am–7pm; no visits during religious services; 922 59 01 86).*

Icod de los Vinos
On the north coast of the island, 60km/37mi W of Santa Cruz de Tenerife via the TF 5.
The heart and hub of Tenerife's wine district, the peaceful town of Icod de

los Vinos, 26km/16mi west of Puerto de la Cruz, is a patchwork of charming squares surrounded by elegant colonial houses with their characteristic Canarian pine balconies.

The Casa Museo del Vino (Plaza de la Pila 4) operates a tasting facility where Canary Island wines and cheeses may be tasted and purchased.

Near Icod de los Vinos on the coast road (C 820), don't miss the 3 000-year-old **Dragon Tree** towering 17m/57ft over the shore. The Guanche civilization worshipped these trees as sources of wisdom and fertility, using the sap, which turns red on contact with the air, in healing ceremonies. Said to be petrified former dragons, the *Dracaeno draco* or dragon tree is the official symbol of the Canary Islands.

ADDRESSES

☜ STAY

⊜⊜ **Finca Salamanca** – *Ctra. Puertito, Sureste 1.5km/1mi Güimar. ℘922 51 45 30. www.hotel-fincasalamaca.com. 20 rooms. Restaurant⊜⊜⊜.* Set among the avocado trees of a former plantation estate, this hotel offers comfortable lodging in various buildings and in different kinds of rooms.

⊜⊜ **Hotel Aguere** – *Obispo Rey Redondo (Calle Carrera) 55, La Laguna. ℘922 25 94 90. www.hotelaguere.es. 23 rooms.* One of the few hotels on the island to retain its seigniorial charm. The wooden door provides access to a large, patio-style open hall area around which are all the rooms. The wooden floors, antique furniture and somewhat antiquated bathrooms provide further old-world charm. Highly recommended.

⊜⊜⊜ **Hotel Monopol** – *Quintana 15, Puerto de la Cruz. ℘922 38 46 11. www.monopoltf.com. 92 rooms. Restaurant⊜.* This attractive four-storey whitewashed building adorned with wooden balconies stands in a pedestrianised street in a lively shopping district near the seafront. Comfortable rooms, arranged around a Canarian-style patio.

⊜⊜⊜ **Senderos de Abona** – *La Iglesia 5, Granadilla de Abona. ℘922 77 02 00. www.senderosdeabona.com. 17 rooms. Restaurant⊜⊜.* Rustic atmosphere, with serene patios. Friendly and polite staff.

⊜⊜⊜⊜ **Hotel San Roque** – *Esteban de Ponte 32, Garachico. ℘922 13 34 35. www.hotelsanroque.com. 32 rooms. Restaurant⊜⊜⊜.* This luxury desgner-boutique hotel is tucked away in a quiet street in the centre of Garachico. It combines traditional Canarian design with contemporary style, fittings and all mod cons.

⊜ **Victoria** – *Hermano Apolinar 8, La Orotava. ℘922 33 16 83. www.hotelrural victoria.com. 14 rooms. Restaurant⊜⊜⊜.* A traditional Canary country house with country cooking to match.

☗/EAT

⊜ **Los Cuatro Postes** – *Emilio Calzadilla 5, Santa Cruz de Tenerife. ℘922 28 73 94. Closed Sun, Aug.* Exceptional dining featuring Spanish cuisine in a classical contemporary setting with views into the show kitchen.

⊜⊜ **Régulo** – *San Felipe 16, Puerto de la Cruz. ℘922 38 45 06. www.restaurenteregulo.com. Closed Sun, Mon lunch, fortnights in Jun and Jul.* This traditional island house retains all its charm, with a lovely patio and dining areas on two floor. Antiques and plants are prominent in the décor.

⊜⊜ **Solana** – *Pérez de Rozas 15, Santa Cruz de Tenerife. ℘922 24 37 80. www.solanarestaurante.es. Closed Sun, Mon, Aug 7–31.* Minimalist décor and contemporary cooking using top-quality local products.

⊜⊜⊜ **La Tasca de la Bodega** – *Av. San Sebastián 57, Santa Cruz de Tenerife. ℘922 22 39 09. Closed a week in Feb, Sat for dinner, Sun.* A renovated restaurant in an antique building, with a tapas bar by the entrance, a wine shop and various cosy dining rooms decorated with farming and wine-growing equipment, noted for its Canarian cuisine.

⊜⊜⊜ **Los Limoneros** – *Los Naranjeros, Crtra General del Norte 447, Tacoronte. ℘922 63 66 37. Closed Sun dinner.* One of the area's established favourites offers Spanish dishes made with local produce.

Gran Canaria★★

Gran Canaria is often described as a continent in miniature on account of its many diverse landscapes. Almost half of its area is a UNESCO Biosphere Reserve. From the Pozo de las Nieves (1 949m/6 393ft) at its centre, ravines fan out in all directions. The mountain barrier divides the wetter landscapes of the north and west from extensive semi-desert-like areas in the south. The north and west coast are steep and rocky; on the accessible south coast are long golden sand beaches and throbbing man-made resorts.

SIGHTS
LAS PALMAS DE GRAN CANARIA★

Las Palmas de Gran Canaria, founded in a palm grove in 1478, is nowadays the biggest city in the Canaries and also one of Spain's major ports. It was the most fashionable resort on the island for many decades but over the past 20 years or so it has lost its position to the burgeoning resorts of the sunnier south. Nonetheless, it is still easily the most interesting place to stay on Gran Canaria.

The old city, **Vegueta**, dates from the Conquest; **Puerto de la Luz** and **Las Palmas** compose the tourist district, flanked by the harbour and Alcaravaneras beach in the east and Canteras beach in the west; between them lies residential **Ciudad Jardín**.

Vegueta – Triana★
Allow 2hr.
These two districts form the historic centre of Las Palmas.

Plaza de Santa Ana
The palm-bordered square is overlooked by the town hall (1842) on one side, and the Cathedral on the other.
To the side are the Bishop's Palace (Palacio Episcopal, 17C), with an *alfiz*-decorated portal showing clear Mudéjar influence, the Renaissance-style Casa del Regente and the Archivo Histórico Provincial (archives). During the Corpus

▸ **Population:** 829 597
▪ **Info:** Las Palmas: León y Castillo 17. ☎928 21 96 00; Playa del Inglés: Avenida España. ☎928 77 15 50. www.grancanaria.com.
▸ **Location:** Gran Canaria, the third-largest Canary Island (area: 560sq km/602sq mi), is wedged between Tenerife and Fuerteventura.

Christi procession, the square is carpeted with flowers, sawdust and salt.
Catedral – *Pl. de Santa Ana.* ⓘ*Open for Mass Mon–Fri 7.15am–10am, Sat 10am–2pm, Sun and public holidays 8am–2pm, 6–8pm.* ⓢ*No charge.* ☎928 33 14 30.
The Cathedral, begun in the early 16C, was not completed until the 19C. It has three elegant aisles with tierceron vaulting. In the transept are statues by Canarian sculptor **José Luján Pérez** (1756–1815).

Museo Diocesano de Arte Sacro
Entrance in Pl. Espíritu Santo. ⓘ*Open Mon–Fri 10am–5pm, Sat 10am–1.30pm.* ⓢ€3. ☎928 31 49 89.
The museum of sacred art, in buildings around the 16C Patio de los Naranjos, contains 16C–19C engravings and gold and silverwork. In the chapterhouse is a mosaic from Manises (Valencia).

Casa de Colón★
Colón 1. ⓘ*Open Mon–Fri 9am–7pm, Sat–Sun 9am–3pm.* ⓘ*Closed public holidays.* ⓢ*No charge.* ☎928 31 23 84. www.casadecolon.com.
The palace of the island's first governors, where Columbus stayed in 1502, houses a museum. Maps and instruments evoke Columbus' expeditions. Note the fine *artesonado* ceilings. On the upper floor are 16C–19C paintings.
The **Iglesia de San Antonio Abad** *(Pl. San Antonio Abad 4)*, on the site where Columbus attended Mass, has a fine Baroque interior.

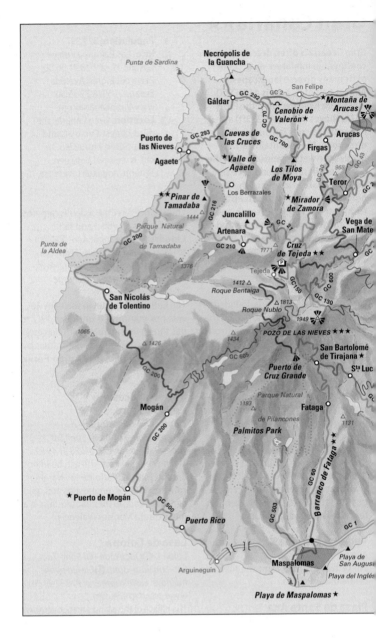

Centro Atlántico de Arte Moderno

Balcones 9–11. ⏰*Open Tue–Sat 10am–9pm, Sun 10am–2pm.* ⏰*Closed public holidays.* 🎫*No charge.* ☎*902 31 18 00. www.caam.net.*

Along **Calle de los Balcones** in one of several 18C buildings with fine doorways is this art centre, renovated by the architect Sáenz de Oíza, with works by 20C artists from the Canary Islands, the Spanish mainland and abroad.

This museum displays a collection of artefacts from pre-Hispanic culture, including mummies, idols and skins. **Don't miss:** the collection of Guanche skulls some of which have been trepanned; terracotta seals *(pintaderas)* found only on Gran Canaria, whose purpose remains a mystery; a re-creation of Gáldar's Cueva Pintada, the island's most important archaeological site.

Adjacent are two picturesque squares, **Plaza del Espíritu Santo** and **Plaza de Santo Domingo**.

Casa-Museo Pérez Galdós

Cano 2 and 6. ◔*Open Tue–Fri 10am–2pm, 4–8pm, Sat–Sun and public holidays 10am–2pm.* ◔*Closed 1 Jan, Shrove Tue, 22 May, 25 Dec.* ✆*No charge.* ℘*928 36 69 76. www.casamuseoperezgaldos.com.* Manuscripts, photographs and objects belonging to Pérez Galdós (1843–1920) are displayed in the house where the writer was born.

Parque de San Telmo

Calle Mayor de Triana, leading from this park, is the main street in the old town. The small **Iglesia de San Bernardo** is full of character with its Baroque altars and paintings. An unusual Modernist kiosk stands in a corner of the park.

MODERN TOWN

Allow 2hr.

▷ *Drive along avenida Marítima del Norte, skirting the town.*

Parque Doramas

In this park are the Santa Catalina Hotel with its casino, and **Pueblo Canario**, a Canary Island village created by painter Néstor de la Torre (1887–1938; ◔*open Tue–Sat 10am–8pm, Sun 10.30am–2.30pm;* ◔*closed 1 Jan, Holy Thu, Good Fri, 25 Dec;* ✆€*3;* ℘*928 24 51 35*).

Folklore festivals are held in the complex, which includes craft shops and the **Museo Néstor** (◔*open Tue–Sat 10am–8pm, Sun and public holidays 10.30am–2.30pm;* ✆€*3;* ℘*928 24 51 35; www.museonestor.com*).

GRAN CANARIA

0   10 km

0   5 miles

Museo Canario★

Doctor Verneau 2. ◔*Open Mon–Fri 10am–8pm, Sat–Sun and public holidays 10am–2pm.* ◔*Closed 1 Jan, 25 Dec.* ✆€*4.* ℘*928 33 68 00. www.elmuseocanario.com.*

Christopher Columbus

It is often maintained that, but for the Canary Islands, Columbus (1451–1506) would never have reached America. His persistence in trying to convince the sovereigns of Portugal, England, France and Castile of the existence of a westerly passage to Asia is well known. Eventually their Catholic Majesties of Castile provided three ships – the *Niña*, the *Pinta* and the *Santa María* – for an expedition to the Indies. He set sail westward from Palos in August 1492 but was forced to put into Las Palmas and La Gomera for repairs to the *Pinta*. On 12 October 1492 he spied land and set foot for the first time on the American continent – on the Caribbean Island of San Salvador. On each of his three subsequent voyages he landed at Las Palmas de Gran Canaria or on La Gomera before going on to discover the other islands of the Antilles (1493), the Orinoco delta (1498) and the shores of Honduras (1502).

Parque Santa Catalina

The park, in **Puerto de la Luz**, includes the Museo de la Ciencia y Tecnología (Science and Technology Museum; ⏱ *open Tue–Sun 10am–8pm;* ◉ *€5 (including cinema and planetarium); €1 robocoaster; www.museoelder.org*) and the Miller cultural centre.

Nearby streets are lined with restaurants and bars. Bazaars sell electronics at duty-reduced prices.

Playa de las Canteras★

This superb 3.5km/2mi beach is sheltered by a line of rocks offshore and backed by a pleasant promenade with restaurants and cafés. At its southeastern end, the **Auditorio Alfredo Kraus** (⏱ *guided tours (50min) Mon–Fri noon, Sun 11.30am;* ◉ *€3; www.auditorioalfredokraus.com*) hosts an opera season. It is the site of the Canaries Music Festival (*www.festivaldecanarias.com*).

Castillo de la Luz

Juan Rejón. ⚬ *Closed for restoration.* ℘*928 46 47 57.*
The 15C fort is an exhibition locale.

Paseo Cornisa

This avenue in the modern neighbourhood Escaleritas provides a fine **panorama**★ of Puerto de la Luz and La Isleta.

Vegueta-Triana

The Vegueta and Triana neighbourhoods in the city's southern section are the historic centre of Las Palmas, with lovely medieval architecture and museums such as the **Casa de Colón** and the **Museo Canario**.

🚗 DRIVING TOURS

THE NORTH COAST

From Las Palmas to La Aldea de San Nicolás

128km/79mi. Allow 1 day.
⏱ *See map p540.*

▷ *Leave Las Palmas on the GC 2, heading W. Take exit 8.*

Arucas

Arucas is the third-largest town on the island. A narrow road leads up **Montaña de Arucas**, shaped like a sugar loaf, offering a **panorama**★ to Las Palmas de Gran Canaria. The black-rock church below stands out against white houses.

▷ *Take the C 813. At Buenlugar, 6km/3.7mi beyond Arucas, turn left.*

Firgas

This is the source of a popular sparkling mineral water. The Paseo de Gran Canaria pays a picturesque homage to the island's communities.

▷ *Return to the main road.*

Los Tilos de Moya

Los Tilos is a protected area with a wood of wild laurel trees.

▷ *At Guía, turn right to join the C 810. Head towards Las Palmas for a few metres, then turn off to Cenobio de Valerón.*

Cenobio de Valerón★
Cuesta de Silva, Santa María de Guía. ◔*Open Tue–Sun Oct–Mar 10am–5pm; Apr–Sept 10am–6pm.* ◔*Closed 1, 6 Jan, 1 May, 25 Dec.* ⊜*€2.50.* ✆*618 60 78 96. www.cenobiodevaleron.com.*
Tradition has it that native girls were prepared in caves hollowed out of tufa for their role as Sacred Virgins. In fact this was merely a granary. Above it, chiefs met in council *(tagoror)*.

▷ *Return to the C 810 and head towards Gáldar.*

Gáldar
At the foot of Mount Gáldar the Guanche king held his court *(guanarteme)*. Outside the heritage centre is the **Cueva Pintada**, a cave with **mural paintings**★. Guanche objects are displayed *(Audiencia 2;* ◔*open Tue–Sat 9.30am–8pm, Sun 11am–8pm, 24, 31 Dec 9.30am–3pm;* ◔*closed 1, 6 Jan, 1 May, 25 Dec;* ⊜*€6; booking required* ✆*928 89 57 46;* ✆*928 89 54 89; www.cuevapintada.org).*

Necrópolis de la Guancha
2km/1.2mi N of Gáldar on coast. ▯✆*928 21 94 21.*
Excavations have brought to light a Guanche settlement and a necropolis of circular constructions of great blocks of lava and a large burial mound.

▷ *Return to Gáldar; take the C 810 S.*

Cuevas de las Cruces
Halfway between Gáldar and Agaete. These are attractive caves in the tufa.

Agaete
In this charming white-walled village is an important burial site, being readied for visitors.
On 4 August the village celebrates the **Fiesta de la Rama**, one of the island's most popular festivals.

Los Berrazales Road★
SE of Agaete.
The road parallels the verdant **Agaete Valley**★ sheltered by mountains.

Puerto de las Nieves
1.3km/0.8mi W of Agaete.
This little fishing harbour once shipped bananas. From the quay there is a good view of what remains of the **Finger of God** *(Dedo de Dios)*, a heavily eroded pointed rock. The hermitage **(ermita)** contains an interesting 15C Flemish triptych by Joos van Clave *(*◔*visits by prior arrangement;* ✆*928 55 43 82).*

La Aldea de San Nicolás
A spectacular road follows cliffs and crosses several ravines to La Aldea de San Nicolás, a village in a fertile basin growing sugar cane and tomatoes.

THE CENTRE OF THE ISLAND
156km/97mi. Allow 1 day.
◔*See map p540–541.*

▷ *Leave Las Palmas on the GC 110, heading S.*

Tafira
A holiday resort favoured by islanders, the town is the site of a university.

Jardín Canario★
Camino del Palmeral. ◔*Open daily 9am –6pm.* ✆*928 21 95 80. www.jardin canario.org.*
The largest botanical garden in Spain (27ha/67 acres) is devoted to Canarian flora, with more than 500 species.

▷ *In Monte Lentiscal turn left.*

Mirador de Bandama★★
A road leads to the summit of Bandama (569m/1 867ft) and a superb view of the enormous Caldera de la Bandama, a crater with its eruption formations intact. The **panorama** takes in Tafira, the Montaña de Arucas and Las Palmas to the north, the crater, and the Real Club de Golf (the oldest in Spain) and Telde to the south. In the caldera are old incised drawings.

Return to the C 811.

Santa Brígida
This village sits close to a ravine planted with palms. A plant and flower market is held weekends. The Casa del Vino de Gran Canaria sells wines *(Calvo Sotelo 26;* ⏰ *open Tue–Fri 10am–6pm, Sat–Sun and public holidays 10am–3pm;* ℘*928 64 42 45; www.museosdelvino.es).*

Vega de San Mateo
A large fruit and vegetable market is held Saturdays and Sundays. The **Casa-Museo Cho Zacarías** *(Av. Tinamar 17;* ⏰ *open Mon–Sat 9am–1pm;* ✆ *€3.60;* ℘*928 66 17 97),* in a series of traditional houses, displays pottery, furniture, textiles, traditional implements, etc.

 Continue along the C 811 for 6km/3.7mi, then bear left.

Pozo de las Nieves★★★
From the summit (1 949m/6 394ft), which is sometimes snow-capped, there is a spectacular **panorama**★★★ of the island. On a clear day, Mount Teide (Tenerife) stands on the horizon.

Cruz de Tejeda★★
NW of Pozo de las Nieves.
Near the parador at the top of the pass (1 450m/4 757ft) lies the village of **Tejeda** in a huge volcanic basin. Out of the chaotic landscape rise the peaks of Roque Bentaiga and Roque Nublo, both venerated by the indigenous people.

 Bear W to Artenara along the GC 110.

The drive includes **views**★ of the troglodyte village of **Juncalillo** where most people live in lava caves.

Artenara
This village is the highest on the island (1 230m/4 035ft). In the enchanting **Ermita de la Cuevita**, a hermitage dug into the rock, is a statue of the Virgin with Child. The **panorama**★ is impressive. From the edge of the village, there is a superb **view**★ of Roque Bentayga.

The most comfortable place to view this from is the Mesón de la Silla restaurant *(*℘*928 66 61 08),* but there is also an adjacent viewing area.

Pinar de Tamadaba★★
The road passes through Canary pines extending to the edge of a cliff which drops sheer to the sea.

 Continue to the end of a tarred road, to the Zona de Acampada, then park and walk 200m/220yd.

On a clear day, the **view**★★ of Agaete, Gáldar and the coast, with the Pico del Teide on the horizon, is superb.

 Return by the same road and turn left onto the GC 110 to Valleseco.

Mirador de Zamora★
Just north of Valleseco there is an attractive **view**★ of Teror.

Teror
Teror has fine mansions with wooden balconies. The 18C **Basílica de Nuestra Señora del Pino** houses a statue of Our Lady of the Pine Tree, the island's patron, who is said to have appeared in 1481 *(Pl. Nuestra Señora del Pino;* ⏰ *open Mon 1–8.30pm, Tue–Fri 9am–1pm, 3–8.30pm, Sat 9am–8.30pm, Sun 7.30–7.30pm;* ✆ *€0.60 (treasury);* ℘*928 63 01 18).* Thousands gather on 8 September to present their gifts and join in worship.
On Sundays *(8am–2pm)* a lively market is held, at which you'll find nuns selling hand-made sweets.

THE SOUTH COAST
Las Palmas to Maspalomas
59km/37mi. Allow about 2hr.
👉 *See map p540.*

 Leave Las Palmas along the GC 1, and then take exit 8 (Telde).

Telde
This was a Guanche kingdom. In the lower town is the 15C **Iglesia de San Juan Bautista** *(Párroco Morales 2;* ℘*928*

60 00 92), a church rebuilt in the 17C and 18C, which contains a 16C Flemish retable depicting the Life of the Virgin.

▶ *Take Calle Inés Chimida.*

The road leads to the quiet **San Francisco district**, known for its traditional craftwork.

▶ *Follow the C 813 towards Ingenio. Beyond the junction with the C 816 turn left, immediately after some cottages, into a rough track; the last 250m/270yd is on foot.*

Yacimiento Arqueológico de Cuatro Puertas★

6km/3.7mi S of Telde. ℘928 68 13 36. The cave, which has four openings *(cuatro puertas)*, is where the indigenous council *(tagoror)* used to meet. The east face of the mountain is riddled with caves where the Guanche embalmed their dead. The summit (to the east) is a sacred site, Almogarén.

Maspalomas/Playa del Inglés/ Playa de San Agustín

This is one of Spain's largest resort areas, a sprawl of apartments and residential zones *(urbanizaciones)* with shopping/ recreation areas *(centros commerciales)*, spread along the sandy coastline. Maspalomas has developed around its spectacular dunes and **beach★**, part of a 400ha/990-acre protected zone, including a palm grove.

Puerto de Mogán★
38km/24mi NW.
This is a picturesque man-made resort in typical Canarian style, built around an attractive marina.

San Bartolomé de Tirajana★
48km/30mi N on the GC 520.
The way up passes through the **Barranco de Fataga★★**, a beautiful ravine. San Bartolomé is set in a magnificent green mountain cirque.

▶ *Return to San Bartolomé and take the C 815 going SE.*

ADDRESSES

🛏 STAY

🍽🍽 **Hostal Escuela Santa Brígida** – *Real de Coello 2. ℘928 47 84 00. www.hecansa.com. 40 rooms. Restaurant*🍽🍽. Set in a cosy garden with traditonal rooms and a restaurant, Satautey, this is a good choice for both lodging and dining.

🍽🍽 **Tenesoya** – *Sagasta 98, Las Palmas de Gran Canaria. ℘928 46 96 08. www.hotel tenesoya.com. 42 rooms.* ⊠€6.50. Just a step from the beach with comfortable rooms and updated, well-equipped bathrooms.

🍽🍽🍽 **Casa de Los Camellos** – *Progreso 12 (on the corner of Retama), Agüimes. ℘928 78 50 03. www.hecansa.com. 11 rooms. Restaurant*🍽🍽🍽. This small hotel, in the old part of Agüimes, has been restored in a welcoming, rustic style, with wooden floors and furniture, and pleasant, attractive bedrooms. Good restaurant.

🍽🍽🍽 **Hotel Rural El Refugio** – *Cruz de Tejeda. ℘928 66 65 13. www.hotel ruralelrefugio.com. 10 rooms.* ⊠€6. *Restaurant*🍽🍽. Extraordinary setting in an area of lush vegetation deep in the interior. An excellent base for excursions through the centre of the island. Cosy bedrooms with wooden floors and attractive furniture.

🍴 EAT

🍽 **Deliciosamarta** – *Pérez Galdós 23, Las Palmas de Gran Canaria. ℘928 37 08 82.* Creative cuisine and minimalist décor set the tone for this contemporary spot in the traditional neighbourhood of Triana.

🍽🍽 **El Arrosar** – *Salvador Cuyás 10, Las Palmas de Gran Canaria. ℘928 27 26 45.* Galician cooking at manageable prices and an easy combination of bar space and intimate dining rooms make this a popular spot in Las Palmas.

🍽🍽🍽 **Casa de Galicia** – *Salvador Cuyás 8, Las Palmas de Gran Canaria. ℘928 27 98 55.* High-quality Galician cuisine where the emphasis is on freshness. A good position between the Playa de las Canteras and the Parque de Santa Catalina.

🍽🍽🍽 **Mesón de la Montaña** – *La montaña de Arucas. ℘928 60 14 75. www.mesonarucas.es.* Traditional Canarian cuisine served at large round tables in a pleasant location offering good views.

Lanzarote★★★

Lanzarote, designated a Biosphere Reserve, is by far the most unusual and intriguing of the Canary Islands. With an area of 846sq km/326sq mi, its lava-black landscape is dotted with oases of bright green vegetation and crops and dazzling white houses. Unlike many parts of Gran Canaria and Tenerife it has retained a vernacular style and local identity; there are no high-rise hotels, neither advertising boards nor pylons, nor many of the other familiar accretions of modern life and mass-market tourism. This is mostly a result of the tireless conservation work of island champion César Manrique (1919–92), modern artist and landscaper extraordinaire. Wherever you go on Lanzarote you will be confronted with his works and philosophy.

LANDSCAPE AND TRADITION

In 1730, a massive series of eruptions occurred in the area now known as the **Montañas del Fuego** (Mountains of Fire). These lasted six years with 26 volcanoes covering one third of the island in lava. In 1824 a new volcano, Tinguatón, engulfed fields and houses.

Lava fields *(malpaís)* and thick black ash and pebbles are pitted with over 100 craters. In **La Geria**, where volcanic pebbles *(lapilli)* are plentiful, vines are protected by low semicircular walls. The grapes produce an excellent light white wine – Malvasía – with a distinctive bouquet. Throughout the island the fields are covered with a deep layer of the *lapilli* to retain moisture from the evening and morning dew, on an island where it rarely rains.

A BIT OF HISTORY

From the 14C to the present – The island owes its name to Lanceloto Malocello from Genoa, who landed in the 14C. In 1401 the Normans **Gadifer de la Salle** and **Jean de Bethencourt** captured the island for the King of Castile. Lanzarote was a base for expeditions against the other islands and became prey to marauding slavers.

SIGHTS

Arrecife

This important port was originally defended from pirates by the **Castillo de San Gabriel** (○open Tue–Fri 10am–1pm, 4–7pm, Sat 10am–1pm), built in the 16C on an islet and linked to the town by two bridges.

Recently given a makeover by the island authorities to entice more visitors to come here for a day trip, the island capital has good shopping, a pleasant beach, promenade and a picturesque lagoon, the Charco de San Ginés, where fisherman tie up small boats.

To the north is the 18C **Castillo de San José**. Restored by César Manrique, it houses the **Museo Internacional de Arte Contemporáneo** (Carretera de Naos; ○open daily 11am–9pm; ᴗ€2.50; ✆928 81 23 21).

West of Arrecife via the LZ-2, the former house of Nobel laureate José Saramago has been converted into a museum (Calle Los Topes 2; ○ open Mon–Sat 10am–2pm; ᴗ€8; ✆928 81 30 53).

EXCURSIONS

Each tour departs from Arrecife.

THE CENTRE OF THE ISLAND

○ *62km/39mi through the island's centre.*

Fundación César Manrique★

Taro de Tahíche, Villa de Teguise.
○*Open Jul–Oct Tue–Sat 10am–7pm, Sun 10am–3pm; Nov–Jun Mon–Sat 10am–6pm, Sun 10am–3pm.*
○*Closed 1 Jan.* ᴗ€8. ✆928 84 31 38.
www.fcmanrique.org.

> **Population:** 127 457
> **Info:** Arrecife: Blas Cabrera Felipe. ✆928 81 17 62. www.turismo lanzarote.com.
> **Location:** Lanzarote lies 100km/62mi from North Africa.

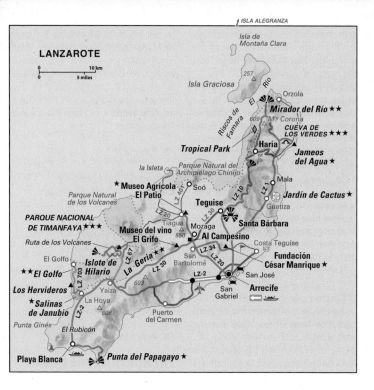

The foundation devoted to the greatest Lanzaroteño is in a remarkable and quite unique house that sits atop five volcanic bubbles. César Manrique chose this location to live – his extraordinary home is open to the public – and to demonstrate the bond between architecture and nature.

Monumento al Campesino

This monument near **Mozaga**, by César Manrique, marks the centre of the island, and pays homage to the peasant farmers of Lanzarote. Next to it is the **Casa-Museo del Campesino** (🕐*open daily 10am–6pm;* ✆*no charge;* 📞*928 52 01 36)*, a characteristic country house.

Museo Agrícola El Patio★

Echeyde 18, Tiagua. 🕐*Open Mon–Fri 10am–5.30pm, Sat 10am–2.30pm.* ✆*€6 (including wine tasting and one tapa).* 📞*928 52 91 34.* *www.museoelpatio.com.*
Exhibits of rural life on the island and Malvasía wine tastings.

Museo del Vino El Grifo

El Islote 121, San Bartolomé.
🕐*Open daily 10.30am–6pm.* ✆*€3.*
📞*928 52 49 51. www.elgrifo.com.*
This 18C is the oldest in the Canaries and a museum of traditional winemaking.

La Geria★★

La Geria lies between Yaiza and Mozaga in a blackish desert pockmarked with craters. The village is a wine centre.

🚗 DRIVING TOUR

The South of the Island
Round-trip of 124km/77mi from Arrecife.

Parque Nacional de Timanfaya★★★

🌀*Guided tours of the park by coach are available from 9am; last tour at 5pm.* ✆*€9 (including volcano circuit).* 📞*928 84 02 38.*
The range, which emerged in the 1730–36 eruptions, stands out sometimes red,

sometimes black, above cinder and slag. It is the major natural attraction on the island. The **Montañas de Fuego** form the centre of this massif.

Dromedaries, once common beasts of burden on Lanzarote, wait by the roadside 5km/3mi north of Yaiza to provide a swaying and jolting ride up the mountainside, from where there is a good view of the next crater. Although the volcanoes have not erupted since 1736, their fires burn and bubble still. To demonstrate the point, at the visitor centre, twigs are dropped into a shallow hole (by the park ranger) and instantly catch fire; water poured into a pipe set into the lava steams immediately because of the subsoil temperature (140°C/284°F at 10cm/4in, over 400°C/752°F at 6m/19.6ft), and in the El Diablo restaurant, food is cooked using the heat of the earth as a giant barbecue. There are fine views from the restaurant.

Buses from here follow the 14km/8.7mi **Ruta de los Volcanes**. A lookout affords a view over an immense lava field stretching to the sea.

Los Hervideros

In the caverns at the end of the tongue of lava, the sea boils (*hervir*: to boil) in an endlessly fascinating spectacle.

El Golfo★★

A lagoon is filled with vivid emerald-green water; a steep cliff of pitted black rock forms an impressive backdrop.

Salinas de Janubio★

Deep blue seawater entering a crater is harvested to leave gleaming white pyramids of salt in square pans.

Playa Blanca

This pleasant resort has a promenade between old fishermen's houses and the white beach.

Punta del Papagayo★

The Rubicón region is where Bethencourt settled. The only trace is the Castillo de las Coloradas, a tower on the cliff edge. Dusty roads lead from Playa Blanca

to the protected **Reserva Natural de los Ajaches** (○*open daily 9am–7pm;* ◎*€4 vehicle fee;* ℘*928 17 34 52*), which leads to the isolated uncommercialised white-sand Papagayo beaches, the finest on the island. From here there are fine **views**★ of Playa Blanca and Fuerteventura .

▷ *Take the LZ 2.*

Museo de Cetáceos de Canarias (Whale Museum)

Antiguo Varadero Building, Puerto Calero. ○*Open Tue–Sat 10am–6pm, last admission at 5.15pm.* ○*Closed 1, 6 Jan, 25 Dec.* ◎*€9.* ℘*928 84 95 60. www.museodecetaceos.org.*

One of the best European whale collections uses replicas, skeletons, explanatory panels, sound and images to tell the story of these mammals.

▷ *Return to Arrecife via the LZ 2.*

THE NORTH OF THE ISLAND

Round trip of 77km/47mi from Arrecife. About half a day.

Jardín de Cactus★

Ctra General del Norte, Guatiza. ○*Open daily 10am–7pm.* ◎*€5.* ℘*928 52 93 97.*

This cactus garden displays many species from the Canary Islands, America and Madagascar, on terraces in an old quarry. In this area are prickly pears, a cactus which attracts cochineal beetles, once crushed to obtain a crimson dye.

Cueva de los Verdes★★★

Haría. ◁*Guided tours (1hr) daily 10am–7pm, last admission 6pm.* ◎*€8.* ℘*928 84 84 84.*

At the foot of the Corona volcano are volcanic galleries where the Guanches once took refuge from marauding pirates. There are 2km/1mi of illuminated passages at different levels.

Jameos del Agua★

Carretera de Orzola, Haría. ○*Open daily 10am–7pm; Tue, Fri, Sat 7pm–2am, including a folklore show at*

11pm. €8 (day), €9 (evening).
🕾 928 84 80 20.

A *jameo* is a cavity formed when the top of a volcanic tube collapses. César Manrique has turned two *jameos* into an extraordinary fantasy grotto, regarded by most people as his *tour de force* on Lanzarote. Quite separately, a lagoon in the cave is the habitat of a minute, blind albino millenary crab, only found here. The **Casa de los Volcanes** on the upper level is an excellent exhibition and study centre on volcanism. By night the Jameos del Agua becomes a small stylish leisure complex with a restaurant, bar, dance floor and auditorium.

Mirador del Río★★

Carretera del norte, Ye. 🕔 *Open daily 10am–7pm.* €5. 🕾 928 52 65 48.

At the north end of the island stands a steep isolated headland, **Riscos de Famara**. The belvedere commands a superb **panorama**★★ across the azure waters of the **El Río** strait to La Graciosa and its neighbouring islands; immediately below are salt pans. A **passenger ferry** (🚢*Orzola to La Graciosa (25min): see website for schedule;* €20 round-trip; 🕾 902 40 16 66; www.lineas-romero. com) operates between Orzola and La Graciosa.

🏞 Tropical Park, Guinate

▶ *From Haría, take the LZ 202 via Mirador del Río.* 🕔 *Open daily 10am– 5pm.* €14; child €6. 🕾 928 83 55 00. www.guinatepark.com.

These gardens are devoted to exotic birds and feature parrot shows and penguins.

Haría

From afar Haría resembles a typical North African village, set in a lush valley replete with palm trees. The best view is from the Mirador de Haría★, some 5km/3mi south.

Teguise

Teguise, once the capital, is a beautifully restored and very atmospheric town with some of the finest colonial buildings in the archipelago. Several of these have been tastefully converted to restaurants, bars and shops. Teguise is most famous nowadays for its **Sunday Market** (🕔*open 9am–2pm*), which draws coach tours from all over the island.

In the nearby **Castillo de Santa Bárbara,** built in the 16C on the Guanapay volcano, is the **Museo del Emigrante** (🕔*open Mon–Fri 10am–6pm, Sat–Sun 10am–4pm;* 🚫*no charge;* 🕾 928 84 59 13), which documents the often poignant tales of the emigration of Canary Islanders to America. There are excellent views of the town and surrounding countryside from here.

ADDRESSES

🛏 STAY

🍽 **Hotel Miramar** – *Coll 2, Arrecife.* 🕾 928 81 26 00. www.hmiramar.com. 85 rooms. 🍴€6. Restaurant🍽. Although this 1980s-style building is lacking in architectural charm, its location, by the sea and opposite the Castillo de San Gabriel in the centre of Arrecife, couldn't be better. Bedroom balconies offer good sea views, although the bedrooms themselves are on the basic side with antiquated furniture.

🍽 **Finca de las Salinas** – *La Cuesta 17, Yaiza.* 🕾 928 83 03 25. www.fincasalinas.com. 17 rooms. 2 restaurants🍽. An 18C mansion with an attractive façade and rustic rooms located in a lively neighbourhood.

🍴 EAT

🍽 **Amura** – *Pas. Marítimo, Puerto Calero.* 🕾 928 51 31 81. www.restaurante amura.com. Closed Mon. This restaurant in an attractive colonial-style octagonal building has a spectacular terrace. Its location opposite the marina, surrounded by palms, is outstanding.

🍽 **La Cañada** – *César Manrique 3, Puerto del Carmen.* 🕾 928 51 04 15. Closed Sun. This restaurant is located on a small hill. It has a lovely terrace and dining room, and a kitchen that takes pride in the quality of its ingredients.

Fuerteventura

Fuerteventura has a captivating elemental beauty thanks to its bare landscape and beaches of white sand with turquoise water all around. Strong winds and a calm sea on the east coast make this island ideal for sailing, diving, fishing and, in particular, kitesurfing and windsurfing.

LANDSCAPE AND CLIMATE

Arid Fuerteventura is dotted with bare crests and extinct volcanoes. It was described as a "skeletal island" by its most famous native, the poet and writer **Miguel de Unamuno**, exiled here in 1924. The harsh terrain is only suitable for grazing goats, which outnumber humans. Villages are marked by palm trees and windmills.

Fuerteventura shares the climate of nearby Africa; sand, blown across the sea, formed an isthmus, El Jable, between the once-separate islets of Maxorata and Jandía.

DRIVING TOUR

North to South

Corralejo★

This likeable one-time fishing village, now the island's main tourist resort, is at the northern tip of the island beyond the *malpaís*.

Crystal-clear water laps at the immense beautiful white dune **beaches** of the Parque Natural Dunas de Corralejo and the Isla de Lobos, a Robinson Crusoe island, accessible by ferry. Lanzarote is visible north.

▷ *Leave Corralejo along the FV 101.*

La Oliva

The **Centro de Arte Canario** (◷*open Mon–Sat 10.30am–6pm, 5pm in winter; ✆admission charges vary; ✆928 86 82 33)* is the island's best art gallery, devoted to Canarian art. Opposite stands the landmark **Casa de Coroneles**, a grand

▶ **Population:** 74 983

ℹ **Info:** Corralejo: Plaza Grande de Corralejo. ✆928 86 62 35. www.fuerteventura turismo.com.

▷ **Location:** Fuerteventura lies 100km/62mi NW of the coast of Africa. Immediately N is Lanzarote.

👫 **Kids:** Oasis Park.

18C house; once the residence of the governor of the island, it is now an arts and cultural centre.

▷ *Continue on the FV 10 passing the Guanche's sacred Mount Tindaya on your right. Just before you turn right onto the FV 207 look for the large hillside statue of Miguel de Unamuno. Pass through Tefía.*

Ecomuseo de la Alcogida

La Alcogida, Tefía. ◷*Open Tue–Fri, Sun 9.30am–5.30pm.* ✆*€5.* ✆*928 85 14 00. www.majorero.com/laalcogida.*

This is the island's most engaging museum, depicting rural country life around 50 to 100 years ago, scattered among seven houses and farms.

Betancuria★

This pretty valley town (in fact no bigger than a small village), was once the island capital, founded in 1404 by island conqueror Jean de Bethencourt.

Betancuria retains a ruined Franciscan monastery and an ancient **cathedral**, with white walls and a picturesque wooden balcony, now called the **Iglesia de Santa María la Antigua**. The baptistery contains an interesting crucifix; the sacristy has a fine panelled ceiling.

On the south side, a small **Museo Arqueológico** displays Guanche artefacts (*Roberto Roldán;* ◷*open Tue–Sat 10am–6pm;* ◷*closed public holidays;* ✆*€2;* ✆*928 87 82 41).*

The road south provides an attractive contrast between the wide horizon of bare rose-tinted peaks and the village

FUERTEVENTURA

0   10 km

0   5 miles

Punta de la Ballena
o de Tostón

★ **Corralejo**

Los Lobos

269

Playas de
Corralejo

FV 10

El Cotillo

FV 101

Parque
Natural

308

529

La Oliva

**Casa de
los Coroneles**

332

Casillas del
Angel

FV 10

**Puerto
del Rosario**

625

FV 30

FV 20

Valle de
Stª Inés

Playa Blanca

★ **Betancuria**

593

724

Antigua

Ermita de Nª Sª
de la Peña

Vega de
Río Palmas

494

FV 2

Pájara

Tiscamanita

382

Tuineje

Malpaís
Grande

FV 605

FV 20

691

FV 4

482

FV 2

464

Gran Tarajal

El Jable

Tarajalejo

Playa de Barlovento
de Jandía

Costa Calma

Parque Natural

Playa de Sotavento

435

Península de Jandía

Punta de
Jandía

Morro Jable

---

of **Vega de Río Palmas** nestling in its green valley-oasis.

▶ *Head SW along the FV 617, turn left onto the FV2 coast road, then NE for a short distance.*

🧍🧍 La Lajita Oasis Park
Ctra General de Jandia, La Lajita.
🕐 *Open daily from 10am.* 🎟 *€24 (€10 camel ride); child €12 (€6 camel ride).*
📞 *902 40 04 34. www.lajitaoasis park.com.*

Located at the gateway to the Jandía Peninsula, Oasis Park is quite literally an oasis of beautiful botanical gardens and exotic animals amid the parched southern landscape. This zoo park includes over 200 species of birds and hundreds of small animals, and is most famous for its camel rides (these were common

beast of burden on the island as recently as the mid-20C). There are also shows featuring sea lions, birds of prey, parrots and crocodiles. Here you will also find a large African area with giraffes elephants, hippos, cheetahs etc.

▶ *Head back SW on the FV2.*

Península de Jandía
The leeward (southern) side of this protected southernmost part of the island is famous for its magnificent beaches. These are largely uncommercialised though a number of low-key resorts popular with German and Scandinvian visitors have grown up over the last three decades. This is the main centre for windsurfing and kitesurfing on the island and world championships are staged here.

La Gomera★

La Gomera, with an area of 378sq km/146sq mi, is ideal for visitors seeking peace, contact with nature and outdoor activities. This round island rises from coastal cliffs, cut by deep ravines, to a *meseta* with a single peak, Mount Garajonay (1 487m/4 880ft). Black beaches are reminders of volcanic activity as are the dramatic basalt cliffs known as Los Órganos, which are only visible by boat. The fertile red soil is carefully husbanded and picturesque terraces are a feature of the island.

SIGHTS

San Sebastián de la Gomera

Christopher Columbus stayed here during his first voyage. His route can be traced down the main street from the corner house where he took on water *(ask to see the well, el pozo, in the patio)*, past the **Iglesia de la Asunción** *(Medio; ℘922 87 03 03)*, where he heard Mass, to the **Casa de la Aguada**, a small house located before the post office, where he is said to have slept.

🚗 DRIVING TOUR

▷ *15km/9.3mi. Leave San Sebastián de la Gomera on the TF 711.*

The road emerges from the first tunnel in the **Hermigua Valley★★** amid white houses, palms and banana plantations.

Agulo★

19km/11.8m NW from San Sebastián.
This small villages enjoys a picture-postcard seaside location with Tenerife clearly visible on the horizon.
In the adjacent pretty village of **Las Rosas** demonstration of *El Silbo*, the unique whistling language invented by the islanders in order to communicate with each other across Gomera's many ravines, are given at the Las Rosas restaurant.

▶ **Population:** 21 952
ℹ **Info:** Calle Real 4, San Sebastián de La Gomera. ℘922 14 15 12. www.gomera-island.com.
◐ **Location:** La Gomera is a 35min ferry ride from Los Cristianos on Tenerife.

Parque Nacional Garajonay★★

Juego de Bolas visitor centre.
🕒*Open daily 9.30am–4.30pm.*
🚶*Guided walking tours on Sat by prior arrangement. ℘922 80 09 93. http://reddeparquesnacionales.mma.es.*
This national park is covered by laurels, traces of the Tertiary era, and giant heathers, punctuated by rocks. Mist caused by trade winds lends an air of mystery.

Valle Gran Rey★★

55km/34mi from San Sebastián de la Gomera on the TF 713.
The road ascends the slopes to the south; the climb to the central *meseta* in the park is less steep.
Chipude– Attractive potters' village.
Arure – After the bridge there is a good **panorama★** of Taguluche.
Barranco del Valle Gran Rey★★ – The most spectacular ravine on the island.

View of Valle Gran Rey

© Imagebrokers.net/Photoshot

El Hierro

This small remote windblown island, just 278sq km/107sq mi, sees very few visitors. Those who come witness fertile farmland, spectacular cliffs plunging into the sea, volcanic cones, fields of lava carpeted in laurel, and an underwater world popular with divers.

EXCURSIONS

The excursions below depart from **Valverde**, the capital of the island, at an altitude of 571m/1 873ft.

Tamaduste

▸ *8km/5mi NE.*

A large sandbank by the small seaside resort forms a lagoon.

El Golfo★★

▸ *8km/5mi W.*

There is a fine **view**★★ of El Golfo from the **Mirador de La Peña**. The rim of a crater is covered with laurels and giant heather; the level floor is cultivated. La Fuga de Gorreta, near the Salmor rocks *(NE)*, is the habitat of a primeval lizard.

TOUR THROUGH LA DEHESA

▸ *105km/65mi. Head S from Valverde along the TF 912.*

Tiñor – Pyramid-shaped formations of ash among fertile fields denote this area. Until 1610, when it was blown down, a Garoé tree was venerated by natives.

Sabinosa – A spa-hotel treats skin and digestive diseases.

La Dehesa – A track 3 km/1.8mi further on crosses the arid La Dehesa region and provides extensive **views**★ of the south coast where the fiery red earth, pitted with craters, slopes to the sea.

Punta de Orchilla – Orchilla Point was the zero meridian before Greenwich. Beyond the lighthouse are sabine trees, conifers with twisted trunks found only on El Hierro.

Ermita de Nuestra Señora de los Reyes – In this hermitage is a statue of the Virgen de Los Reyes, patron saint of

▸ **Population:** 10 162

▸ **Info:** Calle Dr Quintero 4, Valverde. ✆922 55 03 02. www.elhierro.es.

▸ **Location:** El Hierro is in the far southwest of the archipelago.
Ferries run to neighbouring islands (✆902 100 107; www.fredolsen.es).

the island. Every four years since 1741, it is carried in procession to Valverde *(Bajada Virgen de los Reyes)*. It will next take place on the first Saturday of July in 2013.

El Pinar – An aromatic **pine forest**★ extends all over this central region of the island. A shaded picnic area at **Hoya del Morcillo** offers a respite from the bright Canary Island sunlight.

With barbecue pits, picnic tables, toilets, a football field and a playground for children, camping is permitted in this convenient base camp for hikes through the mountainous wooded wilderness at the heart of the El Hierro. Camping permits must be solicited previously in Valverde (✆922 55 00 17).

ADDRESSES

STAY

⊜⊜⊜ **Parador de El Hierro** – *Las Playas.* ✆922 55 80 36. www.parador.es. *45 rooms.* ⊑€17 *Restaurant*⊜⊜. In the Las Playas beach district 20km/12.5mi SW of Valverde, this restful parador built on a ledge of volcanic rock has panoramic views, handsome colonial furnishings and a restaurant specialising in Canarian cooking.

EAT

⊜⊜ **La Higuera de Abuela** – *Valverde 38900.* ✆922 55 10 26. *Closed Tue.* A family operation in Echedo 5km/3mi NE of Valverde, this friendly and rustic spot serves local specialties prepared with care at good value.

La Palma★

With a surface of just 706sq km/272sq mi and its highest peak rising to 2 426m/7 962ft, La Palma has the highest average altitude of any island in the world. Rain is more abundant than in the rest of the Canaries, resulting in numerous streams and springs. It is called, justifiably on both counts, the "Beautiful Island" and the "Green Island" because of its woods of laurel and pine and numerous banana plantations. La Palma has distanced itself from major tourist development and appeals to nature-lovers, walkers, and those seeking peace and quiet.

A BIT OF HISTORY

The Caldera de Taburiente, a huge mountain arch curiously shaped like a crater, spreads over 10km/6.2mi. A chain of peaks, Las Cumbres, extends south; ravines produce an indented coastline. In the mountains, rainwater is collected to irrigate the lower terraces.

SIGHTS
SANTA CRUZ DE LA PALMA

The administrative centre was founded in 1493 by the conquistador Alonso Fernández de Lugo. In the 16C, with rising sugar exports and the expan-

▶ **Population:** 85 932

🛈 **Info:** Avenida Blas Pérez Glez, Santa Cruz de la Palma. ℘922 41 21 06. www.lapalmaturismo.com.

▷ **Location:** La Palma is located in the far northwest of the archipelago.

sion of the naval yards, Santa Cruz was one of the Spanish Empire's major ports (third only to Sevilla and Antwerp) and prey to pirates; now it is a peaceful city where elegant façades line the seafront. Its most famous native is Manolo Blahnik.
At Playa de Los Cancajos *(5km/3mi S)* the beach and rocks are black.

Plaza de España

Several buildings date from the Renaissance. The 16C **Iglesia de El Salvador** has beautiful ceilings with **artesonado ornament**★; the sacristy has Gothic vaulting. Opposite stand the 16C town hall and houses in colonial style.
Walk uphill to the delightful **Plaza de Santo Domingo**.
Next to a college stands the **chapel** of a former monastery with beautiful Baroque altars.
To visit the chapel, ask for the keys at the Iglesia de El Salvador, ℘922 41 32 50.

View from the Caldera de Taburiente, with a view of Pico del Teide in the background

© Michael Runkel/age fotostock

Observatorio Roque de los Muchachos

© quintanilla/Bigstockphoto.com

🚘 DRIVING TOURS

The two tours suggested below both depart from Santa Cruz de la Palma.

The North of the Island

Observatorio Roque de los Muchachos★★★
36km/22.3mi NW of Santa Cruz de la Palma. Allow 1hr45min for the ascent.
Laurel bushes and pine trees line the winding road which offers extensive views as it climbs to the **astrophysical observatory**, at 2 432m/7 981ft, including the William Herschel Telescope, one of the largest in the world with a 4.2m/13.7ft mirror *(Apartado de Correos 50; ✆guided tours by prior arrangement; ℘922 405 500; www.iac.es)*.
From the Roque de los Muchachos the **panorama**★★★ encompasses the Caldera, Los Llanos de Aridane, the islands of El Hierro and La Gomera, and Mount Teide on Tenerife.

Punta Cumplida
36km/22.3mi N. – There are fine views of the coast from the cliff road which crosses deep ravines *(barrancos)* in the Los Tilos Biosphere Reserve. Note the impressive number of craters.

La Galga
(15km/9.3mi N off LP 1) – North of the village, after the tunnel, the road crosses a steep and well-wooded **ravine**★.

San Andrés
(22km/13.6mi N off LP 1) – In the church is a beautiful Mudéjar ceiling in the chancel.

Charco Azul
– Natural seawater pools.

Puerto Espíndola
– A fishing village where boats are drawn up onto a shingle beach in a breach in the cliff face.

Punta Cumplida
– Walk round the lighthouse to see waves breaking on basalt rock piles. The attractive Fajana swimming pools are north of here.

Los Sauces
(2km/1.2mi W of San Andrés) – The main agricultural centre in the north of the island.

Los Tiles★
Detour up Agua Ravine to the lime tree forest. **Los Tiles Interpretation and Investigation Centre** (🕐 *open daily Jul–Oct 9am–5.30pm; Nov–Jun 9am–5pm; ℘922 45 12 46)* interprets the flora in the reserve.

The Centre and South of the Island

Via Los Llanos and Fuencaliente
190km/118mi.

▷ *Head N out of Santa Cruz. After the ravine, take the first left.*

Punta de Rabisca

Punta Cumplida

Bárlovento

Puerto
Espíndola

982

C 830

Los Sauces ○ ▲ Charco Azul
✛
San Andrés

Punta
Gorda

★ *Los Tilos* ▲

★ *Barranco* ○ ▲ La Galga

△ 1209

★★★ ROQUE DE
LOS MUCHACHOS
2426

2351 *Parque Natural*
de las Nieves

Punta
Salinas

Puntagorda ○

★★★ CALDERA
DE TABURIENTE
PARQUE NACIONAL

C 830

1926 △

la
Cumbrecita

Roque de Idafe

Nª Sª de
Las Nieves

Sta Cruz
P
de la Palma

Barranco de
las Angustias

★★★ LOMO DE
LAS CHOZAS

△
2044

★★ *El Time* ▲

Los Llanos
de Aridane

1435 △

La Concepción ★

Puerto de
Tazacorte ○

El Paso

Breña Alta

TF 812

Tazacorte

Parque Natural

C 832

1505 △

San Nicolás

Cueva de
Belmaco

Puerto Naos

C 832

de

C u m b r e   V i e j a

1949 △

C 832

Cumbra Vieja

1249 △

C 832

★ *Volcán de* ○ ▲ Fuencaliente ★
San Antonio ⚠ de la Palma

LA PALMA

0 _____ 6 km
0 _____ 3 miles

★ *Volcán*
de Teneguía

Punta de Fuencaliente

On the seafront of Santa Cruz, stands the **Castillo de Santa Catalina**, built to fend off pirate raiders in the 17C.
In the **Barco de la Virgen** *(the Virgin's Boat)*, a curious cement reproduction of Columbus' Santa María, is a small **naval museum** *(Pérez Galdós 18; ✆922 42 00 07)*. The road passes the **Fuerte de la Virgen**, a 16C fortress.

Las Nieves
At the foot of Pico de las Nieves, shaded by laurel trees, the **Real Santuario de Nuestra Señora de las Nieves** houses the statue of the island's patron saint.

Every five years (the next will be in 2015) it is the centrepiece of a grand parade.

La Concepción★
The summit of the Caldereta commands a wonderful **bird's-eye view**★ of Santa Cruz de la Palma, the harbour and the mountains.

▷ *Take the TF 812 westwards.*

Parque Nacional de la Caldera de Taburiente★★★
4km/2.5mi W of the tunnel on the right is the **Centro de Visitantes** *(Ctra.*

General de Padrón, no. 47, El Paso;
℘922 49 72 77), with information on
marked footpaths.

Ahead, turn right for La Cumbrecita.

The **Cumbrecita Pass** (1 833m/6 014ft)
and the **Lomo de las Chozas Pass**
(1km/0.6mi further on) provide a splendid **panorama**★★★ of the Caldera de
Taburiente, dotted with Canary pines
and crowned by rose-tinted peaks.

Los Llanos de Aridane
The island's second largest town is in a
plain of bananas and avocado trees.

El Time★★
The top of El Time cliff affords a remarkable **panorama**★★ of the Aridane plain,
a sea of banana palms, and of the Barranco de las Angustias, a rock fissure
which is the only outlet for the Caldera
de Taburiente.

Puntagorda
This fine landscape is particularly beautiful in spring, when the almond trees are
in blossom.

Return to El Time.

Puerto de Tazacorte
Alonso Fernández de Lugo landed in this
small harbour in 1492. In 1585, Francis
Drake raided this town on his way to the
Caribbean. Nicknamed "París chiquito"
(little Paris), the small beach is popular
on Sundays.

Puerto Naos
Descend through lava fields from the
1949 eruption and then through thhe
lush avocado and banana plantations
irrigated by La Caldera de Taburiente, to
the Puerto with its large beach of black
volcanic sand.

San Nicolás
The lava stream from the Nambroque
volcano cut the village in two in 1949.

Fuencaliente de la Palma★
Before reaching Fuencaliente, look
back from the Mirador de las Indias for
a **glimpse**★ of the coast through the
pines. A hot water spring disappeared
during the eruption of **San Antonio
volcano**★ in 1677. Circle the volcano
to see the craters of **Teneguía volcano**★, which appeared in October 1971,
and the lava stream which separated the
lighthouse from the village.

Cueva de Belmaco
5km/3mi from the airport fork.
The cave of Guanche King Belamaco. At
the back of the cave are rocks with
inscriptions.

ADDRESSES

🛏 STAY
Pensíon La Cubana – *Calle O'Daily 24.*
℘922 41 13 54. 6 rooms. This tiny pension
in a traditional townhouse ten minutes
from the beach offers excellent value for
budget lodging.

Parador de la Palma – *Crtra. El
Zumacal. ℘922 43 58 28. www.parador.es.
6 rooms. ⊏€17. Restaurant*. The views
from this Parador-promontory on the San
Antonio to Breña Alta road 6km/4 mi SE
of town are extraordinary. Public spaces
are open and ample and guest rooms
are spacious.

🍴 EAT
La Placeta – *Placeta de Borrero 1,
Santa Cruz de La Palma. ℘922 41 52 73.
www.laplaceta.es. Closed Sun, Aug.* Set in an
18C mansion in a picturesque part of town
with views of the typical balconies, this
carefully managed favourite serves fine
local and international cuisine.

Las Nieves – *Plaza de las Nieves 2,
Santa Cruz de La Palma. ℘922 41 66 00.
Closed Thur.* Cooking over coals is the
speciality at this comfortable and rustic
dining spot. Roast rabbit and goat are
favourites here.

Bodegón Mambrino – *Av. del
Puente 19, Santa Cruz de la Palma. ℘922 41
18 73. Closed Sun dinner.* For grass-fed beef
carefully prepared and served with the
typical potato dish *papas arrugadas*, this is
a safe bet in Santa Cruz de la Palma.

INDEX

INDEX

INDEX

INDEX

INDEX

INDEX

INDEX

🛏 STAY

🍽 EAT

MAPS AND PLANS

MAP LEGEND

	Sight	Seaside resort	Winter sports resort	Spa
Highly recommended	★★★	≜≜≜	✱✱✱	‡‡‡
Recommended	★★	≜≜	✱✱	‡‡
Interesting	★	≜	✱	‡

Selected monuments and sights

◉ ▭	Tour - Departure point
🏛 ♦	Catholic church
🏛 ♦	Protestant church, other temple
✡ ▣ ▤	Synagogue - Mosque
▭	Building
■	Statue, small building
♰	Calvary, wayside cross
◎	Fountain
—●—▪	Rampart - Tower - Gate
⋈	Château, castle, historic house
⁖	Ruins
◡	Dam
✿	Factory, power plant
☆	Fort
∩	Cave
▭	Troglodyte dwelling
⚲	Prehistoric site
▼	Viewing table
ᴪ	Viewpoint
▲	Other place of interest

Sports and recreation

🏇	Racecourse
⛸	Skating rink
≋ ▭	Outdoor, indoor swimming pool
🎬	Multiplex Cinema
⛵	Marina, sailing centre
⌂	Trail refuge hut
▫▪▫▪▫	Cable cars, gondolas
▫+++++▫	Funicular, rack railway
▭🚂	Tourist train
◆	Recreation area, park
🎪	Theme, amusement park
☥	Wildlife park, zoo
⊛	Gardens, park, arboretum
☯	Bird sanctuary, aviary
🚶	Walking tour, footpath
☺	Of special interest to children

Abbreviations

G, POL	Police (Federale Politie)	**P**	Local government offices (Gouvernement provincial)
H	Town hall (Hôtel de ville ou maison communale)	**ℙ**	Provincial capital (Chef-lieu de provincial)
J	Law courts (Palais de justice)	**T**	Theatre (Théatrē)
M	Museum (Musée)	**U**	University (Université)

Additional symbols

ℹ	Tourist information	⊗	Post office
═══ ═══	Motorway or other primary route	◎	Telephone
❶ ❶	Junction: complete, limited	▭	Covered market
⇥⇥ ═══	Pedestrian street	⁺✕⁺	Barracks
ɪ═══ɪ	Unsuitable for traffic, street subject to restrictions	△	Drawbridge
▭▭▭	Steps – Footpath	∪	Quarry
🚆 🚉	Train station – Auto-train station	✕	Mine
🚌 🚉SNCF	Coach (bus) station	**B** **F**	Car ferry (river or lake)
—▪—	Tram	🚤	Ferry service: cars and passengers
⌒	Metro, underground	⇋	Foot passengers only
P R	Park-and-Ride	③	Access route number common to Michelin maps and town plans
♿	Access for the disabled	Bert (R.)...	Main shopping street
		AZ B	Map co-ordinates

The Michelin Adventure

It all started with rubber balls! This was the product made by a small company based in Clermont-Ferrand that André and Edouard Michelin inherited, back in 1880. The brothers quickly saw the potential for a new means of transport and their first success was the invention of detachable pneumatic tires for bicycles. However, the automobile was to provide the greatest scope for their creative talents. Throughout the 20th century, Michelin never ceased developing and creating ever more reliable and high-performance tires, not only for vehicles ranging from trucks to F1 but also for underground transit systems and airplanes.

From early on, Michelin provided its customers with tools and services to facilitate mobility and make traveling a more pleasurable and more frequent experience. As early as 1900, the Michelin Guide supplied motorists with a host of useful information related to vehicle maintenance, accommodation and restaurants, and was to become a benchmark for good food. At the same time, the Travel Information Bureau offered travelers personalised tips and itineraries.

The publication of the first collection of roadmaps, in 1910, was an instant hit! In 1926, the first regional guide to France was published, devoted to the principal sites of Brittany, and before long each region of France had its own Green Guide. The collection was later extended to more far-flung destinations, including New York in 1968 and Taiwan in 2011.

In the 21st century, with the growth of digital technology, the challenge for Michelin maps and guides is to continue to develop alongside the company's tire activities. Now, as before, Michelin is committed to improving the mobility of travelers.

MICHELIN TODAY

WORLD NUMBER ONE TIRE MANUFACTURER
- 70 production sites in 18 countries
- 111,000 employees from all cultures and on every continent
- 6,000 people employed in research and development